The Metaphysical Thought of Godfrey of Fontaines

The Metaphysical Thought of Godfrey of Fontaines

A Study in Late Thirteenth-Century Philosophy

by John F. Wippel

The Catholic University of America Press
Washington, D.C.

Library of Congress Cataloging in Publication Data

Wippel, John F
The metaphysical thought of Godfrey of Fontaines.

Bibliography: p.
1. Godefroid de Fontaines, 13th cent.—Metaphysics.
2. Metaphysics. I. Title.
B765.G594W56 111 80-16900
ISBN 0-8132-0556-5 (cl.)
ISBN 0-8132-0965-X (pa.)

Contents

Acknowledgements

My thanks are due to all who have assisted me in bringing this volume to completion. Among these, special mention must be made of Professor Fernand Van Steenberghen of the University of Louvain who many years ago directed my attention to Godfrey of Fontaines as a fruitful area of investigation and under whose guidance the first seeds of the present work appeared as a doctoral dissertation. Particular thanks are also due to Professors Edward P. Mahoney, William A. Wallace and Allan B. Wolter, each of whom has read greater or lesser parts of my manuscript and offered valuable suggestions; to Professor Stephen F. Brown for his generous assistance with paleographical problems encountered at various stages in my research; to Dr. Thomas C. O'Brien for his careful reading and copy editing of the text; to Catholic University librarians Carolyn T. Lee, David J. Gilson, the late Dorothy King, and Bruce Miller for their gracious help in obtaining many scattered sources; and to Dr. Thérèse-Anne Druart, Catherine Boyd, and Joseph Portolano for assisting in various ways in the final stages of the book's production.

I must also express my gratitude to the National Endowment for the Humanities for a fellowship which enabled me to return to this project a number of years ago; to The Catholic University of America for two sabbatical leaves which I devoted to the same; to The American Catholic Philosophical Association for a subsidy which has assisted in defraying the publication costs; and to Dean Jude P. Dougherty of the Catholic University of America's School of Philosophy who has frequently drawn upon his administrative skills in order to make it possible for me to complete this study.

I also wish to thank the editors of *Traditio* and of *Studia Anselmiana* for permission to use in revised form substantial portions of articles which originally appeared in their respective publications.

Finally, I am deeply grateful to Professor Van Steenberghen and to the authorities and other faculty members of the *Institut Supérieur de Philosophie* of the *Université Catholique de Louvain* (Louvain-la-Neuve) for having invited me to present this work for the degree *Maître-Agrégé á l'Ecole Saint Thomas d'Aquin*.

Abbreviations used in the Notes and in the Bibliography

CCSL *Corpus Christianorum. Series Latina*
CSEL *Corpus Scriptorum Ecclesiasticorum Latinorum*
PB *Les Philosophes Belges*
PG Migne, *Patrologiae cursus completus, Series Graeca*
PL Migne, *Patrologiae cursus completus, Series Latina*
Q 2, q. 2 Quodlibet 2, question 2

Introduction

The final quarter of the thirteenth century was marked by intensive philosophical and theological discussion in the Latin West, and especially so at the University of Paris. Owing in no small measure to the commanding and enduring influence of Thomas Aquinas (d. 1274), on the one hand, and of John Duns Scotus (d. ca. 1308), on the other, scholarly interest has tended to pass over leading figures of the intervening decades until relatively recent times. Nonetheless, as ongoing investigation continues to show ever more clearly, powerful philosophical minds were to be found at Paris, and especially in the Theology faculty there, during this interval. Figures such as Henry of Ghent, Giles of Rome, James of Viterbo and Godfrey of Fontaines are now receiving more attention, and deservedly so.

Henry of Ghent, a secular or diocesan priest, served as Regent Master in the Theology faculty at Paris from 1276 until ca. 1292 and during that period delivered the courses which resulted in his *Summa* of Ordinary Questions and his fifteen Quodlibetal Questions. It seems likely that even before that time he had lectured in the Arts faculty, perhaps around 1270.[1] Giles of Rome, an Augustinian, had studied at Paris during Thomas's final teaching period there (1269–1272) and lectured as a Bachelor in theology (1276–1277) and later as Master in that faculty from 1285 until ca. 1291. During the stormy aftermath of the famed prohibition by Bishop Stephen Tempier of some two hundred and nineteen propositions in 1277, Giles himself had encountered some difficulties within the Theology faculty and was "exiled" therefrom in 1278, being permitted to return only in 1285.[2] James of Viterbo held the

[1] For Henry's life and career see F. Ehrle, "Beiträge zu den Biographien berühmter Scholastiker. I. Heinrich von Gent," *Archiv für Literatur-und Kirchengeschichte* 1 (1885), pp. 365–401; 507–08; J. Paulus, *Henri de Gand. Essai sur les tendances de sa métaphysique* (Paris, 1938), pp. xiii–xix; "Henry of Ghent," *New Catholic Encyclopedia* 6 (1967), pp. 1035–37; F. Cunningham, "Some Presuppositions in Henry of Ghent," *Pensamiento* 25 (1969), pp. 104–06. For the suggestion that Henry was already teaching in the Arts faculty in the 1260s see J. P. Zwaenepoel, *Les Quaestiones in Librum de causis attribuées à Henri de Gand* (Louvain-Paris, 1974), p. 18.

[2] On Giles's life and career see P. Nash, "Giles of Rome," *New Catholic Ency-*

Augustinian chair in Theology at Paris from ca. 1293 until 1296 and during that time delivered his only recently edited Quodlibetal Questions.[3] Granted that the Ordinary and Quodlibetal Questions produced by these men during the period in question resulted from their professional duties as Masters in the Theology faculty, nevertheless their writings are filled with philosophical discussions, so much so that it is clear that each of them had worked out a distinctive and highly original underlying philosophy as well. The same may be said, of course, for Thomas Aquinas or Duns Scotus. And the same will also obtain, as we shall see below, for Godfrey of Fontaines.

As B. Xiberta observed some fifty years ago, Godfrey himself is a striking illustration of the arbitrary character of fame.[4] Marked though his influence had been in the final decades of the thirteenth century and onward into the early fourteenth, he subsequently fell into almost total obscurity. The fact that his works remained unedited until the beginning of the twentieth century silently testifies to this. As J. Hoffmans has observed, apart from the rather general bias against medieval scholasticism that prevailed in scholarly circles in the sixteenth century, more particular reasons appear to have contributed to Godfrey's neglect.[5]

---

clopedia 6 (1967), pp. 484–85; "Giles of Rome, Auditor and Critic of St. Thomas," *The Modern Schoolman* 28 (1950–51), pp. 1–2. For discussion as to why he was "exiled" from the Theology faculty at Paris see P. Mandonnet, "La carrière scolaire de Gilles de Rome," *Revue des sciences philosophiques et théologiques* 4 (1910), pp. 484–91; and especially, E. Hocedez, "La condamnation de Gilles de Rome," *Recherches de Théologie ancienne et médiévale* 4 (1932), pp. 34–58. Also see R. Zavalloni, *Richard de Mediavilla et la controverse sur la pluralité des formes* (Louvain, 1951), pp. 489–91.

[3] For James's life and career see D. Gutiérrez, *De B. Iacobi Viterbiensis O.E.S.A. vita, operibus et doctrina theologica* (Rome, 1939); E. Ypma, "Recherches sur la carrière scolaire et la bibliothèque de Jacques de Viterbe †1308," *Augustiniana* 24 (1974), pp. 247–82. For some reservations about the 1293 date proposed by Ypma for James's promotion as Magister and the suggestion that late 1292 is a possibility see our "The Dating of James of Viterbo's Quodlibet I and Godfrey of Fontaines' Quodlibet VIII," *Augustiniana* 24 (1974), pp. 348–86. But even if James was promoted late in 1292, his first Quodlibet would still more than likely not be prior to the Lenten session of 1293.

[4] "Godofred de Fontaines és un dels casos més colpidors de l'arbitrarietat de la Fama. . . . I, no obstant, ell és indiscutiblement un dels quatre o cinc doctors per mèrit dels quals la segona meitat del segle XIIIè és l'edat d'or de l'Escolàstica." See his "Les Qüestions ordinàries de Godofred de Fontaines retrobades parcialment en un manuscrit de Barcelona," *Criterion* 4 (1928), p. 339.

[5] See his "La table des divergences et innovations doctrinales de Godefroid de Fontaines," *Revue Néoscolastique de Philosophie* 36 (1934), p. 412. Along with Xiberta (see n. 4 above), Hoffmans (see pp. 412–14) and Grabmann emphasize the

Like Henry of Ghent he was a secular Master at the University of Paris. And like Henry Godfrey also had strongly resisted the special privileges accorded the Franciscan and Dominican Orders during that time. It would have been highly unlikely under the circumstances that either Godfrey or Henry would be promoted by the Franciscans as were Bonaventure and Duns Scotus or by the Dominicans as were Albert the Great and Thomas Aquinas.[6] It is not surprising that many of Giles of Rome's works were published during the early days of printing, since he had been singled out by the Augustinians during his own lifetime as their official Master.[7] Henry of Ghent was fortunate enough to be "adopted," as it were, by the Servite Order in the sixteenth century, and as a consequence different editions of his works came to be published thereafter.[8] But Godfrey was not so lucky.

Relatively unknown, therefore, even to students and teachers of philosophy apart from a few specialists at the turn of the present century, Godfrey appears to be coming into his own once again today. This is due in no small measure to the editing of his major works by M. De Wulf, J. Hoffmans, A. Pelzer, and O. Lottin. For it was only with the publication of his fifteen Quodlibetal Questions in the series *Les Philosophes Belges* earlier in this century that the way was opened for deeper study of this Belgian thinker. (Three of his Ordinary Questions have also been published in that same series.)[9] In more recent decades a growing number of articles and even some dissertations have been devoted to certain aspects of his thought. But a survey of such work prior to 1960 or thereabouts reveals that interest in Godfrey's doctrine had been confined in large measure to his psychology (theory of knowledge and theory of choice), moral philosophy, and certain aspects of his theology.[10]

---

high esteem in which Godfrey was held in his own time and for some period thereafter. For Grabmann see his "Die Eröterung der Frage, ob die Kirche besser durch einen guten Juristen oder durch einen Theologen regiert werde, bei Gottfried von Fontaines (†nach 1306) und Augustinus Triumphus von Ancona (†nach 1328)," in *Festschrift Eduard Eichmann zum 70. Geburtstag* (Paderborn, 1940), p. 1. For further indications of this see B. Neumann, *Der Mensch und die himmlische Seligkeit nach der Lehre Gottfrieds von Fontaines* (Limburg/Lahn, 1958), pp. 1–2.

[6] See Hoffmans, "La table des divergences . . . ," p. 412; Neumann, *Der Mensch* . . . , p. 2.

[7] See Nash, "Giles of Rome, Auditor and Critic . . . ," p. 1, n. 1. On his works see G. Bruni, *Le opere di Egidio Romano* (Florence, 1936).

[8] See Paulus, "Henry of Ghent," pp. 1036–37.

[9] These appeared in volumes 2, 3, 4, 5, and 14 in *Les Philosophes Belges* and will be listed more fully in Section B of this Introduction, treating of Godfrey's writings.

[10] See, for instance, A. Stohr, "Des Gottfried von Fontaines Stellung in der Trinitätslehre," *Zeitschrift für katholische Theologie* 50 (1926), pp. 177–95; "Die Hauptrichtungen der spekulativen Trinitätslehre in der Theologie des 13. Jahrhunderts,"

By that time it had become clear that a general study of his metaphysical thought was sorely needed, and one that would not only present this for its own sake but correlate it insofar as possible with that of his immediate predecessors and his contemporaries.[11]

Since about that time much of our own research has ultimately been aimed at meeting this need.[12] The present volume is an attempt to draw upon all of this and to present a general study of Godfrey's metaphysical thought within

---

Tübinger theologische Quartalschrift 106 (1925), pp. 113–35; O. Lottin, "Le libre arbitre chez Godefroid de Fontaines," *Revue Néoscolastique de Philosophie* 40 (1937), pp. 213–41; "Le thomisme de Godefroid de Fontaines en matière de libre arbitre," *op. cit.*, pp. 554–73; *Psychologie et morale au XIIe et XIIIe siècles* (Louvain, 1942), T. I, pp. 304–39, essentially the same as the two previously mentioned articles; also in the last named work see T. II (Louvain, 1948), pp. 267–69 (on synderesis and conscience); T. IV (Louvain, 1954), pp. 575–99 (on the connection of the acquired and moral virtues); pp. 682–83 (on the gifts of the Holy Spirit); J. Leclercq, "La théologie comme science d'après la littérature quodlibétique," *Recherches de Théologie ancienne et médiévale* 11 (1939), pp. 357–60; P. Bayerschmidt, *Die Seins- und Formmetaphysik des Heinrich von Gent in ihrer Anwendung auf die Christologie* (Münster, 1941), esp. pp. 105–16, 248–49, 266–79; J. de Blic, "L'intellectualisme moral chez deux aristotéliciens de la fin du XIIIe siècle" (Giles of Rome and Godfrey of Fontaines), in *Miscellanea moralia in honorem ex. Dom. Arthur Janssen, Ephemeridum theologicarum Lovaniensium Bibliotheca,* Ser. I, Vol. 2 (Louvain, 1948), pp. 45–76; M. Grabmann, *Die theologische Erkenntnis- und Einleitungslehre des heiligen Thomas von Aquin* (Freiburg in der Schweiz, 1948), pp. 313–29; R. J. Arway, *Potency and Act in the Human Intellect according to Godfrey of Fontaines,* unpublished doctoral dissertation (Louvain, 1957); P. Stella, "Teologi e teologia nelle 'reprobationes' di Bernardo d'Auvergne ai Quodlibeti di Goffredo di Fontaines," *Salesianum* 19 (1957), pp. 171–214; B. Neumann, *Der Mensch und die himmlische Seligkeit* . . . ; P. Langevin, "Nécessité ou liberté, chez Godefroid de Fontaines," *Sciences ecclésiastiques* 12 (1960), pp. 175–203; P. Tihon, *Foi et théologie selon Godefroid de Fontaines* (Paris-Bruges, 1966). Also see G. de Lagarde, "La philosophie sociale d'Henri de Gand et de Godefroid de Fontaines," *Archives d'Histoire Doctrinale et Littéraire du Moyen Age* 14 (1943–1945), pp. 73–142; *La naissance de l'esprit laïque au déclin du moyen âge,* 2nd ed. Vol. 2 (Louvain, 1958), pp. 161–213. For a helpful survey of many of the above see R. Arway, "A Half Century of Research on Godfrey of Fontaines," *The New Scholasticism* 36 (1962), pp. 192–218. H. Rüssmann's *Zur Ideenlehre der Hochscholastik under besonderer Berücksichtigung des Heinrich von Gent, Gottfried von Fontaines und Jakob von Viterbo* (Freiburg im Breisgau, 1938) treats of some points which are pertinent to Godfrey's metaphysical thought, but must be used only with caution.

[11] As Neumann comments: "Dennoch steht eine umfassende und gewiss sich lohnende Darstellung seiner Metaphysik und Philosophie noch aus" (*Der Mensch* . . . , p. 4).

[12] See Wippel, *Fundamental Metaphysical Themes in the Quaestiones Quodlibetales of Godfrey of Fontaines,* unpublished doctoral dissertation (Louvain, 1963), which concentrated on Godfrey's metaphysical thought simply as contained in his

its historical context. Apart from the fact that his metaphysics is distinctive and powerful enough to merit consideration for its own sake, it is hoped that this study will also provide additional information with respect to the main streams of metaphysical thought that were current at Paris during the final part of the thirteenth century. For anyone who would more fully appreciate the influence of Thomas Aquinas in the years immediately following his death, or the roles of men such as Giles of Rome, Henry of Ghent, and James of Viterbo, or more of the background for the development of Duns Scotus's philosophical thought, some acquaintance with the metaphysics of Godfrey should prove rewarding.

A. GODFREY'S LIFE

De Wulf's *Un théologien-philosophe du XIIIe siècle* still presents the best general account of Godfrey's life.[13] Prior to the appearance of this work considerable legend had been intermingled with the relatively few known facts. For instance, it had been suggested that Godfrey was born in France, or even that he was English by birth. He had been confused with other

---

Quodlibets and considered in itself rather than in comparison with that of his contemporaries; "Godfrey of Fontaines and the Real Distinction between Essence and Existence," *Traditio* 20 (1964), pp. 385–410; "Godfrey of Fontaines," *New Catholic Encyclopedia* 6 (1967), pp. 577–78; "Godfrey of Fontaines: The Date of Quodlibet 15," *Franciscan Studies* 31 (1971), pp. 300–69; "Godfrey of Fontaines and the Act-Potency Axiom," *Journal of the History of Philosophy* 11 (1973), pp. 299–317; "Godfrey of Fontaines: Disputed Questions 9, 10 and 12," *Franciscan Studies* 33 (1973), pp. 351–72, an edition of these three Questions; "The Dating of James of Viterbo's Quodlibet I and Godfrey of Fontaines' Quodlibet VIII," *Augustiniana* 24 (1974), pp. 348–86; "Godfrey of Fontaines and Henry of Ghent's Theory of Intentional Distinction between Essence and Existence," *Sapientiae procerum amore. Mélanges Médiévistes offerts à Dom Jean-Pierre Müller O.S.B., Studia Anselmiana* 63 (Rome, 1974), pp. 289–321; "The Relationship between Essence and Existence in Late Thirteenth Century Thought: Giles of Rome, Henry of Ghent, Godfrey of Fontaines, and James of Viterbo," forthcoming in *Ancient and Medieval Philosophies of Existence,* ed. by P. Morewedge (New York: Fordham University Press, 1981).

[13] *Un théologien-philosophe du XIIIe siècle. Etude sur la vie, les oeuvres et l'influence de Godefroid de Fontaines* (Brussels, 1904). Also see De Wulf's "Un preux de la parole au XIIIe siècle," *Revue Néoscolastique de Philosophie* 11 (1904), pp. 416–32; *Histoire de la Philosophie en Belgique* (Brussels, 1910), pp. 80–116; "L'intellectualisme de Godefroid de Fontaines d'après le Quodlibet VI, q. 15," *Beiträge zur Geschichte der Philosophie und Theologie des Mittelalters,* Supplementband I (1913), pp. 287–96; *Histoire de la philosophie médiévale,* 6th ed., Vol. 2 (Louvain, 1936), pp. 293–97.

personalities such as Godfrey, Bishop of Cambrai in the 1220s and 1230s, or with Godefroid de Brie, a Franciscan who was at Paris in the early 1240s. He was thought by some to have served as Chancellor of the University of Paris. De Wulf's findings have indicated that none of these claims is true.[14]

Godfrey was born in present-day Belgium in the principality of Liège and probably at the chateau of the noble family to which he belonged, that is to say, at Fontaines-les-Hozémont.[15] The exact date of his birth remains unknown, but it must have been not too long before 1250. Thus in 1285 he conducted his first quodlibetal debate at the University of Paris and must, therefore, have been *Magister regens* in theology there by that time. But according to the statutes laid down for the Theology faculty by Robert Courçon in 1215, one would have to be at least thirty-five before becoming a Master of Theology. This brings us back to 1250 or earlier as a possible date for his birth.[16]

While we know nothing of his life prior to his appearance as a student in Paris, the same statutes required that one must have studied theology for at least eight years before becoming a Master. Hence we may conclude that Godfrey was already in Paris and studying theology there by 1277. But there is good reason to believe that he had already been at the University for some time and had pursued philosophical studies in the Arts faculty in the early 1270s, perhaps from 1270 until 1272. For a valuable student notebook belonging to Godfrey and apparently dating from that period has been preserved. Not only does it seem likely that he himself was responsible for compiling this interesting collection of writings during his days as a student

---

[14] *Un théologien-philosophe* . . . , pp. 4–6, 11–14. As regards the claim that Godfrey was at one time Chancellor of the University, De Wulf argues against this because of the lack of any positive evidence for it (*op. cit.*, pp. 30–31). C. Balič cites documentation referring to Godfrey's participation in the disputations *in vesperis* and *in aula* on the occasion of the conferring of the doctoral (*Magister*) degree on Giles of Ligny at Paris in 1304. He concludes from this that Godfrey was at that time either Chancellor or acting Chancellor of the University. See "Henricus de Harcley et Ioannes Duns Scotus," in *Mélanges offerts à Etienne Gilson* (Toronto-Paris, 1959), pp. 98–101; and "The Life and Works of John Duns Scotus," in *John Duns Scotus, 1265–1965, Studies in Philosophy and the History of Philosophy* 3 (Washington, 1965), p. 13. We are inclined to interpret this as meaning simply that Godfrey represented or took the place of the Chancellor at this particular function. See Balič, "Henricus de Harcley . . . ," p. 101 (". . . vel Cancellarii vices gerens").

[15] De Wulf, *Un théologien-philosophe* . . . , pp. 4–8, 10–11; Arway, " A Half Century . . . ," p. 193.

[16] See H. Denifle-A. Chatelain, *Chartularium Universitatis Parisiensis*, T. 1 (Paris, 1889), pp. 78–79; De Wulf, *Un théologien-philosophe* . . . , p. 16; Arway, "A Half Century . . . ," p. 193.

in Arts but, according to Glorieux, he copied a number of the works contained therein with his own hand.[17] It follows from this that Godfrey was a student at the University for the greater part of Thomas's second teaching period there (1269–1272), and that he was a first-hand witness to the controversies revolving around the philosophical positions of certain members of the Arts faculty during the period between Bishop Stephen Tempier's Condemnation of thirteen propositions in December, 1270, and his sweeping prohibition of two hundred nineteen propositions in 1277.[18]

Interestingly enough, the earliest extant copy of Thomas Aquinas's *De aeternitate mundi* is preserved in Godfrey's student notebook, along with other works by Aquinas, Siger of Brabant, Boethius of Dacia, Giles of Rome, Gerard of Abbeville, and others.[19] The presence in this same collection of Giles of Rome's *Theoremata de corpore Christi* might lead one to believe that Godfrey did not complete the compilation of his notebook until after 1272, the date proposed by Glorieux. For students of Giles usually place this work in 1275 or 1276. Glorieux himself would account for this by suggesting

---

[17] On this see Glorieux, "Un recueil scolaire de Godefroid de Fontaines," *Recherches de Théologie ancienne et médiévale* 3 (1931), pp. 37–53. This is contained in a Paris manuscript, *Bibl. Nat. lat. 16.297,* and its importance is widely recognized not only for its implications for Godfrey's early career but for the critical value of many of the writings contained therein. See for instance the references given below in n. 19. For Glorieux's evidence that Godfrey was responsible for the compilation of this notebook and that some of its contents are copied in his own hand see pp. 44–45.

[18] For a general discussion of these two Condemnations see our "The Condemnations of 1270 and 1277 at Paris," *The Journal of Medieval and Renaissance Studies* 7 (1977), pp. 169–201. In addition to the references given there two further and important discussions have even more recently become available: F. Van Steenberghen, *Maître Siger de Brabant* (Louvain-Paris, 1977), pp. 74–79, 139–58; and R. Hissette, *Enquête sur les 219 articles condamnés à Paris le 7 mars 1277* (Louvain-Paris, 1977).

[19] High value has been assigned to Godfrey's copy of the *De aeternitate* by the Leonine editors in their critical edition of Thomas's opusculum. See *Sancti Thomae de Aquino Opera omnia* T. 43 (Rome, 1976), pp. 71, 73, and n. 193 of Ch. III of the present study. A number of the other works contained in Godfrey's notebook have now been edited. See, for instance, the short version of Siger's *Quaestiones in Metaphysicam,* ed. by C. A. Graiff in *Siger de Brabant. Questions sur la métaphysique* (Louvain, 1948), with Godfrey's version appearing at the bottom of the page; Siger's *Impossibilia,* critically edited by B. Bazán in *Siger de Brabant. Ecrits de logique, de morale et de physique* (Louvain-Paris, 1974), pp. 67–97, where Godfrey's copy serves as the principal text; Siger's *De necessitate et contingentia causarum,* as edited by P. Mandonnet in his *Siger de Brabant et l'Averroïsme latin au XIIIe siècle,* 2nd ed., Vol. 2 (Louvain, 1908), pp. 109–28 (although Duin's critical edition of Siger's work should now be used, as found in his *La doctrine de la providence dans les écrits*

that Giles's treatise appeared in two redactions, the first of which would be that included in Godfrey's notebook and date no later than 1272, and the second which would have appeared some time thereafter.[20] Duin, however, has rejected this proposal that Giles's work appeared in two redactions, and has assigned a 1271–1274 dating to Godfrey's notebook.[21]

There is also extrinsic evidence suggesting that Godfrey must have completed his formal studies in the Arts faculty by early 1274. A catalog of the students of the Sorbonne indicates that he was enrolled there during the time of Robert of Sorbon, who died August 15, 1274. Since the Sorbonne itself was founded for students in theology it would seem that Godfrey must have begun his theological studies by early 1274 at the very latest. Hence if his student notebook was completed during his period as a student in Arts at Paris, it will then follow that its *terminus ante quem* can be no later than 1274.[22] In any event, Godfrey's notebook indicates that he was quite interested in and conversant with many of the views then being proposed by Siger of Brabant and Boethius of Dacia, leading representatives of the radical Aristotelian movement in the Arts faculty at that time. And as we shall see frequently enough below, he was well aware of Tempier's Condemnation of 1277, not to mention the later prohibitions directed against the doctrine of

---

de Siger de Brabant [Louvain, 1954], pp. 14–50); *Quaestiones super libros I, IV et VIII Physicorum*, ed. by A. Zimmermann, *Ein Kommentar zur Physik des Aristoteles aus der Pariser Artistenfakultät um 1273* (Berlin, 1968), attributed to Siger by Duin (*op. cit.*, pp. 176–205), though Zimmermann does not regard this as certain (pp. XXX–XXXVII). Also see an abridged version of Boethius of Dacia's *Quaestiones super librum Topicorum*, ed. by N. Green Pedersen and J. Pinborg in *Boethii Daci Opera, Opuscula De aeternitate mundi, de summo bono, de somniis, Corpus Philosophorum Danicorum Medii Aevi*, Vol. VI, p. II (Hauniae, 1976), pp. 393–434 (see pp. 435–56 of the same for editions of abridgments of Boethius's *De aeternitate mundi, De summo bono*, and extracts from his *De somniis*, all contained in *Bibl. Nat. lat. 15.819*, another of the manuscripts left by Godfrey to the Sorbonne); and an abridgment of Boethius's *Modi significandi* ed. by J. Pinborg and H. Roos in the same series, Vol. IV (1969), pp. 311–65.

[20] For a 1276 dating of Giles's work see Paulus, *Henri de Gand* . . . , p. 281; G. Trapé, "L''esse' partecipato e distinzione reale in Egidio Romano," *Aquinas* 12 (1969), p. 455. A. Pattin places it ca. 1275–76 in his "Gilles de Rome, O.E.S.A. (ca. 1243–1316) et la distinction réelle de l'essence et de l'existence," *Revue de l'Université d'Ottawa* 23 (1953), p. 85*. See Glorieux, "Un recueil scolaire . . . ," pp. 51–52.

[21] *La doctrine de la providence* . . . , pp. 274–75, 292.

[22] On this see Duin, p. 272, n. 64. Duin dates Robert's death April 15, 1274. But for the August 15 dating see P. Glorieux, *Aux origines de la Sorbonne. I. Robert de Sorbon* (Paris, 1966), pp. 66 and 171. Also see C. Graiff, *Siger de Brabant. Questions sur la Métaphysique*, pp. XXII–XXVI; Zimmermann, *Ein Kommentar* . . . , p. XIV.

unicity of substantial form in man by John Peckham, Archbishop of Canterbury, in 1286.

A remark in the *Domus Sorbonicae historia* indicates that Godfrey studied theology under Henry of Ghent and Gervais of Mt. St. Elias.[23] Of these two Henry was surely the more important figure, and as we shall continually see below, Godfrey was not only quite familiar with but frequently reacted against his philosophical positions. It is certain that for a number of years, that is, from 1285 until ca. 1292, he and Henry both served as Masters in the Theology faculty. Godfrey himself functioned there as Regent Master from 1285 until 1298 or 1299, and then reappeared at the University in the same capacity ca. 1303/1304.[24] His major writings, in the form of his fifteen Quodlibets, resulted from this period, as did his less extensive Ordinary Disputed Questions. But more will be said below about his works.

As we have already mentioned above in passing, Godfrey, along with other secular Masters such as Henry, strongly opposed the Mendicant orders, and especially so in the disputes resulting from certain privileges accorded them by Pope Martin IV in a bull of December, 1281. The controversy appears to have become particularly acute at Paris in December, 1286. According to a letter from William of Mâcon, Bishop of Amiens, which refers to certain aspects of the dispute as they had developed at that time, Godfrey, along with Henry of Ghent, Gervais of Mt. St. Elias, and Nicholas du Pressoir had all sided against the mendicants in their respective quodlibetal sessions of that year (1286). For they had all determined that those who had confessed to mendicants by reason of the privileges granted to the latter by Pope Martin's bull were still bound to confess the same sins once again to their own priests.[25] In Quodlibet 3, q. 7, which dates from the Advent quodlibetal

---

[23] See De Wulf, *Un théologien-philosophe,* p. 17, for the reference to this (Ms. *Arsenal* 1022, p. III, p. 81) and for discussion of the degree of credence to be given to it (Godfrey could have studied under both Henry and Gervais before becoming their colleague, p. 19). For some general remarks about this source also see Glorieux, *Aux origines de la Sorbonne. I . . . ,* p. 72.

[24] For Henry's career see the references given in n. 1 above. In addition, for the dating of his Quodlibets and *Summa* of Ordinary Questions, see J. Gómez Caffarena, "Cronología de la 'Suma' de Enrique de Gante por relación a sus 'Quodlibetos'," *Gregorianum* 38 (1957), pp. 116–33; for the dating of his Quodlibets also see Glorieux, *La littérature quodlibétique de 1260 à 1320,* Vol. 1 (Paris, 1925), pp. 88–93. For the dates of Godfrey's Quodlibets see below (Section B of this Introduction).

[25] For discussion of this general and ongoing controversy between the seculars and mendicants at Paris during the second half of the thirteenth century see Y. Congar, "Aspects ecclésiologiques de la querelle entre mendiants et séculiers dans la seconde moitié du XIIIe siècle et le début du XIVe," *Archives d'Histoire Doctrinale et Littéraire du Moyen Age* 28 (1961), pp. 35–151 (see the references in nn. 19–21); D.

period of 1286, Godfrey had indeed considered this very question. Unfortunately the text of his reply has not been preserved. The reader is simply referred to the "response in the Master's book."[26]

During his years as Regent Master in Paris Godfrey also held certain ecclesiastical offices, such as Canon of Liège, Canon of Tournai, probably Canon of Paris, and Provost of St. Severin in Cologne (1287–1295).[27] Another sign of the prestige which he enjoyed among his contemporaries was his appointment in 1292 to a commission charged with settling a dispute between the Arts faculty and the Chancellor of the University, Berthaud of St. Denys.[28] In addition, he was selected as bishop of Tournai in 1300 but gave up his claim, apparently because the election was contested.[29] He seems to have been absent from Paris for a time between his fourteenth Quodlibet of 1298/1299 and his final one in 1303/1304.[30] A great lover of books, he evidently enjoyed sufficient material resources so as to acquire a valuable library. Thus he left a fine collection of manuscripts to the Sorbonne, thirty-seven of which still survive.[31] The year of his death remains uncertain, al-

---

Douie, *The Conflict Between the Seculars and the Mendicants at the University of Paris in the Thirteenth Century* (London: Aquinas Papers, n. 23, 1954). For discussion of Godfrey's specific role therein see De Wulf, *Un théologien-philosophe . . .*, pp. 52–55. For William's letter see *Chartularium . . .*, T. 2, p. 13.

[26] "Utrum confessus ab aliquo habente potestatem audiendi confessiones et absolvendi confitentes virtute privilegii Martini IV teneatur eadem peccata proprio sacerdoti iterum confiteri." See *Les Philosophes Belges*, Vol. 2, pp. 214–16. See p. 216: "In libro magistri responsio."

[27] For this see De Wulf, *Un théologien-philosophe . . .*, pp. 25–30; Arway, "A Half Century . . .," p. 195.

[28] See the letter from Pope Nicholas IV in March 1292, to the Bishops of Senlis and Auxerre, the Dean of Paris, and Godfrey, in *Chartularium . . .*, T. 2, p. 53. On this see De Wulf, *Un théologien-philosophe . . .*, pp. 56–57; Glorieux, *Aux origines de la Sorbonne. I . . .*, p. 125.

[29] See De Wulf, *Un théologien-philosophe . . .*, p. 30. He was present at a meeting in Paris treating of certain internal affairs of the Sorbonne, February 26, 1304. See Glorieux, *Aux origines . . .*, p. 206 for this text; also see De Wulf, p. 31, who rather places this meeting in 1303. Granted that the text itself states 1303, this would be according to the old calendar, since the new year (1304) would not yet have begun by that reckoning. See below for our discussion of the date of Quodlibet 15.

[30] See our remarks in the following Section about the date of Quodlibet 15. De Wulf notes that he is cited as a senior member of the Sorbonne until 1306 (*Un théologien-philosophe*, p. 31).

[31] De Wulf, *op. cit.*, pp. 24–25. For a detailed study of the contents of a number of these see J. Duin, "La bibliothèque philosophique de Godefroid de Fontaines," in *Estudios Lulianos* 3 (1959), pp. 21–36, 137–60. For reference to studies of the contents of some of the others see nn. 4 and 5 of the same. Note especially the

though the Obituary of the Sorbonne lists the date as October 29. It seems likely that his death occurred ca. 1306 or perhaps in 1309.[32]

B. GODFREY'S WRITINGS

Godfrey's most important contribution to philosophical and theological literature is, as has already been indicated, his series of fifteen quodlibetal questions.[33] Quodlibets were formal exercises conducted by Masters in theology only at certain reserved times, that is to say, before Christmas (during the second or third week of Advent) and before Easter (near or during the fourth week of Lent). Thus they are often referred to as the Christmas or Easter Quodlibet of a given Master for a given year.[34] Since they were open to all Masters, Bachelors and students, and even to others who cared to attend, other lectures in the faculty would be suspended while they were being held. Their name derives from the fact that a question could be directed at the Master by anyone (*a quolibet*) about any reasonable topic (*de quolibet*).[35] Needless to say, considerable learning and skill would be required on the part of the Master who conducted these sessions. In fact, it seems that not all Masters were prepared to take upon themselves this exacting task. It is also evident that a Bachelor might be assigned to offer a preliminary

---

examination of mss. *16.080* and *16.583* (collections of Aristotle) in *Aristoteles latinus* 1 (1939), pp. 553 and 575.

[32] For the Sorbonne Obituary see Glorieux, *Aux origines de la Sorbonne. I. . . .* , p. 176. For the 1306 or 1309? date see Glorieux, *Répertoire des maîtres en théologie de Paris au XIIIe siècle*, Vol. 1 (Paris, 1933), p. 396.

[33] These have appeared in *Les Philosophes Belges* in the following order: Vol. 2: *Les quatre premiers Quodlibets de Godefroid de Fontaines*, ed. by M. De Wulf and A. Pelzer (Louvain, 1904); Vol. 3: *Les Quodlibets cinq, six et sept*, ed. by De Wulf and J. Hoffmans (Louvain, 1914); Vol. 4: *Le huitième Quodlibet* (Louvain, 1924), *Le neuvième Quodlibet* (Louvain, 1928), *Le dixième Quodlibet* (Louvain, 1931), ed. by J. Hoffmans; Vol. 5: *Les Quodlibets onze et douze* (Louvain, 1932), *Les Quodlibets treize et quatorze* (Louvain, 1935), ed. by Hoffmans; Vol. 14: *Le Quodlibet XV et trois Questions ordinaires de Godefroid de Fontaines*, ed. by O. Lottin (Louvain, 1937).

[34] For general discussion of the Quodlibets see especially Glorieux, *La littérature quodlibétique de 1260 à 1320*, Vol. 1, pp. 11–95; "Où en est la question Quodlibet?" *Revue du Moyen Age Latin* 2 (1946), pp. 405–14; "Quodlibeti" in *Enciclopedia Cattolica*, Vol. 10 (Vatican City, 1953), col. 436–438. On the time of year for holding these sessions in the theology faculty see *La littérature . . .* , Vol. 1, pp. 83–86; "Où en est la question . . . ?" p. 407. Note that the practice of holding quodlibetal debates also spread to other faculties at Paris and to other Universities. See "Quodlibeti," col. 437.

[35] *La littérature . . .* , Vol. 1, p. 21.

response to the objections that had been raised. But after this initial discussion it was the Master himself who analyzed in detail the question proposed and then presented his solution.[36]

The Master would have an opportunity on some following day to discuss the same questions again with his students and to rearrange them according to some more logical or at least coherent order. For many different questions would normally be proposed during the original public session, and without any predetermined order. In this second session the Master would present his final *determinatio* or definitive solution to each of the questions raised.[37] And subsequently, more than likely during the following year, he would also prepare his final written version for release to the public. This means, of course, that one should distinguish between three possible types of written recordings of a quodlibetal debate. First of all there might be a *reportatio* of the first day's discussion taken down by some eyewitness, perhaps by an assistant or by a student. Secondly, there could also be a similar *reportatio* of the Master's *determinatio* as presented orally in the following review session. Or finally, there might be the Master's written and definitive *determinatio* which would be prepared over a more extended period of time and eventually released by him to be copied for public circulation. A *reportatio* of the second day's oral determination by the Master would reflect his reordering as well as his more leisurely and deliberate reflections on these matters, but would still be written down by someone else. And the final written determination prepared by the Master himself would enjoy even greater critical value as an expression of his personal thought. As Glorieux has indicated, written versions of all three types have survived.[38]

These solemn quodlibetal debates should also be distinguished from the Ordinary Disputed Questions which resulted from a Master's regular teaching duties and in cooperation with his Bachelors. These discussions were not open to everyone and also differed from quodlibetal sessions in that the Master himself could establish both the questions to be examined and the order in which they were to be considered.[39] As we shall see, some of

---

[36] *Op. cit.*, pp. 30–35; "Quodlibeti," col. 436.

[37] On these two sessions see Glorieux, *op. cit.*, pp. 18–20, 39–51; "Le Quodlibet et ses procédés rédactionnels," *Divus Thomas* (Piacenza) 42 (1939), pp. 61–93 (esp. 61–66); "L'Enseignement au Moyen Age. Techniques et méthodes en usage à la Faculté de Théologie de Paris, au XIIIe siècle," *Archives d'Histoire Doctrinale et Littéraire du Moyen Age* 35 (1968), pp. 128–32.

[38] In addition to the last two sources cited in the preceding note see Glorieux, *La littérature . . .*, Vol. 1, pp. 51–53.

[39] See Glorieux, "L'Enseignement au Moyen Age . . . ," pp. 123–32; and "Quodlibeti," col. 436.

Godfrey's Ordinary Disputed Questions have also been preserved, although their value for us in studying his metaphysical thought will be considerably less than that of his Quodlibets.

Glorieux has attempted to date Godfrey's Quodlibets and with some modifications his proposed chronology is still acceptable. It may be helpful to the reader for us to summarize here the essentials of his reasoning. First of all, Quodlibet 14 must be prior to 1304 since the official University stationer's list of February 25th of that year apparently includes Godfrey's Quodlibets 5 through 14.[40] And at the other end of the spectrum, Glorieux reasons that Quodlibet 1 must be subsequent to the death of King Philip III (October 5, 1285), since in question 11 Godfrey discusses the issue as to where the King's heart should be buried without naming him in so many words. Quodlibet 3 should be placed in Advent, 1286, since it contains the question referred to by Bishop William of Mâcon in his letter to the Archbishop of Rheims.[41] Quodlibet 2 must be prior to this, therefore, but no earlier than the Lenten session of 1286, since in it Godfrey is still unaware of John Peckham's Prohibition of April 30, 1286. This is referred to at length in Quodlibet 3, q. 5.[42] A remark in Quodlibet 4, q. 13 indicates that it must be a year later than Quodlibet 3 and dates, therefore, from 1287.[43] Because of interdependencies between Godfrey's Quodlibets 5, 6, and 7 and Henry of Ghent's Quodlibets 12 and 13, Glorieux concludes that the former fall into 1288, 1289, and 1290 respectively, either at Christmas or Easter.[44]

In his effort to date the subsequent Quodlibets Glorieux observes that Quodlibet 12, q. 4 shows knowledge of the abdication of Pope Celestine V of December 13, 1294, and should therefore be placed in 1295.[45] Quodlibet 13 must be prior to 1297, since in q. 7 it refers to certain legislation which was in force from the time of Gregory X until it was modified by Boniface VIII in his *Cum ex eo quod filius* of March 3, 1298.[46] Finally, if one assumes,

---

[40] *Chartularium* . . . , T. 2, p. 109 (n. 642). For this see Pelzer's clever deduction from the number of *peciae* indicated in that list (*Les Philosophes Belges*, Vol. 14, pp. 239–44).

[41] See notes 25 and 26 above.

[42] See *Les Philosophes Belges*, Vol. 2, pp. 205–08, cited hereafter as PB 2.205–08.

[43] See PB 2.276, where Godfrey appears to refer both to his Quodlibet 3, q. 7 and to certain meetings of the bishops in December 1286, all relating to the controversy concerning the mendicants.

[44] For all of this see Glorieux, *La littérature* . . . , Vol. 1, pp. 149–50.

[45] PB 5.96–99.

[46] For this see Glorieux, *La littérature* . . . , Vol. 1, p. 150; Pelzer, "Godefroid de Fontaines. Les manuscrits de ses Quodlibets conservés à la Vaticane et dans quelques autres bibliothèques," *Revue Néoscolastique de Philosophie* 20 (1913), p.

as does Glorieux, that with the exception of his first academic year as a Master Godfrey conducted only one Quodlibet every year, one may fill out the series by placing Quodlibet 8 in 1291, Quodlibet 9 in 1292, Quodlibet 10 in 1293, Quodlibet 11 in 1294, Quodlibet 12 in 1295 (after Celestine's abdication), and Quodlibet 13 in 1296. Quodlibet 14 then naturally falls into 1297.[47]

Our efforts on another occasion to resolve an apparent anomaly resulting from Godfrey's citation of James of Viterbo's Quodlibet 1 in his own Quodlibet 8 have led us to propose some modifications for Glorieux's dates for Quodlibets 8 through 14. According to such scholars as Ypma and Gutiérrez, James was promoted as Master only ca. Easter 1293, and could not have succeeded Giles of Rome as Regent Master until the following September. Hence he could not have conducted his first quodlibetal dispute until December 1293, somewhat late for Godfrey to have cited this in 1291. We have offered some evidence to suggest that James could have been promoted somewhat earlier, perhaps late in 1292, and could therefore have held his first Quodlibet in the Easter session (Lent) of 1293. Even so, this of itself will still not entirely resolve the difficulty.[48]

Reexamination of Glorieux's case for the 1291 dating of Godfrey's Quodlibet 8 caused us to question two of his major assumptions. First of all, he had reasoned that because in Quodlibet 12 Godfrey knows of Celestine's

---

503. There Pelzer cites a marginal note in *Vat. lat. 1032* which adverts to the new legislation. Hoffmans points to a similar reference in a Paris manuscript and notes its importance in enabling Pelzer to date Quodlibet 13 no later than 1297 (see PB 14.160). For Godfrey see PB 5.232. For Boniface's constitution see *Liber Sextus Decretalium d. Bonifacii Papae VIII,* I, 6, c. 34, in A. E. Friedberg, ed., *Corpus Iuris Canonici* (Leipzig, 1879), 964–65.

[47] Glorieux, *op. cit.*, pp. 150–51.

[48] See our "The Dating of James of Viterbo's Quodlibet I and Godfrey of Fontaines' Quodlibet VIII," pp. 362–72 (on the textual dependency); 348–49, 372–74, 380–83 (for discussion of the date of James's first Quodlibet). Also see E. Ypma, *Jacobi de Viterbio O.E.S.A. disputatio prima de quolibet* (Würzburg, 1968), pp. v and vi and n. 10; *Jacobi de Viterbio O.E.S.A. disputatio secunda de quolibet* (Würzburg, 1969), p. vi; *La Formation des Professeurs chez les Ermites de Saint-Augustin de 1256 à 1354* (Paris, 1956), pp. 83–84; D. Gutiérrez, *De B. Iacobi Viterbiensis O.E.S.A. vita, operibus, et doctrina theologica* (Rome, 1939), pp. 15, 33. Also see Ypma, "Recherches sur la productivité littéraire de Jacques de Viterbe jusqu'à 1300," *Augustiniana* 25 (1975), p. 249, n. 55 and p. 274, n. 147, where he continues to regard Christmas 1293 (or Easter 1294) as the earliest date for James's first Quodlibet. He remains unconvinced by our defense of late 1292 as a possible date for James's promotion (p. 249, n. 55) although he appears to be more open to this in a second reference to our study (p. 274, n. 147). In any event he there offers no further evidence for his own case nor any refutation of ours.

abdication of December, 1294, he could not have conducted another Quodlibet between the time of that event and Quodlibet 12 itself. But it seems just as likely to us that he might have held a quodlibetal debate sometime thereafter, for instance, Easter 1295, at which no one raised this particular question for his consideration. The fact that it was discussed in 1296 by Peter of Auvergne in his first Quodlibet suggests that it was still regarded as a timely topic then.[49]

Secondly, Glorieux assumes that because Quodlibet 13 does not refer to Boniface's Constitution of March 3, 1298, it must be prior to 1297. But the most that can safely be deduced from this is that Quodlibet 13 cannot be later than 1297, as Pelzer had suggested many years ago. In fact, one might press this point even further and suggest that because of the time required for news to pass from Rome to Paris, knowledge of Boniface's action of March 3 may not have reached Parisian circles before the quodlibetal session for Easter 1298. This seems especially likely if one recalls that Easter fell on April 6 of that year and that the Easter quodlibetal debates were probably held around the fourth week of Lent. In any event, there seems to be nothing precluding one from dating Godfrey's Quodlibet 13 in the 1297/1298 academic year, either at Christmas or Easter.[50]

In light of the above, therefore, Godfrey's preceding Quodlibets might be redated as follows: Quodlibet 12 will be placed in the academic year 1296/1297; Quodlibet 11 in 1295/1296; Quodlibet 10 in 1294/1295; Quodlibet 9 in 1293/1294; and Quodlibet 8 in 1292/1293. We have been unable to specify any more precisely whether they would fall into the Christmas or Easter sessions of each of these respective school years. But if James did conduct his first Quodlibet in Lent 1293, and if Godfrey's Quodlibet 8 does fall into the 1292/1293 academic year, it would be possible for the latter to date from the same Lenten quodlibetal period as the former. Hence if James held his debate a day or so before Godfrey conducted his, Godfrey might very well have known of it and even attended it. On the other hand, if James's first Quodlibet dates only from Advent of the 1293/1294 academic year or even from the Lenten session of that same year, it is possible that Godfrey's oral presentation of Quodlibet 8 antedates it but that he was able to take it into account in the written version of his *determinatio* which he would presumably have been preparing for public release during that same academic year.[51]

---

[49] See Wippel, "The Dating of James of Viterbo's Quodlibet I . . . ," pp. 374–78. Glorieux himself places Peter's first Quodlibet in 1296 (see his *La littérature* . . . , Vol. 1, pp. 257–59; also Vol. 2 [Paris, 1935], p. 375).

[50] See Wippel, *op. cit.*, pp. 378–79. For the reference to Pelzer see n. 46 above.

[51] See Wippel, pp. 379, 383–84. As we indicate in that same context (see pp.

A word remains to be said about Quodlibet 15. Prior to 1934 only fourteen of Godfrey's Quodlibets were known. In an article published at that time, Lottin announced that a fifteenth had been discovered in a Louvain manuscript. Although he was able to establish Godfrey's authorship of this quodlibet in that article, Lottin acknowledged his inability at that time to date it.[52] In a note appended to his 1937 edition of this same Quodlibet he indicated that as a result of comparisons with other manuscripts known to have been transcribed by Godfrey himself he was now satisfied that the Louvain manuscript of Quodlibet 15 was in fact an autograph, coming from Godfrey's own hand.[53] And in 1938 Glorieux managed to date this Quodlibet because of some references therein to Gonsalvus of Spain's Disputed Questions 11 and

---

384–86), one cannot entirely rule out the possibility that Godfrey may have retouched some of his Quodlibets at a later point in his career. Thus even if his Quodlibet 8 dates from 1291 and James's Quodlibet 1 from 1293, Godfrey could have incorporated reference to it in his later retouched version. But this would be a more extreme solution to the problem and one which we do not favor in the present case. On the other hand, appeal to such an explanation seems to be necessary if one is to account for explicit references in Godfrey's Quodlibet 1, q. 11 to the bull of Boniface VIII, *Detestandae*. These references have already been noted by F. Delorme, "Autour d'un apocryphe scotiste. Le *De rerum principio* et Godefroy de Fontaines," *La France franciscaine* 8 (1925), p. 295, n. 1; and by P. Tihon, *Foi et théologie selon Godefroid de Fontaines*, p. 202, n. 5. Delorme's suggestion that Quodlibet 1 be redated from 1285 until after the Bull of February 1299 (1300 according to Delorme) can hardly be accepted since it would involve a radical modification of the relative order of Godfrey's Quodlibets. For Godfrey's text see PB 2.30–33. Apparent references by Godfrey in Quodlibet 10, q. 12 to Peter of Auvergne's Quodlibet 1, q. 21 have been pointed out by G. Cannizzo, and pose another problem. See his "I 'Quodlibeta' di Pietro d'Auvergne," *Revista di filosofia neo-scolastica* 56 (1964), pp. 495, 497, n. 14a; and 57 (1965), p. 68 and nn. 1 and 2. Cannizzo suggests that the date for publication of Godfrey's Quodlibet 10 be placed after 1296. If, as we have suggested, Quodlibet 10 falls into the 1294/1295 academic year and especially if it was disputed in Lent 1295, publication of its final written determination could have been delayed long enough to take into account Peter's Quodlibet 1 of December 1296. But we do not believe that the original oral presentation of Quodlibet 10 should be placed after the academic year 1294/1295 because one should not date Quodlibet 13 any later than the 1297/1298 academic year. And we are not completely convinced that Godfrey is here following Peter's Quodlibet 1, q. 21, as Cannízzo claims.

[52] "Une question quodlibétique inconnue de Godefroid de Fontaines," *Revue d'Histoire Ecclésiastique* 30 (1934), pp. 852–59. See p. 859. Quodlibet 15 was contained in the Louvain manuscript *G 30* (fol. 241r–253r), but this manuscript was lost in the Louvain University Library fire of 1940. It should be mentioned that D. De Bruyne had first noted the inscriptions at the beginning and at the end of this work which attribute it to Godfrey. It was at his request that Lottin then examined it and established its authenticity (also see PB 14.305).

[53] PB 14.76, "Addendum."

13. Since the latter had been debated at Paris in 1302/1303, Glorieux concluded that Godfrey's Quodlibet 15 could be no earlier than Easter 1303, and should more likely be placed in the academic year 1303/1304, either at Christmas or Easter. Since it was apparently not included in the University stationer's list of *exemplaria* of Godfrey's Quodlibets dating from February 25, 1304, Glorieux also suggested that it had not yet been released for public circulation by that time.[54]

If our suggested adjustments to Glorieux's datings of Godfrey's Quodlibets 8 through 13 are accurate, it will then follow that one should place Quodlibet 14 in the 1298/1299 academic year. If, as appears to be the case, Godfrey was absent from the University for a time after 1298/1299, the discovery and dating of his Quodlibet 15 is one more indication that he had returned to Paris by 1303/1304 and had, in fact, resumed his functions as Regent Master in the Theology faculty. Glorieux's dating of Quodlibet 15 has been seriously challenged somewhat more recently by A. San Cristóbal-Sebastián. While he acknowledges the textual similarities already cited by Glorieux between Gonsalvus's Disputed Questions and Godfrey's Quodlibet, he argues that they run in the opposite direction. Gonsalvus was referring to Godfrey's Quodlibet rather than vice versa. Hence Quodlibet 15 will have to be dated prior to 1302/1303 and should, he contends, be placed at Christmas 1286. Since we have examined San Cristóbal-Sebastián's arguments for this radical redating on another occasion and found them wanting, we shall content ourselves here with reasserting our conviction that Glorieux's proposed dating of Quodlibet 15 is to be retained.[55]

As regards the dates for Godfrey's Quodlibets, therefore, both Glorieux's findings and our suggested adjustments may be summed up as follows:[56]

	Glorieux	Wippel
Quodlibet 1	Christmas 1285	Christmas 1285
Quodlibet 2	Easter 1286	Easter 1286
Quodlibet 3	Christmas 1286	Christmas 1286
Quodlibet 4	1287	1287
Quodlibet 5	1288	1288

[54] "Notations brèves sur Godefroid de Fontaines," *Recherches de Théologie ancienne et médiévale* 11 (1939), pp. 171–72.

[55] See San Cristóbal-Sebastián, *Controversias acerca de la voluntad desde 1270 a 1300 (Estudio histórico-doctrinal),* (Madrid, 1958), pp. 109–10, 111–18. For further references and for detailed discussion of all of this see our "Godfrey of Fontaines: the Date of Quodlibet 15," *passim.*

[56] For Glorieux see *La littérature quodlibétique . . .* , Vol. 1, pp. 149–68.

Quodlibet 6	1289 (Christmas, Lottin)[57]	Christmas 1289
Quodlibet 7	1290	1290/1291 or 1291/1292
Quodlibet 8	1291	1292/1293
Quodlibet 9	1292	1293/1294
Quodlibet 10	1293	1294/1295
Quodlibet 11	1294	1295/1296
Quodlibet 12	1295	1296/1297
Quodlibet 13	1296	1297/1298
Quodlibet 14	1297	1298/1299
Quodlibet 15	1303/1304	1303/1304

As one may gather from the above, our modifications would imply that either in the academic year 1290/1291 or else in 1291/1292 Godfrey did not conduct a quodlibetal dispute. And while we would not claim absolute certitude for each of the proposed datings, in the absence of evidence to the contrary we shall accept them for all practical purposes in the present study. The evidence for this as their correct relative sequence is, in our opinion, especially strong.

Some comments are now in order with respect to the form of Godfrey's Quodlibets. As regards Quodlibets 1 through 4, De Wulf has suggested that the long version of the same published in *Les Philosophes Belges* is really a *reportatio* taken down by someone else rather than a direct copy of Godfrey's final written determination.[58] Since the particular questions in each of these Quodlibets do appear in ordered sequence, it will follow that these *reportationes* are not based on the first day when each was conducted but rather on Godfrey's review or *resumptio* on some following day. Moreover, shorter versions of Quodlibets 3 and 4 have also been preserved and have been edited after the longer versions of the same.[59] One might wonder whether Godfrey himself was directly responsible for these abbreviated versions or whether they were summarized in their present form by someone else. Since Lottin has identified Quodlibet 15 as an abbreviated version and even as Godfrey's autograph, he has suggested that Godfrey must have authored the original version of the *abbreviationes* of Quodlibets 3 and 4 as well.[60] Hoffmans has proposed that the same is true of the abridgments of

[57] See his "Le libre arbitre chez Godefroid de Fontaines," *Revue Néoscolastique de Philosophie* 40 (1937), p. 217, n. 3.

[58] PB 2.V, XI, XV–XVI; also see his *Un théologien-philosophe . . .* , pp. 64ff.

[59] For these see PB 2.301–54. For De Wulf's discussion of these see PB 2.XIV–XVI. Note that he regards the short versions as *reportationes* as well. Also see Arway, *op. cit.*, pp. 199–200.

[60] "Une question quodlibétique inconnue . . . ," p. 857 and n. 1. But Lottin does

other Quodlibets which are present in some manuscripts and which remain unedited.[61] But P. Stella has questioned this conclusion and has suggested that Hervé of Nedellec is the person responsible for summing up Quodlibets 3 and 4 in their shorter versions.[62] In our opinion, the issue is still open.

Consequently, it seems wiser to give greater interpretative weight to Quodlibets 5 through 15 than to Quodlibets 1 through 4 in the event of any possible conflict between them, although we have found few examples of such. And one cannot rule out the possibility that Godfrey's thinking on certain points may have developed over the course of his years as Regent Master. Secondly, if Lottin and Hoffmans are correct in attributing the present form of the shorter versions of Quodlibets 3 and 4 to Godfrey, then it would seem that somewhat greater interpretative value should be assigned to these than to the longer versions of the same. But as we have mentioned above, this point is disputed. Whether or not the shorter versions owe their present form to Godfrey, both the longer and shorter versions are at the very least *reportationes* and/or *abbreviationes* of Godfrey's Quodlibets and therefore important sources for his thought. In certain instances the shorter versions of particular questions within Quodlibets 3 and 4 are more tightly organized than the longer versions. Because of this, we shall at times turn to them for assistance in interpreting the longer versions. We have found few if any significant doctrinal discrepancies between the two as regards Godfrey's metaphysical thought, although at times certain points present in one will be missing from the other.

Scholars have also wondered about the literary form represented by Quodlibet 14. It does not seem to fit easily into the traditional mold of a quodlibetal debate. In fact, it is sometimes referred to as the "long Question" or the "Disputed Question" which comes after Quodlibet 9 (meaning thereby Quodlibet 13). But on other occasions, and especially in the earliest manuscripts, it is simply identified as Quodlibet 14. Given this, Pelzer indicates that Lottin eventually confided to him in a private communication that in his opinion it is not a Quodlibet at all, but rather a Disputed Question.[63] And since it does not quite fit into the classical mold for Disputed Questions either, Glorieux went on to suggest that it might be a new kind, perhaps the

---

not state that we now possess Godfrey's autograph of the short versions of Quodlibets 3 and 4, as one might perhaps conclude from an imprecise remark in our "Godfrey of Fontaines and the Real Distinction . . . ," p. 387.

[61] PB 14.305.

[62] "Teologi e teologia nelle 'reprobationes' di Bernardo d'Auvergne ai Quodlibeti di Goffredo di Fontaines," *Salesianum* 19 (1957), pp. 185–86.

[63] On this see Pelzer, PB 14.223–24.

Sorbonique, about which relatively little is known.[64] But it is apparently included in the University stationer's list of 1304 along with Quodlibets 5 through 13.[65] Without attempting to resolve this issue of its proper form, therefore, here we shall continue to refer to it as Quodlibet 14 for the sake of convenience.

Reference has been made to the fact that Godfrey also conducted Ordinary Disputed Questions. Three of these have been edited together with the text of Quodlibet 15 in *Les Philosophes Belges.*[66] In addition, a number of "Disputed and Abbreviated Questions" have survived. Many of these are included in two manuscripts, Bruges *Stadsbibliot. 491,* and Vatican, *Borghese 122.*[67] Some of these have also been edited either in whole or in part, while many are still unedited. The numbering of these questions differs in the two manuscripts in which most are found and another numbering is provided by an important alphabetical table of contents in the Vatican manuscript *Borghese 164.*[68] Here we shall follow the numbering provided by *Borghese 164* in referring to these questions, with the exception of two which are not mentioned there. In these cases we shall simply cite them according to the manuscript(s) in which they are located.

Although in 1913 Pelzer assigned these questions to Hervé of Nedellec rather than to Godfrey, he subsequently changed his mind.[69] That they are to be attributed to Godfrey is generally acknowledged today and this on the strength of two explicit and independent testimonies. Thus, as Pelzer himself has shown to great effect, the table in *Borghese 164* names seventeen of them

[64] "Notations brèves . . . ," pp. 170–71; *Aux origines de la Sorbonne . . . I,* pp. 131–32.

[65] See n. 40 above.

[66] PB 14.77–138.

[67] For descriptions of the Bruges manuscript see A. Dondaine, in A. De Poorter, *Catalogue des manuscrits de la Bibliothèque publique de la ville de Bruges* (Paris, 1934), pp. 561–70; Pelzer, PB 14.293–300. For Pelzer's description of the Borghese manuscript see PB 14.279–89. Also see A. Maier, *Codices Burghesiani Bibliothecae Vaticanae, Studi e Testi* 170 (Città del Vaticano, 1952), pp. 159–60; also see p. 213 for a description of *Borghese 164* which will be referred to below. In a table at the end of *Borgh. 122* fifteen of the twenty questions contained in that manuscript are listed under the title *Quaestiones Godefridi disputatae et abbreviatae* (fol. 175ra). See fol. 175rb for the titles of these fifteen questions.

[68] For a valuable analysis of this manuscript insofar as it lists and identifies seventeen of Godfrey's Disputed Questions see Pelzer, PB 14.259–61. There he has also transcribed these references to Godfrey's questions which are themselves identified by the manuscript as "Disputed Questions."

[69] See "Godefroid de Fontaines. Les manuscrits . . . ," p. 530; PB 14.285–86.

and assigns them to Godfrey.[70] Sixteen of these are included in *Bruges 491*.[71] Moreover, fifteen of the twenty questions included in the series contained in *Borghese 122* are explicitly attributed to Godfrey by a table at the end of that manuscript.[72] And as we have already indicated, many of these questions are found both in *Borghese 122* and in *Bruges 491*. Certain questions which are not present in *Borghese 122* will not, of course, be assigned to Godfrey by the table with which that manuscript concludes. But since they are attributed to him by *Borghese 164* and are at the same time associated with other Godfridian questions in *Bruges 491*, their authenticity is also assured.[73] Further support for their authenticity can be offered in individual cases on the strength of internal evidence.[74]

Since those individual Disputed Questions which have been edited are widely scattered, it may be helpful to the reader for us to list them here according to their numbering in *Borghese 164*.[75]

1. "Utrum virtutes insint nobis a natura" (Neumann, *Der Mensch* . . . , pp. 155–59).

4. "Utrum morales sint priores intellectualibus" (Lottin, *Psychologie et morale aux XIIe et XIIIe siècles*, T. IV, 3rd pt. [Louvain, 1954], pp. 581–88).

5. "Utrum virtutes sint connexae" (Lottin, *op. cit.*, pp. 591–97).

7. "Utrum homo consequatur finem per operationem intellectus vel (voluntatis)" (Neumann, *Der Mensch* . . . , pp. 162–64).

8. "Utrum visio sit principalior in beatitudine" (Neumann, *op. cit.*, pp. 165–66).

9. "Utrum operationes angelicae mensurentur tempore" (Wippel, "Godfrey of Fontaines: Disputed Questions 9, 10 and 12," pp. 356–61).

---

[70] PB 14.260–61.

[71] PB 14.286–87. Note the helpful chart on p. 287 which correlates the questions contained both in *Bruges 491* and *Borgh. 122* with those questions listed in the table of *Borghese 164*. As Pelzer also indicates in the same context, at least thirteen of the questions included in the table of *Borgh. 164* are preserved in *Borgh. 122*.

[72] See n. 67 above.

[73] See Pelzer's chart (PB 14.287). And see our "Godfrey of Fontaines: Disputed Questions 9, 10 and 12," pp. 352–54.

[74] See, for instance, the similarity in doctrine and in argumentation that obtains between Disputed Question 12 and Godfrey's Quodlibets as indicated below in Ch. IV.

[75] Since there are slight variations in the titles as they appear in *Bruges 491*, in *Borghese 122*, and as they are listed in *Borghese 164* we shall here follow the last mentioned source. For which see Pelzer, PB 14.260–61. Note too that not all of these have been edited either *in toto* or critically.

10. "Utrum tempus mensurans operationes angelorum componatur ex indivisibilibus" (Wippel, *op. cit,* pp. 361–65).

11. "Utrum praeter acquisitas oportet ponere infusas" (Lottin, *Psychologie et morale* . . . , T. III, 2nd pt. [Louvain, 1949], pp. 497–502; according to a longer and a shorter redaction).

12. "Utrum anima sit immediatum principium suae operationis" (Wippel, pp. 365–72).

13. "Utrum habitus sit in anima secundum essentiam vel secundum potentias" (Neumann, pp. 152–54).

15. "Utrum sit aliquis habitus in voluntate" (Neumann, pp. 160–61; continuation in J. Koch, *Durandi de S. Porciano O.P. Tractatus de habitibus. Quaestio Quarta* [Münster, 1930], pp. 60–66).

17. "Utrum circumstantiae plurificent actum in esse moris" (J. Gründel, *Die Lehre von dem Umständen der menschlichen Handlung im Mittelalter, Beiträge zur Geschichte der Philosophie und Theologie des Mittelalters* 39, 5 [Münster, 1963], pp. 655–60; but cited as Quodlibet 15, q. 6).

19. "Utrum vere virtutes acquisitae possint esse sine theologicis" (Lottin, in *Recherches de Théologie ancienne et médiévale* 21 [1954], pp. 114–22).

It is difficult to establish precise dates for these Disputed Questions. In treating of a number of these which he describes as *Quaestiones de virtutibus,* Lottin has suggested that they pertain to the period between 1285 and 1290.[76] If this is exact and if the same general dating may be extended to the others including those which are not *Quaestiones de virtutibus,* then all would belong to the earlier part of Godfrey's career as Regent Master. But as we have indicated elsewhere, a fairly lengthy section of Disputed Question 12 is reproduced in the *reportatio* of Bk I of John of Paris's Commentary on the *Sentences.* Since John's editor, J.-P. Müller, dates this work no later than 1296, one may conclude that Godfrey's Disputed Question 12 is prior to that date.[77] And as we shall see below in Chapter VIII while examining Godfrey's views on dispositions and seminal reasons, at least one of two other Disputed Questions which are not mentioned in *Borghese 164* but which are numbered 11 and 12 in *Borghese 122* suggests knowledge of a theory developed by James of Viterbo in his Quodlibet 2 of 1294 (or possibly 1293).[78] These two

---

[76] *Psychologie et morale* . . . , T. III, 2nd pt., p. 502, n. 1; T. IV, 3rd pt., p. 598, n. 1.

[77] See "Godfrey of Fontaines: Disputed Questions 9, 10 and 12," pp. 354–55. The text on p. 354, 3rd line from the bottom, should be corrected so as to read: "Compare p. 370, line 22—p. 371, 1.5 . . ."

[78] To distinguish these from Disputed Questions 11 and 12 as listed in *Borghese 164* we shall refer to these respectively as Disputed Question 11 (Bo 122) and Disputed

final points would lead one to place at least some of Godfrey's Disputed Questions in the early to mid-1290s. Once all of these have been critically edited and gathered into one place, more precise dating may become possible.[79] As will become clearer below, some of these are of value for our study of Godfrey's metaphysical thought, although the majority are of greater interest to students of his moral philosophy and moral theology.

Before concluding this survey of Godfrey's works mention should be made of his Sermon for the Second Sunday after Epiphany which has now been studied and edited by Tihon.[80] In addition, certain marginal notations or *scholia* in a manuscript belonging to Godfrey and containing copies of Thomas Aquinas's *Summa contra gentiles* and an abbreviated version of the *Prima pars* of his *Summa theologiae* have elicited considerable comment. The *scholia* on the *Summa contra gentiles* were published under Godfrey's name by Uccelli in 1878.[81] De Wulf refers to these and expresses some doubts as to whether they were in fact written down by Godfrey himself.[82] Grabmann also casts doubt on their Godfridian authorship and cites doctrinal divergencies from Godfrey's position as presented in his Quodlibets.[83] Glorieux seems to have been convinced of Godfrey's authorship of the same.[84]

Question 12 (Bo 122). Also note that what Pelzer and we ourselves refer to as Disputed Question 11 according to *Borghese 164* is in fact mentioned there as Disputed Question 41. Pelzer's suggestion that the number 41 really means 11 seems to be correct (PB 14.261).

[79] As we have indicated elsewhere, it is our hope one day to complete this editing project. Since we have already transcribed these questions from manuscript we shall use some of them in their still unpublished form in the present study. See our "Godfrey of Fontaines: Disputed Questions . . . ," p. 352.

[80] See his "Le Sermon de Godefroid de Fontaines pour le deuxième dimanche après l'Epiphanie," in *Recherches de Théologie ancienne et médiévale* 32 (1965), pp. 43–53. As Tihon indicates, this must fall into the period 1281–1283.

[81] These are contained in Paris *Bibl. nat. 15.819*. For Uccelli's edition see his *S. Thomae Aquinatis Summa de Veritate Catholicae Fidei Contra Gentiles* (Rome, 1878), "Appendix" (pp. 1–31).

[82] De Wulf first discusses the series of "philosophical questions" located at the end of this manuscript (fol. 305–12) and refers to the suggestion that these were set down by Godfrey's own hand as an ingenious hypothesis which is no more than that. He adds that if they were indeed autographs, then the same would apply to the *scholia* or marginal notations on the *Summa contra gentiles* in the same manuscript. *Un théologien . . .* , p. 68.

[83] "Doctrina S. Thomae de distinctione reali inter essentiam et esse ex documentis ineditis saeculi XIII illustratur," in *Acta Hebdomadae Thomisticae* (Rome, 1924), p. 150.

[84] See his "Un recueil scolaire de Godefroid de Fontaines," p. 44 (numerous annotations, three questions at the end of the manuscript, and perhaps even the entire

Neumann has studied this question rather thoroughly and concludes that they are neither to be accepted nor rejected *en masse* as having been written down by Godfrey, but require individual evaluation. Not all come from the same hand and some may indeed be due to him.[85] Duin regards many of these as being from Godfrey's own hand but also identifies a number of those contained in the final folios as excerpts from or *abbreviationes* of works by other authors such as Siger of Brabant, Boethius of Dacia, Thomas Aquinas, etc.[86]

Given all of this, Neumann and even more recently Tihon have not cited these notations or *scholia* as reliable sources of Godfrey's own thought.[87] We concur with them in this restraint and for two reasons. First of all, the authenticity of many of them is still open to question, so much so in fact that detailed comparison of each notation with known instances of Godfrey's writing would be required to resolve this. Secondly, and even more crucially, in our opinion, it would be misleading to assign to Godfrey every opinion expressed in these or for that matter in every marginal notation or *scholion* preserved in other manuscripts from his library. Even if one can establish with certainty that a given remark comes from Godfrey's own hand, one cannot without further ado assume that it expresses his personal position. Often enough such notations merely summarize or clarify the thought of the main text itself. As has been mentioned, many of these in the present manuscript are taken from works by other authors.

Before bringing this Introduction to a close, a word is in order concerning the method we have chosen to employ in presenting Godfrey's metaphysical thought. The nature of the sources upon which one must draw in reconstruct-

---

abridgment of the *Prima pars* are all in Godfrey's hand); *Répertoire des maîtres en théologie de Paris au XIIIe siècle*, Vol. 1 (Paris, 1933), p. 396 (where he lists both the *scholia* on the *Contra Gentiles* and those on the *Summa theologiae* as Godfrey's works); Lottin evidently regarded the marginal notations on the *Prima pars* as in Godfrey's hand since he cites examples therefrom (fol. 237r, 268v–273r, 294v, 300v–312r) to support his claim that the text of Quodlibet 15 in *Louvain G 30* is (was) also an autograph (see PB 14.76).

[85] *Der Mensch* . . . , pp. 9–11.

[86] "La bibliothèque philosophique de Godefroid de Fontaines," pp. 27–28 (where he assigns the marginal notations on both of Thomas's *Summae* to Godfrey); 29–36, 137–45 (for a description and identification of the various works excerpted or abbreviated in the final part of the manuscript, and according to Duin in the main by Godfrey's own hand).

[87] Neumann, *Der Mensch* . . . , p. 12; Tihon, *Foi et théologie* . . . , p. 10, n. 1. R. A. Gauthier also concurs in this (see *Bulletin Thomiste* 10 [1959], p. 868, #1894).

ing his thinking—Quodlibetal Questions and, to a lesser extent, Disputed Questions—reflects the wide-ranging interests of the times in which these Questions were debated and the equally wide-ranging concerns of those who proposed topics for Godfrey in his quodlibetal sessions. Because of this we have frequently judged it advisable to indicate something of the broader thirteenth-century philosophical background that set the stage for Godfrey's consideration of given issues. We have also attempted to establish for the reader the proximate context for many of these discussions within Godfrey's particular Quodlibetal and Disputed Questions. When the same issue is discussed by Godfrey at different points in his career, we have endeavored to bring out any variation in doctrine, presentation, or nuance by following him as he develops his position in his different works. Where no such differences appear, we have often adopted a more synoptic mode of presentation.

Chapter I.

Preliminary Notions

As has already been indicated, the primary sources for any attempted reconstruction of Godfrey's metaphysical thought are first and foremost his series of fifteen Quodlibetal Questions and then, to a lesser extent, his Ordinary or Disputed Questions. In none of these sources does Godfrey offer a complete presentation of his metaphysics, a fact that is not surprising when one bears in mind that he was by profession a theologian and that his Quodlibetal and Disputed Questions resulted from his official activities in that capacity. Nonetheless, a well-defined current of metaphysical thinking underlies these Questions. It is, of course, our purpose to recapture, as it were, and to present in ordered fashion this metaphysical thought. On many occasions he addresses himself to strictly philosophical topics. On other occasions he introduces a considerable amount of philosophical and metaphysical thinking in order to develop his answer to more explicitly theological matters. In our effort to recover Godfrey's metaphysical thought, we shall feel free to draw upon all of the above-mentioned sources and contexts as the occasion demands.

Since we shall be concerned here with presenting an exposition of his metaphysics, purely psychological, moral, and theological problems will not be considered as such, except insofar as this is necessary or helpful for a better understanding of his views on related metaphysical issues. The relative amount of attention devoted by Godfrey to different metaphysical topics has enabled us to divide the following exposition of his thought into three major parts as indicated by the table of contents, treating respectively of his metaphysics of essence and existence, his metaphysics of substance and accident, and his metaphysics of matter and form. As will gradually become more evident, if there is one underlying theme that runs throughout Godfrey's metaphysics, it is surely the Aristotelian theory of act and potency. In each of the three major parts of this study we shall find Godfrey appealing to this same doctrine, but in decreasing degree of generalization. But before taking up these three main parts, we shall devote this opening chapter to some preliminary notions which are also essential for any proper understanding of his metaphysical thought. With this in mind, we shall now consider his views on: A. The Nature of Metaphysics; B. The Divisions of Being; C. Analogy of Being; D. Being and the Transcendentals.

A. THE NATURE OF METAPHYSICS

In Quodlibet 14, q. 5 Godfrey refers to two ways in which sciences may be compared with one another. While the second of these concentrates on the relationship between subalternating and subalternated sciences,[1] the first has to do with the distinction between those that are prior, more general, and simpler and the other sciences. Sciences that are prior, more general, and simpler treat of beings that are in some way prior to the other sciences. In

---

[1] In terms of context Godfrey is here replying to an objection raised against the possibility of there being some general virtue that would be distinct from other virtues without destroying their character as virtues. The objection affirms that the general virtue would be related to the particular virtues as a subalternating science is related to a subalternated science. Since a subalternated science is not distinguished from its corresponding subalternating science so as to be a science *simpliciter* but only *secundum quid* and *ex suppositione,* so too the particular virtue will not be distinguished from the general virtue *simpliciter* but only *secundum quid* and *ex suppositione*. In reply Godfrey first proposes the method of division analyzed in our text. In this case he defends the genuinely scientific character of the special sciences. Then he proposes another division in terms of subalternation. This division arises insofar as different sciences may consider the same thing but in different ways. Thus one will have knowledge of the particular principles that are proper to it (in distinction from absolutely first and self-evident principles) *quia sunt* but not *propter quid* (knowledge of the fact but not knowledge of the reasoned fact). If another science also has *propter quid* knowledge of these same principles, then it is subalternating with respect to the former which itself is described as subalternated. However, so long as the lower and subalternated science does have certain and evident knowledge of its principles *quia sunt,* it will still be a science *simpliciter* and properly speaking, granted that it lacks the *propter quid* knowledge of the same possessed by the higher science. (PB 5.398–401). For more on Godfrey's theory of subalternation see Quodlibet 4, q. 10 (PB 2.260–64 and 335–36 short version); *Quaestio ord.* III (PB 14.127–28); Tihon, *Foi et théologie . . . ,* pp. 35–36; 120–31.

addition, they do so in a manner that is distinctive, that is, in a general way. Thus, if they also consider things dealt with by other and more particular sciences, they do so in their own manner rather than in that proper to the latter. It is in this respect that metaphysics is general in relationship to all the other sciences. Finally, Godfrey observes that because things that are posterior are not perfectly and fully known unless those that are prior are also known, full and perfect knowledge of the things studied by the special sciences will require knowledge of these first beings studied by metaphysics.[2]

This passage is interesting in that it suggests several points of distinction between metaphysics and the other sciences. First of all, metaphysics treats of things that are prior to the other sciences, "first beings" (*prima entia*). Secondly, it does so in more general fashion. Thirdly, in some way knowledge of these first beings studied by metaphysics is necessary for a full and perfect knowledge of the things investigated by the particular sciences. However, further questions may be raised with respect to these. First of all, what are these first beings with which metaphysics is concerned? Secondly, what is this general mode of consideration that is proper to metaphysics? Thirdly, in what way does complete and perfect knowledge of the things studied in the special sciences presuppose knowledge of these first entities considered by metaphysics? Unfortunately, there is no detailed treatment of these points for their own sake in Godfrey's texts. Nevertheless, we shall attempt to reconstruct his answers in light of the limited indications given there. We shall then be in better position to appreciate more fully his application of the terms "prior," "more general," and "simpler" to metaphysics itself.

It is clear enough that Godfrey did accept the general Aristotelian theory according to which theoretical philosophy may be divided into three parts—physics, mathematics, and metaphysics. Thus he notes that natural philosophy (*scientia naturalis*) treats of changeable body and that its subject is changeable body insofar as it is changeable.[3] And a passing reference in

---

[2] PB 5.399. "Dicendum quod in scientiis ordo multiplex invenitur; quia quaedam sunt priores, generaliores et simpliciores aliis, quae scilicet considerant de entibus prioribus respectu aliarum et aliquo modo, scilicet in generali, de his quae ad eas pertinent, ita tamen quod de his quae ab aliis scientiis considerantur, non considerant in propria forma; et secundum hoc metaphysica est generalis respectu omnium scientiarum aliarum. Et quia posteriora plene et omnino perfecte non cognoscuntur nisi primis cognitis, ideo ad plenam et perfectam cognitionem eorum quae in scientiis specialibus considerantur, requiritur cognitio primorum entium quae in metaphysica considerantur."

[3] PB 2.10. "Subiectum tamen scientiae naturalis, ut nata est esse de corpore mobili, est ipsum corpus mobile secundum se sub ratione qua mobile est simpliciter." See Q 9, q. 20 (PB 4.291): "Cum enim in scientia naturali sit subiectum corpus mobile secundum quod mobile. . . . ;" also see Q 11, q. 1 (PB 5.4 – 5).

Quodlibet 2, q. 7 indicates that he was aware of the distinctive character of mathematical abstraction, that is, the abstraction of a form from sensible matter.[4] Since in each of these cases being (material being, to be sure) is considered from a particular point of view, as mobile or as quantified, one would also expect to find Godfrey accepting the notion that metaphysics is the science that treats of being under no such particular aspect, but simply as being. As already indicated by the passage from Quodlibet 14, q. 5, metaphysics treats of that which it studies in a more general way than does any particular science.

In Quodlibet 10, q. 11 Godfrey explicitly states that the science of metaphysics has as its object being as being or every being under this general and analogous notion of being as being. He makes this point in order to strengthen his contention that one and the same intellectual power can serve as speculative and as practical intellect. In support of this position he has just appealed to the unity of the object of the intellect, which object he also describes as being as being, or each and every particular being as included under this universal and analogous notion precisely as being. Different objects and different kinds of objects, materially considered, will all be included under this formal object of the intellect insofar as they fall under the notion of being as being.[5] This passage is important, then, in that it not only presents meta-

---

[4] PB 2.105. "Praeterea, si genus et species et differentia dicerent diversas formas, non differret abstractio mathematica quae est abstractio formae a materia sensibili ab abstractione logica quae est universalis a particulari, quia utrobique differret re illud quod abstrahitur ab eo a quo abstrahitur quantum ad formas a quibus nomina imponuntur." Here he is criticizing a particular type of theory of plurality of forms which would multiply substantial forms to correspond to the generic and specific nature of the individual (see p. 97 for this theory). Godfrey's distinction between the abstraction of the form that characterizes mathematics and the abstraction of a universal from the particular (which he calls logical abstraction) parallels one made by Thomas Aquinas in his Commentary on the *De Trinitate* of Boethius, Q. 5, art. 3 (*Sancti Thomae de Aquino expositio super librum Boethii de trinitate,* ed. B. Decker [Leiden, 1959], pp. 185:20–186:24). While Thomas does not refer to the second as logical abstraction, he does call it the abstraction of the universal from the particular and notes that it pertains to physics and that it is common to all sciences. Cf. also his *In De anima,* III, lect. 12, ed. A. Pirotta (nn. 781–84).

[5] PB 4.349. ". . . quoniam intellectus ratione suae abstractionis et immaterialitatis pro obiecto habet ens secundum quod ens sive quodcumque particulare ens sub hac ratione communi analoga secundum quod ens; et sic ratio communis entis etiam est forma vel ratio obiecti intellectus, sicut etiam scientia metaphysicae, quae habet pro obiecto ens secundum quod ens sive omne ens sub hac communi ratione analoga, est una scientia simpliciter." See also Q 7, q. 11 (PB 3.379): "Prout in unaquaque scientia de subiecto oportet praecognoscere si est vel quia est, quod quidem si est . . . dicit notitiam rei quantum ad eius entitatem maxime confusam et indistinctam

physics as the science that has being as being as its object or subject, but it also identifies this general and analogous notion of being as being with the object of the intellect.

Godfrey analyzes the notion of being in some detail in Quodlibet 6, q. 6, while developing his notion of truth. The concept of being, and of each and everything as being, is first and simplest. Given this, he reasons, there can be no real addition to that which is signified by the name being. In the case of judgments there must be some first principle that is known first and per se and to which other judgments or principles are reduced, if there is to be no infinite regress. The same must be true of simple concepts. There must be one that is absolutely first and best known to the intellect, in which or to which all other concepts are reduced and which is itself included in all others. This is the concept of being as being, as is clear from a remark by Avicenna in his *Metaphysics*.[6] In this same passage Godfrey goes on to observe that

---

sub ratione etiam maxime communi sive entis sub unitate analogiae quam importat ens ad decem praedicamenta et prout est unum subiectum metaphysicae." For further references to the unity of the formal object of the intellect see *Quaest. ord.* II (PB 14.101) and *Quaest. ord.* III (PB 14.126).

[6] PB 3.137. "Cum autem conceptus entis et uniuscuiusque secundum quod ens sit primus et simplicissimus, ei quod nomine entis intelligitur et significatur, non potest fieri aliqua realis additio. Sicut enim in intellectu complexo oportet esse aliquod principium omnino primum et etiam intellectui per se notum in quod vel ad quod omnes conceptus complexi sive omnia principia posteriora reducuntur—aliter esset processus in infinitum—sic in intellectu incomplexo in quo cognoscitur quid est rei oportet esse aliquod unum omnino primum et intellectui notissimum in quo vel ad quod omnes alii reducuntur et qui in omnibus aliis includitur. Et est ille conceptus entis in quantum ens, prout patet per Avicennam, primo *Metaphysicae* . . ." Compare with Avicenna, *Metaphysica* (Venice, 1508), I, c. 6 (fol. 72rb): "Dicemus igitur quod ens et res et necesse talia sunt quod statim imprimuntur in anima prima impressione, quae non acquiritur ex aliis notioribus se; sicut credulitas quae habet prima principia, ex quibus ipsa provenit per se, et est alia ab eis, sed propter ea . . . similiter in imaginationibus sunt multa quae sunt principia imaginandi quae imaginantur per se. . . . Si autem omnis imaginatio egeret alia praecedenti imaginatione procederet hoc in infinitum vel circulariter." If one understands *credulitas* and *imaginatio* as judgment and concept respectively, the parallel between Avicenna's procedure and that found in Godfrey is clear. For this interpretation as based on the Arabic equivalents see F. Rahman, "Essence and Existence in Avicenna," *Mediaeval and Renaissance Studies* 4 (1958), p. 4, n. 2. For more on the Latin Avicenna's usage of *imaginatio* (and *formatio*) to refer to the first operation of the mind—simple apprehension—and of *credulitas* (and *fides*) to refer to its second operation—judgment—see A. Lobato, *De influxu Avicennae in theoria cognitionis Sancti Thomae Aquinatis* (Granada, 1956), pp. 86–88. Godfrey's argumentation here is so close to that of Thomas in *De veritate* 1, 1c, that we are inclined to think that Godfrey also had his text in mind as well, granted that both also explicitly refer to the text of Avicenna.

being is that whereby each and everything is what it is in its nature and essence taken absolutely, without any condition or addition. Consequently, nothing can be added to this first concept which would be other than being. Every other concept adds something to this notion of being, something, however, which does not really differ from being itself. This is so because the notion of being enters into every other.[7]

These two passages from Quodlibet 10, q. 11, and Quodlibet 6, q. 6, clarify Godfrey's meaning in describing metaphysics as a general science and suggest his answer to the second question raised above: what is the general mode of consideration that is proper to metaphysics? According to Quodlibet 10, q. 11, metaphysics has being as being as its object (or subject). In Quodlibet 6, q. 6 he states that the notion of being is first and simplest and also that it enters into every other concept. In other words, it is the most general notion, one that is truly transcendental. Consequently, Godfrey is justified in describing metaphysics as the most general science (and apparently also as the simplest) because it has as its subject the most general and simplest notion, being itself. And it studies this most general or universal subject from the most general or universal point of view, without limiting itself to the more particular points of view characteristic of the special sciences. Rather than consider its subject as material, whether as mobile or as quantified, it investigates it simply insofar as it is being. On this point, therefore, Godfrey's thought corresponds with that of Aristotle in *Metaphysics* IV, c. 1, where he states that there is a science that studies being as being and that which pertains to it per se. There, too, Aristotle contrasts this science with the particular sciences, in that none of these treats in general of being as being but each one limits itself to a particular part of being and studies the attribute of that part.[8]

At first sight, however, it appears to be more difficult to determine Godfrey's answer to the first question raised above: what are those first beings

---

[7] *Op. cit.*, PB 3.137–38. ". . . et hoc est id quo unumquodque est id quod est in natura et essentia sua absolute absque omni condicione et additione, ita quod nihil potest addi huic conceptui primo quod sit res alia, sed omnis alius conceptus rationem aliquam addit super huiusmodi rationem entis quae tamen non potest esse alia ab ente, quia ratio entis omnes rationes subintrat." Note the similarity with Thomas's remarks in *De veritate*, q. 1, a. 1: "Unde oportet quod omnes aliae conceptiones intellectus accipiantur ex additione ad ens. Sed enti non potest addi aliquid quasi extranea natura, per modum quo differentia additur generi, vel accidens subiecto, quia quaelibet natura essentialiter est ens . . ." (R. Spiazzi, ed. [Turin-Rome, 1953], p. 2).

[8] 1003a 21–26. For a similar contrast between the science that considers being *simpliciter* or as being and the others, see *Metaphysics* VI, c. 1 (1025b 3–10). Also see *Metaphysics* XI, c. 7 (1063b 36–1064a 5).

with which metaphysics is concerned? According to the passage from Quodlibet 14, q. 5, it is apparently because metaphysics studies these first beings that it is said to be prior to the other sciences. Moreover, a knowledge of these same first beings studied by metaphysics is required for a completely full and perfect knowledge of the things studied by the special sciences. Our analysis to this point has indicated that because metaphysics has being as being as its object or subject, it may be described as more general than the particular sciences. But it is not yet clear how Godfrey correlates "first beings" and being as being.

Godfrey also refers to the object of the intellect as being as being (*ens secundum quod ens*) in Quodlibet 2, q. 8. As he explains there, whatever shares in the notion of being and quiddity in some way falls under the intellect's object. A few lines farther on he observes that being as being is primarily affirmed of first substance and of all else insofar as it may be attributed to first substance. He then describes the intellect's object as "first being" (*primum ens*) and all other things insofar as they participate in first being and are attributed to it. He concludes that the object of the intellect is that being which is substance, especially first substance, and all else insofar as it is ordered or attributed to first substance.[9]

This passage is helpful for our purposes in that Godfrey readily passes here from "being as being" to "first being" to "first substance." By describing the object of the intellect as first being (and all other things insofar as they participate in it and are attributed to it) and then as first substance (and all else insofar as it is ordered and attributed to it), he has in effect identified first being and first substance. Consequently, it would seem that the first beings referred to in the text from Quodlibet 14, q. 5 as proper to metaphysical speculation might also be identified as first substances. Moreover, in his description of the object of the intellect and the object of meta-

[9] PB 2.135–36. "Et sic obiectum eius est ens secundum quod ens; et omne quod habet rationem entis et quidditatis aliqualiter habet rationem obiecti respectu huius intellectus. . . . Sed cum nec hoc obiectum habeat unam rationem omnino univocam (quia ens secundum quod ens quod dicitur esse obiectum intellectus non est quid univocum sed analogum, per prius dictum de prima substantia et de omnibus aliis per attributionem ad ipsam),—ita videtur quod etiam primum et per se obiectum intellectus sit primum ens et omnia alia in quantum quodammodo participant rationem primi entis et attributionem habent ad ipsum; ut sic et per se obiectum intellectus sint ens quod est substantia, et praecipue substantia prima, et omnia alia entia secundum hunc ordinem et attributionem." Note that in Quodlibet 2, q. 8, Godfrey is rejecting the view that really distinct powers should be posited in the intellect insofar as it is directed to the study of things necessary and things contingent. Also see Q 2, q. 5, for the view that being as being is the object of every intellectual substance (PB 2.86).

physics as being as being in Quodlibet 10, q. 11, Godfrey must also have first substance in mind. In each of these cases, of course, the universal character of this object is preserved insofar as it includes both first substance and everything else as ordered to or attributed to it.[10]

But one might still wonder whether the expression "first beings" as used in Quodlibet 14, q. 5 and his references elsewhere to first being or first substance as the prime analogate of being as being could be understood to refer first and foremost to the divine. Then metaphysics would be first philosophy because it treats of the divine primarily and would still be universal in some way insofar as it considers all else as related to or caused by the divine. Here we have in mind one proposed way of uniting the universal science of being as being of Aristotle's *Metaphysics* IV, cc. 1–2, with the first philosophy or theology of *Metaphysics* VI, c. 1.[11] The proper understanding of these passages continues to be debated by Aristotelian scholars,[12] but diversity of interpretation on this point was also well known by Godfrey's time. If Avicenna was often cited as one for whom the subject of metaphysics is being as being, Averroes was rather thought to have made God and the intelligences its subject. Metaphysics would be universal only in a secondary sense, in that by studying God it would study the First Cause (First Form and Ultimate End) of other beings.[13]

---

[10] For the view that being is primarily affirmed of substance and of everything else insofar as it is in some way related to it, see Aristotle, *Metaphysics* IV, 2 (1003a 33–1003b 19). Cf. *Metaphysics* XI, 3 (1061a 7–10).

[11] For an apparent attempt to unite these two perspectives in one science by Aristotle himself, see *Metaphysics* VI, c. 1 (1026a 23–32).

[12] For a review of recent contributions to this discussion, see I. Düring, *Aristoteles* (Heidelberg, 1966), pp. 594–99; also, E. König, "Aristoteles' erste Philosophie als universale Wissenschaft von den APXAI," *Archiv für Geschichte der Philosophie* 52 (1970), pp. 226ff.

[13] For interesting discussions of the solution to this problem proposed by a number of medieval thinkers see A. Zimmermann, *Ontologie oder Metaphysik? Die Diskussion über den Gegenstand der Metaphysik im 13. und 14. Jahrhundert, Texte und Untersuchungen* (Leiden-Köln, 1965); J. Doig, "Science première et science universelle dans le 'Commentaire de la métaphysique' de saint Thomas d'Aquin," *Revue philosophique de Louvain* 63 (1965), pp. 41–96 (on Avicenna, Averroes, Albert, and especially on Thomas); *idem, Aquinas on Metaphysics* (The Hague, 1972), pp. 172–213; S. Brown, "Avicenna and the Unity of the Concept of Being: The Interpretations of Henry of Ghent, Duns Scotus, Gerard of Bologna and Peter Aureoli," *Franciscan Studies* 25 (1965), pp. 117–50 (on the closely related question concerning the unity of the concept of being and its application to God). It is interesting to note that Duns Scotus devotes q. 1 of Bk I of his *Quaestiones super libros Metaphysicorum Aristotelis* to this question: "Utrum subjectum Metaphysicae sit ens inquantum ens, sicut posuit Avicenna? vel Deus, et Intelligentiae, sicut posuit commentator Aver-

Although there is no detailed treatment of this point in Godfrey's texts, it is clear enough that he did not accept this more "theological" or Averroistic notion of metaphysics. His references to first being and first substance in Quodlibet 2, q. 8 appear in a discussion of the proper object of the human intellect. He certainly admitted of no natural direct vision of the divine substance in this life. It is in this same context that he applies the terminology being as being to each of these, that is, to first being and to first substance. This in itself makes it most unlikely that he would mean by first substance or first being God or divine substance when he refers to being as being as the object of the human intellect and as the object or subject of metaphysics.[14]

In addition, in a brief reference in Quodlibet 1, q. 5 he explicitly considers

---

roes?" (Vivès ed., T. 7, p. 11). For the basic texts in Avicenna see in particular *Metaph.* I, cc. 1–2 (Venice, 1508), fol. 70r–71r, for explicit rejection of God as the subject of metaphysics and defense of its subject as *ens inquantum est ens*. In addition to the treatments of Avicenna on this point by Zimmermann (pp. 108–16), Doig ("Science première . . . ," pp. 73–82), and Brown (pp. 117–19), see E. Gilson, "Avicenne et le point de départ de Duns Scot," *Archives d'Histoire Doctrinale et Littéraire du Moyen Age* 2 (1927), pp. 91–99; A.-M. Goichon, *La distinction de l'essence et de l'existence d'après Ibn Sina (Avicenne),* (Paris, 1937), pp. 3–5. For texts from Averroes on this see *In IV Metaph.* (Venice, 1562), Vol. 8, fol. 64r–71v; *In VI Metaph.*, fol. 144r–147r; *In I Phys.* (Venice, 1562), Vol. 4, fol. 47rb–47va; *In II Phys.*, fol. 56va–57ra. For treatments of Averroes on this see Zimmermann, pp. 116–17; Doig, "Science première . . . ," pp. 53–60; Gilson, pp. 93ff; also by Gilson, "L'objet de la métaphysique selon Duns Scot," *Mediaeval Studies* 10 (1948), pp. 66–67, and *Jean Duns Scot. Introduction à ses positions fondamentales* (Paris, 1952), pp. 77–78.

14 PB 2.135–36, cited in n. 9 above. For further confirmation of this see Q 13, q. 1. Here, while discussing the nature of sacred theology, Godfrey contrasts its unity (or lack of unity) with that enjoyed by other sciences, in particular by metaphysics: "Sed cum ista ut sic principaliter considerantur [the things considered by theology], non possint considerari sub una ratione speciali ut pertineant ad aliquam scientiam specialem quae simpliciter et proprie sit una, *nec etiam habeant sic attributionem ad aliquid unum nec unum sic attribuatur alteri quod possint etiam proprie pertinere ad unam scientiam communem sive aliquo modo universalem, sicut dicitur de metaphysica;* quia et moralia et etiam speculabilia praedicta sub propriis et distinctis rationibus per se et principaliter considerantur; *nec unum illorum habet attributionem ad aliud sicut entia communiter ad ens primum quod est substantia,* secundum hoc videtur quod theologia in quantum comprehendit considerationem talium non possit esse vere et proprie sic una scientia sicut est una scientia quaecumque alia scientia humana . . ." (PB 5.175). As the lines we have italicized indicate, Godfrey here assumes that the things studied by metaphysics are ordered or attributed to something in such fashion as to assure its unity as a general or universal science. To illustrate this he then cites the way *entia* are generally ordered to that *ens primum quod est substantia*. Again we take this to refer to first substance as the prime analogate for the notion of being, which notion serves as the subject of metaphysics.

God's relationship to metaphysics. Although God is not to be regarded as the subject of metaphysics, the metaphysician does treat of him, not under some particular aspect but simply and as such (*simpliciter et absolute*). If a purely human science cannot know what pertains to God except by reasoning from creatures, nevertheless, as is clear from Aristotle's procedure in *Metaphysics* XII, it can at least do this.[15] In stating that the metaphysician can arrive at knowledge of God simply and as such rather than under some particular point of view, Godfrey is by implication contrasting metaphysical knowledge of God with that offered by a more particular science such as natural philosophy. Thus in Quodlibet 11, q. 1 he observes in passing that the metaphysician's knowledge of God in himself and as such (*secundum se et absolute*) is more eminent and more perfect than that of the natural philosopher, who considers him merely as mover of the first movable sphere. This is so even though God is also a mover in terms of all that which he is in himself.[16] In any event, Godfrey's statement in Quodlibet 1, q. 5 that God is not to be regarded as the subject of metaphysics is clear enough. When he describes the object of metaphysics as being as being he does not mean thereby a particular being or realm of being, the divine, and then only other things insofar as they are caused by the divine. He rather has in mind the analogous and transcendental notion of being as such.

---

[15] PB 2.11–12. "Item, constat quod licet Deus non ponatur subiectum in metaphysica, tamen metaphysicus considerat de Deo non sub ratione aliqua determinata, sed simpliciter et absolute. Quamvis enim scientia humana non possit cognoscere de Deo quae ei conveniant nisi ex creaturis, tamen non est negandum quin ex illis deveniat in cognitionem Dei quantum ad ea quae sibi conveniunt secundum se et absolute, sicut patet per ea quae traduntur in duodecimo Metaphysicae. Et secundum hoc metaphysica verius esset dicenda scientia et verius et universalius considerare de Deo quam illa quae considerat de Deo solum secundum quod glorificator vel defectuum suppletor." As is clear from the final remarks, Godfrey is here criticizing a particular view of theology defended by Giles of Rome, according to which it would not have God as its object (or subject) viewed *simpliciter* and *absolute*, but only under some particular aspect such as term of our glory and principle of our redemption. For more on Godfrey's critique of this theory in Q 1, q. 5, and for references to Giles, see Tihon, *op. cit.*, pp. 202–06. As Tihon points out, Godfrey easily passes from the terminology "object" of theology to "subject" of theology even in this same question without making any observable distinction between them (*op. cit.*, p. 202, n. 4). The same applies to his discussions of the "subject" or "object" of metaphysics. See the texts cited in notes 5 above and 17 below. We have used them interchangeably even as Godfrey does.

[16] PB 5.3 "Unde eminentior et perfectior est consideratio metaphysici de Deo secundum se et absolute quam naturalis considerantis de ipso secundum quod motor primi mobilis, licet secundum totum id quod est secundum se sit etiam motor." For more details on man's natural knowledge of God see Ch. III, sections A and B.

On the other hand, Godfrey does not exclude God from this notion of being. In Quodlibet 9, q. 20, while considering sacred theology's right to be called a science, he writes that the term theology can be taken in two different ways. According to one usage metaphysics itself is called theology. Although it does not have God as its subject but rather being as being, nonetheless God himself is the first and principal being. Therefore, knowledge of God and of those things that can be known of him by natural reason belongs to metaphysics more so than does knowledge of any other particular being. Godfrey distinguishes this kind of theology from that which is grounded on Sacred Scripture. The last-mentioned theology does not deal with being as being but primarily and directly with God himself insofar as he can be known by faith. As to our knowledge of God based on natural evidence, for instance, that because he is the first being he is simple, that he is being in act, intellectual being, etc., such does not pertain properly to the theology that presupposes revelation but to metaphysics.[17] It follows from this that, along with all other being, God, too, is included under that notion of being as being that serves as the subject of metaphysics.[18]

It seems, therefore, that we must leave somewhat undetermined Godfrey's answer to the first question raised above with respect to the passage from Quodlibet 14, q. 5. The "first beings" with which metaphysics is there said to be concerned might be identified with first substances and thus with the prime analogate of his notion of being as being. Metaphysics would thus be prior to the other sciences because it studies being as being (first substance

---

[17] PB 4.288. See in particular: "Sic enim metaphysica dicitur theologia, quia licet non sit de Deo praecise ut de subiecto, sed de ente secundum quod ens, primum ens tamen et principale est Deus. Propter quod ad illam scientiam pertinet cognitio Dei et eorum quae de ipso naturali ratione sciri possunt principalius quam cuiuscumque alterius entis. Sed loquendo de theologia proprie dicta quae traditur in sacra scriptura et quae non sic est de ente secundum quod ens, sed per se et primo de Deo non autem quocumque modo cognoscibili, puta per solum lumen naturale rationis, sed secundum quod per fidem in via est cognoscibilis, ista enim scientia dicitur scientia fidei . . . sic non est proprie scientia et sic nunc loquimur de theologia."

[18] Godfrey is here in close agreement with Siger of Brabant. For Siger's denial that God is the subject of metaphysics see his *Quaestiones in Metaphysicam,* ed. by C. A. Graiff (Louvain, 1948), *Introductio,* q. I, pp. 2–4. Note that one version of this question is contained in Godfrey's student notebook and was apparently transcribed by Godfrey himself. (See Graiff, *op. cit.,* pp. XVIII–XXI). For Siger's conclusion according to that version, see Graiff, p. 4: "Cum ergo ratio subiecti debeat esse universalis, Deus non debet dici subiectum." For more on this and for Siger's inclusion of God within the subject of metaphysics, being as being, see Zimmermann, *Ontologie . . . ,* pp. 181–86. It is interesting to note that Siger also refers to substances as distinguished from accidents (and from change and from privation) as *entia prima* (*op. cit.,* Bk IV, p. 186:10).

and all else as ordered to it). But one might also see in the expression "first beings" reference to the separate substances, God and the intelligences. In that event, rather than describe metaphysics in terms of its subject, being as being, in this particular passage Godfrey would have singled out the highest instances that fall under that subject. Because these, too, are included within its subject and because these are prior to all other substances, metaphysics, the science that also studies these, would be prior to or nobler than any other philosophical science. Or, since for Godfrey metaphysics studies being as being (as its subject) as well as separate substances (included within but not identical with its subject), it may be that the formula "first beings" in the text from Quodlibet 14, q. 5 applies both to first substances and to separate substances.

This final suggestion brings us to the third question raised at the beginning of this chapter with respect to this same passage. In what way is knowledge of these "first beings" studied by metaphysics required for perfect knowledge of the things investigated by more particular sciences? As Godfrey indicates within that same context, this suggested dependency of the particular sciences upon metaphysics is not intended to deprive them of their status as sciences. In a particular science one considers a particular realm or kind of being in terms of its own principles and causes. Since such knowledge is possible within that science itself, it truly deserves to be regarded as a science. But Godfrey immediately adds that knowledge concerning things investigated by such a particular science in terms of the principles and causes proper to that science will not be as perfect and certain as knowledge concerning these same things when they are also known in terms of their relationship to the things, presumably the "first beings," established in the higher science. Nor will such a lower science in itself be as certain as is that higher science in which things pertaining to the lower science are rendered more fully known and more certain.[19]

As far as metaphysics is concerned, then, in this passage Godfrey implies that the things proper to the particular sciences will be more perfectly and fully known when they are also grasped in terms of the "first beings" studied by metaphysics than when they are simply known in terms of their particular principles and causes. In light of our suggested interpretations of the expression "first beings" as employed in this same context, one might see in Godfrey's remarks the implication that one will have fullest and most perfect knowledge of the kind of being or subject (*ens determinatum*) studied by a particular science only when one has correlated this with the "first beings" or first substances that serve as the prime analogates of being as being, the

---

[19] PB 5.399.

subject of metaphysics. Thus one will have fullest knowledge of being as changeable or as quantified only when one understands it in relation to being as such. Or Godfrey may be implying that one will arrive at a fuller and more perfect knowledge of the changeable beings investigated by physics, for instance, only when one has in some way also understood them in relationship to the separate substances or "first beings" studied by metaphysics. Unfortunately, Godfrey himself does not explain his meaning here more fully. Instead he then moves on to consider another way in which certain sciences may be compared with others, that is, as subalternating and as subalternated, a discussion that need not concern us here.[20]

In his *Quaestio ordinaria* II Godfrey again distinguishes between the first and supreme beings studied by wisdom, on the one hand, and the particular beings (*entia determinata*) investigated by more particular sciences, on the other.[21] Here he is examining the virtues or habits of the theoretical (*scientificus*) intellect, and has just distinguished between intuition (*intellectus*), whereby one grasps principles; science, whereby one reasons to conclusions; and wisdom, whereby one knows first beings.[22] He observes that both intuition and science are multiplied in accord with formally distinct objects. Thus the science of physics is not the same as the science of mathematics and neither, therefore, is it by one and the same habit of intuition that one grasps the principles of these two sciences. But wisdom is not so divided and multiplied. If there are different sciences (and intuitions) in accord with the formally different kinds of beings studied in each, there is only one wisdom. This wisdom treats of the first and supreme beings which are causes and principles of all the others. And it also considers the things investigated by the particular sciences, although not according to their particular formalities.[23]

In referring here to the beings studied by wisdom as first and supreme, Godfrey seems to have in mind separate substances. In fact, in the following

---

[20] See n. 1 in this chapter.

[21] PB 14.109.

[22] PB 14.107. Note in particular: ". . . et sapientia quae est habitus cognitivus primorum entium."

[23] PB 14.108–09. See in particular: ". . . omnes alii habitus sunt respectu aliquorum entium determinatorum in quibus bene invenitur formalis differentia ab invicem, et ideo possunt tales habitus plurificari secundum speciem; sicut patet quod plures sunt scientiae; sapientia autem est de omnino primis et supremis entibus quae sunt causae et principia omnium entium determinatorum; et ideo etiam est de omnibus de quibus etiam sunt quaecumque aliae scientiae, non secundum eorum proprias rationes prout a nobis in via nata sunt cognosci naturali lumine rationis; et ideo non possunt esse plures sapientiae."

paragraph, while contrasting the mode of knowing characteristic of wisdom with that of the particular sciences, he again refers to these "first beings" and even describes them as separate.[24] If he does not identify wisdom and metaphysics in this passage in so many words, he does so by implication. And since he has assigned the study of "first beings" to wisdom here and to metaphysics in Quodlibet 14, q. 5, for one to see some reference to separate substances in his usage of this expression in Quodlibet 14, q. 5 will surely not do violence to his thought. At the same time it should here be noted that in *Quaestio ordinaria* II he also assigns to wisdom and hence by implication to metaphysics the consideration of the primary and most universal features of being, including the most general principles of reasoning that follow from being as such.[25] This observation, of course, squares nicely with his stress on the non-particular or general character of metaphysics in Quodlibet 14, q. 5, and in those other texts to which reference has been made where he describes its subject or object as being as being.

In sum, therefore, it is clear from the above that for Godfrey metaphysics is that branch of philosophy that has being as being as its subject. Being as being is the most general notion and is primarily affirmed of first substance and of all else as in some way ordered to first substance. Because it studies being as being, metaphysics is most general or universal in terms of its subject (being) and is distinctive in terms of its point of view (*as* being, rather than as changeable or as quantified). According to Godfrey's description in Quodlibet 14, q. 5, it is prior to and distinct from the other sciences because it studies "first beings," because its point of view is general rather than particular, because it enjoys greater certitude than the other sciences even when it treats of things also considered by them, and because it is in some way presupposed by the lower sciences without thereby destroying their nature as sciences. Two ways have been suggested in which knowledge of the "first beings" studied by metaphysics is also presupposed by these more

[24] ". . . quia, cum sit de primis entibus et sit considerativa primarum et communissimarum rationum, demonstrationes per causam differentes [read: dicentes, as suggested by Tihon, *op. cit.*, p. 173, n. 2] propter quid non habent ibi locum; quia etiam non inveniuntur sic proprii effectus quod possint ducere in propriam cognitionem separatorum secundum eorum proprias rationes . . ." (PB 14.109).

[25] PB 14.109. In addition to the text cited in note 24 above see in particular: ". . . quia non solum est cognoscitiva ostensorum ex principiis, sed etiam omnium principiorum sic, scilicet, quod est circa ipsa veridica, id est veritatis declarativa, non quidem per demonstrationem vel per viam syllogisticam directe ostensivam, sed in quantum ad sapientem considerantem communissimas entium rationes pertinet omnia declarare ducendo ad inconveniens vel impossible; patet enim IV *Metaphysicae* quomodo haec potest sapiens facere . . ." For Aristotle see *Metaphysics* IV, cc. 3–4.

particular sciences. Full knowledge of the particular kinds of being that serve as their subjects presupposes some awareness of being as such (and hence of first substance) as constituting the subject of metaphysics. Moreover, full knowledge of the particular beings studied in the particular sciences presupposes knowledge of their relationship to and dependence upon the separate substances considered by metaphysics. These two ways need not be regarded as mutually exclusive, since both are operative in Godfrey's view of metaphysics. Finally, he has also indicated that investigation of certain principles common to all the sciences in some way falls within the scope of wisdom and hence of metaphysics. This would appear to be particularly true of those that are based on the most general or transcendental notions, such as that of being itself.

B. THE DIVISIONS OF BEING

In Quodlibet 8, q. 3 Godfrey prefaces his presentation of his way of dividing being with this remark: Because essence and existence are really one and the same, whatever is true of or known of the essence of a thing is also true of or known of its existence.[26] He then proposes a division of being (*esse*) according to which a thing can be said to have being in two ways: being in the mind or cognitive being (*esse cognitum*), which he describes as a lesser kind of being (*entitas diminuta*); and true and real being (*esse verum et reale*), by which he means being outside the mind or knower.[27] A thing

---

[26] PB 4.37. "Quia ergo hoc pro principio est supponendum quod essentia et esse essentiae et existentia et esse existentiae sint id ipsum realiter . . . unde quantum est vel cognoscitur de essentia vel de esse essentiae rei, tantum est vel cognoscitur de existentia vel de esse existentiae eius." See Ch. II below for Godfrey's views on the relationship between essence and existence. The context for this division of being in Q 8, q. 3 is suggested by the title of the question: "Utrum creatura rationalis antequam sit in effectu sit capax gratiae sive cuiuscumque accidentis" (PB 4.34). In order to answer this Godfrey must determine if and in what way a thing can be said to enjoy being before it actually exists.

[27] PB 4.38. "Ad cuius evidentiam est considerandum quod, ut supra dictum est, secundum Philosophum, sexto Metaphysicae, res dupliciter habet esse: unum quod est esse cognitum sive secundum considerationem, quod dicitur diminuta rei entitas; aliud quod est esse verum et reale, et dicitur esse extra animam vel cognoscentem . . ." Godfrey develops his division of being in the course of refuting another one defended by Henry of Ghent. Here we have simply extracted Godfrey's division from that context, since Henry's theory and Godfrey's refutation of the same will be considered in detail in CC. II and III below. For Aristotle see *Metaphysics* VI, cc. 2–4. In c. 2 (1026a 33ff.) he distinguishes different meanings of being, including the

enjoys cognitive being only insofar as it is known by some mind. So true is this, apparently, that its cognitive being is to be identified with the knowledge of it possessed by that mind.[28] And real being, which here is identified with the total thing in terms of its essence and existence, is further divided into potential being and actual being. For a thing to enjoy being in potency is for it to have being in terms of its causes. For it to enjoy actual being is for it to have being according to its own nature with its completed or perfected form.[29] Finally, a thing may enjoy being in potency or being in terms of its causes in two ways: according to its intrinsic cause; and/or according to its extrinsic cause(s). A thing has potential being by reason of an intrinsic cause when such a cause, matter, for instance, preexists and can enter into its inner structure. It will have potential being by reason of extrinsic causes insofar as extrinsic causes exist that can bring it into real and actual being. Godfrey

---

accidental, the true, the categories, and also being as potential and actual. (By the accidental here he means that which is neither always nor usually the case.) After discussing being as accidental in cc. 2 and 3 he considers being as truth and not-being as falsity in c. 4. He notes that truth and falsity are not in things but in thought and then concludes: ". . . that which *is* accidentally, and that which *is* in the sense of being true must be dismissed. For the cause of the former is indeterminate, and that of the latter is some affection of the thought, and both are related to the remaining genus of being, and do not indicate the existence of any separate class of being" (1027b 33ff.), Ross transl. in R. McKeon, *The Basic Works of Aristotle* (New York, 1941), p. 782. For a helpful discussion as to how "the remaining genus of being" as found in this passage became the "diminished genus of being" in the Arabic translation of the *Metaphysics* and then in the Latin translation of that Arabic text and Averroes's Commentary on it, see A. Maurer, "Ens Diminutum: a Note on its Origin and Meaning," *Mediaeval Studies* 12 (1950), pp. 216–17. As a result, a number of the Latin scholastics applied the expression *ens diminutum* to being as accidental and/or to being as true (*op. cit.*, pp. 217–22).

[28] *Op. cit.*, p. 34. ". . . duplex sit esse: quoddam diminutum, quod dicitur esse cognitum, quo res est tantum apud animam per suam cognitionem, quod nihil aliud est quam rei cognitio. . . ." Although Godfrey is here presenting the opposed division referred to in note 27 above, he too accepts the first part of that division. In the article cited in note 27 above Maurer appeals to texts from Q 4, q. 2 (PB 2.234–35) and Q 2, q. 2 (PB 2.61) to show that for Godfrey "diminished being is that produced by the created intellect in judgment" (*op. cit.*, p. 220). However, in the text cited from Q 8, q. 3 and in that quoted in note 27 above *esse cognitum* is not explicitly restricted to that which is produced by the created mind through judgment. Here Godfrey appears to think that it is enough for it to be known by the intellect without specifying whether through simple apprehension or judgment. Moreover, he does not limit it to knowledge of something by a created intellect. See PB 4.39–40 for references to *esse cognitum* resulting from divine knowledge, and the remarks in our text immediately below about the *esse cognitum* of a rose and a chimaera.

[29] PB 4.38.

offers as an example a rose that does not now actually exist, but will come into actual being at some future time. Prior to the creation of the world and therefore prior to the creation of matter, it possessed real potential being only by reason of its extrinsic cause, God. Since the creation of the world it also possesses real potential being by reason of its intrinsic cause, matter. It may also possess real potential being by reason of a finite extrinsic cause as well, assuming that such a natural cause exists at this given moment. Finally, both prior to and after the creation of the world it will enjoy cognitive being insofar as it is known by the divine mind. In contrast with this a chimaera enjoys nothing but cognitive being both at the present moment and prior to the world's creation.[30]

In Quodlibet 14, q. 5 Godfrey repeats the same division of being in part but with different precisions. This time he notes that being *(ens)* is divided into mental being and extramental being. (This is further justification for our having treated his division of *esse* in Quodlibet 8, q. 3 as a division of being, the other justification being his explicit identification of essence and existence in that context.) Mental being is described as that to which it belongs to be what it is solely according to some consideration of the mind.[31] Extramental being is divided into being *per se* and being *per accidens*. Being *per accidens* is here taken as that which arises from the concurrence or coming-together of other beings which are not themselves essentially related or connected with one another. Considered as such, beings *per accidens* do not fall under the consideration of any science, and in particular not under the consideration of metaphysics.[32] Being *per se* is that to which it belongs by its very nature to be a determined thing in the order of reality. And being *per se* is divided into the ten supreme genera.[33] Consequently, under being *per se* one may

---

[30] PB 4.38–40. Also cf. Q 2, q. 2 (PB 2.63–65) and Q 4, q. 2 (PB 2.237–38).

[31] Godfrey proposes this division in the midst of a discussion of certain divine attributes and their relationship to and distinction from the divine essence. "Circa hoc autem plenius intelligendum est quod quicquid est in rerum natura est ens aliquod; ens autem dividitur in ens secundum animam et in ens extra animam, sive in ens cui convenit esse id quod est solum secundum aliquam animae conceptionem et in ens cui convenit esse secundum se in rerum natura absque animae conceptione" (PB 5.427).

[32] *Ibid.* "Ens autem extra animam dividitur in ens per se et in ens per accidens; ens autem per accidens est quod contingit ex concursu aliquorum entium ad se invicem essentialiter non connexorum sive habitudinem essentialem et per se inter se non habentium, quod sub nullius artis consideratione consistit. Propter quod ad considerationem Metaphysicae quae est scientia universalissima omittitur." (The context seems to demand *universalissima* rather than *vilissima,* as appears in *Les Philosophes Belges*.)

[33] *Ibid.*

distinguish substance (being *simpliciter*) and the nine genera of accidents (*entia diminuta* with respect to substance and "of being" *simpliciter* rather than being *simpliciter*).[34] Extramental being, therefore, together with its subdivisions, is contrasted with mental being. For the sake of comparison one may summarize these two divisions of being as follows:

According to Quodlibet 8, q. 3:

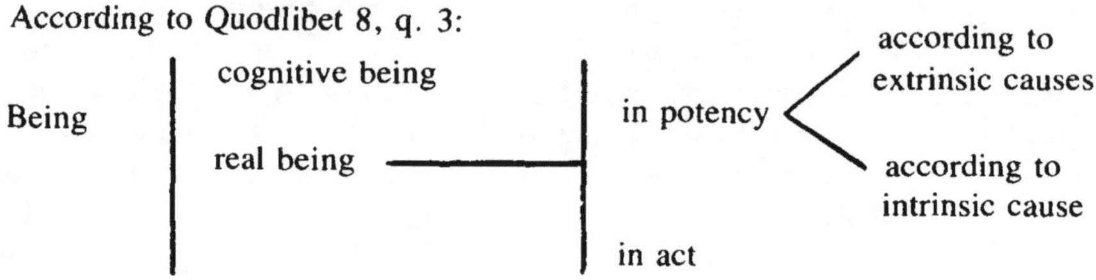

According to Quodlibet 14, q. 5:

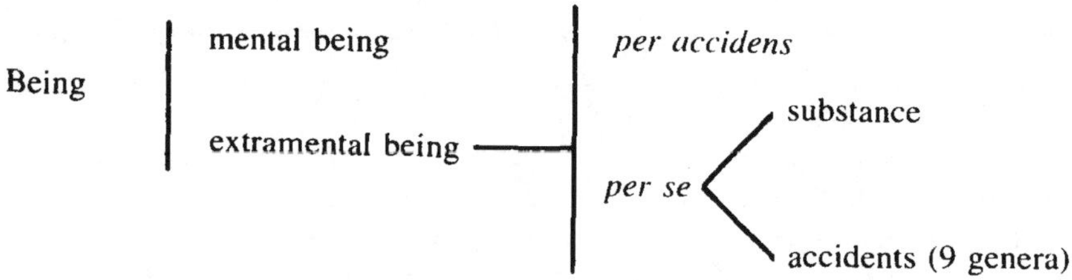

It seems that the cognitive and real being of the first division more or less correspond to the mental and extramental being of the second. In Quodlibet 8, q. 3 cognitive being is also described as being *secundum considerationem*, and real being is also referred to as being outside the mind.[35] However, in that context Godfrey has also considered the situation where something enjoys some kind of real being in addition to its cognitive being. This possibility is not raised in the discussion in Quodlibet 14, q. 5, presumably because Godfrey is there interested in stressing the distinction between these two orders. Be that as it may, the divisions are in agreement to this extent, that a thing enjoys cognitive or mental being only insofar as it depends on the mind's

---

[34] *Ibid*. Note in particular: "Quaedam autem sunt entia, quia sunt quaedam habitudines et dispositiones entis simpliciter quod est substantia. Talia autem entia sunt novem genera entium quae possunt dici modi reales substantiae respectu cuius sunt entia diminuta." This word order seems preferable to that found in *Les Philosophes Belges:* "Quaedam autem sunt entia, quia sunt entis simpliciter; quaedam habitudines et dispositiones quod est substantia." The *entia diminuta* referred to here (accidents) are not to be confused with the *diminuta entitas rei* applied to *esse cognitum* in the division according to Q 8, q. 3. See note 27.

[35] See the text cited in note 27.

consideration.[36] If it should also happen to have real or extramental being, this will be for completely different reasons. Finally, the division of real being into potential being and actual being could be applied to both parts of the extramental being of the second classification, that is, to both substance and accidents.[37]

C. ANALOGY OF BEING

According to certain passages already cited above in our discussion of the nature of metaphysics, Godfrey holds that the intellect has as its object being as being, or each and every particular being under this general and analogous formality of being as such. Consequently, each and every being will in some way be included under this single formal object of the intellect. At the same time we have seen that Godfrey also refers to the object (or subject) of metaphysics as being as being. Hence, the unity of this general and analogous notion of being must be sufficiently great to account for the possibility of one's including every particular entity under this subject and, therefore, of its consideration by the metaphysician.[38] For instance, in the passage from Quodlibet 2, q. 8 referred to above, Godfrey has noted that when being as being is described as the object of the intellect, being is not taken univocally but analogically. It is primarily affirmed of first substance and then of all else as ordered to or attributed to first substance. Granted, then, that substance and accident differ in genus, each will be included under being as being.[39]

---

[36] See PB 5.427. "Circa ens ergo secundum rationem est intelligendum quod in ente per se vel circa ens per se nihil ponit, sed tota eius entitas quae est ex consideratione animae est in ipsa anima realiter non in ipsis rebus conceptis."

[37] For such an application see Q 2, q. 2 (PB 2.64). "Sicut enim unumquodque genus praedicamenti dividitur in actum et potentiam, ut substantia in substantiam actu et substantiam in potentia, ita et unumquodque pertinens ad unumquodque genus ut homo in actu et homo in potentia et cetera . . ."

[38] In addition to the passages from Q 2, q. 8 and Q 10, q. 11 cited above in notes 9 and 5 respectively, note the following from *Quaestio ord.* II (PB 14.101): ". . . ita una sola est potentia quae dicitur intellectus possibilis receptiva omnium intelligibilium; hoc enim convenit sibi ratione suae abstractionis et immaterialitatis, ratione cuius non habet ens sub aliqua ratione determinata pro primo et per se obiecto sive pro obiecto formali, sed *ens sub ratione generali et analoga;* propter quod omnia entia sive necessaria sive contingentia sive quocumque modo aliter differentia non arguunt aliquam diversitatem realem potentiarum in intellectu, quia quodlibet ens est per se, et una et eadem ratione formali, sic tamen generali, ut dictum est, obiectum intellectus . . ." (italics mine).

[39] PB 2.135–36, cited in note 9. For the assertion that while substance and accident differ in genus, they fall under this one analogous object of the intellect, see p. 136.

Finally, from what has already been seen one might infer that for Godfrey the concept of being is not general or universal in the way in which a generic concept is, but that it is transcendental. This would seem to follow from his contention that nothing can be added to the notion of being that is not itself being in some way.[40] In other words, the concept of being will not only apply to that which is common to all beings, but also to the differences that distinguish them from one another.

In Quodlibet 3, q. 1 Godfrey attempts to establish the analogical character of the notion of being by showing that it is neither univocal nor merely equivocal. In order to prove that it is not univocal or simply one in meaning in its various predications and realizations,[41] he counters that if such were true it would then be a genus. But as Aristotle himself has shown, being is not to be regarded as a genus.[42] Godfrey offers two arguments in support of this. First of all, if being were a genus it would then be like a third and undetermined notion distinct from those determined notions into which it is divided immediately and per se. It is in this way that the notion of a genus is distinct from that of its species. But just as the notion of a given species is outside of and distinct from that of its respective genus, in like manner every particular and determined being would be outside this generic notion of being. Such a conclusion must be rejected, however, since only nonbeing or nothingness itself can be excluded from the notion of being.[43]

Secondly, just as the determined species of a given genus are not included within the notion of that genus itself, so too, the notion of a genus is not included within the notion of that which determines it to a given species, that is to say, the *differentia*. (Here Godfrey appeals to the principle that the notion of that which is determined is not included under the notion of that which determines, and vice versa.) Consequently, just as the determined aspects of particular beings would not be included under a universal and undetermined generic notion of being (as the first argument has shown), so too such a generic notion of being would not itself be included within the formal content of those factors that determine it to particular beings and

---

[40] See Q 6, q. 6 (PB 3.137–38), cited in notes 6 and 7.

[41] PB 2.161–62. "Declarato igitur primo articulo, declarandum est secundum, scilicet quod . . . de universitate entium non contingit esse aliquam unam rationem talem solum intellectam, ita quod ens, entitas, essentia, esse non est aliquid unum secundum intellectum quod de universitate rerum dicatur aut omnibus entibus conveniat." Or as he phrases it on p. 160: "Secundo declarandum est quod esse non est aliquid unum secundum rationem vel intellectum in omnibus, sed quod est in diversis diversum secundum rem et nomen."

[42] PB 2.162. For Aristotle see *Metaphysics* III, c. 3 (998b 22ff.).

[43] PB 2.162.

modes of being. Once again, one is left with the unacceptable consequence that factors such as individuating notes and more particular modes of being would not themselves include being in their formal content. Therefore, just as a genus cannot be predicated per se of its *differentia,* being could not be predicated of these.[44]

Godfrey concludes that the idea of being is a concept that is divided per se and immediately into all of those aspects according to which being itself is divided (whether primarily or by way of consequence) into its determined modes and various parts. So true is this that no aspect of a given being can fall outside the notion and meaning of being. Not only does this notion apply to the totality of beings in terms of the generic and specific features in which they share, but it also applies to the various differences between beings, including their individual differences. Precisely because nothing can fall outside the notion of being, therefore, Godfrey concludes that being cannot be univocal.[45]

So forceful is his rejection of any single, universal, and generic notion of being that would apply to particular beings and modes of being by being limited thereto through the instrumentality of specific and individual differences, however, that one might wonder whether he has not fallen into the opposite extreme and reduced being to the purely equivocal. Then its meaning would be completely different in its various applications without being grounded on any similarity in the real order.[46] Godfrey himself is aware of this danger, for he then protests that being is not purely equivocal, but falls

---

[44] *Ibid.* See in particular: "Secundum hoc ergo, sicut extra rationem entis communem et indeterminatam sunt rationes particularium entium determinatae, ita etiam extra rationem determinantium ens ad particularia entia determinata et modos entium determinatos erit ratio indeterminata communis entis. Et sic ut prius essent aliqua in entibus, extra quorum rationem esset ens, de quibus etiam ens essentialiter et per se non praedicaretur, sicut genus etiam per se [non] praedicatur de differentia."

[45] *Ibid.* "Secundum hoc ergo ponendum est quod intellectus entis est mentis conceptus divisus per se et statim in omnes rationes entium, secundum quas dividitur ens primo, vel ex consequenti in determinatos modos vel diversas partes, ita quod nulla ratio determinati entis cadit extra rationem et significationem entis, ut non tantum sit significatum entis universitas entium secundum rationes generales et speciales vel generum vel specierum quibus entia communicant et conveniunt ad invicem, sed secundum rationes differentiarum omnium usque ad individua. Cum ergo nihil potest esse extra rationem entis, sub nulla una ratione significat ens id quod significat."

[46] Cf., for instance, the following remarks: "Rationes ergo omnium entium quas propter communitatem vocis ens non determinat nec distinguit, communicant in ente quantum ad id quod est esse significatum in nomine tantum et modo significandi nominis grammatice loquendo, et non in aliqua ratione una qua contrahatur ad diversa genera per diversas generum differentias vel modos" (PB 2.163).

between the purely equivocal and the univocal. In fact, contends Godfrey, the name being may be applied to individual entities only insofar as they are connected with one another and stand in some kind of ordered relationship to some prime instance of being. This ordered relationship may itself be described as a kind of proportion and analogy and obtains both in the order of reality and in the order of meaning. Because of this, being cannot be regarded as purely equivocal in its various applications.[47]

Here Godfrey seems to have in mind a point already mentioned. If substance and accident, for instance, both fall under the concept of being, this is because there is a certain order and proportion between them. Being is primarily affirmed of substance, especially of first substance, and of all else insofar as it is ordered and attributed to it. But when one turns back to Aristotle's description of the various ways in which being can be predicated in *Metaphysics* IV, c. 2, and in particular to his example of health, one might wonder whether being itself is intrinsically and formally present in its secondary instances. These are so named only insofar as they are in some way related to being in its primary instance—substance. Thus if one asserts that a given climate is healthy only because it contributes to the health of the body, one is not really attributing health to climate as an intrinsic quality.

Certain remarks in Quodlibet 15, q. 3 indicate that Godfrey was well aware of this difficulty. There he considers an objection which asserts that truth and goodness will not belong to God formally and being will not be realized in accidents in the formal sense. Underlying the objection is the contention that if an attribute is predicated of a thing only because of that thing's relationship to something else, then it will not belong to the first thing formally. Hence, if truth and goodness are affirmed of God only because of his relationship to them as they are found in creatures, these perfections will not belong to him formally or intrinsically. And if an accident is described as being only because of its relationship to substance, being will not be formally present in the accident.[48]

In reply Godfrey first comments that when a name is formally affirmed of a thing, the name must point to a form that is truly present in that thing. Thus

---

[47] *Ibid.* "Nec tamen ens est pure aequivocum, sed medium inter pure aequivocum et univocum. Nam entia id quod sunt sub nomine entis participant ordinata et connexa [et: delete] ad aliquid unum cui attribuuntur, quae ordinata habitudo dicitur quaedam proportio et analogia entium et in essendo vel in significando, quod non convenit pure aequivocis." For the short version see PB 2.303. "Secundo sciendum est quod ens non est nomen univocum omnibus entibus. . . . Nec tamen est pure aequivocum, sed analogum. Nam inter entia est quaedam analogia et proportio sive ordo et in essendo et in significando, quia et in esse et in significari quaedam eorum dependent ab aliis."

[48] PB 14.13.

the form in question may inhere in that thing (as whiteness in a stone) or it may be essentially identical with it (as deity in God). Because the divine essence is goodness and entity, it follows that the goodness whereby God is referred to as good and the entity whereby he is referred to as being belong to him intrinsically and formally. But if something is named in a given way not by reason of a form that is really present in it but only because of its relationship to something else, then the name is not applied to that thing formally but only by extrinsic predication. Such would be true of urine when it is said to be healthy only because it bears some relationship to health as found in an animal.[49]

Godfrey now replies to the contention that accident cannot be described as being formally since it is so named because of its relationship to substance. Something can receive a given name because of its relationship to something else in two different ways. It may be that the perfection from which the name derives is found only in that other thing, the primary point of reference. (Consider, for instance, urine when it is said to be healthy. And, according to Godfrey, such will also be true of the sun when it is said to be hot because of the heat it produces, since it is not formally hot in itself.) But it may be that a thing which receives its name because of its relationship to something else also possesses the perfection in question intrinsically and formally. Thus all things are called beings because of their relationship to God as their efficient cause. Nonetheless, the being they receive from God is formally theirs. So too, an accident is described as being because of its relationship to the substance that sustains it as its subject. But to admit this is not to deny that the accident also possesses being intrinsically and formally, although in diminished and dependent fashion.[50]

Godfrey's discussion in Quodlibet 15, q. 3, therefore, sheds further light on his general theory of analogy. If he has refused to reduce being to the level of the purely equivocal in Quodlibet 3, q. 1, he there grounded this refusal on an ordered relationship or proportion that obtains between being's various realizations in the order of reality as well as in the order of meaning. And if being is primarily affirmed of first substance and then of all else as ordered to it, his reflections in Quodlibet 15, q. 3 indicate that it is also formally and intrinsically realized in these secondary instances as well. Precisely because being is intrinsically and formally present in its various instantiations, the term being cannot be regarded as purely equivocal. Because there is analogy and proportion of being in the order of reality, there is analogy rather than equivocity in the order of meaning as well. In other

[49] PB 14.18–19.
[50] PB 14.20.

words, the concept of being is itself analogical. In Quodlibet 15, q. 3 Godfrey has also indicated that being is formally present in God and creatures. It will follow from all of this, then, that for Godfrey the concept of being applies analogically to all levels of being, to the various modes of being, to all individual beings, and to the differences between beings.[51]

As we have also seen, Godfrey refuses to admit that the perfection being is found in the same way in different individual beings. To defend this position would, in his opinion, destroy analogy by reducing it to univocity, univocity in the order of reality and, consequent upon this, univocity in the order of meaning and predication. According to Godfrey one rather has to do with a proportional ordering of being to being, not with univocal presence of one and the same perfection (being) in all, which would simply be applied in greater or lesser degree to various species and individuals by determinations not included under the notion of being itself.[52]

D. BEING AND THE TRANSCENDENTALS: UNITY, TRUTH, AND GOODNESS

One does not find a systematic derivation of the transcendentals in Godfrey's writings such as that developed by Thomas Aquinas in his *De veritate*, q. 1, art. 1. Nevertheless, Godfrey does defend the position that there are certain fundamental properties of being which are really identical and convertible with it. Thus in Quodlibet 3, q. 1 he observes that the one, the good, and being are convertible. In his effort to show that being itself is not really

---

[51] See the texts cited from Q 3, q. 1, in notes 45 and 46 above. For an interesting correlation between the four types of unity distinguished by Aristotle in *Metaphysics* V, c. 6 (1016b 31–35) and different types of predication, see Q 7, q. 7 (PB 3.350–51). Note in particular that generic unity results in univocal predication while unity by way of analogy or proportion normally results in analogical predication. For more on the correlation between these types of unity (analogical, generic, specific, numerical) and the varying degrees in which a thing can be known see Q 7, q. 11 (PB 3.378–82).

[52] This point is brought out again by the following text from Q 13, q. 3 (PB 5.207). "Hoc patet sic: quia constat quod isti termini generales: ens, essentia et esse, non sunt termini univoci; nec respondet eis aliquid unum pro significato; nec unum quidem secundum rem; nec unum etiam secundum conceptum; quia non sunt nomina generum nec etiam specierum, sed sunt termini aequivoci non plura significantia casu quae nullam habent attributionem ad invicem; et ideo dicuntur analogi. Unde istis nominibus non respondet aliquod unum significatum in communi; sed unumquodque ens speciale est significatum per se per illa." Here univocity is rejected on the level of being, the level of meaning, and even on the level of the concept. We do not see in

distinct from that of which it is affirmed, he argues from its similarity with the one. While the one involves an aspect that differs in some way (logically) from that of which it is affirmed, it is universally acknowledged that it does not entail any real addition thereto. And since being does not even add anything in the logical order to that of which it is affirmed, he concludes that both being and the one are really identical with that of which they are predicated and with one another. In other words, being and the one are convertible with one another.[53]

In Quodlibet 6, q. 16 Godfrey distinguishes two types of the one or of unity: (1) the one that is convertible with being; (2) the one that serves as a principle of number. He notes that in a way every unity is a principle of number. This is so because every multitude implies some number and, although Godfrey does not explicitly make this point here, multitude arises from the multiplication of units. The one referred to in the second part of this division, however, is limited to that kind of number that is based on discrete quantity.[54] For the sake of clarity in terminology, we will distinguish with Godfrey between numerical unity in the broad sense (the kind that is convertible with being), and numerical unity in the strict sense (the kind

---

this remark a denial that there is a concept of being, but rather a denial that there is a single generic and univocal concept that would only subsequently be divided into its parts by means of differences added from without. Compare with Godfrey's references to the concept of being in Q 6, q. 6 and Q 3, q. 1, cited in notes 6 and 7 and note 45 above. But as Godfrey notes in the latter reference, this concept of being is divided per se and immediately into those aspects into which being itself is divided. Therefore, just as every particular being in the concrete order will either be substance or in some way ordered to it, so too the mind cannot stop in its knowledge of a particular thing with the confused notion of analogous being, but must know it as substance or as accident if it is to know it as *ens reale* (whether potential or actual) rather than merely as *ens cognitum*. For this see Q 7, q. 11 (PB 3.379, 1st full paragraph).

[53] PB 2.163–64. "Cum enim unum et bonum et ens convertantur, nec magis videtur unum importare aliquid additum ei de quo praedicatur quam ens aut e converso, immo etiam unum dicit aliquam rationem aliam ab eo de quo dicitur, non sic autem ens, et unum secundum omnes non dicit aliquam rem additam. . . . Unde nec videtur posse melius probare intentum quam per Philosophum et Commentatorem quarto Metaphysicae, ubi ostendit Philosophus quod ens et unum inter se sunt eadem re omnino, quia addita alicui nullam diversitatem habent ad illud, ergo nec inter se. Idem enim est dictum: homo et unus homo, et homo et ens homo. . . ." For Aristotle see *Metaphysics* IV, c. 2 (1003b 26–35). For Averroes, see *In IV Met.* (Venice, 1562), Vol. 8, fol. 66vb–67ra.

[54] PB 3.256. Note that q. 16 is concerned with this problem: "Utrum si corpus humanum resurgeret sine quantitate esset idem numero quod prius" (p. 254). For this same distinction in Thomas, see *In IV Met.*, lect. 2 (M.-R. Cathala–R.M. Spiazzi, ed. [Turin-Rome,1950]), n. 560. There Thomas criticizes Avicenna for having failed

based on quantity). Since the first type is found wherever there is concrete being, we may also describe it as transcendental unity or the transcendental one.

According to Godfrey, a thing is one or enjoys unity insofar as it is not divided from itself and is divided or distinguished from everything else. If a thing's very being is not divided from itself and is divided or distinguished from everything else, that thing will enjoy numerical unity in the broad sense, or the kind that is convertible with being.[55] This will be true, however, only insofar as that thing exists or subsists in such a way so as not to be subject to further division either as a genus into species or as a species into individuals. This type of unity will apply to every subsisting substance and to every accident that exists in such a substance. It will also apply to every subsisting angel, adds Godfrey, even if such an angel is unique within its species. As has been noted above, this is why such unity can be described as transcendental.[56] Finally, unity of this type is identical with the individual being (substantial or accidental) in question. In the order of formal causality it belongs to such a being by reason of that form whereby it is what it is and undivided in itself and divided from all else. It does not result from the addition of some other positive factor to being. Otherwise, since the principle added to account for such unity would itself also possess the unity that is convertible with being, another principle would have to be added to account for its unity, *ad infinitum*.[57]

In addition to the one Godfrey considers the true and the good in some detail. In Quodlibet 6, q. 6 he prefaces his discussion of truth with some observations about the priority and simplicity of being. As we have already seen above, he insists that there can be no real addition to being as such. Every other concept adds some aspect to being which cannot, however, be

---

to make this distinction (*ibid.*, nn. 556ff.). For other references to this distinction in Thomas see L. Oeing-Hanhoff, *Ens et unum convertuntur. Stellung und Gehalt des Grundsatzes in der Philosophie des hl. Thomas von Aquin* (Münster Westf., 1953), p. 131, n. 1. See also pp. 125–40 on the transcendental one and the numerical one. For Averroes's criticism of Avicenna for having failed to distinguish between the one that is predicated of all the predicaments and the one that is the principle of number see his *In IV Met.* (Venice, 1562), Vol. 8, fol. 67rb.

55 PB 3.256.

56 PB 3.256–57. For Thomas on this see *In X Met.*, lect. 3, n. 1975.

57 PB 3.257. For the same argument see Q 3, q. 1 (PB 2.164). For Averroes see *In IV Met.*, fol. 67va. For a similar argument see Thomas, *In IV Met.*, lect. 2, n. 555.

really distinct from it. This is so because the notion of being enters into every other notion.[58] Consequently, the true or truth can add nothing real to being. Because of this, reasons Godfrey, truth can only add to being a kind of modality or relationship, that is to say, a relationship to mind or intellect. Thus a thing is said to be true not simply insofar as it is viewed in terms of itself, but insofar as it is recognized as being capable of manifesting itself or making itself known to mind or intellect by reason of that which it is in itself.[59]

In attempting to develop this analysis of truth more fully, Godfrey returns to the point that being as such is the object of the intellect. Hence truth need not be superadded, as it were, to being in order for being itself to be understood. But when a given thing is understood by the intellect, it produces something in the intellect itself, that is to say, an assimilation or adequation of the intellect to the thing that is known. This assimilation or adequation of the intellect to the object known really depends upon that object and is, therefore, really related to it. At the same time, there results from this real relationship of the intellect to the thing a logical relationship of that thing itself to the intellect. Given this, and given the fact that the adequation or assimilation of the intellect to its object may be described as truth, one may then extend the meaning of this same term, truth, so as to apply it to the thing itself that produces truth in the intellect. Because being, as the proper object of the intellect, produces truth in the intellect that knows it, being itself may be described as true when it is so viewed.[60]

In like fashion, observes Godfrey, when one refers to a thing as intelligible one does not imply that intelligibility is a distinctive and superadded formality in that thing which enables it to move the intellect. One rather means that the thing is such by its very entity that it can make itself known to mind or to intellect. The same holds for something when it is described as true. Therefore, an object will first be recognized or understood as being before it is understood as intelligible or as true. It is only by recognizing it as something that can move the intellect that one also grasps it as intelligible or as true.[61]

In light of the above, one might wonder whether and to what extent Godfrey assigns truth to being or defends what is sometimes known as ontological

---

[58] See notes 6 and 7 above.

[59] PB 3.138.

[60] *Ibid.*

[61] PB 3.139. Note in particular: "Unde prius intelligitur obiectum aliquod sub ratione entis quam intellectus apprehendat circa ipsum rationem intelligibilitatis vel veritatis. Ex hoc enim quod cognoscitur quod est motiva intellectus apprehenditur ratio intelligibilitatis suae."

truth. He has maintained that truth is not in things or in beings when they are simply considered in themselves but only insofar as they are considered in relationship to mind or intellect.[62] And he holds that a given entity does not actually enjoy this relationship to intellect except insofar as it is actually capable of moving the intellect to know it. But material entities, as distinguished from separate substances, can move the intellect only insofar as they are subjected to the abstracting activity of the agent intellect and considered apart from their individuating conditions. Consequently, material things, when they are considered according to their being as individuals, are true in the sense just described only in potency. But when they are considered in terms of their essential being taken "absolutely," because they can then actually move the intellect and render it conformed to themselves, they are actually true.[63]

By referring to the possibility of considering something according to its essential being and "absolutely," Godfrey apparently has in mind a frequently cited distinction taken from Avicenna. We shall see more of this same distinction in Ch. II while considering Godfrey's reaction to Henry of Ghent's theory of intentional distinction between essence and existence. As Godfrey presents this Avicennian doctrine in the present context, a thing may enjoy being in two ways, that is to say, in reality and in the mind. But such a thing may be considered in three different ways: (1) according to its being in the mind insofar as it is actually understood; (2) according to its being in reality insofar as its quiddity is particularized in an individual existent; (3) according to its quiddity simply (*absolute*) considered in itself without adverting to whether it exists in reality or in the mind.[64] While Godfrey will

---

[62] *Ibid.* "Cum ergo secundum praedicta verum non addat supra rem quam denominat rem aliquam . . . , patet quod veritas non est in re secundum se et absolute, sed ex aliquo respectu ad intellectum . . ."

[63] PB 3.139–40. See in particular p. 140: ". . . sed ipsae secundum suum esse quidditativum absolute consideratae, quia ut sic habent rationem formalis obiecti intellectum actu moventis et sibi adaequantis, hoc modo sunt verae actualiter . . ."

[64] PB 3.140. "Ut secundum hoc, prout dicit Avicenna, cum res duplex habeat esse, scilicet in re et intellectu, et triplicem considerationem: scilicet secundum esse quod habet in intellectu quod est ipsum intelligere intellectus, et secundum esse quod habet in re quod est ipsam quidditatem esse contractam et particulatam in supposito, et secundum id quod est absolute quidditas quaedam secundum se quae, licet sic non sit aliquid in rerum natura secundum se existens praeter esse in singulari re extra vel praeter esse intellectum in anima, quia nihil habet aliquod esse nisi in re vel in intellectu, tamen nec hoc esse nec illud includit nec determinat secundum se. Unde ut sic non est proprie in aliquo ut in subiecto sed solum est aliquid ut secundum se et absolute consideratum." For this distinction in Avicenna see his *Metaph.* V, 1–2 (Venice, 1508), fol. 86v–87v and his *Logica* I, fol. 2rb.

always insist that a thing can never exist as such except in the mind or in reality, he apparently agrees with Avicenna that it can be considered in this third way or "absolutely." One might wonder whether a thing is to be described as only potentially true or as actually true according to each of these three modes of consideration. As has been noted, when such a thing (at least a material thing) is viewed in the second way, that is to say, as an individual and extramental existent, it is only true in potency. When it is considered in the third way, simply as a quiddity in itself and as disposed by the agent intellect so as to move or actualize the possible intellect, it enjoys actual truth. Finally, insofar as it is viewed in the first way, as actually informing the intellect and rendering it conformed to itself, it may also be said to be true in some way and, presumably, actually so.[65]

With these distinctions in mind Godfrey is now prepared to introduce a further precision into his theory of truth. He does so in direct response to the question explicitly raised in Quodlibet 6, q. 6: Is truth in the formal sense to be assigned to a thing that is present to the mind insofar as it immediately moves the intellect to its act of understanding or insofar as it informs and perfects it as its subject? In other words, when a thing is considered in the first of Avicenna's three ways, it may be regarded as informing the mind or intellect as a quality that inheres in its subject. But when it is considered in the third way or "absolutely," it is not viewed as inhering in or informing any subject, whether the intellect or the concrete particular. Nonetheless, it may still be viewed as an object that moves the intellect to act. (Otherwise, Godfrey might have added, it could hardly be known and discussed by philosophers.) If, as appears to be the case, Godfrey assigns actual truth to such a thing when it is considered in either of these two ways, is truth in the formal sense to be assigned to it according to each mode of consideration?[66]

Godfrey begins his reply by referring to "some" who maintain that truth in the formal sense belongs to the thing insofar as it actually moves the intellect and renders it conformed to itself rather than insofar as it informs the intellect and inheres in it as in its subject. In other words, this position, apparently defended by Henry of Ghent, would assign truth in the formal

---

[65] PB 3.140.

[66] PB 3.141. "Sed restat videre cui istorum formaliter et essentialiter conveniat ratio veritatis et cui participative et denominative solum." See p. 133: "Utrum veritas de re quae est apud intellectum se habeat in ratione informantis vel moventis" and p. 136: ". . . utrum veritas habeat esse formaliter in eo quod est apud intellectum, sic scilicet ut immediate movens et ad actum inducens vel sic ut intellectum informans et perficiens . . ."

sense to the thing only when it is considered absolutely and in itself or according to Avicenna's third mode of consideration.[67]

Godfrey rejects Henry's position and subscribes to what he here calls the more common view.[68] Truth in the proper and formal sense is not to be assigned to a thing when it is considered simply in itself or absolutely. Truth may be assigned to it "virtually" when it is so considered, but this is only to say that the thing considered in itself or absolutely causes truth in the intellect. In order to illustrate he draws upon the by now familiar example of health. Food is described as healthy only because of the health it can produce in the body of an animal. Hence it is said to be healthy virtually, not formally or properly. So too, a thing may be described as true because of something it produces in the intellect, namely, an adequation and conformity of that intellect to the thing itself. Since this adequation and conformity of the intellect to the thing is really another way of describing the intellect's knowledge of that thing, and since such knowledge resides in the intellect as in its subject, it follows that truth itself formally resides in the intellect as in its subject rather than in the thing viewed as moving the intellect.[69]

---

[67] PB 3.141. Certain textual similarities strongly suggest that Godfrey is here referring to Henry of Ghent, *Summae quaestionum ordinariarum* (Paris, 1520), art. 34, q. 5, where he is attempting to determine whether truth more perfectly resides in the divine essence or in the divine intelligence and argues by analogy from that which we know to be the case in creatures (fol. 210v and 217v). Compare, for instance, the following: ". . . quia hac veritate dicitur intellectus verus in quantum est quodam modo conformis ipsi rei tanquam suo exemplari, sicut tabula per imaginem in ea depictam conformis et similis dicitur rei exemplari ad quam depicta est tanquam exemplatum quoddam" (Godfrey, p. 141) and: "Unde et hac veritate dicitur intelligentia vera inquantum ipsa est quodammodo conformis rei extra tanquam suo exemplari primo, sicut tabula per imaginem in ea depictam conformis et similis dicitur rei exemplari ad quam depicta est in ea tanquam exemplatum quoddam" (Henry, fol. 216v–217r). And again: "Et sic quia veritas rei non dependet a veritate notitiae cuiuscumque creaturae, sed e converso, verius autem et dignius est unumquodque in ente absoluto quam dependenti, videtur quod veritas perfectius habet esse in re dicto modo, in quantum scilicet est actu movens et conformans sibi intellectum quam in intellectu" (Godfrey, p. 141) and "Ita quod secundum hoc veritas rei nullo modo dependet a veritate huiusmodi cuiuscumque intelligentiae creatae, sed e converso: verius et dignius est unumquodque in esse absoluto quam dependenti . . ." (Henry, fol. 217r). However, Henry's theory as presented here is far more complicated than Godfrey's summary might lead one to believe.

[68] PB 3.141.

[69] PB 3.142–43. For this same example of health in Thomas Aquinas see his *In I Sent.*, d. 19, q. 5, a. 1 (P. Mandonnet, ed. [Paris, 1929], Vol. 1, p. 486). There Thomas uses this example in order to show that while the *esse* of a thing (as distinguished from its quiddity) is the cause of truth, the formality of truth as such is

If we may apply all of this to the Avicennian distinction of the three ways in which a thing may be considered, truth in the formal and proper sense can be assigned actually to a thing only when it is considered in the first way, that is to say, as present in the intellect. Truth in the virtual or causal sense may be assigned actually to a thing considered absolutely, that is, in Avicenna's third way. Truth can be assigned to the individual existent, the thing considered in the second way, neither formally nor actually, but only virtually and potentially.[70]

In the above discussion Godfrey has been defining truth strictly, as involving an adequation between intellect and thing in such fashion that the thing manifests and declares itself to the intellect by rendering the latter conformed to itself. But in this same general context Godfrey has also referred to a more general and broader definition of truth. According to this usage truth implies an adequation of things to one another in such fashion that one is passively related to the other so as to depend upon it and be measured by it. Godfrey finds this notion in St. Anselm's *De veritate*, wherein truth is described as a kind of "rectitude" and is attributed to all things, even to actions, insofar as each has or does that which it ought to have or do. According to Godfrey, in using the term "rectitude" Anselm really has in mind conformity. Given this, there is truth in all things and actions insofar as they are conformed to the uncreated truth and being, that is to say, to their respective divine ideas.[71] Moreover, adds Godfrey, when truth is defined in

---

primarily in the intellect. Farther on in this same article, after having cited a number of definitions of truth, he appeals to that of Anselm as a general one that includes all the other meanings: "Quaedam autem datur de veritate, comprehendens omnes veritatis acceptiones, scilicet: Veritas est rectitudo sola mente perceptibilis" (p. 487). For more on this in Anselm and for Godfrey's usage of it see below. For the example of health in a similar context cf. *De veritate,* q. 1, art. 2. On Thomas's discussion of truth in his *In I Sent.,* d. 19, q. 5, art. 1, see J. Vande Wiele, "Le problème de la vérité ontologique dans la philosophie de saint Thomas," *Revue philosophique de Louvain* 52 (1954), pp. 545–49; F. Ruello, *La notion de vérité chez Saint Albert le Grand et Saint Thomas d'Aquin* (Louvain-Paris, 1969), pp. 177–227. On the discussion in *De veritate,* q. 1, see Vande Wiele, *op. cit.,* pp. 549–54. On Thomas's usage and interpretation of the Anselmian definition cf. M. J. Lapierre, "Aquinas' Interpretation of Anselm's Definition of Truth," *Sciences ecclésiastiques* 18 (1966), pp. 413–41.

[70] While this explicit application is ours, for support see Godfrey, PB 3.142–43, 145–46.

[71] PB 3.141–42. For Anselm see *Sancti Anselmi opera omnia,* ed. by F. S. Schmitt, Vol. 1 (Edinburgh, 1946), ch. 5 (pp. 181–82) on truth in actions; ch. 7 (pp. 185–86) on truth of the "essences" of things, that is, truth of being; ch. 11 (p. 191) for his definition of truth: ". . . veritas est rectitudo mente sola perceptibilis."

this general and Anselmian way, it can even be assigned to things that we ourselves cause insofar as they conform to that within us which serves as their cause. When truth is taken in this broader sense, therefore, it can be assigned to things themselves, it would seem, and not merely insofar as they inform the intellect that knows them. But when truth is taken in the strict sense it cannot be formally assigned to things simply considered in themselves, but only insofar as they are present in the intellect and known by it.[72]

In his discussion of truth in Quodlibet 6, q. 6, Godfrey has greatly emphasized what is often known as logical truth, that is, truth of the intellect insofar as it is adequated to the thing. This is not surprising in light of the specific topic proposed for examination there. In emphasizing the point that truth in the formal sense is to be assigned to the intellect as adequated to the thing and thus to the thing only insofar as it informs the intellect as its subject, Godfrey was probably influenced by a current of thought going back to Aristotle's *Metaphysics* VI, c. 4, according to which truth (and falsity) are not in things but in the intellect.[73]

At the same time, Godfrey's reference to the more general and Anselmian definition of truth indicates that he was also aware of and apparently accepted the notion of truth of being or ontological truth, meaning thereby the truth enjoyed by beings insofar as they are conformed to their respective divine ideas. In one passage he speaks of a real relation that runs from a thing that is measured to its measure and contrasts this with the purely logical relation that runs from the measure to that which is measured. Since he introduces this notion in connection with this more general definition of truth, one would appear to be justified in applying it to the truth of being enjoyed by things insofar as they are measured by their divine ideas.[74] It will follow from this that things are really related to and conformed to their divine ideas as their measure. But the relationship that runs from divine ideas to things, that of measure to measured, will only be logical.[75] And truth in this sense is to be

---

[72] PB 3.142, 144–45. See the latter context for discussion and application of these two definitions of truth to the practical intellect and its products.

[73] See 1027b 25ff. For Godfrey see PB 3.146: "Praedicta patent per Philosophum dicentem, sexto Metaphysicae, quod verum est in intellectu, bonum in rebus." For more on this see our discussion of transcendental goodness below.

[74] PB 3.143. It must be acknowledged that Godfrey himself does not here make this application. Instead he quickly returns to a discussion of truth taken strictly and his contention that when so defined it exists formally only in the intellect and virtually or causally in the thing.

[75] For fuller discussion of Godfrey's views on the divine ideas see Ch. III, Section C.

assigned to things only when it is defined broadly in the Anselmian way, not when it is defined strictly.

At the risk of some oversimplification, one may distinguish two great traditions as regards the philosophy of truth prior to Godfrey's time. One is Neoplatonic and stresses the truth of being. This was well known to Godfrey and his contemporaries through the writings of Augustine, Anselm, and Avicenna. The other, the Aristotelian, stresses logical truth, the adequation of mind to being.[76] Godfrey was obviously conversant with both of these traditions and to some extent, at least, incorporated each into his own thinking on the nature of truth. Nonetheless, he has just as obviously placed greater emphasis on the Aristotelian tradition.

Finally, we shall conclude this discussion of Godfrey's philosophy of truth by asking whether or not truth itself is transcendental for him, that is, whether every being to the extent that it is a being is also true. In replying one must again bear in mind his different definitions of truth. When truth is defined strictly as an adequation of mind to thing, Godfrey maintains that it is actually and formally present only in the intellect and not in the thing, either when the latter is considered as existing extramentally or when it is considered absolutely in itself as an object that moves the intellect. Truth in the strict and formal sense is not transcendental, therefore, but will only apply to beings insofar as they inform an intellect that is thereby adequated to them-

[76] For helpful historical background on these two traditions prior to Aquinas see Vande Wiele, *op. cit.*, pp. 522–27 (on Aristotle); pp. 527–31 (on Augustine); pp. 532–35 (on Avicenna); and p. 543 for a useful resumé of his findings on this point. Within the Neoplatonic current he distinguishes two lines on this, pure Neoplatonism in Augustine, for instance, and Avicenna's Neoplatonic Aristotelianism. We would, however, put greater stress on Anselm's role as a source for the theory of the truth of things (ontological truth) than does Vande Wiele. This is certainly the case with respect to Godfrey, and also appears to be so with respect to other thirteenth-century thinkers such as Albert and Thomas. See Ruello, *op. cit.*, pp. 130–34 (on Albert); Lapierre, as cited in note 69 above. In light of certain similarities between Godfrey's analysis of truth and that found in Thomas's *De veritate*, q. 1, art. 1–2 and *In I Sent.*, d. 19, q. 5, art. 1, Thomas himself is a likely source for Godfrey here. If Thomas also holds that truth is primarily to be assigned to the intellect and then to things, Godfrey's treatment is distinguished by his explicit connection of this discussion with the Avicennian threefold way in which a thing can be considered and his insistence that it is not the thing considered as an extramental existent but rather as abstracted and moving the intellect as an object that is to be described as *actually* true in the virtual and causal sense. On the other hand, one does not find in Godfrey's discussion explicit indication that truth is primarily realized in judgment as distinguished from simple apprehension (see Thomas, *De veritate*, q. 1, art. 2; *In I Sent.*, d. 19, q. 5, a. 1, ad 7; ST I, q. 16, a. 2).

selves. It would seem, though, that when one extends the meaning of this term to that which causes truth in the intellect, that is, to beings themselves insofar as they are intelligible and capable of manifesting themselves to mind, truth taken in this virtual sense is as broad in extension as being itself and will therefore be transcendental. Thus truth may be applied virtually and actually to things considered absolutely in themselves and virtually but only potentially to individual material existents. As Godfrey phrases it, when it is stated that the true and being are convertible, this is correct if truth is referred to that which causes truth.[77]

On the other hand, if one defines truth more broadly in the Anselmian way, it would seem to be in accord with Godfrey's thought to conclude that every created being will be true in this way. For every such being will be conformed to its respective divine idea. But while Godfrey would hold that the divine being itself is also known by the divine intellect and really identical with it, he could not admit that it is in any way measured by or causally dependent on divine ideas. Hence, if truth is to be applied to God, it will have to be in some analogous fashion and not so as to imply that his being is measured by anything, not even by divine ideas.

Reference has already been made to a text from Aristotle's *Metaphysics* wherein truth and falsity are said to be not in things but in the intellect. Godfrey cites this text in order to contrast the true and the good. As he interprets the passage, it means that while truth is formally in the intellect alone and only in the thing as its cause, goodness is formally in the thing itself. Granted that the act of the appetite (the will) is caused by and measured by that which is desirable in a given thing even as truth in the intellect is caused and measured by the object as it manifests itself to the intellect, nonetheless goodness is not merely in the object in this causal way but formally and really.[78]

---

[77] PB 3.148. "Cum vero arguitur quod verum et ens convertuntur dicendum est quod verum est de veritate causaliter."

[78] PB 3.146. For Godfrey's citation of Aristotle see n. 73 above. It should be noted that Aristotle's Greek text does not say in so many words that "goodness is in things." Nonetheless Aquinas finds this implied by the text, whether or not this was explicitly stated in the Latin version of Aristotle upon which he was then commenting (see *In VI Met.*, lect. 4, nn. 1230–34). And the point is explicitly stated in the medieval Latin translation of the Arabic text which was also surely known both to Thomas and to Godfrey along with Averroes's *Commentary* on the same. For this see Averroes, *In VI Met.* (Venice, 1562), Vol. 8, fol. 151vb–152ra: "Verum enim et falsum non

The two situations differ because in the case of intellection the act of understanding is completed once the object understood is intentionally present in the intellect. Thus the act of understanding may be described as a kind of movement of thing to mind which terminates in the intentional presence of the object in the mind.[79] But in volition the desirable object does not perfect the appetite merely by being desired. It rather produces a kind of inclination in the appetite toward the desirable object that will be perfected only when the object is attained. Therefore the object's exercise of causality with respect to the appetite or will of the one desiring does not terminate in the act of desiring itself or in the being which that object enjoys in the one desiring. It is completed only when the object is itself attained by means of another power and another act on the part of the one desiring—in other words, by the latter's actual possession of that which is desired. Because of this Godfrey describes the act of volition as a quasi-reflexive kind of movement that runs from the thing desired to the appetite or will and then back again to the thing itself.[80]

From this it follows that if a thing may be described as true by reason of the truth that it causes in the intellect that knows it, it will not be described as good by reason of goodness that it produces in the appetite. On the contrary, the will or its act of willing is to be described as good because of goodness found in the thing itself. A thing is recognized as good because of its capacity to draw toward itself the appetite or will of the one who desires. And if truth as such does not imply any real addition to the being that is said to be true, neither does goodness involve any real addition to the being that is said to be good.[81]

In the light of this contrast between truth and goodness, one might suspect that they are not convertible with one another but really distinct. In Quodlibet 15, q. 3 Godfrey touches on this point. When truth is taken in the strict sense as adequation or conformity of the intellect to the thing, then goodness is broader in extension than truth. For truth when so defined is an instance of goodness and every truth will be good. But the converse will not hold. Goodness is realized in certain entities to which truth when so defined does

---

sunt in rebus, sicut bonum et malum, ut verum sit sicut bonum et falsum sicut malum, sed sunt in cognitione." For Averroes's *Commentary* on this see fol. 152rb–152va.

[79] PB 3.146–47. Note in particular: "Propter quod dicitur quod intelligere est motus rei ad animam et est quasi motus rectus, quia actio intelligibilis terminatur in existentia eius apud intellectum secundum actum cognitionis."

[80] PB 3.147. Note in particular: ". . . et ideo est quidam motus quasi reflexus a re ad animam et rursus ab anima in rem et ibi completur in re ipsa."

[81] PB 3.147–48.

not apply.[82] As we have already indicated, truth presupposes actual knowledge of a given thing by a created intellect, and consequently is not transcendental in the fullest sense. Goodness, on the other hand, is really identical with being and is truly transcendental.[83] Granted, then, that every instance of truth will also be ontologically good, truth and goodness differ logically. And this logical distinction is grounded on a real differentiation, namely, that situation wherein an entity is ontologically good without enjoying truth in the strict sense.

If, on the other hand, one extends the meaning of truth to the being of each thing insofar as it can adequate the intellect to itself and thereby cause truth in the strict sense, then truth and goodness will be really identical and, we would presume, convertible. If we may paraphrase Godfrey's concluding remark from Quodlibet 6, q. 6, truth and goodness are convertible when truth is applied to that which serves as its cause. But even then truth and goodness will be logically distinct. This logical distinction will be based on the difference between viewing something in relationship to the intellect, and therefore as true, and viewing it in relationship to the will and therefore as good.[84]

---

[82] PB 14.17–18.

[83] See the text from Q 3, q. 1, cited in n. 53 above. Also see Q 15, q. 3 (PB 14.18) for the statement that being and goodness differ only logically. There he comments that this logical distinction between them can be traced back to a real distinction, not in the sense that there can be any being which is not also good in some way (ontologically) or vice versa, but insofar as something might also inform something else as an entity without being good for it, for instance, excessive heat in the human body. But this would not be to deny that the heat was still ontologically good in itself.

[84] Q 15, q. 3 (PB 14.18). For the quotation from Q 6, q. 6, see n. 77 above.

Part I

The Metaphysics of Essence and Existence

Chapter II.

The Relationship Between Essence and Existence

As will become clearer in subsequent chapters of this study, Godfrey's position with respect to the relationship between essence and existence in beings other than God exercised considerable influence on his proposed solutions to a number of other metaphysical problems. At the same time, his fairly frequent reference to diversity of opinion on this point indicates that it was a much contested issue during his career as a Master in Theology at Paris, and especially so during his earlier years in that capacity.

A definitive history of the thirteenth-century controversy concerning the essence-existence relationship in creatures remains to be written. The remote origins of the doctrine that defends real distinction between essence and existence are still somewhat obscure.[1] It will be sufficient for our purposes to recall that the issue arises in large measure from the efforts of various medieval thinkers to account for the radically contingent, caused, and composite character of all beings apart from God. Various thirteenth-century thinkers such as Thomas Aquinas, Siger of Brabant, and James of Viterbo saw in Avicenna a proponent of an extreme kind of distinction between essence and existence. According to their reading of Avicenna, he had not only distinguished between essence and existence in creatures, but had

[1] For some helpful remarks with respect to the origins of this doctrine and for further references see F. Van Steenberghen, *Maître Siger de Brabant* (Louvain-Paris, 1977), pp. 280–82. Among these references see in particular Paulus, *Henri de Gand . . .* , pp. 260–91; also see M.-D. Roland-Gosselin, ed., *Le 'De ente et essentia' de s. Thomas d'Aquin* (Paris, 1948), pp. 137–205.

viewed existence as if it were superadded to essence in the manner of an accident.[2] Averroes was well known for having criticized Avicenna's teaching on this point and was frequently cited by those who argued against any such real distinction.[3]

In the thirteenth century Thomas Aquinas is usually thought to have defended some kind of real composition and distinction of essence and existence (*esse*) in all creatures.[4] But it is equally clear that he had criticized the position

---

[2] In addition to explicit discussions of Avicenna's position in the studies by Paulus and Roland-Gosselin cited in the preceding note see Thomas, *In IV Met.*, lect. 2, nn. 556–58; *Siger de Brabant. Questions sur la Métaphysique*, qu. 7, C. Graiff, ed. (Louvain, 1948), pp. 12 and 18; *Jacobi de Viterbio, O.E.S.A., Disputatio prima de quolibet*, qu. 4, E. Ypma, ed. (Würzburg, 1968), p. 46:102–07. On Siger's understanding of Avicenna's position see A. Maurer, "*Esse* and *Essentia* in the Metaphysics of Siger of Brabant," *Mediaeval Studies* 8 (1946), pp. 78ff. But for recent defenses of Avicenna based on his Arabic text against the charge of having viewed existence as if it were an accident see F. Rahman, "Essence and Existence in Avicenna," *Mediaeval and Renaissance Studies* 4 (1958), pp. 1–16; "Ibn Sīnā," in M. M. Sharif, *A History of Muslim Philosophy*, Vol. 1 (Wiesbaden, 1963), pp. 483–86; P. Morewedge, "Philosophical Analysis and "Ibn Sīnā's 'Essence-Existence' Distinction," *Journal of the American Oriental Society* 92 (1972), pp. 425–35.

[3] For Averroes see *In IV Metaphy.* (Venice, 1562), Vol. 8, fol. 67rab. For Siger of Brabant's usage of the Averroistic critique see qu. 7 of his *Quaestiones in Metaphysicam*, p. 18 (as cited in n. 2 above). For James of Viterbo's reference to the same discussion in Averroes see his Q 1, q. 4, p. 53:325–27.

[4] For some discussions by those who find this view in Aquinas see N. del Prado, *De veritate fundamentali philosophiae Christianae* (Fribourg, 1911), pp. 23–79; J. de Finance, *Etre et agir*, 2nd ed. (Rome, 1960), pp. 94–111; C. Fabro, *La nozione metafisica di partecipazione*, 2nd ed. (Turin, 1950), pp. 212–44; E. Gilson, *History of Christian Philosophy in the Middle Ages* (New York, 1955), pp. 420–27; *Being and Some Philosophers*, 2nd ed. (Toronto, 1952), pp. 171–78; M. Grabmann, "Doctrina s. Thomae de distinctione reali inter essentiam et esse ex documentis ineditis saeculi XIII illustratur," *Acta hebdomadae Thomisticae Romae celebratae 19–25 Novembris 1923 in laudem S. Thomae Aquinatis* (Rome, 1924), pp. 131–90; L. Sweeney, "Existence/Essence in Thomas Aquinas's Early Writings," *Proceedings of the American Catholic Philosophical Association* 37 (1963), pp. 97–131; J. Owens, "Quiddity and Real Distinction in St. Thomas Aquinas," *Mediaeval Studies* 27 (1965), pp. 19–22; J. Wippel, "Aquinas's Route to the Real Distinction: A Note on *De ente et essentia*, c. 4," *The Thomist* 43 (1979), pp. 279–95. For some who deny that Thomas defended the real distinction see M. Chossat, "Dieu," *Dictionnaire de théologie catholique*, Vol. 4, pt. 1, col. 1180; "L'Averroïsme de saint Thomas. Note sur la distinction d'essence et d'existence à la fin du XIIIe siècle," *Archives de Philosophie* 9 (1932), pp. 129[465]–177[513]; F. Cunningham, "Distinction According to St. Thomas," *The New Scholasticism* 36 (1962), pp. 279–312; "Textos de Santo Tomas sobre el esse y esencia," *Pensamiento* 20 (1964), pp. 283–306; "The 'Real Distinction' in John Quidort," *Journal of the History of Philosophy* 8 (1970), pp. 9–28.

defended by Avicenna and, therefore, that his understanding of the composition and distinction of essence and existence cannot be identified with or reduced to that of the Muslim thinker.[5] His well known contemporary at Paris, Siger of Brabant, had himself defended real identity of essence and existence while lecturing there in the Arts Faculty in the early 1270s. But Siger had also distinguished Thomas's teaching on this point from that of Avicenna (and Albert), while acknowledging his own inability to understand fully Aquinas's position.[6] And some decades later around the turn of the century Duns Scotus would also reject any kind of real distinction or real composition of essence and existence in created beings, whatever may have been his own view as to their exact relationship.[7]

Already during Godfrey's student days at Paris and especially during his earlier years there as a Master in the Theology faculty, a bitter controversy had developed between Henry of Ghent and Giles of Rome concerning this same issue.[8] Thus in his first Quodlibetal debate of 1276 Henry of Ghent reacted sharply against a theory that defends real distinction between essence and existence. While it is admittedly difficult today to determine with cer-

---

[5] See his *In IV Met.*, lect. 2, n. 558. For helpful discussion of this important text in Aquinas see Van Steenberghen, *Maître Siger . . .* , pp. 286–87.

[6] See Siger's *Quaestiones in Metaphysicam*, qu. 7, p. 14 (Albert); p. 16 (where he presents Thomas's position as intermediary between that which identifies existence with essence and that which regards it as a superadded accident). For Siger's reaction to Thomas's position see Van Steenberghen, *Maître Siger . . .* , pp. 287–89. For Siger's own position in this writing (ca. 1273, for which dating see pp. 218–20), see pp. 289–91. But for an apparent move toward Thomas's position in Siger's recently discovered and edited later work, his *Quaestiones super librum de causis*, see Van Steenberghen, pp. 291–92, and A. Marlasca, ed., *Les Quaestiones super librum de causis de Siger de Brabant* (Louvain-Paris, 1972), p. 21, n. 20.

[7] See A. Wolter, "The Formal Distinction," *Studies in Philosophy and the History of Philosophy*, Vol. 3: *John Duns Scotus, 1265–1965* (Washington, 1965), pp. 54–59; A. J. O'Brien, "Duns Scotus' Teaching on the Distinction Between Essence and Existence," *The New Scholasticism* 38 (1964), pp. 61–77; W. Hoeres, "Wesen und Dasein bei Heinrich von Gent und Duns Scotus," *Franziskanischen Studien* 47 (1965), pp. 170–71.

[8] On this controversy between Giles and Henry see E. Hocedez, "Gilles de Rome et Henri de Gand sur la distinction réelle (1276–1287)," *Gregorianum* 8 (1927), pp. 358–84; "Le premier quodlibet d'Henri de Gand (1276)," *Gregorianum* 9 (1928), pp. 92–117; "Deux questions touchant la distinction réelle entre l'essence et l'existence," *Gregorianum* 10 (1929), pp. 365–86; *Aegidii Romani Theoremata de esse et essentia. Texte précédé d'une introduction historique et critique* (Louvain, 1930), pp. (82)–(84); J. Paulus, *Henri de Gand . . .* , pp. 280–82; "Les disputes d'Henri de Gand et de Gilles de Rome sur la distinction de l'essence et de l'existence," *Archives d'Histoire Doctrinale et Littéraire du Moyen Age* 13 (1940–42), pp. 323–58.

tainty what precise written source or sources Henry then had in mind, it seems likely that Giles of Rome was his primary target. Some have even suggested that a number of arguments presented there by Henry in support of the real distinction not only reflect Giles's position but possibly even his oral intervention in that particular session.[9] Be that as it may, it is quite clear that Henry and Giles were to engage in a running battle concerning this same matter shortly after Giles's return to the Theology faculty ca. 1285. And while considerable work remains to be done concerning the presence or absence of this theory in Giles's writings prior to 1275, certain remarks in his *Commentary on Bk I of the Sentences* as well as in his *Theoremata de corpore Christi* suggest that by 1275 or 1276 he had already begun to develop his definitive personal position.[10]

---

[9] For Henry see his Quodlibet 1, qu. 9 (Paris, 1518), Vol. 1, fol. 6v–7v: "Utrum creatura ipsa sit suum esse." On Giles as Henry's target in this question and on the possibility that Giles himself was a participant in the original discussion see Hocedez, "Le premier quodlibet . . . ," pp. 100–01, 104; Paulus, *Henri de Gand* . . . , p. 281.

[10] For further studies of Giles's position on the essence-existence relationship (in addition to those cited above in n. 8) see: A. Pattin, "Gilles de Rome, O.E.S.A. (ca. 1243–1316) et la distinction réelle de l'essence et de l'existence," *Revue de l'Université d'Ottawa* 23 (1953), pp. 80*–116*; G. Suárez, "El pensamiento de Egidio Romano en torno a la distinctión de esencia y existencia," *La ciencia tomista* 75 (1948), pp. 66–99, 230–72; P. Nash, "Giles of Rome on Boethius' 'Diversum est esse et id quod est'," *Mediaeval Studies* 12 (1950), pp. 57–91; "The Accidentality of Esse According to Giles of Rome," *Gregorianum* 38 (1957), pp. 103–15; and a series of articles by G. Trapé either treating directly of the essence-existence distinction in Giles or of related themes in his metaphysics: "Il Platonismo di Egidio Romano," *Aquinas* 7 (1964), pp. 309–44; "Il Neoplatonismo di Egidio Romano nel commento al 'De causis'," *Aquinas* 9 (1966), pp. 49–86; "La dottrina della partecipazione in Egidio Romano," *Aquinas* 10 (1967), pp. 170–93; "Caratteristiche dell' 'esse' partecipato in Egidio Romano," *Lateranum* 34 (1968), pp. 351–68; "Causalità e partecipazione in Egidio Romano," *Augustinianum* 9 (1969), pp. 91–117; "L' 'esse' partecipato e distinzione reale in Egidio Romano," *Aquinas* 12 (1969), pp. 443–68. On the chronology of his development of this doctrine and of his debates with Henry of Ghent see Paulus, *Henri de Gand* . . . , p. 281; Trapé, "L' 'esse' partecipato e distinzione reale . . . ," p. 455. Both Paulus and Trapé date Giles's *Commentary on I Sentences* and his *Theoremata de corpore Christi* in 1276 and prior to Henry's Quodlibet 1 of Advent 1276. Pattin follows Suárez in placing the *Commentary on I Sentences* ca. 1275 ("Gilles de Rome . . . ," p. 82*). He dates the *Theoremata de corpore Christi* ca. 1275–76 (p. 85*). On the presence or absence of this doctrine in Giles's earlier works see the doctoral dissertation on essence and existence in Giles now being completed by M. Quaresma at the Catholic University of America. For this doctrine in Giles's *Commentary on I Sentences* see his *In I Sent.*, d. 8, p. 2, pr. 1, q. 2 (Venice, 1521), fol. 52v, and *In I Sent.*, d. 8, p. 2, pr. 2, q. 1, fol. 53vb–54rb. Also see his *Theoremata de corpore Christi* (Bologna, 1481), fol.

Giles is often criticized for having defended an extreme version of the real distinction according to which essence and existence differ from one another as "thing" and "thing" (*res et res*). It can hardly be denied that such terminology appears in his exposition of his theory, as, for instance, in his detailed defense of the same in his *Theoremata de esse et essentia* (probably written between 1278 and 1280) and in his *Quaestiones disputatae de esse et essentia* (1285–1287).[11] The consequences of such a position were not lost on Giles's immediate critics, as we shall see below while considering Godfrey's reaction thereto. If we may abstract from the historical situation for a moment, let us suppose that one appeals to a composition of essence and existence in order to account for the contingent, the participated, and the nonsimple or composite character of all created entities. If one correlates essence and existence as if they were "things" or beings in themselves, one will thereby explain nothing. One will then have to account for the contingent, participated, and nonsimple character of each of these constituting "sub-things" by postulating further composition of essence and existence in each of them, *ad infinitum*.

In all fairness to Giles, however, it must be acknowledged that already in his *Theoremata de corpore Christi*, while he does there favor some kind of

---

119rb–120ra. For further discussion and references see our "The Relationship between Essence and Existence in Late Thirteenth-Century Thought: Giles of Rome, Henry of Ghent, Godfrey of Fontaines, and James of Viterbo," in P. Morewedge, ed., *Ancient and Medieval Philosophies of Existence* (Fordham University Press, New York), forthcoming in 1981.

[11] Note the following texts from his *Theoremata de esse et essentia:* "Esse autem quod causatur a forma totius . . . est *res* differens ab ipsa forma" (p. 101);". . . et etiam hic ostendetur quod esse et essentia sunt duae *res* . . . " (p. 127); "Et, sicut materia et quantitas sunt duae res, sic essentia et esse sunt *duae res* realiter differentes" (p. 134). Also see his *Quaestiones disputatae de esse et essentia* (Venice, 1503), q. 9: "*Res* ergo ipsa quae est esse est in genere substantiae. Habet tamen ipsum esse quemdam modum accidentalem actualem inquantum est superadditum substantiae" (fol. 20vb); and q. 11: ". . . et per consequens intelligitur quod esse sit alia *res* ab essentia" (fol. 24vb). (Italics mine.) There is some disagreement as to the date of the *Theoremata de esse et essentia*. Thus Paulus simply places it between 1278 and 1286 ("Les disputes d'Henri . . . ," p. 328) and here follows Hocedez (*Aegidii Romani Theoremata de esse* . . . , p. (12)). For the 1278–1280 dating see Suárez, "El pensamiento de Egidio . . . ," p. 80; Pattin, "Gilles de Rome . . . ," p. 91*. Trapé places it in 1278 ("L' 'esse' partecipato e distinzione reale . . . ," p. 453). Z. K. Siemiatkowska would date it somewhat earlier, that is to say, before Giles's "exile" and thus sees it as directly attacked by Henry in 1276. See her "Avant l'exil de Gilles de Rome: Au sujet d'une dispute sur les 'Theoremata de esse et essentia' de Gilles de Rome," *Mediaevalia Philosophica Polonorum* 7 (1960), pp. 4–5, 31, 48.

real diversity or distinction between essence and existence, he refuses to liken this diversity to that which obtains between two essences.[12] And in later discussions, while defending his theory against the objection that existence when distinguished from essence can be neither substance nor accident and must, therefore, be nothing, Giles counters that existence in some way does belong to the category of substance, but only by reduction insofar as it is the act of substance or of essence.[13] At the same time, as we have already seen, he does distinguish between essence and existence as between *res* and *res*. And he does emphasize the "separability" of existence from essence, though he does not thereby intend to suggest that either could exist in separation from the other.[14] Not surprisingly, he is often accused of having "reified" or turned into things Thomas's principles of being, that is to say, essence and existence. By so doing he would have created that "monstrosity" that was to scandalize subsequent critics such as Duns Scotus and Suarez.[15]

Given all of this, one can understand why Giles continues to have his critics and defenders today.[16] Rather than attempt here to resolve this continuing controversy about his true thought on the matter, we shall content

---

[12] *Op. cit.*, fol. 119vb–120ra. Note in particular: ". . . videtur enim absurdum quod essentia et esse dicantur duae essentiae." Giles here acknowledges that further precision is needed as regards the kind of distinction that obtains between essence and *esse*, and promises to develop this more fully on a subsequent occasion. For which see his *Theoremata de esse et essentia*. For more on this see our "The Relationship . . . ," as cited in n. 10.

[13] For this see his *Quaestiones disputatae de esse et essentia*, q. 9, fol. 20vb; *Theoremata de esse et essentia*, pp. 155–59.

[14] For the point that separability is the best proof of real distinction between essence and *esse* see the *Theoremata de esse et essentia*, Th. XII, pp. 67–68. For his denial that essence can ever exist in fact without its *esse* see in the same work, Th. VI (p. 29), Th. VII (p. 37), Th. X (p. 57). Also see other passages as cited by Pattin, "Gilles de Rome . . . ," pp. 102* – 105*; Suárez, "El pensamiento de Egidio . . . ," pp. 252–54, 270.

[15] See Hocedez, *Aegidii Romani theoremata de esse . . .* , pp. (62)–(65), and (117) where he comments: "Gilles est l'inventeur du monstre qui a effarouché Scot et Suárez." For the same see Paulus, *Henri de Gand . . .* , pp. 283–84. For others who also stress the difference between Giles and Thomas on this point even more so than Hocedez and Paulus see the articles by Nash cited above in n. 10 together with his "Giles of Rome," *New Catholic Encyclopedia* 6 (1967), pp. 484–85; Wm. Carlo, *The Ultimate Reducibility of Essence to Existence in Existential Metaphysics* (The Hague, 1966), pp. 14–17, 19, 31, 66, 67, 83.

[16] See Suárez, "El pensamiento de Egidio Romano," pp. 251–54 and 270–71 (separability of essence and existence does not imply that either can exist in separation from the other); pp. 262–63 and 266–68 (the terminology of *res* and *res* need not imply "reification"); Pattin, "Gilles de Rome . . . , p. 90* (Giles's real distinction need not be interpreted as being in opposition to real distinction between principles

ourselves with the following observations. Whatever may have been his original intent in applying the words "thing" and "thing" to essence and existence, his choice of terminology was unfortunate. It left him open to charges and interpretations such as those to which reference has been made above, and those we shall find Godfrey himself raising against the theory. Moreover, another point clearly emerges when one studies this controversy during the closing decades of the thirteenth century. Giles's terminology as well as his way of defending the real distinction became standard in his own time and for quite some time thereafter.

If Thomas and Giles defended somewhat different versions of the real distinction between essence and existence, Henry of Ghent proposed an unusual theory according to which they differ "intentionally."[17] Godfrey himself was obviously quite familiar with each of these general positions. For instance, in Quodlibet 2, q. 2, while attempting to determine whether the essence of a creature is indifferent to existence and nonexistence, he connects this question with that concerning the essence-existence relationship. Either essence is really identical with existence and differs from it only logically or intentionally, or else existence is a distinct thing (*res*), that is to say, the act of essence and really distinct from essence.[18]

Again, in Quodlibet 4, q. 2 Godfrey considers the question as to whether the view according to which predicamental things are eternal in terms of their quidditative being also implies that the world is eternal. Within this context Godfrey once more outlines three different opinions on the essence-existence relationship. Some maintain that existence (*esse*) is really distinct from (*aliud ab*) essence and joins with it in real composition. Yet neither is separable from the other. If a thing lacks its existential being (*esse existentiae*), it will likewise lack essential being (*esse essentiae*). According to another position, clearly that of Henry of Ghent, essence and existence are really one and the

---

of being); pp. 102* – 106* (granted Giles's extreme realism or Platonism, this should not be exaggerated). Also see Trapè, "L' 'esse' partecipato . . . ," pp. 455ff., 467 – 68; "Il Platonismo de Egidio Romano," pp. 309 – 44.

[17] All parties in the discussion referred to above will admit that Giles's terminology, at least, differs from that of Thomas. For more on Henry's theory see Section B of this same chapter.

[18] For Q 2, q. 2 see PB 2.53: "Utrum essentia creaturae sit aliquid indifferens ad esse et non esse." For his reference to the different theories on essence and existence see p. 60: "Ad cuius intellectum est considerandum quod essentia sic se habet ad esse existentiae eius quod est aut idipsum realiter cum ipso differens ratione vel intentione, aut esse dicit *rem aliam* ab ipsa essentia. Si autem esse dicat *rem aliam* quae sit actualitas essentiae realiter alia ab ipsa essentia . . ." Italics mine to indicate Godfrey's reference to existence (*esse*) as a *res* according to the theory of real distinction.

same but differ intentionally. Because of this intentional distinction it is asserted that they enter into composition with one another in some way. Finally, Godfrey refers to those who maintain real identity of essence and existence. While they acknowledge that the two differ in the purely logical order or by a distinction of reason, they deny that they enter into composition in creatures. To the extent that something is or remains in terms of its essential being or its essence, to that extent does it continue to be in terms of its existence.[19]

Because much of Godfrey's metaphysical thinking on the essence-existence relationship is developed in direct confrontation with the theories that defend real distinction and then merely intentional distinction between essence and existence, we shall divide this chapter into the following sections: A. Godfrey and the Real Distinction between Essence and Existence; B. Godfrey and Henry of Ghent's Theory of Intentional Distinction between Essence and Existence; C. Godfrey's Position: Real Identity of Essence and Existence.

A. GODFREY AND THE REAL DISTINCTION BETWEEN ESSENCE AND EXISTENCE

Godfrey's treatment of the real distinction will be presented according to the following order: (1) theory of and argumentation for the real distinction; (2) argumentation against the real distinction; (3) his reply to argumentation for the real distinction.

1. Theory of and Argumentation for the Real Distinction

In his Quodlibet 3, q. 1 of 1286 Godfrey asks whether a creature may be called a being by reason of its essence when it is not such by reason of its existence.[20] He replies that one's answer will depend upon one's understanding of the relationship between essence and existence. If they differ in some way, one might then at least hesitate in denying that such a nonexisting creature may be styled a being by reason of its essence. But if they differ in

---

[19] PB 2.235. Godfrey accepts the third opinion, as is clear from the following: "Sed mihi videtur quod esse existentiae et essentia omnino sint idem secundum rem et differunt solum secundum rationem et modum intelligendi et significandi, nullam omnino compositionem facientia, sicut nec currere et cursus vel huiusmodi. Et ideo in quantum manet res secundum esse essentiae, manet etiam secundum esse existentiae et e converso, et in quantum intelligitur de uno intelligitur de alio et e converso . . ."

[20] PB 2.156. "Utrum creatura possit dici ens ratione suae essentiae, cum ipsa est non ens quantum ad esse existentiae."

no way, it must be held as certain that such cannot be the case. Godfrey then considers a theory according to which there is real distinction between essence and existence. Existence will be the act of essence just as form is the act of matter. Just as matter is in potency to form and its privation, so will essence be in potency to existence and its privation. As Godfrey himself presents the theory, "existential being (*esse existentiae*) is something (*aliquid*) that really differs from essence or from essential being (*esse essentiae*)."[21]

Godfrey's usage of the term *aliquid* here to designate existence should be noted. For one must wonder whether the theory of real distinction which he presents and then criticizes was that of Thomas Aquinas or rather that of Giles of Rome. As usual, Godfrey does not name his adversary. But if the second suggestion is correct, it will follow that Godfrey is really rejecting a theory that distinguishes between essence and existence as between "thing and thing" (*res* and *res*), however one may wish to interpret that doctrine in Giles himself. Difficult though it may be to pronounce definitively on this point, Godfrey's employment of terms such as "something" (*aliquid*) and "thing" (*res*) to signify existence strongly suggests that his understanding of the theory was heavily influenced by Giles.[22] Again, as will be seen below, the close correlation of the matter-form distinction with that between essence

---

[21] PB 2.158. ". . . esse existentiae est aliquid differens realiter ab essentia sive etiam ab esse essentiae, et est actualitas ipsius essentiae, sicut forma est actualitas materiae. Sicut enim materia de se est in potentia ad formam et ad privationem eius, sic essentia quantum est de se est in potentia ad esse et ad privationem eius." As may be seen from this passage and from others Godfrey easily moves from *esse* to *esse existentiae* and from *essentia* to *esse essentiae* in discussing their relationship. For all practical purposes he takes *esse* (existence) and *esse existentiae* (existential being) as synonyms. The same applies to *essentia* (essence) and *esse essentiae* (essential being). We shall feel free to do the same. Hence one may speak of the distinction between or identity of essence or essential being and existence or existential being.

[22] See the text cited from Q 2, q. 2 in n. 18 above, as well as the following from the short version of Q 3, q. 1: "Quantum ergo ad primum, dicunt quidam quod esse et essentia sunt diversae res in creatura, ita quod essentia est potentia susceptiva ipsius esse et esse est actus eius" (PB 2.302). Since Godfrey's Q 3 dates from Christmas 1286 and since Giles of Rome had prepared qq. 1 – 11 of his *Quaestiones disputatae de esse et essentia* before that date, Godfrey was probably familiar with Giles's detailed treatment of essence and existence in qq. 9 and 11 of the same. For this same judgment see Paulus, *Henri de Gand. . .* , p. 321, n. 2, and Hocedez, "Gilles de Rome et Henri de Gand . . . ," p. 381. Hocedez considers it certain that Godfrey had Giles's doctrine in mind and highly probable that he had direct access to his text (p. 381, n. 2). Also see his discussion of the same in *Aegidii Romani theoremata de esse et essentia,* p. (12). On the dating of Giles's *Quaestiones disputatae de esse et essentia* see Hocedez, "Gilles de Rome et Henri . . . ," pp. 360, 365; Pattin, "Gilles de Rome . . . ," p. 96* and n. 63.

and existence is characteristic of Giles's exposition of his theory. Further indications will also be cited which suggest that Giles's terminology and argumentation in defense of the real distinction played a major role in shaping Godfrey's understanding and appreciation of the same.

To return to Godfrey's discussion in Quodlibet 3, q. 1, he then presents some arguments that may be offered in favor of the theory of real distinction. The first connects the possible existence and nonexistence of a creature with our knowledge of its essence. The argument as it appears in the long version of Godfrey's text is somewhat involved, but may be considered according to the following steps.

(1) A created essence can either exist or not exist. (2) Existence and nonexistence are not included in one's notion or concept of a created essence. If existence were included therein, the creature could never fail to exist and would be a necessary existent. Such, however, is true of God alone. If nonexistence were included in one's concept of a creaturely essence, that essence could never be brought into being by any agent. It would be of its essence not to exist. (3) Therefore, the essence of a creature is to be regarded as a kind of possible existence, that is, as a possibility to exist. This implies that it is a potency with respect to existence as to something which is really distinct from itself.[23]

Proof of this final point (the transition from possible existence to potency with respect to a really distinct existence): Whenever one finds that a thing can be understood without taking another thing into account and even with the contrary of that other thing, one may conclude that the former is really distinct from the latter. But a created essence can be understood without taking its existence into account and even with the contrary of existence, since it can be understood as not existing. Consequently, one must conclude that existence really differs from essence, and that essence is a kind of potentiality with respect to existence, its actuality.[24] When one turns to the short version of this same argument one finds it reduced to its essentials. Again essence is presented as a potency which receives existence as its act. The same principle is fundamental to both the long and the short versions: that which is not included in one's understanding or concept of an essence but is such that the essence can be known without it and even with its opposite

---

[23] PB 2.158. Note in particular: ". . . ergo essentia creaturae intelligitur ut quoddam possibile esse, sive ut quaedam potentia ad esse tanquam ad aliquid re differens ab ipsa."

[24] *Ibid*. See in particular: "Cum ergo omnis essentia creaturae possit intelligi non cointellecto esse eius vel sine esse, immo etiam cum contrario ipsius quia potest intelligi non esse, oportet quod esse sit aliud ab essentia et non sit de eius ratione . . ."

is really distinct from that essence. But such is true of existence since an essence can be understood as not existing.[25]

The similarity between this argument and a well-known passage from Thomas's *De ente et essentia* is rather striking, at least at first sight. There Thomas reasons that every essence or quiddity can be understood without anything being known of its existence. For I can understand what a man is or what a phoenix is and still not know whether it exists in reality. Therefore, it is clear that existence is other than essence or quiddity.[26]

Godfrey's version of this argument goes farther, however, since it maintains that a given essence may be known even as nonexisting. Giles of Rome had made this same point in his *Quaestiones disputatae de esse et essentia*. In q. 11 he lists six truths that cannot be safeguarded without the real distinction. The first of these is precisely this, that the essence of any creature can be understood with the opposite of its existence. He goes on to comment that nothing can be understood with the opposite of itself. Consequently, that which can be understood with the opposite of something else is really distinct from that latter thing. In short, then, because essence can be understood as nonexisting (with the opposite of existence), essence cannot be identified with existence. And so, concludes Giles, essence is really distinct from existence.[27] It seems more likely, therefore, that Godfrey had Giles's version of this argument in mind rather than that proposed by Thomas in his *De ente*.

Although it is somewhat difficult to determine precisely where the above argument ends and the second one begins in Godfrey's long version, by using his short version as a guide one may present the latter as follows:

> Secondly, because . . . that which participates (in something) is not to be identified with that in which it participates. But in creatures essence participates in existence (*esse*). Otherwise many unacceptable consequences would result.[28]

---

[25] "Primo quia illud quod non solum non est de intellectu essentiae sed etiam tale quod sub eius opposito potest essentia intelligi, non est idem re cum essentia. Sed esse non est de intellectu essentiae creatae et essentia potest intelligi sub opposito eius, quia potest vere intelligi non esse" (PB 2.302).

[26] See *Le 'de ente et essentia' de s. Thomas d'Aquin*, M.-D. Roland-Gosselin, ed., c. 4 (Paris, 1948), p. 34.

[27] See *op. cit.*, q. 11 (fol. 24vb): "Primum est quod omnis essentia cuiuslibet creaturae potest intelligi cum opposito ipsius esse . . . Nam nihil potest intelligi cum opposito sui ipsius. Quicquid ergo potest intelligi cum opposito alicuius [text: aliter] est realiter differens ab ipso. Erit ergo essentia realiter differens ab esse." Also see q. 9 (fol. 20va). On this argument in Giles see Suárez, "El pensamiento . . . , " pp. 230–32.

[28] "Secundo quia . . . participans non est ipsum participatum. Sed in creaturis

The more complicated presentation in the long version may be analyzed as follows. The argument presupposes a number of principles: No agent can do that which cannot be done. *Esse* is the actuality of a created essence just as form is the actuality of matter. One must admit a composition of essence and existence in every creature as between that which participates and that in which it participates. (Otherwise many difficulties would follow, according to the argument.) Finally, the underlying principle of this presentation is the same as that found in the shorter version: that which is in potency to something so as to receive it and participate in it cannot be identified with it.

The argument then goes on to apply these principles in the following way:

(A) Since every created essence is in potency to exist, this potency could not be actualized unless there were an act-potency composition within the creature. In order to establish the first part of this proposition—that every created essence is in potency to exist—the argument reasons as follows. If such an essence were of itself act, it could never become or be brought into being. It would always be. If it were neither act nor in potency to exist, then it could never be actualized or brought into being by any agent. Hence it would never be, since the impossible cannot be effected by any agent (see the principles presupposed as listed above).

In order to prove the second part of proposition (A), that is, that a creaturely essence's potency to exist could never be actualized unless there were an act-potency composition within the creature, the argument continues. This follows because a creature is neither act alone nor potency alone. Here the reasoning offered immediately above reappears. If the creature were act alone, it would not be in potency to exist and could never be nonexistent. If it were potency alone, it would never actually be. Therefore, a creature must be composed of act and potency so as to be able to exist and not exist.

(B) Consequently, concludes the argument, one must admit that *esse* adds some "thing" (*rem aliquam*) to essence. Just as the potency, matter, is not actualized except by something that is superadded to it, that is, form, so too the potency, essence, will not be reduced to act or actualized except by something that is superadded to it, namely, existence (*esse*). The underlying principle is that indicated above: that which is in potency to something so as to receive it and participate in it cannot be identified with it. Therefore, the argument concludes, existence differs from essence even as form differs from matter.[29]

---

essentia participat esse, alioquin sequerentur multa inconvenientia ut dictum est. Ergo et cetera" (PB 2.302).

[29] PB 2.158–59. Although the text is too long to be quoted in full, the following should be noted: "Sed quod est in potentia ad aliquid, potens scilicet illud participare

Comparison of this presentation with the shorter version reveals that the notion of participation is taken as given in both. According to each version the distinction between essence and existence is grounded on a real distinction between that which participates (essence) and that in which it participates (existence). In the longer version, moreover, the parallel between matter and form, on the one hand, and essence and existence, on the other, is stressed. The argument based on participation, the parallel between matter-form and essence-existence, and the reference in the longer version to *esse* as a "thing" all remind one of Giles of Rome's version of the real distinction.[30]

Godfrey's formal presentation of arguments in favor of the real distinction concludes in the long version with an application to the case of simple creatures, that is to say, created beings in which there is no matter-form composition. In order to safeguard the difference between any such creature and God, pure actuality and pure *esse*, the argument contends that one must postulate the reception and limitation of *esse* in creatures. This approach

et recipere, non est illud" (p. 158); ". . . —cum inquam ita sit, ut iam dictum est, necesse est dicere quod esse addit *rem aliquam* super essentiam. Sicut ergo potentia materiae non reducitur ad actum nisi per aliquid additum, scilicet per formam, ita et potentia essentiae non reducitur ad actum nisi per aliquid additum, scilicet per esse. Ergo esse est aliud ab essentia sicut forma est aliud a materia" (p. 159). Italics mine.

[30] For an argument based on the distinction between that which participates and that in which it participates as well as for the notion that existence unless limited by essence will be unlimited (cf. immediately below for the next argument as presented by Godfrey), see Giles's *Quaestiones disputatae de esse et essentia*, q. 11 (fol. 24vb–25ra). On this general argument for the real distinction from participation in Giles see Suárez, "El pensamiento . . . ," pp. 232–38. In this context, however, Giles stresses the point that unless one admits of the real distinction one could not account for the limited presence of existence (*esse*) in limited and participating beings. See especially fol. 25ra. In q. 9 of this same work Giles argues that without real composition of essence and existence one cannot account for the fact that a creature merely participates in existence without being subsistent existence. See fol. 19ra. As Giles sums it up there: "Si ergo creatura esset ipsum esse non participaret esse." Earlier in the same column he observes: "Nam quicquid participat aliquo est aliquid aliud praeter illud." In this same question Giles develops an argument based upon a close parallelism between the matter-form couplet and the essence-existence couplet, and a similar analogy between substantial change and creation. Above all in the case of spirits, one would not be able to account for their created character without the act-potency composition of existence and essence whereby essence receives existence as its act. See fol. 20vb–21va, and in particular: ". . . sicut generatio facit scire materiam aliud esse a forma, sic creatio facit nos scire essentiam esse aliud ab esse" (fol. 20vb–21ra). As will be seen below, this reasoning was also well known to Godfrey, even though he does not present it as a distinct argument for the real distinction in the opening pages of Q 3, q. 1. On this parallelism see Paulus, *Henri de Gand*. . . , p. 318.

seems to accept as given the notion that existence (*esse*) is an act which would be infinite or unlimited in itself if it were not received and limited by a really distinct principle, essence. It accepts as given the simple character of certain created essences, presumably angels and separated souls. From these presuppositions it concludes to a more fundamental composition in all such creatures, that of essence and existence.[31]

Godfrey is also aware, of course, that the theory of real distinction may be applied to matter-form composites as well as to purely simple created beings. In the case of a matter-form composite the essence which is so composed is itself a potency with respect to substantial existence. Thus the essence receives and participates in existence from the First Cause, which itself is pure and unparticipated *esse*.[32] According to the theory of real distinction as it is presented by Godfrey, then, there must be a real composition of essence and existence in every creature, whether its essence itself is simple or composite.[33]

This, then, is Godfrey's understanding of the theory of the real distinction between essence and existence. He is familiar with arguments in its defense, arguments which have appeared frequently enough since his time in the Thomistic tradition: an argument based on one's notion or concept of essence; an argument based on the participated character of created beings; finally, a possible approach grounded on the distinction between finite and simple creatures, on the one hand, and the perfectly simple and unlimited being of God, on the other. Godfrey is also familiar with the notion that *esse* is an act that is received by, participated in, and limited by a really distinct essence or potency in all creatures. Granted that these themes and arguments have long been associated with the metaphysical thought of Thomas Aquinas,[34] considerable evidence has been offered above to suggest that Giles of Rome's presentation of this theory strongly influenced Godfrey in his understanding of the same. As has been indicated, Godfrey's terminology in presenting the

---

[31] PB 2.159. "Si enim ens quod non est compositum ex materia et forma productum in esse per generationem, sed ens simplex in essentia in esse productum per creationem non esset tale quod in eo necessario aliquid esset receptum a creante illud, esset actus purus et esse purum, et esset suum esse, et sic esset infinitum et illimitatum et per se necesse esse. Sed hoc est falsum."

[32] PB 2.159.

[33] PB 2.160.

[34] For a helpful collection and analysis of texts from Aquinas on the real distinction see C. Fabro, *La nozione metafisica di partecipazione*, pp. 212–44. Also see J. de Finance, *Etre et agir*, pp. 94–111; L. Sweeney, "Existence/Essence in Thomas Aquinas's Early Writings," *Proceedings of the American Catholic Philosophical Association* 37 (1963), pp. 97–131.

theory strongly reflects that used by Giles. Secondly, if Godfrey's arguments for the real distinction are not verbatim reproductions of those offered by Giles, they are similar. Finally, at the time of Quodlibet 3 (Christmas 1286), Godfrey could hardly have been unaware of the debate then being waged by Henry of Ghent and Giles of Rome with respect to the real distinction.[35]

2. *Arguments against the Real Distinction*

Godfrey prefaces his presentation of these arguments with two fundamental presuppositions: (1) the denial of any universal *esse* that would exist in itself outside the mind and apart from individual entities; (2) the analogy of being. Godfrey offers two arguments in support of his first presupposition, that is, to show that there can be no subsisting being in general or universal *esse*. If no other universal exists as such, as universal, in the order of real and actual being, the same must apply with even greater force to that which is most general and most universal, that is to say, to being, the one, the good, etc., or in other words, to that which is transcendental. Universality is a condition that is realized in the intellect of the one who understands rather than in the existing thing itself. Secondly, if such an absolute and universal *esse* were

---

[35] See n. 22 above. In his *Quaestiones disputatae de esse et essentia* Giles responded to Henry's rejection of the real distinction in his Quodlibet 1, q. 9, of 1276. Henry's reply to this refutation is to be found in his Q 10, q. 7 of Christmas 1286 (see Paulus, *Henri de Gand. . .* , p. 281). One might also seek for parallels between Godfrey and Giles's *Theoremata de esse et essentia*. But while listing the sources Godfrey seems to have in mind in his Q 3, qq. 1 – 2, Paulus does not cite it (see *Henri de Gand . . .* , p. 321, n. 2). Moreover, in his article treating of the debate between Henry and Giles ("Les disputes d'Henri . . . et de Gilles . . . ," p. 328), he states that Henry did not have the *Theoremata* available. One might suspect, then, that the same was true of Godfrey. Granted that the date of this work is disputed (see n. 11 above), none of the proposed dates would preclude Godfrey's usage of it in Q 3 (Christmas 1286). Hocedez seems to be of the opinion that Godfrey did have access there to Giles's *Theoremata*. See his *Aegidii Romani theoremata . . .* , pp. (12) and (103). One does find similarities between the argumentation presented by Godfrey and that in Giles's *Theoremata*. Thus, for the analogy between generation and creation, and between matter-form composition and essence-existence composition see Theorem V, pp. 19ff. (Theorem VI notes this parallel again but points out certain differences between matter-form composition and that of essence and existence. See pp. 26 – 30.) For the real distinction as necessary to account for the contingent character of the separate intelligences see Theorem XII, pp. 74 – 77. For the need of the same distinction to safeguard the limited and participated character of finite being, see Theorem V, pp. 25 – 26; Theorem XX, pp. 141 – 42. For an argument based on the possibility of knowing created essences without knowing their existence, see Theorem XII, pp. 67 – 70, 73.

to subsist apart from its realization in individual beings, all that is would have to be identified with this universal *esse*. But, as Parmenides once reasoned, nothing can be distinguished or divided from being. It would follow, then, that all things would be identical with this subsisting universal being, and hence, that all things would be one.[36]

Godfrey grants, of course, that there is one first being which is the measure and the cause of all others and that it itself is unparticipated being. But he absolutely refuses to identify this being with being in general or being taken as universal in the order of predication. One may describe this entity as "universal" virtually, which is to say that its causal influence extends to all other beings. But insofar as it is the cause of all else, it must be a formally distinct being in itself, not some kind of universal being that would be predicated of everything else. One should not seek as the cause of all things a being which is existence alone (*esse solum*) therefore, but which is rather itself a given being (*aliquod ens*).[37] In like manner, reasons Godfrey, one should not seek for something in its effects which would be existence alone. An effect is not produced by this first cause either in terms of its existence alone or in terms of its essence alone, but in terms of the determined being it enjoys in the order of reality. In other words, Godfrey insists that one cannot distinguish the first cause from the creature by holding that the former is nothing but existence itself, while only the latter would be a given being with a given mode of being.[38]

Godfrey's second presupposition is that being is analogical. As we have already seen in our discussion of analogy in Ch. I above, he arrives at this conclusion by contending that being is neither univocal nor purely equivocal.

---

[36] See PB 2.302–03 (short version); 160–61 (long version).

[37] PB 2.161 (long version); PB 2.303.

[38] PB 2.161, 163. For the short version see p. 303: "Secundum, quod in rerum natura non est aliquid in rebus creatis quod sit tantum esse nec ut participans nec ut participatum [quod sit effectus primi entis, et alia agentia causent essentias quantum ad formas], quia nihil est in rerum natura quod super esse [absolute dictum] non addat aliquam determinatam rationem essendi." According to *Vat. ms. Borghese* 298 as cited by A. Pattin, the bracketed texts should be omitted. See his "La structure de l'être fini selon Bernard d'Auvergne, O.P. († après 1307)," *Tijdschrift voor Filosofie* 24 (1962), p. 690. Granted this, the thought conveyed by the first bracketed text corresponds to that found in the long version, pp. 161 and 163. One is here reminded of Siger of Brabant's refusal to distinguish essence and *esse* in creatures in such fashion that *esse* would be caused by the first cause while essence would not. See his *Quaestiones in Metaphysicam,* q. 7, p. 14. Siger attributes such a view to Albert the Great in connection with his defense of a theory of real distinction and counters that all that is found in the thing is the effect of the first cause. See p. 15 for the same according to the shorter version as preserved in Godfrey's student notebook.

Consequently, reasons Godfrey, being applies to all things that exist in terms of their individuating notes as well as their generic and specific aspects, and according to a real ordering and proportion that obtains between the analogates (different beings) themselves.[39]

In the short version Godfrey presents five arguments against the real distinction between essence and existence. Although the same argumentation is present in the long version, but in more scattered fashion, we shall follow the plan of the short version.

Argument 1: Being involves less addition to that of which it is affirmed than does the one. An aspect of being is included in every other, while the notion of the one or unity in some way adds to being. Yet the one adds nothing real to the essence of that of which it is affirmed. Consequently and a fortiori, neither does being (*ens*) and therefore neither does existence (*esse*) add anything real to the essence of which it is predicated.[40]

Argument 2: Godfrey appeals to Aristotle's contention in *Metaphysics* IV that being and the one are really identical. Neither adds anything to that in which it is realized. Thus man, man considered as being (*ens homo*), and man considered as one (*unus homo*) are really one and the same. This would not be so if being (*ens*) added anything real to the essence of which it is affirmed.[41] Again the argument assumes that if such is true of being (*ens*) and essence, if being implies no real addition to essence, then the same will hold for existence (*esse*) and essence. Existence will likewise imply no real addition to essence.

Argument 3: Godfrey's third argument in the short version is much like the first two. Each and everything is being either of itself or by reason of something which is added. But if it is being only by reason of some factor which is superadded, the same alternative arises again. This factor itself is being either of itself or by reason of something further which is superadded. If it is being of itself, one should have admitted this of the first case. If it is being only by reason of something further which is superadded, the same question and the same process will be repeated indefinitely, to infinity. To avoid this one must rather admit that each and every thing is being (*ens*) of itself and not by reason of something superadded, that is, not by reason of a really distinct *esse* or existence.[42]

---

[39] See PB 2.161–63 (long version) and 303 (short version). For fuller discussion of this see our Ch. I, pp. 20–22.

[40] PB 2.303.

[41] *Ibid*. For Aristotle see *Metaphysics* IV, c. 2 (1003b 26–33).

[42] PB 2.303. In both the short and the long versions of this argument (PB 2.164) Godfrey attributes it to Averroes. For which see *In IV Met.*, Vol. 8, fol. 67va.

Since these three arguments are closely related, and especially so in the long version, they may be discussed together.[43] First of all, they seem to be directed against a theory of real distinction wherein existence (*esse*) would be superadded to essence from without, almost, as it were, as an accident. Far from being the theory defended by Thomas Aquinas, he had attributed this position to Avicenna and, as we have already seen, had sharply criticized it.[44] And Godfrey's own argumentation against this theory is evidently heavily influenced by Averroes's refutation of Avicenna.[45] But Giles of Rome's language according to which existence (*esse*) adds some "thing" (*res*) to essence would obviously leave his theory open to criticism of this type, whether or not such terminology accurately reflects his understanding of the real distinction.

Secondly, the present arguments draw a close parallel between *ens* (being), taken as a transcendental, and *esse*, taken as existence. If a thing is not an *ens* or being by reason of something superadded, the same must hold for its *esse*. It will not enjoy existence by reason of something superadded. In other words, because thing (*res*) and being (*ens*) when taken as transcendentals are convertible, then *res*, when taken as essence will be convertible with *ens*, taken as *esse* or existence. Essence and existence will, therefore, be really identical. But a defender of a theory of real distinction would surely challenge this last step. Within the Thomistic theory, in any event, one can hardly equate the transcendental being (*ens*) with existence (*esse*), one of its intrinsic principles, to be sure, but only one. One cannot equate the thing-being (*res-*

[43] Arguments one and two as presented by Godfrey in the short version could be regarded as one argument. All three are loosely joined to form one argument in the longer version. But there the text seems to be misplaced. Instead of appearing in the section where Godfrey presents his arguments against the real distinction, it is to be found near the end of the previous section which treats of analogy (see PB 2.163–64).

[44] See his *In IV Met.*, n. 558, and n. 5 of this chapter.

[45] For Averroes's argumentation against Avicenna see *In IV Met.*, fol. 67ra-va. Note in particular: "Avicenna autem peccavit multum in hoc quod existimavit quod unum et ens significant dispositiones additas essentiae rei" (67ra). For an interesting discussion of Averroes and Siger in their opposition to Avicenna on this see Maurer, "*Esse* and *Essentia* in the Metaphysics of Siger of Brabant," pp. 78ff. Godfrey's arguments 2 and 3 (and by implication argument 1) are anticipated by Siger's presentation of arguments in the *contra* of his q. 7 in his *Quaestiones in Metaphysicam* (*op. cit.*, pp. 13–14). His rejection of the real distinction and his citation of the final argument again in the body of his question (p. 18) indicate his fundamental agreement. Granted the close similarity between these arguments and those presented by Godfrey, it should be noted that they do not appear in the short version of Siger's question, that is to say, in Godfrey's student notebook. There is, of course, no reason to deny that Godfrey could have been familiar with the longer version as well.

ens) couplet with the essence-existence couplet. Granted that being (*ens*) is predicated of a subject by reason of its existence (*esse*) and that thing (*res*) is predicated of it by reason of its essence, yet both being (*ens*) and thing (*res*) apply to the entire concrete subject rather than to existence alone or to essence alone.[46] Godfrey's confusion here between the transcendentals, on the one hand, and essence and existence as intrinsic principles of being, on the other, once more suggests that his understanding of the real distinction was not that of an Aquinas.

Argument 4: In Quodlibet 13, q. 3 Godfrey notes that it is often asserted that essence and existence differ for this reason: that which is signified by essence in the abstract is signified as something fixed and permanent, somewhat like a habit; but that which is signified by existence is taken as something in change and in a state of flux or becoming, as an act which is continuously exercised. But, counters Godfrey, the relation between essence and existence seems to be similar to that which obtains between "heat" and "to heat," "light" and "to give light," "whiteness" and "to whiten," etc. If one finds that with such particular terms that which is signified by the noun is really distinct from that which is signified by the verb, the same will hold for more general terms such as essence and existence. But if such is not true in the first case, it will not apply in the second.[47]

In Quodlibet 3, q. 1 Godfrey presents a similar argument. As he sees it, the concrete noun, the abstract noun, and the verb do not signify really distinct things, granted that they differ in their mode of signification. Just as this is true, for instance of *currens* (one who runs, or running), *cursus* (race), and *currere* (to run), so will it apply to *ens* (being), *essentia* (essence), and *esse* (existence). Nor does it help to reply that when *ens* is taken as a noun (being) it does signify the same thing as essence, but not when it is taken as

---

[46] For this in Thomas see *In IV Met.*, lect. 2, n. 558: "Et ideo hoc nomen ens quod imponitur ab ipso esse significat idem cum nomine quod imponitur ab ipsa essentia." Also see *De veritate*, q. 1, art. 1, for his discussion of *res* and *ens*. There is a similar misconception of the Thomistic theory in Siger. For an interesting criticism of his confusion between the *res-ens* couplet (taken as transcendentals) and the essence-existence couplet see Van Steenberghen, "La composition constitutive de l'être fini," *Revue Néoscolastique de Philosophie* 41 (1938), pp. 515–16; *Siger de Brabant d'après ses oeuvres inédites*, Vol. 2 (Louvain, 1942), pp. 598–99. For an excellent commentary on the Thomistic passage in question see pp. 595–600; and the reference cited above in n. 5.

[47] PB 5.207. It is interesting to note that even at this late date in his career Godfrey's views on the real distinction remain unchanged. In the same context he comments: "Argumentum quod ad aliam partem inducitur non valet; quia falsum supponit, scilicet quod esse sit aliquid differens a substantia rei."

a participle (be-ing). He counters that *legens* whether taken as a noun (one who reads) or as a participle (reading) signifies the same thing as *legere* (to read), granted a difference in the mode of signification. The same will apply, therefore, to being (*ens*) and essence and existence (*esse*).[48] Indeed, continues Godfrey, one must posit for every infinitive a term which, while remaining the same, may serve both as participle and as noun and which signifies the same thing in each case, although in different ways. Since *esse* (or *esse existentiae*, existential being) is an infinitive, it will have such a term corresponding to it. Hence, one must conclude that *ens*, taken either as noun or as participle, and *esse* signify the same thing and therefore that being (*ens*), essence, entity (*entitas*), and existence (*esse*) likewise all signify the same thing in reality.[49]

Argument 5: The final argument is derived from a consideration of the structure of a finite being, particularly of a finite material being, as required by a theory of real distinction between essence and existence. A composition of a really distinct essence and existence must either be a composition of pure potency and unqualified act (*actus simpliciter*), resulting in a being that is essentially one (*unum per se*) or else of potency in a qualified sense (*secundum quid*) and act in a qualified sense (*secundum quid*), resulting in something that is only accidentally one (*unum per accidens*). But consider a purely material entity. If one adopts the first alternative, it will follow that its essence—pure potency by hypothesis—will itself be composed of prime matter and substantial form. There can be no intermediary between pure potency (prime matter) and potency in a qualified sense, a subject which enjoys actuality in itself (*actus simpliciter*) but which is in potency with respect to its accidental acts. According to this first alternative, therefore, the essence itself will be pure potency, and will yet be composed of prime matter or pure potency and substantial form. Moreover, according to this alternative, existence will be unqualified act. But this will amount to identifying existence with substantial form, since unqualified act is substantial form![50]

---

[48] PB 2.303–04. Godfrey finds support here in Boethius and in Aristotle: ". . . sicut patet per Boethium, super illud verbum Perihermenias: verba secundum se dicta nomina sunt, ubi dicit Boethius quod legens nominaliter dictum, et legens participium, et legere verbum idem dicunt. Unde et Philosophus, quinto Metaphysicae, ubi distinguit nomina vult quod quotiens dicitur ens, et esse." For Boethius see *In librum de Interpretatione*, PL 64.309, 310, and 429. For Aristotle see *De interpretatione*, c. 3 (16b 20–21) and *Metaphysics* V, c. 7 (1017a 23–30). For Godfrey's long version see PB 2.164–65 as well as the discussion in Q 13, q. 3 (PB 5.207–08).

[49] PB 2.165 (long version). Note his conclusion: "Esse igitur dicit ipsam essentiam vel entitatem rei."

[50] PB 2.167–68 (long version); p. 304 (short version).

Godfrey rejects the second alternative as equally unsatisfactory. In this case essence and existence will be united as potency in a qualified sense and act in a qualified sense. But just as there is no intermediary between unqualified act and act in a qualified sense, so there is no intermediary between the act which is substantial form and that which is accidental form. Since existence is now being considered as act in a qualified sense, it will be reduced to the level of an accidental form. This will not do, continues Godfrey, since a subject must possess essence and existence in itself before (at least by priority of nature) it can receive any accident or accidental form. If one concedes this last point, it will then follow that an essence will exist "before" receiving its act of existence and by reason of an existence different from that with which it enters into composition.[51] For Godfrey, however, something is in potency to the degree that it is ordered to act or form. To be in potency is to be in potency to a form, whether substantial or accidental. That which is in potency to substantial form is in potency to substantial existence (*esse*). That which is in potency to accidental form is in potency to accidental existence. This is so because essence (*esse essentiae*) and existence (*esse existentiae*) and form and act are really one and the same.[52]

3. Godfrey's Reply to Argumentation for the Real Distinction

Having now offered a series of arguments against the theory of real distinction between essence and existence, Godfrey must respond to the argumentation in favor of that same theory. As will be recalled from our presentation of this argumentation above, one line of reasoning is based on the

---

[51] PB 2.168 (long version); p. 304 (short version). For some improvements in the text of the short version as suggested by Pattin see his "La structure de l'être . . . ," p. 691.

[52] PB 2.168 – 69. There is a certain similarity between some of the above arguments and three arguments directed against the real distinction by Henry of Ghent in his Q 1, q. 9 (fol. 6v – 7r). There Henry likens the case of *esse* to that of unity, truth, and goodness. If the latter are essential properties and are not really superadded to things, the same must be true of *esse*. In showing that being and the one are convertible Henry appeals to the texts from Aristotle's *Metaphysics* IV and Averroes's commentary on the same to which reference has been made above. Henry then argues that if no creature has *esse* by its essence but by reason of something superadded, no creature will be an *unum per se*. Again, if a creature only possesses *esse* by reason of a superadded form, this form itself will be *esse* only by reason of something else that is superadded, *ad infinitum*. Finally, will this superadded *esse* be something substantial or something accidental? Henry finds difficulties with each alternative. In Q 10, q. 7, Henry repeats these arguments (see fol. 416v – 417r). The latter Quodlibet dates from the same period as Godfrey's Q 3, that is, Christmas 1286.

possibility of knowing or understanding an essence without its existence or even as nonexistent. Godfrey questions the central assumption of this argument. If essence and existence are really identical, he counters, essence can neither be known nor be realized with the opposite of its existence. Essence in act cannot be realized or be known as such without actual existence. And essence in potency can neither be nor be known except with potential existence. He acknowledges that an essence can be understood not to be when it does not actually exist. In that case neither the essence nor its existence is actual. But whatever applies to one applies to the other. Whatever is true of essence is true of existence, since there are as many existences as essences.[53] In other words, Godfrey acknowledges that one may understand a given essence as not actually existing or without actual existence, for instance, when one recognizes it as only potentially existing. But in that case it will also be recognized as only potential in the line of essence as well or, as he puts it, with *non-esse essentiae* as well as with *non-esse existentiae*. For that which is only potential in the order of existence is only potential in the order of essence. The argument in question does not lead, therefore, to real distinction between essence and existence, but rather to a distinction between essence and essence, essence in act and essence in potency, or between being and being, being in act and being in potency.[54]

Godfrey makes a similar point in Quodlibet 4, q. 2. There he comments that when one knows the nature of a man by way of a simple concept (and hence only through the intellect in its first operation, simple apprehension), one will not yet have judged that the man exists or does not exist. But he will know the man's existence insofar as he knows his essence. For the two are really one and the same.[55]

---

[53] PB 2.305.

[54] PB 2.171. Note in particular: "Et ideo dicendum quod non potest intelligi essentia sub non esse existentiae nisi sicut potest intelligi sub non esse essentiae . . . Unde hoc non arguit quod esse sit aliud ab essentia, sed etiam quod ipsa essentia est alia a se ipsa, sicut ens in potentia est aliud a se ipso ente in actu et cetera." Also see Q 13, q. 3 (PB 5.208–09). Note in particular: "Non ergo potest dici quod essentia in actu sit indifferens ad esse et non esse. Immo includit esse, quia est id ipsum quod est illud sub alio modo intelligendi et significandi. Nec etiam essentia in potentia est indifferens ad esse et non esse. Immo excludit esse et includit non esse. Quantum ergo convenit alicui enti de essentia, tantum competit ei de esse; et e converso. Et cum essentia in potentia fit essentia in actu, esse in potentia fit etiam esse in actu." Also see the long version of Q 3, q. 1 for a somewhat related argument against the real distinction based on the unhappy consequences that will follow, according to Godfrey, from holding that an essence even when actual may be conceived of as not existing (PB 2.165–66).

[55] PB 2.235.

A second line of argumentation concluded to the real distinction on the basis of the diversity that must obtain between essence, an intrinsic passive principle or potency which participates, receives, and limits existence, and existence, its corresponding act and that in which it participates. Godfrey replies by distinguishing. Something may be in potency in one of two ways. On the one hand, it may be an intrinsic principle such as matter which receives its corresponding act or form. In such cases the subject will be prior to the form (at least in the order of nature) and will be capable of receiving it. But something may be in potency simply insofar as it preexists in the power of another and does not involve intrinsic contradiction in itself. In this sense an essence which does not now actually exist may be said to be in potency insofar as it can be brought into being by its cause. It is to be distinguished from a mere chimera since the latter, because it implies self-contradiction, cannot be brought into being by any cause.[56]

As regards the proposed argumentation for the real distinction, one can readily anticipate Godfrey's refutation. Essence is not to be described as potency in the first sense, that is, as an intrinsic receiving principle. It is not to be regarded as an intrinsic passive principle such as matter which would receive existence as its act. It is potential in the second way since, because of its conformity to its divine idea and consequent lack of intrinsic contradiction, it can be brought into being by its cause. Existence (*esse*) may be understood as the same essence insofar as it is an actual object and terminus of the divine creative activity. If one will speak of participation, the essence itself insofar as it is a divine likeness produced by God is also a certain participated existence, that is, an actual if inadequate likeness of the divine perfection.[57] Participation by composition of a really distinct *participans* (essence) and *participatum* (existence) is to be rejected.

As we have seen, Godfrey's formal presentation of arguments for the real distinction concludes in the long version of Quodlibet 3, q. 1 with an appeal to it as necessary to safeguard the difference between creatures and the Creator. Unless created *esse* is received and limited by a distinct essence, there

---

[56] PB 2.305 (short version).

[57] PB 2.169–71 (long version). Also see p. 305 for the short version. For a similar refutation of the argument based on participation see Henry of Ghent, Q 10, q. 7 (fol. 418r). There he distinguishes these two different ways of understanding participation. The verbal similarity between Henry's description of these and Godfrey's text in his long version is great enough to suggest that he may here be following Henry's text. Compare Godfrey's text (p. 170, 2nd par.) with Henry's description of the second way in which one may understand participation. Henry had already exposed this theory in his Q 1, q. 9 of 1276, but the verbal similarity between that exposition of the same and Godfrey's text is not so great. For Henry see fol. 6v.

will be no principle of limitation in simple finite beings. Consequently, there will be no way of distinguishing between them and the infinite being or God. Though one finds no direct reply to this argument in the long version, the short version approaches the problem from the standpoint of simplicity. In order to maintain that a created essence is less simple than the divine it is not necessary to posit plurality of really distinct principles therein, whether essence and existence or substance and accident. Granted that in every creature there is some accident in addition to its substance, this does not establish composition of the creature's essence as such. The finite essence is rather said to be participated and to be more composite or less simple than the divine by reason of one and the same principle, which is act in one respect and potency in another. A less perfect essence is always potential when compared with one that is more perfect, and yet actual to the extent that it actually exists.[58] More will be said about this theory in Section C of this chapter, where Godfrey's positive teaching on essence and existence will be considered.

One might attempt to reason from the fact that a creature is caused to a real composition therein of existence (*esse*) and a distinct principle that receives it. The point is important, since Giles of Rome had insisted that without the real distinction one cannot safeguard the doctrine of creation.[59] Although Godfrey does not offer this as a separate argument while presenting the case for the real distinction in the opening pages of Quodlibet 3, q. 1, he does recognize its importance and its close connection with the others.[60]

As one might expect, he categorically rejects any such contention. To say

---

[58] PB 2.306.

[59] On this in Giles see Gilson, *History of Christian Philosophy . . .* , p. 423; Hocedez, *Aegidii Romani theoremata . . .* , pp. (32)–(33); Suárez, "El pensamiento de Egidio Romano . . . ," pp. 240–47; Carlo, *The Ultimate Reducibility. . .* , p. 14; Trapé, "Causalità e partecipazione . . . ," p. 108. For Giles's own stress on this point see his *Theoremata de esse . . .* , Th. XIX: "Quia tota causa quare nos investigamus quod esse sit res differens ab essentia ex hoc sumitur ut possimus salvare res creatas esse compositas et posse creari et posse esse et non esse . . . " (p. 129); and in his *Quaestiones disputatae de esse et essentia*, q. 9: " . . . sic creatio facit scire quod essentia esset [read: est] aliud ab esse quia ex hoc est creatio inquantum essentia acquirit esse" (fol. 21rab).

[60] "Et ulterius et consequenter et quarto declarandum est quod ratione productionis rei per quam ipsa res potest recipere esse, non oportet ponere compositionem ipsius esse ad rem sive essentiam rei sicut quibusdam videtur oportere dicere. Nam ad hanc rationem possunt fere omnes rationes reduci quibus probatur diversitas ipsius esse ad essentiam secundum rem aut per intentionem, et necessitate huius rationis amota videntur dissolvi omnes aliae rationes pro illa parte aut saltem difficiliores" (PB 2.160).

that a thing is caused or created is not to imply that really distinct principles must be found therein, one an essence which would receive the other, its corresponding act, existence. He refers to the "philosophers" who had admitted that an effect could be coeternal with its cause as in the case of separate substances without appealing to any such intrinsic composition of the effect itself. Hence those who maintain that things have been created from nothing without any kind of change in their cause can surely defend the created character of such effects without presupposing any such composition therein of essence and existence. If one would argue from the conditions required for an effect-cause relationship, the only possible reason suggesting the need for such composition in the effect might seem to arise from a consideration of its efficient cause. One might think that the efficient cause needs a subject on which to exercise its causal activity. But this will apply only to a cause that acts by changing something that preexists, not to a creative cause. The Creator needs no such subject in which its effect would be realized. In Godfrey's opinion, therefore, one should not attempt to establish a parallel between generation and creation or between the matter-form relationship and that of essence and existence. Once again he finds no need to conclude to real distinction of essence and existence.[61]

Godfrey resolutely decides, therefore, for real identity of essence and existence. Not only has he found the arguments advanced in favor of the real distinction wanting. He has attempted to show by counterarguments that the theory leads to insurmountable difficulties. His theory of identity of essence

---

[61] PB 2.166–69, 171–73. Note that Godfrey inserts here (pp. 167ff.) in the longer version argument five of the shorter version against the real distinction. As already indicated, we have chosen to follow the plan of the shorter version for the sake of greater clarity. For criticism of any argument based on a strict parallel between essence and existence and matter and form, joined with further criticism of any argument grounded on the created or caused character of finite being, see pp. 171–73. Here a new development appears. Before its creation (or in an eternal world, by priority of nature) the matter of a stone, for instance, will be in potency to its *esse essentiae* before actually realizing it, as well as to its *esse existentiae*. Or to apply this to an angel which is to be created, since it does not yet exist either as regards actual *esse essentiae* or actual *esse existentiae*, it will be in potency to both. Consequently, according to the underlying principle of this argument, the nature in question will not only be really distinct from its *esse existentiae* which it "later" receives. It will also be in potency to its *esse essentiae*, since it does not yet possess this either. Hence it should also be distinct from its *esse essentiae*. But, argues Godfrey, it is clear that *essentia* and *esse essentiae* do not really differ. Consequently, the argument does not point to the alleged distinction between *essentia* and *esse existentiae* with any greater force. From the fact that an essence is in potency to exist, one cannot conclude to a real distinction between essence and existence.

and existence now enables him to answer the question originally raised at the beginning of his treatment of their relationship in Quodlibet 3, q. 1: Can a creature be called a being by reason of its essence when it is not such by reason of its existence?[62]

If one holds for the real distinction and if one also holds that matter can continue to exist without any form, then one might argue that essence can be without existence. Even this hypothesis should be qualified, however. If one maintains that essence retains some actuality of itself (though not enough for it to exist in fact without the addition of existence), then a given essence either is or is not determined to a given existence. If it is, then one cannot say that the essence in question can be understood not only without its existence but even as nonexisting. (It will be recalled that Giles of Rome had contended that an essence can be understood even as nonexisting.) If the essence is not determined to a given existence, then that same essence could successively receive different existences, as is true of matter with respect to different forms. In this event the essence would always be joined to some existence just as matter is always found with some form. Nonetheless, when something is not by reason of its existence, it might still be such by reason of its essence insofar as the latter remains subject to another existence. But for Godfrey the answer is clear. When something is not being by reason of its existence then it is likewise not being by reason of its essence. Insofar as it is virtually contained within its cause and can be brought into being, it is in potency both as regards its essence and its existence. Whatever is true of essence is true of existence and vice versa.[63]

---

[62] PB 2.156, quoted in n. 20.

[63] PB 2.174–75. Note p. 174 in particular: "Sed quia magis probabile est dicere quod non differt realiter esse et essentia, ideo dicendum quod re non ente secundum esse existentiae, ipsa nihil est actu in se ipsa nec in aliqua realitate secundum esse essentiae, sed solum est virtualiter in sua causa et est secundum hoc aliquid secundum esse essentiae et existentiae in potentia, ut semper quantum contingit alicui de esse essentiae vel de essentia, tantum de esse existentiae vel existentia." Godfrey's usage here of "magis probabile" should not deceive the reader, as it seems to be merely a rhetorical device. In the light of his detailed refutation of the arguments for the real distinction, his presentation and unreserved acceptance of the arguments against it, and his rejection of Henry of Ghent's theory of intentional distinction (see PB 2.175–77 and our text below), there can be no doubt as to his personal conviction. He returns again and again throughout his career to the theme that whatever is true of essence is true of existence. This theme is, of course, anchored in the real identity of essence and existence. Moreover, as will be seen below, real identity of essence and existence serves as a controlling principle in his solution to the problem of subsistence and in his attribution of accidental existence to accidental forms as distinguished from the existence of substance. Finally, in addition to the passages already

In Quodlibet 3, q. 2, Godfrey entertains practically the same question. This time he asks: Is essence created before existence?[64] If one holds for the real distinction then both essence and existence will arise simultaneously with the creation of the composite. However, one might argue that essence is prior to existence from the standpoint of origin (presumably because according to the theory of real distinction essence receives existence), while existence is prior to essence from the standpoint of dignity and perfection. Godfrey would qualify this suggestion. If essence and existence differ as potency *simpliciter* and act *simpliciter*, the above will stand. But if they differ as potency *secundum quid* and act *secundum quid*, then that which is in potency (essence) will be prior to its act *secundum quid* not only in terms of origin but in terms of actuality and perfection. In other words the essence will possess its substantial being before receiving its act *secundum quid* (existence). Under this hypothesis, therefore, essence will be created "before" existence, at least by priority of nature.[65] But since essence and existence are really identical for Godfrey, there is no real priority of essence over existence. Essence cannot be created before existence.[66]

In conclusion, it should be noted that Godfrey has proposed a rather extreme version of the theory of real distinction between essence and existence as a necessary condition for giving an affirmative answer to the questions raised by Quodlibet 3, q. 1 and Quodlibet 3, q. 2. According to the discussion in Quodlibet 3, q. 1, essence would not be determined to a given act of existence but could receive different existences in succession. According to

---

quoted or referred to above, Godfrey concludes Q 3, q. 1 with the following: "Hoc igitur modo loquendo de esse [intentional distinction] et quocumque alio modo quo ponitur differentia ipsius esse ad essentiam secundum rem aut per intentionem relicto, teneamus ut praedictum est quod esse et essentia id idem sunt, ita quod quantum intelligitur de essentia tantum intelligitur de esse" (PB 2.177). Near the end of Q 3, q. 2 he comments: "Et ideo secundum praedicta dicendum est quod cum omnino sint idem secundum rem esse et essentia . . ." (PB 2.179). Also, note his comment in Q 7, q. 11: "Hoc enim verum est in omnibus, scilicet quod esse non dicit aliquam rem additam essentiae . . ." (PB 3.386). In Disputed Question 18 (according to the numbering of the table in *Borghese 164*) one finds the following according to the two versions: "Sed ista positio non potest stare, primo quia supponit falsum, scilicet quod essentia realiter differat ab esse" (*Borghese 122*, fol. 159vb); "Sed ista positio non potest stare, primo quia supponit falsum, ut tenetur pro verissimo ab aliquibus, scilicet quod essentia realiter differat ab esse, quod alii firmissime tenent esse falsum" (*Bruges 491*, fol. 226rb–226va).

64 PB 2.177. "Utrum prius creetur essentia quam esse."

65 PB 2.178–79, 306.

66 PB 2.179. See pp. 306–07: "Sed quia, ut probatum est supra, esse et essentia non differunt re, ideo unum non creatur prius alio nec unum praecedit aliud origine vel dignitate secundum rem."

the argumentation in Quodlibet 3, q. 2, essence and existence would differ only as potency *secundum quid* and act *secundum quid*. Neither a Thomas Aquinas nor a Giles of Rome would subscribe to either of these qualifications as they stand. Nor would Godfrey himself regard either of them as acceptable.[67] But given his identification of essence and existence, he cannot find any version of their real distinction acceptable.

B. GODFREY AND HENRY OF GHENT'S THEORY OF INTENTIONAL DISTINCTION BETWEEN ESSENCE AND EXISTENCE

As we have already indicated, in Quodlibet 4, q. 2 Godfrey outlines three different theories with respect to the relationship between essence and existence. According to the second theory, that of Henry of Ghent as we shall now see, they do not differ really but only intentionally. Because of this intentional distinction, essence and existence are said to join in composition with one another in some manner. Therefore, when a thing is corrupted as regards its existence (*esse existentiae*), its essence likewise ceases to be in the extramental order. Nevertheless, it continues to be in terms of its essence or essential being (*esse essentiae*) in some way.[68] As may be gathered from this text, there is a close relationship between Henry's theory of essential being (*esse essentiae*) and his defense of an intentional distinction between essence and existence. Consequently, in presenting Godfrey's understanding of and reaction to this theory, we shall consider: (1) Henry's theory of *esse essentiae* and Godfrey's reaction thereto; (2) Henry's theory of intentional distinction between essence and existence and Godfrey's reaction thereto.

1. *Henry's Theory of* Esse Essentiae *and Godfrey's Reaction*

As we have also seen above, in Quodlibet 6, q. 6 Godfrey refers to Avicenna's position according to which something may be considered in terms

---

[67] See argument 5 above for Godfrey's criticism of the view that essence and existence are joined as potency *secundum quid* and act *secundum quid*. There he finds uniting them as potency and act *simpliciter* equally unacceptable. For apparent rejection of the view that one and the same entity could receive different essences in succession see Q 2, q. 2 (PB 2.60): ". . . cum corrupta re creata quantum ad eius esse existentiae quod est actualitas realis ipsius essentiae, non maneat huiusmodi essentia sub alia actualitate essendi sive existendi, alioquin una et eadem essentia numero posset esse plurium successive, sicut contingit de materia."

[68] See our text, pp. 45–46, and PB 2.235.

of its existence in the mind, its existence as an individual thing, or "absolutely," that is to say, in terms of its quiddity viewed in itself. While Godfrey acknowledges that things may be considered in this third way, he insists that they can exist only in the mind or in the individual.[69] Godfrey's warning might lead one to suspect that some had carried Avicenna's division farther and posited a third kind of existence to correspond to this third or absolute way of considering things.

In Quodlibet 8, q. 3 Godfrey considers a division of being according to which cognitive being is distinguished from real being. Real being is in turn divided into essential being (*esse essentiae*) and existential being (*esse existentiae*). Essential being refers to that whereby a thing is what it is in itself and absolutely, without reference either to its existence in the mind or to its extramental existence as an individual, its *esse existentiae*.[70] According to this theory a thing will enjoy eternal cognitive being insofar as it is always known by God. But its essential being or *esse essentiae* will also be eternal. Such is not true of its existential being. As Godfrey presents this theory, it is because such things are known from eternity by God that an eternal essential being must be assigned to them. And this essential being is something in addition to a thing's merely cognitive being, granted that it can never be realized without the latter, that is to say, without God's knowledge of it.[71] Because of their essential being, therefore, things fall under the predicaments even when they possess no actual existence or existential being. In addition to their purely cognitive being and apart from their existence as individuals, they enjoy a certain quidditative content in themselves, again by reason of their *esse essentiae*. Needless to say, Godfrey rejects this division of being and proposes the one we have already considered above in Ch. I.[72]

Such a theory does show, however, where an overly pressed interpretation of Avicenna's view of nature or essence considered absolutely may lead.[73]

---

[69] See pp. 28–29 of our text above and PB 3.140, cited in Ch. I, n. 64. Note the following from Avicenna: "Essentiae vero rerum aut sunt in ipsis rebus aut sunt in intellectu; unde habent tres respectus. Unus respectus essentiae est secundum quod ipsa est non relata ad aliquod tertium esse, nec ad id quod sequitur eam secundum quod ipsa est sic. Alius respectus est secundum quod est in his singularibus. Et alius secundum quod est in intellectu." *Logica* I, fol. 2rb.

[70] PB 4.34–35.

[71] PB 4.35.

[72] PB 4.36–38. See our text, pp. 15–18.

[73] For a nuanced presentation of this notion of the essence or nature taken absolutely in the light of its Avicennian origins as well as in Henry of Ghent, see J. Paulus, *Henri de Gand . . .* , pp. 69–74. In Avicenna see especially his *Metaphysica* V, 1–2, fol. 86va–87vb. For evidence of Henry's close dependence upon Avicenna

It should be remembered that Avicenna himself does not seem to have posited a threefold state of existence to correspond to this threefold consideration of essence. For him the nature will never be realized in fact except in the mind or in the thing.[74] But there is danger in a theory which moves from the order of the possible to the order of the real that such a threefold consideration of essence may ultimately lead one to postulate a corresponding threefold *esse*. In such an event the third *esse* (*esse essentiae*) may be granted priority over cognitive being as well as over existential being.

As we shall now see, such a doctrine of essential being seems to have been of central importance in the metaphysics of Henry of Ghent and an innovation within Latin scholasticism itself.[75] Godfrey was quite familiar with Henry's views on this point and appears to have had the latter in mind in his discussion of and rejection of the division of being cited above from Quodlibet 8, q. 3. As is suggested there and as is quite clear from Godfrey's detailed examination of the same theory in Quodlibet 2, q. 2, he closely connects Henry's views on *esse essentiae* with his reading (misreading, according to Godfrey) of Avicenna's three ways in which an essence or nature may be considered. (Paulus compliments Godfrey for his accurate exposition of Henry's views in Quodlibet 2, q. 2.)[76]

Godfrey's Quodlibet 2 dates from Easter 1286, as does Henry's Quodlibet 9. But in Quodlibet 2, q. 2 Godfrey describes Henry's theory of *esse essentiae*

---

with respect to the same see his Q 3, q. 9, fol. 60v–61r. Also see J. Gómez Caffarena, *Ser participado y ser subsistente en la metafísica de Enrique de Gante* (Rome, 1958), pp. 26–27; W. Hoeres, "Wesen und Dasein bei Heinrich von Gent und Duns Scotus," *Franziskanische Studien* 47 (1965), pp. 122–23.

[74] Note the *certitudo*, tentatively described as *esse proprium*, which appears to correspond to the essence considered absolutely in the following passage from Avicenna's *Metaphysica* I: "Unaquaeque enim res habet certitudinem qua est id quod est, sicut triangulus habet certitudinem qua est triangulus, et albedo habet certitudinem qua est albedo, et hoc est quod fortasse appellamus esse proprium. Nec intendimus per illud nisi intentionem esse affirmativi, quia verbum ens signat etiam multas intentiones, ex quibus est certitudo qua est unaquaeque res, et est sicut esse proprium rei. . . . Quoniam cum dixeris quod certitudo talis rei est in singularibus vel in anima vel absolute ita ut communicet utrisque, erit tunc haec intentio apprehensa et intellecta" (fol. 72va). See Paulus, *op. cit.*, pp. 77, 82–83.

[75] Paulus, *op. cit.*, p. 84.

[76] Paulus, *op. cit.*, pp. 123–25. On p. 124 Paulus observes that in Q 2, q. 2 Godfrey puts his finger on a point often missed by exegetes of Henry's doctrine of *esse essentiae*. Godfrey rightly notes that the notion of *esse essentiae* rises for Henry from an examination of human knowledge and of the different situations regarding our knowledge of genuine possibiles, on the one hand, and mere chimeras, on the other. Then only does Henry appeal to the theory of a twofold divine causality, one formal and the other efficient (also see p. 124, n. 2).

especially as it is found in the latter's Quodlibet 3, q. 9.[77] Here Godfrey raises the question whether the essence of a creature is indifferent to existence and nonexistence.[78] He begins by noting that some maintain that such is true for this reason, that science can only be had concerning that which is a true quiddity and essence, or a true predicamental reality (*res*). But for there to be science in the proper sense about a given thing, it is not necessary for that thing to exist in actuality. Its capacity to exist suffices, as is the case, for instance, with an eclipse or with rain. Therefore, according to this position, actual existence is not required for something to be a true essence or to enjoy quidditative being. In other words, an essence or quiddity of this kind may be said to be indifferent with respect to existence and nonexistence.[79]

After a brief reference to the opposed position, the denial that essence is indifferent to existence and nonexistence,[80] Godfrey returns to the first theory in the corpus of Quodlibet 2, q. 2. From his remarks there it is clearly Henry that he has in mind. As he observes, some account for the fact that such nonexistents can be known by holding that they correspond to exemplar ideas in the divine intellect. These nonexistents are to be distinguished from others which not only do not now exist in fact as individuals but will never be capable of so doing. The latter, chimeras, cannot be objects of science in any proper sense. This is so, according to defenders of this theory (Henry), because they do not correspond to formal exemplars in the divine mind. Since the former, genuine possibles, can be objects of science even before they actually exist as individuals, Henry maintains that in some way their essence is and remains indifferent to existence and nonexistence. The kind of indifference will be determined more precisely later in this chapter. Consequently, according to this theory, when a thing is corrupted in terms of its individual

---

[77] As Paulus observes, Godfrey's description reflects views found in Henry's Q 8, qq. 1–2, and may also have in mind Henry's Q 9, q. 2 (*op. cit.*, pp. 123–24, n. 2). However, the textual similarity is especially striking between Godfrey's Q 2, q. 2 and Henry's Q 3, q. 9.

[78] "Utrum essentia creaturae sit aliquid indifferens ad esse et non esse" (PB 2.53).

[79] PB 2.53–54.

[80] Here Godfrey cites a text from Augustine's *De Trinitate* in support of the contrary view: ". . . sicut ab eo quod est sapere dicta est sapientia et ab eo quod est scire dicta est scientia, ita ab eo quod est esse dicta est essentia." Godfrey comments: "Essentia ergo se habet ad esse sicut sapientia ad sapere. Sed nulla sapientia se habet per indifferentiam ad sapere et non sapere, quia omnis sapientia determinate se habet ad actum sapiendi. Quare et cetera." (PB 2.54). For Augustine see *De Trinitate* V, c. 2 (PL 42.912; CCSL 50.207–08). For reference to the same text in Augustine and precisely the same commentary on it as an argument for the contrary view, see Henry, Q 3, q. 9, fol. 60v. There Henry is discussing the question: "Utrum sit ponere aliquam essentiam per indifferentiam se habentem ad esse et ad non esse."

existence, it will not be corrupted in terms of its essential being (*esse essentiae*).[81]

Fundamental to Henry's theory as Godfrey here presents it are two points. First of all, the need to account for our ability to have true knowledge or science of nonexisting possibles, on the one hand, but not of mere chimeras, on the other, leads him to distinguish between a creature insofar as it is merely dependent on God in the order of formal exemplary causality and insofar as it is also dependent on him in the order of efficient causality. Secondly, Henry finds support for his understanding of *esse essentiae* by offering a particular interpretation of Avicenna's description of the threefold way in which an essence or nature may be considered. In the subsequent pages of Quodlibet 2, q. 2, Godfrey exposes Henry's views on each of these issues in considerable detail and then criticizes them.

As regards the first point and in accord with the description we have already seen both in Quodlibet 8, q. 3 and in the opening part of Quodlibet 2, q. 2, Godfrey notes that according to Henry (always unnamed) it is precisely because a creature has a formal exemplar in the divine intellect that it may be said to be something in itself or a true predicamental entity (*res*). This kind of dependency also accounts for the fact that true knowledge or science can be had of it even when it does not exist as an individual. But it is because a creature is dependent on the divine will in the order of efficient causality that it exists as an individual in fact and has existential being.[82] Moreover, if a creature enjoys a real relation to God in time as to its efficient cause, it will also enjoy a real relation to him from eternity in the order of

---

[81] PB 2.54–55. Note the following remark: ". . . de talibus potest dici esse scientia quae non est non entium, sed entium, eo quod obiectum intellectus est quod quid est sive vera rei quidditas, et cum de talibus sit scientia, hoc non contingeret nisi apprehenderentur vere praedicata essentialia de ipsis sive ipsis convenire, utpote pluvia non existente vere habetur scientia de ipsa, non autem nisi cognoscendo eius materiam et formam ad eius essentiam pertinentia et praedicata essentialia de ipsa, ut quod est aqua gradatim cadens, et per se passiones et cetera. . ." The passage is interesting in that it indicates how *scientia* is being understood by Godfrey in this context, that is to say, strictly, as implying knowledge of a thing in terms of its essential principles and necessary properties.

[82] PB 2.55–56. For Henry see Q 1, q. 9: "Primum esse [esse essentiae] habet essentia creaturae essentialiter . . . inquantum habet formale exemplar in Deo et per hoc cadit sub ente quod est commune essentiale ad decem praedicamenta . . . et est illud esse rei definitivum quod de ipsa ante esse actuale solum habet existere in mentis conceptu, de quo dicitur quod definitio est oratio indicans quid est esse. Secundum esse [esse actualis existentiae] non habet creatura ex sua essentia, sed a Deo, inquantum est effectus voluntatis divinae iuxta exemplar eius in mente divina" (fol. 7r). Also Q 3, q. 9: "Et ut dicit Avicenna, cap. octavo, hoc esse proprie dicitur

formal exemplary causality.[83] Or as Godfrey expresses Henry's view in Quodlibet 8, q. 3, insofar as the essences of creatures correspond to ideas (*rationes*) found in God and are thus caused and constituted by him in the order of formal exemplary causality, they are related to him by a real relation of the first mode, by way of reduction. Insofar as their existence is efficiently caused by him, they are related to him by a real relation of the second mode.[84]

If this view leads Henry to defend the indifference of a created essence to being and nonbeing, Godfrey now rightly notes that this is affirmed by Henry only with certain qualifications. One might interpret this to mean that such a thing is indifferent to *esse* or *non esse essentiae*, that is to say, to its essential being. It is not this kind of indifference that Godfrey finds Henry defending. If this *esse* or essential being were lost, a thing's status as a thing (*res*) or nature would also be destroyed.[85]

On the other hand, a created essence might be said to be indifferent with respect to its actual existence. In this sense, it would retain its *esse essentiae* even without its individual actual existence; this, of course, because of its continued reference to and dependence on its exemplar in the divine intellect.[86] To say that such an essence is indifferent to actual existence and nonexistence is not, concedes Godfrey, to suggest that it will ever be found without either one or the other. It is rather to hold that the essence is not so determined to its state of nonexistence when it does not enjoy actual existence that it could not receive existence from an agent acting as its efficient cause.

---

definitivum esse, et est dei intentione. Quod intelligo: quia tale esse non convenit alicui nisi cuius ratio exemplaris est in intellectu divino, per quam natum est fieri in rebus extra, ita quod sicut ex relatione et respectu ad ipsam ut ad causam efficientem habet quod sit ens in effectu, sic ex relatione quadam et respectu ad ipsam ut ad formam extra rem habet quod sit ens aliquod per essentiam" (fol. 61r). Also see Q 9, q. 2, fol. 345v.

83 PB 2.56. For Henry see Quodlibet 9, q. 1 (fol. 341v): "Ex consideratione enim divini intellectus circa divinam essentiam ut est intellecta ab ipso sunt in ipso rationes ideales . . . quae sunt relationes ex hoc in deo secundum rationem ad ipsas essentias creaturarum, quae ex hoc sunt aliquid secundum essentiam quae respondent rationibus idealibus in deo existentibus. Et ratione ipsius essentiae earum habent *relationem realem* ad deum." (Italics mine). Also see Paulus, *Henri de Gand . . .* , pp. 293–95.

84 PB 4.36. See *Metaphysics* V, c. 15 (1020b 26–1021b 11), where Aristotle distinguishes three ways in which things may be described as relative. For detailed discussion of this by Henry and for his application to the relationship between God and creatures and creatures and God see Q 9, q. 1 (fol. 343r–344r). Also see Paulus, *op. cit.*, pp. 301–02.

85 PB 2.56.

86 For Godfrey see Q 2, q. 2 (PB 2.56), where he appears to be following Henry's Q. 3, q. 9 very closely. See fol. 61v–62r.

Moreover, when it does receive actual existence from an efficient cause, it is not so committed to existence that it would not fall into nonexistence were such a cause to stop communicating existence to it. It is this kind of indifference that Godfrey finds Henry defending.[87]

Godfrey now turns to the second critical point in Henry's theory, his interpretation of Avicenna's threefold way in which a nature or essence can be considered and, in particular, the implications which he draws from viewing the essence or nature absolutely. Godfrey joins this discussion to Henry's qualification cited above according to which an essence, while being indifferent to actual existence and nonexistence, cannot be realized in fact apart from one state or the other. He now notes, still following Henry's text closely, that such an essence can nonetheless be regarded as indifferent to *esse* and *non esse* in the conceptual order in that it can be conceived without one's taking into account either its actual existence or nonexistence. Such a concept would simply be that of the essence or quiddity of the thing viewed in itself or absolutely.[88]

As Godfrey then observes, Henry cites passages from Avicenna's *Metaphysics* in support of this interpretation. In these passages Avicenna appears to hold that the essence or the intelligibility (*certitudo*) of a given essence admits of an absolute concept whereby one knows what the thing is without

---

[87] "Sed loquendo de non esse quod negat esse secundum unam rationem essendi, scilicet esse actualis existentiae extra in singularibus . . . hoc modo bene est ponere essentiam et naturam creaturae per indifferentiam se habere ad esse et non esse. Non quod de facto neutrum ei conveniat, cum sint contradictoria, sed quod non ita de natura sua determinat sibi unum, quin possit habere alterum. *Essentia enim creaturae non ita determinat sibi non esse actualis existentiae quin possit illud recipere ab alio effective, nec sic habet esse ab alio quin relictum sibi caderet in non esse*" (PB 2.56). Compare with the following from Henry: "Isto secundo modo essentia cuiuslibet creaturae inquantum creatura est, per indifferentiam se habet ad esse et non esse. *Non enim ita determinat sibi non esse existentiae actualis quin potest esse recipere ab alio efficiente. Nec sic habet esse ab alio, quin relictum sibi cadit in non esse*" (fol. 61v). (Italics mine, to indicate the close similarity between the passages.)

[88] For Godfrey see Q 2, q. 2 (PB 2.56–57). Compare with Henry's Q 3, q. 9 (fol. 61v–62r). Note that in the immediate context Godfrey also cites Algazel's *Logica*: "Cum intelligis quid est homo et quid animal, non potes intelligere hominem sine intellectu animalis. Sed cum intelligis quid est homo, non est necessarium intelligere ipsum esse, vel esse album, quia esse accidentale est omnibus quae sunt, animal vero est essentiale homini. Unde potest quaeri quae res posuit hominem esse vel habere esse; sed non est vera interrogatio qua quaeritur quae res posuit hominem esse animal, sicut nec hominem esse hominem: homo enim est homo et animal essentialiter" (PB 2.57). Cf. "*Logica Algazelis:* Introduction and Critical Text," Ch. Lohr, ed., *Traditio* 21 (1965), pp. 247–48. Godfrey has simply excerpted a number of sentences from a fuller discussion in Algazel's text.

taking into account its existence either in the intellect or as an individual entity. Moreover, it is argued from Avicenna's text that this absolute consideration, for instance, of animal as animal, is prior in *esse* both to animal as individuated through its accidents and to animal taken universally as existing in the intellect, just as that which is simple is prior to what is composite and a part is prior to a whole.[89] It is true that animality of itself must either be realized as universal or as particular. Nevertheless, simply considered in itself, it is not determined to one or the other situation, but is indifferent to both.[90]

As Godfrey also reports, Henry draws upon a key passage from Avicenna's *Logica* for added support for his thesis. In this passage Avicenna holds that the essences of things have a twofold *esse*, that is to say, in singular things in extramental reality and in the intellect. But they admit of a threefold consideration: (1) one simply insofar as they are viewed in themselves; (2) another insofar as they are viewed as in singular things; (3) another insofar as they are viewed as in the intellect.[91] Then, in what is perhaps his chief grievance against Henry's interpretation of Avicenna, Godfrey notes that some go on to hold that the quiddity or essence of a thing enjoys these three modes of consideration in accord with three ways in which it has being or

---

[89] For Godfrey see PB 2.58–59, where he cites texts from Avicenna, including: *Metaphysics* I, c. 6 (fol. 72va); *Metaphysics* V, c. 1 (fol. 87ra; 86vb). For Henry's citation of these same texts see Q 3, q. 9 (fol. 60v; 61r). Both Henry himself and Godfrey in his summary of Henry note that one should not postulate a separate state of existence to correspond to the nature considered absolutely. Thus Henry: "Non autem dico quod quantum est de se habet esse absolutum absque eo quod habet esse in intellectu vel singularibus, tanquam sit aliquid separatum" (fol. 60v); Godfrey: ". . . hoc tamen quod sic habet conceptum absolutum non ponit rem habere aliquod esse separatum, quia non habet esse nisi in anima et universale, vel in re extra et singulare" (PB 2.58). For the priority of essence or nature considered absolutely vis à vis its realization in the mind as universal or in the individual as singular, see Avicenna (fol. 87ra), cited and commented on by Henry (fol. 61r) and Godfrey (PB 2.58–59). Note the following from Godfrey's citation of Avicenna: "Ergo haec consideratio secundum quod est animal praecedit in esse et animal quod est individuum per accidentia sua et universale, quod est in istis singularibus et intelligibile, sicut simplex praecedit compositum et sicut pars totum" (PB 2.58). The comma which we have inserted between *universale* and *quod* appears to be necessary in order to convey Avicenna's thought.

[90] PB 2.58–59. "Quamvis enim animalitas non sit nisi universalis vel particularis, tamen ex ratione suae essentiae sive secundum se ut est animalitas neutrum sibi determinat, sed est indifferens ad utrumque."

[91] PB 2.59, citing Avicenna's *Logica* I (fol. 2rb). For Avicenna's text see in this chapter, n. 69.

esse, namely, in the extramental thing, *esse naturae*; in the intellect, *esse rationis;* and simply in itself, *esse essentiae*.[92]

Godfrey is now in position to begin his criticism of Henry's theory. Whatever degree of probability might be assigned to it on the basis of the Avicennian texts,[93] and this too Godfrey will challenge in due course, his most fundamental objections are of a metaphysical nature. Still arguing within the context of a proposed indifference of essence to existence and nonexistence in Quodlibet 2, q. 2, Godfrey considers two possible situations. One may hold that existence is the act of essence and therefore a thing (*res*) that is really distinct from it or one may maintain that *esse* is really identical with essence and differs from it only logically or intentionally.[94] While we have already seen above that Godfrey ends by emphatically rejecting any theory of real distinction between essence and existence, here he proceeds cautiously and considers each alternative.

If one holds for real distinction between essence and *esse*, the proposed indifference of essence to *esse* (and *non esse*) may be taken in either of two ways. It may be understood to mean that the essence of a creature can remain after the creature's existence has been lost. In this sense corruption of a thing with respect to its existence would not entail loss of its essential being, taken as something distinct from its cognitive being. According to Godfrey, however, such indifference of essence to existence is to be rejected even within the framework of a theory of real distinction between them. Otherwise numerically one and the same essence could successively receive different existences. But one can also understand this indifference of essence in a different sense, that is, as indifference in the order of consideration. In this sense a thing would be said to be indifferent to *esse* or *non esse* insofar as it may be considered in itself and absolutely, without one's taking into account its actual existence or nonexistence. Such indifference would not imply a third *esse* (*esse essentiae*) corresponding to this state of consideration and distinct from cognitive being and from actual existence. It would rather be like the indifference of matter insofar as it may be considered in itself as the common subject of contrary forms and privations, without one's taking into account any given form or privation. Within the context of a theory of real distinction

---

[92] PB 2.59. "Sed ulterius aliqui dicunt quod ipsa quidditas et essentia rei habet huiusmodi tres respectus vel considerationes secundum tres modos quos habet in esse: unum quidem habet extra in rebus quod dicitur esse naturae, alium in intellectu quod dicitur esse rationis, tertium vero habet secundum se quod dicitur esse essentiae." Here Godfrey is clearly referring to Henry's Q 3, q. 9, fol. 61r.

[93] PB 2.59.

[94] PB 2.60.

between essence and existence, such indifference in the order of consideration may be admitted.[95]

If one rejects real distinction between essence and existence (which view Godfrey here cautiously refers to as more probable), with even greater reason is it to be denied that essence is really indifferent to *esse* and *non esse*.[96] Not only is this true in the order of being, it is also true in the order of consideration. When a thing is brought from a state of nonexistence into actual existence, it is also brought into being as regards its essential being. When it is corrupted or loses its actual existence, it also loses its essential being. This is so precisely because of the real identity of essence and existence. Because of such identity, whatever is true of one is true of the other. Moreover, whatever is known of the essence of a thing is known of its existence.[97] Hence indifference in the order of consideration is also to be ruled out, at least as regards a really existing essence. Given this identity of essence and existence, Godfrey argues that it is not possible for someone really to understand what the thing is in itself or according to its essential being without knowing that it is in the order of existence as well.[98] If a thing possesses essence in act, it also possesses existence in act. And if it possesses essence potentially and virtually in terms of its cause(s), it will possess existence in the same way and to the same degree. Thus if something is a man in actuality, it also exists in actuality, and if only a man in potency, then it exists only

---

[95] *Ibid.*

[96] PB 2.60–61. "Si autem esse existentiae, ut dicitur probabilius, non sit res alia ab ipsa essentia, sed differt ab ea solum ratione vel intentione sive respectu (aliter etiam quam differunt in Deo essentia et esse solum ratione, propter quod etiam nulla creatura ita dicitur suum esse sicut dicitur de Deo), multo magis est dicendum quod ipsa essentia creaturae realiter non possit esse indifferens ad esse et non esse." On Godfrey's reference to rejection of the real distinction as the more probable view, cf. n. 63 in this chapter.

[97] PB 2.61.

[98] *Ibid.* "Cum enim haec non sint diversae res sed una, non potest dici quod intelligatur essentia quin etiam intelligatur esse, esse quidem rei verum et reale extra in seipsa sub ratione incomplexi, licet non esse diminutum quod dicitur esse verum in anima et sub ratione complexi; prout dicit Commentator quarto Metaphysicae, quod hoc praedicatum: est, cum dicitur res aliqua est, potest esse et praedicatum essentiale per modum generis vel accidentale sive de accidente." For the same point see Q 4, q. 2 (PB 2.235). In brief, Godfrey is here referring to our knowledge of a thing's real being, not to mere being in the mind which it would enjoy only as a result of some mind's knowledge of it as expressed through judgment. For Averroes as referred to in the first passage see *In V Met.* (Venice, 1562), fol. 117rb–117va. Note his comment on fol. 117va: "Et intendebat distinguere inter hoc nomen ens, quod significat copulationem in intellectu, et quod significat essentiam quae est extra intellectum." Also see Siger of Brabant, *Questions sur la Métaphysique*, p. 13.

in potency. This point should be kept in mind, for it will frequently reappear in Godfrey's metaphysics. Whatever is true of essence is true of a thing's existence and *vice versa*.[99]

As regards indifference of essence to existence and nonexistence, therefore, Godfrey's view is straightforward. Within a framework of real distinction of essence and existence, such indifference is to be rejected in the order of being, though it may be admitted in the order of consideration. Within a system of real identity of essence and existence, essence is not indifferent to existence in either sense. Apparently, Godfrey would say the same within the framework of Henry's theory of real identity and intentional distinction of essence and existence.[100] But, as will be seen later, he is extremely critical of this entire theory.

Godfrey now returns to the texts of Avicenna from which Henry had argued in favor of indifference of essence to existence and nonexistence in the sense indicated above. As regards things, especially material things, which do not merely enjoy cognitive being but extramental reality as well, Godfrey suggests that one may assign a twofold or even a threefold *esse* to them. Thus such an existent enjoys an *esse existentiae* that is appropriate to it insofar as it is viewed in itself and essentially, in other words, a substantial existence which is distinct from the existence of any of its accidents. (Godfrey's views on the existence of accidents will be examined in Ch. V.) Consequently, such an existent may be considered: (1) insofar as it has its own substantial existence in distinction from the existence of its accidents; (2) insofar as it exists with its own substantial existence and in union with the existence of one or more accidents. Thus, comments Godfrey, according to Avicenna this existing humanity may be considered simply insofar as it is existing humanity or insofar as it is joined with this existing quantity, a particular accident. In the second case it will be considered together with something which "happens" to it and accompanies it. So viewed, this humanity may be regarded as a part of that whole which humanity forms in union with its accident(s). Therefore, one may speak of such a substantial existent as having a twofold *esse* or a twofold consideration.[101]

Godfrey goes on to suggest that such an existing thing may also be regarded in a third way, insofar as it has being in the intellect, that is to say, according

---

[99] PB 2.61.

[100] Note that in the present section Godfrey rejects indifference of essence to existence both in the order of being and in the order of thought as following from a theory of real identity of essence and existence, whether the two differ only *ratione vel intentione sive respectu*. By the expression *vel intentione sive respectu* he seems to have Henry's intentional distinction in mind. (PB 2.60–61, cited in n. 96).

[101] PB 2.61–62. For Avicenna see *Metaphysica* V, c. 1 (fol. 86vb and 87ra).

to its cognitive being (*esse cognitum*). So viewed, the actual existence of an animal, for instance, just as it is distinct from the existence of those proper accidents without which it is never realized in actuality, is also distinct from this *esse* in the mind (*esse consideratum*). Further, this cognitive or mental being is not to be identified with the actual essence itself, nor does it inhere in the latter as in its subject. Nor are the two found in any one thing as in their subject. Rather this cognitive being refers to the actual existent as to its object, but inheres in the intellect as its subject. Finally, it is to be distinguished from those accidents which follow upon the being of an animal insofar as it enjoys such cognitive being, such as to be universal, or a genus, or a subject, or a predicate.[102]

In sum, then, Godfrey has admitted of a threefold consideration, even of a threefold *esse*, for such an existing essence: (1) substantial existence as such; (2) substantial existence as realized together with its proper accidents; (3) *esse cognitum*. But then, apparently returning to his attack against Henry, he warns that if such an individual ceases to exist as an individual with its proper accidents in extramental reality, then it will no longer retain its actual essential being. Thus if no individual men were to exist at a given time, the essence of man would not continue to be according to any actual *esse essentiae*. It would remain in cognitive being, however, which is merely to say that true knowledge of it would still be possible. And those things which follow from its cognitive being would also remain. Thus it would still be true that it was a universal. That is to say, there would still be a universal term and a species corresponding to it so that it could be known abstractly and universally as a nature that could be realized in individuals. It is in this sense, then, that Godfrey would understand the texts from Avicenna.[103]

As Godfrey has indicated above, Henry had argued for a real indifference of essence to existence and nonexistence in order to account for the possibility of one's knowing certain essences which do not enjoy actual existence and describing them as true quiddities or things (*res*) or predicamental entities.

---

[102] PB 2.62. Note in particular: "Et tunc etiam ipsum esse existentiae animalis secundum se sicut est aliud ab esse existentiae accidentium particularium sine quibus tamen non habet suum proprium et reale esse existentiae, ita etiam est aliud ab hoc esse considerato quod non est ipsa essentia, nec etiam in ipsa subiective, nec etiam ambo simul sunt in uno secundum esse ut in subiecto, sed huiusmodi esse cognitum est ipsius objective sive ut obiecti, et est in intellectu subiective, et est etiam aliud ab accidentibus quae consequuntur hoc esse animalis secundum hoc eius esse cognitum ut est cognitum sive eius cognitionem vel conceptum in intellectu, ut esse universale, genus, subiectum, praedicatum" (note that we have added the final four commas).

[103] PB 2.63. Cf. Godfrey's remarks in Q 14, q. 5 (PB 5.429–30).

Godfrey, too, concedes the possibility of there being knowledge of such nonexistent essences. It now remains for him to account for this and to indicate why such does not obtain in the case of mere chimeras. Not surprisingly in the light of what we have seen, he rejects Henry's explanation in terms of any real and actual *esse essentiae* which such possibles would enjoy because of their correspondence to their divine ideas in the order of formal exemplary causality.[104] Rather than pursue his criticism of Henry on this point here, however, we shall reserve further discussion of this for the following chapter.

In order to resolve this issue within the framework of his own metaphysics, Godfrey now has recourse to the same division of real being that we first encountered in Ch. I while presenting his general division of being.[105] In Quodlibet 8, q. 3, it will be recalled, he divides real being into being in act and being in potency. At times things exist formally and in act, at times only virtually or potentially by reason of their cause or causes. As he also explains in Quodlibet 2, q. 2 and with some added precisions in Quodlibet 4, q. 2, it may happen that a given thing exists only potentially by reason of the preexistence of something else that may serve as its intrinsic principle or cause. Because of the preexistence of such a principle, the thing in question may itself be said to enjoy real being, not actual being, to be sure, but potential being. Witness vapor which may become rain or a seed that is proximately disposed to become a rose.[106] Even if such proximately disposed matter does not preexist, one may still ascribe real but potential being to such a thing by reason of the preexistence of more remote matter, for instance, earth or some other element that can become rain or a rose as the result of a series of transformations. Given this, reasons Godfrey, knowledge can be had of such actually nonexistent entities insofar as one may know them in terms of the potential being they enjoy in their intrinsic cause or causes.[107]

As we have also seen, Godfrey assigns virtual or potential being to nonexistent possible things by reason of a preexisting extrinsic cause, and even when there are no preexisting material principles that might enter into their

---

[104] PB 2.67.

[105] See Ch. I, pp. 16–18.

[106] Q 2, q. 2 (PB 2.63–64); Q 4, q. 2 (PB 2.237–38); Q 8, q. 3 (PB 4.38). In Q 4, q. 2, Godfrey refers to Aristotle's discussion of potency in *Metaphysics* IX (see c. 7). The example of the rose would appear to go back at least as far as Abelard who had added a fourth question to the well known three raised by Porphyry and passed on by Boethius to the Latin West in his second commentary on Porphyry's *Isagoge*. For Abelard see *Logica "Ingredientibus,"* B. Geyer, ed. (*Beiträge zur Geschichte der Philosophie und Theologie des Mittelalters* 21, 1933), pp. 8 and 30.

[107] See Q 4, q. 2 (PB 2.238).

intrinsic constitution. Such would be true of things which can be created by divine agency prior to their actual existence and prior to the existence of matter. Such things may still be said to have real potential being in God virtually as in their cause, since he has the *virtus* or the capacity to produce them. Consequently, at least God will have true knowledge of them by reason of his exemplar ideas.[108] Because mere chimeras can never be realized in actual existence, they enjoy no real being, whether actual or potential. Hence essential knowledge or science cannot be had of them. At best an imaginary or cognitive being can be assigned to them.[109]

Godfrey sees no need, therefore, to postulate a distinctive essential being (*esse essentiae*) that might be viewed as another sector of real being and distinguished from *esse existentiae* (existential being). Application of his division of real being into actual being and potential being suffices for him to account for the possibility of there being knowledge of nonexistent possibles. Controlling his thinking on this matter and his firm rejection of Henry's position is his conviction that essence and existence are really identical. Whatever is true of one is true of the other. If an essence is realized in actuality, then the existence with which it is really identical is also given in actuality. If an essence is real only in potentiality, then its existence is likewise only potential.[110]

2. *Henry's Theory of Intentional Distinction between Essence and Existence and Godfrey's Reaction*

As has been noted above, Henry's theory of *esse essentiae* entails some kind of distinction within a creature insofar as it is dependent on God in the order of formal exemplary causality, on the one hand, and insofar as it is so

---

[108] Q 2, q. 2 (PB 2.64); Q 4, q. 2 (PB 2.238); Q 8, q. 3 (PB 4.38–39).

[109] Q 2, q. 2 (PB 2.65); Q 4, q. 2 (PB 2.238); Q 8, q. 3 (PB 4.40).

[110] Q 4, q. 2 (PB 2.235–36): ". . . et pro quanto aliquid est res praedicabilis et habet esse in genere secundum esse essentiae, pro tanto etiam habet hoc secundum esse existentiae et e converso." As Paulus has noted, Siger of Brabant had already criticized Henry's theory for dissociating too sharply between *esse essentiae* and *esse existentiae*. On this point there is close similarity between Godfrey and Siger in their rejection of Henry's theory. See Paulus, *op. cit.*, pp. 123–25. See Siger's "Quaestio utrum haec sit vera: homo est animal, nullo homine existente," in *Siger de Brabant, Ecrits de logique, de morale et de physique*, B. Bazán, ed. (Louvain-Paris, 1974), p. 54:52–66. See Q 4, q. 2 (PB 2.238–41) for an interesting application of these distinctions in order to determine in what ways things may be said to belong to a genus. Q 4, q. 2, is directed to this question: "Utrum ponere res praedicamentales esse aeternas secundum esse quidditativum sit ponere mundum esse aeternum" (PB 2.233). In brief, things which exist formally in themselves as extramental realities

dependent in the order of efficient causality, on the other. In the present section we shall concentrate on the implications of Henry's theory with respect to the metaphysical structure of created beings insofar as this position is exposed by and then criticized by Godfrey.

In the passage from Quodlibet 4, q. 2, wherein Godfrey outlines three different positions as to the relationship between essence and existence, Henry's theory of intentional distinction is described as follows. According to this position essence and existence are one and the same thing in reality. That is to say, Henry rejects any real distinction between them. (Godfrey here speaks of the relationship of *esse existentiae* to essence or to *esse essentiae*, evidently regarding essence and *esse essentiae* as synonymous for the purposes of his immediate discussion.)[111] Secondly, Godfrey observes that essence and existence are said to differ intentionally. Thirdly, because of this intentional distinction, they are said to enter into some kind of composition. Therefore, when a thing is corrupted in terms of its existence, its essence itself is corrupted in this sense that it can no longer be said to exist without qualification. For instance, when the existence of Fido is lost, one

---

belong to a genus in the proper sense (*simpliciter*). Things which are real potentially and by reason of intrinsic principles may be said to belong to their genus potentially and in virtue of these same principles, as well as by reason of proper and particular extrinsic principles pertaining to the same genus if such already exist. Things which are potentially real only by reason of extrinsic principles not included within the same genus belong to the genus less properly and with greater qualification, since no principle entering into their essential constitution or even belonging to their genus actually exists. Chimeras do not belong to a genus in any way at all. In what appears to be a slight effort at reconciliation with Henry's position, Godfrey then notes that a nonexistent possible may be said to have an *esse essentiae* insofar as it implies a given degree of imitation of the divine perfection and therefore enjoys potential being insofar as it can be brought into actual being by its cause. However, he hastens to add that as regards real being it exists only in potency, both as regards it *esse essentiae* and its *esse existentiae* (PB 2.239–40). See J. Paulus, *op. cit.*, pp. 124–25. Note also that Godfrey here takes genus not as a second intention but rather as signifying directly the underlying reality, that is to say, as a natural rather than as a logical genus (PB 2.241 and short version, PB 2.323). As to the question raised by Q 4, q. 2, Godfrey replies as follows. To hold that a thing enjoys predicamental reality from eternity in either the first or second sense (see the three ways in which something may be said to belong to a genus) is to defend an eternal world, although not so in the third way (short version, PB 2.325, long version, PB 2.241). Note that the short version makes this application more explicit.

[111] "Quia vero de hoc alias diffusius est tractatum, quantum ad praesens propter primum articulum est repetendum quod circa habitudinem esse existentiae ad essentiam sive ad esse essentiae est diversus modus ponendi" (PB 2.234–35). On Henry's vacillation as to whether there is merely a logical or an intentional distinction between essence and *esse essentiae* see n. 119.

can no longer simply say that Fido or Fido's essence "is" or "exists." Nonetheless, the essence in question does remain in such fashion that it continues to enjoy real being and to belong to its appropriate genus or predicament. In this way, when a thing no longer exists in terms of its existential being, it is said to continue to be in terms of its essential being (*esse essentiae*). Because of this, one can continue to say "it is a substance" or "it is an animal." Here, too, Godfrey observes that defenders of this view (Henry) argue from the fact that science can be had concerning such nonexisting entities.[112]

In Quodlibet 3, q. 1, after his detailed exposition and refutation of the theory of real distinction between essence and existence, Godfrey also turns to Henry's view that they are intentionally distinct. As will be recalled, the general question at issue is this: whether a creature can be described as a true and real being by reason of its essence when it is not such by reason of its existence.[113] As Godfrey presents Henry's theory within this context, something may be said to be in terms of its *esse essentiae* insofar as it is a quiddity or essence and is thus indifferent to existence and nonexistence. Actual existence is assigned to it only by reason of its dependence on an efficient cause which determines it actually to be. Because of this, some kind of composition of *esse* and essence is found in the creature, and hence some degree of distinction from the divine simplicity. In other words, its essence is not its *esse* (existence). Although they are not really distinct, they do differ intentionally, just as a relation differs from its foundation. In fact, existence signifies this relationship of a creature to God insofar as it is efficiently caused by him. Essence signifies the thing or quiddity in itself and therefore something else than this same relationship (existence). Consequently, when a thing does not actually exist because it lacks this relationship to its efficient cause, it is still a real being (*ens reale*) by reason of its essential being (*esse essentiae*).[114]

In light of these descriptions of Henry's theory and in light of some subsequent remarks by Godfrey in Quodlibet 4, q. 2,[115] one can draw the following comparison between the two as to their views on the essence-existence relationship. According to both, essence and existence are really the same in reality, in that they are not really distinct. According to Godfrey, they can

---

[112] PB 2.235. Note the following: ". . . Et sic secundum aliquos res dicitur habere esse rei praedicabilis et esse in genere secundum esse essentiae et non esse existentiae."

[113] PB 2.156.

[114] PB 2.175.

[115] PB 2.235.

therefore only differ logically, while according to Henry they therefore differ intentionally. According to Godfrey they do not enter into composition with one another. According to Henry they do enter into composition with one another. Presumably this composition, corresponding to the intentional distinction itself, is less than real but more than purely logical. Further, to say that essence and *esse* differ intentionally is to say that they differ as a relation differs from its foundation. In fact, Henry holds that *esse* (existence) really is the relationship of a created entity to God insofar as it is actually and efficiently caused by him. As will be seen below, Godfrey refuses either to distinguish between existence and essence as between a relation and its foundation or to identify existence with such a relationship of a thing to God as its efficient cause.

Before taking up Godfrey's critical reaction to Henry's theory of intentional distinction between essence and existence, further reference should be made to one aspect of his description of the same. According to Godfrey's presentation in Quodlibet 4, q. 2, Henry maintains that essence and existence are one and the same thing in reality, although they differ intentionally. According to his exposition in Quodlibet 3, q. 1, Henry holds that a created essence is not its existence. Yet they do not differ really but only intentionally. If essence and existence are one and the same thing, why not say that essence is existence? One might suspect that Godfrey (or his reporter) has not accurately presented Henry's thought here. On the other hand, it may be that these two statements nicely capture an important nuance that Henry is attempting to develop through his theory of intentional distinction.

Examination of some of Henry's texts indicates that the latter suggestion is correct. Thus in Quodlibet 1, q. 9, Henry seeks to determine whether or not a creature may be said to be its own *esse*.[116] After presenting three arguments against a theory that would really distinguish existence from essence as something superadded to it,[117] he returns to the question at issue. On the one hand, it should not be said that the essence of a creature is pure subsisting *esse*. Such is true of God alone. On the other hand, it should not be completely denied that a creature is its *esse* since, contends Henry, its *esse* is not really distinct from its essence. Even so, he questions the appropriateness of simply stating that a creature is its *esse*. He resolves the question by appealing to his distinction between *esse essentiae* and *esse existentiae*. Here he distinguishes between them in that the first *esse* is said to pertain to a creature essentially but by participation insofar as it depends on God as its

---

[116] "In generali autem erat quaestio: utrum creatura ipsa sit suum esse" (fol. 6v).
[117] *Op. cit.*, fol. 6v – 7r.

formal exemplary cause, whereas the second pertains to a creature only insofar as it is efficiently caused by the divine will.[118]

Henry then observes that if one takes *esse* in the first way, as *esse essentiae* (essential being), since such only differs logically from the essence itself, one may then say that a created essence is its *esse*. If one takes *esse* in the second way, as *esse existentiae* (actual existence), then one should not say that the essence of a creature is its *esse*. This is so because, while such *esse* (existence) does not really differ from a created essence, neither does it merely differ from it logically, but also intentionally.[119] Henry then illustrates this by citing some other examples, such as "one who runs" (*currens*), "race" (*cursus*), and "to run" (*currere*), or "light" (*lux*), "that which gives light" (*lucens*), and "to give light" (*lucere*). Although such terms signify one and the same thing in reality, one cannot say without qualification that "race" (*cursus*) is "to run" (*currere*), or that "light" (*lux*) is "to give light" (*lucere*). So too, one cannot say that a being (*ens*) is its existence (*esse*), even though they are one and the same in reality.[120]

---

[118] "Et est hic distinguendum de esse secundum quod distinguit Avicenna in quinto in fine Metaphysicae suae, quod quoddam est esse rei quod habet essentialiter de se, quod appellatur esse essentiae, quoddam vero quod recipit ab alio, quod appellatur esse actualis existentiae. Primum esse habet essentia creaturae essentialiter, sed [following Macken's edition, p. 53:69] tamen participative, inquantum habet formale exemplar in deo." (fol. 7r).

[119] *Op. cit.*, fol. 7r–7v. Note in particular: "Si loquamur de primo esse creaturae, illud sola ratione differt ab essentia creaturae, nec potest ei abesse quia non habet illud ab alio effective sed solum formaliter. Unde . . . potest dici de essentia creaturae quod ipsa est suum esse participatum formaliter licet non effective. . . . Si vero loquamur de secundo esse creaturae, illud, licet non differt re ab essentia creaturae non tamen differt ab illa sola ratione . . . sed etiam differt ab illa intentione . . . et ideo de tali esse non potest concedi quod essentia creaturae est esse suum; quia esse essentiae nunc existens in actu potest esse non ens, sicut prius fuit ens. In solo autem deo verum est quod de tali esse loquendo ipse est suum esse." At times during his career Henry seems to have held for an intentional distinction between essence and *esse essentiae*. In his first *Quodlibet* he admits only a logical distinction between them (see the text just cited in this note). Then he seems to have introduced an intentional distinction in this case as well, but ended by returning to his original position, that they are not intentionally distinct. See Paulus, *Henri de Gand* . . . , pp. 311–14; W. Hoeres, "Wesen und Dasein bei Heinrich von Gent und Duns Scotus," *Franziskanische Studien* 47 (1965), p. 146, n. 77; p. 156, n. 14; F. A. Cunningham, "Some Presuppositions in Henry of Ghent," *Pensamiento* 25 (1969), p. 129.

[120] "Sufficit autem ad praesens quod non possit dici in creaturis quia essentia earum sit earum esse, quia sunt diversa intentione licet sint idem re, ut dictum est. Ut clarius videmus in exemplis: Idem enim sunt omnino re et idem significant currens, cursus, et currere; lux, lucens, lucere; vivens, vita, et vivere, sicut ens, essentia, et esse, et

Again in Quodlibet 10, q. 7 (Christmas 1286 and therefore contemporary with Godfrey's Quodlibet 3 and prior to his Quodlibet 4), while replying to certain criticisms raised by Giles of Rome, Henry stresses the point that *esse* is not something absolute that is added to the essence of a creature. Not only is this true of *esse essentiae* (essential being), as even Giles would admit, but also of *esse existentiae* (existential being). *Esse existentiae* adds nothing but a relationship to God as creative cause or signifies the created essence insofar as it is actually so related. In brief, Henry once more writes that the essence of a creature or the creature itself is not simply to be identified with its existence. At the same time, there is no real distinction between them but rather intentional distinction. In the course of his continuing refutation of Giles, he replies to the latter's complaint that he has been unable to understand Henry's proposed intentional distinction. Henry comments that between rational animal and man there is only a logical distinction (distinction of reason), as between a definition and that which is defined. Between substance and accident there is real distinction, as between that which is rational and white. But what of the distinction between rational and animal when they are taken as difference and genus? Since they do not differ in a merely logical way and yet are not really distinct, some intermediary kind of distinction must be admitted. Henry insists that this is not to imply that two (or three) of these, for instance, the logical and the intentional, are merely different degrees of the same kind of distinction. On the contrary, three specifically different kinds of distinction are at issue here, the logical, the intentional, and the real.[121]

Henry carefully presents his position once more in Quodlibet 11, q. 3. There he notes that while existence (*esse existentiae*) does not add anything

---

tamen non possum dicere cursus est currere vel lux est lucere. Similiter etiam non possum dicere ens est suum esse, licet idem sint in re." (fol. 7v). On this discussion in Q 1, q. 9, see Gómez Caffarena, *Ser participado . . .* , pp. 72–74.

[121] Fol. 417r–418r. For more details on this particular question of Henry in reaction to Giles's *Quaestiones disputatae de esse et essentia*, 9 and 11, see Paulus, *Henri de Gand . . .* , p. 250, n. 2; his "Les disputes d'Henri de Gand et de Gilles de Rome . . . ," pp. 334–42; and Hocedez, "Gilles de Rome et Henri de Gand . . . ," pp. 365–69. On the theory of intentional distinction according to Henry, see Paulus, *Henri de Gand . . .* , pp. 220–36; Hoeres, "Wesen und Dasein bei Heinrich von Gent und Duns Scotus," pp. 129–40. On his application of this distinction to the question of essence and existence see Paulus, *op. cit.*, chap. 5 and especially pp. 284–91; Hoeres, *op. cit.*, pp. 144–50; F. A. Cunningham, "Some Presuppositions in Henry of Ghent," pp. 103–37. Cunningham finds a good summary of Henry's general position on this issue in his *Summa . . .* , a. 28, q. 4, which he has presented in English translation on pp. 138–43. Also, see Gómez Caffarena, *Ser participado . . .* , pp. 65–92.

real to essence, it does not follow from this that the essence of a creature is its existence (*esse*). Such is true only of God. Existence rather adds to essence a relationship which involves a distinctive intelligible content (*intentio*). Since existence adds this *intentio* to essence as something accidental, that is to say, not as a real accident but as an "intentional" accident, it follows that a creaturely essence is not its existence.[122]

In sum, then, one can understand why Godfrey has stated that in creatures, according to Henry's theory, essence and existence are one and the same thing in reality and yet that essence is not simply to be identified with existence. When Godfrey portrays him as holding that essence and existence signify one and the same thing, he is conveying the point that they do not signify different "things" (*res*) in the sense defended by Giles of Rome. When Godfrey presents him as denying that a created essence is its existence (*esse existentiae*), he is allowing for Henry's application of intentional distinction to essence and existence rather than purely logical distinction.

In the light of Godfrey's criticism of Henry's theory of *esse essentiae*, one is not surprised to find him rejecting Henry's proposed intentional distinction between essence and existence. To begin with, Godfrey judges the very notion of an intentional distinction to be indefensible. For instance, in *Disputed Question* 12 he quickly dismisses this as a special kind of distinction. To differ intentionally is really the same as to differ logically. This is so, continues Godfrey, because being is adequately divided into what he there describes as *ens rationis* (apparently meaning thereby cognitive being) and real being. This leaves no room for an intermediary "intentional" being and therefore undermines the ontological foundation for any distinctive type of intentional distinction.[123]

In Quodlibet 3, q. 1, Godfrey directs a series of criticisms against Henry's theory of intentional distinction of essence and existence. As we have seen, the theory is considered in this context insofar as it might justify the contention that when something lacks actual existence it is still a real being by reason of its essential being.

First of all, counters Godfrey, a thing does not acquire substantial being by reason of a relationship, but only relative being. Nor does the operation

[122] Fol. 441r–441v.

[123] "Nec potest dici quod virtus illa sit res intentionis ita quod differat a substantia rei non secundum rem neque secundum rationem sed secundum intentionem quia non est aliud differre ratione et intentione. Cuius ratio est quia ens sufficienter dividitur tanquam per differentias primas et immediatas per ens diminutum et incompletum quod est ens rationis et per ens completum et perfectum quod est ens reale habens esse ratum in natura. Unde non est ibi medium ens intentionis." (Wippel, ed., "Godfrey of Fontaines: Disputed Questions 9, 10 and 12," p. 368.)

of an agent terminate in something that is merely relative. But the creative activity of God does terminate in the existence (*esse*) of the creature. The unexpressed conclusion is this, that the existence of a creature is not purely relative or a mere relationship.

Secondly, reasons Godfrey, the existence (*esse*) of a relation presupposes the existence of its foundation. Therefore, an essence must first be understood to exist before it can be understood as related to existence. In brief, apart from any relationship whereby an existing essence is actually related to its efficient cause, there must be something within it whereby it is formally constituted in its substantial existence. Again the conclusion is the same, that existence is not to be regarded as a real relation that is grounded in essence and enters into composition with it.[124]

Thirdly, Godfrey argues from the implications of a theory of real identity of essence and existence. He suggests that it is contradictory to hold that essence and existence are really one and the same, as does Henry, and then to maintain that when a thing does not exist by reason of its existential being it may still be (real) by reason of its essential being. One might counter that such can be true of relative things. Even though a relation does not really differ from its foundation, the relation can be absent while the foundation remains. For instance, while the relation of similarity is really identical with whiteness, its foundation, something may continue to be white even when its relationship of similarity with something else no longer obtains.[125] The implication would be that in the present case when the relation, existence, is not actually realized, the foundation, the essence, may still remain in some sense.

Godfrey finds two difficulties with this counterproposal. First of all, a relation presupposes the reality of both its term and its foundation in order for it itself to be real. So too, the nonexistence of the relation presupposes

---

[124] PB 2.175. Note that we have interpreted the first clause of the following sentence as pertaining to the first argument, with the remainder belonging to the second argument: "Operatio autem creatoris terminatur ad esse creaturae, et omnis relatio in suo esse praesupponit naturaliter esse sui fundamenti, et sic oportet praeintelligi essentiam esse antequam intelligatur aliquis respectus eius ad esse et cetera." The two arguments emerge more clearly from the text of the short version, although in reverse order: ". . . hoc non valet. Primo quia esse simpliciter praesupponitur ei quod est esse ad aliquid. Sed respectus ille dat tantum esse ad aliquid. Ergo praesupponit esse simpliciter; et sicut talis, respectus non constituit esse simpliciter. Secundo quia actio semper terminatur necessario ad aliquid absolutum, actio autem Dei terminatur ad esse creaturae. Ergo et cetera" (PB 2.302; revised according to Pattin, "La structure. . . , p. 690).

[125] PB 2.176. On Henry's denial of real distinction between a relation and its foundation, see Paulus, *Henri de Gand* . . . , pp. 163–72 (especially 171–72); 303–08; Hoeres, *op. cit.*, pp. 125, 167–68; Gómez Caffarena, *Ser participado* . . . , pp. 131–32.

the nonexistence either of its foundation or of its term. As regards the example of similarity between two white things, the similarity will remain so long as whiteness remains both in the foundation and in the term. So too, according to Henry a created essence will always remain in terms of its essential being, which is the foundation for the relation, existence. Since God himself will also always remain as the term of this relationship, it will follow that the relation itself, the creature's existence, must always remain as well. Thus, argues Godfrey, defenders of this view fall into the very position they so strenuously strive to avoid, that is to say, assertion of the eternal existence of creatures. Such a consequence would be especially galling for Henry since, as we shall see in the following chapter, he denies the very possibility of any eternally created being. Secondly, Godfrey simply notes in passing that it does not seem to be true in creatures that a real relation is completely and really identical with its foundation.[126]

In another criticism of Henry's theory Godfrey returns to his own views on essence and existence. He recalls one of his reasons for rejecting real distinction between them. Existence does not signify a distinct "thing" (*res*) or even a distinct intelligible content (*ratio*) apart from essence, just as being (*ens*) does not signify a distinct *res* or *ratio* apart from that of which it is predicated.[127] Hence, he concludes that existence does not signify a distinctive real relationship either. For every real relationship also falls under being (*ens* or *esse*). Just as no created substance nor any other accident can be *esse* or *ens* without some qualification or specification, neither can there be any real relation which is nothing but unqualified existence. Rather, every real relation must participate in *esse* according to its proper modality. For instance, a white thing is said to be white by reason of whiteness, and to be related to something else by reason of a given relationship. But it is not said to exist by reason of any such relationship. So too, every creature is what it is by reason of its formal entity. It enjoys a particular relationship by reason of the corresponding relation. Such relations are themselves realized in their formal entity in the manner in which relations have existence. Granted, therefore, that every creature is really related to God insofar as it is efficiently caused by him, whether this relation be described as creation taken passively or as something else, Godfrey does not believe that it can be identified with existence. Rather existence itself appears to be presupposed by all those things that pertain to a thing only insofar as it exists.[128]

---

[126] PB 2.176.

[127] See the first three of Godfrey's arguments against the real distinction as presented in Section A of this chapter. For the specification that *ens* does not even involve a distinct *ratio* from that of which it is affirmed see PB 2.163.

[128] PB 2.176–77.

In still another criticism of Henry's theory Godfrey argues that within the context of intentional distinction between essence and existence, essence can be understood as not existing. In support of this he returns again to the case of the relation of similarity between white things. Such a white thing can be understood and can exist as dissimilar to something else even while retaining its own reality. This is so, adds Godfrey, because neither similarity nor any other relation confers existence on the thing in which it (the relation) is found. In like fashion, according to Henry an essence can be understood as not existing and therefore, urges Godfrey, could exist without its existence. Needless to say, Godfrey is attempting to refute Henry's position by reducing it to an absurdity, the admission that an essence could exist without its existence. Given this consequence Godfrey again denies that existence is to be regarded as a real relation of the essence.[129] Presupposed for this argument is the admission that an essence can be conceived of as not existing. As will be recalled, in *Disputed Questions* 9 and 11 Giles of Rome had rested one argument for the real distinction of essence and existence on this very point. In Quodlibet 10, q. 7, Henry carefully shows that his theory of intentional distinction allows for this same possibility.[130] Godfrey has attempted to show that if such is admitted, and if existence is treated as a relation, then the absurd consequence will follow. He himself admits neither that essence in act can be known without existence in act nor that existence is a relation.

Finally, by reasoning once more within the terms of Henry's theory, Godfrey again attempts to reduce to absurdity the view that existence is a relation. If, as the theory asserts, a real relation is not really distinct from its foundation, then it can have no existence other than that of the foundation. But just as the foundation is prior in nature to the relation, so is the foundation's existence prior to the relation's existence. If one holds that existence itself is such a relation, there will be one single existence for the essence (the foundation) and the existence (the relation). This single existence will belong to the essence itself before it belongs to the existence. Again one ends in the absurd position of holding that essence exists before it has existence, "before" at least by priority of nature.[131]

---

[129] PB 2.177. Note in particular: ". . . ita etiam ipsa essentia posset solum intelligi sub non esse sive sub opposito ipsius esse, sive sic posset esse simpliciter et sic essentia esset sine esse. Non videtur ergo quod esse sit realis respectus in essentia, quia, ut dictum est, esse praesupponeret esse."

[130] For Giles see his *Quaestiones disputatae* . . . , fol. 20va and 24vb, cited in n. 27 of the present chapter. For Henry see fol. 420r (*ad secundum principale*). Henry notes that such would not be possible if essence and *esse* only differed logically. Also see Paulus, "Les disputes . . . ," p. 339.

[131] PB 2.177.

Having already excluded real distinction between essence and existence, and having now rejected Henry's theory of intentional distinction, Godfrey resolutely opts for real identity. As we have seen above, in rejecting the theory of real distinction as it was presented by Giles of Rome, Godfrey was in agreement with Henry of Ghent. A certain similarity in their argumentation against real distinction of essence and existence has also been noted. Godfrey's negative reaction to Henry's theory of their intentional distinction was prepared for both by his critique of Henry's theory of *esse essentiae* as a distinctive mode of being and by his own identification of essence and existence. For Godfrey, essence enjoys no greater reality than does existence. Whatever is known with respect to essence, so much is known with respect to existence. To return again to the question originally asked in Quodlibet 3, q. 1, if a thing does not actually exist or is not being by reason of its existence, it cannot be described as being by reason of its essence (*esse essentiae*).[132]

While differing sharply from Giles on the question of real distinction of essence and existence, Godfrey is in agreement with him in refusing to admit of an intentional distinction between them. Both Giles and Godfrey reject Henry's intentional distinction as a distinctive type in addition to the purely logical and the real.[133] Both find insurmountable difficulties with the notion that existence is to be regarded as a relationship to God as efficient cause.[134] But if Henry's intentional distinction between essence and existence implies too little difference between them in Giles's eyes, it implies too much difference and too much composition in Godfrey's judgment.

C. GODFREY'S VIEW: IDENTITY OF ESSENCE AND EXISTENCE

In the previous sections of this chapter we have presented Godfrey's thought on the relationship between essence and existence in light of his direct confrontation with theories that defend either their real or intentional

---

[132] PB 2.177.

[133] For this in Giles see his *Quaestiones disputatae de esse et essentia*, q. 9, fol. 19vab.

[134] For Giles's criticism of this point see *op. cit.*, q. 9, fol. 19rab and 19vb. There is some similarity between Giles's contention here that operation does not terminate in something relative but in something absolute and the operative principle in Godfrey's first argument against Henry in Q 3, q. 1, as presented above; also between Giles's point that nothing can lose or acquire a relationship unless it loses or acquires something absolute (*aliquid*) and Godfrey's first criticism of the counterproposal to his third argument. Also, Giles draws an analogy between this case and the relationship of similarity between white things: "Sic itaque imaginabimur quod sicut corpus acquirit albedinem quam acquirendo acquirit similitudinem quae fundatur in albedine,

distinction. In so doing we were, of course, reflecting his own development on this point as it emerges from his quodlibetal debates. At the same time we have, by following Godfrey's own procedure, concentrated more on what the proper relationship between essence and existence is not, in his opinion, than upon what it is. But from the above considerations it has become clear enough that Godfrey does reject both real and intentional distinction between them and defends their real identity.

Thus, as regards the ontological order he has insisted throughout his discussion that whatever is true of essence is true of existence and *vice versa*.[135] And if one would account for one's ability to be aware of something as a possible existent even when it does not actually exist, one need not, insists Godfrey, postulate two really or even two intentionally distinct principles, essence and existence, within that thing itself. Recourse to his understanding of act and potency will suffice. Thus one should indeed distinguish between being in act and being in potency. But it is not by reason of its essence that something is to be regarded as potential and by reason of a really or intentionally distinct existence that it is actual. If something is merely potential in terms of its essence, then it is potential and only potential in terms of its existence as well. If it is actual with respect to its essence, then so too with respect to its existence. This point bears repeating, since it is the cornerstone of Godfrey's thinking on the essence-existence relationship: whatever is true of one is true of the other.[136]

Insofar as Godfrey has here appealed to his theory of act and potency, his position on this matter might well be viewed as Aristotelian in inspiration. And in his rejection of the real distinction he has drawn upon and developed certain arguments found in Averroes. Granted this, Godfrey himself has applied the act-potency theory much more broadly than did the Stagirite, so much so in fact that one may describe a not yet existent prior to its creation and, for that matter, even prior to all creation as enjoying real but potential being by reason of God, its extrinsic efficient and creative principle.[137] Again, Godfrey is well aware of the distinction between signifying something concretely whether by means of a verb (*esse*) or a concrete noun (*ens*), on the

---

sic etiam essentia creaturae a primo agente acquirit esse et habet esse quod acquirendo acquirit habitudinem et respectum ad ipsum agens. Esse igitur non est ipse respectus" (fol. 19vb). However, Godfrey's argumentation is considerably more detailed than that offered here by Giles on this particular point.

[135] See, for instance, the texts cited in n. 63 of this chapter.

[136] See in this chapter, pp. 59–60, 78–79.

[137] See Q 4, q. 2 (PB 2.238), and our remarks in n. 110 of this chapter.

one hand, and signifying it abstractly by means of an abstract noun (*essentia*), on the other. But he insists that such distinction in the order of signification is only that and does not imply really distinct ontological principles within the entity in question. In this context he has also appealed to Aristotle (as well as to Boethius) for support.[138]

At the same time, Godfrey must come to grips with the classical problem of the One and the Many. Having rejected any theory of real metaphysical composition of essence and existence in finite beings, how is he to account for the fact that being is realized in many different individuals in limited fashion and this in spite of the admitted unity of being? He has, of course, defended an analogous notion of being and has also rejected any view according to which one might postulate the existence of some kind of subsisting universal *esse*. Nonetheless, one may still wonder how he is to account for the distinction of beings, the many, from God the supreme being, and from one another.

We have already touched on his view on this matter in considering his refutation of argumentation for real distinction between essence and existence. According to the shorter version of Quodlibet 3, q. 1, Godfrey denies that one need have recourse to real distinction and real composition of essence and existence in order to maintain the participated and nonsimple character of creatures. The essence of a creature may be regarded as participated and as more composite than the divine essence if one views one and the same thing, the creature or creaturely essence, as potential insofar as it is less perfect than any more perfect being, especially God, and yet as actual insofar as it enjoys some degree of actuality in itself.[139]

Godfrey returns to this same theory in other contexts, especially in Quodlibet 3, q. 3 and in Quodlibet 7, q. 7. In Quodlibet 3, q. 3 he rejects an argument that was sometimes offered in support of matter-form composition of angels. According to this argumentation an angel must be composed of act and potency if it is not to enjoy the same degree of simplicity as does God. But to say that the angel is composed of act and potency amounts to holding that it is composed of matter and form.[140] Thomas Aquinas had, of course, considered and refuted such reasoning by positing composition of essence and *esse* in such simple substances.[141] Godfrey can hardly do this

---

138 See Q 3, q. 1 (PB 2.164–65 and 303–04); also see Q 13, q. 3 (PB 5.207–08).

139 See PB 2.306 as well as p. 62 in this chapter.

140 In Q 3, q. 3 Godfrey considers this question: "Utrum natura angelica sit composita ex vera materia et vera forma" (PB 2.179). For the argument in question see p. 180 (long version) and p. 307 (short version).

141 See, for instance: *Le 'De ente et essentia' de s. Thomas d'Aquin*, Roland-Gos-

since he has so emphatically rejected any theory of real or intentional distinction of essence and existence. He replies by questioning the very presuppositions of such argumentation. It is not by appealing to composition of essence and *esse* or of matter and form that one meets this difficulty. It is not the composition of an essence with something else that is at issue here, but the composition of such an essence viewed in itself. If composition with something else were sufficient to distinguish any creaturely essence from the divine simplicity, then it would be enough to appeal to the substance-accident structure. But already in Quodlibet 3, q. 1 Godfrey had considered and rejected recourse to substance-accident composition as insufficient to establish composition within the essence of the creature.[142]

Godfrey then points to some further flaws in such reasoning. It is not by postulating a collection (*aggregatio*) of different things (*res*) that one distinguishes a created essence from the divine simplicity. If such were the case, then the created form in question would be as simple as God, presumably because it would still be simple in itself even if united with a distinct *esse* or a distinct matter or a distinct accident. Or else the form in question would itself be composed of distinct factors, each of which would in turn have to be further composed *ad infinitum*. It would then follow that that which is farthest removed from God's simplicity is that which is composed of more things. But then a simple element would be less removed from the divine simplicity than a man and the man would be less perfect than the element. Therefore, apparently hearkening back to his earlier presentation of this same theory, Godfrey concludes that one must rather account for the nonsimplicity of such a creaturely essence not by positing distinct things (*res*) therein but by holding that while such an essence is not itself really composed, it still includes both potentiality and actuality.[143]

It is in Quodlibet 7, q. 7 that Godfrey develops this final point more fully. There he is attempting to show that even though angels are not composed of

---

selin, ed. (Paris, 1948), c. 4, pp. 29–36; SCG II, cc. 52 and 53; *Treatise on Separate Substances*, ch. 8, reply to the fourth argument (F. Lescoe, ed., West Hartford, 1963), pp. 79–82; ST I, q. 50, a. 2, and 3; *De spiritualibus creaturis*, q. 1, a. 1. For our interpretation of the text from the *De ente* see our "Aquinas's Route to the Real Distinction. . . ," as cited in n. 4 of this chapter.

[142] Q 3, q. 3 (PB 2.186), long version. For the short version see p. 309. For the same point in Q. 3, q. 1 see PB 2.306 (short version).

[143] See PB 2.186 (long version) and p. 309 for the shorter version. The argument is more fully developed in the shorter version. Note the concluding remark in that version: "Et ideo dicendum quod ille recessus, sicut alias dictum est, non est includere diversas res sed includere potentialitatem cum actualitate defectiva in eadem re simplici quantum ad compositionem realem."

matter and form, in some way they do fall within the genus of substance and in some way have this in common with corporeal substances.[144] After considering a series of arguments that would militate against including angels within a genus, Godfrey replies that their presence therein must be admitted. Not to be included in any genus is something that should be reserved for God alone and this because of his supreme degree of actuality. Godfrey adds that "we" (Christians, presumably) do not attribute so much actuality and simplicity to angels as did the philosophers who seem to have regarded their separate substances almost as if they were gods.[145]

In order to allow for the presence of angels in the genus of substance in some way, Godfrey appeals to the distinction between a natural or real genus, on the one hand, and a logical or rational genus, on the other. In developing this distinction he observes that the notion of genus implies something potential and undetermined but determinable, something which the notion of species signifies as actual and as determined by a form or *differentia*. In other words, to the extent that something may be viewed as potential and determinable and yet as determined by some actuality, it can be included within a genus. If different individuals are composed of a real potential principle and a really distinct actuality, that is, of matter and form, then they will fall within the same real or natural genus. Godfrey warns that this should not be thought to imply that the intellect derives the notion of genus simply from matter. It rather develops this notion from the composite consisting both of matter and of form, by viewing it as determinable and without focusing on a given form whereby it is determined.[146]

Simple entities will not be included under a natural or real genus, and this because they lack a real potential principle, or matter, distinct from their forms. Still, maintains Godfrey, if one finds sufficient potentiality and actuality therein to enable one to view them as undetermined under one aspect but as determined under another, it will be possible to apply a logical genus to them.[147] Godfrey now attempts to show that there is some minimum degree of potentiality and actuality within such simple entities.

---

[144] PB 3.349: "Utrum essentia angeli sit composita ex genere et differentia."

[145] For the arguments against inclusion of angels within any genus see PB 3.351–53. For Godfrey's own view see PB 3.353.

[146] PB 3.353–54. Godfrey's final remark bears quotation since it will be essential for his subsequent argumentation: "Et hoc dicitur communitas generis, non quia sumatur ab illa re potentiali quae est materia sic communis secundum se, sed a toto composito ex ipsa et forma qua perfectibilis est absque cointellectu alicuius formae determinatae qua specificabilis et determinabilis est" (PB 3.354).

[147] PB 3.354–55.

He first considers and dismisses one attempt to account for this that would appeal to composition of the angelic essence with its existence (*esse*), its properties, and its accidents. With respect to each of these the angelic essence would be viewed as potential. Godfrey objects that the notions of genus and difference should be derived from something found within the very essence of the thing in question. But since the potentiality of an angelic essence with respect to its accidents and properties does not meet this criterion, such will not establish the intrinsic potentiality of the essence nor suffice to ground its presence within a genus. Moreover, suppose that some separate entities were to be created according to differing degrees of actuality and perfection, but without any kind of accidental perfections. Then logical genus if so derived could not be applied to them. But this Godfrey rejects as unfitting, again because only God is to be completely excluded from presence in a genus.[148]

In accord with indications we have already seen in Godfrey's Quodlibet 3, q. 1 and Quodlibet 3, q. 3, he now attempts to show that there is some kind of actuality and potentiality within the essence of simple creatures. Already somewhat earlier in Quodlibet 7, q. 7 he had remarked that in such simple entities one and the same thing may be viewed both as potential and as actual. Thus all such entities share in the notion of potentiality in some way because they cannot be identified with that first being which is Pure Act. Each of these is a participated being and as such cannot account for its own existence.[149] As he now develops this same theme he stresses what one might refer to as the hierarchy of being. Insofar as one kind of being enjoys greater perfection than another, the latter may be said to be less perfect than the former and hence potential. But insofar as any such being is higher or more perfect than another, to that degree it may be viewed as including actuality. Given this, one then may derive the notion of genus with respect to such a being insofar as it is viewed as potential and the notion of difference therefrom insofar as it is regarded as actual. Granted that the potentiality and

---

[148] PB 3.356–57. According to the anonymous author of a table of Godfrey's Quodlibets, Godfrey may here be referring to James of Viterbo, Quodlibet 1, q. 6. See "La table des divergences et innovations doctrinales de Godefroid de Fontaines," J. Hoffmans, ed., *Revue Néoscolastique de Philosophie* 36 (1934), p. 429. But for our reservations about the accuracy of this attribution see our "The Dating of James of Viterbo's Quodlibet I and Godfrey of Fontaines' Quodlibet VIII," *Augustiniana* 24 (1974), pp. 350–54.

[149] PB 3.355. ". . . ita etiam in separatis est accipere unum et idem secundum rem sub ratione potentialitatis et sub ratione actualitatis; et sic etiam omnia conveniunt in ratione potentialitatis sic quod unumquodque secundum se potentialitatem includit in quantum non est ens primum quod sit actus purus, sed est ens per participationem ex se non habens entitatem vel esse in actu sed in potentia tantum . . ."

actuality found in such entities will not be sufficient for them to be placed in a natural or real genus, it will allow for their inclusion in a logical genus.[150]

In further defense of this "composition" Godfrey now appeals to proposition II of Proclus's *Elementatio theologica*: "That which participates in the One is both one and not one" (*omne quod participat uno est unum et non unum*).[151] There, Godfrey notes approvingly, Proclus proves that anything that is not identical with the One itself, that is to say, with God or Pure Act, is therefore something other than the One. This is so, he continues, because something cannot fall short of the One except by approaching (*accessus*) the not-One. Thus that which participates in the One is not the One itself or in the primary sense, but only in some secondary fashion and by receding (*recessus*) from the same. Hence any such entity is both one and not one, that is to say, both one in one respect and not one or many in another. Godfrey then likens the differing degrees of being to the different kinds of numbers. Just as a given number does not fall short of the unit except by approaching multitude, so too within the realm of being different entities do not fall short of the First One except by approaching things possessed of multitude according to a greater or lesser degree.[152]

More perfect beings such as the angels, continues Godfrey, recede from or fall short of the First One without including composition of really distinct factors within their essence. Actuality and potentiality are found therein, nonetheless, not by way of real composition, but rather by reason of the fact that they possess a kind of intermediary nature and hence by "assimilation" of their nature to different points of reference, that is, to that which is higher and more actual, and to that which is lower and more potential. For purposes of illustration Godfrey now draws another analogy, this time with air and lighter and heavier elements. Air is said to have an intermediate nature insofar

---

[150] PB 3.357–59. See the same for further discussion of the minimum prerequisites for presence in a logical genus.

[151] PB 3.359. For the medieval Latin translation of Proclus's *Elementatio theologica* see C. Vansteenkiste, "Procli Elementatio theologica translata a Guilelmo de Moerbeke," *Tijdschrift voor Philosophie* 13 (1951), prop. 2, p. 265. For the Greek text see the edition by E. R. Dodds, *The Elements of Theology* (2nd ed., Oxford, 1963), prop. 2, pp. 2–3.

[152] PB 3.359–60. Note in particular: ". . . quia, ut ibi probatur, omne quod non est ipsum unum, id est primo unum quod est Deus quod est actus primus et purus, est aliquid aliud existens quam unum, eo quod a primo uno non est recedere nisi per accessum in non unum seu in aliquid aliud quam unum; quia omne participans uno non est ipsum unum sive primo unum, sed secundario et per quendam defectum et recessum ab eo. Ergo est unum et non unum, id est non sic unum quin aliquo modo multa, quia est unum uno modo et non unum alio modo" (p. 359).

as it falls between the heavy and the light, not in that it is composed of these two, but rather because when compared with fire air is said to be heavy and when compared with earth it is said to be light. So too, then, insofar as an angelic nature falls short of the actuality of the First Being and approaches potentiality, some kind of composition is to be assigned to it, not real composition to be sure, but a logical composition of act and potency. And then, perhaps in anticipation of the obvious objection that might be raised against his theory, Godfrey hastens to add that this logical composition is not purely imaginary, but that it applies to the thing in question by reason of its twofold comparison to different points of reference, the higher and the lower. Because there is nothing higher than God to which he could be compared, no such notion of potentiality can be assigned to him and hence no such logical composition of actuality and potentiality. Even though the mode of existing in one's self rather than in something else or the mode of substance does apply to God, the genus of substance does not.[153]

While Godfrey's primary concern in Quodlibet 7, q. 7 has been to show that there is sufficient "composition" of actuality and potentiality within angels to account for their presence in the logical genus of substance, the theory he has developed in support of the same is quite important for a proper understanding of his metaphysical solution to the problem of the One and the Many. In sum, then, he does allow for a metaphysics of participation, to be sure, not by composition of really distinct principles within the essence of simple created entities, but by viewing them both as assimilated to God as the highest being and pure actuality and as assimilated to lower beings. The resulting potency-act composition of such beings is not that of really distinct things or principles, according to Godfrey, and yet it is not purely fictitious. That is to say, it really pertains to such entities insofar as they are compared to really diverse points of reference.

---

[153] PB 3.360. Note in particular: ". . . ita etiam in natura angeli, recedendo ab actualitate primi et accedendo ad potentialitatem simpliciter habet quodammodo compositionem, non rei, sed rationis ex potentia et actu; non quidem fictae rationis, sed rei convenientem secundum comparationem ad superius . . . et secundum comparationem ad inferius." In q. 11 of his *Quaestiones disputatae de esse et essentia* Giles of Rome had already considered and rejected a similar analogy between air, viewed as intermediary between fire and water without being composed of fire and water or of the heavy and the light, and an angelic substance viewed as being both potential and actual without being composed of essence and *esse*. Giles replies that air could not enjoy this intermediary status unless it were composed of matter and form. So too, an angel could not be viewed as more actual than bodies and more potential than God unless it were really composed of potency and act, that is, of essence and *esse* (fol. 25rab).

One might still wonder whether such logical composition really succeeds in allowing Godfrey to account for the fact that there are many different beings and different kinds of being and to maintain that created separate substances do, indeed, fall short of the divine simplicity. If he himself has rejected the potency-act composition entailed by the substance-accident structure of such entities as inadequate to account for this because it would not be intrinsic but extrinsic to the essences in question, one wonders how reference to really distinct but extrinsic points of reference can ground intrinsic potentiality and actuality. Within a metaphysical perspective such as that of Aquinas wherein *esse* itself is viewed as the actuality of all acts and the perfection of all perfections, only real composition of *esse* and a distinct receiving principle will suffice to account for this.[154] But on this point Godfrey is surely not a follower of Aquinas.

In Godfrey's own solution there is an interesting blending of the Aristotelian and the Neoplatonic. Here again he has appealed to the Aristotelian doctrine of act and potency, but once more he has extended its application to separate entities. In other contexts he will also give credit to Aristotle for the analogy between the different kinds of beings and different kinds of numbers.[155] But at the same time he has explicitly cited Proclus as his source for his view that what participates in the One is both one and not one. And as we shall see in the following chapter in considering his metaphysics of creation, there are strong Neoplatonic currents in his doctrine of the approach towards (*accessus*) and falling short (*recessus*) of other beings with respect to God, the supreme One.[156]

Although some elements of Godfrey's solution, especially the last mentioned point (*accessus* and *recessus*), may be found in a number of other earlier and contemporary scholastics, Siger of Brabant appears to be his most likely source for the "composition" of act and potency that he has here defended in angels. In considering the essence-*esse* relationship in his *Quaes-*

---

[154] In addition to the references in n. 141 above see Thomas's *De potentia Dei*, q. 7, a. 2, ad 9: "Unde patet quod hoc quod dico esse est actualitas omnium actuum, et propter hoc est perfectio omnium perfectionum," in *Quaestiones disputatae*, R. Spiazzi, ed. (Turin-Rome, 1953), Vol. 2, p. 192.

[155] See, for instance, Q 2, q. 7 (PB 2.102); Q 2, q. 10 (PB 2.140), referring to Aristotle's *Metaphysics* VIII. See there 1043b 33ff. This analogy was drawn by many of the scholastics. On this see A. Maier, *Zwei Grundprobleme der scholastischen Naturphilosophie. Das Problem der intensiven Grösse. Die Impetustheorie*, 2nd ed. (Rome, 1951), pp. 11ff.

[156] See, for instance, Q 4, q. 3 ("Utrum in perfectionibus essentialibus rerum sive ordinem essentialem habentibus sit processus in infinitum"), PB 2.242–47, and especially pp. 245–46 for citations from Proclus and from the *Divine Names* of Pseudo-Dionysius.

tiones in Metaphysicam Siger refers to an argument in support of their distinction based on the claim that all things with the exception of the First Being must be composed. But since some of these beings are not composed of matter and form, it seems that they must be composed of essence and *esse*. Siger observes that this argument was decisive for Thomas.[157] Earlier in this same question Siger had presented and then criticized Thomas's viewpoint as found in the latter's *Commentary on the Metaphysics*.[158] Now he must come to terms with the objection to which we have just referred. In so doing he proposes two possible replies. According to the long version of his text he does not present the first as definitive. But in the shorter version of this same text, that is to say, in the version in Godfrey's student notebook, only Siger's first reply appears, and this without any qualifications.[159]

According to Siger's first reply, those things that are distinct from the First Being fall short of it (*recedendo*) and are multiplied by reason of the fact that they approach (*accessus*) the potential. But this does not imply any real composition of essence and *esse* in them. Rather, potency is to be assigned to them by reason of the fact that none of them attains to the pure actuality proper to the First Being. The similarity with Godfrey's reasoning is apparent, although he develops the act-potency "composition" of such entities in far greater detail than does Siger. Siger then goes on to observe that such entities participate in the First Being to a greater or lesser degree, because the closer they are to the First Being, the more do they participate in being. Just as no two numbers that differ in kind can be equidistant from the unit, so it is with substances. Since the First Being is the measure of all other beings, no two substances that differ in nature can approach the First Being to an equal degree.[160]

---

[157] See *Siger de Brabant, Questions sur la Métaphysique*, C. A. Graiff, ed. (Louvain, 1948), p. 13:50–54 (for the objection); p. 20:25 (for the reference to Thomas). For a detailed study of the doctrine of *accessus et recessus* in a number of medieval thinkers see E. P. Mahoney, "Metaphysical Foundations of the Hierarchy of Being According to Some Medieval and Renaissance Philosophers," in *Ancient and Medieval Philosophies of Existence*, P. Morewedge, ed. (New York: Fordham University Press, forthcoming).

[158] *Op. cit.*, p. 16:21–39, longer version; pp. 16–17, (14)–(21), for the shorter version contained in Godfrey's student notebook.

[159] "Dicendum quod haec ratio duplicem habet solutionem. Primum tamen modum non assero" (pp. 20:25–21:27).

[160] For the longer version see p. 21:30–44. For the shorter version see p. 21, (60)–(64). Also see "Die *Questiones metaphysice tres* des Siger von Brabant," J. Vennebusch, ed., *Archiv für Geschichte der Philosophie* 48 (1966), pp. 177–82.

In the second reply, found only in the longer version, Siger contends that even if one agrees that what falls short of the simplicity of the First Being must be composed, it does not follow that things lacking matter-form composition must be composed of essence and *esse*. They fall short of the divine simplicity in another way, in that every such being understands only by means of species that are distinct from it.[161] In other words, in this second argument Siger has recourse to substance-accident composition in order to safeguard the nonsimple character of such entities.

As we have seen, Godfrey rejects any appeal to substance-accident composition as inadequate to account for the nonsimple character of such essences in themselves. Instead, he attempts to show that there is some kind of logical composition of actuality and potentiality therein. But Siger's first argument appears to have been accepted and developed by Godfrey. This is striking both because it is the only one to appear in the shorter version found in Godfrey's student notebook and because Siger's longer version expresses some reservations with respect to the same. Interestingly enough, certain remarks in Siger's somewhat later *Quaestiones super librum de causis* suggest that he may have ended by moving towards Thomas's doctrine of real composition of essence and *esse* in the intelligences.[162] But there is no reason to think that Godfrey ever did or that he ever rejected as inadequate the logical composition of act and potency that we have seen him defending. For him, this theory goes hand in hand with his defense of the real identity of essence and existence.

---

[161] *Op. cit.*, p. 22:47–52. Cf. "Die *Questiones metaphysice tres. . .* ," p. 182. On this see Van Steenberghen, *Maître Siger de Brabant*, pp. 289–91.

[162] See *Les Quaestiones super Librum de causis de Siger de Brabant*, A. Marlasca, ed. (Louvain-Paris, 1972), p. 21, n. 20, for these texts, and Van Steenberghen, *Maître Siger de Brabant*, p. 292, for discussion.

Chapter III.

Uncreated Being and Creation

As we have already seen in Chapter I, according to Godfrey the subject of metaphysics is being as being. Although God himself is not to be regarded as the subject of metaphysics but only of sacred theology, still he is in some way included within that being that serves as subject of this philosophical discipline. Thus Godfrey observes that knowledge of God and of that which can be known about him by natural reason belongs to metaphysics more properly than does knowledge of any other particular being.[1] We have already found it necessary to make some reference to God in presenting Godfrey's metaphysics of essence and existence and especially when considering his rejection of Henry of Ghent's theory of intentional distinction of the same. Thus Godfrey has defended the nonsimple character of all finite beings, including angels, in contrast with the divine simplicity and this in spite of his assertion of real identity of essence and existence in such entities. If in some of the discussions examined above Godfrey seems to have taken God's existence as given, this is understandable not merely because he conducted his quodlibetal debates in his formal capacity as a Master of Theology, but also because he was convinced that unaided human reason in its own right can demonstrate the existence of the divine. Given this, it is now incumbent upon

---

[1] See Ch. I, pp. 4–6; for Godfrey's text see Q 9, q. 20 (PB 4.288), cited in Ch. I, n. 17.

us to examine Godfrey's views with respect to metaphysical knowledge of God. Having done this, we shall then be in position to present his metaphysics of creation.

With this in mind the present chapter will be divided into the following parts: A. Philosophical Knowledge of God's Existence; B. Philosophical Knowledge of the Divine Essence and the Divine Attributes; C. The Procession of Creatures from God.

A. PHILOSOPHICAL KNOWLEDGE OF GOD'S EXISTENCE

Reference has been made in Chapter I to the disputed issue as to whether the subject of metaphysics is God or being as being. As we have suggested there, in holding that the subject of this discipline is being as being and that God is included under the notion of being, Godfrey appears to be in fundamental agreement with Siger of Brabant.[2] Closely connected with this question in the texts of Avicenna and Averroes, and therefore in the minds of many thirteenth-century participants in the discussion, was another issue: To which part of philosophy, physics or metaphysics, does it belong to establish the existence of God? The problem obviously originates from the texts of Aristotle and in large measure from the difficulty in determining the precise relationship between the First Mover of *Physics* VII and VIII and the Unmoved Mover of *Metaphysics* XII.[3] Avicenna had strongly argued that philosophical demonstration of God's existence belongs to metaphysics and only to metaphysics. If he himself had touched upon this issue in his own presentation of physics or of natural philosophy, he explains in his *Metaphysics* that such discussion was really foreign to natural philosophy. He had introduced it there only to encourage the reader to hurry on to study this matter in first philosophy, that is to say, in metaphysics.[4] Averroes, on the other hand,

---

[2] See Ch. I, n. 18.

[3] See, for instance, M. De Corte, "La causalité du premier moteur dans la philosophie aristotélicienne," *Revue d'Histoire de la Philosophie* 5 (1931), pp. 105–46. J. Paulus, "La théorie du premier moteur chez Aristote," *Revue de Philosophie* n.s. 4 (1933), pp. 259–94 and 394–424.

[4] *Metaphysica* (Venice, 1508), fol. 70rb. See in particular: "Iam etiam significavi tibi in naturalibus quod deus est non corpus, nec virtus corporis, sed est unum separatum a materia et ab omni commixtione omnis motus. Igitur inquisitio de eo debet fieri in hac scientia [scientia divina], et quod de hoc apprehendisti in naturalibus erat extraneum a naturalibus quia quod de hoc tractabatur in eis non erat deus [according to the manuscript in Godfrey's library, *Paris, Bibl. Nat. 16.096*, fol. 2ra: "non erat de eis"]. Sed volumus per hoc accelerare hominem ad tenendum esse primum principium, ut per hoc augeretur desiderium addiscendi scientias et perveniendi ad locum in quo certius possit cognosci."

sharply rejected this Avicennian position and, in conjunction with his view that metaphysics has as its subject divine being, maintained that God's existence could be proved in physics and only in physics.[5]

When one turns to thirteenth-century thought on this matter, one finds that scholarly opinion is divided today with respect to certain aspects of Thomas Aquinas's position, especially as regards the role of the argumentation in the *Physics* and hence of the proof from motion in his understanding of Aristotle's procedure and in his personal thought as well. According to one interpretation, Thomas's argumentation for God's existence is metaphysical and only metaphysical. Purely physical argumentation will not lead to the existence of God.[6] According to another view, in proving the existence of the First Mover in the *Physics* Aristotle had, in the eyes of Aquinas, demonstrated the existence of God.[7] Rather than dwell here on this problem in Thomistic scholarship, it will be more advantageous for us to turn once more to the text of Siger of Brabant.

---

[5] See *In I Phys.* (Venice, 1562), Vol. 4, fol. 47rb–47va. See in particular: "Sed notandum est quod istud genus entium, esse scilicet separatum a materia, non declaratur nisi in hac scientia naturali. Et qui dicit quod prima Philosophia nititur declarare entia separabilia esse peccat. Haec enim entia sunt subiecta primae Philosophiae. . . . Unde Avicenna peccavit maxime cum dixit quod primus Philosophus demonstrat primum principium esse." See also *In II Phys.*, fol. 57ra; *In XII Metaphys.* (Venice, 1562), Vol. 8, fol. 293ra–295rb. If it pertains to the natural philosopher to establish the existence of the First Mover, it will belong to the metaphysician to show that this same First Mover is also the first form and the ultimate end and not merely of substance insofar as it is mobile, but of substance as substance or as being (fol. 293vb; 294vb; 295rab). Also see Zimmermann, *Ontologie oder Metaphysik?*, pp. 116–17; Doig, *Aquinas on Metaphysics*, pp. 35–46; W. Dunphy, "The *Quinque Viae* and some Parisian Professors of Philosophy," *St. Thomas Aquinas: 1274–1974 Commemorative Studies* (Toronto, 1974), Vol. 2, pp. 76–77.

[6] See, for instance, J. Owens, "Aquinas and the Proof from the 'Physics'," *Mediaeval Studies* 28 (1966), pp. 119–50, especially pp. 132–37 and 149; also "The Conclusion of the Prima Via," *The Modern Schoolman* 30 (1953), pp. 33–53; 109–21; 203–15. Also J. Paulus, "Le caractère métaphysique des preuves thomistes de l'existence de Dieu," *Archives d'Histoire Doctrinale et Littéraire du Moyen Age* 9 (1934), pp. 143–53.

[7] See A. Pegis, "St. Thomas and the Coherence of the Aristotelian Theology," *Mediaeval Studies* 35 (1973), pp. 67–117. Both Owens and Pegis acknowledge the importance of the following text from SCG I, 13, in interpreting Aquinas on this point: "Sed quia Deus non est pars alicuius moventis seipsum, ulterius [that is, after completing the argumentation of the *Physics*] Aristoteles, in sua *Metaphysica*, investigat ex hoc motore qui est pars moventis seipsum, alium motorem separatum omnino, qui est Deus." See in Thomas's discussion of the *secunda via* the paragraph "Sed quia." (Ed. *Leonina manualis* [Rome, 1934], p. 14).

In his *Quaestiones in metaphysicam* Siger refers to the disagreement between Avicenna and Averroes not only as regards the subject of metaphysics but also as regards the physical or metaphysical nature of argumentation for God's existence. While rejecting the view that God is the subject of metaphysics, Siger offers what one might term a compromise position on the second issue. To establish a given conclusion, on the one hand, and the middle term whereby that same conclusion is proven, on the other, need not belong to one and the same science. Thus the middle term whereby God's existence is established is physical. But this middle term was utilized by Aristotle himself in *Metaphysics* XII. Here, then, Siger seems to imply that while the argumentation for God's existence is physical in nature, it may be employed in metaphysics as well.[8] And as Van Steenberghen has recently shown, Siger also offered other and more obviously metaphysical arguments for the existence of God.[9] But Siger's compromise interpretation should be kept in mind as we now turn to Godfrey's discussion, especially since the shorter version of Siger's text is preserved in Godfrey's student notebook.

Godfrey seems to assign some knowledge of God as First Mover to physics, but then reserves more complete study of the divine to metaphysics. Thus in a passing remark in Quodlibet 11, q. 1 he observes that the metaphysician's consideration of God as viewed in himself is more eminent and more perfect than that of the natural philosopher, who simply considers him as mover of the first movable being.[10] But Godfrey also adds that God is the First Mover in terms of his total being. In other words, Godfrey here implies that one should not distinguish two Gods or two entities, the First Mover of the *Physics* and the God of the *Metaphysics*.[11]

In Quodlibet 5, q. 11 Godfrey considers the following question: Can the human intellect by reasoning from natural things know that God is the efficient cause of creatures? Here he appears to have in mind knowledge of God not only as First Mover but also as creative principle. Godfrey replies that one can reason from creatures to a knowledge of God as that first being that depends upon no other and subsists in himself, and hence, as causal and

---

[8] Siger de Brabant, *Questions sur la métaphysique*, p. 4:41 – 50 (longer version); p. 4:(27) – (35), for the shorter version. Note in particular: "Medium autem quo Deus ostenditur naturale est, quo Aristoteles utitur XII° huius quasi hoc supponens ex physicis" (p. 4:46 – 47). On this see Dunphy, "The *Quinque Viae* . . . ," p. 78.

[9] *Maître Siger de Brabant*, pp. 296 – 301. As Van Steenberghen indicates, in these other and clearly metaphysical arguments Siger is concerned with establishing the fact that there is *one* supreme being which is the cause of the being of all other things.

[10] PB 5.3. See Ch. I, n. 16 for citation of the same.

[11] ". . . licet secundum totum id quod est secundum se sit etiam motor." (*ibid.*).

productive principle of all other things.[12] And as has been noted, in Quodlibet 9, q. 20 Godfrey observes that it belongs more properly to metaphysics to treat of God and that which can be known about him by natural reason than to treat of any other being. Shortly thereafter within the latter context he lists certain things that can be known by human reason with certitude about God: that because God is the first being he is therefore simple; that he is being in act; that he is an intellectual being. All these things, continues Godfrey, are proven in metaphysics. Interestingly enough, there is no reference to physics in this discussion.[13]

Godfrey's position is more fully presented in Quodlibet 7, q. 11. There he is attempting to determine whether by natural reason one can not only know of God that he is but also what he is to some degree.[14] Before replying Godfrey develops at some length his understanding of the difference between

---

[12] PB 3.40. "Utrum intellectus humanus ex naturalibus possit cognoscere Deum esse principium effectivum creaturarum." In Godfrey's reply note in particular: "Ex creaturis autem hoc potest intelligi de Deo, scilicet quod oportet ponere aliquod ens primum a nullo dependens, sed a quo omnia dependent et sic ut in se subsistens et ut habens rationem alicuius suppositi et ideo poterit Deus ex naturalibus intelligi esse principium causativum vel productivum rerum omnium" (PB 3.41). A theological difficulty is then raised. If one knows God as subsisting and hence as a supposit, one appears to be affirming an absolute supposit of him. Yet this is precluded by Christian belief in the Trinity, according to which only relative supposits can be assigned to God. Hence, apart from faith, it would seem that one cannot assign any kind of supposit to God. Godfrey replies that God is not known in philosophy as a supposit in the sense of relative supposits, but only as a supposit without further qualification in some general and vague fashion and without explicit indication as to whether he exists in himself as relative or as absolute supposit (" . . . id est non determinate ut subsistens ad se solum, nec determinate ut subsistens ad alium, sed in generali" [p. 41]). Even this general but indefinite notion of "absolute" supposit is not assigned by natural reason to God *ex parte rei intellectae* but only with reference to our mode of understanding. It is in this way that the philosophers have known that God exists and subsists. And at times even believers think of God in this way without explicit reference to the Trinity of Persons, as, for instance, when they say that God created the world. Godfrey concludes by warning the philosophers not to enter into the intricacies of the Trinity unless they wish to fall into error as Averroes once did in commenting on *Metaphysics* XII (PB 3.41–44). For Averroes see *In Metaphys. XII*, fol. 322va.

[13] PB 4.288. "Quantum ad ea ergo, quae de Deo certitudinaliter et evidenter cognoscuntur, puta quod quia Deus est primum ens, ideo est simplex; item est ens in actu; item est ens intellectuale et cetera; dicendum quod talia non pertinent proprie ad scientiam theologiae prout nunc de ea intendimus. . . . Constat enim quod talia probantur et declarantur in metaphysica, quae est scientia lumini naturalis rationis innitens."

[14] "Utrum eadem cognitione cognoscatur de Deo si est et quid est" (PB 3.377).

knowing "what something is" *(quid est)* and knowing "that it is" *(si est* or *quia est)*. In acknowledged dependency upon Aristotle's *Posterior Analytics* Godfrey begins by introducing a distinction between preexistent knowledge or foreknowledge *(praecognitio)*, on the one hand, and knowledge that must in some way be established by investigation *(quaestio)*, on the other. This distinction may be applied both to knowledge as to "what something is" *(quid est)* and to knowledge "that it is" *(quia est* or *si est)*. Thus when one merely understands the meaning of a term but does not know whether or not there is anything real that corresponds to it, one has foreknowledge as to what something is, or purely nominal knowledge *(quid nominis)*, of the same. This kind of merely nominal knowledge is the most primitive that one may have with reference to something and is prior to one's awareness either as to whether that thing enjoys real being or as to what its real quiddity is. But when knowledge *quid est* is directed towards the essence of a thing, it is no longer merely foreknowledge but rather the kind that must be grounded or established in some way by investigation *(quaestio)*.[15]

The same distinction may be applied to knowledge "that it is" *(si est* or *quia est)*. Thus in the case of indemonstrables, that is to say, things that are prior to others and not themselves capable of being justified by any reasoning process, one's knowledge of these is not acquired by investigation *(quaestio)* but is rather foreknowledge *(praecognitio)*. Such things can only be known by simple apprehension following upon sense experience. And because one must know such things in order to be able to reason or conclude from them to others, such knowledge is appropriately entitled foreknowledge. Godfrey cites as examples one's understanding of being insofar as such constitutes the subject of metaphysics, or of mobile being insofar as such constitutes the subject of natural philosophy. In each case as soon as one understands the meaning of the name in question and thus arrives at nominal knowledge, one also immediately becomes aware of the corresponding "if it is" or "that it is" of being or of mobile being.[16] But when knowledge "if it is" or "that it is" is directed toward things that do not enjoy such priority in reality but must be discovered by reasoning from other things that are prior to them

[15] PB 3.377–78. Here Godfrey refers to the beginnings both of Bk. I and of Bk. II of the *Posterior Analytics*. See Bk. I, c. 1 (on the need for preexistent knowledge); Bk. II, cc. 1–2 (on the four kinds of "questions" that may be asked). Godfrey also finds support in Aristotle for his description of purely nominal knowledge: "Prout enim dicitur secundo Posteriorum, significare est per nomen ea quae non sunt sicut ea quae sunt; et ideo hoc modo accipiendo quid est sic est praecognitio quod nullo modo potest esse quaestio, sed antecedit omnem quaestionem" (*ibid.*). For Aristotle see *Post. Anal.* II, c. 7 (92b 29–30).

[16] PB 3.378.

either in being or at least in the order of discovery, then such knowledge is not foreknowledge but rather the kind that must be grounded or justified (*quaestio*). Godfrey observes that there is a certain order among the things that are known by us, as well as among the sciences. Thus it may happen that something that was first established by investigation in one science is accepted as given or as foreknowledge by another science and hence may serve as subject of the latter.[17] This is, of course, in accord with the generally accepted axiom that no science can establish the "if it is" of its own subject.[18]

Godfrey now attempts to determine more precisely the meaning of knowledge "if it is" or "that it is." Whether such is simply given as foreknowledge (*praecognitio*) or is in fact established by investigation (*quaestio*), it implies knowledge of something in terms of real being, but knowledge that is extremely confused and indistinct or, as he also describes it, knowledge of something in terms of the kind of unity being implies insofar as it is divided into the predicaments and constitutes the subject of metaphysics. But, continues Godfrey, if the intellect is to grasp something as enjoying real being it cannot stop with this confused notion of analogous being, but must understand the thing in question either as substance or as accident. In brief, then, knowledge "that it is" with respect to a thing is knowledge of it as belonging to its most general genus, that is to say, knowledge of it as substance or as accident.[19]

---

[17] PB 3.378–79.

[18] This axiom played a central role in the dispute between Averroes and Avicenna as to the subject of metaphysics, and as to whether it belongs to physics or to metaphysics to prove the existence of God. Frequent recourse to it is found among the various thirteenth-century participants in the same discussion. For references see those listed above in Ch. I, n. 13, and notes 4 and 5 of the present chapter. For this in Aristotle see *Post. Anal.* I, c. 10 (76b 3–22). Also see *Metaphys.* VI, c. 1 (1025b 7–18). Interestingly, Owens suggests that Aristotle himself restricted this principle to the particular sciences but did not apply it to first philosophy. See "The Conclusion of the Prima Via," p. 203 and note 115.

[19] PB 3.379. Until this point in his discussion there is some similarity between Godfrey's treatment and that found in Henry of Ghent in his *Summae quaestionum ordinariarum* (Paris, 1520), a. 24, q. 3, fol. 138r–138v. But Henry adjusts his treatment to his general theory of *esse essentiae*. Thus once one arrives at nominal knowledge of a thing, one immediately wonders as to whether or not it is a *res*, that is to say, endowed with *esse essentiae*. Then, by arriving at *si est* knowledge of the same one grasps it as a *res*, or as enjoying *esse essentiae*, but without further determining it as creator or creature, or as substance or as accident. For Godfrey, to recognize it as real (to know "that it is") is to grasp it in terms of its supreme genus, that is, as substance or accident. On Henry see Paulus, *Henri de Gand . . .*, pp. 29–43; Gómez Caffarena, *Ser participado y ser subsistente . . .*, pp. 44–47.

In contrast with merely nominal knowledge of a thing (*quid est nominis*), knowledge as to what it really is (*quid est rei*) is perfect and determined awareness of it in terms of its species, the kind that is discovered by a discursive process and expressed in a definition. For Godfrey such awareness is not to be termed foreknowledge (*praecognitio*) but is rather acquired by investigation (*quaestio*).[20]

In order to illustrate more fully his understanding of these different types of human knowing Godfrey then turns to *Metaphysics* V wherein Aristotle distinguishes four different kinds of unity: numerical, specific, generic, and unity of analogy or proportion.[21] Corresponding to these are four different kinds of human knowing, Godfrey comments.[22] Thus one may know a thing by analogy or proportion to the extent that it enjoys proportional or analogical identity with something else. But knowledge by analogy or proportion can itself be twofold. One kind corresponds to the analogy of one being to another when the two do not fall within the same genus and when, therefore, a single (and presumably univocal) concept cannot be formed of both. Thus it is that one understands accident as pertaining to and implying substance, which itself is being in the primary sense. But knowledge by analogy or proportion can be realized in another and broader sense, when the analogy is no longer grounded on the relationship of one being to another but rather on that of nonbeing to being. It is because nonbeing is in some way attributed to being that it can in some way be known.[23]

Knowledge based on this second kind of analogy or proportion is sufficient for one to impose a name or term. But it does not imply knowledge of the being or the nonbeing of the thing in question. Hence, continues Godfrey, neither does merely nominal knowledge as to what something is.[24] He has obviously correlated the latter kind of *quid est* knowledge with that based on analogy or proportion in the broadest and weakest sense. He then goes on to correlate knowledge "if it is" or "that it is" with that grounded on generic unity. Once one has arrived at the weakest and most primitive kind of knowledge as to what something is (*quid est nominis*), then one immediately wonders whether it is a being, that is to say, whether it really falls under that genus of being that was first signified by the name or term. Once one knows

---

[20] PB 3.379.

[21] *Met.* V, c. 6 (1016b 31 – 1017a 2).

[22] PB 3.379. ". . . est intelligendum quod quadruplex est rei cognitio, sicut etiam quadruplex est rei entitas sive unitas, scilicet numero, specie, genere, analogia sive proportione, secundum Philosophum, quinto Metaphysicae."

[23] PB 3.379 – 80.

[24] PB 3.380.

this, presumably either as a precognition or as established by investigation, then one grasps the thing in terms of its most universal genus.[25]

Godfrey adds two important precisions with reference to this. First of all, in accord with his notion of potential being as analyzed above, he warns that knowledge *si est* of a thing does not imply that it is understood as actually existing in itself extramentally. It may so exist or it may exist only potentially in terms of its principles. To illustrate he again cites the example of a non-existing rose, on the one hand, and a chimera, on the other. One may have such knowledge "that it is" with respect to the former, not with respect to the latter.[26] Secondly, Godfrey remarks that to know "that something is" in the strict sense is already to know to some degree "what it is," that is, at least in terms of its most general genus. Thus in the *Posterior Analytics* Aristotle can write that knowledge "that it is" is a part of knowledge "what it is," and that to the degree that we know of something "that it is," to that degree we also know "what it is."[27]

What Godfrey has here done, therefore, is to treat knowledge "what it is" and "that it is" respectively as more confused knowledge and less confused knowledge. In the order of discovery one moves from knowledge that is more confused to that which is less confused. And just as generic unity comes after and presupposes analogical or proportional unity when the latter is defined in the broader sense so as to apply to being and to nonbeing, so too does knowledge "that it is" follow after and presuppose purely nominal knowledge "what it is."[28]

Finally, Godfrey correlates knowledge as to what a thing really is (*quid est rei*) with knowledge of it in terms of specific unity or in terms of its proximate species. Since this kind of knowledge is more determined and less confused than merely generic knowledge, it comes after knowledge "that it

---

[25] PB 3.380–381.

[26] PB 3.380. "Hoc tamen non est sic intelligendum quod cognitio de aliquo si est includat quod illud sciatur esse sic in rerum natura quod existat extra in actu in propria forma et materia; immo sufficit quod habeat esse in rerum natura vel dicto modo in actu vel in potentia et in virtute suorum principiorum, prout rosa non existente in actu . . . "

[27] PB 3.381. "Unde cognoscere aliquid si est proprie est cognoscere quid est illud, saltem sub ratione generis generalissimi; propter quod, sicut genus generalissimum pertinet ad quidditatem rei, ita cognitio si est pertinet ad cognitionem quid est. Unde dicit Aristoteles, secundo Posteriorum, quod cognitio si est est pars cognitionis eius quod quid est et quantum habemus de re si est tantum habemus de ea quid est; et haec cognitio si est sequitur cognitionem quid est nominis sicut cognitio minus confusa magis confusam." For Aristotle see *Post. Anal.* II, c. 8 (93a 20–28).

[28] PB 3.381.

is." And just as knowledge of something in terms of its species presupposes knowledge of its genus, so too one cannot understand what a thing really is (*quid est rei*) without having already understood "that it is." Here Godfrey finds support in a well-known quotation from the *Posterior Analytics* to this effect, that one cannot know what something is without knowing that it is.[29] One might wonder how Godfrey will fit the fourth kind of unity, numerical, into this scheme. In fact he explicitly refuses to do so, contenting himself with the observation that none of the modes of intellectual cognition under discussion corresponds to numerical unity, because things enjoying such unity are not intelligible of themselves and can only be grasped by the senses.[30]

After this rather lengthy, if interesting, digression Godfrey is now in position to respond to the original question: Is it by one and the same cognition that one knows of God both "that he is" and "what he is"? Godfrey prefaces his reply by distinguishing between a natural, direct, and quasi-intuitive knowledge, on the one hand, and discursive knowledge, on the other. In accord with remarks he has already made, he comments that while the first is not derived from anything prior, the second does presuppose something more fundamental and ultimately rests on knowledge of the first kind. Moreover, the first kind of direct and quasi-intuitive knowledge is not subject to error, whereas the second may indeed be.[31]

As regards man's knowledge of God, he will enjoy knowledge of the first type in the life to come in the beatific vision. And in that eventuality it will be by one and the same cognition that he knows of God "that he is" and "what he is."[32] But in this life one must have recourse to knowledge of the

---

[29] "Et ex his ulterius patet quod cognitio quid est rei qua cognoscitur res complete et determinate secundum rationem speciei, et hoc est per rationem diffinitivam dicentem quid est res, sequitur alias duas cognitiones praedictas sicut magis determinata magis confusas; et sicut cognitio generis tanquam magis confusa praecedit cognitionem speciei magis determinatam, ita cognitio si est praecedit cognitionem quid est; et sicut cognitio speciei non potest esse sine cognitione generis, ita nec cognitio quid est sine cognitione si est. Unde dicitur, secundo Posteriorum: impossibile est scire quid est ignorantem si est, quia de eo quod non est non contingit scire quid est" (*ibid.*). For Aristotle see *Post. Anal.* II, c. 8 (93a 19–20). For a similar interpretation of this doctrine in Aristotle see J. Owens, *The Doctrine of Being in the Aristotelian Metaphysics*, 2nd printing (Toronto, 1957), pp. 170–72.

[30] PB 3.381–82.

[31] PB 3.382.

[32] PB 3.382–83. Godfrey warns that this is not because God's essence is his existence (*esse existentiae*), for, as we have seen, he rejects any real or even intentional distinction between essence and existence in creatures as well. It is rather because, to the extent that God is known immediately as he is in himself, there is no possibility of one's moving from a general quasi-generic knowledge of him (*si est*)

second type, that is to say, to rational investigation, in one's effort to arrive at some knowledge of the divine. Given this, some have concluded that one cannot in any way know of God "what he is." Thus certain remarks by John Damascene seem to imply that we are unable to know what God is, but only what he is not. Hence some conclude that one can only know of God that he is.[33] And even in this cognition the "is" that one discovers is not the being whereby God subsists in himself but only that of the proposition: "God is." Although Godfrey does not name him here, certain remarks in the texts of Thomas Aquinas come to mind.[34]

Godfrey finds this position too restrictive. First of all, both the efforts of the philosophers and the interpretation of certain texts from Scripture by "holy men" indicate that they were striving for something more in their discussions of man's knowledge of God. Far from contenting themselves with offering motives to prove the truth of the proposition asserting that God is, they were attempting to arrive at some more specific knowledge of the divine.[35]

Furthermore, Godfrey argues that one cannot recognize the truth of the propositon "God is" unless one has some knowledge "that he is" in the sense defined above. There, it will be recalled, Godfrey contended that knowledge "if it is" or "that it is" is not directed to a thing's actual existence but is rather one phase in one's knowledge of its essence or entity. Godfrey's point in the present discussion appears to be this. If one is to recognize the truth of the proposition "God is" one must be able to assign some meaning to the subject of that proposition, that is, to the name "God." But, he

---

to a more determined quasi-specific knowledge (*quid est*). Both knowledge *si est* and *quid est* are directed to his essence and will in the beatific vision be one and the same cognition. Also see pp. 386–87.

[33] PB 3.383. For John Damascene see his *De fide orthodoxa*, E. Buytaert, ed. (St. Bonaventure, N.Y., 1955), Bk. I, c. 2 (pp. 14–15) and c. 4 (pp. 19–20). Godfrey also cites "Gregorius super Ezechiel," but the editors refer rather to his *Moralia* V, c. 36, 169 (PL 75.716).

[34] The anonymous doctrinal table also sees Godfrey as here referring to Thomas, ST I, 3, 4, ad 4 (which is fairly exact, although it should read ad 2). See J. Hoffmans, "La table des divergences et innovations. . . ," p. 429. For another reference in Aquinas on this same point see *De potentia dei*, q. 7, a. 2, ad 1. For discussion of this position in Thomas see E. Gilson, *The Christian Philosophy of St. Thomas Aquinas* (New York, 1956), pp. 109–10. For more on the "negative theology" of Aquinas see pp. 107ff., and Gilson's stress on the text from SCG I, 30: "Non enim de Deo capere possumus quid est, sed quid non est, et qualiter alia se habeant ad ipsum. . ." Also see A. D. Sertillanges, *Les grandes thèses de la Philosophie Thomiste* (Paris, 1928), pp. 67–80. For a different reading of Aquinas on this see J. Maritain, *The Degrees of Knowledge* (New York, 1959), Appendix III, pp. 422–29.

[35] PB 3.383–84.

reasons, purely nominal knowledge of this subject will not be sufficient since such knowledge may apply both to being and nonbeing. Therefore, at least some knowledge "that it is" will also be required of this subject, or God. But he has also maintained above that knowledge "that it is" shares in some way in knowledge as to what something is (*quid est*) because it involves recognition of it as enjoying real being in some way, whether substantial or accidental. In sum, then, Godfrey argues that one cannot recognize the truth of the proposition "God is" without also having at least the minimal awareness as to what he is required for knowledge *si est* or *quia est* of the subject of that proposition.[36]

Moreover, Godfrey contends that one will not know what things are to be denied of God unless one also knows what is to be affirmed of him. But this is to know in some manner that which pertains to his nature or quiddity. Hence Godfrey concludes that in this life we can in some way know of God "what he is."[37] He quotes Augustine in support of his position and suggests that authorities such as those cited above in favor of the opposite view be interpreted as denying that we can have any kind of immediate or intuitive knowledge of God's quiddity in this life. Such authorities may also be taken to mean that while one can know in this life with perfect certainty the truth of the proposition asserting "God is," one cannot know with certainty and in perfect fashion "what he is." Just as in propositions more is required for *propter quid* knowledge than for knowledge *quia*, so too as regards the present discussion, more is required for knowledge *quid est* than for knowledge *si est*.[38]

Godfrey now proceeds to trace out in greater detail the path that one must follow in one's effort to arrive at rational knowledge of God. One first attains to purely nominal knowledge of God (*quid nominis*) on the strength of some kind of analogy or proportion with that which one observes in the world of sensible things. Thus one finds among lower beings that some are principal causes with respect to others and that some are governed by others such as the family by its father and a servant by his master. One then applies this name "God" to signify something in the universe that is the first and unique

36 PB 3.384.

37 *Ibid.*

38 *Ibid.* See Q 11, q. 5 (PB 5.27), where the same text from Augustine is cited: "Unde Augustinus *De Orando Deum, ad Probam*: si omnino Deum quid sit nesciremus, omnino eum non amaremus. Sed verum est quod quid est Dei secundum eius propriam rationem et in eius propria forma a viatore sciri non potest, sed tantum in quibusdam generalibus attributis, scilicet sub ratione puri actus et summi boni." For Augustine see *De Orando Deum, Ad Probam. Epistula* 130, c. 15, 28 (PL 33.505–506), but cited as c. 1 (PL 33.494) in PB 3.409.

cause of all things and than which nothing greater can be thought. But at this juncture one does not yet know whether or not that which is signified by this name "God" enjoys real being, that is to say, one does not yet possess knowledge *si est* of God.[39]

Godfrey suggests that one may now reason to *si est* knowledge of God, as did Aristotle in *Physics* VII, by showing that one cannot regress to infinity in moved movers and hence that there must be one First Mover, or God. Such *si est* knowledge does not yet yield *quid est* knowledge of God. Thus in *Physics* VIII Aristotle also concluded to the fact that the First Mover is perpetual and pure act without potentiality.[40] But, continues Godfrey, it was in the *Metaphysics* that Aristotle arrived at more precise knowledge of God and investigated his quiddity (*quid est*). Taking God's *si est* as established, Aristotle concluded to the presence therein of certain noble characteristics to an eminent degree. In fact, Godfrey suggests that Aristotle treated these characteristics as quasi-differences and thereby moved from knowledge "that he is" to knowledge "what he is" as if he were proceeding from confused and quasi-generic knowledge to determined and quasi-specific knowledge.[41]

Two points should be noted now in our effort to understand Godfrey's thought on man's philosophical knowledge of God. First of all, he here assigns *si est* knowledge of God to the *Physics* and reserves more perfect or *quid est* knowledge to the *Metaphysics*. This bears out our earlier suggestion that Godfrey himself seems to assign some knowledge of God to natural philosophy, but more perfect knowledge to metaphysics. Secondly, he finds support from Aristotle's procedure for his own view that one moves from vague and confused awareness of God to more exact and precise knowledge, so much so that he uses the language "quasi-generic" and "quasi-specific." Godfrey is well aware, of course, that God falls under no genus or species and has qualified these expressions accordingly. Thus he remarks that this diversity between *si est* and *quid est* knowledge of God arises solely from the side of the human mode of knowing.[42]

---

[39] PB 3.384–85. Godfrey's usage of the Anselmian formula "quo maius cogitari non possit" to illustrate merely nominal knowledge of God and his judgment that such is inadequate to establish anything about the reality of the divine might be taken as a veiled refutation of Anselm's argument. In any event we have found nothing in Godfrey's corpus to indicate that he would have accepted that approach as probative.

[40] PB 3.384–85. Presumably, at this point in the argumentation Godfrey is assuming that one has established the fact that the First Mover does, in fact, exist. Such knowledge presupposes, he has contended, *si est* awareness of the subject of the proposition "God is." See the text referred to in note 36.

[41] PB 3.385.

[42] PB 3.385–86.

With this last-mentioned qualification in mind, Godfrey retraces once more the steps through which man should pass in his reasoned investigation of God. Once one has gone beyond the level of purely nominal knowledge of God, one arrives at a very confused and quasi-generic knowledge *si est* of him, presumably by knowing him as a substance. Then one specifies this knowledge slightly and it becomes a more precise knowledge as to what God is. Thus one now knows him as a living, incorporeal substance. As more precisions are added the knowledge becomes more exact. For instance, one may know him as an intelligent, living, and incorporeal substance.[43]

Before leaving Godfrey's treatment of this issue, it is interesting for us to note that he now refers to two of the articles condemned by Stephen Tempier in 1277, two which at first sight appear to him to be mutually exclusive. According to article 36 it is an error for one to say that we can know God in this life by his essence. But article 215 cites as erroneous the claim that one can only know of God that he is, or his existence. Writing in 1290 or thereabouts, Godfrey states that the condemnation of the first article cannot be reconciled with that of the second unless one distinguishes in some way concerning knowledge of God through his essence. This distinction, he suggests, he himself has clarified in the present discussion. Some years later in Quodlibet 12, q. 5 (ca. 1296 or thereafter) Godfrey turns to these same prohibited articles again. There his attitude towards the 1277 prohibitions is considerably more critical, especially insofar as some of the condemned propositions appear to touch on the views of Aquinas. He cites these two as illustrations of prohibited articles that appear to be in contradiction with one another.[44] And in the present discussion (Q 7, q. 11) he offers a final clarification. Granted that in God existence (*esse*) and quiddity are one and the same, we are unable in this life to know him directly as he is in himself, but only by

---

[43] PB 3.386.

[44] "Et ex praemissis patet quomodo intelligendi sunt quidam articuli ab Episcopo Parisiensi condemnati qui tamen praedictis contrarii videntur. Unus enim sic dicit: Deum in hac vita intelligere possumus per essentiam; error alius dicit: de Deo non potest cognosci nisi quia est sive ipsum esse. Error primus enim non potest stare cum secundo nisi aliquo modo distinguatur de cognitione qua cognoscibilis est Deus per essentiam et haec distinctio ex praedictis satis est manifesta" (*ibid*). See Denifle-Chatelain, *Chartularium* . . . , I, p. 545 (n. 36); p. 555 (n. 215); nos. 9 and 10 according to Mandonnet's numbering in his *Siger de Brabant* . . . , Vol. II, p. 177. For more on the condemnation of 1277 see our "The Condemnations of 1270 and 1277 at Paris," *The Journal of Medieval and Renaissance Studies* 7 (1977), pp. 169–201. In addition see F. Van Steenberghen, *Maître Siger de Brabant*, pp. 139–58; R. Hissette, *Enquête sur les 219 articles condamnés à Paris le 7 mars 1277* (Louvain-Paris, 1977), especially pp. 30–34, on these two propositions. For Godfrey's treatment in Q. 12, q. 5, see PB 5.101.

reasoning from creatures. Hence we can arrive at certain knowledge as to his existence, since an equivocal effect (one that differs in kind from its cause) does clearly manifest the existence of its cause. But precisely because such an effect is equivocal, it does not perfectly reflect the quiddity of its cause. Hence it is not possible for man in this life to arrive at perfect and certain knowledge of God's quiddity.[45]

B. PHILOSOPHICAL KNOWLEDGE OF THE DIVINE ESSENCE AND ATTRIBUTES

It is clear from our discussion in the preceding section of this chapter that Godfrey defends man's ability to arrive at philosophical knowledge of God's existence by reasoning from effect to cause as well as his capacity to arrive at some imperfect knowledge of the divine quiddity (knowledge *quid est rei*). To that extent, then, we have already touched on his view with respect to the possibility of philosophical knowledge of the divine essence. Now it remains for us to determine more precisely his position with respect to knowledge of the divine attributes. In q. 1 of this same Quodlibet 7, and therefore also dating ca. 1290, Godfrey addresses himself to the following question: Does the distinction between the various divine attributes arise simply from God's view of himself with reference to himself alone, or only from his view of himself with reference to perfections found in creatures?[46]

Along with his contemporaries, of course, Godfrey defended the absolute simplicity of the divine essence. This we have already seen in his efforts to show that even created separate entities, while lacking both matter-form and essence-existence composition, are not so simple as is God. At the same time, Godfrey also predicates certain names and attributes or perfections of the divine. In the present discussion, then, he will attempt to identify the ultimate ontological foundation for such predication. Is such grounded on God's knowledge of himself as he is in himself or in his knowledge of himself viewed in relationship to perfections found in creatures?

Godfrey proposes to consider this issue in three steps. First of all, he will introduce some clarifications with respect to the meaning of the term "attribute." Secondly, he will argue for plurality of attributes in God. Thirdly, he will address himself to the more fundamental issue to which reference has just been made and to which this quodlibetal debate is expressly directed.[47]

---

[45] PB 3.386.

[46] "Utrum distinctio attributorum divinorum accipiatur per comparationem ad intrinseca vel respectu ad extrinseca sive ad ea quae reperiuntur in creaturis" (PB 3.264).

[47] PB 3.264–65.

As regards the meaning of attribute, Godfrey suggests that this term may be taken in two different ways. On the one hand, one may understand thereby a given divine perfection in this sense that something found in creatures without implying any imperfection or limitation of itself is then assigned to God to an eminent degree.[48] By this first usage, therefore, Godfrey appears to have in mind what is often referred to as a pure or simple perfection. On the other hand, one might take attribute to signify that whereby something is perfected in some accidental way rather than in its substantial being. When so understood a divine attribute signifies a kind of disposition that again implies no imperfection of itself and that is attributed to the divine substance as a "quasi-quality" perfecting the divine substance in "quasi-accidental" fashion. It is in this second sense, observes Godfrey, that attributes are usually affirmed of God. Thus in the *De trinitate* Augustine refers to him as eternal, living, wise, powerful, full of beauty (*speciosus*), just, and as a spirit. Augustine then comments that only the last named of these seems to signify substance, whereas the others appear to designate qualities of substance.[49] Since neither Godfrey nor Augustine would assign substance-accident composition to God, one can understand why Godfrey has used the expression "quasi-quality."

Godfrey now returns to his second point, that is, to show that there are many attributes in God. He reasons that there are many such quasi-qualities that perfect God in a quasi-accidental way, and therefore, many attributes. This is so because there are many attributes in creatures that imply no imperfection in their formal content. Hence they are to be assigned to God in more eminent fashion since every such perfection found in creatures is present in God more eminently, and this because of his infinite perfection.[50] Here one

---

[48] PB 3.265: ". . . uno modo sic quod intelligatur aliqua divina perfectio eminens, ex eo quod perfectionem simpliciter et absolute absque defectu et limitatione importat in creatura, ipsi Deo in quo omnis perfectio creaturarum eminentius invenitur tributa."

[49] *Ibid.* See in particular: ". . . et secundum hoc attributum in Deo dicitur id quod in ipso intelligitur ut quaedam dispositio quae simpliciter et absolute absque aliqua limitatione perfectionem nobilem importans ipsum quasi in esse secundo et in bene esse perficit, et hoc modo in Deo dicuntur communiter esse attributa; unde, attributa divina significant quasi quasdam qualitates divinae substantiae ipsam quasi accidentaliter et in bene esse perficientes secundum quod dicit Augustinus, libro decimo quinto, de Trinitate, capitulo sexto, ut si dominus aeternus, vivus, sapiens, potens, speciosus, iustus, spiritus, sic horum omnium novissimum quod posui tantummodo videtur significare substantiam, cetera vero huius substantiae qualitates." For the text from Augustine see his *De trinitate* XV, c. 5 (*Oeuvres de Saint Augustin*, Desclée de Brouwer, Vol. 16, p. 438; CCSL 50a.470).

[50] PB 3.265. In support of this final point Godfrey cites Pseudo-Dionysius, *De Divinis Nominibus*: "Hoc autem contingit Deo ratione suae perfectionis infinitae et illimitatae, scilicet quod omnium entium perfectiones in se continet eminenti modo,

has an application of the familiar *via eminentiae* of scholasticism, presupposing, presumably, both the *via causalitatis* and the *via negationis*. A slight problem remains for us here, however, in interpreting Godfrey. Granted that he has argued for a multiplicity of divine attributes when they are taken in the second sense defined above, what of attributes when they are understood in the first way? His argumentation would seem to imply the multiple character of these as well, although he does not explicitly draw this conclusion here. And such is also indicated by some remarks he makes in the subsequent discussion, as we shall now see.

Godfrey next addresses himself to the third issue, that is, to determine how distinction of attributes arises in God. He begins by stressing the point that because of God's absolute simplicity and unity divine attributes signify perfections which are in fact really identical with the divine essence itself. Hence the distinction (and plurality) of attributes in God is not real but only logical, that is to say, something that arises from the intellect's consideration. Thus the intellect apprehends in some way the one and simple divine essence and views it as containing in potency, as it were, many perfections, and then formally and actually distinguishes them. By this Godfrey means that it is through the intellect's operation that the potential logical distinction and plurality of attributes becomes an actual but logical distinction and plurality. It is because of this intellectual operation that God can be recognized as good or as wise, etc.[51]

But the major question still remains. One may wonder whether such distinction and plurality of attributes arises from the intellect's view of God simply as he is in himself, or only as a result of some comparison with such perfections as they are found in creatures. Godfrey replies by hearkening back to the two meanings he has assigned to attribute. If one takes an attribute in the first way (as implying that every simple or pure perfection found in creatures is to be applied to God to an infinite degree), then the answer is

---

prout dicit Dyonisius, quinto capitulo, de Divinis Nominibus: Deus non quodammodo est existens, sed simpliciter et incircumscripte, totum in se ipso esse coaccepit et simpliciter quicquid utique est in ante existente et est et intelligitur et salvatur." For this see *De Divinis Nominibus*, c. 5, nn. 4–5 (PG 3.817,820). Also cf. the Latin version in the Marietti edition of Thomas's Commentary: *In librum Beati Dionysii De divinis nominibus expositio*, C. Pera, ed. (Turin-Rome, 1950), pp. 229–30.

[51] PB 3.266. Here again he refers to Pseudo-Dionysius: "Unde dicit Dionysius, ubi supra, quod omnia in divino esse continentur immensurate et convolute et unite. Etenim, in monade omnis numerus uniformiter quidem ante subsistit et omnis numerus unite quidem in monade; et in tota omnium natura omnium naturae secundum singulas rationes convolutae sunt per unam et inconfusam unitatem." For this see PG 3.821; Pera, *op. cit.*, pp. 230–31; also see PL 122.1149.

clear. In this case the intellect, especially the created intellect, does not arrive at such logical distinction and multiplicity of divine attributes except by reasoning from perfections in creatures. As we have seen above, according to Godfrey such an intellect cannot directly grasp the divine essence as it is in itself and as it contains all perfection in itself. Hence man must reason from perfections in creatures to knowledge of the divine perfection on the ground that effects bear some likeness to their cause. Thus pure perfections, which are found in creatures as really distinct from one another, are grasped by the created intellect through distinct concepts. By reasoning from these perfections as realized in creatures the human intellect arrives at some knowledge of the divine perfection. But while the divine essence is itself one and simple, the human intellect, by using such distinct concepts derived from really diverse perfections in creatures, grasps that essence under one aspect as containing one perfection and under another aspect as containing another (and logically distinct) perfection. Obviously, such logical distinction of attributes by the human intellect presupposes knowledge of pure perfections as realized in creatures.[52]

Godfrey observes that it is in the above mentioned way that attributes are usually distinguished and assigned to God and that few *doctores* consider their distinction insofar as God understands himself simply as he is in himself. Still, the divine intellect can surely grasp in one simple act of understanding whatever any created intellect can apprehend. And as Godfrey himself has just explained, the human intellect can arrive at knowledge of the divine attributes as logically distinct from one another. Hence, some maintain that it is unreasonable to hold that the divine intellect, apart from any reference to really distinct perfections as present in creatures, could not apprehend the divine attributes as logically distinct simply by considering the divine essence in itself. Here then, with obvious reference to Henry of Ghent, Godfrey reports that according to this position, insofar as the attributes are taken in the second sense defined above, plurality and distinction of the same can be grasped by God insofar as he views himself directly and without reference to creatures. In other words, it is not because of some "prior" awareness of really distinct perfections in creatures that God can grasp himself under these logically distinct aspects or attributes.[53]

---

[52] PB 3.266–67.

[53] PB 3.267. As will be clear from what follows Godfrey is here referring to Henry's treatment in Quodlibet 5, q. 1, of Christmas 1280 or Easter 1281. See Gómez Caffarena, *Ser participado . . .*, p. 270. For a general discussion of this doctrine in Henry with reference to his treatment of the same in other contexts, see Paulus, *Henri de Gand . . .*, pp. 243–48. For Henry's Quodlibet 5, q. 1 see fol. 150v–154r.

Godfrey presents a number of arguments that may be offered in defense of this theory, arguments too numerous for us to present in detail here. We shall consider only a sampling of these for the purpose of illustration. According to one such argument, taken literally from Henry's Quodlibet 5, q. 1, just as wisdom and goodness differ logically in God, so do the divine essence and divine wisdom. But it is hardly fitting to maintain that the divine essence and the logically distinct divine wisdom are not present in God except as a result of their being compared with really distinct instances of wisdom and essence in creatures. In that eventuality deity itself could not be described either as essence or as wisdom except by reason of such a comparison with creatures. If wisdom could not be affirmed of the deity except by reason of some reference to created wisdom, then neither could essence apart from some such comparison.[54]

Another interesting argument rests on the distinction between divine ideas and divine attributes. The distinction of ideas in God results from a comparison by the intellect that apprehends the divine essence with the essences of creatures. But if the distinction of the divine attributes also rests on this same kind of comparison, it will follow that the divine attributes do not differ from the divine ideas. This is rejected as unfitting.[55]

Finally, in the course of replying to an argument offered for the opposite position, Godfrey reproduces Henry's view as to how plurality and multiplicity ultimately proceed from God's knowledge of himself. The divine intellect views itself and in so doing first conceives the different attributes as logically distinct. From its view of these different attributes there then follow the really distinct emanations of the divine persons. (Henry has here, of course, introduced a central theological notion.) By means of or as a result of these really distinct emanations of the divine persons, the universe of creatures then proceeds from the divine essence. Far from conceding that the distinction of divine attributes derives from God's vision of really distinct perfections in creatures, then, Henry's view defends the contrary position.[56]

Henry there addresses himself to this question: "Utrum scilicet pluralitas et distinctio attributorum essentialium accipienda sit penes respectum et comparationem ad aliquid extra ut ad creaturas an ad comparationem ad aliquid intra." (fol. 150v). Cf. Godfrey's text, pp. 267 bottom and 268 top for a literal and almost verbatim reproduction of one of Henry's theological arguments (fol. 152r, lines 15–22). Godfrey has eliminated some unessential expressions in Henry's text for the sake of brevity. Also see Henry's Quodlibet 9, q. 2, fol. 345r.

54 PB 3.268. For Henry see Quodlibet 5, q. 1, fol. 153r.

55 PB 3.268. For Henry see fol. 152r (near the bottom) and 153r (near the bottom).

56 PB 3.269. For Henry see fol. 154r. Here again Godfrey has reproduced almost literally a section of Henry's text, running from line 19 to line 23.

Godfrey is unimpressed by such argumentation. Such a position runs counter to a principle that he appears to regard as axiomatic, namely, his conviction that it is impossible for both unity and plurality to be derived from a single thing that is simply one both in reality and in conception. Henry's theory does violence to this principle, for it implies that one and the same thing in the order of reality, the divine essence, could be viewed by God as including logically distinct divine attributes, and this without its being compared with anything else that differs from it. Thus both unity and plurality would be derived from God's knowledge of the divine essence as it is in itself. But when it is so viewed, argues Godfrey, it is one and simple not only in reality but also in the logical order. And such knowledge of the divine essence will not suffice, he insists, for the divine intellect to view the divine essence as wise under one aspect and as good or as intelligent under others. Because the divine essence is perfectly one and simple, logical distinction of divine attributes therein cannot be admitted without some reference on the part of the divine intellect to other beings in which real or at least logical diversity of such perfections obtains.[57]

In fact, to strengthen his case, Godfrey distinguishes two "moments" as it were, in one's discovery of logically distinct things. If they are to be recognized as logically distinct from one another, this presupposes that they have "first" been constituted as logical beings. In other words, in the first moment the intellect constitutes such things in their logical or rational being; then in a second moment or operation the intellect compares them with one another and distinguishes them. Just as two things in nature must be distinct instances of real being before they can be compared with one another, so too rational or logical entities must already enjoy rational or logical being before they can be distinguished from one another.[58]

In accord with this precision, Godfrey reasons that if the divine intellect is to grasp the divine essence as logically distinct from the divine attributes and the attributes themselves as logically distinct from one another in the

---

[57] PB 3.270. Note in particular: "Quod enim in uno omnino simplici et indistincto secundum rem ponantur aliqua plura et distincta pure secundum rationem absque comparatione ad aliqua, quae aliquo modo differunt ab eo in quo huiusmodi distincta sola ratione ponuntur, est impossibile, alioquin ab uno eodem modo se habente secundum rem et secundum conceptionem sumeretur unitas et pluralitas." We might note in passing that what we have here described as Godfrey's "principle" is consistent with his attempt to account for the nonsimple character of angels or of separate substances. As we have seen in Ch. II above, he maintains that they may be regarded as potential when they are compared with God or other higher beings and as actual insofar as they are compared with lower entities within the hierarchy of being.

[58] PB 3.271.

way proposed by Henry, then they must first actually be logically distinct in themselves and from one another. But this Godfrey rejects as unfitting, presumably because it would introduce too much distinction into the divine being. Hence he insists that this logical distinction can only result from the divine intellect's knowledge of the divine essence in comparison with other things wherein such distinction and diversity are actually present. In fact, Godfrey suggests that this may serve to illustrate the difference between real and logical distinction. Things that differ when they are viewed in themselves without being compared with other things are really distinct from one another; but things that can be distinguished only insofar as they are compared with others that are really distinct are themselves only logically distinct.[59]

In order better to illustrate his position Godfrey draws an analogy between the divine ideas and the divine attributes. Divine ideas arise from God's understanding of his essence as containing virtually the limited and determined perfections of creatures insofar as the latter can imitate the divine essence in varying degrees. Thus God understands his essence, which is of course really one and simple, as being in some way many in the logical order insofar as it is imitated (or can be imitated) in one way by one creature and in another way by a different kind of creature. These distinctive ways in which the divine essence is viewed by the divine intellect as being capable of such imitation by creatures are the divine ideas. And once they are so described, it is clear that they result from some reference by God to really differing degrees of perfection actually or at least potentially present in creatures. According to Godfrey these same divine ideas or exemplars then serve both as that whereby God knows creatures and that whereby he produces them.[60]

So too, then, as regards the divine attributes, argues Godfrey. When the divine intellect contemplates the divine essence as containing virtually but eminently the pure and simple perfections found in creatures, it understands that essence as really one but as perfected by logically distinct perfections or attributes. But if it did not understand that a creature enjoys really distinct perfections insofar as it is good and insofar as it is wise, for instance, it could not understand the divine essence as perfected in one way by goodness and in another but logically distinct way by wisdom. In other words, God's

---

[59] PB 3.271. Note in particular, as regards the last mentioned point: "Quaecumque enim differunt aut habent differentiam secundum se sive ex se ipsis formaliter per illud quod sunt secundum se ipsa absque comparatione ad alia differentia, talia differunt secundum rem; alia autem sunt quae habent pluralitatem sive differentiam ex comparatione ad aliqua realiter differentia et ista differunt ratione."

[60] PB 3.272.

awareness of the real distinction between wisdom and goodness as realized in creatures is a necessary condition for him to grasp their logical distinction within himself.[61]

Implied in the above is Godfrey's answer to Henry's charge that such a theory will be unable to safeguard the distinction between the divine ideas and the divine attributes. By divine ideas Godfrey understands the divine essence insofar as it is viewed as capable of being imitated by creatures in limited fashion. Hence divine ideas do not signify the divine perfection as it is in itself and without qualification. But by divine attributes Godfrey rather has in mind the divine essence insofar as it is viewed as enjoying pure and simple perfections to an unlimited degree. Granted that Godfrey has insisted that some reference to perfections as realized or realizable in creatures is required both for God's knowledge of the divine ideas and of the divine attributes, there is this further difference between them. According to Godfrey, when God understands himself as perfected by the divine attributes, he does not thereby view himself as causing these perfections in creatures, but as possessing in himself most eminently the pure and simple perfections found in creatures. But when he views himself in terms of the divine ideas, he then understands himself as the cause of creatures. This point is important for another reason, contends Godfrey, for it enables him to maintain that God is wise not merely in the sense that he produces wisdom in creatures, but also in the sense that he himself possesses to an eminent degree that perfection signified by the name wisdom.[62]

As regards the first argument for Henry's position that we have reproduced above, Godfrey rejects the analogy between God's grasp of himself as an essence or entity and his awareness of himself as wise or as good. In order for something to be grasped by intellect it must in some way enjoy essence or being. Hence if God is to know himself at all he cannot do so without grasping himself as essence or entity, and this is possible even without any reference to creatures. In this understanding of himself as essence or quiddity, continues Godfrey, God knows his goodness and wisdom, etc., that is to say, all the pure and simple perfections, but only as one and in implicit fashion. In order for him to apprehend them as actually though logically distinct from the divine essence and from one another, he must advert to their real distinction in creatures.[63] It is interesting to observe that Godfrey draws support for his position from Averroes's Commentary on *Metaphysics* XII,

---

[61] PB 3.272–73.

[62] PB 3.277 (''ad quintum . . .''); also see p. 273.

[63] PB 3.277. Also see p. 276.

not only here in Quodlibet 7 but also in a later discussion of the same in Quodlibet 14, q. 5 (dating from ca. 1298 or thereafter).[64]

In that last-mentioned question Godfrey continues to defend the same view. Moreover, he there points out that this position does not imply that goodness, wisdom, etc., belong to God only insofar as his essence is viewed by some intellect as perfected by these attributes. On the contrary, by reason of his unlimited perfection God in fact possesses in simple and perfect unity those pure perfections that are really distinct in creatures. Hence he acquires no new perfection by being viewed explicitly as wise or as good. Still, reference to these perfections as realized in creatures is required for him to be understood as perfected in one way by wisdom and in a logically distinct way by goodness.[65] Godfrey defends the same position in Quodlibet 15, q. 3 as well, his final quodlibetal debate dating from 1303/1304.[66]

---

[64] PB 3.276. Here in Q 7 Godfrey summarizes Averroes's explanation of the way in which perfections such as life, wisdom, etc., are said of God. Averroes argues that in the case of separate entities there is no real distinction between a disposition that is affirmed of such a being and that being itself. Still the intellect introduces a logical distinction in such cases so as to be able to affirm such a predicate of the subject with which it is really identical, without thereby formulating a tautology. The intellect can do this by treating such an entity according to some likeness (*secundum similitudinem*) with the categorical propositions that it formulates about material entities and their dispositions. See *In Metaphys. XII*, fol. 322va–323ra. As Godfrey puts it: "Secundum hanc igitur intentionem Commentatoris, attributa omnia significant unam rem omnino indistinctam extra intellectum, sed distinctam secundum respectus vel rationes diversas in intellectu per operationem intellectus modo supradicto" (PB 3.276). In the discussion in Q 14, q. 5, Godfrey again briefly refers to Averroes's insistence that perfections such as goodness, wisdom, etc., do not really differ in God. Godfrey also refers to Averroes's criticism of certain *fideles* who thought they could conclude to the doctrine of the Trinity by reasoning from the distinction between attributes. Godfrey agrees that such believers are to be criticized for any such effort to prove the mystery of the Trinity and suggests that such a misguided effort may in fact detract from the truth of the faith. See PB 5.428. For this in Averroes see *op. cit.*, fol. 322va. For another reference to this see Q 5, q. 11 (PB 3.44), referred to in note 12 in this chapter. For Henry of Ghent's citation of this same Averroistic defense of real identity and only logical diversity of the divine attributes, see his Quodlibet 5, q. 1, fol. 152v.

[65] PB 5.428–29. See in particular: "Ab intellectu autem non causantur huiusmodi perfectiones in Deo, sed ipsae quae in Deo sunt una res simplex ab intellectu apprehenduntur sub diversis rationibus ex comparatione eminentis perfectionis divinae unius et simplicis ad perfectiones creaturarum multiplices et distinctas" (p. 429).

[66] PB 14.18–19. See in particular: ". . . nam esse bonum vel ens non convenit Deo ex habitudine ad creaturas; sed esse differens ratione secundum ista convenit Deo ex diversitate creaturarum cointellecta; et ideo non potest concludi quod esse bonum et ens non praedicentur de Deo formaliter, sed tantum potest concludi quod esse

C. THE PROCESSION OF CREATURES FROM GOD

In the two preceding sections of this chapter we have concentrated on Godfrey's position with respect to philosophical knowledge of God's existence and essence, including his discussion of the divine attributes. In the present section we shall consider his philosophical analysis of the procession of the created universe from God, its creative source. In so doing we shall present: (1) Godfrey's theory of the divine ideas; (2) his knowledge of and reaction to Henry of Ghent's metaphysics of creation; (3) Godfrey's own account of creation or of the procession of creatures from God; (4) more particular applications of Godfrey's metaphysics of creation including his views with respect to: (a) the possibility of annihilation; (b) the possibility of an eternally created universe.

1. Godfrey's Theory of the Divine Ideas

As we have seen above in considering Godfrey's discussion of philosophical knowledge of God's existence, it is in metaphysics that one arrives at some awareness of God as intelligent.[67] For Godfrey as well as for Aristotle in *Metaphysics* XII this means, of course, that God understands himself. But for Godfrey this also implies that God knows all other things. Thus in Quodlibet 2, q. 5, in the course of considering the angelic mode of knowing, Godfrey observes that in knowing his own essence which is, in fact, an adequate likeness of all else, God knows all other things as well. Godfrey also remarks within this same context that it is necessary for us to postulate divine ideas (*rationes ideales cognoscendi*) within the divine essence in order to account for God's knowledge of each and every distinctive species of being.[68] He refers in passing to the view of some according to which distinct divine ideas are not to be posited to correspond to genera but only to species, since genera do not imply forms that really differ from those forms implied by species. According to this position, then, divine ideas are to be distin-

differens secundum rationem per ista non praedicatur de Deo formaliter, sed denominatione extrinseca" (p. 19).

[67] See Ch. III, section A, pp. 105 (discussing Q 9, q. 20); 112–14 (on Q 7, q. 11).

[68] PB 2.87: ". . . ut, sicut Deus in intelligendo suam essentiam quae est sufficiens omnium similitudo intelligit omnia alia a se . . ." Also see: "Nam cum in una re simplici divina sit aliquo modo ponere diversas rationes ideales cognoscendi, ita quod oportet respectu uniuscuiusque entis specifici ponere propriam rationem vel ideam, et saltem quot natae sunt esse species . . ." (PB 2.87–88).

guished in the logical order only insofar as the forms and essences of creatures are really distinguishable.[69]

In the preceding section of this chapter we have found Godfrey defending the distinction between the divine attributes and the divine ideas. Neither the attributes nor the ideas are really distinct from the divine essence, of course, but only differ logically therefrom. Nonetheless, when God views himself as perfected by a divine attribute, the attribute in question is present in God to an unlimited or infinite degree. But when God considers his essence as capable of being imitated by creatures, that is, in terms of his ideas, such imitation and participation can only be finite. Godfrey's passing remarks in Quodlibet 2, q. 5 raise two further questions with respect to his own understanding of the divine ideas. First of all, one might wonder whether Godfrey himself agrees with those who deny that divine ideas are to be multiplied to correspond to genera as well as to species. Secondly, one wonders whether he himself allows for distinct divine ideas for individual members of species or only for the species as such.

Godfrey offers further precisions with respect to his theory of the divine ideas in Quodlibet 4, q. 1. In fact, this question is explicitly addressed to the second issue just raised above. There he asks: "Whether in God there is a proper and distinct idea for every individual."[70] This discussion dates from 1287 and is especially interesting since one of the most conservative theologians of the time, Henry of Ghent, had himself defended the negative position on this point in his Quodlibet 7, qq. 1-2 of Christmas 1282. In fact, Henry had denied that there are distinctive divine ideas for any of the following: second intentions, relations, artefacts, genera, differences, individuals, privations, and numbers.[71]

Godfrey prefaces his reply to this question by recalling his understanding of a divine idea. A divine idea is nothing but the divine essence itself insofar as it is the exemplar form of a thing, that is to say, insofar as the divine

---

[69] PB 2.88.

[70] PB 2.229. "Utrum in Deo sit idea propria et distincta respectu cuiuslibet singularis."

[71] For this date see Gómez Caffarena, *Ser participado . . .* , p. 270. For Henry see Quodlibet 7, qq. 1–2, fol. 255r–257r. Note in particular fol. 256v: "Dicimus igitur breviter recolligendo quod isti viii modi entium proprias ideas in deo non habent: intentiones secundae, relationes, artificialia, genera, differentiae, individua, privationes, et numeri. Restat igitur quod proprias ideas solummodo habent specificae rerum essentiae. . . ." For discussion of Henry's position see J. Paulus, *Henri de Gand . . .* , pp. 371–75; H. Rüssmann, *Zur Ideenlehre der Hochscholastik unter besonderer Berücksichtigung des Heinrich von Gent, Gottfried von Fontaines und Jakob von Viterbo* (Freiburg im Breisgau, 1938), pp. 61–64.

essence is viewed as capable of being imitated by a creature. In this description as well as in the shorter version's account of the same the notion of exemplarity predominates.[72] But as will be recalled from Godfrey's discussion in Quodlibet 7, q. 4, he there refers to the divine ideas as that which accounts both for God's knowledge and his production of creatures (*ratio cognoscendi . . . et ratio producendi*).[73] As we shall now see, this cognitive element is also included in Godfrey's understanding of divine ideas in the present question. And as we shall also see, in other contexts Godfrey argues that an intelligent agent cannot act as formal cause of creatures without serving as their efficient cause as well. In fact, he will state that insofar as the divine ideas are formal exemplar causes of creatures they also serve in some way as their efficient causes.[74] Hence one can understand why he refers to them in Quodlibet 7, q. 4 as principles for God's production as well as for his cognition of creatures.

In the present question (Quodlibet 4, q. 1) Godfrey proceeds to reason from his definition of divine ideas to the conclusion that they are not to be multiplied so as to correspond to individual members of species but only to species themselves. He stresses the point that a divine idea is the expression of a distinctive way in which the divine essence may be imitated by creatures. Insofar as God's essence may be viewed in different ways, to that extent there will be different divine ideas. If a number of individuals imitate the divine essence in the same way or according to the same form, one divine idea will be sufficient to allow for this. But such, observes Godfrey, appears to be true of the individual members of a species. They possess the same form essentially speaking (*per se*), granted that it is multiplied in individuals

---

[72] PB 2.229: ". . . idea in Deo non sit nisi ipsa essentia divina ut est exemplaris forma rei secundum quod apprehenditur ut est imitabilis a creatura. . . ." For the shorter version see PB 2.321: ". . . cum ideae non sint nisi quaedam imitabilitates essentiae divinae a creaturis." Note that here it appears within the argument for the *Contra*. For fundamentally the same also see the *Contra* of the longer version (PB 2.229).

[73] See Section B of the present chapter, p. 121 as well as PB 3.272: ". . . istae autem distinctae imitabilitates quae in Deo apprehenduntur ab eius intellectu ex tali comparatione et habitudine ad diversitatem realem creaturarum dicuntur ideae sive formae exemplares quae sunt et ratio cognoscendi diversas res et ratio producendi easdem . . ."

[74] See, for instance, Q 8, q. 3 (PB 4.44): "Sic ergo istae ideae in Deo sunt rationes formales exemplares creaturarum; et quicquid circa creaturas constituitur, hoc etiam per eas efficitur. Unde sicut ex eis constituuntur rerum essentiae sive res ut sint id quod sunt secundum essentiam, sic etiam ab eis efficiuntur . . . nihil ponitur in Deo habere rationem temporalis causae formalis exemplaris ad constituendum aliquid, nisi ratio idealis quae est etiam ratio effectiva accedente voluntate."

in accidental fashion (*per accidens*).[75]

In order to strengthen the above argumentation Godfrey next draws an analogy with number. In fact this analogy appears as a distinct and second argument in the shorter version. Just as the unit is the measure of all numbers, so is the divine essence by reason of its ideas the measure of all creatures. But the unit measures all numbers of the same kind or species in the same way. Thus it measures all fours in the same way, but not fours and threes. So too, then, does the divine essence serve as measure and as principle of knowledge with respect to all individual members of one and the same species through one single divine idea.[76]

Godfrey's second and third arguments of the longer version appear as the third argument in the shorter version. Divine ideas should stand in some kind of logical order with respect to one another. But the different individual members of a given species are not so ordered to one another with a prior and a posterior. Hence only one idea is needed to apply to all the members of such a species. The third argument of the longer version then specifies this reasoning by applying it to order in terms of perfection. Insofar as a divine idea is the principle for measuring and knowing something that is more perfect, then it is to be regarded as a more perfect idea, although only in the logical order. Given this, the divine essence cannot be imitated in different ways except insofar as one way is more perfect than another. But such perfection is realized in beings by reason of their specific forms. In other words, because individual members of the same class or species do not thus vary in degree of perfection, they do not imitate the divine essence in different ways. Therefore, one divine idea will suffice for all of them.[77]

Godfrey's fourth argument draws a parallel between species, difference, and genus, on the one hand, and species and individuals, on the other. Since it is the ultimate species that implies of itself a form that is essentially distinct from all other forms, there is no need to postulate distinctive ideas to correspond to differences and to genera as well. Through the perfect idea of the

---

[75] PB 2.230. Note in particular: "Et quia secundum diversas formas nata sunt imitari divinam essentiam diversas ideas habent, ideo ea quorum non est nisi una forma per se (si autem multiplicentur hoc est per accidens), videntur habere unam ideam quae est illius formae primo et per se et ex consequenti omnium in quibus reperitur." For the shorter version see PB 2.321.

[76] PB 2.230. For the shorter version see PB 2.321. Note that in the latter version of this argument the divine idea is explicitly referred to both as measure and as principle of cognition with reference to individuals in a species (". . . essentia divina est mensura et ratio cognoscendi respectu omnium individuorum eiusdem speciei per unam ideam").

[77] PB 2.230. For the shorter version see PB 2.321–22.

species the genus may be understood as something incomplete and the difference as that which completes it. So too, then, *mutatis mutandis,* Godfrey reasons that the individual does not add anything essential or formal to that which is already contained in the idea of the species. Therefore, one and the same idea which applies to the species directly and *per se* also applies to all individuals included therein. Thus an individual man, Peter, for instance, does not imitate the divine essence immediately and directly insofar as he is Peter or this man, but insofar as he is man. And insofar as it happens that the perfection signified by the idea of humanity is realized in this individual man, or Peter, then the divine idea of the former will also apply to the latter.[78]

Although this argument is not primarily designed to resolve the first of the two questions we raised in connection with Godfrey's remarks in Quodlibet 2, q. 5, yet in supporting his answer to the second question he has also stated his position with respect to the first. He agrees with those who deny that divine ideas are to be multiplied to correspond to genera and differences as well as to species. And because of this he has here argued again in support of his contention that there are no distinct divine ideas for individual members within species.

In the long version Godfrey offers a final argument based on an analogy with angelic cognition. If it is conceded that an angel can know a species as well as the individual members of that same species by means of one and the same idea, with even greater reason is this to be said of God. This follows because neither the angel nor God would have full knowledge of the species without also understanding all those things that are related to the nature of that species and accidentally multiply it.[79]

---

[78] PB 2.231–32. Godfrey appeals to a text from one of Augustine's letters to Nebridius for added support for his contention. For the shorter version see PB 2.322. There Augustine's letter is cited only after all of the arguments have been presented. In the text in question Augustine draws a parallel between the idea (*ratio*) of a mathematical figure such as an angle or square which will apply to all such figures, on the one hand, and the divine idea of man which should apply to all men, on the other. One finds another more general reference to this text in Henry's Quodlibet 7, q. 5, where it appears as a preliminary argument in the *sed contra* ("in oppositum"). See fol. 255r. For Augustine's text see *Ad Nebridium, Epist.* XIV (PL 33.80), reproduced in PB 2.232, n. 1. Also see CSEL, Vol. 34.1, pp. 34–35. This highly interesting passage which Godfrey has carefully reproduced could, it would seem, be interpreted to mean that it is by means of one divine idea that God creates all men. See in particular: "*ita quilibet homo una ratione, qua homo intelligitur, factus est.*" Note, however, that Augustine is speaking tentatively here. For an English translation of the same see *The Fathers of the Church*, Vol. 12 (*Saint Augustine. Letters*, v. 1), p. 35.

[79] PB 2.232–33. For the same see arguments five and six of the shorter version

In this final argument Godfrey is especially concerned with defending the cognitive role of divine ideas. And along with his stress on their role as exemplars, this defense of their cognitive character has also been apparent in much of the earlier argumentation. Without maintaining this cognitive aspect of the divine ideas, of course, Godfrey would find it difficult to defend divine knowledge of particulars and divine providence. Hence in the present discussion he now reiterates this point, that one must account for God's distinctive cognition of all things, both singular and universal. One must do this by positing only the minimum degree of distinction and multiplicity of divine ideas required for the same.[80] In sum, then, an overriding but implicit concern in the foregoing discussion has been this: to account for divine knowledge of all things, including singulars, and this without multiplying unnecessarily the divine ideas, even though the latter are only logically distinct from one another and from the divine essence. But, Godfrey contends, one can account for God's perfect knowledge of the individual members of a species simply by postulating one divine idea for that species. Perfect knowledge of the species will imply knowledge of all the individual members in which the specific perfection is multiplied in accidental fashion. Divine knowledge of the specific perfection apart from knowledge of the individuals that share in the same would not be, in Godfrey's eyes, perfect knowledge of the species itself.[81]

As we have already suggested, in denying that distinctive divine ideas are to be posited to correspond to individual members of a species apart from the idea of the species itself, Godfrey is in agreement with a position already defended by Henry of Ghent. In addition, both Godfrey and Henry reject divine ideas for genera and differences apart from ideas of species.[82] It seems less likely, however, that Godfrey would support Henry's rejection of different divine ideas to correspond to the different kinds of numbers. In fact, one of Godfrey's arguments for restricting divine ideas to species is based on an analogy between species and numbers. Moreover, as we have already indicated in the preceding chapter and shall shortly see again, Godfrey will

---

(PB 2.322). On angelic knowledge of singulars through their knowledge of the corresponding species see Q 2, q. 5 (PB 2.88).

[80] "Sed quicquid sit de hoc, dicendum ut prius, salvando perfectam et distinctam cognitionem in Deo omnium tam singularium quam universalium et ponendo minimam distinctionem et multitudinem idearum in ipso. Negare enim Deum cognoscere singularia distincte est inconveniens, sed ponere quod hoc fiat per unam ideam rationale videtur" (PB 2.233).

[81] In addition to our remarks above see Godfrey's reply to the argument for the opposite position (PB 2.233).

[82] See the references in n. 71.

never acknowledge that any greater degree of reality is to be assigned to a creature's *esse essentiae* than to its *esse existentiae* by reason of God's eternal cognition of the former. On this central metaphysical issue he will always be most critical of Henry. Hence it is all the more interesting for one to find the two denying that there are distinctive divine ideas for individuals within one and the same species. In defending this position they were surely espousing the minority view for their times, and a position that Thomas Aquinas had attributed to Plato.[83] Finally, one may still wonder whether such a theory can, in fact, allow for God's knowledge of singulars.[84]

2. *Godfrey's Knowledge of and Reaction to Henry of Ghent's Metaphysics of Creation*

In Chapter II we found it necessary to study Godfrey's views on the essence-existence relationship within the context of his knowledge of and reaction to theories that defended either their real or intentional distinction. In order better to appreciate his metaphysics of divine creative causality, we shall now turn to Henry of Ghent's position and to Godfrey's reaction to it. Once more Godfrey develops his personal thought in direct confrontation with Henry, and to a lesser extent with James of Viterbo.

As we have already seen in Chapter II, Godfrey has thoroughly undermined Henry's attempt to defend the priority or indifference of essence with respect to existence by reason of their alleged intentional distinction. Interestingly enough, however, Godfrey concludes the longer version of Quodlibet 3, q.

---

[83] See ST I, 15, 3, ad 4: "Individua vero, secundum Platonem, non habebant aliam ideam quam ideam speciei: tum quia singularia individuantur per materiam, quam ponebat esse increatam, ut quidam dicunt, et concausam ideae; tum quia intentio naturae consistit in speciebus, nec particularia producit, nisi ut in eis species salventur. Sed providentia divina non solum se extendit ad species, sed ad singularia, ut infra [q. 22, a. 2] dicetur." Also see *De veritate*, q. 3, a. 8. On the divine ideas in Augustine, Thomas, Bonaventure, and Scotus, see the remarks in Gilson, *The Spirit of Mediaeval Philosophy* (London, 1950), pp. 153–60.

[84] For Paulus's critique of Henry on this point see pp. 374–75. In his exposition of this theory Godfrey acknowledges the need for different divine ideas to correspond with the different ways in which the divine essence may be imitated. Since individuals within a species imitate the divine essence in essentially the same way, one idea will suffice for God's knowledge and production of them. Still, one might counter, individual differences are also real, real enough for Godfrey to include them under his analogous notion of being. Should not the logic that leads him to postulate plurality of ideas in accord with specific differentiation also lead him to posit the same in accord with numerical differentiation?

2 by observing that if one should opt for this intentional distinction between essence and existence, it would then follow that essence is created before existence just as a relation's foundation is prior to that relationship itself. Godfrey, of course, will have none of this.[85]

As has also been indicated above, Henry of Ghent's theory of the intentional distinction between essence and existence is closely connected with his rather unusual view of divine efficient and divine formal (exemplar) causality and their interrelationship. One finds this same theory of divine causality exposed by Godfrey in Quodlibet 2, q. 2; Quodlibet 8, q. 3; and in Quodlibet 9, q. 2. Thus in Quodlibet 2, q. 2 Godfrey introduces Henry's doctrine in connection with a theory that would defend the real indifference of essence with respect to existence and nonexistence.[86] Godfrey considers this same view of divine causality again in Quodlibet 8, q. 3 in the course of his effort to determine whether a rational creature might be capable of receiving grace or any other accident before it actually exists.[87] In Quodlibet 9, q. 2 he will conclude that acceptance of this same theory should lead to the denial that God really produces things from nothing in creating them and hence to the denial that anything can really be annihilated.[88]

As will be recalled from our discussion in Ch. II, Section B, according to Godfrey Henry maintains that God may be considered both as efficient and as formal exemplar cause of creatures. His formal causality is directed to their essences (*esse essentiae*), while his efficient causality has to do with their actual existence. In support of this distinction it is argued that the essences of creatures are eternally present to the divine knowledge as objects of that knowledge. As objects thereof true essential being (*esse essentiae*) is to be assigned to them. Since they cannot enjoy this kind of being of themselves, it must be caused in them by something else. The kind of causality at issue here is not efficient, since that is rather directed towards the actual existences of things. But the essences in question need not yet actually exist. Hence God communicates essential being to such things by means of his

---

[85] PB 2.179. In this question Godfrey has been seeking to determine whether essence is created before existence (*esse*). Note his final comment on p. 179: "Si etiam differrent intentione, prius crearetur essentia quam esse, sicut prius fundamentum respectus ut album similitudine, sed ex hoc etiam sequerentur inconvenientia supra dicta et cetera."

[86] See Ch. II–B, pp. 69–70.

[87] "Utrum creatura rationalis antequam sit in effectu sit capax gratiae sive cuiuscumque accidentis" (PB 4.34).

[88] In Q 9, q.2 Godfrey addresses himself to this question: "Utrum aliqua actio Dei possit in nihilum terminari sive utrum Deus possit aliquid in nihilum redigere" (PB 4.189).

divine ideas as their formal exemplar cause, and this without the intervention of the divine will. This divine cognition, in and of itself, accounts for the fact that such essences enjoy predicamental being or may be described as predicamental realities (*res*) even before they acquire actual existence. They will be realized as concrete individual entities only when they receive actual existence due to the intervention of the divine will operating as an efficient cause of the same.[89]

In other words, Henry's theory sets up a kind of parallelism between the orders of divine exemplar causality and the reception of essential being (*esse essentiae*) by a creature, on the one hand, and divine efficient causality and the creature's reception of actual existence (*esse existentiae*), on the other. In fact, in both Quodlibet 2, q. 2 and in Quodlibet 8, q. 3 Godfrey draws upon a text from Boethius's *De consolatione philosophiae* to illustrate this point, a text that is quoted by Henry himself in his development of his position in his own Quodlibet 9, q. 2. Both in his presentations in Quodlibet 2 (Easter 1286) and Quodlibet 8 (ca. 1293) Godfrey appears to be following closely Henry's discussion in Quodlibet 9 (also Easter 1286).[90]

As Godfrey understands Henry's theory, the essential being of a possible creature, prior to its reception of actual existence, is already something distinct from its cognitive being (*esse cognitum*) in the divine mind, that is to say, distinct from God's cognition of it. In knowing his essence as capable of being imitated by a creature in a given way, that is, in terms of the appropriate divine idea, God also knows the creaturely essence itself as dis-

---

[89] See Q 2, q. 2 (PB 2.55); Q 8, q. 3 (PB 4.35).

[90] Q 2, q. 2 (PB 2.55–56); Q 8, q. 3 (PB 4.35). Godfrey's citation in Q 2, q. 2 reads: "Et secundum modum et formam secundum quam creatura sic habet esse id quod est per essentiam in scientia interiore ut a causa exemplari, per voluntatem ut a causa efficiente, habet esse in existentia exteriore, secundum illud Boetii tertio de Consolatione: tu cuncta superna ducis ab exemplo pulchrum, pulcherrimus ipse mundum mente gerens similique in imagine formans." Compare with Henry's Quodlibet 9, q. 2: "A scientia enim tali ipsa scita alia habent esse id quod sunt. Primo enim ab huiusmodi scientia habent esse id quod sunt per essentiam in cognitione interiori ut a causa exemplari; et deinde per voluntatem per efficientiam, ut a causa efficiente in existentia exteriori, secundum formam et modum quo habent esse in scientia interiori, secundum quod dixit Boetius tertio de consolatione: Tu cuncta superno Ducis ab exemplo, pulchrum pulcherrimus ipse Mundum mente gerens, similique imagine formans" (fol. 345v). For another citation of this text from Boethius see Henry's *Summae quaestionum ordinariarum*, a. 68, q. 5, T. 2 (fol. 230v–231r). For Boethius see *Boethii Philosophiae consolatio* III, 9 (L. Bieler, ed., *Corpus Christianorum. Series Latina*, vol. 94 [Brepols, 1957], p. 52:6–8). For other texts in Henry which bring out this parallelism, see Q 1, q. 9 (fol. 7r) and Q 3, q. 9 (fol. 61r), cited in Ch. II, n. 82.

tinct in some way both from his essence and from his knowledge of it. As Godfrey phrases it in Quodlibet 8, q. 3 in a passage that is almost literally taken from Henry's Quodlibet 9, q. 2, insofar as such essences exist in the divine cognition their being is not so minimal that they are not also something in themselves.[91] This is why Henry can assign predicamental reality to such essences, of course, prior to their realization as concrete individual existents. Godfrey also observes both in Quodlibet 2, q. 2 and in Quodlibet 8, q. 3 that according to Henry's theory, such creaturely essences prior to their reception of actual existence are already and from all eternity really related to God as their formal exemplar cause according to the first mode of relation and by reduction. When they actually exist in concrete entities they are also related to him as their efficient cause according to the second mode of relation.[92]

---

[91] See Q 8, q. 3 (PB 4.35–36). For the text where Godfrey appears to have Henry's Quodlibet 9, q. 2 before his eyes see PB 4.36: "Unde entia existentia sic in divina cognitione non sunt sic diminuta entia, quin ex isto esse cognito sint aliquid in se per essentiam . . . praedicamentum est contentivum rerum, non secundum quod sunt in esse cognito neque secundum quod sunt in esse existentiae extra in rerum natura, sed secundum quod sunt aliquid simpliciter per indifferentiam se habens quantum ad illud quod est per essentiam ad utrumque illorum esse." Compare with Henry: "Ista autem non sunt sic diminuta respectu entis quod deus est et existentia in esse cognito quin in illo esse sint aliquid ad se per essentiam. . . . Est enim praedicamentum contentivum talium rerum non secundum quod sunt in esse cognito, neque secundum quod sunt in esse vero, sed secundum quod sunt aliquid simpliciter; per indifferentiam se habens quantum ad illud quod est per essentiam, ad utrumque illorum esse dicente Simplicio exponendo intentionem libri praedicamentorum. Ipsa dictio substantiae symbolum est existens substantiae quae est in entibus suis: sive sit in hypostasi, sive penes intellectum existat. Nihil enim hoc quantum ad praedicamentum differt. Non enim secundum quod in hypostasi sunt res significatae a praedicamento, sed secundum quod concipiuntur vel existentes vel tanquam existentes" (fol. 345r). For the same citation from Simplicius see Godfrey in the paragraph following the text just cited. For further discussion by Godfrey of this passage from Simplicius, see Q 4, q. 2 (PB 2.240–41). For that passage itself see the edition by A. Pattin, *Simplicius. Commentaire sur les catégories d'Aristote. Traduction de Guillaume de Moerbeke*, T. 1 (Louvain, 1971), pp. 14–15, lines 32–36. For further discussion of Henry's passage in terms of the immediate context see Gómez Caffarena, *Ser participado* . . . , pp. 31–32.

[92] Q 2, q. 2 (PB 2.56); Q 8, q. 3 (PB 4.36). In the latter text note in particular: "Et dicitur ulterius quod, quia essentiae creaturarum ex hoc sunt aliquid secundum essentiam quia respondent rationibus idealibus quae sunt in Deo, et aliquid causatum et constitutum ab ipso, secundum hoc creaturae rerum secundum suas essentias, antequam sint, referuntur reali relatione ad Deum: hoc secundum modum primum relationis, in quinto Metaphysicae, per quandam reductionem; secundum autem suas existentias referuntur ad Deum secundum modum secundum relationis." For Aristotle

In light of the above one might wonder about the relationship between divine ideas and the essential being (*esse essentiae*) of creatures prior to their actual creation in extramental reality. According to Henry both the divine ideas and the creaturely essential being are realized from all eternity, and both are intimately connected with divine knowledge. But according to Henry's texts and according to Godfrey's understanding of the same theory, essential being (*esse essentiae*) accrues to a possible creature only as a result of God's cognition. The divine ideas are simply distinctive ways in which God views his essence as capable of imitation by creatures. Far from identifying the creaturely essential being (*esse essentiae*) with God's knowledge of the same, or with God's idea, Henry rather holds that the former, the essential being, depends upon the latter, the divine idea, as upon its exemplar cause.[93]

Thus in Quodlibet 9, q. 2 Henry distinguishes different objects of divine cognition, when one understands by "object" that which terminates God's knowing activity. The primary object of God's cognition is the divine essence itself. Secondary objects of divine knowledge, the possibles, may be understood simply as virtually present in God and hence as identical with his essence, or as enjoying some degree of reality in themselves in distinction from God, although as still dependent upon his knowledge. In order to account for God's knowledge of such objects in this final way, Henry distin-

---

see *Metaphysics* V, c. 15 (1020b 26–1021b 11), where he distinguishes three ways in which things may be described as relative, based on number, on active and passive potency, and on measure. Henry correlates three kinds of causality with these, that is, formal, efficient, and final causality respectively. For detailed discussion of this by Henry and for his application of the same to the relationship between God and creatures and vice versa see Quodlibet 9, q. 1, fol. 343r–344r. On the real relation of such not yet existent essences to God see Henry, Q 9, q. 1 (fol. 341v) as cited in Ch. II, note 83. Also see Paulus, *Henri de Gand* . . . , pp. 293–94, and J. Benes, "Valor 'possibilium' apud S. Thomam, Henricum Gandavensem, B. Iacobum de Viterbio," *Divus Thomas* (Piacenza) 30 (1927), pp. 107–08. Benes also cites some other texts wherein Henry speaks of this real relationship.

[93] See, for instance, Quodlibet 9, q. 2 (fol. 344r–347r). Note in particular: "Illa autem ratio in divina essentia secundum quam sua essentia est ratio qua cognoscit alia a se nihil aliud est quam imitabilitas quae ab aliis imitetur, quam vocamus ideam . . . " (fol. 344v); "Et est talis haec dei cognitio in cognoscendo se secundum rationem formae exemplaris; a quo secundum rationem causae formalis habent esse aliquid per essentiam ipsa exemplata in esse suo cognito" (*ibid.*); ". . . quemadmodum divina essentia secundum rationes ideales est forma exemplaris qua essentiae creaturarum sunt id quod sunt ut quaedam exemplata" (fol. 345v). Also see Benes, *op. cit.*, pp. 107–10; Gómez Caffarena, *Ser participado* . . . , pp. 30–32; Paulus, *Henri de Gand* . . . , pp. 87–88; 293–94; Hoeres, "Wesen und Dasein bei Heinrich . . . ," pp. 154–55.

guishes different logical "moments" within God's cognitive activity. In a first moment God simply knows himself as such. In the second moment he knows himself as capable of being imitated by creatures or in terms of his ideas. But in knowing himself in this second way God also knows and constitutes the possibles as such, that is to say, creaturely essences in terms of their essential being. Insofar as these are understood as determined essences in themselves they acquire a certain essential being (*esse essentiae*) or reality as essences and thus stand, in some curious way, on the side of creation with reference to God. So true is this that, as we have seen, Henry states that by reason of their essential being and before they actually exist in the extramental world, they are in some way really related to God.[94]

That Godfrey also understands Henry's theory in this way is clear, for instance, from the first of several arguments that he presents in support of the same in his own Quodlibet 9, q. 2. There he notes that defenders of this position reason that God must have true and perfect knowledge of the essences of things before he brings them into actual existence. Granted that he knows himself as the first and primary object of his intellect, still, by knowing himself as admitting of imitation in various ways by creatures he also knows the quiddities of all creatures as a quasi-secondary object. Thus in this way and from all eternity God himself is the exemplar cause of all such things. Hence one must assign some reality to these (possible) essences themselves, and this in distinction from that of their exemplar cause. This must be conceded because it is unfitting for the divine idea itself to be identical with that which depends on it (*ideatum*) or for the divine exemplar to be identical with that which is modelled upon it (*exemplatum*).[95] In this same general context

---

[94] Fol. 344r–344v. See in particular: "Obiectum primarium . . . non est nisi ipsa divina essentia, quae per se intelligitur a Deo, et nihil aliud ab ipso. . . . Obiectum autem secundarium est aliud a se. . . . Sed aliud a se ut obiectum secundarium suae cognitionis potest cognoscere dupliciter. Uno modo cognoscendo de creatura id quod ipsa est in Deo. Alio modo cognoscendo de ipsa id quod ipsa habet esse in seipsa aliud a Deo, quamvis non habeat esse extra eius notitiam. . . . Hoc [primo] modo deus cognoscit alia a se ut sunt in sua essentia idem quod ipsa, et sic non ut alia. . . . Secundo autem modo cognoscit alia a se vere. . . . Sic autem sua essentia qua cognoscit se cognoscit alia a se . . . ut ipsa essentia est ratio et habet rationem respectus quo respicit alia a se, non ut quae sunt per existentiam aliquid extra in seipsis, sed ut quae sunt per essentiam aliquid in divina cognitione, videlicet in eo quod divina essentia est ratio et forma exemplaris illorum." See Paulus, *Henri de Gand* . . . , pp. 88–92.

[95] PB 4.190–191. See his concluding remark: "Quare oportuit eas importare aliquam realitatem, quae esset obiectum verum et reale intellectus divini realiter differens a suo exemplari; quia inconveniens est quod ipsa idea sit ideatum et exemplar sit exemplatum."

Godfrey has also observed that according to this theory the essence of a creature is not only an essence in potency but in actuality in terms of its *esse essentiae* (essential being).[96]

In light of Godfrey's rejection of Henry's view of *esse essentiae* and his intentional distinction between essence and existence, one can readily anticipate his reaction to the latter's theory of creative causality. Thus in Quodlibet 8, q. 3 Godfrey comments that if one wishes to distinguish between essential being (*esse essentiae*) and existence (*esse existentiae*) and to hold that things may be constituted in essential being as objects of divine knowledge from all eternity, then one should say the same of their existence. If, as defenders of this view sometimes argue, God knows things he has created in the same way that he knows things he is to create, then it should follow that he knows their existence as well as their essential being from eternity. In other words, as we shall see in greater detail, Godfrey here attempts to refute Henry's position by showing that it leads to a defense of the eternity of all things, past, present and future, both as regards their essences and their existences.[97] Godfrey himself then appeals to his own view that essence and existence are really identical, differing neither really nor intentionally. If essence and *esse essentiae* and existence and *esse existentiae* are all really one and the same, whatever is true of a thing's essence must be true of its existence. To the extent that its essence is known, so must its existence be known.[98]

In replying to the general question under discussion in Quodlibet 8, q. 3 ("Whether a rational creature is capable of receiving grace or any accident before it actually exists"), Godfrey observes that a thing is capable of possessing accidents to the same degree that it enjoys being. He then proposes an alternative to Henry's theory by drawing upon the division of being we have already seen him defending in our Chapters I and II.[99] To recapitulate, real being is to be divided into real being in act and real being in potency rather than into *esse essentiae* and *esse existentiae*. Hence a particular entity does not possess real being except in potency prior to its actual existence. Thus a rational nature before its actual existence cannot be said to enjoy any distinctive real being or *esse essentiae* in addition to its being in the mind (*esse cognitum*) except potentially, that is, by reason of its formal exemplar and efficient cause, or God. Insofar as it is eternally known by God it has

---

[96] ". . . sicut ipsa realitas et essentia vel quidditas creaturae ab aeterno etiam non solum est essentia et quidditas realis in potentia et in esse cognito, sed in actu secundum esse essentiae reale et quidditativum" (PB 4.190).

[97] PB 4.37.

[98] PB 4.37–38.

[99] See Ch. I, pp. 15–17; Ch. II–B, pp. 78–79.

cognitive being, of course, and insofar as God has the capacity to produce it as its exemplar and efficient cause, it enjoys real being potentially, but only potentially. But since the divine knowledge (by reason of which a created nature is said to have cognitive being) and the divine perfection (by reason of which it has real being potentially) are one and the same, one may say that the thing's cognitive being and its potential being are in fact one and the same prior to its actual existence. Since neither cognitive being nor real potential being pertains to the very nature of the not yet existent entity as it is in itself, when it is so viewed it is said to possess "diminished" or minimal being.[100]

Given this explanation, then, Godfrey concludes that it is absurd to postulate some additional and absolute being or *esse essentiae* in the sense defended by Henry.[101] His point is that one may adequately account for the ontological status of a not yet existent possible simply by appealing to his division of being into cognitive being, on the one hand, and real potential being, on the other. Recourse to this same division will also enable one to account for the distinction between a possible entity and a mere chimera, since the latter lacks real being even in potency. And as we have already noted, Godfrey applies this same division in order to account for the possibility of genuine knowledge of nonexistent possible entities.[102]

Godfrey offers a series of arguments against Henry's position both in Quodlibet 8, q. 3 and in Quodlibet 9, q. 2, arguments too extensive for us to present here in their entirety. We shall rather concentrate on a few of these insofar as they reveal more about Godfrey's own metaphysics of creative causality. In Quodlibet 8, q. 3, after rephrasing certain objections to Henry's theory following from the essence-existence relationship in creatures,[103] God-

---

[100] PB 4.38–39. Here Godfrey also discusses the *esse cognitum* of things insofar as they are objects of a created intellect. As regards natural entities, their *esse cognitum* implies the real being neither of these entities themselves nor even of their extrinsic cause. As regards artefacts, however, their *esse cognitum* does imply the real being of their cause. Godfrey also introduces a distinction with respect to the term "diminished" being. Such applies with greater force to nonexisting essences which can originate only through creation than to those which can come into being through generation. The former neither preexist in themselves nor in terms of intrinsic principles. The latter may be said to be real potentially both by reason of some preexisting intrinsic principle as well as by reason of a preexisting extrinsic cause.

[101] PB 4.39.

[102] PB 4.39–41. See Ch. II–B, pp. 78–79. Also see Q 9, q. 2 (PB 4.198–99).

[103] PB 4.41–42. In brief Godfrey here reasons that one interpretation of Henry's view seems to imply that essence and existence can be separated from one another. Thus, if they are separable, one might hold that a thing is eternally constituted with

frey introduces a new line of attack based on an unusual feature of his own general theory of causality. Henry's position ultimately assumes that something may serve as exemplar cause with respect to something else without at the same time being its efficient cause. Thus from all eternity creaturely essences would depend on God and his ideas as upon their exemplar cause, but God would not serve as their efficient cause until he communicated actual existence to them in time. This raises the question as to the proper place of the exemplar within the traditional division of the causes. The reader may be familiar with attempts within the scholastic tradition to include the exemplar under the formal cause and other attempts to place it under the final cause.[104]

Godfrey's view is distinctive, however, in that he maintains that in intelligent agents the exemplar or extrinsic formal cause is really identical with the efficient cause. In support of this he reasons that one should not distinguish the exemplar from the efficient cause on the grounds that the former simply causes in the order of exemplarity and the latter in the order of efficiency. They are rather to be distinguished for this reason, that there are two kinds of agents, intelligent agents on the one hand, and purely natural or noncognitive agents, on the other. Intelligent agents act both as efficient and formal exemplar causes. Purely natural agents act only as efficient causes, not as exemplar causes. One should distinguish two kinds of forms by reason of which agents act. The form in question may be that knowledge

---

respect to its essence and only in time with respect to its existence. But then, counters Godfrey, one will fall into contradiction by suggesting that such an eternally constituted essence enjoys some reality prior to and apart from its own actual existence (*esse existentiae*). On the other hand, if one denies that essence and existence are separable, Godfrey regards his refutation of Henry as given. One can then hardly say that essence enjoys some reality apart from and prior to its existence. Finally, if one holds that essence and existence are really one and the same but that existence adds some relationship to God as to its efficient cause while essence merely bespeaks relationship to him as to an exemplar, efficient causal production of such an entity will not involve acquisition of any new and unqualified reality. Nothing but a new relationship will be acquired through creation, a view which Godfrey rejects as false because a relation as such can never be the per se *terminus* of action. For more see p. 42, and compare with Godfrey's arguments against Henry's theory of intentional distinction of essence and existence as exposed in Q 3, q. 1. See Ch. II–B, pp. 85–88.

[104] For a brief but interesting discussion of the position of the exemplar cause in relation to the formal, efficient and final causes in Aquinas see F. Meehan, *Efficient Causality in Aristotle and St. Thomas* (Washington, D.C., 1940), pp. 178–81. Also see T. Kondoleon, "Exemplary Causality," *New Catholic Encyclopedia* (New York, 1967), Vol. 5, pp. 715–16; C. Hart, *Thomistic Metaphysics: An Inquiry into the Act of Existing* (Englewood Cliffs, N.J., 1959), pp. 321–22; G. Girardi, *Metafisica della causa esemplare in San Tommaso d'Aquino* (Turin, 1954), pp. 97–100.

according to whose likeness the effect is to be modelled or it may simply be a natural form or quality which renders the agent capable of acting as an efficient cause. Because both kinds of forms are found in intelligent agents, such agents are both efficient and exemplar causes.[105]

Here Godfrey hearkens back to the traditional division of the causes into four kinds. He maintains that the exemplar is not to be placed under the formal cause except insofar as the latter is included under the efficient cause. Therefore the extrinsic exemplar cause falls under the efficient cause. Otherwise there would not be four but five supreme genera of causes. Given this understanding of the exemplar cause, then, Godfrey reasons that if something depends upon something else as upon its exemplar cause, it also depends on it as upon its efficient cause. The converse need not hold, however, since a purely natural agent acts as efficient cause of a given effect without being its exemplar. But if an intelligent agent serves as formal exemplar cause of a given effect, it will also be its efficient cause.[106]

While many would agree that the idea or the exemplar is to be located in the mind of the agent when that agent is intellectual, Godfrey is saying more than this. In such agents the exemplar and the efficient cause are one and the same. This is not surprising, of course, in light of the immediate context, since Godfrey is here attempting to show that something cannot be an exemplar cause of a given effect without at the same time being its efficient cause. Once this principle is granted, Henry's position is thoroughly undermined. It will not be possible for creatures to be eternally dependent on God as exemplar cause of their *esse essentiae* and only temporally dependent upon him as efficient cause of their *esse existentiae*.[107]

---

[105] PB 4.43.

[106] PB 4.43. Note in particular: "Propter quod hoc, scilicet esse causam exemplarem formalem et esse causam efficientem est omnino idem in tali causa agente, scilicet per cognitionem. Unde illud quod producitur vel constituitur ab aliquo secundum rationem formae exemplaris producitur secundum rationem artis." Godfrey here turns to a theological point, the emanation of divine persons. Because this takes place not according to art but according to nature, the Divine Word itself does not proceed from the Father according to any exemplar form or idea. Rather the Word itself is the *ars* in which all the formal and exemplar ideas (*rationes*) of creatures are contained, as Augustine says in *De trinitate* VI, c. 10 (CCSL 50.241). Lest one think that the divine ideas themselves are constituted in God in accord with more fundamental exemplar ideas Godfrey also notes that they themselves are not constituted after the manner of art, but naturally. Here he finds support in Anselm, *Monologium*, c. 33:"Deus uno eodemque verbo dicit se et quaecumque fecit" (F.S. Schmitt, ed., *Opera Omnia*, Vol. 1 [Edinburgh, 1946], p. 53). See PB 4.44.

[107] PB 4.44. Also see Q 9, q. 2 (PB 4.195) and Q 2, q. 2 (PB 2.67–68). For a similar refusal to regard the exemplar as distinct in genus from the efficient cause see

Godfrey acknowledges that the divine ideas serve as formal exemplars of creatures. But he also insists that whatever is constituted by them in the order of formal exemplarity must also be efficiently produced by them to that same degree and in conjunction with the divine will. Here he draws an analogy with the art of medicine and with the idea of a house that is to be produced insofar as they exist in the mind of the doctor and the builder respectively. Just as these human ideas serve both as exemplar causes and as efficient causes of their effects in cooperation with the human will, so too a divine idea (*ratio idealis*) serves as exemplar cause and as efficient cause of its effect (both of *esse essentiae* and *esse existentiae*) only in cooperation with the divine will. For Godfrey, of course, this exercise of divine exemplar and divine efficient causality is realized in fact only in time. Prior to their creation creatures do not enjoy real actual being of any kind, whether essential or existential, but only cognitive being (*esse cognitum*) plus real being in potency in the sense described above.[108]

In what one may single out as another line of attack, Godfrey also attempts to show that Henry's theory leads to the denial that creatures are really created from nothing. If the creature enjoys true essential being (*esse essentiae*) distinct from that of the divine essence before it receives actual existence or is created, then it is not really created from nothing. Nothingness indicates the complete negation of any reality in the thing itself, including its essential being.[109] This point is developed as a major theme in Quodlibet 9, q. 2 where, it will be recalled, Godfrey attempts to show that Henry's theory should lead to the denial that God produces things from nothing in creating and hence to the denial that anything can be annihilated.[110] Here Godfrey interprets Henry as implying that essential being is assigned to a not yet existent creature in such fashion as to be actually and not merely potentially distinct from the divine essence. But, insists Godfrey, such an actually distinct essential being cannot be described as nothing. Therefore a creature

---

Duns Scotus, *Ordinatio* I, d. 2, pars 1, qq. 1–2, n. 40 (Vat., 1950), T. 2, p. 149; and *Ordinatio* I, d. 36, q. un., n. 23 (Vat., 1958), T. 6, pp. 279–80. In the latter context this is one of a series of arguments directed by Scotus against Henry's position. For others in Scotus that have already been anticipated by Godfrey see *op. cit.*, pp. 276–77.

[108] PB 4.44–45. In this same context Godfrey appeals to authority. He has found no trace of support for Henry's view in Augustine or in any other recognized authority. Here and again in Q 9, q. 2 (PB 4.195) he explicitly refers to q. 46 of Augustine's *De diversis quaestionibus*. See CCSL 44A.71.

[109] PB 4.45. Also see pp. 45–46 for Godfrey's citation of certain texts from Anselm's *Monologium* in his support, in particular from cc. 9, 34, and 35.

[110] PB 4.190.

such as an angel cannot be described as nothing prior to its reception of existence. One might counter that it is a true being (*ens*) only in the sense that one can say of it "it is a substance," but not in the sense that one can say "it is (exists)." To this Godfrey replies, that which is a substance is something (*aliquid*), and that which is something is not nothing.[111]

In like manner, continues Godfrey, even if an angel should be corrupted so as to lose its existence, its essential being would still remain. Since this essential being is not nothing, the angel will not have been annihilated. If one protests that such an essence is really nothing before its creation in terms of its existence although not in terms of its essence, the difficulty is simply compounded. This would be to hold that the preexisting essence is nothing only in a qualified sense, but not in the absolute sense since, according to Henry, existence adds nothing absolute to essence but only a certain mode and relationship. Godfrey concludes, therefore, that if one is to preserve the doctrine of creation from nothing, one must regard the angelic essence before its actual creation as completely and totally nothing apart from the potency of God, its extrinsic cause.[112] Godfrey would, of course, acknowledge that material things that arise by generation from preexisting matter also enjoy real potential being by reason of their intrinsic cause, matter, prior to their actual production.

In another major criticism of Henry's position, Godfrey charges that acceptance of the same is inconsistent with his (Henry's) rejection of the possibility of creation of the world from eternity. Henry admits that it is not repugnant for the essence of a creature to be eternally constituted in its essential being (*esse essentiae*) by God as its exemplar cause. In fact his theory assumes this to be the situation of all possibles. But as Godfrey well knew, as early as 1276 Henry had denied that a creature can be eternally constituted in actual existence (*esse existentiae*) or eternally created.[113] And

[111] PB 4.191. See in particular: ". . . angelus enim creandus, si est verum ens secundum realem quidditatem substantialem ut vere sit substantia rationalis, licet non dicatur secundo adiacens quod sit, dicitur tamen tertio adiacens quod sit substantia, non potest dici nihil; quod enim est substantia est aliquid, et quod est aliquid non est nihil." Also see PB 4.192, where Godfrey reasons: ". . . ergo si est substantia, est" (punctuation corrected).

[112] PB 4.191–92. For further arguments against the view that *esse existentiae* (and for that matter, the *esse* of *esse essentiae*) may be described in terms of relationship see PB 4.192–94 and Q 8, q. 3 (PB 4.46). See also PB 4.194 for Godfrey's reiteration of the point that whatever is true of essence is true of existence and his denial that any support can be found in recognized authority for Henry's view that a thing may be said to have *esse essentiae* in one way and *esse existentiae* in another.

[113] For Henry see Quodlibet 1, qq. 7–8. For an edition of these questions as well

for this Godfrey taxes him with inconsistency. Godfrey counters that God is no less powerful to cause in the order of efficiency than in the order of exemplarity. Moreover, from the side of the creature and within the framework of Henry's theory, there is no incompatibility between a creature's essential being and its actual existence that might prevent the two from always being realized together in a given entity. From both points of view, contends Godfrey, it therefore follows that as soon as an essence is constituted in its essential being (*esse essentiae*), it either is or may be constituted as actually existing. But by rejecting the possibility of eternal creation Henry has in effect denied this final point, and for this Godfrey labels his position as irrational.[114]

Then, in obvious reference to another favored theme in Henry, Godfrey observes that according to him that which is of itself purely nothing cannot attain to real being without undergoing some change (*mutatio*).[115] Without pausing here to discuss the adequacy of so describing creation, that is, as a kind of change, Godfrey prefers to argue once more from within the confines of Henry's position. According to Henry the essence of a creature considered simply in itself and apart from divine exemplar causality would be nothing, not merely in terms of its actual existence but in terms of its essential being (*esse essentiae*). It is only constituted in essential being by God, its exemplar cause, and this from all eternity. To that extent it may be described as being "changed" from nothingness to something, according to Henry's language. In fact, argues Godfrey, only this process whereby it is constituted in essential

---

as a lengthy study of the same see R. Macken, "La temporalité radicale de la créature selon Henri de Gand," *Recherches de Théologie ancienne et médiévale* 38 (1971), pp. 211–72. For an earlier version of part of the same see his "De radicale tijdelijkheid van het schepsel volgens Hendrik van Gent," *Tijdschrift voor Filosofie* 31 (1969), pp. 519–71.

[114] PB 4.196–97.

[115] "Dicitur enim ab istis quod illud, quod de se nihil est, non potest consequi esse reale sine mutatione; mutatio autem de non esse in esse non potest fieri circa id quod semper habet esse et cetera" (PB 4.197). For Henry see Q 1, qq. 7–8: ". . . actus creationis, etsi non sit vera transmutatio, ut est illa quae est naturalis, quia tamen est de non esse in esse, modum mutationis habet" (Macken ed., p. 265, 12–13). Macken wonders if the similarity between Henry's position and the condemnation of the opposite some months later by Stephen Tempier was not more than coincidental, given Henry's role as a member of the bishop's commission. See proposition 217: "Quod creatio non debet dici mutatio ad esse.—Error, si intelligatur de omni modo mutationis" (*Chartularium* . . . II, p. 555); Mandonnet, *op. cit.*, pr. 187 (p. 189). See Macken, *op. cit.*, pp. 236, 253; also p. 220, n. 46 (on Henry's membership in Stephen's commission). See the final section of this chapter for Godfrey's reaction to Henry's argumentation to prove that the world could not be eternal.

being or in *esse essentiae* will be true creation, for this alone marks a transition (*mutatio*) from nothing to something.[116] In other words, the creature's reception of existential being in time due to God's efficient causality is not really creation. And its essence will in fact have been eternally created.

Godfrey makes this same point by reasoning from a slightly different perspective. Henry's position assumes that because a creaturely essence can be known before it actually exists and from eternity, some distinctive reality must be assigned to it and also from eternity. But, objects Godfrey, the existence of such a creature is also eternally known by God. As Augustine has stated, God knows things he has produced in the same way he knows things he is to produce. Hence according to Henry's own logic it will follow that because God eternally knows a thing in terms of its existence, it must also actually possess such existence from eternity.[117] For Godfrey, of course, neither follows. It is enough for him to assign potential being to such an entity by reason of the divine causal power to account for God's eternal knowledge of it both in terms of its essence and its existence.[118]

It is by appealing to this same theory of act and potency that Godfrey responds to the argument we have seen him offering above in Quodlibet 9, q. 2 in defense of Henry's position. According to that argumentation one might reason that it is unfitting for a divine exemplar to be identical with that which is modelled upon it or for a divine idea to be identical with that which depends on it. Hence one should distinguish between the divine ideas and the possible essences that depend on them from all eternity. Godfrey counters that prior to the actual creation and resulting actual existence of any creature there is only a potential distinction between its appropriate divine idea or exemplar, on the one hand, and the creature itself as modelled upon or imitating the same, on the other. In fact they are really identical. It is true that the creature will be really distinct from its divine idea or exemplar once it has been brought into actual existence. But one need not and should not assign any distinct and actual reality to its essence (or to its existence) prior to its creation in time in order to account for the possibility of its being known by God.[119]

---

[116] PB 4.197.

[117] *Ibid.* Godfrey cites Augustine: ". . . nec enim Deus aliter novit facta quam fienda, creata quam creanda." See *De trinitate*, XV, c. 13 in *Oeuvres de Saint Augustin* (Desclée de Brouwer, 1955), Vol. 16, p. 486 and CCSL 50.A, 495. "Nec aliter ea scivit creata quam creanda. . . ." Also see pp. 197–98 for further variations of the argument just presented.

[118] PB 4.198–99.

[119] See p. 135 of this chapter for Godfrey's presentation of the argument. For his

In sum, then, in addition to having rejected Henry's theory because of its intimate connection with an alleged intentional distinction between essence and existence, Godfrey finds his position unacceptable for at least three additional reasons. It rests on a faulty understanding of the exemplar cause. It leads to the denial that creatures are in fact created from nothing. And it is inconsistent with Henry's claim that the world could not have been created from eternity.

Near the end of Quodlibet 8, q. 3 Godfrey refers to another theory, one that is found in James of Viterbo's Quodlibet 1, q. 5.[120] Reference has been made above to the careful way in which Godfrey here follows and abbreviates James's text and to the implications following from this textual interdependency for the dating of the two Masters' respective quodlibets. It is at least clear that both texts date from the early 1290s.[121] According to Godfrey's reproduction of James's theory, and according to the latter's text as well, he distinguishes two ways in which a not yet existent creature may be said to be present in God's knowledge. In one way God simply knows the thing as present in his essence and as identical with it. In another way he knows it as present in his essence insofar as the latter is a potency or power.[122]

When God views such nonexistent essences or possibles in the first way, he does not understand them as distinguished from himself. But when he knows them in the second way he does view them as distinct from himself. Known in this second way then, and as distinct from God, such nonexistent but possible creatures may be described as things (*res*), not without qualification, to be sure, but in this sense, insofar as they are objects of God's cognition. For something to be an object of God's knowledge, reasons James, it must be something in itself. If it were pure nothingness, it could not be known by God as distinct from himself. Hence James concludes that before such a creature actually exists it may be referred to as a real thing or *res*.

---

reply see PB 4.201–02. Also see Q 8, q. 3 (PB 4.46–48).

[120] For James see *Jacobi de Viterbio O.E.S.A. Disputatio prima de quolibet*, E. Ypma, ed. (Würzburg, 1968), p. 63: "Quinto quaeritur: Utrum essentia creaturae antequam habeat esse in effectu sit verum ens reale." For Godfrey see PB 4.48.

[121] See our *Introduction*, pp. xxivff. For more detailed illustration of this textual interdependency see our "The Dating of James of Viterbo's Quodlibet I and Godfrey of Fontaines' Quodlibet VIII," *Augustiniana* 24 (1974), pp. 366–72. It should be noted that James's Quodlibet I was included in Godfrey's library. See Duin, "La bibliothèque philosophique de Godefroid . . . ," pp. 23–24, with reference to *Paris: Bibl. Nat. lat.* 15.350 (fol. 291ra–337rb). Duin assigns the marginal notes in the same to Godfrey's own hand (p. 24). Ypma rather wonders if they are by Godfrey himself (*op. cit.*, p. xi).

[122] For Godfrey see PB 4.48. For James see *op. cit.*, 62:25–63:30.

Both Godfrey and James note the similarity between this theory and that defended by Henry insofar as the latter would insist that for something truly to depend on or to imitate a divine idea or exemplar, it must enjoy some reality in itself.[123] (Of course they do not cite Henry by name, just as Godfrey has not referred to James by name.)

Not surprisingly in light of his detailed criticism of Henry's theory, Godfrey is no more sympathetic to that proposed by James. First of all, he rejects the suggested distinction. If God really knows creatures before their actual existence, then he must know them in some way as distinct from himself. To maintain that God can know them in the first way that James has proposed is to imply that God does not thereby understand them actually and formally and distinctly at all, but only virtually and in universal and confused fashion and in potency.[124] Secondly, Godfrey again appeals to his theory of act and potency. Prior to their actual existence God does know creatures, to be sure, and as distinct from himself, but only as potentially existing and hence only as potentially distinct from himself (and from one another). Hence there is no need to conclude that they must actually be things or *res* in themselves and actually distinct from God prior to their creation. Granted that absolute nothingness cannot be known, potential being can be. And such is enjoyed by possible creatures prior to their actual creation.[125]

3. *Godfrey's View of the Procession of Creatures from God*

In the preceding section of this chapter we have concentrated on Godfrey's reaction to Henry of Ghent's metaphysics of creative causality and then to that of James of Viterbo. Granted that Godfrey's discussion was somewhat polemical in tone, a positive metaphysical doctrine clearly emerges from his

---

[123] For Godfrey see PB 4.48–49. For James see *op. cit.*, pp. 63:33–65:112. Note in particular: "Quare creatura, antequam sit in effectu, est res aliqua ut obiectum cognitum, etiam ut est a Deo alia et distincta" (65:101–102). For explicit identification of the final view mentioned in our text as that of Henry of Ghent also see Benes, "Valor 'Possibilium' . . . ," p. 350.

[124] PB 4.49.

[125] PB 4.49–50. See Q 9, q. 2 (PB 4.204–05) where Godfrey again refers to James's theory. In addition to summarizing much more briefly the first part of Q 1, q. 5 which he had followed in Q 8, q. 3, he also cites James's subsequent reference to a not yet existent object of divine cognition as being distinct from God and a true *res* only insofar as it is a possible. For James see p. 65:113–125 and p. 68:204–210. For Godfrey's almost verbatim citation of part of the last text see PB 4.205. Godfrey is still unsatisfied with what he now seems to regard as James's attempt at compromise: ". . . non multum valet quod quidam, qui nituntur quadam via media circa praemissa procedere, dicunt. . ." (PB 4.204).

texts. As we have seen, this doctrine ultimately rests once more on his application of the metaphysics of act and potency to the division of being. Real being is contrasted with merely cognitive being. Real being itself may be either actual or potential. Prior to the creation of particular entities, then, God views his essence as capable of being participated in by creatures in various ways. Corresponding to his knowledge of himself in these different ways or his divine ideas is his knowledge of creatures, but only as potentially distinguishable from him prior to their actual creation. According to Godfrey there is no need to postulate any additional essential being that would in some way be distinct from God and really related to him prior to its realization as an existing entity. As a potential object of God's creative activity any possible existent may be described as potentially dependent upon God from all eternity as upon its exemplar and efficient cause and as potentially distinct from him. But it is only when such a possible or potential entity is actually created that it is actually distinguished from God and actually depends upon him either as its exemplar or as its efficient cause.

In other contexts Godfrey introduces some further elements that are of interest to us in our effort to reconstruct his metaphysics of creation. First of all, he raises the question of divine final causality. Secondly, in describing the procession of creatures from God he uses language that is heavily indebted to Neoplatonism and especially to Proclus. We shall now consider each of these points in turn.

Godfrey considers the first issue in Quodlibet 10, q. 1, which dates from ca. 1294/1295 and, therefore, after the detailed treatments of divine creative causality that we have just considered in Quodlibet 8 and Quodlibet 9. In Quodlibet 10, q. 1 he explicitly addresses himself to this question: "Whether in producing the universe God intended the more important parts to a greater degree than the less important parts."[126] In preparing his reply Godfrey observes that God serves as exemplar cause, efficient cause, and final cause of all things. He immediately warns that this must not be taken to imply that one may distinguish really diverse factors in creatures to correspond to this threefold exercise of divine causality. Perhaps he is also thinking of Henry's intentional distinction of essential being and existential being to correspond to God's exercise of exemplar and efficient causality. Godfrey contends that to the extent that anything is brought into being it depends upon God according to this threefold causal order. He recalls that because God is pure act, separate, and immaterial, he is endowed with intellect and will. Hence

[126] "Utrum in producendo universum magis principaliter intenderit Deus partes magis principales quam minus principales" (PB 4.297).

he always acts in accord with the order that follows from his knowledge and wisdom and it is in accord with this that the order of things to be produced by him is to be understood. Thus it is because there are divine ideas or exemplar forms in the divine mind that God is not merely an efficient but also an exemplar cause of things.[127]

Godfrey now turns directly to the issue of divine finality. Because God is the supreme good and dependent on no other and is both willing and able to communicate some participation of his goodness to others, nothing else apart from God himself can serve as the end of his creative activity. He himself therefore is the end or goal of all other things that participate in his goodness and perfection. In other words, in creating God cannot intend to acquire anything from that which he produces. He rather intends to communicate his goodness or perfection to others. Each and every creature tends to realize its own perfection and this is, in fact, a likeness and imitation of the divine goodness and perfection. Thus it is that every creature ultimately tends toward the divine goodness and perfection.[128]

Godfrey now introduces another familiar theme. He has just stated that God produces creatures in order to communicate his goodness to them and in order for this to be reflected in them. But no single creature can adequately represent or reflect the divine goodness. Given this, God has established a universe, that is to say, many creatures, so that what is lacking to one in its representation of the divine perfection may be, to some extent, supplied for by others. Because the entire universe more fully participates in the divine goodness and hence represents it more adequately than does any particular creature, Godfrey concludes that God intended more primarily to produce the whole universe than to produce any particular creature therein. And since more perfect creatures more adequately reflect the divine goodness, he also concludes that God intended more primarily to produce these than less perfect beings.[129]

Godfrey then offers an important qualification. Even though he has sug-

---

[127] PB 4.297–98.

[128] PB 4.298. Also see Q 8, q. 5 (PB 4.61–62): "Quia supponendum est quod Deus res modo congruentissimo et in se ipsis et in ordine ad fines suos disposuit quae ad hoc congruunt, providendo et disponendo; secundum autem ordinem agentium sive motionum est ordo finium; ad ultimum finem autem converti habet homo per motionem primi agentis vel moventis, ad finem autem proximum per motionem alicuius inferiorum moventium; cum ergo Deus sit primum movens simpliciter, ex eius motione est quod omnia in ipsum convertuntur secundum communem intentionem boni, per quam unumquodque intendit assimilari Deo secundum suum modum."

[129] PB 4.298.

gested that certain creatures are intended less primarily or to a lesser degree than others, he does not wish to imply thereby that there are really distinct "intentions" in God. It is rather because we find really distinct degrees of perfection in creatures that we speak of one as being intended to a greater degree than another and as if there were such distinct intentions in God. In fact, however, in God these can be no more than logically distinct and are really identical with one another and with God, something that we have also found Godfrey maintaining with reference to the divine ideas. But from man's point of view one may say that the nobler and more perfect creature is intended by God to a greater extent, just as one may say that God wills to give glory more than he wills to give grace (the means to glory).[130]

Recent scholars have identified two descriptions of finality in Thomas Aquinas's account of the order of the universe, finality by assimilation and finality by intellectual knowledge and love. In assessing Godfrey's understanding of the divine purposiveness in creating and the resulting finality of the universe, he appears to stress finality by assimilation—whereby creatures achieve their end by imitating and reflecting the divine goodness and perfection. Thus he assigns this kind of finality to every creature on its own level. Yet, insofar as he allows for the subordination of one creature to another he has at least left a place for the other kind of finality whereby all things return to God through knowledge and love of him, intellectual creatures directly and others by means of intellectual creatures by serving as their instruments in this same return.[131]

In Quodlibet 4, q. 3 Godfrey offers some further precisions with respect to his understanding of the procession of created being from God. In the course of this discussion he develops again the analogy between numbers and the species of things and supports his general theory with a series of citations from Neoplatonic sources. In this particular question he is explicitly concerned with this issue: to determine whether regress to infinity is possible in the essential perfections of things or in perfections that are essentially ordered to one another.[132] In formulating his answer he immediately likens the species of things to number. Just as one number cannot be unequal to another unless

---

[130] PB 4.298–99.

[131] On man as primarily intended see Q 2, q. 3 (PB 2.80). For a discussion of these two kinds of finality in Aquinas see J. de Finance, *Etre et agir dans la philosophie de Saint Thomas* (Rome, 1960), pp. 315–25; J. Wright, *The Order of the Universe in the Theology of St. Thomas Aquinas* (Rome, 1957) pp. 45–63, and the many references to Aquinas given there.

[132] "Utrum in perfectionibus essentialibus rerum sive ordinem essentialem habentibus sit processus in infinitum" (PB 2.242).

it differs from the latter in species, so too within a given species of being, one individual cannot differ essentially from another and still belong to the same species as the first. And just as there can be no instance of the number two that does not include the essential perfection of that species of number, so must one say the same of any individual entity within a given species of being. Every such individual must possess the essential perfection of its species.[133]

But, continues Godfrey, this same analogy between the species of being and number leads some to conclude that just as one can increase any number to infinity, so may one allow for ever more perfect species of being to infinity. Defenders of this view appeal to the infinite "distance" that must obtain between the "unlimited sea" of divine perfection and the limited and determined degree of perfection found in any creature. This infinite "distance" does not run between two finite extremes, but between one that is finite (any creature) and one that is infinite (God). Given this, they contend that it is possible for creatures to proceed from the finite side toward the infinite in ever increasing degree of perfection without thereby attaining to the infinity of God.[134]

Godfrey reacts rather cautiously to this theory and suggests that he will only indicate what seems probable to him without attempting to offer a definitive solution. He then presents a series of arguments against the proposed extension to infinity of increasing degrees of perfection in creatures. Here we shall limit ourselves to one of these arguments, since in presenting it Godfrey reveals something more of his understanding of the procession of creatures from God.[135]

---

[133] PB 2.242 (long version); PB 2.325. For some other texts on the analogy between number and the differing degrees of being see Ch. II–C, p. 95 (commenting on Q 7, q. 7); and p. 127 of the present chapter (commenting on Q 4, q. 1). Also see Q 2, q. 7 (PB 2.102), on unicity vs. plurality of substantial forms; Q 2, q. 10 (PB 2.140), on intension and remission of forms; Q 9, q. 7 (PB 4.231), on whether two specifically different beings may stand in equal relationship to God (Godfrey thinks not). Also see *Disputed Question* 18 (*Bruges 491*: fol. 226va): "Sed secundum istos illud verbum philosophi quarto Metaphysicae, quod formae sunt sicut numeri, non est intelligendum de omnibus formis sed solum de non habentibus tales gradus. Sed hoc stare non potest primo quia non videtur verisimile quod verbum philosophi sit particulare cum ibi intendat loqui generaliter de esse quidditativo et specifico cuiuscumque rei generaliter quod, scilicet, esse quidditativum secundum rationem speciei consistit in indivisibili."

[134] Q 4, q. 3 (PB 2.242–43). For the short version see PB 2.325. For the view that God can create an ever more simple being see Giles of Rome, *De mensura angelorum* (Venice, 1503), fol. 40rab.

[135] PB 2.243. "Sed nihil circa hoc determinando sed probabiliter coniecturando,

This argument is based on the order of the universe, that is to say, on the order of beings therein to one another and to God. Since every multitude in some way participates in a one, all parts of any essentially ordered multitude must participate in ordered fashion in such a one. Infinity within a multitude would preclude any such ordered relationship. Hence if there is no creature (actual or possible, presumably) that is first in dignity and perfection, there will be no others, for any essential ordering of the multitude of creatures will require that they be referred to such a first creature. The essential order that obtains between different numbers requires that one come to a halt with one first number that is immediately derived from the unit and that admits of no other number between itself and the unit. So too the order of beings in the universe requires that there be one creature that is closest to the first and divine Unity, and that can admit of no other creature that is more perfect than itself or closer to God.[136]

Godfrey also reasons that one does not account for the order found in numbers by relating them to something that is indefinitely distant from the unit but rather by reason of the degree to which they approach and recede from the unit itself. Again, he contends, the parallel holds in the order of entities. The essential order of all created beings is determined by their relationship to the first Unity, that is, to the supreme simplicity and perfection of the divine essence. Because this supreme Unity is pure act, it is the principle of all other things which fall short of it and thereby approach composition and multiplicity. Godfrey paraphrases the by now familiar proposition 2 from Proclus's *Elementatio theologica:* All that participates in the One is in some way one and not-one. Godfrey insists that one cannot account for the order that obtains between beings by reversing one's perspective and relating them to some lowest being. If something may be described as imperfect as it approaches such a lowest entity, this can only be because it falls short of and recedes from the first and highest being. In like fashion, if *per impossibile* one could arrive at an ultimate number, one would not measure other numbers by their degree of proximity to it but by reason of their relationship to the unit.[137]

---

videtur posse poni contrarium. . . ." For the same hesitation see the short version (PB 2.325). Godfrey offers four general arguments against this position: 1) one based on the natural appetite of created being for perfection; 2) another following from the finite nature of creatures and the requirement that all be contained in genera; 3) the argument from order presented in our text; 4) a final one grounded on the infinite "distance" that must be maintained between God and creation. See PB 2.243–47 (long version) and 325–27 (short version).

[136] PB 2.244 (long version); PB 2.326.

[137] PB 2.244–45 (long version); PB 2.326–27. See our Ch. II–C, p. 95 and n.

Then as added support for his contention that the order of things in the universe derives from their distance from and proximity to the first being or God, Godfrey cites both Pseudo-Dionysius and Proclus. He paraphrases the former to this effect, that in God all things are, as it were, precontained in undivided fashion and are distinguished and multiplied only by proceeding from the one. According to Proclus in the *Elementatio theologica* all order begins from the one and proceeds to a corresponding many (prop. 21). And that which produces brings into being its like before its unlike (prop. 28). Again, all procession is effected through the similitude of things that are secondary to that which is primary (prop. 29). Finally, according to proposition 36, when things are multiplied in terms of procession, those that are primary are more perfect than those that are secondary, and those that are secondary are more perfect than those that come after them, and so on throughout the series. Godfrey concludes from these passages that to allow for extension of the perfection of created beings to infinity would be to eliminate the possibility of any ordered procession of the many from the one.[138]

From this general line of argumentation as well as from the others that he also offers in the same context it is clear that Godfrey favors the view that a series of essentially ever more perfect creatures cannot be created. At the same time he has advanced this point of view as only probable, and continues to be extremely cautious in referring to this in other contexts.[139] But it is interesting to see him likening the procession of created beings from God to a Neoplatonic flow of the many from the one. In so doing, of course, he is incorporating the Neoplatonic account into a creationist setting wherein all lower beings are *freely* created by God and depend upon him as their efficient,

151 for the reference to Proclus.

[138] PB 2.245–46. For Pseudo-Dionysius see PL 122.1149. The citations by Godfrey are not quite literal. For Proclus see Vansteenkiste, "Elementatio theologica . . . ," pp. 275–80. For the Greek see E. R. Dodds, *The Elements of Theology*, pp. 24 (prop. 21); 32 (prop. 28); 34 (prop. 29); 38 (prop. 36). Godfrey's Proclus citations are literal.

[139] See Q 4, q. 4 ("Utrum supposito quod Deus posset facere angelum angelo perfectiorem in infinitum, oporteret quemlibet pertinere ad aliquam determinatam hierarchiam nunc existentium") for this same cautious attitude with respect to the issue discussed in Q 4, q. 3. See PB 2.247–50 and PB 2.329. Also see Q 7, q. 12 (PB 3.389): "Sed, sicut alias dixi, ita adhuc etiam dico, non asserendo tamen ita esse, sed recitando, me non videre quod possibilis sit processus in infinitum secundum gradus perfectionum naturalium in diversis speciebus." Here he is discussing the possibility that charity might be increased to infinity in a rational creature. Also see Q 7, q. 8 (PB 3.365), and our "The Dating of James of Viterbo's Quodlibet I . . . ," pp. 357–58.

exemplar, and final cause. Thus Godfrey immediately warns that one must not conclude from the above that God could not produce a lower creature before he created a higher one. Nor should one think that God has in fact produced the noblest creature that can be brought into being.[140] But he is obviously very sympathetic to and much influenced by this Neoplatonic model of the procession of the many from the one.

Godfrey concludes his discussion in Quodlibet 4, q. 3 by introducing another precision. One should not imagine that the really distinct perfections found in creatures imitate correspondingly distinctive degrees of perfection in God himself. It is rather one and the same supremely simple divine essence that serves as the standard for every creature, insofar as one shares in multiplicity to a greater degree than another and is thereby farther removed from the divine unity. Logical distinction is therefore introduced into God, the supreme One, not insofar as his essence is viewed as it is in itself, but only by reason of his knowledge of himself as capable of being imitated by different creatures in different ways or in terms of his divine ideas.[141]

4. *Applications of Godfrey's Metaphysics of Creation*

a) The Possibility of Annihilation—As we have already observed while considering Godfrey's criticisms of Henry's theory of creative causality, one of his major objections to the same rests on his contention that it would undermine the doctrine of creation from nothing. To this same degree, argues Godfrey in Quodlibet 9, q. 2, Henry's doctrine also eliminates the possibility of annihilation. If creation as described by Henry simply consists in the reception of actual existence by an already real essential being, then annihilation can be no more than loss of that same actual existence. But the real essential being of any creature would have been realized from all eternity and would be realized for all eternity by reason of its dependence upon God as its formal exemplar cause.[142]

Having rejected Henry's theory, in this same Quodlibet 9, q. 2 Godfrey proceeds to discuss the possibility of annihilation in terms of his own metaphysics of creative causality. If one is content to speak of God's absolute power, then just as he brings every creature into being, so too can he reduce the same to nonbeing. If such a creature has been produced from "nothing," then it can be reduced to "nothing." Godfrey observes that creatures are not

---

[140] PB 2.246.

[141] PB 2.247 (long version); PB 2.327 (short version).

[142] See pp. 140–41 and the references given there.

only created by God but are also conserved in being by divine action. Just as God has freely created all beings, by reason of his absolute power he could simply withdraw this conserving action and permit them to fall into nothingness or to be annihilated.[143] As Godfrey explains farther on in this same question, annihilation would not really entail any action on the part of God. It would rather be the cessation of his conserving action. Nor is "nothing" something that would be produced through annihilation. It would simply be the negation of something that had been created and conserved.[144] While admitting the possibility of annihilation by God in terms of his absolute power, Godfrey quickly dismisses ill-advised attempts to find factual illustrations of this. Thus one should not cite the loss of grace or charity in the human soul as an example of annihilation.[145]

b) The Possibility of an Eternally Created Universe—As is well known, the eternal or noneternal character of the universe had long been contested prior to Godfrey's time. Philosophers such as Aristotle among the Greeks and Averroes and Avicenna within the Arab-speaking world had defended the eternity of the universe and many of their texts were available to thirteenth-century thinkers in Latin translation. In his *Guide of the Perplexed* Moses Maimonides had attempted to show that neither argumentation for or against the eternity of the world was demonstrative and, therefore, that from the standpoint of purely human reason, the question remained open. His position was also well known to the Latin scholastics of the thirteenth century.[146] In the thirteenth century itself classical positions were developed by

---

[143] PB 4.189–90.

[144] PB 4.205–06.

[145] PB 4.206–07.

[146] See E. Behler, *Die Ewigkeit der Welt . . . Erster Teil: Die Problemstellung in der Arabischen und Jüdischen Philosophie des Mittelalters* (Munich, 1965), pp. 45–53 (Aristotle); 110–14 (Avicenna); 192–94 (Averroes). For Maimonides see *The Guide of the Perplexed* II, c. 16 (Chicago, 1963), pp. 293–94. For the Latin translation see *Dux neutrorum seu dubiorum* (Paris, 1520), II, c. 17 (fol. 48v–49r). For other references and for commentary see Behler, pp. 254–61. For one illustration of the Latin thinkers' acquaintance with the views of Aristotle, Avicenna, Averroes, and Maimonides on this topic see Giles of Rome, *Errores philosophorum*, J. Koch, ed. (Milwaukee, 1944). Koch dates this work between 1268 and 1274 and more likely ca. 1270 (see pp. lv–lix). For Aristotle see c. 1, items 1, 2, 3, 4, 6, 7, 8; c. 2 for repetition of these in summary form; on Averroes see c. 4 where all of Aristotle's errors are assigned to him; for Avicenna see c. 6, items 2, 3, 5, 6; c. 7 for repetition of these in summary form; on Maimonides' disagreement with Aristotle on the eternity of the world see c. 12, introductory paragraph. On this treatise by Giles see Van Steenberghen, *Maître Siger . . .* , pp. 71–74; Wippel, "The Condemnations of 1270 and 1277 . . . ," p. 181.

St. Bonaventure, on the one hand, and by Thomas Aquinas, on the other. According to Bonaventure not only was the world in fact created with a temporal beginning, as Christians believe, it could not have been created from eternity. In support of this final point Bonaventure offered a series of six arguments in his *Commentary on the Sentences*, dating from the early 1250s.[147] And if at that time he had been in doubt as to Aristotle's true thought on this matter, by the time of the doctrinal crises and controversies of the late 1260s and the 1270s all such hesitation had disappeared from his mind. Aristotle had indeed defended the eternity of the world and on this point as on others had fallen into error.[148]

Thomas Aquinas treated this same question on various occasions throughout his career, beginning with his own *Commentary on the Sentences* in the 1250s.[149] As is also well known, he continuously maintained that one cannot

---

[147] *In II Sent.*, d. 1, p. 1, a. 1, q. 2, in *Doctoris Seraphici S. Bonaventurae . . . Opera Ominia*, 10 Vols. (Quaracchi, 1882–1902), Vol. 2, pp. 20–22. On Bonaventure and the eternity of the world see Van Steenberghen, *La philosophie au XIIIe siècle*, pp. 225–26; "Saint Bonaventure contre l'éternité du monde," *S. Bonaventura 1274–1974* (Grottaferrata, 1973), T.3, pp. 259–78 (also for references to many other studies of the same); A. Coccia, "De aeternitate mundi apud s. Bonaventuram et recentiores," *op. cit.*, pp. 279–306; B. Bonansea, "The Impossibility of Creation from Eternity According to St. Bonaventure," *Proceedings of the American Catholic Philosophical Association* (Washington, D.C., 1974), pp. 121–35; "The Question of an Eternal World in the Teaching of St. Bonaventure," *Franciscan Studies* 34 (1974), pp. 7–33.

[148] For his earlier hesitation on this point see *In II Sent.*, d. 1, p. 1, a. 1, q. 2, pp. 22–23. He refers to the view of certain *moderni* who maintain that Aristotle did not intend to prove that the world did not begin, but that it did not begin by natural motion, a point which Bonaventure refuses to settle here. For his later view (1267) see his *De decem praeceptis* II n. 28, in *Opera Omnia*, Vol. 2, p. 515. On this see Van Steenberghen, *La philosophie au XIIIe siècle*, pp. 220–21, 225–26; *Maître Siger . . .*, pp. 36–37. For a slightly different interpretation of the text from the *Commentary on the Sentences* see J. Quinn, *The Historical Constitution of St. Bonaventure's Philosophy* (Toronto, 1973), pp. 595–601.

[149] For central texts on this see *In II Sent.*, d. 1, q. 1, a. 5 (between 1252–1256, hence ca. 1253); *Summa contra Gentiles* II, cc. 31–38 (1261 or thereafter); *De potentia dei* q. 3, aa. 14 and 17 (1265–1266); *Summa theologiae* I, 46, 1 and 2 (1266–68); Quodlibet 3, q. 14, a. 2 (Easter 1270); *De aeternitate mundi* (probably spring 1270); *Compendium theologiae* cc. 98–99 (1269–1273). See J. Weisheipl, *Friar Thomas d'Aquino* (New York, 1974), pp. 358–405 for the dating of Thomas's works. For the Latin texts and discussion of many of these see A. Antweiler, *Die Anfangslosigkeit der Welt nach Thomas von Aquin und Kant*, 2 Vols. (Trier, 1961). For English translations of these texts as well as important selections from Bonaventure and Siger of Brabant on this topic and discussion of the same see C. Vollert, L. Kendzierski, P. Byrne, *St. Thomas Aquinas, Siger of Brabant, St. Bonaventure, On the Eternity of the World* (Milwaukee, 1964). For some other recent discussions

demonstrate either the eternity of the world or its creation in time. Like all orthodox Christians of his day he accepted the temporal beginning of the world as an article of religious belief. But for him it could only be that and not a matter for philosophical demonstration. Arguments claiming to prove the noneternal character of the universe were both faulty and ill advised. Presentation of these as demonstrative by Christians runs the risk of bringing derision upon the faith on the part of unbelievers who can easily perceive the flaws in such reasoning.[150]

As regards Aristotle's own position, Aquinas attempted to give him the most favorable interpretation possible from the standpoint of religious orthodoxy. While the Stagirite had indeed offered arguments in favor of the eternal character of the universe in his *Physics, Metaphysics,* and *De caelo,* still a curious passage in his *Topics* suggested to Thomas that Aristotle may not, in fact, have regarded such argumentation as demonstrative.[151] This more benign reading of the Philosopher does not seem to have finally won the day in Thomas's mind any more than it has today among contemporary Aristotelian scholars.[152] It is also interesting to find Aquinas in one of his finest treatments of this issue (*De aeternitate mundi*) devoting almost all of his

---

of this see Van Steenberghen, *La philosophie au XIIIe siècle*, pp. 458–64 (also p. 346, n. 69 for treatment and criticism of Thomas's position); "Le mythe d'un monde éternel," *Revue philosophique de Louvain* 76 (1978), pp. 157–79; F. Kovach, "The Question of the Eternity of the World in St. Bonaventure and St. Thomas—A Critical Analysis," in *Bonaventure and Aquinas*, R. Shahan and F. Kovach, ed. (Norman, Oklahoma, 1976), pp. 155–86.

150 On this last point see, for instance, SCG II, c. 38; ST I, q. 46, a. 2; and especially Quodlibet 3, q. 14, a. 2.

151 See *In II Sent.*, d. 1, q. 1, a. 5 (ed. Mandonnet, Vol. 2, pp. 33–34): "Dico ergo quod ad neutram partem quaestionis sunt demonstrationes, sed probabiles vel sophisticae rationes ad utrumque. Et hoc significant verba Philosophi dicentis, I *Top.*, cap. vii, quod sunt quaedam problemata de quibus rationem non habemus, ut utrum mundus sit aeternus; unde hoc ipse demonstrare nunquam intendit. . . ." For Aristotle see *Topics* I, c. 11 (104b 12–17). Thomas's apparent source for this reading was Moses Maimonides. See his *Guide* . . . , II, c. 15, p. 292; and c. 16, fol. 48v for the Latin. Within the same immediate context Thomas also explicitly cites an example taken from the *Guide*. For the English translation see c. 17, p. 295; for the Latin, c. 18, fol. 49r. On this text in Aristotle and its interpretation by Maimonides see Behler, *Die Ewigkeit der Welt*, pp. 54–55, 260–61. For later appeal to this same text from the *Topics* see *Summa theologiae* I, q. 46, a. 1. On Aristotle also see R. Macken, "La temporalité radicale de la créature . . . ," pp. 211–12 and his reference in notes 3 and 4 to Prezioso and Pépin.

152 See *In VIII Phys.*, lect. 2. (P.M. Maggiòlo, ed. [Turin-Rome, 1954]). Note in particular n. 986. See also *In XII Met.*, lect. 5, especially n. 2496. Thomas himself does not regard these arguments as demonstrative but only as probable. See n. 2497. Weisheipl places the Commentary on the *Physics* in 1269–70 and that on the *Metaphysics* in 1269–72; see *op. cit.*, pp. 375, 379.

attention to those Christians who claimed that they could demonstrate the noneternity of the world rather than to those who had argued in favor of its eternal character. It has recently been suggested that in this writing Thomas had in mind as his special target the Neo-Augustinian, John Peckham.[153] And shortly after this exchange in early 1270, articles on the eternity of the world would be included among those condemned by Stephen Tempier, Bishop of Paris, in December of that same year.[154]

Eternity of the world was also a favorite topic for discussion by some of the best known Masters of the Arts faculty during this period, namely, Siger of Brabant and Boethius of Dacia. Siger treated of this in two works prior to 1270, in his *Quaestio utrum haec sit vera: homo est animal, nullo homine existente,* and in his *Quaestiones in tertium de anima*. In the first of these he affirms the eternity of the human species without any hesitation, while in the second he presents as the more probable opinion Aristotle's assertion of the eternity of the unique intellect for all mankind.[155] After the 1270 Condemnation Siger treats of this problem with greater circumspection, presumably because he was now only too well aware that eternity of the universe could not be reconciled with Christian religious belief. Thus in his *De aeternitate mundi,* while he is obviously impressed by the argumentation for the eternity of the human species, he constantly qualifies his presentation of the same by referring to it as the view of the philosophers or of Aristotle. In one passage he explicitly states that he is not attempting to prove the eternity of the human species, but to reveal the weakness of argumentation for the opposite.[156] And

---

[153] See I. Brady, "John Pecham and the Background of Aquinas's *De Aeternitate Mundi*," in *St. Thomas Aquinas 1274–1974. Commemorative Studies* (Toronto, 1974), Vol. 2, pp. 141–78, including evidence for this conclusion and the edition of two questions by Peckham on the eternity of the world.

[154] *Chartularium* I, pp. 486–87. See propositions 5 ("Quod mundus est eternus") and 6 ("Quod nunquam fuit primus homo"). On the Condemnation of 1270 see our "The Condemnations . . . ," pp. 179–83; Van Steenberghen, *La philosophie au XIIIe siècle*, pp. 472–74; *Maître Siger . . .* , pp. 74–79.

[155] For the first see *Siger de Brabant. Écrits de logique, de morale et de physique*, B. Bazán, ed. (Louvain-Paris, 1974), pp. 57–59; for the second see *Siger de Brabant. Quaestiones in tertium de anima, De anima intellectiva, De aeternitate mundi*, B. Bazán, ed. (Louvain-Paris, 1972), qq. 2–5, pp. 4–17. On the dating of the first work see Bazán's *Introduction* to the same, pp. 25 and 39, and Van Steenberghen, *Maître Siger . . .* , pp. 50–51. For the dating of the second see Bazán's *Introduction* to his edition of the same, p. 74*, and Van Steenberghen, *Maître Siger . . .* , pp. 51–52.

[156] For the most recent critical edition of this see B. Bazán, *Siger de Brabant . . . ,* (1972), pp. 113–36. For such qualifications see p. 116:36–37; p. 117:43, 47–48; p. 118:10–13; p. 119:29–32, 44–46; p. 131:66–70; p. 132:85–86. It is interesting to observe that many of these qualifying expressions are missing from ms.

in many other works dating after 1270, one finds this same curious combination of sympathetic presentation of argumentation for the eternity thesis joined with Siger's careful refusal to espouse it as his own doctrine. On more than one occasion he also explicitly adverts to the fact that the eternity thesis cannot be reconciled with the faith.[157]

Another important although only recently discovered and edited treatment of this same theme is contained in Boethius of Dacia's *De aeternitate mundi.*[158] Herein Siger's colleague in the Arts Faculty presents a carefully nuanced position and avoids contradicting Christian religious belief not only by distinguishing between faith and reason but also by distinguishing within the field of reason itself between the different methodologies of natural philosophy, mathematics, and metaphysics. He contends that neither the natural philosopher nor the mathematician nor the metaphysician can demonstrate that the world began to be.[159] His discussion of the role of the natural philosopher is especially interesting, since Boethius insists that the student of any science must operate in accord with the principles of that science. But nature itself is the principle of natural things. And in studying nature one can account for a new motion only by appealing to another and preceding motion that serves as its cause. Hence the natural philosopher *qua* natural philosopher cannot affirm an absolute temporal beginning for motion or for the universe

---

B, that is to say, from *Paris: Bibl. Nat. lat. 16.297*, Godfrey's scholarly notebook. On the relative value of this ms. for establishing the text of Siger's *De aeternitate mundi* see Bazán, *op. cit.*, pp. 49* – 56*. Finally, see p. 120:58 – 60: "Non conamur autem hic oppositum conclusionis ad quam arguunt ostendere, sed solum suae rationis defectum, qui apparet ex praedictis" (also missing from B).

[157] For this see Van Steenberghen, *Maître Siger . . .*, pp. 310 – 11, and the many references given there.

[158] On Boethius see Van Steenberghen, *La philosophie au XIIIe siècle*, pp. 402 – 12. On his writings see G. Sajó, *Un Traité récemment découvert de Boèce de Dacie De mundi aeternitate* (Budapest, 1954), pp. 20 – 25; Sajó, "Boetius de Dacia und seine philosophische Bedeutung," in *Die Metaphysik im Mittelalter, Miscellanea Mediaevalia*, 2 [1963], pp. 454 – 63; J. Pinborg, "Zur Philosophie des Boethius de Dacia. Ein Überblick," *Studia Mediewistyczne* 15 (1974), pp. 165 – 85 (see pp. 182 – 85 for further bibliography).

[159] Here we will follow Sajó's 2nd edition: *Boetii de Dacia. Tractatus de aeternitate mundi* (Berlin, 1964). See pp. 43:303; 48:451 – 50:485 (mathematics); 50:486 – 501 (metaphysics). For his citation of the text from the *Topics* to support his claim that neither side can be definitively established by reason see p. 51:511 – 13. On the dating of this work see Sajó, *Un traité . . .*, pp. 50 – 53; and R. Hissette, "Boèce de Dacie et les Questions . . . ," *Recherches de Théologie ancienne et médiévale* 39 (1972), pp. 71 – 81, especially p. 73, n. 7. The work falls between 1270 and 1277 and probably after April 1272.

or for mankind. Nor can he ever consider the doctrine of creation, since his principles do not extend to this.[160]

One might counter that the natural philosopher should not deny truths to which his principles do not extend if such truths rest on a higher authority, revelation. It is in replying to this objection that Boethius offers his most interesting precision. To the extent that such truths are contrary to the principles of natural philosophy, the natural philosopher *qua* natural philosopher should deny them. And such applies to the Christian's belief that the world began to be. Taken in the absolute sense, then, the natural philosopher's conclusion that the world did not begin to be is false. But this contention does follow from the principles of his science and in denying that this is possible in terms of natural causes and principles he speaks the truth. Still the Christian believer asserts the absolute truth in affirming that the world began to be, and this because he accepts a power and authority superior to nature.[161] Were Boethius to state that both contentions are true without qualification, then he would have defended the double-truth theory. But this he has carefully avoided. The noneternity of the world is to be accepted as a matter of religious belief, but not as something that can be demonstrated philosophically.[162]

Enough evidence has now been marshalled to show that during Godfrey's student days at the University of Paris eternity of the world was a much discussed topic. Hence one is not too surprised to find in Godfrey's personal library copies of Thomas's *De aeternitate mundi* as well as of the treatises by Siger and Boethius which bear that same title and to which reference has been made above.[163] Nor is one surprised to find Henry of Ghent addressing

---

[160] *Op. cit.*, pp. 43:306–46:384.

[161] *Op. cit.*, pp. 46:385–48:450. See in particular: "Unde conclusio in qua naturalis dicit mundum et primum motum non esse novum, accepta absolute, falsa est, sed si referatur in rationes et principia ex quibus ipse eam concludit, ex illis sequitur" (pp. 47:430–48:433). Also: "Sic verum dicit christianus, dicens mundum et motum primum esse novum, et primum hominem fuisse . . . verum etiam dicit naturalis qui dicit hoc non esse possibile ex causis et principiis naturalibus" (p. 48:435–41).

[162] After having established to his own satisfaction that neither the natural philosopher nor the mathematician nor the metaphysician can prove that the world began to be, Boethius also comments that by no human argumentation can it be shown (definitively, we presume) that the world is eternal. For he who would demonstrate such a conclusion would have to demonstrate something that depends solely on divine choice (p. 51:509–10). On the absence of a double-truth theory in this work see in addition to the references cited by the scholars listed above in n. 158 our "The Condemnations of 1270 and 1277 . . . ," pp. 196–97 and the references given there in n. 64.

[163] Both Thomas's *De aeternitate mundi* and that of Siger are contained in God-

himself to this same question in his Quodlibet 1 of 1276 and defending therein the more conservative position. According to Henry one can prove that the world could not have been created from eternity.[164] Finally, it should be noted that a number of the articles condemned in 1277 touch on the eternity of the world. At least two of these had endorsed the probative character of Aristotle's argumentation for the same.[165]

With this background in mind we shall now turn to Godfrey's own discussion of this problem. As we have seen, in refuting Henry's metaphysics of creative causality in Quodlibet 9, q. 2 Godfrey argues that such a theory really entails asserting the eternity of creatures by reason of their essential being (*esse essentiae*).[166] But in his much earlier Quodlibet 2, q. 3 of 1286 Godfrey had already explicitly addressed himself to this very issue, that is, the possibility that the world or any creature might have existed from

---

frey's student notebook. See *Paris: Bibl. Nat. lat. 16.297*, fol. 68ra – 69rb (Thomas); fol. 78vb – 80va (Siger). On this see Glorieux, "Un recueil scolaire . . . ," pp. 38, 48ff., and J. Duin, *La doctrine de la providence* . . . , pp. 133 – 34. An abbreviated version of Boethius's *De aeternitate mundi* is included in another manuscript belonging to Godfrey's library, *Paris: Bibl. Nat. lat. 15.819*, fol. 300v – 301r. For an edition of this see Sajó, *Boetii de Dacia. Tractatus* . . . , pp. 65 – 70. For discussion of this ms. see *op. cit.*, pp. 6 – 7, 19 – 27; Duin, "La bibliothèque philosophique de Godefroid de Fontaines . . . ," pp. 29 – 31. Both Sajó and Duin regard this as Godfrey's autograph. For an interesting comparison between this *abbreviatio* by Godfrey and the fuller and critically edited text of Boethius's treatise, see P. Wilpert, "Ein Compendium des 13. Jahrhunderts (Gottfried von Fontaines als Abbreviator)," *Mittellatèinisches Jahrbuch* 2 (1965), pp. 165 – 80.

[164] See Quodlibet 1, qq. 7 – 8, where Henry considers together these two questions: "Utrum creatura potuit esse ab aeterno. . . . Utrum repugnat creaturae fuisse ab aeterno." See T. 1, fol. 4r – 6r. For a critical edition of this see R. Macken, "De radicale Tijdelijkheid van het Schepsel volgens Hendrik van Gent," *Tijdschrift voor Filosofie* 31 (1969), pp. 546 – 70, as well as his "La temporalité radicale de la créature selon Henri de Gand," pp. 257 – 72. See the latter for a detailed study of the same, pp. 221 – 56.

[165] For the text of the 1277 prohibitions see Denifle-Chatelain, *Chartularium* . . . , I, pp. 543 – 61; Mandonnet, *Siger de Brabant* . . . , Vol. II, pp. 175 – 91. For some propositions touching on the eternity of the world see 4 – 87, 87 – 85, 89 – 89, 91 – 80, 98 – 84, 99 – 83, 101 – 91, 107 – 112, 202 – 111, 205 – 88 (with the *Chartularium* numbering listed first). See in particular prop. 89 – 89: "Quod impossibile est solvere rationes philosophi de eternitate mundi, nisi dicamus, quod voluntas primi implicat incompossibilia;" and prop. 91 – 80: "Quod ratio Philosophi demonstrans motum celi esse eternum non est sophistica; et mirum, quod homines profundi hoc non vident." On the 1277 Condemnation and the eternity of the world see R. Hissette, *Enquête sur les 219 articles condamnés* . . . , pp. 147 – 60.

[166] See in this chapter, pp. 142 – 43.

eternity.[167]

In beginning his reply Godfrey observes that if admission of the possibility of an eternally created universe involves intrinsic contradiction, this can only be either because God must be prior in duration to any creature or because it is essential to creatures to receive being after nonbeing.[168] Godfrey then connects this discussion with the controversy concerning the essence-existence relationship in creatures. According to his own position, of course, essence and existence are not really distinct. Given this, he can easily admit the Christian position according to which God is in fact prior in duration to all creatures. Thus he holds that creatures enjoy neither essential nor existential being from eternity in actuality, granted that they do so in potency. Godfrey observes that it does not follow, as some would have it, that one must affirm real distinction of essence and existence in creatures in order to allow for the fact that God is prior to them in duration.[169] Perhaps Godfrey has Giles of Rome in mind, since he had insisted that one must defend the real distinction in order to safeguard the possibility of creation in any true sense.[170] In any event, Godfrey concludes that if one does defend real distinction between essence and existence and if one then concedes that a creature can be eternal in terms of its essential being, one should also admit the same with respect to its actual existence.[171] Apparently his purpose in this digression is twofold: to show first, that his theory of real identity of essence and existence can be reconciled with Christian belief that the world was created in time and, secondly, that to the degree that one allows for the eternal being of creatures in terms of their essential being, one should do the same with respect to their actual existence.

Godfrey now turns his attention to the second of the two proposed ways in which defense of the possible eternity of the world might involve contradiction. Perhaps it is essential to creatures to receive being after nonbeing.[172] Here he seems to have in mind one of Henry of Ghent's arguments as found in the latter's Quodlibet 1, qq. 7–8. There Henry had contended that while the essence (*quod quid est rei*) of a creature when taken in the absolute sense abstracts from the here and now, its actual existence does not always so

---

[167] "Utrum mundus sive aliqua creatura potuit esse vel existere ab aeterno" (PB 2.68).

[168] PB 2.69. For the same procedure see Thomas, *De aeternitate mundi*, in *Opuscula philosophica*, R. Spiazzi, ed. (Turin-Rome, 1954), n. 298, p. 106.

[169] PB 2.69–70.

[170] See Ch. II, n. 59.

[171] PB 2.70.

[172] PB 2.71–72.

abstract. Thus while one cannot reason from one's understanding of the essential being of a creature such as a lunar eclipse to its here-and-now existence, one can reason from one's understanding of its actual existence to its existence here and now and hence one may conclude that it can enjoy actual existence only after having previously not existed. Godfrey counters that to the extent that one may abstract such a quiddity (e.g., an eclipse) from the here and now in terms of its essential being, one may also do so in terms of its existential being. Whatever is true of one is true of the other. If such a creature may enjoy essential being without presupposing its previous nonbeing, then it may enjoy existential being without having been previously nonexistent. In other words, Godfrey taxes Henry with inconsistency because he denies the possibility of an eternal world and still allows for the eternity of things in terms of their essential being.[173]

As to the claim that a creature can receive being only after nonbeing, Godfrey introduces a distinction. It is not necessary for a creature to have being *after* nonbeing when the term "after" is taken in the temporal sense. It need only have being *from* nothing (*ex nihilo*), which is to say, not from something. A creature may be said to have being "after" nonbeing in the order of nature, to be sure, but this simply means that if it were solely dependent upon itself, it would not enjoy being at all. It does so only insofar as it receives being from God, its cause. In this sense one may say that nonbeing is more proper to a creature than is being. Hence if one concedes that a creature may enjoy being from eternity, one will still say that it has being "after" nonbeing in the order of nature, but not in the order of time. Nor would admission of this possibility imply that such a thing enjoyed being and nonbeing at the same time and in the same respect. Since its nature is such that it would be nothing at all if it did not receive being from its cause, a creature existing here and now may be said to have being from another and nonbeing of itself. In sum, then, Godfrey does not find this objection against the possible eternity of the universe particularly difficult.[174]

But what of the first alleged point of contradiction? Perhaps eternal creation

---

[173] For Henry's text see Quodlibet I, qq. 7–8, fol. 4v–5r. For the critical edition see Macken, "La temporalité de la créature . . . ," p. 263:20–30. Here Godfrey is citing Henry almost verbatim. Henry in turn is replying to an argument that he appears to have taken from Aquinas (ST I, q. 46, a. 2). According to that argument one cannot prove that creatures did not always exist because the essence of a creature (*quod quid est creaturae*) abstracts from all duration. See p. 263:12–14. For a comparison of Henry's text with that of Thomas see Macken, *op. cit.*, pp. 231–34. For Godfrey see PB 2.70–71.

[174] PB 2.71–72. Again Godfrey's reasoning is very similar to that found in Thomas's *De aeternitate mundi* (*op. cit.*, nn. 303–305, p. 107).

is impossible because God as cause must be prior in duration to any and all of his effects. Godfrey replies that if an agent acts by means of successive operation or even by an instantaneous operation that results from successive operation, then it must be prior in duration to its effect. But neither of these qualifications applies to God's creative activity. Still one might insist that there is some other reason requiring that God be prior to his effects in duration. Thus certain causes are so imperfect in themselves that they depend upon something else in order actually to produce their effects. Others produce their effects only through motion. And others do not produce their entire effects, but require some passive subject upon which to operate. None of these restrictions applies to God, however, since his power is unlimited, his causal activity is neither successive nor divisible, and in creating he produces the total being of his effects.[175] Hence God need not precede his effects in duration. Godfrey also offers another argument in support of this same contention, one that is literally taken from Thomas's *De aeternitate mundi*. In the case of instantaneous action the beginning and the end are simultaneous and, in fact, one and the same. Hence in whatever instant the agent produces its effect, the *terminus* of that activity may also be realized. But the *terminus* of the causing activity is simultaneously given with the existence of the effect. In sum, then, there is no contradiction involved in holding that such a cause need not be prior in duration to its effect.[176]

Godfrey also observes that the fact that God freely creates in no way implies that he must be temporally prior to his effects. If he were compelled to create by natural necessity, the world would be both eternally and necessarily produced. But divine freedom does not detract from divine power. Hence the fact that he is free should not diminish his capacity to produce an effect from eternity.[177]

Godfrey concludes, therefore, that there is no intrinsic contradiction involved in suggesting that a creature that is made from nothing could nonetheless eternally receive its being from God. As an instantaneously acting cause, God need not be temporally prior to his effects. And granted that creatures are produced *from* nothing, this need not imply that they are produced *after* nothing when "after" is taken in the sense of duration. Godfrey concludes the body of this question by two appeals to authority, similar to appeals also present in Thomas's *De aeternitate mundi*. If the notion of eternal creation is self-contradictory, one must surely marvel at Augustine's

[175] PB 2.72–73. Compare with Thomas, *op. cit.*, nn. 300–301, p.106.

[176] See Godfrey PB 2.73 (middle paragraph) and Thomas, *op. cit.*, n. 299, p. 106.

[177] PB 2.73–74. Here Godfrey has expanded upon a point found in Thomas, *op. cit.*, n. 302, p. 106.

failure to appeal to the same in his effort to show that the world is not eternal in the *City of God*. And one must also marvel at the philosophers' failure to have detected this contradiction.[178]

Godfrey now replies to some further objections to the possibility of eternal creation, objections which appear to have been raised at the beginning of this quodlibetal debate. According to the first of these, if the world could possibly have existed from eternity, then in that eventuality it would never have been capable of not existing. Just as a thing necessarily is when it is and just as that which was necessarily was when it was, so too that which always was necessarily always was. Or as others formulate this objection, God would have been unable not to produce an eternally existing world since he could not fail to produce it in the same instant that he produced it. And there would have never been an instant in which he was not producing it.[179]

Godfrey counters that God was capable from all eternity either of producing or not producing the world. And if the world had been produced from eternity, God would have always been free to produce or not to produce it. The objection trades upon a certain ambiguity in the term "necessary," and Godfrey does not fail to notice this. He resolves this by distinguishing between absolute necessity and hypothetical necessity (*ex suppositione*). Given the supposition that God has determined to create the world in time, one may say that in light of that divine decision the world had to be created in time. But this does not imply that its creation is absolutely necessary, since it is necessary only under the supposition that God has so willed. Likewise, if the world had existed from eternity, this could only be because God had freely so willed. Given that divine choice or under that supposition, one could say that the world had necessarily existed from eternity, not by absolute necessity, however, but only by hypothetical necessity (*ex suppositione*). Thus one may say of something that exists now that, under the supposition that it exists, it necessarily exists. Just as this does not entail the absolute necessity of that existing thing, neither would eternal existence of the world entail its absolute necessity from eternity.[180]

A second objection would reject the possibility of an eternally created world on the grounds that the creature would then be equal to the creator in

---

[178] PB 2.75–76. Compare with Thomas, *op. cit.*, pp. 108–09, nn. 306–07. For Augustine see *De Civitate Dei* X, c. 31 (CCSL 47.308–09); XII, cc. 15–16 (CCSL 48.369–72).

[179] For this objection see PB 2.68. For a similar but more fully developed argument in Henry see Macken, *op. cit.*, pp. 267:28–268:34. For Macken's commentary on this see pp. 239–41.

[180] PB 2.76–77.

terms of duration. Thus both the creator and the creature would be eternal and God's eternity would not exceed or encompass the duration of the creature. To this it may be replied that only God's duration is eternity in the strict sense, meaning thereby the kind of duration that is simultaneous, total, and supremely simple and undivided. The duration of the world would be "eternal" only in that it lacked beginning and end, not in that it was simultaneous, total, and indivisible. Its duration would in fact still be successive. Thus the divine eternity would surpass it in simplicity and perfection and would encompass the successive parts of this "eternal" time in one and the same simple fashion.[181]

As Godfrey here presents the final objection, the possibility of an eternal world would carry with it the possibility of an actually infinite body. If the world were eternal, an infinity of days would have preceded the present one and God could have created an object such as a stone every day and kept each of them in existence. This would result in an actual infinity of stones here and now. Granted that each would be finite in quantity, God could now combine them so as to form one infinite body. But since an actually infinite body must be rejected as an impossibility, it must also be impossible for there to be an infinity of finite bodies that exist simultaneously. Because admission of the possibility of an eternally created world leads to such impossible consequences, this possibility itself must be rejected.[182]

Godfrey prefaces his reply with the observation that such arguments based on an infinity of stones or of revolutions of the sun, etc., do not of themselves disprove the possibility of an eternally created universe. Nonetheless, he is obviously troubled by this kind of objection. Granted that God could make one stone after another to infinity and granted that whatever he can bring into being in successive fashion he can also produce at one and the same time, Godfrey also concedes that there could never be an actual infinity of stones. If God can divide the continuum to infinity, it can never come to pass that the continuum has actually been so divided as to render further division impossible, at least in principle. Godfrey also suggests that one need not restrict this objection to stones and pieces of wood, etc., since one can make

---

[181] This objection does not appear at the beginning of Godfrey's question. Since the text that we have is a *reportatio*, it is possible that the objection in question was omitted, especially so since Godfrey appears to supply this answer for the respondent: "ut probabiliter dicebat respondens." On the other hand, Thomas touches on a similar objection near the end of his *De aeternitate mundi* and this could also account for Godfrey's development of it here. For Godfrey see PB 2.77–78. For Thomas, *op. cit.*, n. 309, p. 108.

[182] For the objection see PB 2.68–69.

the same point more forcefully by discussing human souls, had the world been created from eternity.[183]

Central to Godfrey's discussion is a distinction between the infinite in complete actuality, on the one hand, and the infinite in act in only a qualified sense, on the other. The second kind of infinite in act is still in potency in some sense. He acknowledges that the first kind of actual infinite is indeed an impossibility. Here he appears to take the term "infinite" in the Aristotelian sense, as signifying that beyond which something more is always to be admitted. Given this understanding of the infinite, one can see why Godfrey rejects the actual infinite in the first sense, that is to say, a completely actualized infinity of stones or trees or what have you. When the infinite is taken in the second or qualified sense, further addition or division will always be possible. Since purely successive beings (those that come to be and pass away while new ones come into being) do not survive indefinitely, they can never unite to constitute an infinite totality in actuality. For instance, an infinitely extended or beginningless series of dogs begotten by other dogs from eternity would never result in a completely actualized infinity of dogs here and now. At any given moment only a finite number would exist. Hence Godfrey allows for the possibility of an infinite succession of such entities, nonpermanent ones, both as regards the past and as regards the future.[184]

But he is much more concerned about allowing for the possibility of an infinity of permanent beings. Even here he concedes that there might be such extending into the future. Thus if the continuum were divided continuously in the future, further division would always be possible, at least in theory. One would never arrive at a completely actualized infinity. Godfrey also allows for the possibility that God might make one stone today and another tomorrow, *ad infinitum*. Since more stones could always be added, this will never result in an actual infinite. But why not allow for the same with respect to the past? Thus God would have made one stone yesterday and another the day before, extending into a beginningless past. Although initially sympa-

---

[183] PB 2.78.

[184] *Ibid*. For this see Q 10, q. 2, where he comments: ". . . quod infinitum est ens in potentia, sic scilicet quod infinitum non potest esse in actu completo et determinato . . . sed in actu semper potentiae permixto et ut secundum successionem et una pars eius sit post alteram. . . ." There he refers to Aristotle's definition: ". . . infinitum est cuius semper est aliquid extra accipere quia est modo praedicto in potentia" (PB 4.302). For Aristotle see *Physics* III, c. 6, especially 207a 1ff. Godfrey also observes that if one asserts that a whole is infinite in such a way that nothing further remains to be reduced to act, one will then have accepted another and erroneous definition of the infinite as that outside of which there is nothing ("extra quod nihil est"). Again he cites Aristotle, *loc. cit.*

thetic to this view, Godfrey ends by rejecting it. An infinite series of permanent beings extending into the future will never result in a completely actualized infinity of things. But an infinite series of permanent entities extending into the past will result in an actualized infinity of such beings here and now, and this because of their permanent nature. And this is to be rejected, in Godfrey's opinion, because it is repugnant to the definition of the infinite.[185]

Finally, Godfrey turns to the case of man. An eternal world peopled by human beings created successively in an infinitely extended past would, it would seem, result in an actualized infinite multitude of souls here and now, and this because of their immortality. Thomas Aquinas had repeatedly grappled with this objection against the possibility of an eternal world. Thus in his *De aeternitate mundi* he acknowledges that this is a serious objection, but replies by suggesting that the world could have been eternal without having been inhabited by man from eternity. Then there would be no resulting actual infinity of souls. He also remarks that it has not yet been demonstrated that God could not produce an actual infinity (of souls, presumably), a point on which he had wavered during his career.[186] Godfrey is apparently convinced not only here in Quodlibet 2 but later in Quodlibet 10 that one must reject the possibility of an actual infinity whether of species or of individuals within species and whether of material or of immaterial beings. Given this, Thomas's final suggested escape is not open to him.[187]

---

[185] PB 2.78–79.

[186] See Thomas's *De aeternitate mundi*, near the end, where he comments: "Et praeterea adhuc non est demonstratum, quod Deus non possit facere ut sint infinita actu" (*op. cit.*, n. 310, p. 108). Thomas had long recognized the difficulty of this objection. See *In II Sent.*, d. 1, q. 1, a. 5, ad 6; also SCG II, c. 38, where he observes that according to some it is not unfitting for there to be an infinite multitude when the things in question are not ordered to one another. See SCG II, c. 81, for the observation that admission of an actual infinity of souls is not contrary to Aristotle's principles, although he never pronounced on this point. In ST I, q. 46, a. 2, ad 8, he refers to Algazel's view that an infinity of souls in act is possible, but notes that he himself has already rejected this (see ST I, q. 7, a. 4). In both his commentaries on the *Physics* and the *Metaphysics* he presents and criticizes argumentation against the possibility of an infinite multitude that is based on the nature of number. While number is a species of discrete quantity, multitude rather pertains to the transcendental. See *In III Physic.*, lect. 8, nn. 351–52. For somewhat similar criticism of this argumentation, see *In XI Met.*, lect. 10, n. 2329. It seems clear that there was doubt in Thomas's mind as to the possibility of an actual infinite multitude of souls.

[187] See Q 10, q. 2: "Utrum Deus posset producere in actu completo infinitum quod se tenet ex parte materiae sive multitudinem aliquorum entium infinitam" (PB 4.300). See in particular p. 301 (on species); pp. 302–04 (on material individuals); pp. 305–06 (on immaterial beings).

Godfrey remarks that this objection is sufficient to indicate that the world as we now know it, that is, as peopled by men who are destined to enjoy beatitude in soul and body in the life to come, could not have been created from eternity. Still, other dispensations are possible. Thus one could allow for a world that has been populated by man from eternity by appealing to a theory of circulation or transmigration of souls from body to body. A finite number of souls would be sufficient to account for an unending series of men extending into the past, and this without resulting in an actual infinity of souls here and now. Godfrey also observes that Augustine's only reason for rejecting such a theory in Bk XI of his *City of God* appears to be his need to allow for man's reward and punishment in the life to come. But, continues Godfrey, in a purely natural dispensation wherein souls are ordered only to their natural perfection, this would not seem to be impossible. Godfrey does not quite say that such circulation would be possible, but only that it does not seem that one can decisively establish its impossibility.[188]

He also counters that this argument based on souls and stones does not prove that the world taken as such could not have been eternal in terms of some of its parts, or in terms of another order, or that another world could not have been. But since in our world man seems to be intended primarily and before lower beings, if man himself could not have been created from eternity according to the present disposition of things, one may argue with probability that this world itself could not have been so created in terms of God's ordained power. In other words, because man as we know him is ordered to a supernatural end, the impossibility of an actualized infinity of souls seems to show that he could not have been made from eternity. Hence, concedes Godfrey, it is probable that this world wherein man is primarily intended could not have been so created. But, he repeats, this does not prove that no creature could have existed from eternity.[189] And, we might comment, since the argument rests in large measure upon man's being ordered to a supernatural destiny, it is not purely philosophical in nature. Without positively defending the possibility of circulation of souls in another and purely natural dispensation, Godfrey has not seen fit to reject such an alternative as impossible.

Given all of this, then, Godfrey arrives at a fairly cautious conclusion. He refuses to determine that either side is necessarily true or necessarily false and impossible. He rather regards each position as only probably true or

---

[188] PB 2.79. For Augustine see *De Civitate Dei*, XI, c. 4 (CCSL 48.323–25). For simple reference to circulation of souls as a view held by some, see Thomas SCG II, c. 38; ST I, q. 46, a. 2, ad 8.

[189] PB 2.80.

probably false. Hence either position may be defended as a matter of opinion but not as something demonstrable, and neither is to be condemned as erroneous. In sum, then, one may defend as probable both the position according to which the world could have existed from eternity and that according to which it could not have done so. Neither can be demonstrated.[190]

In drawing this cautious conclusion, Godfrey clearly differs from the more conservative position defended by Masters such as Bonaventure, John Peckham, and Henry of Ghent. According to them, one can demonstrate the impossibility of an eternally created universe. At the same time he agrees with Masters such as Aquinas, Siger, and Boethius of Dacia in maintaining that one cannot demonstrate the impossibility of eternal creation. But in his refusal to claim to have demonstrated the possibility of an eternally created universe, he may also have been influenced by certain precisions to which Giles of Rome refers in his *Commentary* on Bk II of the *Sentences*. As Hocedez has suggested, these precisions may have resulted from Giles's effort to meet certain conditions laid down for his readmission to the Theology faculty at Paris in 1285.[191]

Giles distinguishes three positions that might be defended with respect to the possibility of an eternal world: (1) one might maintain that the world could have existed from eternity; (2) one might only claim that one cannot demonstrate the impossibility of an eternally existing world; (3) or one might merely state that the impossibility of an eternal world has not yet been demonstrated. Giles here insists that he does not defend the first and strongest proposition, even though some of his earlier remarks might have given that impression. That is to say, he does not claim that an eternal world is possible. Nor does he even defend the second and weaker proposition, according to which the impossibility of an eternal world cannot be demonstrated. He decides for the third and weakest position, the claim that an eternal world has not yet been shown to be impossible.[192]

As we have now seen, according to Godfrey neither the possibility nor the impossibility of an eternal world can be demonstrated. Therefore he does not

---

[190] "Et ideo neutram partem determinando tanquam verum necessarium, neutram etiam reprobando tanquam falsum impossibile sed tanquam probabile sive probabiliter verum vel falsum, potest dici quod utraque pars per modum opinabilis sive etiam credibilis, *non demonstrabilis*, potest sustineri, et neutra erronea" (PB 2.80). (Italics mine.) It will be recalled that the precise question being examined was this: whether the world or any creature could be or exist from eternity (PB 2.68).

[191] E. Hocedez, "La condamnation de Gilles de Rome," *Recherches de Théologie ancienne et médiévale* 4 (1932), pp. 42–46. Also see Macken, "La temporalité de la créature . . . ," pp. 243–47.

[192] For Giles see *In Secundum Librum Sententiarum*, d. 1, p. 1, q. 4, a. 2 (Venice, 1581), pp. 57, and 70. For the citation of the latter passage and commentary see both Hocedez, *op. cit.*, p. 45, and Macken, *op. cit.*, 244. Hocedez concludes that Giles

defend the first and strongest claim. He does defend the third and weakest statement, to be sure, but also seems to defend the second proposition, that is, the claim that an eternal world cannot be shown to be an impossibility. Hence, while Godfrey does take a bolder position than does Giles by defending the second proposition, he is still proceeding very carefully in his discussion in Quodlibet 2, that is to say, in the spring of 1286. If Giles's alleged defense of the possibility of an eternal world had indeed been partially responsible for his "exile" from the theology faculty in 1278 and if clarification of this point was required for his readmission thereto in 1285, one can appreciate why Godfrey would have treated it with such circumspection in his discussion of Easter 1286. This is not to deny, of course, that difficulties following from his rejection of the possibility of an actualized infinite multiplicity of human souls also weighed heavily upon him in his refusal to defend the possibility of an eternal universe.[193]

---

had in fact been condemned for having defended the possibility of eternal creation (see position 1), along with a number of other propositions.

[193] It would be interesting to direct these same three propositions to Thomas Aquinas in order to determine his reaction to each. Macken suggests that Thomas did not defend the first and strongest proposition, according to which the world could have existed from eternity (*op. cit.*, p. 256). This bears further investigation, but there is one passage from his *De aeternitate mundi* which, according to some readings, seems to indicate the opposite: "Videndum est ergo utrum in his duobus repugnantia sit intellectuum, quod aliquid sit creatum a Deo et tamen semper fuerit. Et quidquid de hoc verum sit, non est haereticum dicere quod hoc possit fieri a Deo ut aliquid creatum a Deo semper fuerit. Tamen credo quod, si esset repugnantia intellectuum, falsum esset. *Si autem non est repugnantia intellectuum, non solum non est falsum sed etiam possibile; aliter esset erroneum, si aliter dicatur.*" See *Opuscula omnia*, J. Perrier, ed. (Paris, 1949), pp. 54–55. Since Thomas does go on to establish the lack of incompatibility between saying that something could be created by God and have always existed, here he does appear to defend the possibility of an eternally created world. But in the Spiazzi edition the text italicized above reads differently: "Si autem non est repugnantia intellectuum, non solum non est falsum, sed etiam est impossibile aliter esse, et erroneum, si aliter dicatur" (n. 297, p. 106). As the editors of the recently published Leonine critical edition indicate, the manuscript tradition for this passage is troubled. They propose the following reading: "si autem non est repugnantia intellectuum, non solum non est falsum sed etiam [non est] impossibile: aliter esset erroneum, si aliter dicatur" (with the *non est* to be inserted mentally as indicated). This reading is that found in Godfrey's student notebook (to which they assign a privileged position in the manuscript tradition), and also implies that it is not impossible for something to be made by God and always to have existed, and hence, it would seem, that an eternal world is possible. See *Sancti Thomae de Aquino opera omnia* . . . , T. 43 (Rome, 1976), pp. 79–80 for discussion of this, for the variants in the manuscript tradition, and for the preferred text (p. 79), and p. 86, for the text again. For more on this see Wippel, "Did Thomas Aquinas Defend the Possibility of an Eternally Created World? (The *De aeternitate mundi* Revisited)," forthcoming in the *Journal of the History of Philosophy*.

Part II

The Metaphysics of Substance and Accident

Chapter IV.

Relationship Between Substance and Accident

Having now completed our consideration of Godfrey's metaphysics of uncreated being and of the procession of creation from God, we are in position to return to his metaphysical description of finite reality, this time in terms of his theory of substance and accident. Here again we shall find him frequently having recourse to his theory of act and potency. With this in mind we shall divide the present chapter into the following parts: A. Preliminary Definitions; B. Substance as Cause of Accidents; C. Created Substance and Immediate Operation; D. The Relationship between the Soul and its Powers.

A. PRELIMINARY DEFINITIONS

In his first Quodlibet of 1285 Godfrey already gives some indications of his understanding of substance. There, while explicitly addressing himself to the question whether it can belong to an accident in the natural course of events to exist apart from any subject,[1] he remarks that being is divided primarily and directly into substance and accident. He identifies substance as being that exists without qualification, and accident as being to which it belongs to be attributed to something else. Given this, he immediately adds

[1] "Utrum alicui accidenti conveniat per naturam habere esse sine subiecto" (PB 2.43).

that accident is to be described as being only insofar as it is a disposition of substance, and hence it is not so much being (*ens*) as "of being" (*entis*).[2] In support he cites Aristotle's *Metaphysics* and observes that for something to be a substance is for it to have a separate entity to which it belongs to exist in itself and not in something else.[3] Not surprisingly, then, he concludes that for anyone to suggest that in the natural order an accident could be distinct from substance and yet not inhere in another as in a subject would be to make of it both a substance and an accident at one and the same time. With all due allowance for divine intervention as in the case of the Eucharist, he emphatically rejects any suggestion that in the natural order an accident can exist apart from its subject.[4]

In reading Aristotle's description of the manifold ways in which being may be predicated according to *Metaphysics* IV, c. 2, one might wonder whether secondary instances of being such as accidents enjoy any reality in themselves. Godfrey is well aware of this difficulty, as is indicated by certain remarks in his final Quodlibet 15. As we have already noted in Chapter I,[5] Godfrey acknowledges that accidents are referred to as being because of their relationship to and dependency upon that substance by which they are sustained or supported. Yet they still possess being in some way in the formal and intrinsic sense, granted that they do so only in dependent and diminished fashion.[6] And in Quodlibet 7, q. 5 he remarks that it does not belong to accidents to subsist in themselves but to inhere in a subject.˙ But he also suggests that a substance itself may be said to participate in its accidental perfections. In other words, by reason of its union with accidents a substance shares in these accidental perfections without exhausting them. Hence Godfrey's usage of the term "participate" to describe this, a usage that one already finds in Thomas Aquinas.[7]

---

[2] ". . . cum ens primo et per se dividatur in ens secundum rationem essendi absolutam dictum ut substantia, et in ens secundum rationem essendi ad aliud attributum ut accidens, quod est non ens, nisi quia entis quod est substantia dispositio" (PB 2.43).

[3] ". . . secundum Philosophum septimo Metaphysicae, ita quod habere entitatem separatam et rationem essendi non in subiecto est habere rationem substantiae . . ." (PB 2.43). For Aristotle see *Metaphysics* VII, c. 1 (1028a 18–20; 30–31; 33–34).

[4] PB 2.43–44. He also refers to Aristotle's description in the *Categories*. See there c. 2 (la 20–25); c. 4 (lb 25–26).

[5] See Ch. I, pp. 22–23.

[6] See PB 14.20

[7] ". . . quia etiam accidens dicit naturam sive formam non in se natam subsistere, sed in eo et ex eo cuius est perfectio et quod natum est illud participare ex illa unione consequitur subsistentiam substantiae et suam etiam existentiam sive entitatem quam

It is clear, then, that Godfrey accepts the usual Aristotelian division of being into substance and the other predicaments and that he regards substance as primary in the ontological order. He also at times refers to the other categories as nine in number, thereby implying his acceptance of the traditional division of being into ten supreme genera.[8] But on at least one occasion he remarks that it is difficult to determine the precise number of predicaments.[9] Perhaps it is for this reason that he does not attempt any deduction or derivation of the predicaments comparable to that proposed by Thomas Aquinas in his *Commentary on Metaphysics* V.[10] Much more important for our understanding of Godfrey, however, is his unequivocal acceptance of the division of being into substance and accident.

From what has already been stated it is evident that for Godfrey substance enjoys the twofold role of center of existence in itself and support or subject of accidents. Because of this second role, of course, substance may be said to be potential with reference to its accidents and the latter may be viewed as secondary perfections or actualities of substance.[11] Still, Godfrey also implies that the first role is primary and essential to substance as such, whereas the second is not. Thus in *Disputed Question* 12 he observes that it does not pertain to substance as substance to serve as the subject of accidents. Otherwise every substance would support accidents, something that is not true of God.[12] Hence one must conclude that the second role, to serve as substratum or subject of accidents, is restricted to and characteristic of created substances alone. But since our primary concern in the present chapter is

---

in se sine substantia non haberet nisi miraculose . . ." (PB 3.313). For Thomas see *In de Hebdomadibus,* 1.2 (in *Opuscula theologica,* Vol. 2, R. Spiazzi-M. Calcaterra, ed., [Turin-Rome, 1954], pp. 396–97): ". . . similiter etiam subiectum participat accidens . . ."

[8] See Q 14, q. 5 (PB 5.427): "Ens autem per se quod est ens cui convenit ex natura suae speciei esse aliquid determinatum in natura se ipso formaliter est quod per se dividitur in decem rerum genera."

[9] See Q 7, q. 7 (PB 3.349–50). See especially: "Sed, quia modus et distinctio praedicamentorum non est res multum manifesta et quia sumitur secundum quosdam modos essendi rerum secundum quos diversimode intelliguntur et significantur res et naturae diversorum praedicamentorum, haec autem magis quandam probabilitatem quam evidentem certitudinem praebent, ideo perscrutationem talium relinquendo et supponendo quod solum sunt decem genera praedicamentorum et solum unum genus substantiae, ut philosophi supposuerunt . . ." (p. 350).

[10] See *In V Met.,* lect. 9, nn. 890–92 (*ed. cit.,* pp. 238–39).

[11] See Q 7, q. 5 (PB 3.313).

[12] ". . . ita substantia ut substantia est non potest esse subiectum accidentis quia sic substantia omnis accidenti subjiceretur quod est falsum de Deo" (Wippel ed., p. 367).

with created substance, we may wonder in what sense it may be said to serve as the cause of its accidents. This question, then, leads to the next section of the present chapter.

B. SUBSTANCE AS THE CAUSE OF ACCIDENTS

Godfrey explicitly addresses himself to this issue in Quodlibet 8, q. 2. There he asks whether a subject (substance) can be an immediate cause, especially an immediate efficient cause, of its accidents.[13] And in attempting to determine whether or not the soul itself is an immediate principle of its operations in *Disputed Question* 12, he first judges it necessary to resolve this same problem.[14] In Quodlibet 8, q. 2 he observes that this question may be understood in a general way, in that one may seek to determine whether any created substance can be the immediate efficient cause of its accidents. But it may also be raised on a more particular level, in that one may ask whether the soul can be the efficient cause of its operations.[15] Given this, he first treats this matter in more general fashion both in Quodlibet 8, q. 2, and in *Disputed Question* 12. We shall follow Godfrey's procedure in presenting his views on this point and shall reserve consideration of his discussion of the soul and its operations for the following section of this chapter.

In both Quodlibet 8, q. 2 and in *Disputed Question* 12 Godfrey reduces this more general question to an even more fundamental metaphysical issue. As he puts it in the former context, to inquire whether any created substance may be the efficient cause of its accidents is really to ask whether one and the same thing can be active and passive with respect to the same thing. He accepts it as given that a subject or substance is in some way passive with respect to its own accidents.[16] To suggest that it could efficiently cause these same accidents would be to hold that it is also active with reference to them. In order to show that nothing can be active and passive at the same time and in the same respect, Godfrey refers to one of his favorite passages from Aristotle's *Metaphysics* V (and IX). According to the Stagirite an active power is a principle of change in another insofar as it is other. Godfrey cites with approval Averroes's comment that Aristotle does not describe such a power as a principle of change in itself, since nothing can act on itself.

---

[13] "Utrum subiectum possit esse immediatum principium praecipue effectivum alicuius sui accidentis" (PB 4.18).

[14] *Op. cit.*, pp. 365–66.

[15] PB 4.18.

[16] *Ibid.*

Aristotle also describes a passive power as that which receives change in itself from another insofar as it is other. Again Averroes points out that it does not receive this change from itself, since it is evident that nothing can receive from itself. Hence, observes Godfrey, the general question would appear to be resolved.[17] Presumably he means that because nothing can be

---

[17] PB 4.18–19. For Aristotle see *Metaphysics* IX, c. 1 (1046a 10–13): ἥ ἐστιν ἀρχὴ μεταβολῆς ἐν ἄλλῳ [ἢ] ᾗ ἄλλο. ἡ μὲν γὰρ τοῦ παθεῖν ἐστὶ δύναμις, ἡ ἐν αὐτῷ τῷ πάσχοντι ἀρχὴ μεταβολῆς παθητικῆς ὑπ' ἄλλου [ἢ] ᾗ ἄλλο. (brackets mine). Note that in his edition of the Greek text and in his translation of the same Ross has inserted the ἢ into the Bekker text on the authority of a number of codices. Hence his translation runs: ". . . which is an originative source of change in another thing [or in the thing itself] *qua* other. For one kind is a potency of being acted on, i.e., the originative source, in the very thing acted on, of its being passively changed by another thing [or by itself] *qua* other" (brackets mine). See W. D. Ross, *Aristotle's Metaphysics. A Revised Text with Introduction and Commentary* (Oxford, 1924), Vol. 2; and *The Works of Aristotle Translated into English*, 2nd ed. (Oxford, 1954), Vol. 8. As J. E. Royce has noted, this addition was apparently not included in the Latin translation of this passage available to Aquinas. See "St. Thomas and the Definition of Active Potency," *The New Scholasticism* 34 (1960), p. 432. For Thomas's commentary on the same see *In IX Met.*, lect. 1, *ed. cit.*, n. 1776 (where he describes active potency as: "principium transmutationis in alio inquantum est aluid") and n. 1777 (where he refers to passive potency as "principium [per] quod aliquid moveatur ab alio, inquantum est aliud"). Nor was it included in the version of Aristotle on which Averroes was commenting, if one may judge from the Latin translation of the same. See *In IX Met.*, c. 2 (Venice, 1552), Vol. 8, fol. 227ra: ". . .[Aristoteles] descripsit potentiam actionis et passionis, et dixit: et est illud, quod est principium transmutationis, etc., id est, potentia agens est illud, quod est principium transmutationis in aliud, secundum quod est aliud, non in se, cum sit manifestum quod nihil agit in seipsum. Deinde dixit: Potentia enim passionis, etc., id est et ideo potentia passiva est illud quod recipit transmutationem in se ex alio, secundum quod est aliud, cum etiam sit manifestum quod nihil patitur a seipso." It was also obviously missing from the text to which Godfrey was referring, as is clear from the following: "Secundum Philosophum enim, quinto et nono Metaphysicae, potentia activa est illud quod est principium transmutationis in aliud secundum quod aliud; Commentator: non in se, cum sit manifestum quod nihil agit in se ipsum. Et ex hoc patet quid sit potentia passiva. Unde subdit: potentia passiva est illud quod recipit transmutationem in se ex alio secundum quod est aliud; Commentator: non a se, cum sit manifestum quod nihil patitur a se ipso" (PB 4.19). The version available to Godfrey would make it much less likely that one could interpret Aristotle as allowing for action on oneself. Also see Aristotle, *Metaphysics* V, c. 12 (1019a 15–20). For other citations of these same definitions by Godfrey see Q 1, q. 7 (PB 2.19); Q 6, q. 7 (PB 3.152–53); Q 13, q. 3 (PB 5.192–93); and *Disputed Question* 12 (p. 366). For fuller discussion of Godfrey's argumentation in each of these contexts see our "Godfrey of Fontaines and the Act-Potency Axiom," *Journal of the History of Philosophy* 11 (1973), pp. 302–08.

active and passive at the same time and in the same respect, no created substance can be the active or efficient cause of its accidents. Insofar as it supports these accidents, it is their passive principle. And Godfrey's major reason for accepting Aristotle's contention that nothing can be active and passive at the same time appears to rest on his conviction that to allow for this would be to violate the theory of act and potency. It would, in fact, be equivalent to holding that something could act on itself.[18]

In this same context in Quodlibet 8, q. 2, Godfrey offers some supporting argumentation to show why something cannot be active and passive at the same time. He observes that act and potency are contraries. Hence, if something is in potency with respect to something else so as to lack it, it cannot actually possess that thing at one and the same time. And that which actually possesses a given perfection cannot be in potency to receive the same, for this would imply that it did not actually possess it.[19] One of a series of arguments offered in support of the same in *Disputed Question* 12 makes this point more forcefully. One and the same thing cannot be in act and potency at the same time (with reference to the same thing), for it would then follow that it would enjoy being and nonbeing and would be in act and not in act simultaneously. Hence it is impossible for something to communicate accidental perfection to itself, for this would entail the following contradiction. The thing in question would actually possess the perfection insofar as it actively caused it and yet would not actually possess it insofar as it received it.[20]

Godfrey also defends this position by arguing from Aristotle's theory of the four causes. According to *Physics* II the causes are so ordered to one another that the form and the intrinsic end may be numerically the same and the form and the efficient cause may fall into the same species (in cases of

[18] For a detailed examination of Godfrey's various arguments in support of the act-potency principle or the contention that nothing can reduce itself from potency to act, see our "Godfrey of Fontaines and the Act-Potency Axiom," pp. 299–317. Rather than reduplicate that study here we shall limit ourselves to Godfrey's argumentation insofar as it directly bears on our immediate topic, his views on the substance-accident relationship.

[19] PB 4.19. Also see Q 6, q. 7 (PB 3.152). Also see p. 151. His immediate purpose in Q 6, q. 7 is to prove that the will cannot move itself.

[20] *Op. cit.*, p. 367: "Praetera, nihil idem potest esse simul actu et potentia quia sic sequeretur quod simul esset ens et non ens, actu et non actu. . . . Si ergo aliquid facit seipsum tale secundum aliquod accidens oportet ipsum esse tale secundum illud accidens. Sed inquantum est tale iam est actu. Inquantum autem fit tale non est actu quia quod fit non est. Ergo unum et idem simul est actu tale et non actu [tale] quod est contradictoria simul esse vera . . ."

univocal causation, presumably). But the material cause or subject can never be really identified with the others. How then, asks Godfrey, can that substance which is the subject and material cause of its accidents also serve as their efficient cause?[21] And as he has already noted in this same Quodlibet 8, q. 2, Averroes observes in commenting on *Metaphysics* IV that the various predicaments are attributed to substance not because it is their agent (efficient cause) or their end but because it is their subject and they are constituted by it.[22]

In sum, Godfrey insists that no substance can serve as efficient cause of its accidents, for this would be to suggest that it could be active and passive with respect to them at one and the same time. And that suggestion would, in turn, violate the fundamental law of being according to which nothing can act on itself or reduce itself from potency to act. So fundamental is this law of being, maintains Godfrey, that it is as all embracing as is the division of being into act and potency. If it applies to material entities, it applies with equal force to spiritual entities as well. No exceptions can be made to such a certain and universal principle in order to resolve alleged and more particular problems. In fact, contends Godfrey, to allow for any exception would be to undermine the entire principle.[23]

Both in his defense of the universality of this act-potency principle and in his application of it to the causal relationship between substance and accident, Godfrey surely has in mind Henry of Ghent. Along with others, Henry had argued for some exception to the act-potency axiom in the case of man's spiritual activity. Moreover, Henry had suggested that in some way substance may be regarded as an efficient cause of its accidents.

In Quodlibet 8, q. 2 Godfrey appears to be especially concerned with

---

[21] PB 4.23. For Aristotle see *Physics* II, c. 7 (198a 24–26). Also see Q 14, q. 5 (PB 5.387). For fuller discussion of this see our "Godfrey of Fontaines and the Act-Potency Axiom," pp. 309–11.

[22] PB 4.19. For Averroes see *In IV Met.*, Vol. 8, fol. 65va.

[23] Q 8, q. 2 (PB 4.19–20): "Unde cum actus et potentia dividunt et circueunt totum ens, istae rationes aequaliter applicabiles sunt cuilibet enti. Et si per eas probatur et conceditur quod in aliquibus materialibus ita est, per easdem probabitur quod etiam in immaterialibus ita est. Et quia [read: qua] ratione in uno ente quocumque deficiet, et in omnibus." Also see Q 6, q. 7 (PB 3.170): ". . . et ideo quia ex metaphysica hoc scire debemus quod unum et idem non potest esse in actu et potentia et quod illud quod est in potentia ad aliquid non potest se reducere ad actum secundum illud et hoc pertinet ad metaphysicam, quia est commune omni enti, ideo hoc debemus supponere circa angelos et circa animam et, hoc supposito, alia quae ad ipsam animam specialiter pertinent investigare, nec propter ignorantiam vel dubitationem circa posteriora debemus certissima et prima negare." Also see Q 6, q. 7 (PB 3.158, 162).

Henry's Quodlibet 10, q. 9, dating from Christmas 1286. There Henry had inquired as to whether a subject may serve as the efficient cause of its accidents. In brief, Henry distinguishes between accidents that are already present in a subject, and those that may come to be present therein. As regards the first, he suggests that in such cases the efficient cause of the substance is in some way the efficient cause of the proper accidents and operations that follow from the essence of that substance. In addition, he maintains that the substantial form of that same substance, or perhaps more exactly, the composite substance itself by reason of its substantial form, is the proximate efficient cause of its proper accidents. Consider the properties of lightness and heat that follow from the nature of fire. If the extrinsic cause that generates the fire is also an efficient cause of these properties themselves, still their proximate efficient cause is rather the essence or substance of the fire itself. Presumably, Henry feels that here he has not violated the act-potency axiom, since he distinguishes within the composite essence that by reason of which it must receive the accidents (matter) and that by reason of which it must actively produce them (substantial form). He concludes that by reason of its form every subject is the proximate efficient cause of its proper accidents.[24]

As regards accidents that may come to be present in a previously existing subject, Henry suggests that when proper accidents and operations have not yet been realized therein because of some obstacle, the substance has been produced with an aptitude to bring these proper accidents and operations into being once the obstacle is removed. In this case also the substance itself will be the proximate efficient cause of its proper accidents and operations.[25] And when it comes to man's spiritual activities, especially volition, Henry argues that here one must restrict the act-potency axiom. It is possible for a spiritual being to act directly on itself and to reduce itself from virtual act (the proximate capacity to act) to formal act. Just as the sun can produce heat without being formally but only virtually hot, so too can the will produce its respective acts of volition by reducing itself from virtual to formal act. Here again, then, the created substance will be the efficient cause of its operations, and hence of certain accidents, and this time in more direct fashion, it would seem.[26]

---

[24] See *op. cit.*, fol. 425v–426r. In each of these cases Henry is considering substances which have received from their producing principles the capacity to produce their accidents.

[25] *Op. cit.*, fol. 426r.

[26] *Op. cit.*, fol. 426r; 427r (on the will's capacity to move itself; also for the example of the sun being virtually hot in order to illustrate how the will can reduce

In light of what has already been presented, one would expect Godfrey to reject all of Henry's proposed ways in which a subject or substance might serve as efficient cause of its accidents. Thus he insists constantly that nothing can reduce something else from potency to act unless the two differ in reality and in subject (and in place, if the agent and patient are corporeal).[27] In other words, nothing can directly act on itself. As regards proper accidents, he agrees that in matter-form composites the composite substance itself is the material cause of these. But for that very reason it cannot be their efficient cause. Efficient causality must be traced back to the extrinsic principle that functioned as efficient cause of the substance itself.[28] Just as prime matter cannot be described as an efficient cause of its substantial form, neither can the subject or substance be an efficient, albeit instrumental, cause of its accidents. In Godfrey's eyes, therefore, Henry's distinction between the composite viewed as passive by reason of its matter and as active by reason of its form is a subterfuge. In fact it cannot be reconciled with the act-potency axiom.[29]

As regards proper accidents that pertain to a composite essence especially by reason of its form, the essence will serve as their subject, to be sure, but not as their active or efficient principle. So true is this that if the substantial form of such an essence can exist in separation from its matter so as to retain such accidents, it itself will then be their subject and passive principle. Godfrey's point appears to be that even in this case the substance or substantial form cannot be regarded as the efficient cause of such proper accidents. He may have in mind the status of the separated soul and the continuing presence of proper accidents such as intellect and will in the same. In the state of separation such accidents will inhere in the substantial form, that is, in the

---

itself from virtually willing to willing formally); fol. 427v. For more on this see the rest of Quodlibet 10, q. 9 (until 430v); Quodlibet 9, q. 5 (fol. 356r–363v); and the many references to primary and secondary sources listed by R. Macken in his two studies: "La volonté humaine, faculté plus élevée que l'intelligence selon Henri de Gand," *Recherches de Théologie ancienne et médiévale* 42 (1975), pp. 5–51; "Heinrich von Gent im Gespräch mit seinen Zeitgenossen über die menschliche Freiheit," *Franziskanische Studien* 59 (1977), pp. 125–82 (see especially pp. 148–58 and 142–47). Also see R. Effler, *John Duns Scotus and the Principle "Omne quod movetur ab alio movetur"* (St. Bonaventure, N.Y., 1962), pp. 15; 64–67.

27 Q 8, q. 2 (PB 4.26): ". . . immo universaliter est dicendum quod, ubicumque aliquid existens in potentia ad aliquem actum fit in actu secundum illum, oportet quod agens et patiens differant re et subiecto, et cum hoc situ et loco in corporalibus."

28 Q 8, q. 2 (PB 4.28–29). See Q 6, q. 4 (PB 3.116–17).

29 Q 8, q. 2 (PB 4.29, 30–31); Q 6, q. 4 (PB 3.117–18); *Disputed Question* 12, pp. 368–69.

soul. Hence the soul itself is not to be regarded as their active or efficient cause. The efficient causation of such proper accidents must be assigned to the extrinsic cause that produced the composite essence itself.[30]

Granted that certain proper accidents of a material substance may come into being after an obstacle or impediment to their appearance has been removed, as Henry had suggested, in no way does this imply that the substance itself efficiently causes such accidents. Godfrey notes that his opponents cite as counterexamples such changes as the fall of heavy bodies or the cooling of water.[31] Although he would account for these and similar examples in various ways, in none of these cases does he see any exception to the act-potency axiom. Hence none of them is to be interpreted as implying that a substance can efficiently cause its accidents. In fact, in Quodlibet 6, q. 7 Godfrey comments that detailed discussion of such cases pertains more properly to natural philosophy (physics) than to metaphysics.[32]

Spiritual activities are no exception. As we shall see in greater detail in the following section of this chapter, even with respect to these Godfrey

---

[30] Q 8, q. 2 (PB 4.30–31).

[31] Q 8, q. 2 (PB 4.24), for examples such as a physical body consisting of different parts where one part by being hotter might act on another and cooler part; or a living body wherein the soul would act as mover and as agent and the body as moved; or the fall of a heavy body in that by reason of its form it would move the medium and thereby move itself downward; or water which had been warmed and would tend to cool itself.

[32] See Q 8, q. 2 (PB 4.25): all such cases are to be accounted for by appealing to a distinct mover; in a living body there are heterogeneous and integral parts that differ in place and in subject, so that one part can be moved by the soul, and another part by that part, etc. (p. 26); proper accidents are not caused by their substance but by their extrinsic efficient cause (pp. 28–29); if something such as a heavy body is impeded from producing its natural effect (falling), then one must appeal to another agent (*movens per accidens*) in order to allow the heavy body to divide the medium and thus to fall (p. 27); not even this indirect kind of self-motion applies to the cooling of hot water which as a proper accident is rather assigned to its generating cause (p. 28). Godfrey sums up his position: "Et sic substantia nullo modo debet dici proprie agens, nec principale nec instrumentale respectu suorum accidentium" (p. 29). See Q 6, q. 7 (PB 3.167) for further reference to such cases. Note his comment: "Haec autem sunt magis naturalis quam theoreticae speculationis." For further discussion and two possible accounts of the fall of heavy bodies see Godfrey's Q 15, q. 20 ("Utrum sequatur quod si grave movetur effective a generante, quod moveatur effective a forma sua"), PB 14.72–74. On this see our "Godfrey of Fontaines: the Date of Quodlibet 15," pp. 354–58, especially p. 356, n. 84. Here he still denies that a subject is to be regarded as efficient cause of its accidents (p. 73). For Siger's efforts to account for the movement of falling bodies see Van Steenberghen, *Maître Siger . . .*, pp. 330–34.

insists throughout his career that one must maintain in all its force the principle that nothing can reduce itself from potency to act. Not even the will is to be regarded as the efficient cause of its acts. Henry's appeal to the sun to illustrate how something may reduce itself from virtual act to formal act really works against his position. The sun is virtually hot in that it has the ability to render other things formally hot. But it can never make itself formally hot. Far from showing that one and the same thing can be active and passive at the same time, concludes Godfrey, this example has the opposite effect.[33] In sum, then, as Godfrey phrases it in Quodlibet 8, q. 2, no subject whatsoever can be the immediate efficient cause of its accidents.[34]

But if this is true, one might wonder whether or not a substance can serve as immediate passive principle of its accidents. To deny this in all cases would lead to a rather disastrous situation wherein accidents would inhere in other accidents to infinity. Godfrey considers this issue in Quodlibet 2, q. 4 and comments that just as prime matter is the immediate subject of its substantial form without any intermediary entity, so is the composite of matter and form the immediate passive subject for at least some accidents.[35] As he observes in *Disputed Question* 12, one must acknowledge that the substance by reason of its essence is the immediate passive principle of some of its accidents, that is, those that are primary and invariable and follow from that essence. But he also cautions that one should not conclude that the same holds for variable accidents that may or may not be present, such as cognitive operations.[36]

In Quodlibet 6, q. 4 Godfrey again has recourse to this distinction between invariable or connatural accidents, on the one hand, and those that are variable or separable or that come from without ("adventitious"), on the other. Here he suggests that accidents inhere in their substance or subject according to a certain order. Thus substance appears to be in immediate potency to

---

[33] In addition to the above see the rather involved argumentation from Q 15, q. 4 wherein again Godfrey attempts to prove the act-potency axiom: ". . . impossibile est idem et secundum idem primo et per se et immediate movere seipsum" (PB 14.21–23). There Godfrey is especially concerned to show that the axiom is all-embracing and is not to be restricted to corporeal entities. See our "Godfrey of Fontaines and the Act-Potency Axiom," pp. 311–17. For Godfrey's discussion of Henry's theory of virtual act vs. formal act and the analogy with the sun see Q 8, q. 2 (PB 4.22–23). Also see Q 6, q. 7 (PB 3.151, 154) and *Disputed Question* 12, p. 369.

[34] PB 4.31. ". . . subiectum quodcumque non potest esse immediatum principium effectivum accidentis cuius est subiectum."

[35] PB 2.83.

[36] *Op. cit.*, p. 369.

proper and inseparable accidents much more so than to those that are common and separable or variable. This is especially so with respect to the latter when their being is successive and transitory by nature, as with motion, or when it depends upon the constant presence of an object that serves as their efficient cause, as with intellection.[37] As Godfrey explains in Quodlibet 2, q. 4, in the case of a material entity one can introduce a quality such as heat only into a quantified subject. Therefore such an entity would be immediately informed by quantity and only mediately by quality. Or in the case of a spiritual entity such as the soul, intellection and volition can inhere therein only because of the more proximate presence of proper accidents, presumably the intellect and the will. The latter immediately inform the essence of the soul, but the former do not.[38]

C. CREATED SUBSTANCE AND IMMEDIATE OPERATION

The present section of this chapter naturally follows from the preceding one. If, as Godfrey has contended, no created substance can serve as immediate efficient cause of its accidents and if operation itself pertains to the accidental order, how is one to account for the operations or accidents of such substances? What will serve as their efficient cause? Godfrey approaches this issue in Quodlibet 2, q. 4 by asking whether any created substance can be the immediate principle of its operations.[39] In his reply he refers to an opinion that had been defended a few years before by Henry of Ghent in his Quodlibet 3 of Easter 1278.[40] Godfrey's Quodlibet 2 dates from Easter 1286. According to Henry it is possible for a created agent to function as the immediate active or efficient cause of its operations. By this Henry does not mean to say that the essence of such an agent is identical with its operations or that the agent is always in act. He acknowledges that there is a distinction between a created agent and its operations. But he does hold, as Godfrey accurately reports, that such an agent is to be viewed by reason of its substantial form as the immediate and active principle or cause of the effects it

---

[37] PB 3.118–20.

[38] PB 2.83–85. Also see Q 6, q. 4 (PB 3.120).

[39] "Utrum aliqua substantia creata possit esse immediatum principium alicuius operationis" (PB 2.80).

[40] For Godfrey's description of this theory see PB 2.81. In Quodlibet 3, q. 14, Henry addresses himself to this issue: "Utrum substantia animae sit ipsa potentia eius" (*op. cit.*, fol. 66r). For the date of Henry's Quodlibet 3 see Gómez Caffarena, *Ser participado . . .*, p. 270.

produces, and this without appeal to any superadded and distinctive active power in that agent.[41] In like fashion, Henry allows for immediate reception of such action by the appropriate passive principle in a creature. He cites the case of prime matter where it is clear that there is no need to add any distinct thing or accident to matter to account for its ability to receive its form. All one need postulate is some kind of relationship to form in the very essence of matter.[42] By analogy, then, he contends that since the soul may be regarded as quasi-material and as passive with respect to sensible and intelligible objects, it follows that there is no need to regard its powers of sensing and understanding, for instance, as accidents and as really distinct from the essence of the soul itself.[43]

As one would expect, Godfrey decisively rejects Henry's position. In his opinion, no created substance can be identified with its immediate principle of action or operation or, for that matter, even with receptive principles such as the powers of sense and intellect. As we shall see in more detail in the following section, Godfrey will argue for real distinction between any created substance and its powers of operation, including real distinction between the soul and its powers. But for the present we shall concentrate on his arguments against the possibility of immediate operation on the part of any created substance, some of which arguments will apply, according to Godfrey, whether or not one admits of real distinction between such substances and their powers. In Quodlibet 2, q. 4 he proposes three arguments to establish this point with respect to material entities: one based on the nature of the recipient of action in material things; a second grounded on the nature of such agents themselves; and a third that rests on the nature of action insofar as it is realized in material entities.

In his first argument Godfrey appeals to Averroes's *Commentary on the Physics* to support his claim that no created agent can come into immediate contact with prime matter, whether by directly impressing a substantial form upon it, or by immediately removing a substantial form from its matter.[44] A natural agent must rather first change the dispositions of matter, and only by so changing these dispositions can it introduce (literally: induce) a new substantial form therein. Just as matter cannot be acted on by such an agent until contrary dispositions have been introduced into it, so too, is a natural agent unable to act on matter without having recourse to such contrary dispositions.

---

[41] For Godfrey see PB 2.81. For Henry, *op. cit.*, fol. 66v.

[42] For Godfrey, see *loc. cit.* For Henry, *op. cit.*, fol. 66v–67r.

[43] For Godfrey, *loc. cit.* For Henry see fol. 67r–71r.

[44] PB 2.81. For Averroes see *In VIII Phys.* (Venice, 1562), Vol. 4 (fol. 341ra), as indicated by Godfrey's editors. Godfrey's citation here is not literal.

Hence, concludes Godfrey, just as the very reality of prime matter cannot be immediately and directly changed by any natural agent, neither is the mere substance of such an agent sufficient of itself to produce such a change.[45] Presumably, Godfrey's point here is to show that just as one must appeal to really distinct and accidental dispositions in a recipient to account for the fact that matter can be acted on by a natural agent, so must one postulate really distinct powers of operation in the agent itself, and this because potency and its corresponding act should belong to the same genus.

The same conclusion follows, continues Godfrey in his second argument, from the nature of the agent. The action of physical agents is not instantaneous and indivisible but successive and divisible. Thus that which is first introduced into the recipient by the active power of an agent is an accidental form. If such an agent is to introduce (induce) a substantial form, this can only be by means of some such accidental form. But since a natural agent first induces an accidental form and only by means of this the appropriate substantial form, then in corresponding fashion that agent's immediate active principle must also be an accidental form rather than its very essence or its substantial form. Its substantial form is rather that by reason of which its active power can function.[46] Hence Godfrey's conclusion again follows, that no such agent is immediately operative.

Godfrey also reasons from the nature of action itself. Since action on the part of an active power in a creature is itself a kind of change, and since, as he has already contended, every change is immediately directed to some accidental form rather than to the substantial form, then the power which serves as the immediate principle for such a change must also be accidental. Again the unexpressed presupposition appears to be that a power and its proximate actuality belong to the same genus.[47]

Then, as we have already indicated in the preceding section of this chapter, Godfrey adds an important qualification. Just as prime matter is directly informed by its substantial form (once the latter has been introduced by some agent), so too is the matter-form composite itself the immediate passive principle for some of its accidents—quantity, for example, in corporeal entities. In his discussion of the introduction of forms into matter and his denial that any created substance is immediately operative, Godfrey did not wish to deny that some permanent accidents immediately inhere in and inform

---

[45] PB 2.81–82.

[46] PB 2.82. Note Godfrey's comment: "est tamen forma substantialis id in cuius virtute activa potentia accidentalis operatur . . ."

[47] *Ibid.*

their substantial subject.[48] As he indicates farther on in this same question, the argumentation according to which act and potency must fall into one and the same genus is not universally true. Otherwise, the substantial essence itself could not be the immediate recipient of its invariable accidents.[49]

In Quodlibet 6, q. 4 Godfrey again explicitly addresses himself to this same issue.[50] There, in his effort to show that no created substance can be immediately operative, he distinguishes between transitive operation, or that which terminates in something else, and immanent operation, or that which remains within the acting subject. As regards the former he first hearkens back to and summarizes the argumentation from Quodlibet 2, q. 4 that we have just seen.[51] He then extends this to intellectual agents such as souls and angels. Since these do not produce any extrinsic effect except after the manner of art and by means of the practical intellect, and hence by means of intellect and will, it is clear that their acts of understanding and willing are themselves dispositions that are superadded to the intellectual essences themselves. Hence, concludes Godfrey, even if the powers of souls and of angels do not really differ from their essences, still souls and angels do not produce extrinsic effects except by means of something that does differ from them, that is, acts of understanding and willing.[52] This is a rather curious observation on Godfrey's part, for even Henry would admit that there is a distinction between the activities of finite agents and their essences. Still, for him, the created essence itself would be the proximate principle of such activity. But as we shall see, Godfrey in fact holds that the proximate principles of such agency, in this case the intellect and will, are themselves really distinct from the essence of the soul or of an angel.

Godfrey next turns to the case of immanent operations and activities. As will be recalled, he has denied that a created substance can be the efficient cause of its proper and invariable accidents. Efficient causality of these must rather be assigned to the extrinsic agent that produced the substantial essence from which they necessarily follow.[53] As he had already implied in his discussion in Quodlibet 2, q. 4, while such invariable accidents may directly

---

[48] PB 2.82–83.

[49] PB 2.84–85.

[50] "Utrum substantia creata possit esse immediatum principium alicuius sui actus" (PB 3.114).

[51] PB 3.115.

[52] PB 3.116.

[53] *Ibid.* Also note the following: "Accidens ergo connaturale praecipue et inseparabile non efficitur ab ipsa substantia cuius est, sed a causa efficiente ipsam substantiam" (PB 3.117).

inform the substantial essence of their subject, such does not appear to be true of variable accidents such as operations. As regards immanent and spiritual operations such as intellection and volition, the very fact that they can come and go, that the soul does not always actually will or understand, implies that they do not immediately inform the essence of the soul or of an intellectual substance. Precisely because the soul is incorruptible, any accident that is immediately grounded on and inheres in it must also be incorruptible, just as those material accidents that immediately inhere in a material substance are also invariable and remain as long as does that substance itself. Given the nonpermanent character of immanent operations such as intellection and volition, therefore, Godfrey concludes that they cannot immediately inform the essence of the soul or of an intellectual substance. They can be present in it only by means of some inseparable accident or power that does immediately inform it. Rather than admit that such substances could be immediately operative or immediately elicit their acts of intellection and volition, Godfrey concludes that they can do so only mediately, that is, by means of accidental powers, in this case the intellect and the will.[54]

In defending this position Godfrey obviously continues to oppose Henry of Ghent, who had defended immediate operation on the part of such created substances and had denied the need to postulate really distinct powers in which such activities would inhere. Godfrey defends the same position in Quodlibet 6, q. 4, and observes that in so doing he is in agreement with those who hold that the powers of the soul really differ from its substance because potency and act should correspond in genus. Since the soul's operation cannot belong to the genus of substance because of its variable character, the proximate potency for such operation is not to be identified with the substance or essence of the soul. Godfrey here seems to have Thomas Aquinas in mind and again remarks that this position does not imply that no accident can immediately inhere in its subject, but only that variable ones such as operations cannot.[55] Godfrey also argues from the variable nature of such operations to the same conclusion in Disputed Question 12.[56]

Before concluding this section of Ch. IV one more problem remains to be examined. Godfrey has insisted that no created substance can serve as the efficient cause of the accidents that inhere in it. He also holds that no created substance can be immediately operative. If one grants, then, that immanent operations do not immediately inhere in the essence of the substance in

---

[54] See Q 2, q. 4 (PB 2.84–85).

[55] PB 3.119–22. For Thomas see ST I, q. 77, a. 1c and ad 5, as well as the final section of this chapter.

[56] *Op. cit.*, p. 370.

question, how is one to account for the efficient causation of such operations? Though Godfrey assigns efficient causal production of invariable accidents to the extrinsic agent that brought the substance itself into being, he can hardly account for variable accidents and hence for immanent operations in that way. And while he can assign efficient causal production of transitive actions to the substance itself by means of its distinctive powers of operation, can he account for immanent operations in the same way? Since they inhere in the substance itself mediately and immediately in their corresponding passive potencies, their situation is more complicated. To suggest that the substance itself is their efficient cause (by means of its powers) might run counter to Godfrey's metaphysical axiom according to which nothing can be active and passive at the same time with respect to the same thing. As productive of such operations the substance itself would be active, while insofar as they are immanent and remain within it, that same substance appears to be passive.

As we have noted in the preceding section of this chapter, Godfrey resolutely refuses to admit that any finite subject can serve as material and as efficient cause of a given accident or operation at one and the same time. He strongly opposes Henry of Ghent's contention that an exception should be made in the case of spiritual agents and that the will can indeed reduce itself from potency to act or, more exactly phrased, from virtual act to formal act.[57] Thus Godfrey and Henry fall on opposite sides of a widely disputed issue in late thirteenth-century thought, the analysis of free human activity. Full discussion of late thirteenth-century accounts of human activity, especially volition, would carry us far beyond the limits of this study.[58] But at the risk of some oversimplification, we may distinguish between two different ways in which authors of that time attempted to account for this, one more volunta-

---

[57] See pp. 181–83 above of the present chapter.

[58] For some general studies of this see O. Lottin, *Psychologie et morale aux XIIe et XIIIe siècles*, T. 1 (Louvain-Gembloux, 1942), pp. 225–389; A. San Cristóbal-Sebastián, *Controversias acerca de la voluntad desde 1270 a 1300 (Estudio histórico-doctrinal)*, (Madrid, 1958), to be used with considerable caution as we have already indicated in our "Godfrey of Fontaines: The Date of Quodlibet 15" (*passim*) and as R. Macken frequently points out in his general study of Henry's confrontation with his contemporaries on the question of human freedom, "Heinrich von Gent im Gespräch mit seinen Zeitgenossen über die menschliche Freiheit," *op. cit., passim*. In this study Macken gives a helpful overview of discussion of freedom during this period by using Henry as a focal point. Also see E. Stadter, *Psychologie und Metaphysik der menschlichen Freiheit. Die ideengeschichtliche Entwicklung zwischen Bonaventura und Duns Scotus* (München-Paderborn-Wien, 1971); R.-A. Gauthier, "Trois commentaires 'averroïstes' sur l'Ethique à Nicomaque," *Archives d'Histoire Doctrinale et Littéraire du Moyen Age* 16 (1947–1948), pp. 187–336. See in particular pp. 198–99, 220–22, 291–93.

ristic and one more intellectualistic. By the terms "voluntarism" and "intellectualism" one might have in mind those currents of thought that tend to assign greater dignity and priority to the will or to the intellect respectively.[59] But as we shall use the terms here we are rather interested in a more particular and more metaphysical issue, that is, the way in which defenders of each tradition correlate intellect and will in their analyses of the act of volition and the degree to which they apply the Aristotelian act-potency axiom to the same.[60] This is not to deny that the authors to be mentioned below who assign greater activity and self-motion to the will in itself also tend to stress its nobility vis à vis the intellect, while those who differ from them on the former point also tend rather to emphasize the nobility and dignity of the intellect.

Henry of Ghent himself stands out as a leading representative of the voluntaristic position during the period in question. As we have already indicated, he emphasizes the active role of the will in volition and restricts rigid application of the act-potency axiom to corporeal entities. Moreover, he eventually distinguishes between virtual act and formal act in order to make his position more plausible. In so doing he is, of course, opposing doctrines that would assign any directly causal role to the intellect or to the object as presented to the will by the intellect in volition. Any "motion" to be conceded to the object itself in volition can be no more than metaphorical, since the object itself is only a *conditio sine qua non* and not a true cause of the will's activity.[61]

Henry's position may well have been foreshadowed by the Franciscan Master, Walter of Bruges, in his *Disputed Questions* at Paris, which seem to date from the late 1260s. There one already finds a proposed distinction

---

[59] For this usage see Macken, "La volonté humaine selon Henri de Gand," p. 41.

[60] As both Macken (*ibid.*) and Lottin observe (*op. cit.*, p. 275), this priority or preeminence of will or of intellect in the order of dignity may easily be translated into priority in one's analysis of action, here the act of volition itself. For varying assessments of the Aristotelian axiom in thirteenth-century thinkers, see R. Effler, *John Duns Scotus and The Principle "Omne quod movetur ab alio movetur,"* pp. 1–21 ("Introductory Historical Notes").

[61] See, for instance, Quodlibet 1, q. 14 (fol. 11r): ". . . neque adhuc proprie ratio movet, sed ipsum obiectum, movens per se rationem ad cognoscendum et per hoc se ostendendo tamquam bonum, metaphorice movet volentem ad appetendum . . . ;" on this in Henry see Lottin, *op. cit.*, T. 1, pp. 274–77, 305–07; Macken, "La volonté humaine . . . ," pp. 7 (n. 10), 14, 33–35, 45–59; "Heinrich von Gent im Gespräch . . . ," pp. 129–39; 145–46; 152–55 (on the will as *potentia virtualis*); 178ff. Henry first seems to have clearly formulated his distinction between virtual act and formal act in Quodlibet 10, q. 9 (see Macken, *op. cit.*, pp. 152–53). Also see W. Schöllgen, *Das Problem der Willensfreiheit bei Heinrich von Gent und Herveus Natalis* (Düsseldorf, 1927), pp. 47, 77.

between the virtual and the formal, as well as the example of the sun that we have seen Henry using to illustrate his version of this distinction.[62] In any event, Henry clearly developed this doctrine much more fully and would defend it against all challengers.[63] One also finds this tendency to stress the active role of the will in volition in other late thirteenth-century thinkers such as William de la Mare, Richard of Middleton (with some modifications), and Roger Marston,[64] as well as another version of this in James of Viterbo.[65] And as one approaches the beginning of the fourteenth century, one discovers John Duns Scotus developing this position in his own way. It is interesting to note that Scotus does so with explicit knowledge both of Henry's texts and those of Godfrey on this point.[66]

Opposed to the above line of explanation was another held by those who defended more rigid application of the Aristotelian act-potency axiom to the

---

[62] See Macken, "Heinrich von Gent im Gespräch . . . ," pp. 152–53; our "Godfrey of Fontaines: the Date of Quodlibet 15," pp. 362–63; San Cristóbal-Sebastián, *Controversias* . . . , pp. 33–39, 69, 133. Against San Cristóbal-Sebastián's proposed dating of these questions between 1274–76 (p. 37), we prefer to follow Lottin who places them between 1267–69 (see *Psychologie et morale* . . . , T. 1, p. 243). Also see Stadter, *Psychologie und Metaphysik* . . . , pp. 71–78, 283. For Walter's text see his *Quaestiones disputatae du B. Gauthier de Bruges*, PB 10 (Louvain, 1928), q. 4, ad 5 (p. 42), also cited with some other texts in our "Godfrey of Fontaines . . . ," p. 362, nn. 92, 93.

[63] See the references in n. 61 above.

[64] For references to these see Lottin, *Psychologie et morale* . . . , T. 1, pp. 291–92 (William de la Mare); pp. 293–99 (Richard of Middleton); pp. 299–300 (Roger Marston). But on William also see Stadter, *op. cit.*, pp. 241–42, who finds him acknowledging that the will is moved by the *bonum apprehensum*.

[65] On James's position see his Quodlibet 1, q. 7 ("Utrum motus voluntatis in finem sit actus voluntatis vel intellectus"), E. Ypma, ed. (Würzburg, 1968), pp. 79–111 and the long study of the same by F. Ruello, "Les fondements de la liberté humaine selon Jacques de Viterbe O.E.S.A. Disputatio 1ª de Quolibet, q. 7 (1293)," *Augustiniana* 24 (1974), pp. 283–347; 25 (1975), pp. 114–42. See especially pp. 114–24. As Giles of Rome had already attempted some years before, James was trying to develop a *via media* between the more intellectualistic and voluntaristic positions. On Giles see Lottin, *op. cit.*, T. 1, pp. 316–17. But James's position is *sui generis*. On the act-potency or motion axiom also see James's Quodlibet 4, q. 4 ("Utrum idem subjecto posset movere seipsum"), ed. Ypma (Würzburg, 1975), pp. 14–27, especially pp. 25–26.

[66] See Effler, *John Duns Scotus* . . . , *passim*. On his knowledge of Henry and Godfrey see especially pp. 62–67 (Henry); 92–97 (Godfrey); pp. 149–54 (on and against Godfrey's application of the act-potency axiom to intellection; also, pp. 161–63). On Scotus also see W. Hoeres, *Der Wille als reine Vollkommenheit nach Duns Scotus* (München, 1962), especially, pp. 256–74; Stadter, *Psychologie und Metaphysik* . . . , pp. 285–320.

act of choice and thus emphasized to a greater or lesser extent some causal role on the part of the intellect or on the part of the object as it is presented to the will by the intellect. This current is represented in varying degrees by Thomas Aquinas, Siger of Brabant, an anonymous commentary on the *Physics* emanating from the Arts faculty at this time, another anonymous treatise (*tractatus parvus*) that has been reconstructed from Henry of Ghent's citations therefrom, and finally and especially, by Godfrey himself.

Thomas had long assigned some kind of causal influence to the intellect upon the will in volition. Throughout his earlier discussions he had described this influence in terms of finality, but shortly after 1270 or thereabout modified his exposition so as to restrict it to the order of formal causality.[67] This change in Thomas's position was probably due in part to antideterministic concerns being voiced by others at that time, concerns which are also reflected in two of the propositions condemned by Stephen Tempier in 1270.[68] Siger of Brabant also appears to assign considerable causal influence to the object in his *Impossibilia*, and one might conclude from his discussion there that his position was very close to determinism. But he clarifies his thought in his *Tractatus de necessitate et contingentia causarum* so that, while indeed

---

[67] See Lottin, *Psychologie et morale . . .*, T. 1, pp. 228–36 (commenting on *De veritate*, qq. 22 and 24). See especially *De veritate*, q. 22, art. 12: "Unde intellectus movet voluntatem per modum quo finis movere dicitur, in quantum scilicet praeconcipit rationem finis, et eam voluntati proponit" (*op. cit.*, p. 409). Also see Lottin, *op. cit.*, pp. 236–38 (on *Summa contra gentiles*, Bk. IV, c. 19, Bk. II, cc. 47–48); pp. 238–43 (on ST I, q. 82, aa. 1–2). For Thomas's modifications see Lottin, pp. 252–62 (on *De malo*, q. 6, dated by Lottin in early 1271; ST I-IIae, qq. 9–10). In the *De malo* Thomas introduces an important distinction between freedom of exercise and freedom of specification. The free act depends on the will as its efficient *and final* cause in the order of exercise or for its existence, and on the object as presented by the intellect for its determination or specification, and hence only as *formal cause*. Also see Macken, "La volonté humaine. . . ," pp. 43–44; "Heinrich von Gent im Gespräch . . . ," pp. 131–32. On the dating of *De malo* see Weisheipl, *Friar Thomas d'Aquino*, pp. 363–64 (he favors a 1266–67 dating), and p. 366 (where he indicates that q. 6 of the *De malo* was originally an independent dispute and inserted into the *De malo* later by someone). This q. 6, which is of interest here, should be placed in 1270 according to Weisheipl.

[68] *Chartularium*, I, pp. 486–87. Note proposition 3: "Quod voluntas hominis ex necessitate vult vel eligit;" and proposition 9: "Quod liberum arbitrium est potentia passiva, non activa; et quod necessitate movetur ab appetibili." See Lottin for Gerard of Abbeville's concern to obviate any kind of determinism of the will by the object in his Quodlibet 14, qq. 4–5, of December 1269, in *op. cit.*, T. 1, pp. 248–52. On the condemnation of 1270 see Van Steenberghen, *La philosophie au XIIIe siècle*, pp. 472–74; *Maître Siger . . .*, pp. 74–79; our "The Condemnations of 1270 and 1277 . . . ," pp. 179–83.

emphasizing a necessary connection between the motive of action and volition, he submits this motive itself to the free judgment of reason. At the same time, the similarity between one of Siger's key statements in this same context and one of the propositions condemned by Stephen Tempier in 1277 is noteworthy.[69] The anonymous commentary on the *Physics* mentioned above refers to the will as a passive power that is moved by the good insofar as it is understood. Still the "motion" in question here appears to pertain to the order of finality.[70] The *tractatus parvus* reported on by Henry assigns too much passivity to the will and too much causal efficacy to the desired object to meet with his approval.[71] Finally, it should also be noted that a series of propositions condemned by Stephen Tempier in 1277 assign an important causal role to the intellect or the object in choice, or present the will as passive.[72]

---

[69] For important texts in Siger see his *Impossibilia* in *Siger de Brabant. Ecrits de logique, de morale et de physique*, B. Bazán, ed. (Louvain-Paris, 1974) pp. 89–92; *De necessitate et contingentia causarum*, in J. J. Duin, *La doctrine de la providence . . .*, pp. 32–35. On the same see Lottin, *op. cit.*, T. 1, pp. 262–65; Van Steenberghen, *Maître Siger . . .*, pp. 384–86. For the particular text in question see Duin, *op. cit.*, p. 34:55–60, and condemned proposition 131 (*Chartularium*)-160 (Mandonnet). On this see our "The Condemnations of 1270 and 1277 . . . ," p. 192, n. 54. Also see Hissette, *Enquête sur les 219 articles . . .*, pp. 251–53.

[70] See *Siger de Brabant. Questions sur la Physique d'Aristote*, P. Delhaye, ed. (Louvain, 1941), PB 15, pp. 115–20. On this also see Van Steenberghen, *Maître Siger . . .*, p. 387, n. 105; Lottin, *op. cit.*, pp. 266–71. Lottin accepted the Sigerian authorship of this commentary, as did Van Steenberghen for quite some time until more recent discoveries made this attribution very questionable. See Van Steenberghen, *Maître Siger . . .*, pp. 197–99. It seems clear that this commentary along with others of unknown authorship contained in the same Munich manuscript (Clm 9559) emanated from one or more members of Siger's radical Aristotelian group in the Arts faculty at Paris.

[71] For Macken's discussion of and reconstruction of part of this treatise on the basis of literal citations of the same in Henry's Quodlibet 11, q. 6, see Macken, "Heinrich von Gent im Gespräch . . . ," pp. 161–68. The doctrine found there resembles to some extent the Thomistic position without being reducible to it.

[72] For listing and discussion of many of these see Lottin, *op. cit.*, pp. 278–80; our "The Condemnations of 1270 and 1277 . . . ," pp. 192ff.; and most recently, R. Hissette, *Enquête sur les 219 articles . . .*, pp. 241–60, for background. See in particular 157–208, 158–164, 159–134 ("Quod appetitus, cessantibus impedimentis, necessario movetur ab appetibili.—Error est de intellectivo"), 160–131, 161–135 ("Quod voluntas secundum se est indeterminata ad opposita sicut materia; determinatur autem ab appetibili, sicut materia ab agente"), 162–173, 163–163 ("Quod voluntas necessario prosequitur, quod firmiter creditum est a ratione; et quod non potest abstinere ab eo, quod ratio dictat. Haec autem necessitatio non est coactio, sed natura voluntatis"), 164–159, 166–130 ("Quod si ratio recta, et voluntas recta . . .").

With this brief historical survey in mind, we are now in position to return to Godfrey's account of the causal explanation of immanent actions. Consistent with all that we have seen so far, Godfrey insists in Quodlibet 8, q. 2 on applying the act-potency axiom to these as well. In no way is it to be admitted that a passive principle could also serve as an active principle or efficient cause of the accidents or operations that inhere in it. If the act of volition may be regarded as inhering in and informing the will, the will itself cannot be its efficient cause. The will is rather moved by the desired object, insofar as the latter is presented to it by the intellect, of course.[73] And as regards the possible intellect, those acts of understanding or intellection that inform it as their subject cannot be efficiently caused by it. Nor can any species be postulated in the possible intellect by means of which it might then be thought to move itself. In Quodlibet 6, q. 7 he had considered and rejected the suggestion that some disposition might be introduced into the will whereby it could move itself.[74]

In Quodlibet 8, q. 2 Godfrey also remarks that as regards vital actions of the soul such as seeing, hearing, understanding, desiring, willing, and loving, if the individual man who is said to perform these actions is to be regarded as their active principle, then it will be necessary to postulate within him another and distinctive active principle apart from that passive principle in which they reside as in their subject. Thus one might suggest that this applies to the intellect, and even to the will by means of its dependency upon the intellect, in that there is both an agent and a possible intellect. Still, if both the agent and possible intellects are grounded in one and the same simple essence of the soul, one does not act directly and of itself on the other. Rather, the agent intellect acts on the phantasms and the phantasms themselves act on the possible intellect in virtue of the power of the agent intellect. In like fashion one might also postulate an agent sense, as Averroes seems to imply in his *Commentary on the De anima*.[75]

But then Godfrey offers another account, and one that seems to reflect his

---

Here we have first listed the Mandonnet number, then that of the *Chartularium*, as does Hissette in considering them in turn.

[73] PB 4.29–30. See in particular: "Et sic voluntas non movetur nisi ab appetibili; sed non potest moveri ab eo quod est ad finem nisi prius mota fuerit a fine."

[74] PB 4.30. See especially: "Et similiter etiam dicendum de intellectu possibili respectu cuiuscumque actus intelligendi qui habet esse in ipso subiective; scilicet quod respectu nullius habet rationem agentis et efficientis . . ." For Q 6, q. 7 see PB 3.148–72. On the latter see Lottin, *op. cit.*, T.1, pp. 307–11.

[75] PB 4.31–32. For Averroes see *In Aristotelis de anima libros*, Bk. II, com. 60, F. Stuart Crawford, ed. (Cambridge, Mass., 1953), p. 221:50–57.

personal opinion, as we shall shortly see. It might also be suggested that such vital and immanent actions remain in the "agent," not meaning thereby that either the sense or the possible intellect serves as their efficient cause, but that such immanent operations formally perfect the subject in which they inhere. And because their being is, as it were, only transient, they continually depend on their efficient cause, that is to say, upon their respective objects. In fact, continues Godfrey, not only are their objects their efficient causes, but they also serve as the termini of such dependency. Due to a certain trick of language we speak of these immanent actions as if their subjects were their agents or efficient causes, but this is misleading.[76]

Godfrey illustrates this final point by drawing an analogy between statements that express immanent action and those that refer to transitive action. Thus we say: "The eye sees the stone" and also: "Fire heats wood." Since the latter kind of statement expresses true action, we assume that the former also does and assign the efficient causation of such action to the subject of the sentence in each case. But the two situations differ, since the former kind of "action" really remains in the subject, that is, in the power of sight, while the latter type, heating, does not but passes into the wood. In fact, contends Godfrey, in the former case, immanent action, the action itself really inheres in the subject, for instance, in the sense or in the intellect or in the will. And that to which such action looks as to its terminus, e.g., the colored or intelligible or desirable object, is really its active and efficient cause.[77]

Godfrey here seems to offer two possible causal explanations for immanent operations. One might contend that the subject by means of its agent intellect in some way efficiently causes its acts of intellection with the assistance of the phantasm. And one might even postulate an agent sense to allow for a similar explanation of sense perception. On the other hand, one might assign efficient causality of such operations to the object. Yet even according to the first proposed explanation one could hold that the efficient causality in question still derives from the object. Thus it is the object as presented by the phantasm and as illumined by the agent intellect that efficiently moves the possible intellect in its acts of understanding. In this way it would seem that the first explanation is really reducible to the second and that the second is in fact Godfrey's personal choice.[78]

---

[76] PB 4.32.

[77] PB 4.32. For much the same see our discussion below of Godfrey's Q 13, q. 3.

[78] For Godfrey's discussion of the role of the phantasm in intellection and that of the agent intellect with respect to the phantasm itself see Q 5, q. 10 (PB 3.35–40). In order to show how the phantasm which is of itself singular and organic can be rendered capable of acting on the possible intellect (pp. 36–37) he suggests that the

This final point becomes clearer from Godfrey's rather lengthy examination of the same issue in Quodlibet 13, q. 3, which may date from as late as 1297 or even 1298.[79] It is interesting to find Godfrey still defending the same position here. Although this question is explicitly addressed to the possibility of immediate transitive operation on the part of a created substance, Godfrey devotes the greater part of his reply to the possibility of immediate immanent activity. Thus he begins by reiterating his conviction that no substance can be the active or efficient cause of any operation that exists within it, whether by causing this directly or by causing it by means of something else that is superadded. One is reminded of his earlier rejection of attempts to account for this by appealing to some disposition that might be added to the will to enable it to move itself, or to some intelligible species that would enable the possible intellect to produce its cognitive acts as their efficient cause.[80] Again Godfrey counters that precisely because such a substance, even with some superadded disposition, will still be in potency to such perfections or operations and thus will be passive with respect to them, it cannot efficiently cause them. Otherwise it would be in act and in potency and active and passive at one and the same time and with respect to the same thing. In other words, Godfrey's application of the act-potency axiom to immanent operation is as unreserved in Quodlibet 13 as it was in his earlier discussions of the same.[81]

---

agent intellect accounts for this not by introducing any positive disposition into the phantasm but rather by "touching", as it were, only that which pertains to the quiddity of the object in question. By thus removing or separating the substantial quiddity from the individuating conditions which had prevented it from being actually intelligible, the agent intellect renders it actually intelligible and capable of moving the possible intellect. While this abstracting and illuminating activity on the part of the agent intellect is described as active and even as efficient by Godfrey (p. 39), this has to do with the agent intellect's activity on the phantasm. That in turn enables the abstracted intelligible content, the object, to move or to serve as efficient cause of the act of understanding. For confirmation of this final point see Q 9, q. 19 (PB 4.275–76). See especially: "Obiectum ergo intelligibile habet rationem moventis et agentis respectu intellectus possibilis educens ipsum de potentia secundum actum intelligendi ad actum secundum illud, et sic intellectus nec ut agens nec ut possibilis posset dici efficere actum intelligendi in se ipso. Sed obiectum est quod habet rationem efficientis et moventis, licet non habeat quod sit obiectum nisi in virtute eius quod habet rationem intellectus agentis . . ." (p. 276). Also see Q 10, q. 12 (PB 4.361).

[79] "Utrum aliqua substantia creata per se ipsam absque aliquo alio sibi addito possit esse principium immediatum alicuius operationis et praecipue transeuntis extra" (PB 5.190).

[80] PB 5.191. In addition to the references given in n. 74 also see Q 9, q. 19 (PB 4.271, 275); Q 10, q. 12 (PB 4.361).

[81] PB 5.191.

Once more he presents and ultimately rejects some opposed positions that would assign some degree of agency to the subject of immanent operations. One theory appears to be that defended by James of Viterbo in his Quodlibet 1 of the early 1290s.[82] As Godfrey presents this position, certain "aptitudes" are to be postulated in any subject or power that is to be reduced from potency to act. (In fact, these *aptitudines* remind the reader of James's version of a much earlier notion, Augustine's seminal reasons [*rationes seminales*].) When such "aptitudes" are to be actualized, some action on the part of an extrinsic agent is required whereby the subject itself is changed in some way, and this as by an efficient and moving cause. But once the subject has been so changed or "stimulated" (*excitatum*), it will then itself actually realize these same capacities or "aptitudes." And it will do so as their formal cause, though not as their efficient cause. In this way some degree of agency will be assigned to the subject in that it moves itself formally but not efficiently. They (James) argue that this explanation is especially successful in accounting for the soul's immanent activities.[83]

Godfrey also refers to another position according to which that same form by reason of which something enjoys real being also serves as the principle of its immanent operations. According to this view the powers of the soul would function as active but instrumental efficient causes of immanent operations and the soul itself would be their principal efficient cause. Thus the intellect would receive a determined species from a given object and then, as determined by that species to that particular object, the intellect would be

---

[82] On the dating of this see our "The Dating of James of Viterbo's Quodlibet I and Godfrey of Fontaines' Quodlibet VIII," *Augustiniana* 24 (1974), pp. 372–86. On James's doctrine in general see F. Casado, "El pensamiento filosófico del Beato Santiago de Viterbo," *La Ciudad de Dios* 163 (1951), pp. 437–54; 164 (1952), pp. 301–31; 165 (1953), pp. 103–44, 283–302, 489–500. James discusses the general question of origin of forms and the notion of *rationes seminales* in Quodlibet 2, q. 5, E. Ypma, ed. (Würzburg, 1969), pp. 59–96. On this see Casado, *op. cit.*, 164 (1952), pp. 309–13. James applies his general theory of *aptitudines* to the problem of knowledge in Quodlibet 1, q. 12, *op. cit.*, pp. 157–82. For the claim that the intellect is in some way active and in some way passive, the notion of *aptitudines*, and the view that the intellect can move itself *formaliter* though not *efficienter*, see pp. 165–67. There (p. 165:273–75) he refers back to his fuller discussion of the same with respect to the will's self-motion in his Quodlibet 1, q. 7. There see in particular pp. 92–95 (for general discussion and application of the notion of *aptitudo* to the soul and its powers); application to the will as moving itself formally but not efficiently (pp. 95–99). For detailed study of this question see Ruello, "Les fondements de la liberté humaine selon Jacques de Viterbe . . . ," *Augustiniana* 24 (1974), pp. 283–347; 25 (1975), pp. 114–24.

[83] PB 5.191. For references to James see the preceding note.

in position to elicit its corresponding act of intellection as (instrumental) efficient cause of the same.[84]

Not surprisingly in light of all that we have seen so far, Godfrey rejects both of these positions. In fact, he regards the second as extremely irrational and this for a series of reasons similar to those we have noted above in his criticisms of Henry of Ghent. For instance, he argues again that such a position contradicts the definition of a power as presented by Aristotle in *Metaphysics* IX, since it would suggest that such a power could be a principle of action on itself.[85] Moreover, it does violence to the classical fourfold division of the causes, and this time because it would suggest that something could serve as intrinsic form or formal cause of that in which it inheres and as its efficient cause at one and the same time.[86] To the extent that form is a principle of action or operation, it is a principle of operation on something else, not on itself. To deny this would be to contradict first and most general principles that are based on most general terms such as being and nonbeing, act and potency.[87] The immanent operations of the powers of the soul are not efficiently caused by these powers themselves but by their objects. Nor will it do to suggest that species could be efficiently caused by their objects and then that by means of these species the soul itself would efficiently cause its immanent operations.[88] As Godfrey indicates in greater detail in other contexts, he does not defend the reality of intelligible species that are distinct from acts of understanding themselves. But even if one should acknowledge the reality of distinctive species, the object itself would still serve as principal efficient cause both of these species and of the intellectual operations themselves. According to Godfrey, therefore, under no circumstances is it to be admitted that such species might enable the intellect to produce its operations as their efficient cause.[89]

---

[84] PB 5.192–93.

[85] PB 5.193.

[86] *Ibid.*

[87] *Ibid.*

[88] *Ibid.*

[89] PB 5.193–94. According to some interpreters, Godfrey rejected what he regarded as a faulty theory of intelligible species, but still accepted them when they are correctly understood. See De Wulf, *Un théologien-philosophe . . .*, pp. 94–97; Arway, "A Half Century of Research . . . ," pp. 210–11. See Q 1, q. 9 (PB 2.22–23), where Godfrey appears to reject any intelligible species that would inform the possible intellect apart from the very act of understanding itself. Unfortunately, the text there appears to be truncated. But this impression is confirmed by his discussion in Q 9, q. 19 (PB 4.275, 280). No species apart from the act of understanding itself is to be admitted, but insofar as that act of understanding is a formal perfection

Among Godfrey's criticisms of James's position, two should be mentioned here. The first is directed against James's general theory according to which seminal reasons or "aptitudes" are to be posited in matter or in some potential principle which might then be actualized because of stimulation on the part of an extrinsic cause, but also because the subject serves as formal cause of their actualization. If one assigns such efficient causality to the object or to some extrinsic factor, contends Godfrey, then there is no need to assign formal agency to the subject in order to account for their actualization.[90] Another argument is based once more on the traditional fourfold division of the causes. This time Godfrey reasons that just as it is unfitting to hold that something can serve as material cause or subject and as efficient cause of one and the same thing, so is it unfitting to suggest that it could be the intrinsic formal cause and the material cause of the same thing. But according to James's suggestion, the intelligent or willing subject itself would be the material or passive cause of its acts of intellection and volition and would still serve as their active and formal principle.[91]

As Godfrey sums up his position in Quodlibet 13, there are certain perfections that depend upon the continuing presence of their efficient cause for their being. Moreover, they look to that same agent or efficient cause as their terminus but do not inhere in it as in their subject. Such is true of the perfections or operations both of the cognitive and appetitive powers of the soul. Although they are described as operations or as actions of the corresponding powers of the soul, they are really *passiones* since they inhere therein as in their subject. And they denominate these powers in which they inhere, sense or intellect or will, for instance, as if they were their actions

---

that informs the possible intellect, it may be referred to as a "species." Note also his comment in Q 10, q. 12 (PB 4.361): "Loquimur autem nunc de specie, prout dicit quandam dispositionem in intellectu, quae est quaedam rei similitudo alia ab actu intelligendi et ratio formalis secundum quam intellectus possibilis se ipso fit in actu intelligendi. Sic autem nunquam posuit Aristoteles speciem, sed bene dicit ipsum actum intelligendi quandam speciem, in quantum est quaedam similitudo rei per quam etiam intellectus dicitur rei assimilari . . ." Again he goes on to comment that even if one were to allow for such a species, it would still be efficiently caused by the object (PB 4.361–62). Also see Neumann, *Der Mensch und . . .*, pp. 103–04.

[90] PB 5.200. As Godfrey also makes clear, he himself does not accept James's theory of *aptitudines* either as a general account of the possibility of change, or in its application to immanent actions. As we shall see in our discussion of matter-form theory below, he defends the purely potential character of prime matter without assigning any degree of actuality to it in itself or positing any such *aptitudines* or *rationes seminales* in it.

[91] PB 5.200–01.

because of the fact that they are ordered to their object as their terminus. In like fashion, even though they are grammatically predicated of the object as if they were passions of the same, in fact they are rather actions that are efficiently caused by that object itself. Thus we refer to "seeing" as if it were an action performed by the perceiving subject, and we do this because it looks to its object as to its terminus. But in fact "seeing" inheres in the sense power of the perceiver as a passion in its subject and hence is described as immanent rather than as transitive action. And it is not the perceiving subject but rather the "perceived" object that is its efficient cause.[92]

Although more detailed examination of Godfrey's theories of intellection and volition would carry us far beyond the limits of this study and although these applications of his general act-potency theory have been studied by others, it is clear from the above that he does rigorously apply this theory to both of these highly sensitive areas. In intellection, therefore, it is ultimately the object as presented to the possible intellect by means of the phantasm and as illuminated by the agent intellect that is the efficient cause of thinking. And in volition it is the object insofar as it is presented to the will by the intellect that efficiently causes willing.[93] By stressing the dependency of the

---

[92] PB 5.202. For the same and for more detailed discussion of the example of one's vision of a stone, see Q 9, q. 19 (PB 4.276). For discussion and application of the same to intellection and to other instances of immanent operation see pp. 277–80. Also see Q 12, q. 1 (PB 5.82): "Oportet ergo ponere . . . quod causa quare visio non potest esse sine visibili haec est quia visio dependet a visibili ut a causa agente per se, et respicit ipsum visibile ut terminum huiusmodi dependentiae relativae." Here Godfrey is considering the question: "Utrum Deus possit potentias animae passivas reducere in actus suos absque suis obiectis faciendo visionem sine visibili et sic de aliis" (PB 5.79). He replies that this cannot be done.

[93] For study of Godfrey's application of the act-potency axiom to his theory of knowledge see De Wulf, *Un théologien-philosophe* . . . , pp. 90–94; B. Neumann, *Der Mensch* . . . , pp. 99–103; Arway, "A Half Century of Research . . . ," pp. 207–11; O. Lacombe, "La critique des théories de la connaissance chez Duns Scot," *Revue thomiste* 35 (1930), pp. 150–53; Gilson, *Jean Duns Scot. Introduction à ses positions fondamentales* (Paris, 1952), pp. 526–28; B. Martel, *La psychologie de Gonsalve d'Espagne* (Montreal-Paris, 1968), pp. 120–22; Effler, *John Duns Scotus* . . . , pp. 149–53; also, our "Godfrey of Fontaines and the Act-Potency Axiom," pp. 302–04, for Godfrey's discussion in Q 1, q. 7 (PB 2.18–21). For Godfrey's application of his axiom to volition see De Wulf, *op. cit.*, pp. 102–12; Lottin, "Le libre arbitre chez Godefroid de Fontaines," *Revue Néoscolastique de Philosophie* 40 (1937), pp. 213–41; "Le thomisme de Godefroid de Fontaines en matière de libre arbitre," *loc. cit.*, pp. 554–73; *Psychologie et morale* . . . , T. 1, pp. 304–39 (fundamentally the same as the two articles just cited as regards Godfrey); J. de Blic, "L'intellectualisme moral chez deux aristotéliciens de la fin du XIIIe siècle," *Miscellanea moralia in honorem ex. Dom Arthur Janssen, Ephemeridum theologicarum*

will upon the object as presented by the intellect and also by stressing the indeterminacy, even the freedom of the intellect itself, Godfrey insists that he has safeguarded human freedom of choice.[94] Here he clearly sides with the more intellectualistic current in later thirteenth-century thought to which we have referred, and this in spite of the obvious reaction against the same that is evident in a number of the propositions already condemned in 1270 and especially in 1277.

According to Lottin, while Godfrey has indeed carried this intellectualistic tradition farther than Aquinas ever did by assigning efficient causality in volition to the object, and in some other ways as well, still he is not unfaithful to the Thomistic approach.[95] And we should recall in concluding this section that Godfrey identifies the extrinsic formal cause and the efficient cause in the case of intelligent agents. Thus he has denied that such an agent can serve as extrinsic formal cause of something else without also functioning as its efficient cause.[96] As we have seen, Thomas himself had assigned some kind of formal and determining causality to the object insofar as it is presented by the intellect to the will. Given all of this, then, one will not be quite so surprised by Godfrey's references to the object as presented to the will by

---

Lovaniensium Bibliotheca, Ser. I, Vol. 2 (Louvain, 1948), pp. 45–76 (on Giles of Rome and Godfrey); P.-E. Langevin, "Nécessité ou liberté chez Godefroid de Fontaines," *Sciences Ecclésiastiques* 12 (1960), pp. 175–203; San Cristóbal-Sebastián, *Controversias* . . . , cc. 10, 11-A, 13, 14, for many references to Godfrey vis-à-vis Henry of Ghent, John of Murro, and Giles of Rome; Arway, *op. cit.,* pp. 211–16.

94 On this see Lottin, *Psychologie et morale* . . . , T. 1, pp. 310–14. In Godfrey see, for instance, Q 6, q. 10 (PB 3.206–09). Note in particular: "Habet ergo intellectus libertatem suo modo in iudicando; quia ex se non est determinatus circa talia ad unum, sicut voluntas in eligendo; et dependet aliquo modo, sicut dictum est, libertas voluntatis a libertate huiusmodi rationis" (p. 208). For many other references see Lottin, *loc. cit.* See especially Q 8, q. 16 (PB 4.150, 157, 175), commented on by Lottin, pp. 319–23. Note in particular: "Oportet ergo intellectum formaliter liberum esse se ipso, ut est potentia talis naturae; et hoc habet ab illa natura in qua radicatur originaliter. Et similiter dicendum de voluntate" (p. 150). Also see Langevin, *op. cit.,* especially pp. 190–203. For Godfrey's final treatment see Q 15, qq. 2, 3, and 4 (PB 14.6–33), and Lottin's commentary on the same (*op. cit.,* pp. 326–29).

95 *Op. cit.,* T. 1, pp. 331–39.

96 See Ch. III, Section C-2 (pp. 138–40) where Godfrey refutes Henry's theory of divine exemplary causality of creatures solely in terms of their essential being. If with Aquinas he assigns formal causality to the object as presented to the will by the intellect in volition, then it will follow from Godfrey's metaphysics of the causes that such an object may also serve as efficient cause with respect to the same. Lottin has already noted the close connection between the efficient causality assigned by Godfrey to the object in volition and formal causality (*op. cit.,* p. 310, n. 2).

the intellect as the efficient cause of choice. As we have already indicated, in his unbending application of his metaphysics of act and potency to intellection and to volition, Godfrey appeals to what are, at least for him, undeniable metaphysical principles. Even if one may find application of these difficult in certain particular cases, such general principles themselves must be defended in any eventuality. His account of human volition is surely one of these areas where application is more difficult. Even here he insists that no created substance is immediately operative, or can serve as the mediate or immediate efficient cause of any perfection or operation that is found therein.[97] In light of the above considerations, then, we are now in position to turn to Godfrey's position with respect to the relationship between the soul and its powers.

D. THE RELATIONSHIP BETWEEN THE SOUL AND ITS POWERS

Closely connected in Godfrey's mind with his rejection of the possibility of immediate operation on the part of any creature is his defense of real distinction between the soul and its powers. In defending such distinction he is, of course, siding with Thomas Aquinas on this much contested point and once more differing with Henry of Ghent. Thomas had consistently defended this position throughout his career, a position which is well summarized by his discussions in the *Summa theologiae* I, q. 54, a. 3 and q. 77, a. 1.[98] As

---

[97] See Q 13, q. 3 (PB 5.204–05).

[98] For Thomas's view on this see P. Künzle, *Das Verhältnis der Seele zu ihren Potenzen. Problemgeschichtliche Untersuchungen von Augustin bis und mit Thomas von Aquin* (Freiburg, Switzerland, 1956), pp. 171–218. For other positions on this question in high scholasticism see pp. 97–170. One author has surprisingly suggested that Thomas abandoned his doctrine of real distinction between the soul and its intellective power of operation or the intellect, and this around 1270 because of pressure coming from Siger of Brabant: see E.-H. Wéber, *La controverse de 1270 à l'Université de Paris et son retentissement sur la pensée de s. Thomas d'Aquin* (Paris, 1970); "Les discussions de 1270 à l'Université de Paris et leur influence sur la pensée philosophique de s. Thomas d'Aquin," *Die Auseinandersetzungen an der Pariser Universität im XIII. Jahrhundert, Miscellanea Mediaevalia*, Vol. 10 (Berlin-New York, 1976), pp. 297–307. For detailed critical reaction to Wéber's claim see Ch. Lefèvre, "Siger de Brabant a-t-il influencé saint Thomas?" *Mélanges de science religieuse* 31 (1974), pp. 203–15; and especially B. Bazán, "Le dialogue philosophique entre Siger de Brabant et Thomas d'Aquin. A propos d'un ouvrage récent de E. H. Wéber, O.P.," *Revue Philosophique de Louvain* 72 (1974), pp. 53–155. For reference to this controversy and for support of Bazán in his critique of Weber see Van Steenberghen, *Maître Siger . . .*, pp. 357–60; 412–14.

we have already implied, Henry of Ghent's defense of the possibility of immediate immanent operation by creatures is closely connected with his rejection of real distinction between the soul and its powers. This position is already developed by Henry in his Quodlibet 3 of 1278.[99]

As we have also seen, in Quodlibet 2, q. 4 Godfrey had contended that immanent operations such as intellection and volition cannot immediately inform the soul itself, but can do so only by informing accidental powers of the soul, that is to say, the intellect and the will. Already implied in Godfrey's discussion there is real distinction between the soul and its powers as between a substance and its accidents.[100] In Quodlibet 6, q. 4 and in *Disputed Question* 12 Godfrey explicitly connects his denial that creative substances can be immediately operative with his defense of real distinction between the soul and its powers. As he reasons in the former context, it is because the operations of the soul such as knowing and desiring are present to it only by means of certain properties or powers that these latter appear to be "things" (*res*) that are superadded to the substance of the soul.[101] In other words, these powers or properties are distinct *res* or things that are superadded to the essence of the soul, and are, therefore, really distinct from it. And then, in what appears to be a direct reference to Henry of Ghent, Godfrey remarks that it will not suffice to suggest that the powers of the soul are merely relationships on the part of the soul, presumably enabling it to act in given ways. According to Godfrey, a mere relationship is of itself neither an active nor a passive principle. Moreover, nothing can be added to a creaturely substance or essence as a distinctive *res* without itself also being an accident. Hence any real relation that is so added to the substance of the soul would itself be an accident, something that Henry would deny as regards the powers themselves. And, continues Godfrey, for any such real relationship to be added to the soul as an accident, it would have to be grounded in some further and absolute accident, that is, in one that is not a mere relationship.[102]

---

[99] See in this chapter p. 184, and notes 40, 41, 42, and 43 for references to Henry's discussion of this in his Quodlibet 3, q. 14.

[100] See in this chapter, pp. 185–88. For Godfrey see PB 2.84.

[101] PB 3.120.

[102] PB 3.120–21. Godfrey appeals to Simplicius to support his contention that the accident of relation cannot immediately inhere in a substance, but must presuppose some absolute accident, that is, quantity or quality. See *Simplicius: Commentaire sur les Catégories d'Aristote*, A. Pattin, ed., T. 1 (Louvain, 1971), p. 213. As Godfrey puts it: ". . . non solum quantum, sed etiam quale praecedit ad aliquid" (p. 121). For Henry see Quodlibet 3, q. 14, fol. 71r. Also see Macken, "Heinrich von Gent im Gespräch . . . ," p. 156. According to Macken, while defending real identity of

In an apparent reference to Thomas Aquinas, Godfrey also remarks that his position agrees with those who maintain that the powers of the soul really differ from its substance for this reason, that a potency and its corresponding act belong to the same genus. Since the soul's operation does not pertain to the genus substance, neither can the proximate power or potency for such operation.[103]

In *Disputed Question* 12 Godfrey offers three rather extended arguments to show that the essence of the soul really differs from its powers. A first is grounded on the nature of the soul's operations. Because these operations enjoy only a fleeting kind of being that cannot endure without the continuing influence of their cause, they cannot directly inhere in their substantial subject but must presuppose some prior accident that enjoys a permanent and invariable presence in its subject and directly informs the soul. Such permanent accidents, concludes Godfrey, are the powers of the soul and insofar as they too are accidents, they must really differ from the soul's essence. In other words, because of their variable and fleeting character he is arguing that operations such as willing and thinking cannot directly and immediately inform the soul, but can do so only by means of proper accidents or powers such as the will and the intellect which are, therefore, really distinct from the soul's essence.[104]

A second argument is based on the indeterminacy of the soul's essence when it is viewed in itself. By this indeterminacy Godfrey means that the soul of itself is not more determined to one operation than to another. But in fact its various activities are really distinct from one another. Hence, if the soul could act immediately without having recourse to distinctive powers it would be determined to different actions or operations at one and the same time. This Godfrey rejects as impossible. Here again he criticizes a counter-proposal, presumably that of Henry, according to which the soul might be determined to its different acts by different relationships. Once more he

---

the soul and its spiritual powers, Henry allows for intentional distinction between them. Also see his "La volonté . . . ," pp. 28–30.

[103] PB 3.121. One should here recall that neither Godfrey nor Thomas will allow for unlimited application of this principle. Otherwise no accident, not even an invariable and permanent one, could immediately inform a substance or substantial essence. For Godfrey see our remarks on pp. 186–87, 188. For Thomas see Künzle, *Das Verhältniss* . . . , pp. 206–11, for texts and discussion.

[104] *Op. cit.*, pp. 369–70. As we have seen above, Godfrey appeals to fundamentally the same argument in Q 2, q. 4 in order to show that created substances are not immediately operative (see p. 188). Here, however, he explicitly uses it to establish real distinction between the soul and its powers: "Ergo potentia naturalis animae ad tales actus accidens est et ita realiter differt ab essentia" (p. 370).

reasons that such relationships will have to be grounded in something else whereby the soul itself is more determined to one operation than to another. But this is simply to acknowledge that such relationships will be grounded in distinctive powers of the soul. In addition, Godfrey observes that such relationships will have to be either logical or real. Neither alternative will suffice to save Henry's position. Purely logical relationships cannot determine the soul to really distinct operations. And real relations cannot immediately inhere in a substance or in the soul without being grounded in some other really distinct accident, that is, in a power of the soul. Finally, reasons Godfrey, if the power to understand were really identical with the power to see, then the operations of understanding and of seeing would also be identical. In other words, Godfrey here appeals again to real diversity in the soul's operations to establish real distinction of its powers.[105]

Godfrey proposes a third line of argumentation, which rests upon diversity between sense organs. Since matter exists for the sake of form rather than vice versa, where one finds diversity in matter, this must be because of diversity in form. The fact that there are different sense organs implies, therefore, some kind of diversity in the soul. But since the soul of itself is simple, the diversity required therein cannot be realized within its essence itself. Hence, one must conclude to the presence of really distinct powers in the soul, powers that are not only really distinct from one another but from the soul itself.[106]

In Quodlibet 15, q. 3 he returns to this matter again and offers some further precisions as to how the soul's powers are to be distinguished from one another. Something may be distinguished from something else in any one of four different ways: (1) *efficiently*, as when one accounts for the difference between that which is heated and that which is cooled by appealing to the distinction between a cause that heats and another cause that cools; (2) *formally*, as a given form is of itself distinguished from other forms; (3) *materially*, as when things are distinguished by reason of the different subjects in which they are received; (4) in terms of *finality*, as when a saw is distinguished from an axe by reason of their different functions (ends).[107]

---

[105] *Op. cit.*, pp. 370–71.

[106] *Op. cit.*, p. 371. For further development of this line of argumentation see pp. 371–72. For Godfrey's reiteration of his contention that no simple essence such as that of the soul can be the immediate active or passive principle of its operations see Q 8, q. 6 (PB 4.65–66). Here again he considers and rejects Henry's view that the powers are merely relations. He also remarks that at times we mean by the term "intellect" the very substance of the soul, and at other times rather signify thereby the soul's intellective power.

[107] PB 14.16.

Godfrey applies this to the distinction of the powers of the soul from one another. One may distinguish them by reason of their efficient cause, not by appealing to their objects, but to the generating principle that produced both the powers themselves and the soul in which they inhere. He notes that if the objects of such powers are efficient causes of their operations, these objects do not efficiently cause the powers themselves. Godfrey also observes that powers of the soul are formally distinct from one another precisely because they are forms (accidental, to be sure), and hence differ by their very nature from one another. Since these powers are found in one and the same subject, they do not differ from one another materially, that is, by being received in different subjects.[108]

As regards the order of final causality, Godfrey contends that the powers of the soul differ from one another both by reason of their objects and by reason of their operations. Final causality may be assigned both to an object as the thing toward which something tends and to the action whereby such an object is attained. To suggest that the powers of the soul are distinguished by reason of their operations presents no great difficulty for Godfrey, since it is clear that activities such as thinking and willing really differ from one another. Hence, the soul must be disposed in one way in order to be moved toward that which it understands, and in another way in order to be moved toward that which it loves or desires. And according to Godfrey it is so disposed by the distinctive powers of intellect and will.[109] In short, then, Godfrey here echoes the view found in Aquinas according to which powers of the soul are distinguished and specified by reason of diverse operations.[110] And Godfrey obviously has in mind what one might style formal diversity rather than mere material diversity. Two distinct powers are not required to account for two different operations of intellection, for instance, but rather to account for two essentially distinct kinds of operation, such as intellection and volition.

But one might wonder how powers are to be distinguished from one another by reason of diverse objects, since it is possible for someone to understand and to love one and the same physical thing. Godfrey resolves this by appealing to distinctive perspectives under which the same object may be attained. Insofar as the object can move the soul to understand it, one must posit a corresponding power in the soul, the intellect. But insofar as the same

---

[108] *Ibid.* In referring to the powers as forms Godfrey specifies that they are qualities. As regards material diversity he does acknowledge that one power might immediately inform the essence of the soul, and another only by means of the first.

[109] *Op. cit.*, pp. 16–17.

[110] See, for example, ST I, q. 54, a. 3c.

physical object can move the soul to love it, one must posit another and distinct power in the soul, the will. Hence Godfrey seems to mean that the powers of the soul are distinguished by reason of their objects viewed precisely as objects of its operations, or in terms of formal diversity, which is not incompatible with material and physical identity of the objects in question.[111]

In conclusion, then, it is clear that for Godfrey the soul is really distinct from its powers just as substance is distinct from the accidents that inhere in it. In fact, the powers of the soul are accidents and fall under the predicament quality. In addition, the powers of the soul are really distinct from one another, and in three of the four ways he has proposed in Quodlibet 15, q. 3, that is, efficiently, formally, and in terms of final causality.

[111] PB 14.17. See in particular: ". . . et sic obiectum, licet unum realiter, exigit diversas potentias et inquantum facit diversos actus et inquantum est finis quae est res diversis actibus attingibilis."

Chapter V.

The Existence (ESSE) of Accidents

Within his general theory of substance and accident composition, another metaphysical issue arises for Godfrey. Must one assign individual and particular existences (*esse*) to accidents in distinction from and in addition to the substantial existence of the subject in which such accidents inhere? Or to phrase the same question in different terms, is one to admit of only one existence (*esse*) in any given substance or of many, one substantial and the others accidental? Recent studies of this question in Thomas Aquinas reveal that there is still no unanimity on the part of scholars today as to his mind on this point. Thus certain texts in his writings lead some to conclude that he did assign particular existences to individual accidents and that such existences are to be distinguished from the substantial existence of the existing and subsisting subject. But these and other texts are utilized by other commentators to suggest that Thomas did not defend the reality of such accidental existences and that he accounts for the actual existence of accidents by appealing to the single act of existence of their substantial subject.[1]

---

[1] According to Hocedez the majority of Thomists hold that the existence of an accident is really distinct from that of its substance; see his *Aegidii Romani Theoremata . . .* , p. 93, n. 2. Among other texts he there cites SCG IV, c. 14; ST III, q. 17, a. 2; and ST III, q. 2, a. 6, ad 2. He also finds Capreolus and Hugon defending this view. For the same see L. De Raeymaeker, *Metaphysica generalis*, Vol. 1 (Louvain, 1931), pp. 141–42. He also cites *In IV Sent.*, d. 12, q. 1, a. 1, sol. 3, ad 5, and lists Capreolus and Cajetan as defenders of the same. But his reading of Thomas

It is beyond our purposes here to attempt to resolve this disputed point within Thomistic scholarship. We shall content ourselves with the observation that this issue is particularly troublesome for metaphysical systems that defend some kind of real distinction or real otherness of substantial essence and substantial existence (*esse*). Once one has allowed for such distinction or otherness in the substantial order, one may then wonder whether or not this distinction or otherness of essence and *esse* is repeated on the level of accidents as well. One can readily understand why question has been raised as to Thomas's mind on this point. And one will not be surprised to discover that Giles of Rome treats of this quite explicitly. As will be recalled from our discussion of Godfrey's knowledge of and reaction to theories of real distinction between essence and existence, Thomas did defend some kind of real (as opposed to purely logical or intentional) otherness of essence and existence. And Giles of Rome was well known to Godfrey and his contemporaries for having defended a considerably less nuanced version of real distinction between essence and existence in all creatures.[2]

In Giles's *Theoremata de esse et essentia*, dating perhaps from his period of "exile" from the Theology faculty at Paris (1278–1285), he wonders whether the *esse* given by an accidental form to its subject is to be regarded as a distinctive thing (*res tertia*) apart from the subject and the accidental form itself. Giles connects this question with a more specific case of the same, that is, the relationship between extension, on the one hand, and matter

on this seems to have shifted in his *The Philosophy of Being* (St. Louis-London, 1954), pp. 180–81. For a firm denial that Thomas assigned a distinctive and proper *esse* to accidents apart from that of their substance see J. Albertson, "The *Esse* of Accidents according to St. Thomas," *The Modern Schoolman* 30 (1953), pp. 265–78. Among the texts from Thomas that he cites in favor of his reading see ST I-IIae, q. 55, a. 4, ad 1; ST I, q. 90, a. 2; and even though these might be used by others to argue for the opposite position, Quodlibet 9, q. 2, a. 2; SCG IV, c. 14; ST III, q. 17, a. 2; and *De ente et essentia*, c. 6 (analyzed on pp. 277–78). He cites in support of his interpretation, along with others, de Finance, *Etre et agir . . .* , 1st. ed., pp. 241ff. (pp. 248–49 in the 2nd ed.); Gilson, "La notion d'existence chez Guillaume d'Auvergne," *Archives d'Histoire Doctrinale . . .* , 15 (1946), p. 89, n. 1; A. Forest, *La structure métaphysique du concret selon saint Thomas d'Aquin* (Paris, 1931), p. 89. For direct challenge to Albertson's reading of Thomas see F. McMahon, "The *Esse* of Accidents: A Discussion," *The Modern Schoolman* 31 (1954), pp. 125–30 (McMahon stresses ST III, q. 2, a. 6 and ad 2, and ST I-IIae, q. 110, a. 2). For Albertson's reply see *loc. cit.*, pp. 130–32. For McMahon and G. Phelan against Albertson and therefore in defense of the *esse* of accidents see "The *Esse* of Accidents," *The New Scholasticism* 43 (1969), pp. 143–48. Also for explicit refutation of Albertson's interpretation see A. Patfoort, *L'unité d'être dans le Christ d'après s. Thomas* (Paris, 1964), pp. 229–33.

[2] See Ch. II-A.

and quantity, on the other.[3] The extension or *esse* that belongs to matter insofar as it is quantified is not some third thing that differs from matter and from quantity, but a particular mode of being that matter enjoys only insofar as it is conjoined with quantity. In like manner, the existence (*esse*) given by any other accidental form is not to be regarded as a third thing that differs from that accidental form and from its subject. This existence (*esse*) is only a mode of being that the subject enjoys insofar as it is determined by that accidental form.[4] In other words, Giles refuses to assign to accidents a distinctive existence (*esse*) that might be described as a third thing (*res*) in addition to the accidental form and its subject. He does, as we have seen, apply the term "thing" (*res*) to substantial existence insofar as he views it as really distinct from essence.[5]

Giles defends the same position in his Quodlibet 2, q. 2, of Easter 1287 and especially in q. 10 of his *Quaestiones disputatae de esse et essentia* (before Christmas 1286). According to the discussion in Quodlibet 2, q. 2, accidents do not enjoy their own existences (*existere*) but actually exist only because they are present in an existent subject and by reason of its existence.[6] In q. 10 of the *Quaestiones disputatae*. . . , Giles examines this question in greater detail. Again he insists that the existence (*esse*) given by an accidental form to its subject is not another thing (*res*) in distinction from the essence of that form and from the subject that receives it. Just as in a given entity one quantity suffices to account for the extension of matter and of the accidents received in that thing, so it is by reason of one and the same substantial existence that a created substance exists and that its accidents exist. Thus Giles observes that accidents should not be described as existents except insofar as they belong to that which exists (*nisi quia sunt existentis*).[7] Plurality

---

[3] On the dating of the *Theoremata* see Ch. II, n. 11. See *Aegidii Romani Theoremata de esse et essentia*, Th. XV, pp. 92–94. Near the end of Th. XIV, Giles had just concluded that since an accidental form is a kind of essence, some *esse* must flow therefrom (p. 92:9–12). Hence the need for him to discuss the nature of this accidental *esse* in Th. XV.

[4] *Op. cit.*, pp. 94:14–95:3 and pp. 99:22–100:9. For more on this notion of a *modus essendi* see his *Quaestiones disputatae de esse et essentia*, q. 8, ad 6 (fol. 17v); and q. 10 (fol. 22v), also cited by Hocedez in his *Aegidii Romani Theoremata* . . . , p. 94, n. 2.

[5] See above Ch. II, n. 11.

[6] *B. Aegidii . . . Quodlibeta* (Louvain, 1646), p. 50: "Utrum humanitas Christi posset existere per se absque additione alicuius novi esse." See p. 51: "Accidentia autem existunt, non quod habeant per se esse, nec quod habeant proprium existere, sed quia sunt in existente et existunt per existere subiecti." On the date of Quodlibet 2 see Glorieux, *La littérature quodlibétique* . . . , Vol. 1, p. 141.

[7] See his *Quaestiones disputatae de esse et essentia*, fol. 22v–24r. See in partic-

of accidental forms or plurality of substance plus accidental forms within one and the same subject does not result in plurality of existences.[8]

In his Quodlibet 10, q. 8 of 1286 Henry of Ghent also addresses himself to this same question.[9] Since he rejects real distinction between essence and existence while defending their intentional distinction, one would expect him to allow for distinctive accidental existences to correspond to accidental essences. And so he does. But he even goes so far as to assign a distinct *esse* to form and another to matter in a composite entity,[10] a point which will not be quite so surprising when one recalls, as we shall see, that Henry assigns some degree of actuality to prime matter itself. As we shall also see, Godfrey will sharply differ with Henry on this last-mentioned issue.

As regards the question now under consideration, Godfrey, of course, rejects real (as well as intentional) distinction between substantial essence and substantial existence. As we have observed above on different occasions, for him essence and existence are so identical that wherever one finds essence one must also find a corresponding and identical existence. Given this, one can readily anticipate his position with respect to the existence of accidents. If there are distinct accidents or accidental quiddities within a given entity, there must be corresponding existences as well. This will follow because

---

ular: ". . . non est quaestio de esse quod est a forma accidentali quia tale esse non est res alia ab essentia accidentis et substantiae" (fol. 23ra); "Ita possumus dicere quod non sunt existentia nisi quia sunt existentis" (fol. 23rb). Also see Quodlibet 2, q. 2 (p. 52): ". . . quod accidens non sit existens nisi quia est existentis."

[8] See the *Quaestiones disputatae . . .* , fol. 23vb.

[9] See Henry's Q 10, q. 8 (fol. 422r–425v). Although Henry explicitly addresses himself here to our problem, to determine whether or not the *esse existentiae* of accidents is distinct from the actual existence (*esse existentiae*) of the subject in which they inhere, much of his discussion touches on the theological question as to whether one or more than one *esse* is to be admitted in Christ. Insofar as Henry's discussion treats of this latter issue, it has been reproduced in part by E. Hocedez, *Quaestio de unico esse in Christo* (Rome, 1933), pp. 63–72. As Hocedez indicates, much of Henry's discussion is directed against the theory of only one existence per substance that we have just seen in Giles of Rome (p. 63, n. 2).

[10] See in particular: "Quotquot ergo sunt essentiae in eodem, sive de praedicamento substantiae, sive accidentis, tot necessario sunt esse essentiae in eodem et tot esse existentiae. . . . Unde in quolibet composito per se ex materia et forma, sicut sunt duae essentiae, sic sunt duo esse utroque modo [that is, in terms of *esse essentiae* and *esse existentiae*]. Et similiter in composito per accidens ex substantia et accidente, quotquot sunt in eo essentiae diversae substantiae et accidentis, tot sunt in eo esse utroque modo" (fol. 423r). For his explicit connection of this thesis with his earlier rejection of any real distinction between essence and existence see fol. 423v, and his reference there to his discussion in Q 10, q. 7 (where he had defended his intentional distinction of the same).

accidental essence and accidental existence are really identical. Such is clearly implied by Godfrey's discussion in Quodlibet 2, q. 2 of the twofold or even the threefold way in which the essence of a thing, especially a material thing, may be said to have existence (*esse existentiae*). But, as he also warns in that context, this should not be interpreted as implying that any finite essence does in fact exist without some accidents.[11]

As Godfrey explicitly states in the short version of Quodlibet 3, q. 4 (Christmas 1286), in any given finite substance one must posit one substantial existence or subsistence (*esse subsistentiae*) and a plurality of accidental existences (*esse secundum quid*). For him the latter correspond to and are identical with the various accidental forms or essences present there. Thus he reasons that if accidental forms or essences exist by reason of and inhere in the substantial essence, so do accidental existences exist by reason of and presuppose the existence of their substance.[12] Or as he explains in the longer version of the same question, one should distinguish between substantial existence or subsistence, on the one hand, and mere existence (*esse existentiae*), on the other. As we shall see in greater detail in the following chapter, subsistence pertains to substance alone, that is, to that to which it belongs to exist in itself. But existence (*esse existentiae* or *existere*) also pertains to accidents. Hence, while there can be but one subsistence in any given substance, there may be many existences.[13]

In this discussion in Quodlibet 3, q. 4, Godfrey is especially concerned with refuting a theory according to which there can only be one existence in any substantial entity. In obvious reference to Giles of Rome, Godfrey notes that defenders of this view draw an analogy between extension and existence. Just as it is through one and the same quantity or extension that matter is extended by serving as its subject and that accidents are also extended by being received in something that is extended, so it is through one and the same substantial existence that the substantial essence and the accidental forms of one and the same being exist.[14] In another passage that also reminds one of Giles, Godfrey remarks that defenders of this view not only cite Aristotle to this effect, that accidents are beings only because they are "of being"

---

[11] PB 2.62–63. On this passage see Ch. II, pp. 76–77.

[12] In Q 3, q. 4, Godfrey explicitly addresses himself to this question: "Utrum anima separata existat eodem esse quo existit totus homo" (PB 2.186). For the passage in question see the short version, PB 2.311.

[13] PB 2.190. See in particular: "Et hoc modo in uno est tantum unum esse, scilicet quod est esse existentiae simpliciter et esse subsistentiae. . . . Sunt tamen in illo plura esse existentiae . . ."

[14] PB 2.187–88 (long version); PB 2.310 (short version).

(*entis*), they go on to observe that accidents are existents only insofar as they pertain to some existent (*nisi quia sunt alicuius existentis*).[15] And Godfrey comments that defenders of this theory maintain that substantial existence is really distinct from substantial essence.[16]

Godfrey presents a series of arguments offered in support of this position by its defenders. Some of these remind one of reasoning offered by Giles of Rome and of arguments presented by Henry of Ghent in his discussion and refutation of this same theory in his Quodlibet 10, q. 8. Since they appear in more orderly fashion in the shorter version of Quodlibet 3, q. 4, we shall present them according to their sequence there. (1) Existence follows upon the substantial form of a thing and only upon the final and perfecting form, if one holds for plurality of forms. But there can only be one such form in any given substance. Hence there can only be one existence.[17] (2) Things which are one in subject are said to be one in terms of their existence. It is by means of this single existence that the thing in question and all that is present therein are said to exist. But such would not be so if there were many existences in one and the same subject.[18] (3) Again, one should not reason from a multiplicity of accidental natures and essences to a multiplicity of existences within a given subject. Accidents are not said to be except insofar as they are "of being." And they are not existents except insofar as they belong to some existent. This can only be because accidents do not have their proper existences.[19] (4) A final argument is based on the notion of participation. It belongs to existence to be received in and to be participated in by another, not to participate in or to receive something else. But if there are many existences in one and the same thing, then they will have to be ordered

---

[15] For Aristotle see *Metaphysics* VII, c. 1 (1028a 18–20). For Godfrey see PB 2.188 (long version): ". . . ut dicitur in principio septimi Metaphysicae, accidentia non sunt entia nisi quia sunt entis. Ergo similiter nec sunt existentia nisi quia sunt alicuius existentis." For Giles see the texts cited in n. 7. In the citation from his *Quaestiones disputatae* Giles too had referred to *Metaphysics* VII immediately before the passage cited in n. 7 (fol. 23rb).

[16] PB 2.310: ". . . dicunt quidam qui ponunt esse et essentiam re differre in creaturis. . ."

[17] See PB 2.310 (short version) and PB 2.187 (long version). Also see Henry, *op. cit.*, fol. 422v, arg. 2; Giles, *Theoremata* . . . , Th. XVII, pp. 111–17.

[18] PB 2.187 (long version) and PB 2.310 (short version). For Giles see his *Quaestiones* . . . , q. 10, args. 1 and 2 *in contrarium* (fol. 22vb). For Henry see *op. cit.*, args. 3 and 4 for only one *esse* per substance (fol. 422r).

[19] PB 2.188 (long version); PB 2.310 (short version). For Giles see *Quaestiones disputatae* . . . , *loc. cit.*, ("Secunda via . . ."), fol. 23vb. For Henry see *loc. cit.*, arg. 1 for only one *esse* (fol. 422r).

to one another in such fashion that one existence is received in and participated in by another. This would imply that one existence receives and participates in another, something that is repugnant to the very notion of existence.[20]

Godfrey must reject this position on all counts. If one holds, as he himself does, that essence and existence are really identical in creatures, then wherever one finds multiplicity of essences one must also posit multiplicity of existences. But Godfrey makes a stronger claim here. Even if one defends real distinction of essence and existence in creatures, one must still allow for as many existences as there are essences within any given being.[21] In support of this contention Godfrey offers a series of arguments. Since they, too, are presented in more organized fashion in the shorter version of this question, we shall follow the plan of the latter in considering them here.

A first argument rests on the conditions required for a being to enjoy essential unity. If many forms are present in a given being, they cannot unite to constitute essential unity or an *unum per se*. Such can result from the union of distinct factors or principles only when these are ordered to one another as pure potency and as unqualified act (*actus simpliciter*). But if an entity already possesses its specifying and substantial form, it can no longer be regarded as being in pure potentiality. Nor can any subsequent or accidental form that is added communicate substantial being to it or be regarded as its *actus simpliciter*. And since such a being cannot enjoy essential unity with any such added form and thus cannot unite with it to form an *unum per se*, Godfrey reasons that it cannot have merely one existence. This follows because that which does not enjoy such essential unity has only accidental unity or is only an *unum per accidens*. Hence it is really many in some sense. But it can be many only insofar as it has more than one existence, corresponding to the different forms present within it.[22] (One might counter that this final statement really begs the question unless one assumes that there is real identity between essence and existence. One should also note that if Godfrey here describes a substance as enjoying only accidental unity with its accidents, he would not deny that even a composite substance may be re-

---

[20] PB 2.188 (long version); PB 2.310 (short version). For Giles see *Quaestiones disputatae . . .* , *loc. cit.*, ("Tertia via . . ."), fol. 23vb–24ra. For Henry see *loc. cit.*, arg. 2 for only one *esse* (fol. 422r). Both Giles and Henry directly connect this argument with Axiom 3 of Boethius's *De hebdomadibus*. For which see *Boethius. The Theological Tractates*, H. F. Stewart-E. K. Rand, ed. (Cambridge, Mass., 1968), p. 40.

[21] PB 2.188. For the short version see PB 2.310.

[22] PB 2.310 (short version); PB 2.188–89 (long version).

garded as enjoying essential unity in another sense, that is, in terms of the prime matter and substantial form which unite to constitute its substantial essence.)

Godfrey's second argument is based upon Aristotle's distinction in *De generatione* I between substantial generation, which results in the production of a substance, and accidental generation, which rather terminates in the production of an accident. Since all generation terminates in some existence (*esse*), in addition to that existence which is given with any substantial form one must allow for another that follows upon accidental forms as well.[23]

A third argument rests on the view that existence is the act of essence and formally perfects it. If one concedes this, as both Giles and Thomas Aquinas would, then, reasons Godfrey, one should posit as many perfections as there are principles or things to be perfected. If a number of forms or principles within a given being require perfection and actualization, one should allow for as many existences to perfect them. Otherwise, contends Godfrey, these various (accidental) forms would not exist.[24] His point seems to be that within the framework of real distinction of essence and existence, since existence is the act of essence and formally perfects it, without its corresponding existence any given essence will not in fact exist. Rather than restrict this to substantial essence and existence, however, Godfrey urges his opponent to apply the same to accidental essences or forms. They, too, must be perfected by corresponding acts of existence if they are to be realized in actuality.

Godfrey's final argument is theological, but will be mentioned here for the sake of completeness and because it sheds some further light on his understanding of accidental being. According to his interpretation of Eucharistic transubstantiation, once the substance of bread has been changed into the body and blood of Christ, the accidents of bread remain and therefore exist. But one cannot account for the continuing existence of quantity and the other accidents after transubstantiation by appealing to the existence of their substantial substratum, since it is that very substratum that no longer remains. Hence, urges Godfrey, one must concede that such quantity now exists by reason of its own act of existing which formally perfects it and which it already had when it was present in its substantial subject, the bread. Nor will it do to say that in its former state it existed only by reason of the existence

---

[23] PB 2.310–11 (short version); PB 2.189–90. See *De generatione et corruptione* I, c. 3. For fuller discussion of Aristotle's doctrine in this chapter also see Q 3, q. 1 (PB 2.168).

[24] PB 2.311 (short version). See PB 2.191 for similar reasoning, but within the context of Godfrey's refutation of Giles's argument based on the analogy between existence and extension.

of its substantial subject, and that after transubstantiation it continues to exist because of a new existence that now perfects it. Against this, Godfrey replies that if the existence of something is changed, then that thing itself must also be changed either in terms of its species or at least in terms of its numerical identity. Hence numerically the same accident (quantity) would no longer remain, something which he rejects as unfitting.[25] Godfrey's contention—that when the existence (*esse*) of something is changed its numerical identity is also changed—is interesting. Such will follow, to be sure, from his identification of essence and existence—in this case, accidental essence and existence. But such also follows, he implies, if essence and existence are really distinct.

From the above, then, Godfrey's position is clear. Whether or not one holds for real distinction between essence and existence in creatures, one must still admit of plurality of existences therein. Only one of these will be truly substantial existence and can, therefore, be referred to as subsistence. But in addition to this existence, there will be as many accidental existences as there are accidental forms. All of the latter will in some way depend upon and presuppose the former, whether that be taken as essential or as existential being. As he phrases it, just as secondary essence presupposes and depends upon primary or substantial essence, so does secondary existence presuppose and depend upon primary and substantial existence. Since this dependency does not eliminate secondary essences, neither does it eliminate secondary existences.[26]

As regards the arguments offered against multiplicity of existences in any given substance, Godfrey quickly disposes of the first three. According to the first argument, since existence follows upon the substantial form of a thing and since there can only be one substantial form in a substance, or at least one final and perfecting form if one defends plurality of substantial forms, there can only be one existence. Godfrey replies that while this argument does show that there can only be one substantial existence (*esse simpliciter*) in a given substance, it does not prove that there cannot be many accidental existences as well.[27] The second argument, according to which things that are one in subject must only be one in existence, again applies only to substantial existence.[28] As regards the third argument, Godfrey concedes that accidents are not described as existing or as beings except insofar

---

[25] PB 2.311 (short version); PB 2.193 (long version).

[26] PB 2.311 (short version); PB 2.192 (long version).

[27] For this argument and the others see pp. 214–15. For Godfrey's reply see PB 2.311 (short version). Also cf. PB 2.188–89.

[28] PB 2.311.

as they are "of being." But this does not show that they do not have their own existences, but merely that they enjoy such existences only insofar as they inhere in and depend upon the existence of their substantial subject.[29]

The fourth argument reasoned that it does not pertain to existence as such to participate in something else. But if there were many existences in a particular substance, one of these, substantial existence, would participate in the others, that is to say, in accidental existence. Godfrey replies within the framework of his metaphysics of identity of essence and existence. Just as it is not unfitting to hold that one form or essence can participate in another, so may one admit the same of existence. One instance of existence may in fact participate in another. Nor will one avoid this by allowing for only one existence in a subject. Even then, since that existence will be that of the substantial subject, one must acknowledge that the existence of the substance (or the substance itself, since they are identical) participates in its accidents.[30]

Finally, Godfrey criticizes in some detail Giles's alleged analogy between extension and existence. He acknowledges that all that is found in one and the same extended body is extended by participating in one and the same extension, just as all that is found in a white body is white by reason of one and the same whiteness. But Godfrey denies that the same may be said of existence, as Giles would have it. Extension signifies a determined degree of being (quantity) that cannot be essentially multiplied in one and the same subject. Existence, on the other hand, can indeed be multiplied in the same subject or substance just as essence may be.[31] And within the terms of Godfrey's own metaphysics, existence must be multiplied whenever essence is, since they are one and the same. Hence, where one finds many accidental essences, one must also find as many accidental existences.

COROLLARIES

Godfrey addresses himself to two additional questions concerning the existence (and nature) of accidents, questions which we shall now consider as corollary to the above discussion: (1) May an accident exist apart from any subject? (2) May numerically one and the same accident exist in different subjects?

---

[29] PB 2.311 (short version); PB 2.192 (long version).

[30] PB 2.311–12 (short version); PB 2.192–93 (long version).

[31] PB 2.312 (short version); PB 2.191–92. As we have indicated above in n. 12, the immediate occasion for this discussion of multiplicity of accidental existences within an entity was the question whether the separated soul exists by reason of the

Corollary 1: May an Accident Exist Apart from Any Subject?

Since Godfrey does assign individual existences to individual accidents, one can readily see why he would address himself to this question. But as we have already indicated in Ch. IV,[32] and as should also be clear from our consideration of his defense of the individual existences of accidents in the present chapter, he categorically rejects any such possibility within the natural order. As he remarks in Quodlibet 1, q. 20, to admit that an accident could exist apart from any subject would be to assign to it the characteristics of substance. While he allows for the possibility of such separate existence in the case of the Eucharist because of divine intervention, he observes that it is extremely difficult to account for this and expresses his wonder at any theologian who would dare to suggest that an accident could exist apart from its subject in the purely natural order.[33] That this was a timely topic for discussion is also clear from the fact that four propositions which challenge this possibility without allowing for any such exception were included among the articles condemned by Stephen Tempier in 1277.[34]

In Quodlibet 4, q. 22 Godfrey considers a related question: May a given quality exist apart from any subject or apart from quantity?[35] The context indicates that Godfrey here has in mind sensible qualities. Thus one might reason that quantity is as dependent upon substance as whiteness (a sensible quality) is upon its surface or on quantity. But since quantity can exist apart

---

same existence as did the whole man. Godfrey concludes that the separated soul does not retain every existence (*actus essendi*) that was found in the whole man but only substantial existence plus the accidental existences of those accidents that pertain to the soul alone and not to the composite (PB 2.311). Since form gives *esse* to matter and since the form or separated soul continues to exist, one may say that the substantial *esse* of the composite continues to exist, but only in imperfect fashion, in that the soul has a natural aptitude to inform matter and to communicate its *esse* to it. See PB 2.193–94.

[32] See p. 174.

[33] PB 2.43–44.

[34] See propositions 138–199, 139–198, 140–196, 141–197 (with the *Chartularium* number listed first). For the likelihood that at least some of these may have been directed against an anonymous commentary on the *Physics* recently edited by A. Zimmermann and emanating from the Arts Faculty at Paris see Zimmermann, *Ein Kommentar zur Physik des Aristoteles* (Berlin, 1968), pp. xxvii–xxviii; Wippel, "The Condemnations of 1270 and 1277 at Paris," pp. 193–94, n. 56; and most recently, R. Hissette, *Enquête sur les 219 articles condamnés à Paris le 7 mars 1277*, pp. 287–90.

[35] "Utrum aliqua qualitas possit habere esse absque omni subiecto sive sine quantitate" (PB 2.299–300) long version; PB 2.353–54, short version.

from substance—witness the Eucharist again—then whiteness can exist apart from any surface or quantity. Godfrey replies by introducing a distinction. Granted that all accidents essentially depend upon substance, still a certain order obtains among them. Thus some depend more immediately upon substance and therefore participate in its mode of being to a greater degree than do others. This is true of quantity, in that it is presupposed if a material substance is to have certain other accidents, such as to be present in place or to be in a given position or to be subject to sensible qualities such as whiteness or color. Because quantity does participate more fully in the mode of being that is proper to substance, by divine power it can be preserved in being apart from its proper subject. But such does not appear to be true of sensible quality. It does not seem to be separable from quantity in the same way that quantity may be separated from substance, not even by divine intervention.[36]

Corollary 2: May Numerically One and the Same Accident Exist in Different Subjects?

If one agrees with Godfrey that in the purely natural order no accident can exist apart from its subject, still one might wonder whether numerically one and the same accident can be found in two different substances. This question appears to have been of considerable interest in Parisian University circles ca. 1289, since Godfrey explicitly addresses himself to it in his Quodlibet 6, q. 5, of Christmas 1289 and since Giles of Rome had considered the same problem in his Quodlibet 4, q. 9, dating from Easter of that same year.[37] As Godfrey remarks in his discussion of this, one might defend the claim that numerically one and the same accident can exist in different subjects or substances by considering a scar observed on the body of a man before and after the latter's death. Insofar as the senses can determine, the scar remains one and the same. And yet, the man's body will have undergone substantial change, that is to say, death.[38]

---

[36] *Ibid.* Godfrey's conclusion is, it should be noted, rather cautious: "Et ideo non videtur quod ita sit separabilis albedo vel consimilis qualitas a quantitate sicut quantitas a substantia" (PB 2.354). The order that obtains between quantity, quality, and other accidents is brought out very nicely by Thomas Aquinas in his *Expositio super librum Boethii De trinitate*, Q. 5, a. 3 (Decker, ed.), p. 184.

[37] On the date of Godfrey's Quodlibet 6 see Glorieux, *La littérature* . . . , Vol. 1, p. 157 and Lottin, *Psychologie et morale* . . . , T. 1, p. 307, n. 4. For the date of Giles's Quodlibet 4, see Glorieux, *op. cit.*, p. 144.

[38] PB 3.123. Q 6, q. 5 is explicitly addressed to this question: "Utrum aliquod accidens unum numero possit esse in duobus naturis [or subiectis]" (PB 3.122).

Godfrey bases the first part of his reply on the following contention. Just as two or more accidents that are identical in species cannot be found at the same time in one and the same subject, so too is it impossible for numerically one and the same accident to exist simultaneously in two different subjects. As regards the first part of this proposition, if two accidents agree in species, they are not distinguished from one another of themselves. Hence, the fact that they exist in the same subject will not result in their differentiation from one another but in their identity. Thus two points or two instances of whiteness or two lines cannot exist simultaneously in one and the same subject without becoming one point or one whiteness or one line. (It is true that two qualities that differ in species, such as whiteness and sweetness, may be found in one and the same subject simultaneously. But then, reasons Godfrey, they will not remain as two contrary qualities but will intermingle so as to form something intermediary, even though in themselves they are essentially distinct from one another.) So, too, is it impossible for two qualities of the same species to retain their numerical distinction from one another within the same subject. Rather they will unite to form one more or less intense quality.[39]

In like fashion, continues Godfrey, it follows that numerically one and the same accident cannot exist in two different subjects simultaneously. Just as numerical identity of a given subject excludes numerical distinction of accidents inhering therein unless they also differ in species, so does numerical diversity of subjects exclude numerical identity of accidents found in such different subjects simultaneously. Or to phrase the same point in more positive terms, if two subjects are numerically distinct from one another, the accidents that inhere in them simultaneously must also be at least numerically distinct from one another, even if they happen to agree in species.[40]

Still, one might wonder whether numerically the same accident can exist successively in different subjects. In fact, such might appear to be true of the scar on a man's body before and after that man's death. Godfrey replies that this is clearly impossible as regards the kinds of accidents that cannot exist apart from a subject even by divine intervention. When their subject is corrupted, such accidents must also cease to exist. But as we have already

---

[39] PB 3.123. Godfrey observes that this is especially clear for those who hold that habits can undergo intension and remission by being added to one another if they are identical in species. Without committing himself here to this theory Godfrey comments that if such addition is possible, it is clear that it can only be interpreted as meaning that the two qualities when so added together constitute one that is numerically one and the same, but more intense than its components (*ibid.*).

[40] PB 3.124.

seen, considerations relating to the Eucharist had moved Godfrey to defend the existence of another kind of accident. What, then, of those accidents that can, by divine intervention, exist apart from any subject, accidents such as quantity or others that immediately inhere in quantity such as configuration? In this case, suggests Godfrey, it would seem that God could create another substance—similar bread, for instance—and that quantity and the other accidents accompanying it could then inhere in this new substance. This seems especially likely since quantity does not depend upon its subject for its numerical identity, but enjoys this of itself simply by reason of the fact that it is quantity.[41] (We shall see more of this in Ch. IX in our discussion of Godfrey's theory of individuation.)

At this juncture Godfrey raises a further question. If it is possible for an accident to exist successively in different subjects by special divine intervention, is this also possible in the purely natural order? In responding to this Godfrey considers a related issue. If it were true that certain accidents inhere immediately in prime matter, then one might reason that even in the natural order numerically one and the same accident can exist successively in distinct subjects. Thus in the course of substantial change, just as the same prime matter remains, one might then conclude that numerically the same accident can also survive the change and thus continue to exist in the new substance as well as in the old. Godfrey rejects this possibility, however, since he is convinced that within the natural order not even quantity can immediately and directly inform prime matter. Prime matter must first (in the order of nature) be informed by its appropriate substantial form. It is the composite consisting of prime matter and substantial form that is in potency to accidental forms and that serves as their subject.[42]

Godfrey refers to an alternative theory which he regards as more probable than the above. According to this view, certain accidents can pass from subject to subject for this reason, that they do not require only one kind of substantial form and substantial subject but may be found in different subjects and even in different kinds of subjects. Thus one and the same quantity would be present both in that which is corrupted and that which is generated, although its termination or limits would vary in accord with its subject. So, too, certain qualities known as *qualitates symbolae* would be present in both the corrupted and generated subjects, granted that their degree of termination would also vary in accord with the respective substantial forms of these different subjects.[43]

---

[41] PB 3.125.
[42] PB 3.125–26.
[43] PB 3.126–27.

In response to this proposal, Godfrey concedes that there are such accidents that do not of themselves require a particular subject or kind of subject. Thus it is true that quantity and certain other accidents may inhere in different subjects and in different kinds of subjects. Nonetheless, any particular realization of such an accident will depend upon its substantial subject and upon the latter's substantial form not only insofar as it is this determined instance of that accident but for its very existence as well. And when the particular substantial form upon which it depends is corrupted, such an accident will also cease to exist. Hence, this attempt to account for the natural transition of accidents from one subject to another fails. Godfrey adds that any such explanation must be rejected by all who maintain that in substantial change there is resolution of everything pertaining to the corrupted substance back to prime matter itself. It is because of this that nothing pertaining to the substantial form of the corrupted substance can pass over into the newly generated one. Given this understanding of substantial change, which Godfrey apparently accepts as his own, no accidental form of a corrupted substance can continue to exist in a newly generated one, barring special divine intervention, of course.[44]

Finally, Godfrey turns to a theory that had recently been defended by Giles of Rome in his Quodlibet 4, q. 9. According to this view, one should distinguish between those accidents that inhere in a composite substance by reason of its form and those that do so by reason of its matter. Because the substantial form does not endure during the process of corruption or substantial change, accidents of the first-mentioned variety cannot pass over from that which is corrupted to that which is generated. But since prime matter does remain throughout such change, accidents of the second type may do so.[45]

Godfrey rejects this theory on two counts. First of all, he emphasizes the point that every material accident has as its subject a matter-form composite, not prime matter alone. Hence, one cannot reason from the continuing existence of prime matter in two different substances that succeed one another to the numerical identity of any accidents that would be found in both. Secondly, he clarifies the meaning of the distinction to which Giles had

---

[44] PB 3.127–28.

[45] For Godfrey's exposition of this theory see PB 3.129. For Giles see *B. Aegidii . . . Quodlibeta* (Louvain, 1646), Q 4, q. 9, pp. 221–23. There Giles derives this distinction from Avicenna's *Sufficientia*, and applies it to quantity (*quantitas materiae*) and to *qualitas symbola*. Both quantity and the kind of qualities that follow upon matter can retain their numerical identity in that which is corrupted and in that which is generated (p. 223).

referred. To say that certain accidents are in a composite by reason of its form simply means that because of the nature of its form the composite is so determined that it must be informed by such accidents. To say that other accidents inform a composite by reason of its matter is not to imply that they directly inform matter and the composite or form only as a consequence of this. Rather, accidents are so described when the substantial form of a given composite does not so determine its matter that the latter could not receive another accident of the same species when it (the matter) is subsequently informed by a new and specifically different substantial form. Or again, accidents may be so described if the substantial form of the composite essence in which they inhere does not so determine its matter that it (the composite) could not receive another and contrary accident. But Godfrey finds no warrant in either of these usages for concluding that numerically the same accident that pertains to a composite by reason of matter could be found in distinct subjects successively.[46] Once the substantial composite is corrupted, all that inheres in it must also cease to exist.

In concluding, Godfrey returns to the example of the scar on the body of a man before and after death. He insists that the scar and similar accidents really differ numerically insofar as they exist in a living and then in a dead body. But he does acknowledge that they are so similar to one another that the senses cannot detect this numerical distinction. Here he may have in mind Giles's citation of Avicenna to this effect, that a scar as well as an Ethiopian's darkness of skin will remain numerically one and the same in a living and then in a dead Ethiopian.[47]

As regards the question whether numerically one and the same accident can exist in different subjects, then, one may summarize Godfrey's position as follows. Numerically one and the same accident cannot exist simultaneously in two different subjects or substances. By special divine intervention numerically one and the same quantity (or a similar accident) can exist successively in two different substances. But not even this possibility is to be admitted within the purely natural order.

---

[46] PB 3.129–32.

[47] PB 3.132. For Giles see *op. cit.*, p. 223.

Chapter VI.

Subsistence, Supposit, and Nature

In the previous chapter reference was made to a text from Quodlibet 3, q. 4, where Godfrey distinguishes between existence and subsistence. Godfrey there describes subsistence as the existence which a thing enjoys without qualification and in itself rather than dependently in something else. Subsistence belongs only to substance since it is to substance alone that it pertains to exist in this way, that is, in itself and without qualification.[1] As we have also seen, Godfrey assigns existences to accidents as well as to substance and, as a consequence, defends plurality of accidental existences in finite substances along with a single substantial existence or subsistence. In the present chapter, therefore, we propose to examine in greater detail Godfrey's position with respect to subsistence and the supposit or subsisting subject and the relationship that obtains between nature and supposit in finite entities.

In Godfrey's metaphysics, as is generally true of the metaphysical thought of his time, the problem of subsistence arises at least in part from theological concerns. But since its solution involves fundamental metaphysical options, our primary concern here will be with these underlying philosophical notions. Nonetheless, for purposes of illustration and in order to present Godfrey's position more completely, we shall also make some reference to his meta-

---

[1] See Ch. V, n. 13. Also note: "Esse autem subsistentiae quod est esse simpliciter et secundum se et non in alio et ab alio in quo existat dependens, convenit solum substantiae cui convenit et esse simpliciter et per se subsistere" (PB 2.190).

physics of subsistence insofar as he applies it to the theology of the hypostatic union. In Christ, according to the faith that was common to the thirteenth-century schoolmen, two natures, the divine and the human, are united in one supposit or person (an intelligent supposit). Hence, one is not surprised to find Godfrey and others attempting to define more precisely the relationship that obtains between supposit (or person) and nature. With this in mind we shall divide this chapter into the following parts: A. Preliminary Notions; B. The Relationship between Nature and Supposit; C. Subsistence and the Separated Soul; D. Application to the Hypostatic Union (One or More Existences in Christ?).

A. PRELIMINARY NOTIONS

Godfrey accepts as his own the generally received notion that incommunicability is a distinctive characteristic of a supposit.[2] As he observes in Quodlibet 2, q. 1, a thing subsists or is a supposit to the extent that it is separated from every other entity and at the same time is not of such a nature as to exist in something else as a part of the latter.[3] It is also clear from his remarks in that same context that activities or operations are, properly speaking, to be assigned to the supposit. Thus it is really this man, this rational supposit, who wills or thinks or walks or speaks.[4] In Quodlibet 8, q. 1 he remarks that according to Aristotle in *Metaphysics* V substance may be understood in two ways. It may be taken as referring to the supposit itself, which cannot be predicated of anything else. But it may also be applied to the form or specific nature, which can itself be predicated of a supposit.[5] By combining these two passages, one

---

[2] For brief indications of this insofar as it applies to Thomas's metaphysics see L. De Raeymaeker, *Metaphysica generalis,* Vol. 1 (Louvain, 1931), pp. 174ff.; *Philosophy of Being,* pp. 240ff.; L. Vicente, "De notione subsistentiae apud sanctum Thomam," *Divus Thomas* (Piac.) 71 (1968), pp. 404ff., commenting on Thomas's *In I Sent.,* d. 23, q. 1, a. 1.

[3] ". . . quia ratio suppositi consistit in hoc quod res huiusmodi in se separata sit a quocumque alio, nec nata sit secundum suam naturam naturaliter existere in alio ut aliquid eius. Et ideo actio intelligendi et volendi quae sunt actiones suppositi ut suppositum est . . ." (PB 2.50).

[4] *Ibid.* See the final part of the citation in n. 3 above.

[5] ". . . ut dicitur quinto Metaphysicae: substantia dicitur secundum duos modos, scilicet: suppositum quod de aliquo non praedicatur, et forma vel natura speciei quae de supposito praedicatur" (PB 4.9). For Aristotle see *Metaphysics* V, c. 8 (1017b 10ff., 23ff.). For similar citation of this text by Aquinas see *De potentia,* q. 9, a. 1 (beginning of his reply); and ST I, q. 29, a. 2.

may conclude that for Godfrey the supposit is the concrete subject and that it enjoys ontological incommunicability (which is to say that it cannot be assumed by some other entity as a part of the latter).

With this background in mind, it should be clear that for Godfrey more precise understanding of subsistence, or of that which constitutes a supposit as such, and examination of the relationship between nature and supposit are important philosophical concerns. In addition, as we have already suggested, clarification of the same will be of prime importance to him in his theological discussion of the hypostatic union. Not without reason, then, he discusses these issues and related matters in considerable detail in two quodlibetal debates, Quodlibet 7, q. 5 of 1290/91 or 1291/92 and Quodlibet 8, q. 1 of 1292/93.

B. THE RELATIONSHIP BETWEEN NATURE AND SUPPOSIT

In Quodlibet 7, q. 5 Godfrey addresses himself to this question: "Does supposit add any reality *(res)* to essence or to nature?"[6] Before presenting his rather lengthy reply, he introduces an important distinction. Nature and supposit may be contrasted with one another in two different ways. In the first way, nature is taken as that which is signified by an abstract term, as it were in the manner of a simple form to which it belongs to be participated in by something else. When nature is so understood it includes only those things that pertain to a thing's essence, for instance, that which is signified by terms such as humanity or whiteness. All that does not pertain to the essence is not only not included but excluded from its meaning. To nature so understood one may compare the supposit, here taken as that which is signified by a concrete term after the manner of something composed. Granted once more that only that which pertains to the essence or nature of the thing is primarily and directly signified (denoted) by the term supposit when it is so used, still, by connotation, due to the concrete mode of signifying, it includes or at least does not exclude other characteristics of the thing as well. Godfrey illustrates this usage of supposit by terms such as a man or white as realized in a thing. To inquire as to the relationship between nature and supposit when they are so understood is to investigate the relationship between an essence or quiddity (humanity), on the one hand, and that which has such a quiddity (a man) on the other.[7]

---

[6] "Utrum suppositum addat aliquam rem supra essentiam vel naturam" (PB 3.299).

[7] PB 3.300–01. See in particular: "Quaerere ergo quid sit quod addit suppositum sic acceptum supra naturam est quaerere quomodo se habeant quidditas et habens

Essence or nature and supposit may also be contrasted in another way. This time nature is that which is signified by a general or universal term and which, while being one in definition, can be participated in by many individuals. In order to illustrate Godfrey cites man or humanity, white and whiteness. To nature so understood one may oppose the supposit, now taken as a singular or an individual, that is, as something undivided in itself and divided from all other individuals. To ask what supposit when understood in this way adds to nature is to inquire after the principle of individuation, to ask what the individual adds to the universal or what *this* man adds to man or *this* humanity to humanity or *this* whiteness to whiteness.[8]

In this same Quodlibet 7, q. 5, Godfrey addresses himself to each of these ways in which nature and supposit may be compared. We shall return to the problem of individuation and hence to the second way of contrasting them in Ch. IX. For the present we shall restrict ourselves to Godfrey's discussion of the first kind of comparison between nature and supposit, that is, to his effort to determine whether that which is signified by the concrete term, supposit, adds anything real to that which is signified by the abstract term, nature.

Godfrey begins by presenting some reasons that might lead one to think that supposit does add something real to nature. First of all, he notes that one (nature) cannot be predicated of the other (supposit). Thus one cannot say that "man is humanity" or that "a white thing is whiteness." To account for this it is suggested that there must be something in the supposit, in man, for instance, in addition to his accidents, whereby he is really distinguished from humanity. A mere difference in the way in which these terms signify, abstractly versus concretely, would not seem to be enough to prevent predication in terms of identity, granted that it may preclude formal predication of one of the other. Thus, when one treats of divine things, the difference between the abstract and the concrete does not militate against this. Hence one can say: "God is deity."[9]

This same conclusion also seems to follow from the fact that certain things are attributed to supposit which are not attributed to nature. Thus, as we have

---

quidditatem ad invicem, ut per quidditatem intelligatur essentia, per habens quidditatem suppositum."

[8] PB 3.301.

[9] PB 3.301. As D. Trapp has shown, Giles of Rome had directed a similar argument against Henry of Ghent's denial of real distinction between nature and supposit. For this see Giles's *De compositione angelorum,* qu. 5, edited in part by Trapp in his "Aegidii Romani de doctrina modorum," *Angelicum* 12 (1935), p. 451. For Henry see Q 4, q. 4, *op. cit.*, fol. 90v–91v.

already seen Godfrey implying above in his discussion in Quodlibet 2, q. 1, actions are assigned to the supposit but not to nature.[10]

Finally, there is the theological argument. According to Christian belief, the Son of God assumed into the unity of the eternal and divine supposit a human nature, to be sure, but not a human supposit, not a man. Hence it seems that what constitutes a created supposit as such cannot be present in the assumed nature. If the human nature should be separated from the divine supposit so as to exist in itself, then it would be a created supposit. In order to account for this it seems that something would have to be added to it which it now lacks and therefore that it would then really differ from itself as it now exists as an assumed nature.[11]

Such reasons, continues Godfrey, lead some to conclude that if nature and supposit are related as that which is possessed (nature) and that which possesses (supposit), one cannot identify the former—nature and supposit, without identifying the latter—that which is possessed and that which possesses. Since the latter identification is realized only in God, the absolutely simple being, it follows that nature and supposit are not to be identified on the creaturely level.[12]

One might wonder what contemporary figure or figures Godfrey here has in mind. Thomas Aquinas would seem to be one, at least in terms of general background..For as we shall see below, Godfrey immediately presents and criticizes a theory that was defended by Giles of Rome in his *De compositione angelorum* with obvious reference to Thomas's own position, especially as developed in the latter's Quodlibet 2, q. 4.[13] Moreover, there is every likelihood that Godfrey himself was directly conversant with Thomas's position, especially so since the latter's Quodlibet 2 is contained in Godfrey's student notebook.[14]

As regards Thomas's own position, his opinion with respect to a closely related topic, the formal constituent of the supposit or the person (the rational supposit) has been disputed by his students and followers for centuries. Is it existence itself that formally constitutes an individuated nature as a supposit? Or is it a real substantial mode in the line of essence that seals and renders incommunicable that same nature, thereby making of it a supposit? Or is it perhaps neither of these? All three interpretations continue to be defended, perhaps because Thomas does not explicitly address himself to the problem

[10] PB 3.301.
[11] *Ibid.*
[12] PB 3.302.
[13] For Giles's text and commentary see Trapp, *op. cit.*, pp. 451–52.
[14] See *Bibl. Nat. Lat.* 16.297, ff. 32rb–32vb.

under this precise formulation in any great detail.[15]

On a number of occasions, however, Thomas does treat of the topic with which Godfrey is here concerned, that is, the relationship and distinction between nature and supposit. Usually he maintains that in corporeal entities nature and supposit really differ as part and whole. In spiritual beings, including angels and God, they are identical.[16] But in certain contexts, especially in Quodlibet 2, q. 4, Thomas seems to defend a different position. There he is attempting to determine whether nature and supposit differ in angels. He observes that if in any being something can be found in addition to its essence, then in that being nature and supposit will also differ. Thus it is that supposit is signified as a whole, and nature or quiddity as a part of the same. But, continues Thomas, of God alone can it be said that nothing can be found within him in addition to his essence. For in him alone are essence and existence identical. Therefore, only in God are nature and supposit identical. As Thomas goes on to indicate, it will follow from this that even in angels nature and supposit differ, since an angel includes not only its essence but existence and certain accidents as well.[17]

In the same context, while replying to the first objection, Thomas distinguishes two ways in which something may be present within a given being

---

[15] Roughly speaking, one might refer to the first as the Capreolus-Billot interpretation, the second as the Cajetan school, and the third as that proposed by recent defenders of the theory of "pure union" in their effort to indicate why the assumed human nature of Christ is not also a person. For a helpful discussion of each of these and for many references to classical and contemporary literature on the same see O. Schweizer, *Person und Hypostatische Union bei Thomas von Aquin* (Freiburg, Schweiz, 1957), pp. 6–10; 15–17; 23–53. Schweizer ultimately concludes that Thomas defended the theory of "pure union" and hence that for him that which makes an individual nature a person is not something positive but something negative, the absence of union with another supposit. See pp. 114–17. This rather interesting interpretation of Thomas would bring him closer to Duns Scotus on this particular point and, as we shall see below, to the position defended by Godfrey. Needless to say, it is hardly a traditional reading of Aquinas.

[16] See for instance *In III Sent.*, d. 5, q. 1, a. 3 (commented on by Schweizer, pp. 65–67); ST I, q. 3, a. 3; SCG IV, c. 55 ad 4: ". . . quia in homine aliud est natura et persona, cum sit ex materia et forma compositus; non autem in angelo, qui immaterialis est."

[17] See Quodlibet 2, q. 4 in *Quaestiones Quodlibetales,* R. Spiazzi, ed. (Turin-Rome 1956), p. 25. See in particular: "In solo autem Deo non invenitur aliquod accidens praeter eius essentiam, quia suum esse est sua essentia . . . et ideo in Deo est omnino idem suppositum et natura. In angelo autem non est omnino idem . . ." Also see ST III, q. 2, a. 2, where Schweizer finds this same doctrine implied (*op. cit.*, pp. 97–98). Trapp obviously does not, however, interpret this text in this way (*op. cit.*, p. 451, n. 1).

without being included in its essence or definition. It may be that that which is added to the thing's essence determines one or more of its essential principles. Or it may be that it does not do so. In matter-form composites both of these possibilities are realized. Thus an individual man is not only composed of body and soul but of *this* body and *this* soul and hence includes an individuating principle, something that is accidental to man as such or to man taken universally, but determines the essence of this man to be *this* man or to be individual. In other words, to be individuated or to be this individual man is not part of the essence of man as such or of man viewed universally, but would be included in the definition of this individual man if he were to be defined. But other features are present in an individual man which are neither included in the definition of man nor determine any of his essential principles. As an example, Thomas mentions the accident whiteness.[18]

In created spiritual entities, however, Thomas admits only of the second possible way in which something may be present therein in addition to essence. Since for him each angel is a species unto itself, he does not postulate a distinctive principle of individuation within an existing angel. But he does assign a distinct existence to the angel in addition to its essence, along with certain accidents. Admission of this will be sufficient for Thomas to deny that supposit and nature are identical in angels. In fact, as he himself phrases it, supposit and nature are not to be identified in any being whose essence *(res)* is not identical with its existence.[19]

As we have remarked above, in other contexts Thomas seems to restrict distinction between nature and supposit to material entities. One might conclude that his opinion on this point has undergone some change. Or one might attempt to remove the apparent discrepancy by suggesting that he defines supposit differently in Quodlibet 2, q. 4 and in the other texts.[20] Any

---

[18] *Ed. cit.*, pp. 25–26.

[19] *Ed. cit.*, p. 26. See in particular in his reply to obj. 2: "Et ideo, licet ipsum esse non sit de ratione suppositi, quia tamen pertinet ad suppositum, et non est de ratione naturae, manifestum est quod suppositum et natura non sunt omnino idem in quibuscumque res non est suum esse."

[20] For attempts to resolve this see J. Winandy, "Le Quodlibet II, art. 4 de saint Thomas et la notion de suppôt," *Ephemerides theologicae Lovanienses* 11 (1934), pp. 5–29; Schweizer, *op. cit.*, pp. 85–89. According to Schweizer, Thomas at times takes the term supposit to signify an individual substantial nature that is completed in itself, while at other times, especially in Quodlibet 2, q. 4, he uses it in a broader sense, so as to include not only the individual substantial nature but its existence as well. When used in this broader sense as including existence, then, it would differ from nature in all creatures, not merely in material entities. For endorsement of this part of Schweizer's interpretation see *Bulletin thomiste* 10, fasc. 3 (1959),

effort here to resolve this controverted point in Thomistic interpretation would carry us too far afield. But both the passage from Quodlibet 2, q. 4, according to which nature and supposit differ in every creature, and Thomas's more general teaching, according to which nature and supposit differ only in material entities, should be kept in mind as we turn once more to Godfrey's text. Godfrey now presents and criticizes a rather unusual theory that would defend real distinction between nature and supposit, but without postulating the addition of any distinctive thing *(res)* to nature insofar as it is realized in the supposit. This theory was developed by Giles of Rome and especially in his still largely unedited *De compositione angelorum*. Enough of the text has been published by D. Trapp for one to be certain that it is Giles's position and in large measure this very text with which Godfrey is here concerned.[21]

As Godfrey presents Giles's theory, arguments such as those we have considered above lead some to conclude that supposit adds something to nature. But to suggest that supposit merely includes certain accidents in addition to nature does not appear to be sufficient. One would then risk making of supposit itself not a true entity in its own right *(ens per se)* but only an accidental aggregate *(ens per accidens)*. Nor could supposit then be placed in any predicament or category, since it would not enjoy true essential unity. Hence, it seems that supposit should not be defined as including nature and that which is added to nature. Still, it pertains to the supposit to act, not to nature. Given this, it might seem that one should include in one's definition of supposit both existence and those accidents without which a supposit or nature as realized in a supposit could neither exist nor act. In the face of this, Giles proposes a compromise. A supposit implies and signifies a kind of "mode" which follows upon the fact that it is subject to existence and to those properties without which the nature could not exist and the supposit itself could not act.[22]

---

p. 683. But for reservations about his general conclusion as to Thomas's teaching on the formal constituent of the supposit see the preceding review, pp. 678–82.

[21] See n. 9.

[22] PB 3.302. One is here reminded of Schweizer's suggested two ways in which Thomas uses the term supposit (see n. 20). For Giles's text from *De compositione angelorum*, q. 5, see Trapp, *op. cit.*, pp. 470–71. See in particular Giles's argument to show that nature really differs from supposit. If they did not differ, one could be predicated of the other *per identitatem*. Also see part 4 (". . . quod aliquid intraret definitionem suppositi, si definiretur . . .") which Godfrey follows very closely and part of which he reproduces verbatim. Note in particular Giles's comment: "Et licet ea quae sunt extra naturam, ponantur in definitione suppositi, suppositum tamen in suo significato non includeret illa, ita quod natura suppositi includeret naturam et advenientia naturae, sed solum significaret naturam cum quodam modo, quem natura

It is because of this mode, according to Giles's theory, that supposit does not signify another thing *(res)* apart from nature. On the contrary, nature and supposit signify the same thing. Nonetheless, because of this same mode supposit really differs from nature. And as Godfrey accurately reports, Giles appeals to his rather unusual theory of extension to illustrate this point. According to Giles, while extended matter is really distinct from the same matter when it is not extended, extended matter does not signify a distinctive thing *(res)* in addition to or apart from nonextended matter.[23] Matter acquires a real mode by reason of the fact that it is subject to quantity or extended. And insofar as it thereby undergoes true variation in itself, Giles insists that such matter really differs from itself when it is not extended and hence not subject to such variation. As Godfrey also explains, according to Giles's theory matter is itself extended by quantity and not by means of any other extension, just as quantity of itself extends matter. Therefore, the extension of quantity is different from the extension of matter. But the extension of matter is not a distinct thing or essence apart from matter itself. Since matter acquires a real mode by being conjoined with quantity, this mode suffices to make such extended matter really distinct from itself when it is not extended.[24]

In like fashion, Giles concludes that one and the same essence may simply be considered in itself and not insofar as it participates in any added perfections. It is then called nature. But insofar as it is considered as subject to and as participating in added perfections, it is referred to as a supposit. The supposit, therefore, signifies nature together with this mode that the latter acquires insofar as it is subject to existence and to its proper accidents. And supposit when so understood really differs from the nature considered in itself, but does not signify another essence or thing apart from the nature

---

consequitur ex hoc, quod subest ipsi esse et aliis proprietatibus hypostaticis, sine quibus natura actu non existit" (p. 471).

[23] PB 3.302. Giles is aware of the seemingly paradoxical nature of his position: "Et tamen secundum veritatem simul stare possunt. Quod sic patet. Nam quod aliqua dicant eandem essentiam et tamen aliquid cadat in definitione unius quod non cadit in definitione alterius, simul stare potest. . . . Similiter etiam quod aliqua dicant eandem essentiam et tamen realiter differant, quod tamen videtur multum extraneum, simul stare potest. Nam materia extensa differt a seipsa realiter non extensa et tamen non dicit aliam essentiam ipsa extensa a se non extensa . . ." (p. 471).

[24] PB 3.302–03. For more on Giles's theory of modes as well as his distinctive position with reference to matter and extension see Trapp, pp. 457–69; also on his doctrine of extension see Hocedez, *Aegidii Romani Theoremata de esse et essentia*, pp. (8)–(10); Pattin, "Gilles de Rome . . . ," pp. 85*–87*.

itself.[25] Giles here is quite familiar with Thomas's position as expressed in his Quodlibet 2, q. 4. In fact, while somewhat sympathetic to it, Giles is critical of Thomas's way of expressing it, especially so insofar as he seems to imply that existence and other accidents constitute the supposit. Thus, while agreeing with Thomas's position as stated there that nature and supposit differ in all creatures, Giles would account for this in his own way, that is, by the mode that nature receives insofar as it is subject to existence and other accidents.[26]

Godfrey is very critical of any such solution. He counters that one must rather hold that supposit, when considered in its direct and primary meaning, adds nothing real to nature and hence does not really differ from it. As he sees it, this applies to nature and supposit whether they are taken universally (humanity and man) or individually (this humanity as found in this man).[27]

Godfrey then presents a series of counterarguments against Giles's position, some of which we shall now consider. First of all, he judges it contradictory for anyone to suggest that something can really differ from something else and yet neither be nor include a distinct thing *(res)* when compared with that other thing. When things differ only logically, distinct logical aspects or formalities *(rationes)* must be present in them. So true is this, urges Godfrey, that it would be contradictory for someone to hold that one thing could differ logically from another without involving some distinct logical aspect or formality. A fortiori, he reasons, it is clearly contradictory to hold that something (supposit) can really differ from something else (nature) and to deny that it is or at least includes a distinct thing. Godfrey's criticism is of special interest because, if justified, it will undercut Giles's position not only with reference to the relationship between nature and supposit, but also with reference to any more general claim that something may be really distinct from itself without acquiring any new essence or *res*. Hence, one can readily

---

[25] PB 3.304. For Giles see *De compositione angelorum,* q. 5, cited by Trapp, p. 453: "Natura ex hoc quod subicitur esse et proprietatibus, alium modum acquirit et realem modum, per quem modum differt realiter a seipsa ut non est praedictis coniuncta. Iste tamen modus non dicit aliam essentiam a natura ipsa. Suppositum igitur quod dicit naturam cum tali modo, quem natura consequitur ex hoc, quod subicitur esse et proprietatibus, realiter differet a natura ipsa secundum se accepta. Non tamen dicit aliam essentiam ab ipsa natura." The last two sentences are literally quoted by Godfrey (p. 304).

[26] Giles is also familiar with the other view that we have seen in Thomas according to which nature and supposit really differ in material things but not in angels. See Trapp, citing *De compositione angelorum,* pp. 451–52.

[27] PB 3.304 and 318.

anticipate Godfrey's subsequent critical reaction to Giles's theory of extension as well.[28]

Godfrey directs further criticisms against the very notion of such a mode. The mode is either nothing, and therefore as absolute nonbeing cannot ground either real or logical distinction, or else it is something. If it is something, then it either enjoys purely mental reality and cannot serve as the basis for real and extramental distinction or else it exists in itself and independently from the mind's consideration. But if the latter alternative be chosen, then the mode will either be identical with the nature itself or will differ from it in some way. If it is completely identical with the nature, it will not of itself suffice to ground real distinction between the nature and the supposit. If it differs from the nature in some way, then it will either be something absolute in itself or something relative. If it is something absolute, then it will be added to nature as a distinct reality, a conclusion which the theory in question rejects. But if the mode differs from nature as something purely relative, then it will stand as a real relation between a given substance and its accidents. Godfrey's point seems to be that if it is this mode that renders a nature incommunicable and complete in itself, the mode will, as a real relation, come between the substance and the accidents that inhere in it. This, too, he rejects.[29]

On the other hand, as Godfrey observes in another criticism of Giles's theory, since this real mode is supposed to belong to an individuated nature as a consequence of the latter's union with its accidents (and its existence, we might add), it would seem that the mode does not pertain to the definition of the supposit as such but rather follows upon it. If the nature must first be united with its accidents before it can receive such a mode, it must already be constituted as a supposit in itself so as to support these same accidents. Hence, if Giles will not admit that it is the union of a nature with its accidents that constitutes the nature as a supposit, much less should he hold that this could be effected by his proposed mode.[30] Or to phrase it in different terms, Godfrey also contends that if such a mode is indeed that which constitutes and defines a supposit as such, since it presupposes the union of the substantial nature with its accidents, then the accidents themselves will also be included within the definition of the supposit. But this would be to acknowledge that the supposit does add a real essence or *res* to nature, that is to say,

---

[28] PB 3.304 – 05. See Ch. III, pp. 120 – 21, and PB 3.270 – 71.

[29] PB 3.305.

[30] PB 3.306. See in particular: "Sed non potest intelligi esse sub accidentibus nisi habens rationem suppositi in se subsistentis et accidentia sustentantis."

something accidental, which Giles cannot admit.[31]

In sum, then, for these and other reasons Godfrey finds Giles's theory unacceptable. As he puts it, to suggest that such a mode is neither pure nonbeing nor enjoys merely mental reality but that it has extramental reality and yet that it is neither substance nor accident, neither something absolute nor something relative, is really to make of it something purely fictitious. Hence, Godfrey concludes that Giles's position is simply unintelligible and that it is to be rejected in its entirety.[32]

Godfrey is now in position to present his own position. As he sees it, supposit does not differ from nature except in the way in which something concretely considered differs from itself when it is viewed abstractly. That which is primarily signified or denoted by nature and by supposit is one and the same. There is, however, a difference in the way of signifying *(modus significandi)* when something is designated by the abstract term, essence, and by the concrete term, supposit.[33]

In order to show that the primary meaning or denotation of nature and supposit is one and the same, Godfrey appeals to their definitions. That which is signified by a given term in implicit and confused fashion will be expressed by a quidditative definition of the same explicitly and distinctly. But examination of nature and supposit reveals that whatever pertains to the definition of one also pertains to the definition of the other. For instance, whatever is included in the definition of humanity in abstract terms is also found in the definition of man in concrete terms and vice versa.[34]

---

[31] PB 3.306, the following paragraph.

[32] ". . . ideo est omnino irrationalis et penitus est repellenda" (PB 3.307). For some discussion of these criticisms by Godfrey and then by others who repeat Godfrey's argumentation see Trapp, pp. 480–85. He finds Durandus, Guido, Hervaeus Natalis, Petrus Paludanus, and James of Metz contributing little more to Godfrey's critique. He also suggests that Giles himself was probably present for Godfrey's Quodlibetal discussion of this theory and that under the pressure of the latter's attack Giles modified his theory ever so slightly. Thus Godfrey acknowledges that it might be said that the mode in question does not result from the union of a nature with its accidents but that it is a certain mode of subsisting which pertains to a nature only *virtually* complete in the genus of substance, and that it is *actually* given to the supposit by its efficient cause. Godfrey judges this to be no more acceptable. See Trapp, pp. 484–85, and Godfrey, PB 3.307–08.

[33] PB 3.308; also see PB 3.318.

[34] PB 3.308. Godfrey adds that this holds whether one has to do with logical or with natural definition. He also observes that this seems to be Aristotle's meaning in *Metaphysics* VII, c. 6 (1031a 28ff.), where he states that in that which is *per se*, the thing *(res)* and its *quod quid est* are one and the same. Godfrey surmises that by *res* Aristotle may mean supposit and by *quod quid est* the essence.

Thus the term nature signifies an essence abstractly after the manner of a simple form or formal perfection that can be participated in by something else. Granted that such a finite nature, above all, one that is material, will never exist in fact without certain accidents, nonetheless, these are beyond the scope of the essence or nature considered in itself. Hence, nature, which signifies essence abstractly, does so in such fashion as to exclude (precision in the technical sense) all such accidents. It signifies the essence and its essential principles alone. In its denotation or primary meaning the term supposit also signifies one and the same nature, but concretely and as participated in by that which also participates in the accidents. Precisely because it does not signify the essence or nature abstractly but concretely, it does not exclude the accidents, granted that it does not include them in its direct and primary meaning or denotation. That which is indicated by the term supposit, therefore, is signified as a whole. But that which is signified by the term nature is rather taken as a formal part. At the same time, it should also be observed that for Godfrey the term supposit connotes something more, the exclusion of any other subject in which it (the supposit) might inhere or with which it might join as a part.[35]

Godfrey had argued against real distinction between nature and supposit by reasoning that whatever is included in the definition of the one is also included in the definition of the other. In other words, he had shown that in terms of their denotation the terms nature and supposit signify one and the same thing. As he now phrases this point, if one looks only to the primary and principal meaning of these two terms, that is, to their denotation, there

---

[35] PB 3.308–09. Shortly thereafter Godfrey makes it explicit that nature, as designated by the term supposit, is taken as a whole and thus connotes the exclusion of any other subject upon which the supposit might depend or with which it might join in union (see PB 3.311). Also see Q 8, q. 1 (PB 4.16): "Et est dicendum quod subsistentia addit aliquo modo aliquid ad existentiam, non proprie aliquid intrinsecum, sed aliquid extrinsecum quod potest dici connotatum: nam esse dicit actualitatem essentiae vel naturae simpliciter et absolute, non determinando quod ipsa natura existens sit vel non sit alteri innitens, et cetera . . . sed subsistere dicit actualitatem essentiae vel naturae connotando aliquid extrinsecum; nam ex hoc dicitur aliquid subsistere quod habet esse secundum se non innitendo alteri; et sic, ut non est pars vel quasi pars alicuius vel cum alio, sic connotat aliud exclusive sive exclusionem alterius. Non subsistere autem in se, sed subsistere in alio dicitur quod dicit esse innitens alteri et cetera." If one bears in mind Godfrey's identification of essence and existence, then one will not be surprised that he correlates subsistence and existence as he had compared supposit and nature in Q 7, q. 5. Thus existence and subsistence are really identical in a given subsisting subject, but subsistence connotes something more, the exclusion of dependence upon another supposit.

is no real distinction between that which is signified by nature and that which is signified by supposit. But if one looks beyond this to their connotation as well, then one finds that supposit is not really identical with nature. So viewed, supposit does not merely add a mode, as Giles would have it, but true accidental reality, that is, those accidents without which nature can never be realized in concrete existence. Granted, therefore, the complete identity of that which is primarily and principally signified or denoted by these two terms, because of this difference in connotation one cannot be predicated of the other whether by formal predication or by identity.[36]

With this final observation Godfrey has, in effect, already replied to the first of those indications that might move some to defend real distinction between nature and supposit. In order to account for the fact that nature cannot be predicated of supposit, it was suggested that something must be found in the supposit in addition to accidents whereby it is distinguished from nature.[37] Godfrey counters that the difference between signifying essence abstractly or as nature and signifying it concretely or as supposit is sufficient to account for the fact that on the created level one cannot be predicated of the other either by formal predication or by identity. Such will not be true of God, however, since on the divine level that which is concretely signified—God, for instance—does not include even by connotation anything that is really distinct from the nature of deity. Hence, predication of the abstract term "deity" of God is possible by identity, if not by formal predication.[38]

This difference in the mode of signifying essence as nature and then as supposit will also suffice, continues Godfrey, to account for the fact that actions may be attributed to supposit but not to nature. This will be true even in the case of God. One can say that God creates, but not that deity or the divine nature creates. This is so because that which is signified abstractly by nature is taken after the manner of a formal part, while that which is signified concretely by supposit is taken after the manner of a whole which is informed and which exists. Therefore it is signified as that to which operation or activity can also be assigned.[39]

---

36 PB 3.309. See in particular: "Si ergo aspiciatur ad id quod per nomen naturae et suppositi per se et principaliter significatur, non est differentia realis inter naturam et suppositum, sed solum secundum rationem et modum intelligendi et significandi. . . . Sed, si aspiciatur ad id quod ratione modi significandi et intelligendi datur intelligi modo supradicto per nomen suppositi et naturae, sic suppositum non est idem realiter cum natura, quia non solum addit modum quendam, sed veram rem accidentalem. . ."

37 See p. 228.

38 PB 3.309–10.

39 PB 3.310.

Nor does the theological point based on the hypostatic union indicate real distinction between nature and supposit, Godfrey insists. In order to account for the fact that Christ did not assume a human supposit (man) but rather a human nature (humanity), Godfrey appeals once more to the distinction between essence when it is considered abstractly and as a formal part (as nature) and essence when it is considered concretely and as a whole. Because nature and supposit agree in their denotation or primary meaning, they are really one and the same. But because they differ in connotation, the term supposit also implies independence in concrete existence from any other subject upon which the supposit might lean or depend or with which it might tend to unite as a part. Because the human nature has been assumed by the divine supposit in the hypostatic union, the human nature itself does not enjoy this condition of independent existence. Hence, while it retains its own existence, this existence is not subsistence. And for this same reason, the human nature is only a human nature, not a human supposit. But if the human nature were to be separated from the divine supposit and were to continue to exist, then its human existence would become a human subsistence and the human nature itself would be a human supposit.[40]

In other words, insofar as nature is considered concretely as supposit, it is viewed as something whole and perfect and connotes not only the accidents which must be realized in it for it to exist in fact, but also the exclusion of any other supposit upon which it might lean as a support or with which it might unite as a part or even tend so to unite.[41] When the same nature is viewed abstractly, as a formal part, it does not include in its connotation either its accidents or this exclusion of dependence or of aptitude to depend upon or unite with something else. Consequently, the individual human nature as assumed by Christ cannot be called a supposit or person because it does now exist as part of something else and as dependent upon the divine supposit. Hence, it does not possess that independence in existence from any other subject which is necessarily included in the connotation of supposit.[42]

According to Godfrey, therefore, none of these alleged indications points to real distinction between nature and supposit when they are considered in terms of their primary meaning or their denotation. Nor should one appeal

---

[40] PB 3.310–11.

[41] PB 3.311. ". . . ad hoc quod aliquid habeat rationem suppositi et significetur sub ratione suppositi et in concreto, oportet quod res illa intelligatur ut in se et per se existat. Hoc autem requirit quod non apprehendatur sub ratione partis, sive materialis sive formalis, sive ut aliquid alterius vel alteri innitens, vel quo alteri aliquid convenit."

[42] See PB 3.311–12.

to Giles's modal theory in order to account for the fact that a given nature is also a supposit and a center of action. If a substantial nature in fact enjoys independent existence in itself without depending upon any other center of existence as its subject, then it will also enjoy subsistence and will be a supposit. When one concentrates on the primary meaning of the term supposit or its denotation, one finds nothing more included therein than that which is signified by the term nature. But because of the fact that the term supposit signifies concretely, by connotation it will designate something in addition to nature, that is, independent existence in itself and those accidents without which the nature will not be realized in concrete and factual existence.[43]

Godfrey is equally unsympathetic to Giles's appeal to his theory of extension in order to show how something might really be distinct from itself without including any superadded essence or *res*. As already noted, Giles contends that insofar as matter is conjoined to quantity and is thereby extended, this same matter acquires a certain mode. By reason of this mode it undergoes some change or variation within itself whereby it is rendered really distinct from itself when it was not joined to quantity and extended. Thus while the extension of quantity is said to be different from the extension of matter, Giles denies that the extension of matter is a distinct thing apart from matter itself.[44]

Godfrey's refutation of Giles's theory of extension is too detailed for us to consider it at length. In brief, he denies that when distinctive predicamental realities are joined together, the conjoined principles are so changed in themselves as to be rendered really distinct from themselves as they were prior to or apart from such union. Hence, he also flatly rejects the contention that matter as extended may be described as really distinct from itself when it is considered as nonextended, and this without its involving any superadded thing or essence. According to Godfrey, extended matter really includes two things, the essence of matter and the essence of the quantity whereby the matter is extended. At most, therefore, one may say that matter viewed in itself and as nonextended differs from itself when it is extended in the way something simple differs from something composite or a part (the matter) differs from a whole (the matter-quantity composite).[45]

---

[43] See PB 3.312. Also, note Godfrey's comment in Q 8, q. 1 (PB 4.17): "Ideo potest dici variatio circa subsistentiam, sive circa esse subsistentiae, ratione differentis rei quam connotat et includit, scilicet secundum quod alteri unitur vel non unitur modo praedicto, absque hoc quod fiat variatio circa ipsam essentiam vel esse quae hoc non includant vel connotant."

[44] See pp. 233–35.

[45] PB 3.312–14.

Nor will Godfrey admit that the extension of matter is different from the extension of quantity in such a way that, in addition to the quantity which extends matter, matter would also enjoy a certain real mode (extension) in itself. Strictly speaking, counters Godfrey, it is the composite that is extended and the quantity that serves as the formal principle of extension, that is to say, as the very extension of the composite. Hence, one may say that extended matter is really distinct from its extension or quantity, but not that it is really distinct from itself when it is considered without this extending quantity. In sum, then, Godfrey finds no value in Giles's theory of modes in accounting for the extension of matter and, hence, no justification for reasoning by analogy therefrom to a similar mode to account for alleged real distinction between supposit and nature.[46]

In concluding this discussion of Godfrey's position with reference to the relationship between nature and supposit, one may return to the question he had originally raised in Quodlibet 7, q. 5: Does supposit add any reality to essence or nature? As we have now seen in some detail, Godfrey maintains that in terms of their primary and principal meaning or denotation, supposit and nature are really one and the same. Hence, supposit does not add any new reality or new mode to essence or nature. In terms of its connotation, however, the term supposit does signify something more than does the term nature, that is, those accidents without which a nature would not exist in the concrete order, and the exclusion of dependence upon another subject or center of existence.[47]

---

[46] PB 3.314–15; 317–18. For explicit defense of his claim that something can really differ from itself without including an added thing or essence, also see Giles's Quodlibet 5, q. 14 (pp. 306b–310b). There both in the *In contrarium* (p. 306b) and near the end of his reply (p. 310ab) Giles refers to the connection between this discussion and his defense of real distinction between supposit and nature in his *De compositione angelorum*. Here also he offers another fairly detailed defense of his theory of modes, especially as illustrated by the extension of matter. According to Glorieux both Godfrey's Q 7 and Giles's Q 5 date from the year 1290, with the added conjecture that Giles's Quodlibet may date from Easter of that year (*La littérature quodlibétique*, Vol. 1, pp. 140–41, 150–51; Vol. 2, p. 375). He also suggests that Godfrey's Q 7 comes after Giles's Q 5, though this could still be the case even if both date from the same quodlibetal period. But this will be even more likely if one places Godfrey's Q 7 in the academic year 1290/91 (perhaps Easter 1291) or 1291/92 as we have proposed. See, for instance, Giles's appeal (pp. 306b–307b) to a text from Aristotle's *De Generatione* I, c. 1, an appeal which Godfrey sharply contests (PB 3.317–18). What is beyond dispute is the fact that both Giles and Godfrey explicitly refer to or quote from Giles's *De compositione angelorum*.

[47] PB 3.318. See in particular: "Ad quaestionem ergo, cum quaeritur utrum suppositum aliquid addit supra naturam secundum primum modum accipiendi suppositum

As regards Godfrey's agreement or disagreement with his contemporaries on this point, enough has already been said to show that he differs strongly from Giles of Rome and, in fact, develops his position in direct confrontation with him. Insofar as Thomas Aquinas had defended real distinction between nature and supposit in all material entities, and according to the thinking of Quodlibet 2, q. 4 even in created spirits, Godfrey also differs from him. Two further observations should be made with reference to this. Thomas often distinguishes between nature and supposit in material entities because of the presence of individuating principles in material existents.[48] When the problem is presented in these terms, Godfrey would prefer to treat it in connection with the question of individuation. As we shall see in Ch. IX, even in proposing his solution to the problem of individuation Godfrey will refuse to admit that supposit adds any new or distinctive thing to nature. But in the present context he is rather concerned with the relationship between nature and supposit when they are compared as the abstract and the concrete. Secondly, when approaching the problem from the perspective reflected in Quodlibet 2, q. 4, Thomas appeals to the presence of existence *(esse)* as well as of accidents in the supposit in order to differentiate it from nature. Godfrey cannot agree with this, of course, since he does not allow for real distinction between essence and existence.[49]

In his denial that there is real distinction between nature and supposit Godfrey is somewhat closer to the position defended by Henry of Ghent, for instance, in the latter's Quodlibet 4, q. 4. The two Masters formulate the problem in different terms, however, since Henry is especially concerned with contrasting a physical and a metaphysical understanding of a material thing in the course of his discussion.[50] But he does maintain that both in material things and in spirits nature and supposit are identical, although he acknowledges that this is much clearer with respect to spirits. Even in the case of material entities he denies that any reality can be added to an essence

---

et naturam, dicendum est quod sic quantum ad connotatum: sed quantum ad principale significatum dicendum quod non."

[48] See the texts cited in n. 16.

[49] See our text pp. 230–31.

[50] *Quodlibeta, ed. cit.*, fol. 90v–91v. According to Trapp, Giles was concerned in particular with refuting this text of Henry in q. 5 of his *De compositione angelorum* (*op. cit.*, p. 450). According to Henry, a physical understanding (*intellectus*) of a thing involves grasping it in terms of its matter and form, while a metaphysical understanding entails grasping it in terms of those principles of which it is composed in its intentional being, for instance, genus and species. Thus, while the physicist or natural philosopher defines man as composed of body and soul, the metaphysician defines him as a rational animal (fol. 91r).

or nature to make of it a supposit which would thereby differ substantially from itself when it is considered only as a nature.[51] Godfrey's explicit differentiation between the comparison between nature and supposit when they are considered as abstract and concrete and when they are contrasted as universal and individual is, in our opinion, an important clarification and marks an advance in the general discussion. And as regards the first comparison, his distinction between the denotation and connotation of the term supposit is central to his solution.

In passing, we should also like to call the reader's attention to the striking similarity between Godfrey's discussion of the relationship between nature and supposit and the solution proposed shortly thereafter by James of Viterbo for another disputed issue, the relationship between essence and existence. In his Quodlibet 1, q. 4 of 1293, James considers three different positions defended by "modern" *doctores* on this matter, that is to say, theories that defend real identity, real distinction, and finally, intentional distinction between essence and existence. As we have suggested in another context, it is clear that James here has in mind Giles of Rome as a defender of the second position and Henry of Ghent as a proponent of the third. Godfrey's defense of real identity of essence and existence was also surely well known to him.[52]

In proposing his own solution James reasons that *esse* and essence are to one another as the concrete and the abstract. Hence, existence will differ from essence just as the concrete differs from the abstract. If one wonders whether a concrete term signifies the same thing as its corresponding abstract term, James proposes a distinction. An abstract term signifies a form alone, whereas a corresponding concrete term signifies that form together with its subject. But if a concrete term signifies both the form and its subject, it does not do so with equal immediacy. It signifies the form primarily and the

---

[51] *Op. cit.*, fol. 91v.

[52] See *Jacobi de Viterbio. O.E.S.A. Disputatio prima de quolibet*, pp. 45–47. According to Grabmann, James is thinking both of Thomas and of Giles in his presentation of the theory of real distinction (see his "Doctrina S. Thomae de distinctione reali . . . ," pp. 174, 176). But James's later reference to the *Theoremata* (p. 54:379–84) when discussing this same theory makes it clear that he is referring to Giles, presumably to the latter's *Theoremata de esse et essentia*, possibly also to his *Theoremata de corpore Christi*. James also finds some possible adumbration of the third opinion in Robert Grosseteste, but acknowledges that it owes its present form to "others," that is, to Henry of Ghent. For fuller exposition of James's position see our "The Relationship between Essence and Existence in Late Thirteenth Century Thought: Giles of Rome, Henry of Ghent, Godfrey of Fontaines, and James of Viterbo," in *Ancient and Medieval Philosophies of Existence*, P. Morewedge, ed. (forthcoming).

subject only in a secondary way.[53] By applying this precision to the essence-existence relationship, James can conclude that since essence and existence are related as the abstract and the concrete, they are one and the same in their primary meaning. But as regards their secondary meaning they differ, and really so, in creatures. This is to say, that which is signified by the concrete term existence *(esse)* in its secondary meaning includes something in addition to essence. Here James seems to have in mind things such as proper accidents and individuating notes.[54]

There is remarkable similarity between James's proposed correlation of essence and existence and Godfrey's view that nature and supposit are related as abstract and concrete and that what they signify primarily or denote is one and the same. Moreover, James suggests that since existence *(esse)* and being *(ens)* signify the same thing and since being or "that which is" may also be referred to as a supposit, then one may say that essence and existence differ just as do essence and supposit.[55] Since the term supposit signifies the essence primarily and by way of consequence other factors which are united with the essence in the concrete existent, supposit really differs from essence when it is taken in this secondary and consequent meaning just as existence differs from essence. But in terms of their primary meaning essence and existence signify one and the same thing. And it is this primary meaning, or denotation as we might describe it, that is most important in James's eyes.[56]

It seems clear, then, that James's solution to the essence-existence relationship is very similar to Godfrey's position on the relationship between nature and supposit. One might wonder if Godfrey's own position on the essence-existence relationship is itself identical with or reducible to his solution to the nature-supposit relationship. Such does not seem to be the case. We have not found Godfrey applying this secondary meaning or connotation to existence in his discussion of its relationship with essence. Hence, he does not admit that the two may be said to differ really if one should concentrate on the secondary meaning or connotation of existence, as James has proposed. While serving as a possible source for James's interrelationship of essence and existence through his own discussion of nature and supposit, therefore, Godfrey appears to stress the identity of essence and existence to

---

[53] *Op. cit.*, p. 47:146 – p. 48:172.

[54] *Op. cit.*, p. 48:173 – 182.

[55] *Op. cit.*, p. 49:188 – 193. Note in particular: "Et quia id quod est dicitur ipsum suppositum, ideo etiam dici potest quod, sicut differt essentia et suppositum habens essentiam, sic differt essentia et esse."

[56] *Op. cit.*, p. 49:193 – 214; p. 53:350 – p. 54:359.

a greater extent than does James.[57] And James himself is aware that his position on the essence-existence relationship differs from that which admits of no more than logical distinction between the two.[58]

In denying that supposit when taken in its primary meaning or denotation adds anything real or positive to nature, Godfrey has, at least by implication, also indicated his position with respect to the closely related issue, the formal constituent of the supposit or the person (rational or intelligent supposit). It is clear from the above that he will not appeal either to a distinctive act of existence or to a mode in the line of essence (whether as proposed by Giles of Rome, or later, by Cajetan) in order to account for the fact that a given individual nature is also a supposit or a person. On the contrary, it is only in terms of its connotation that supposit can be distinguished from nature, and this because it not only connotes those accidents without which the individuated nature would not be realized in concrete existence, but also the exclusion of dependence upon another supposit as upon its subject or even of an aptitude or inclination so to depend.[59]

This final point reminds one of a theory to be defended shortly thereafter by Duns Scotus, according to which it is the negation both of the actual dependence of a given nature on some other subject and of any inclination so to depend that constitutes a nature as a person. Scotus discusses more explicitly and places greater emphasis upon the final negation—the exclusion of any inclination of the person so to depend—than does Godfrey.[60] Hence,

---

[57] See, for instance, Godfrey's comment in Q 13, q. 3 (PB 5.208): "Inconveniens ergo est dicere quod esse et essentia differant realiter." It is true that in this context he has been considering the principal or primary meaning of expressions such as "light" and "to give light," and essence and *esse*. But he does not state that essence and existence may be said to differ really when one concentrates on the secondary meaning or connotation of existence, something that he has admitted of supposit with reference to nature and something that James has asserted of essence and existence.

[58] See *op. cit.*, p. 54:365–367.

[59] See Q 7, q. 5 (PB 3.311): "Quia enim nomine quo significatur natura sub ratione suppositi significatur quasi sub ratione cuiusdam totius et perfecti connotando exclusive aliud vel cui innitatur vel cum quo sit pars vel *nata sit esse pars,* tali autem convenit agere" (ital. mine). Also see the text cited in n. 41. Godfrey defends the same position in his Q 13, q. 2, dating from 1297 or 1298. See PB 5.188–89, and in particular: ". . . quia sic accipitur ut cum quodam alio connotato exclusive, scilicet aliud cui innitatur in existendo excludendo; et sic dicitur suppositum" (p. 189).

[60] See in particular Scotus's *Quodlibet,* qu. 19, art. 3, par. 19 (Paris, Vivès ed., T. 26, pp. 287–88); also for an improved Latin text see *Cuestiones Cuodlibetales (Obras del Doctor Sutil Juan Duns Escoto),* Felix Alluntis, ed. and tr. (Madrid, 1968), pp. 688–89, nn. 63–68. Also see his *Ordinatio* III, d. 1, q. 1, nn. 5–11 (Vivès ed., T. 14, pp. 16–28); d. 5, q. 2, n. 4 (*ibid.*, p. 228). For fuller discussion

his position can hardly be reduced to Godfrey's. Nonetheless, further investigation of possible Godfridian influence upon Scotus in his development of his own position might prove fruitful.

C. SUBSISTENCE AND THE SEPARATED SOUL

Within a metaphysical system such as that developed by Godfrey, the situation of the separated soul might appear to be paradoxical. For Godfrey, as we shall see in greater detail in Ch. VIII, the human soul is to be regarded as a substantial form, perhaps as the only substantial form, of a human being. But in its state of separation from the body this same substantial principle or form exists in itself and even seems to subsist. At the same time, however, it does not seem to enjoy perfect subsistence. Granted that in its state of separation it does not inhere in another subject, according to Godfrey it does retain its natural inclination to be reunited with its body. Hence, the question may be raised: How can one and the same thing, the separated soul, be said to exist and even to subsist in itself, on the one hand, and to retain its natural inclination or tendency towards its body, on the other?

In Quodlibet 2, q. 1 of Easter 1286, Godfrey wonders whether the soul of Christ during the period between his death and his resurrection was in some way impeded from enjoying the fullness of beatitude because of its separation from his body.[61] And in Quodlibet 9, q. 8 of 1293/94 he discusses a related question, whether the human soul in its state of glory and apart from its body can enjoy greater happiness, even greater essential happiness, than can an angel.[62] In the course of preparing his reply to these theological matters, Godfrey sheds some further light upon his philosophical understanding of the separated soul. As he explains in both of these contexts, the separated soul is, naturally speaking, only a part of a composite whole. Since a part enjoys more perfect being when it exists within its whole than when it exists in separation from that same whole, it follows that the separated soul does not enjoy its full natural perfection in its state of separation.[63]

---

of Scotus's position see H. Mühlen, *Sein und Person nach Johann Duns Scot* (Werl/Westf., 1954), esp. pp. 95–105; L. Seiler, "La notion de personne selon Scot. Ses principales applications en Christologie," *La France franciscaine* 20 (1937), pp. 209–48.

[61] "Utrum anima Christi in triduo fuerit aliquo modo impedita a plenitudine beatitudinis ratione suae separationis a corpore" (PB 2.45).

[62] "Utrum anima humana in gloria sine corpore suo possit esse beatior etiam quantum ad beatitudinem essentialem aliquo angelo . . ." (PB 4.234).

[63] ". . . anima autem non est ens secundum se perfectum omnino et omnem modum

In Quodlibet 2, q. 1, Godfrey goes on to discuss the separated soul's status as a supposit. Strictly speaking, a human being consists both of soul and body. When the soul exists in separation from its body, it always retains its natural aptitude and inclination to exist in that body. So true is this, continues Godfrey, that for it to exist apart from its body is contrary to its nature in this sense that it is contrary to this natural inclination. Hence, it does not then enjoy the full perfection of a supposit but is such only in diminished fashion.[64] As Godfrey explains, it not only belongs to a supposit as such to exist in separation from any other subject, but it does not belong to its nature to be ordered to something else so as to exist in it as a part. In other words, the natural inclination of the separated soul to be united with its body precludes one from describing it as a supposit in the full and perfect sense. And since a person is a rational or intellectual supposit, Godfrey does not hesitate to deny to the separated soul personality in the full and proper sense.[65]

---

perfectionis suae naturalis secundum se habens, quia est pars naturae compositae ex anima et corpore; unaquaeque pars autem habet perfectius esse in toto quam secundum se. . ." Q 2, q. 1 (PB 2.47). See Q 9, q. 8 (PB 4.235). Note especially: ". . . pars autem sine toto non habet omnem modum suae perfectionis quem in toto nata est habere." For fuller discussion of Godfrey's solution to the theological question raised in these two questions see B. Neumann, *Der Mensch* . . . , pp. 125–29. Also see his discussion of and references to studies by Glorieux and Pelster pertaining to Godfrey's proposed textual resolution of an apparent shift in opinion between Thomas's discussion in his Commentary on Bk. IV of the *Sentences* (d. 49, q. 1, a. 4), and his *Summa theologiae* I-IIae, q. 4, a. 5, ad 5 ("Et ideo, corpore resumpto, beatitudo crescit non intensive, sed extensive"). For Glorieux see "Saint Thomas et l'accroissement de la beatitude," *Recherches de Théologie ancienne et médiévale* 17 (1950), pp. 121–25. But for Pelster see his "Das Wachstum der Seligkeit nach der Auferstehung. Um die Auslegung von S. th. 1, 2, q. 4 a. 5 ad 5," *Scholastik* 27 (1952), pp. 561–63. On this also see C. Peter, *Participated Eternity in the Vision of God* (Rome, 1964), pp. 273–80.

[64] ". . . ita quod anima etsi possit esse separata secundum se existens, quia tamen semper nata est existere in alio ut in corpore, et contra suam naturam est et contra eius naturalem inclinationem quod sit extra corpus, rationem perfectam suppositi non habet sed diminuti rationem . . ." (PB 2.50). On the separated soul's natural inclination to be united with its body see Q 9, q. 8 (PB 4.235); also cf. Q 3, q. 4 (PB 2.194); Q 5, q. 6 (PB 3.24); Q 6, q. 16 (PB 3.256).

[65] Q 2, q. 1 (PB 2.50). Note in particular: "Et ideo actio intelligendi et volendi . . . conveniet animae sic secundum se existenti et rationem suppositi diminute habenti . . . cum *causa* non habendi perfectum actum beatitudinis est non tam propter defectum corporis secundum se quam propter defectum personalitatis sive rationis suppositi quam non habet anima sine corpore." Compare with Duns Scotus's *Quodlibet*, qu. 19, art. 3, par. 19 (Vivès ed., T. 26, p. 288; Alluntis, p. 689). ". . . sola negatio actualis dependentiae non sufficit ad hoc quod aliquid dicatur in se personatum vel persona, quia anima Petri habet talem negationem, et tamen non est persona."

Godfrey clarifies the above by assigning to the soul a twofold way of subsisting and of being a supposit. The first is that incomplete and imperfect mode of subsisting that the separated soul continues to enjoy in its state of separation as a consequence of its immaterial nature. (Godfrey's point here is that it is because of its immaterial nature that the soul survives death and separation from the body.) The second is that complete and perfect mode of subsisting that the soul enjoys insofar as it is united with its body and is thus a part of a subsisting whole.[66] In other words, the separated soul is said to be an incomplete supposit precisely because and insofar as it is an incomplete being. It is true that it is not inclined by its nature to unite with something else as an accident with its subject. But it is naturally inclined to be united with its body, the body that it would substantially perfect and with which it would constitute a being that enjoys essential unity.[67]

In Quodlibet 3, q. 4 Godfrey asks whether the separated soul exists by that same existence *(esse)* whereby the whole man had existed.[68] In his reply Godfrey recalls his rejection of any real distinction between essence and existence and reasons that there are as many existences in a given being as there are essences or forms. As will be recalled, he maintains that this conclusion should be defended even if one upholds real distinction between essence and existence.[69] He observes that if there are many forms in a given entity which enjoys substantial unity, it would seem that only one of these can be the substantial form that communicates unqualified existence to that same being. He acknowledges that there may be many accidental existences in a single entity, but insists that there can only be one existence that is also subsistence.[70]

Farther on in this same discussion Godfrey touches on that much contested issue, unicity vs. plurality of substantial form in man. Here he does not decisively commit himself on this point.[71] If one holds for plurality of substantial forms in man, it will follow that there are many existences in man as well. Only that actual substantial existence that belongs to man by reason of his soul will remain in the separated soul. Other "substantial" existences will be corrupted along with the other substantial forms.[72] If, on the other hand, one defends unicity of substantial form in man—the position we shall

---

[66] PB 2.50.

[67] PB 2.51.

[68] "Utrum anima separata existat eodem esse quo existit totus homo" (PB 2.187).

[69] PB 2.188. See Chapter V.

[70] PB 2.188 – 89; 190; 192.

[71] "Supposito ergo quod in homine non sit nisi una forma substantialis, quod tamen non assero . . ." (PB 2.193).

[72] PB 2.193.

find Godfrey hesitantly favoring in Ch. VIII—then further distinctions are required. If one also assumes, as Godfrey himself does, that prime matter is pure potentiality, then when it is subject to its single substantial form, it will enjoy no actual existence except that of its substantial form.[73] Hence, when matter is separated from its substantial form, it will lose that substantial existence, granted that it will receive a new substantial existence from the new form that actualizes it. Given these presuppositions, one may, reasons Godfrey, conclude that the separated soul retains its entire actual substantial existence and therefore the actual substantial existence whereby the whole or composite man had existed. Nonetheless, since both matter and form pertained to the essence of the composite or the whole man, in the soul's state of separation not all that had belonged to the man's essence remains.[74]

Godfrey suggests that one may refer to form as actual being *(esse)* and to matter as potential being *(esse)*. One may say that the entire actual being or existence of the composite remains in the separated soul, as he has already pointed out, because of our usual linguistic identification of being or existence as such with actual existence. But he immediately adds that the total being *(esse)* of the composite cannot be said to be retained by the separated soul except by aptitude, that is, by reason of the soul's inclination to inform its matter and to communicate existence to it once more.[75]

As regards the apparent paradox to which reference was made above, Godfrey's reply is that because of its immaterial nature the human soul survives the body and is, therefore, a separated soul. To that extent it may be said to exist in itself apart from the body. But insofar as it retains its inclination to be reunited with the body, its mode of existence is imperfect and incomplete. Moreover, because of this same inclination or natural desire for its body, it cannot be described as a supposit in the full and perfect sense or even as a person in the complete sense. This apparent paradox is to be resolved, then, by recalling the two modes or ways of subsisting that Godfrey has distinguished for the soul, one imperfect and incomplete and applying to it in its state of separation, the other the complete and perfect mode of subsisting that it enjoys insofar as it is united with its body. Godfrey's reasons for assigning both of these modes to the soul are, it would appear, twofold: his application of Aristotle's hylemorphic theory to the union of soul and body; and his defense of the soul's survival by reason of its immateriality.

---

[73] PB 2.193.

[74] *Ibid.* Note in particular: "Quia tamen ad eius essentiam quae est composita non simplex pertinet materia et forma simul unita, ideo in anima separata non remanet totum id quod pertinet ad compositi essentiam nec tota essentia nec totum esse essentiae."

[75] PB 3.194.

D. APPLICATION TO THE HYPOSTATIC UNION (ONE OR MORE EXISTENCES IN CHRIST?)

In his discussion of this theological problem, Godfrey remains faithful to the theory of subsistence we have just considered as well as to his metaphysics of essence and existence. In fact, it is his metaphysical position that controls his answer to the theological issue. In brief, the question reduces to this. If it is a matter of Christian belief that in Christ there are two natures, a divine and a human, what is one to say of a human existence? Is there a human existence in Christ in addition to the divine existence of the Word? This problem was frequently discussed in Parisian theological circles by the time of Godfrey's explicit treatment of it in his Quodlibet 8 of 1292/1293, and as we shall see, he seems to have been quite familiar with the positions of Thomas Aquinas, Henry of Ghent, and Giles of Rome with respect to the same.

As regards Thomas's position, one of his texts poses a particular difficulty for his interpreters. In most of his discussions of this matter he apparently assigns only one substantial existence to Christ, that of the Word. Not only is this true of earlier treatments such as his *Commentary* on Bk III of the *Sentences* and Quodlibet 9, but also of later works such as the *Summa theologiae*, III, q. 17, a. 2, and the *Compendium theologiae*.[76] In the hypostatic union the existence of the Word is the only substantial existence present in Christ.[77] So true is this that if the Word should put aside the human nature of Christ and if that nature were to continue in existence, then a human existence would be realized therein.[78] But in his Disputed Question *De unione*

---

[76] The key texts are: *In III Sent.*, d. 6, q. 2, a. 2 (1253–1257); Quodlibet 9, a. 3 (1257–1259 or 1265–1267); *Summa theologiae*, III, q. 17, a. 2 (1272–1273); *De unione verbi incarnati* (1272–1273, or perhaps 1269–1272); *Compendium theologiae*, c. 212 (1272–1273, or 1258–1259, or 1265). For these dates see A. Patfoort, *L'unité d'être dans le Christ d'après s. Thomas* (Tournai, 1964), pp. 15–17. As can be seen from the proposed dates and as Patfoort indicates, a number of these are disputed. Weisheipl proposes to date the five as follows: *Commentary on the Sentences*, 1252–1256; Quodlibet 9, Easter 1258; *De unione* . . . , spring 1272; ST III, q. 17, late summer or early fall 1272; *Compendium*, unresolved. See his *Friar Thomas d'Aquino*, "A Brief Catalogue of Authentic Works."

[77] For discussion of these texts see P. Bayerschmidt, *Die Seins-und Formmetaphysik des Heinrich von Gent in ihrer Anwendung auf die Christologie* (Münster i. W., 1941), pp. 46–54, 63–65; Patfoort, *L'unité* . . . , pp. 33–84, 107–49.

[78] See Quodlibet 9, a. 3 (q. 2, a. 2): "Si tamen ponatur humanitas a divinitate separari, tunc humanitas suum esse habebit aliud ab esse divino. Non enim impediebat quin proprium esse haberet nisi hoc quod non erat per se subsistens" (*ed. cit.*, p. 181).

verbi incarnati Thomas appears to defend a different position. There he seems to assign to Christ not only the eternal existence of the Word, but another human existence as well. He denies that this other existence is accidental, and refuses to identify it with the divine existence. In fact he refers to it as a "secondary" existence.[79]

Thomistic scholarship has long been divided in its effort to resolve this apparent dilemma.[80] According to one interpretation, Thomas does indeed postulate a human existence in Christ in this passage. In fact, this represents his final thinking on this matter.[81] According to another approach this text can in some way be brought into harmony with the other passages. Whether this be done by stressing the continuity of Thomas's discussion here with his other treatments of this topic[82] or by acknowledging some development or variation in his thinking, this line of interpretation maintains that at least in his final opinion he defends only one existence in Christ.[83] It thus stands in direct opposition to another reading that has recently developed according to which Thomas never maintained that the divine existence of the Word substituted for a distinct human existence in Christ.[84] Without delaying longer here over this controverted point in Thomistic interpretation, it will be enough for us to observe, as we shall shortly see, that Godfrey associates Thomas with those who defend only one existence in Christ.

In an early consideration of this same question in his Quodlibet 3, q. 2 of 1278, Henry of Ghent had also denied any distinct human existence to Christ apart from that of the Word.[85] While not agreeing with Thomas in all parts

---

[79] *De unione Verbi incarnati,* a. 4: "Est autem et aliud esse huius suppositi, non in quantum est aeternum, sed in quantum est temporaliter homo factum. Quod esse, etsi non sit esse accidentale . . . non tamen est esse principale sui suppositi, sed secundarium" (Calcaterra-Centi, ed. [Turin-Rome, 1953], p. 432). On this see Bayerschmidt, *op. cit.*, pp. 54 – 63; Patfoort, *op. cit.*, pp. 85 – 106.

[80] For some of the literature on this see Bayerschmidt, *op. cit.*, pp. 54, 59 – 62; Patfoort, *op. cit.*, p. 11, nn. 1–2; p. 12, n. 1.

[81] F. Pelster, "La Quaestio disputata de saint Thomas 'De unione Verbi incarnati'," *Archives de Philosophie* 3 (1925), pp. 198 – 245.

[82] See some of the critical reactions to Pelster cited by Bayerschmidt, pp. 59 – 61, and especially F. Synave in *Bulletin thomiste* 1 (1926), 3, pp. [1] – [21], and in particular, p. [20]. Also see authors cited by Patfoort, p. 194, nn. 1–2. Also, L. De Raeymaeker, "La profonde originalité de la métaphysique de saint Thomas d'Aquin," *Die Metaphysik im Mittelalter, Miscellanea Mediaevalia* 2 (1963), pp. 18 – 21.

[83] See Patfoort, *op. cit.*, pp. 150 – 89; Weisheipl, *Friar Thomas d'Aquino,* pp. 311 – 13.

[84] See the references given by Patfoort, *op. cit.*, p. 11, n. 2, especially to the series of articles by H. Diepen in the *Revue thomiste*.

[85] "Utrum in Christo sit tantum unum esse an [Hocedez:vel] plura?" *op. cit.*, fol.

of his exposition, on this particular issue, at least, he does appear to be influenced by the Dominican Master.[86] But in Quodlibet 10, q. 8 of 1286, Henry assigns two existences to Christ. He does so within the general context of his defense of distinctive existences for accidents in addition to the substantial existence of their subjects.[87] As will be recalled, in this context he not only assigns existence to accidents as well as to substance, but to matter as well as to form. In short, there will be as many existences in a given entity as there are "essences," with the latter term being taken so broadly as to apply to essential principles such as matter and form.[88] Because there are two natures in Christ, there must be two existences. Since Henry had rejected any real distinction between essence and existence, this position appears to be consistent with his defense of their intentional distinction. If the Word should set aside the human nature of Christ, then that human nature could continue to exist without acquiring any new human existence.[89]

In Quodlibet 2, q. 2 of Easter 1287, Giles of Rome asks whether the humanity of Christ, should it be put aside by the Word, could exist without receiving a new existence.[90] Both in this context and in his Quodlibet 5, q. 3 of 1290 he rejects multiplicity of existences in Christ.[91] It is true that his position as expressed in his *Commentary* on Bk. III of the *Sentences* appears to have changed, but since this work dates from after 1309, it will not be a factor in our consideration of the background for Godfrey's own position as presented in the early 1290s.[92]

49r–50r, reproduced in large measure by E. Hocedez, *Quaestio de unico esse in Christo a doctoribus saeculi XIII disputata*, pp. 29–34. See in particular: ". . . idcirco absolute dicendum est quod Christus ratione humanae naturae nullum habet ex se esse actualis existentiae, sicut nec accidens quod est in subiecto, vel materia quae est in composito; sed solum habet Christus esse existentiae ratione suae divinae naturae quod communicatur naturae humanae per assumptionem ad ipsam in unitate suppositi. . ." (fol. 49v; Hocedez, p. 33).

[86] See Bayerschmidt, *op. cit.*, pp. 76–80.

[87] Fol. 422r–425v; Hocedez, pp. 63–72.

[88] See Ch. V, n. 10 for an important text. Also see Bayerschmidt, *op. cit.*, pp. 85, 88, 89.

[89] Fol. 423r–424r; Hocedez, pp. 66–69. See Bayerschmidt, *op. cit.*, pp. 90–95.

[90] "Utrum humanitas Christi posset existere per se absque additione alicuius novi esse?" *Quodlibeta*, pp. 50–53. Since he holds that the human nature of Christ does not exist through its own existence but through that of the Word, he concludes that should it be separated from the Word it could not continue to exist without receiving a human existence (see pp. 51–52). See Bayerschmidt, *op. cit.*, pp. 97–100.

[91] "Utrum in Christo sint plura esse?" *op. cit.*, pp. 271–74. See p. 273 and Bayerschmidt, *op. cit.*, pp. 100–02.

[92] See d. 6, p. 3, q. 1, a. 2 ([Rome, 1623], pp. 258b–261b; and Hocedez, *op. cit.*, pp. 79–82). Rather than defend two existences in Christ, he here ascribes an

As we now turn to Godfrey's detailed discussion of this matter in Quodlibet 8, we can easily anticipate his answer. Since both Thomas Aquinas and Giles of Rome admitted some form of real distinction between essence and existence, granted the diversity in their respective formulations of the same, it was possible for each of them to defend unicity of existence in Christ and to deny of him a distinct human existence. Our brief remarks have indicated that both did, in fact, at least in the majority of their discussions of this question, defend this position. Because of his denial of any such real distinction between essence and existence, one would expect Henry of Ghent to reject the theory of a single existence in Christ. And so he does, at least by the time of his Quodlibet 10. Godfrey, of course, categorically rejected both real distinction and Henry's intentional distinction between essence and existence. Because of his great stress on their identity, he can hardly allow for Christ's human essence or nature to be realized without his human existence. In other words, if he is to affirm the presence of two natures in Christ, the divine and the human, he will have to defend two existences there as well.

In Quodlibet 8, q. 1 Godfrey inquires as to whether Christ may be said to be one *(unum)* or many.[93] He immediately comments that when the question is phrased in this way, it might be understood as asking whether Christ is one in supposit, or one in nature, or one in existence. And if, as Godfrey immediately recalls, it is certain according to faith that Christ is one in one way, in supposit, and plural in another, in nature, one may wonder whether in accord with Latin usage one may refer to him as many *(plura)* when the term "many" is neuter in gender.[94] Godfrey contends that when we say Christ is one *(unus:* where "one" is masculine in gender) we refer to his unity in supposit or person. But when we say that he is many *(plura:* where "many" is neuter in gender), we signify that he is many in nature. He defends this position in conscious opposition to Thomas Aquinas, whose argumentation in *Summa theologiae* III, q. 17, a. 1 he here reproduces in some detail.[95] Against Thomas's contention that Christ is not only one according to the masculine gender *(unus)* but also according to the neuter gender

---

actual existence *(esse actuale)* to Christ's human nature; but since he now takes this to imply an existence that is really distinct from essence, he judges it inappropriate to speak of such an actual existence in God. See Bayerschmidt, *op. cit.*, pp. 103–05. Also see Trapp, "Aegidii Romani de doctrina modorum," pp. 489ff.

93 "Utrum Christus sit unum vel plura" (PB 4.5).

94 PB 4.5–6.

95 "'Et quia unus masculine respicit unitatem suppositi, unum neutraliter rationem naturae . . ." (PB 4.7). For the presentation and criticism of Thomas's position see PB 4.7–8.

(unum), Godfrey insists that the presence of two natures in Christ is sufficient to permit one to refer to him as being many *(plura)* according to the neuter gender.[96]

Godfrey now turns to the question of whether there is one or more than one existence in Christ. He begins by carefully reproducing the theory defended by Giles of Rome in his Quodlibet 2, q. 2 of Easter 1287. As Godfrey notes, defenders of this position (Giles) maintain that existence is a thing *(res)* in distinction from essence and superadded to it.[97] Then, in terms that almost literally reproduce parts of Giles's text, Godfrey observes that according to this position existence, insofar as it is ordered to substance, is both existence and subsistence. But when it is ordered to accidents it is existence alone, not subsistence. In a given supposit there can only be one existence which both serves as the subsistence of the supposit and at the same time provides existence for all else found therein. Thus there is only one existence in a substance-accident composite, not distinctive accidental existences. So too, there can only be one existence, that of the divine supposit, in Christ. Granted that the human nature of Christ is not an accident, still in some way it acts after the manner of an accident since it is supported in the divine supposit. Therefore, it exists by reason of the divine supposit's existence. And since the human nature of Christ cannot exist unless it is united with some existence, if it should be separated from the Word then it could not exist at all unless a created existence were communicated to it.[98]

For Godfrey a proper existence must be granted to every essence, since he identifies essence and existence.[99] And as we have also seen, even within the context of real distinction between essence and existence, Godfrey contends that proper existences must be granted to accidents in distinction from the substantial existence of their substance. He argues as forcefully for this conclusion here in Quodlibet 8, q. 1 as he had some years before in his Quodlibet 3, q. 4 of 1286.[100] In short, even if one defends real distinction

---

[96] PB 4.8. See pp. 8–9 for discussion of the question as to whether Christ may be said to be one or two *simpliciter*. In brief, Godfrey insists that one must distinguish in replying. That which is one in supposit is one *simpliciter* insofar as it is a supposit. But that which is plural in nature is plural *simpliciter* in the order of nature. See Bayerschmidt, *op. cit.*, pp. 106–07.

[97] "Et ponunt aliqui esse existentiae dicere rem aliam ab essentia et ei additam" (PB 4.10).

[98] See PB 4.10, 1st par., and Giles, Q 2, q. 2 (*Quodlibeta*), pp. 51a, 51b, 52b. See Bayerschmidt, pp. 107–08, where he has reproduced the texts both from Godfrey and from Giles to illustrate how exactly Godfrey is representing Giles's position.

[99] PB 4.10.

[100] PB 4.10–11. See pp. 11–12 for further arguments against Giles's denial of

between essence and existence, existences must be multiplied just as essences are.

Not surprisingly, Godfrey applies this same conclusion to the question of plurality of existences in Christ. Thus, if one maintains that form gives existence *(esse)* to matter, how can one admit of a substantial form in Christ (the human soul) and deny that it also communicates existence to matter?[101] Then, in lines which paraphrase the opening part of the corpus of Thomas's *Summa theologiae* III, q. 17, a. 2, Godfrey observes that that which pertains to nature in Christ is multiple (dual) while that which pertains to supposit is only one. But existence pertains both to nature and to supposit—to supposit as that which has existence and to nature as that whereby something has existence.[102] Godfrey now departs from Thomas's text in order to draw his own conclusion. Because there are two natures in Christ, the divine and the human, two existences must be admitted therein to correspond to these natures. While he is not especially concerned with this point here, he observes in passing that the same conclusion may also be applied to accidental existences. These are multiplied in Christ just as they are in other men.[103]

In what must surely be a reference to Henry of Ghent's theory, Godfrey explicitly refuses to postulate distinctive unqualified existences to correspond to matter as well as to form. Matter does not enjoy any unqualified existence apart from that of its form. This follows from Godfrey's view that matter is pure potentiality, a point that will be developed in the following chapter of our study.[104] He does acknowledge that insofar as the human nature of Christ is assumed by the preexisting and eternal supposit, its existence may be described as quasi-accidental and secondary when compared with that of the Word. He immediately qualifies this by remarking that this human nature is not something accidental but pertains to the substantial order, and that it does not unite with the Word accidentally but hypostatically.[105]

---

proper existences to accidents. Also see Ch. V, pp. 214 – 17, for Godfrey's discussion of this in Q 3, q. 4.

101 PB 4.12.

102 See PB 4.12. ". . . oportet quod quae ad naturam pertinent in Christo plurificentur, quae autem pertinent ad suppositum sint unum tantum. Esse autem existentiae pertinet ad naturam et ad suppositum; ad suppositum sicut ad illud quod habet esse, quia suppositum significatur ut ens perfectum et formatum; ad naturam sicut quo aliquid habet esse; natura enim significatur per modum formae quae dicitur ens ex eo quod aliquid ea est." Compare with Thomas, ST III, q. 17, a. 2, beginning of his reply.

103 PB 4.12.

104 PB 4.13. For Henry's position see above in this chapter, n. 88.

105 PB 4.13. ". . . oportet ponere plura esse in Christo, sed unum quasi substantiale

Godfrey then returns to Thomas's reasoning in *Summa theologiae* III, q. 17, a. 2. There he finds Thomas arguing against the presence of two existences in Christ for the following reason. If the existence of a given form or nature is not included within the personal existence or the existence of a subsisting supposit, then it cannot be described as existence without qualification but only in a qualified sense. Thus, the existence of the whiteness found in Socrates cannot be assigned to him insofar as he is Socrates but only insofar as he is white. In other words, a twofold existence is realized in the white Socrates, one insofar as he is Socrates and one insofar as he is white. Therefore, continues Thomas, if the human nature had been united with the Word accidentally rather than hypostatically, then a twofold existence would be present in Christ, one insofar as he is God and another insofar as he is man. But since the human nature is united with the Word hypostatically rather than accidentally, it follows that there will be no new personal existence in Christ by reason of his human nature, but only a new relationship of the preexisting personal existence to that human nature.[106]

Godfrey counters that this reasoning will not apply with reference to unqualified existence *(esse simpliciter)*. A real and proper existence pertains to a substantial nature, such as the human nature of Christ, and more so than to any accident. Godfrey here assumes that Thomas does indeed assign proper existences to accidents and that he denies such to the human nature of Christ. But if Thomas has admitted that an accidental nature or form has its proper but accidental existence, how can he deny that the human nature of Christ will also have its proper existence? The above argumentation rather shows that the human nature does not bring with it a merely accidental existence, since it is neither an accident in itself, nor is it another substance that unites accidentally with the Word. It communicates substantial existence, to be sure, even though not independently and in itself, but only in dependence upon the divine supposit. Hence, this substantial existence is not subsistence and the human nature is not a human person.[107]

In sum, Godfrey insists that because there are two natures in Christ, there must also be two existences. This conclusion is to be maintained even if one defends real distinction of essence and existence in creatures. For Godfrey, of course, it is all the more evident in light of his identification of essence

---

et principale et aliud quasi accidentale et secundarium." Bayerschmidt has noted the similarity between Godfrey's terminology here in referring to an *esse* that is "quasi accidentale et secundarium" and that employed by Thomas in his *De unione verbi incarnati*, a. 4. See *op. cit.*, p. 111 and n. 76.

[106] PB 4.13–14, where Godfrey is obviously following Thomas's text very closely. For illustration of this interdependency see Bayerschmidt, *op. cit.*, pp. 111–12.

[107] PB 4.14.

and existence. By assuming a human nature in the Incarnation the Word not only assumed a new nature but a new existence as well. While defending plurality of existences in Christ, Godfrey acknowledges that there can only be one subsistence in any given being. Hence he does concede that if one should restrict the term existence *(esse)* to subsistence, the existence of a supposit, one would have to conclude that there is only one existence (subsistence) in Christ. He even suggests that this might be what those who deny plurality of existences in Christ have in mind. But, as he immediately adds, if one means by existence the actuality of an essence or nature with which essence or nature it is really identical, there can be no doubt. Existence must be multiplied just as is essence. This, of course, is his own position.[108]

Given his assertion of two existences in Christ, Godfrey must face an obvious difficulty. If the human nature of Christ enjoys its proper existence, how is he to avoid the conclusion that that same human nature also enjoys its own subsistence and is, therefore, a human person? In other men he does maintain that essence, existence, and subsistence are one and the same.[109] Godfrey meets this difficulty by returning to the theory he had developed in Quodlibet 7, q. 5. Subsistence does in some way add something to or imply something more than does existence, but only extrinsically and in terms of its connotation. Existence simply signifies the actuality of an essence or nature, without determining whether that nature does or does not depend upon something else. Therefore, variation in its state of depending or not depending upon something else will not change the nature in itself or in terms of its existence. But subsistence signifies the actuality of an essence or nature with the added connotation that it does not depend on something else and thus does not unite with it as a part or quasi-part. Thus, there can be variation in this connotation and variation in subsistence without any corresponding variation in essence and existence. Hence, the human nature of Christ enjoys its proper human existence but cannot be said to have a human subsistence precisely because of the fact that it is united with the Word and depends upon the latter. Should it ever be separated from the Word and yet continue in existence, then its human existence would also be a human subsistence and the human nature would be a human person.[110]

---

[108] PB 4.15.

[109] PB 4.16.

[110] PB 4.16–17. Also see Q 3, q. 4 (PB 2.193): "Cum etiam natura humana in Christo aliquod esse habeat aliud ab esse divino licet non habeat subsistere nisi in supposito divino, unde si deponeret hanc naturam ipsa subsisteret in se ipsa, non tamen haberet novum esse reale, oportet in Christo ponere duo esse aliquo modo." For Godfrey's discussion of this in Q 7, q. 5 see in this chapter, p. 239.

Part III

The Metaphysics of Matter and Form

Chapter VII.

Notion of Prime Matter

In the three preceding chapters we have considered Godfrey's metaphysical description of created reality in terms of his theory of substance and accident (Ch. IV), his application of this to the realm of accidental being (Ch. V) and then to substantial and subsisting being (Ch. VI). In the next three chapters of this study we propose to concentrate on his theory of matter and form and certain ramifications that follow therefrom. Since, as we shall now see, Godfrey limits matter-form composition to corporeal entities, the philosophical positions we are about to study apply, in his opinion, only to the realm of the corporeal. Many of these issues could be considered in a study of his physics or his philosophy of nature. Nonetheless, his discussion of these topics is also important for a fuller understanding of his views with respect to the metaphysical structure of corporeal reality. Hence, it seems appropriate for us to include them in this general treatment of his metaphysical thought.

In the present chapter we shall investigate his understanding of the nature of and the evidence for prime matter. With this in mind we shall proceed according to the following order and shall consider in turn his views with respect to: A. The Nature of Prime Matter; B. The Evidence for Prime Matter; C. The Possibility of the Existence of Prime Matter Apart from Any Form; D. The Possibility of Different Kinds of Prime Matter.

A. THE NATURE OF PRIME MATTER

Common to Godfrey and his scholastic contemporaries was the conviction that corporeal beings in our world are composed of matter and form.[1] But

[1] All of these thinkers were, of course, heavily indebted to Aristotle for their general understanding of matter-form theory, even though they would develop it in

there was considerable diversity of opinion as regards the nature of prime matter. Thus the view that prime matter enjoys some actuality in itself and that God could create it apart from any form, should he so choose, seems to have been fairly widespread, especially among Franciscans from the English province. As A. Wolter has observed, in Thomas's time it had been defended by John Peckham and shortly thereafter was represented again by Richard of Middleton. Somewhat later it would also be proposed by William of Ware, by Duns Scotus, and by Ockham, although within a different philosophical context.[2] On the other hand, another position maintained that prime matter is, in itself, pure potentiality and that as a consequence it cannot exist apart from any and every form. Thomas Aquinas is surely the best known representative of this position, but one also finds it in Giles of Rome and, at least in part, in Siger of Brabant.[3] As we shall see, it is this second position that Godfrey was to champion throughout his career.

---

different ways. For an interesting and challenging article on certain aspects of Aristotle's theory and for many helpful references see R. Sokolowski, "Matter, Elements and Substance in Aristotle," *Journal of the History of Philosophy* 8 (1970), pp. 263 – 88. Also see H. Happ's lengthy study: *Hyle. Studien zum aristotelischen Materie-Begriff* (Berlin-New York, 1971), and his Bibliography, pp. 816 – 24.

[2] See A. Wolter, "The Ockhamist Critique," in *The Concept of Matter in Greek and Medieval Philosophy*, E. McMullin, ed. (Notre Dame, Ind., 1965), pp. 131 – 34. For references to Peckham see D. E. Sharp, *Franciscan Philosophy at Oxford in the Thirteenth Century* (London, 1930), pp. 178 – 82. For Richard of Middleton see Sharp, pp. 220 – 21, and R. Zavalloni, *Richard de Mediavilla et la controverse sur la pluralité des formes* (Louvain, 1951), pp. 303 – 09. On William of Ware see G. Gál, "Gulielmi de Ware, O.F.M., Doctrina philosophica per summa capita proposita," *Franciscan Studies* 14 (1954), pp. 275 – 79. On Scotus and especially on Ockham see Wolter, pp. 131 – 46.

[3] For this in Giles see Hocedez, "Le premier Quodlibet d'Henri de Gand (1276)," p. 96 (referring to Giles's *Theoremata de Corpore Christi*, pr. 30 and pr. 44); Suárez, "La metafísica de Egidio Romano a la luz de las 24 tesis tomistas," *La Ciudad de Dios* 161 (1949), p. 294. See in particular Giles's *Quaestiones de cognitione angelorum*, qu. 8 (Venice, 1503), fol. 98vb: "Quicquid enim est supra materiam, i.e., supra potentiam puram, oportet quod sit ens in actu, quia quod non dicit potentiam puram aliquam actualitatem importat." Also, *Theoremata de esse et essentia*, Th. X, p. 58: "Materia quidem sine forma cum sit pura potentialitas, nec potest intellegi nec existere." Also see Th. VI, p. 26 of the same, and *In I Sent.*, d. 44, p. 4, 1, q. 3 (fol. 227ra). For Thomas see below. For Siger on matter as pure potency see Van Steenberghen, *Maître Siger de Brabant*, pp. 327 – 28, referring to Siger's *Quaestiones in Metaphysicam*, ed. Graiff, VII, 3 (pp. 368 – 69) and VII, 14 (p. 376). Interestingly, though, Siger distinguishes between "potency" taken as that whereby matter is determinable and capable of being ordered to form, on the one hand, and potency insofar as it is the very ordering of matter to form. Taken in the first sense he identifies matter and potency. But taken in the second way, he distinguishes between matter

Since Godfrey's proximate target in his critique of the theory that would assign some degree of actuality to prime matter seems to have been the secular Master, Henry of Ghent, something more should be said about the latter's position. In Quodlibet 1, q. 10 of 1276, Henry addresses himself to the question whether matter can exist in itself apart from and without any form.[4] It has been suggested that the objector in this particular debate was Giles of Rome.[5] Be that as it may, Henry immediately takes the offensive and rejects what he regards as a faulty view of matter according to which it is nothing but a kind of potency which is so close to nonbeing that if it were left even for a moment without some form, it would immediately fall into nonbeing. Henry turns to the authority of Plato, Augustine, and Avicenna for support for his own opinion, that one must assign some minimum degree of reality to matter.[6]

In support of the same contention Henry reasons that matter cannot be so close to nonbeing or so potential as to preclude it from being a kind of nature that is capable of receiving forms. Nor does it receive this capacity for forms directly from the given form that actualizes it, but from God, and in more immediate fashion than forms themselves receive their being from God. So true is this that one might better describe the production of forms in matter as a process of "formation" rather than as creation. As regards God's creative activity, therefore, the existence of matter is prior to that of the form and the composite in the order of nature although not in the order of time.[7]

Henry's point here is that because forms are in some way educed from the potentiality of matter, matter must of itself enjoy some degree of reality that is given to it directly by God. As he puts it, one must not conclude that matter is so weak and so potential in terms of its being that its possibility for existence as such depends upon its form. On the contrary, it receives existence in itself insofar as it has its own proper divine idea within the divine

---

and potency, and apparently regards the latter as pertaining to the accidental category of relation. See his *Quaestiones in Physicam* II, 1 (ed. Bazán), pp. 149 – 50; *Quaestiones in Metaphysicam* V, 5 (pp. 287 – 89). Also see Van Steenberghen's comment on this theory, p. 327, n. 7.

[4] "De materia erat quaestio: Utrum posset existere per se sine forma" (fol. 8r).

[5] See Hocedez, "Le premier Quodlibet . . . ," p. 96, and R. Macken, "Subsistance de la matière première selon Henri de Gand," in *San Bonaventura, Maestro di vita francescana e di sapienza cristiana* (*Atti del Congresso internazionale per il VII centenario di San Bonaventura da Bagnoregio*), T. 3 (Rome, 1976), p. 107.

[6] *Op. cit.*, fol. 8r – 8v. Note Henry's reference to the opposed opinion: "Hic primo oportet excludere falsam imaginationem quam habent quidam de materia, videlicet, quod nihil sit nisi potentia quaedam . . . ita quod in sua natura tantum appropinquat non enti, quod si careat forma, statim cadat in non ens" (fol. 8r).

[7] *Op. cit.*, fol. 8v.

mind. Granted that in the normal course of events matter never exists without some form, still such is possible by reason of God's power. For God is surely no less capable of conserving matter than of creating it, nor any less capable of creating matter in itself than of concreating a form in a composite.[8]

Henry then distinguishes a threefold way or mode in which being (*esse*) is realized in matter. First of all he assigns existence as such (*esse simpliciter*) to matter, and this insofar as it, like every creature, is an effect of God's creative activity. Secondly, matter enjoys a second mode of being insofar as it is by its nature capable of receiving forms. Finally, there is the mode of being that form communicates to matter or, in other words, that matter has only insofar as it is actualized by its form in the composite. It is by reason of this final *esse* which the form communicates to it that matter itself enjoys its actual existence, so much so, in fact, that without this, matter itself would cease to exist in the natural course of events.[9]

But, insists Henry, by direct divine intervention matter could be kept in existence without any form.[10] This is so both because matter enjoys its own existence and nature and because its form does not communicate to it its essence and existence in general, but only the concrete conditions required for their realization in the composite.[11] If matter should be maintained in existence by God and apart from any form, it would then be a kind of imperfect act which would still be in potency to be perfected by another act, its form. Its degree of actuality would not be so complete as it is when it is informed by its appropriate form.[12] As Paulus and Macken have indicated, not long after this discussion in Quodlibet 1, q. 10, Henry bowed to the internal pressure of the theory we have just considered and assigned a kind of existence to matter, another to form, and existence in the full and proper sense (subsistence) to the substantial supposit. This development first clearly appears in art. 27 of his *Summa* of Ordinary Questions, and shortly thereafter in Quodlibet 4, q. 13 of Christmas 1279. The same is also present in his Quodlibet 10, q. 8 of Christmas 1286.[13]

---

[8] *Ibid.*

[9] *Op. cit.*, fol. 9r. On this passage see Paulus, *Henri de Gand* . . . , p. 214, n. 1; Macken, *op. cit.*, pp. 110 – 11.

[10] *Op. cit.*, fol. 9r.

[11] Paulus, *op. cit.*, p. 214, n. 1.

[12] ". . . suus actus proprius est in potentia ad illum actum ulteriorem" (fol. 9r). See fol. 9v.

[13] See *Summa* . . . , a. 27, q. 1 (fol. 163r); Q 4, q. 13 (fol. 113r); Q 10, q. 8 (fol. 423r). On these passages see Paulus, *op. cit.*, p. 219, n. 1; Macken, *op. cit.*, pp. 111 – 13; and most recently, Macken, "Le statut de la matière première dans la philosophie d'Henri de Gand," *Recherches de Théologie ancienne et médiévale* 46 (1979), especially pp. 136–56.

If Henry's theory of prime matter serves as Godfrey's proximate target in his presentation of his own position, Thomas Aquinas's view surely exercised considerable positive influence on him in his development of the same. As is well known, Thomas had contended that prime matter is pure potentiality.[14] Insofar as it is a principle that is required if one is to account for substantial change, it must be in potency with respect to the act or form toward which it is ordered. If one were to assign some minimum degree of actuality to prime matter one would, in Thomas's eyes, undermine the essential unity of the matter-form composite.[15] Thus prime matter must rather be viewed as pure potency in itself, just as God is pure actuality.[16] Every bodily substance is composed of potency and act, that is to say, of prime matter and an appropriate substantial form. Hence it is not possible, according to Thomas, for prime matter to exist in itself apart from and without any substantial form.[17] In fact, strictly speaking, it is not prime matter that should be said to exist, but the composite including both matter and form. Prime matter as such should be said to be concreated with the composite rather than created in itself.[18]

So true is this that Thomas will not allow for a distinctive divine idea for prime matter apart from that of the composite or its form. Just as matter cannot exist in itself apart from any form, so too, it cannot be understood in itself apart from some form toward which it is ordered.[19] At least in his mature works Thomas maintains that prime matter is correlative by its very nature and thereby ordered to form, without admitting that there is any real distinction between matter as such and its ordering or relationship to form.[20]

---

[14] On this in Thomas see A. Forest, *La structure métaphysique du concret . . .*, pp. 210–16; Weisheipl, "The Concept of Matter in Fourteenth Century Science," in *The Concept of Matter . . .*, pp. 151–52; V. E. Smith, *The General Science of Nature* (Milwaukee, 1958), pp. 111–13.

[15] See Smith, *op. cit.*, p. 112. For Thomas see, for instance, *In VIII Met.*, lect. 1 (n. 1689): "Si enim materia prima de se haberet aliquam formam propriam, per eam esset aliquid actu. Et sic, cum superinduceretur alia forma, non simpliciter materia per eam esset, sed fieret hoc vel illud ens. Et sic esset generatio secundum quid et non simpliciter."

[16] ST I, q. 115, a. 1, ad 2: "Sed hoc est materia prima, quae est potentia pura, sicut Deus est actus purus. Corpus autem componitur ex potentia et actu."

[17] SCG II, c. 43: ". . . materia non potest esse absque omni forma." Also see *De potentia Dei*, q. 4, a. 1.

[18] SCG II, c. 43; ST I, q. 7, a. 2, ad 3.

[19] *De veritate*, q. 3, a. 5c. See *In VIII Met.*, lect. 1, n. 1687.

[20] See ST 1, q. 77, a. 1, ad 2; *In I Phys.*, lect. 15, n. 131: "Non igitur potentia materiae est aliqua proprietas addita super essentiam eius; sed materia secundum suam substantiam est potentia ad esse substantiale." But compare with *In I Sent.*, d. 3, q.

With this background in mind, we are now in position to turn to Godfrey's own views on prime matter. If one may refer to the theory defended by Henry of Ghent as a more Augustinian and Neoplatonic reading of Aristotle and to that presented by Thomas as more literally Aristotelian, Godfrey's personal position will have to be regarded as falling within the purer Aristotelian tradition. Thus already in his first Quodlibetal debate of 1285, Godfrey unequivocally defends the purely potential character of prime matter.[21] He does so here within the context of defending Aquinas's claim that matter cannot exist without some form and in specific opposition to Henry of Ghent. Against Henry he counters that according to Aristotle and his commentators matter is not identical with nonbeing or nothingness but enjoys a minimum degree of being. For this reason it may be said to be near to nothingness.[22] Godfrey recalls that being may be divided into being in act (being without qualification) and being in potency. In accord with this division matter must be placed under potential being, not under actual being. He also cites Aristotle's well-known description of matter in *Metaphysics* VII according to which of itself it is neither a quiddity nor a quantity (nor a quality) nor any of the other predicaments.[23] Matter is described as potency or potential being because it is not something to which it belongs to exist in itself, nor even something by reason of which (actual) existence pertains to something else, as is true of form. It is only that by reason of which something *can* exist.[24]

According to Godfrey, prime matter falls between actual being and total nonbeing or nothingness. As he observes in Quodlibet 2, q. 4, prime matter is the first and purely potential principle of a material entity, while substantial form is the first actual principle of the same, that which actualizes matter. Given this, anything that is immediately added to prime matter will have to be substantial form. Just as there can be nothing intermediate between matter or pure potency and being in act or substantial form, so too there is no

---

4, a. 2, ad 4: ". . . tunc materia non est sua potentia, quia essentia materiae non est relatio" (ed. Mandonnet, p. 117). On this point see Forest, *op. cit.*, pp. 215 – 16.

[21] Q 1, q. 4 (PB 2.7): "Utrum materia prima creata fuerit vel creari potuerit omnino informis sive carens omni forma."

[22] ". . . quod non est omnino non ens et nihil, sed minimum habet de entitate, propter quod dicitur quod est prope nihil" (PB 2.8). As Godfrey indicates in Q 2, q. 6, this expression "prope nihil" goes back to Augustine's *Confessions*, Bk. XII, c. 7 (see PL 32, cols. 828 – 29). See PB 2.89 – 90.

[23] PB 2.8 – 9. See in particular: "materia de se nec est quid nec quantum, nec quale, nec aliquod aliorum praedicamentorum." For Aristotle see *Metaphysics* VII, c. 3 (1029a 20–21). Godfrey's citation of Aristotle is not completely literal. Thus the "nec quale" does not appear as such in the Greek original.

[24] PB 2.9.

intermediate stage between prime matter and absolute nonbeing. Anything that falls short of the minimum entity enjoyed by prime matter, therefore, will be absolute nonbeing.[25]

Godfrey's concern is twofold. On the one hand he must not identify prime matter or pure potentiality with absolute nonbeing. On the other hand, he refuses to equate the minimum degree of entity or reality that he has assigned to matter with actuality. He develops each of these points more fully in other contexts, especially in Quodlibet 10, q. 9 of 1294/1295. There he is attempting to show that man is truly composed of matter and form. He begins by acknowledging that if one should allow for the presence of many substantial acts within a given substantial composite, then one might deny that matter is purely potential and assign some minimum degree of actuality to it.[26] But if one maintains, as Godfrey is inclined to do, that there can only be one substantial act in a given substance, then prime matter must be pure potentiality. One must not conclude from this that prime matter is absolute nonbeing. When being is divided into act and potency, this should not be regarded as a division of being into complete actuality and incomplete actuality. From such a division it would follow that anything less than incomplete actuality would have to be regarded as nonbeing. But, counters Godfrey, there is an intermediary between actuality of any kind, on the one hand, and pure nothingness, on the other. This intermediary is, of course, prime matter or pure potentiality. Hence Godfrey insists that one must distinguish three levels: pure nothingness (which exists only in the mind); pure potentiality; and actuality. Strictly speaking, prime matter or pure potentiality is not intermediate between being and nonbeing, but between actuality of any kind and nonbeing.[27]

In this same context Godfrey attempts to show that if prime matter is not to be identified with absolute nonbeing, one should not assign to it any actuality of its own. He does this by arguing that prime matter does not enjoy a distinctive and actual existence (*esse simpliciter*) in and of itself apart from that of its form. Thus it is not prime matter that passes from potentiality to

---

[25] PB 2.83. Also see Q 2, q. 6 (PB 2.90). In the latter context after having described prime matter as "pura potentia" Godfrey comments: ". . . sicut quia quod est infra simpliciter potentiam ut infra materiam est pure non ens, ita quod est supra materiam in genere substantiae est simpliciter ens . . ."

[26] PB 4.336–37. Godfrey comments that such a view of matter, according to which it enjoys some degree of actuality, is not that of Aristotle, but that defended by the "ancients."

[27] PB 4.337. See in particular: "Unde sunt tres gradus: unus secundum conceptionem, scilicet purum non ens et alius secundum quamcumque actualitatem; medius secundum puram potentialitatem." Also see Q 11, q. 2 (PB 5.9): "Est enim materia medium inter non ens simpliciter et ens in actu." Also see Q 14, q. 5 (PB 5.404).

actuality in the course of change, but the composite. Just as this composite enjoys actual being by reason of its form, it has potential being by reason of its matter. The composite may be said to enjoy essential unity precisely because it consists of these two factors or principles (as he describes them in Q 14, q. 5),[28] the one potency as such or matter, the other act or form. To assign any distinctive actuality or actual existence to matter would, insists Godfrey, compromise the essential unity of the composite and reduce it to the level of an accidental aggregate. He finds confirmation for this in Averroes's *Commentary* on Bk II of the *De Anima.*[29]

It is clear from the foregoing that prime matter is pure potency, according to Godfrey, and that it is neither absolute nonbeing nor does it enjoy any actuality in itself. But in Quodlibet 10, q. 9 Godfrey considers an interesting consequence that seems to arise from his metaphysics of essence and existence and his identification of these in all beings. It will follow from his theory that a composite entity will be one or many in terms of its existence just as it is in terms of its essence. And Godfrey repeatedly insists that existence is to be multiplied just as is essence. The difficulty is this: he has admitted that the essence of a composite substance results from the union of matter and form. Insofar as he refuses to identify matter with absolute nonbeing but assigns some entity or reality to it, he seems to account for the reality of the composite essence by appealing to two simpler essential factors or "entities," the one potential, the other actual. Given his identification of essence and existence, it seems to follow that the existence of any such composite will itself be composed of two simpler existences, that of matter and that of form.[30]

Godfrey observes that some conclude from this that the existence of a composite substance is really identical with the form of the same, but not with the entire essence of the composite. While acknowledging the difficulty,

---

[28] See PB 5.404–05: "Non sic autem potest produci de non esse ad esse materia nec etiam forma ut secundum se accepta in esse producatur propter causam praedictam, quia scilicet nullum eorum est aliquid quod sit ens simpliciter vel cui conveniat esse simpliciter; sed ambo sunt *principia* unius entis simpliciter et cui convenit esse simpliciter" (ital. mine).

[29] For this see Q 10, q. 9 (PB 4.337–39). For Averroes see *In II De anima,* com. 7, F. Stuart Crawford, ed. (Cambridge, Mass., 1953), p. 139:39–42; cited by Godfrey, p. 339. Note Godfrey's remark: "Licet enim materia non dicat actualitatem—sic enim, ut dictum est, non esset unum per se sed per accidens ex ipsa et forma—dicit tamen entitatem aliquam, et forma etiam entitatem aliquam. Sed talis est habitudo unius ad alterum secundum rationem potentiae et actus quod ex eis constituitur unum simpliciter" (PB 4.339).

[30] PB 4.339.

Godfrey replies that the existence of a composite substance is really identical with the entire essence of the composite. He can hardly say anything else since for him being, essence, and existence signify one and the same thing in reality, although in different ways. He goes on to apply this doctrine to matter itself. Just as matter is being in potency or that whereby something is being in potency, so it may be said that matter has existence in potency or is that whereby the composite has existence in potency or potential existence. But even potential existence is a kind of existence. And just as the entity or essence of matter as realized in a composite cannot be identified with that of the form, then neither can matter's existence be identified with that of the form.[31]

One might wonder whether Godfrey himself has not here fallen into Henry of Ghent's position, according to which distinctive existences are to be assigned to matter as well as to form. Godfrey immediately distances himself from any such view, however, by stressing the point that the existence he has assigned to matter is not unqualified existence (*esse simpliciter*) but only potential existence. Henry had, it seemed, assigned a minimum degree of actuality to matter and presumably, therefore, to its existence. This Godfrey will not do. He does acknowledge that if one wishes to restrict the term existence so as to signify only that whereby the composite enjoys actual existence, since such is the existence of the form, then one may refuse to identify this existence with the composite essence. It will then be identical only with the form itself. And while he maintains that both matter and form pertain to the essence of a composite substance, he agrees that form does so in foremost fashion.[32]

Still, potential existence is not nothingness. Hence, reasons Godfrey, when existence is taken more generally so as to apply both to actual and to potential existence, it will be identical with the entire essence. He concludes that just as matter by reason of its potential essence enters into composition with form, so does matter's existence (which is really identical with the matter itself) enter into composition with the existence of the form. Such can occur without impairing the essential unity of the entity in question because matter, viewed in terms either of its essence or its existence, is only potential, that is, potential essence or potential existence.[33] Were Godfrey to assign any ac-

---

[31] PB 4.339–40.

[32] PB 4.340.

[33] *Ibid.* See in particular: "Sicut enim materia est essentia vel pars essentiae non secundum actum sed secundum potentiam . . . ita etiam esse materiae est esse non secundum actum sed secundum potentiam." Reference was made in the preceding chapter (p. 255) to a passage in Q 8, q. 1, where Godfrey refuses to assign unqualified

tuality to matter or to its essence or its existence, he would then compromise the possibility of its essential union with form and its essence and existence. But this he has steadfastly refused to do.

In this same Quodlibet 10, q. 9, Godfrey distinguishes two ways in which one might apply the notion of potency and of relation to matter. One may understand by potency a real relationship that differs from the essence of matter, by means of which relationship matter is ordered to a given type of form or a given form. This relationship itself results from the fact that matter is so ordered by reason of certain dispositions found therein. If one applies the notion of potency to this resulting relationship, then potency will indeed be a real relation in addition to and distinct from matter, and thus something accidental. Godfrey acknowledges that if matter were nothing but this kind of potency, then it would be nothing more than a mere relationship.[34] But one may also understand by potency matter itself insofar as it is capable of receiving any material form and serving as its subject. When potency is taken in this second way, it is not a real relationship or anything accidental added to matter, but is in fact identical with matter itself. Hence, to identify matter with potentiality in this second sense, as Godfrey has done, is not to reduce it to the status of a predicamental or accidental relationship.[35]

B. THE EVIDENCE FOR PRIME MATTER

Central to Godfrey's argumentation in Quodlibet 10, q. 9 both for the reality of prime matter and for its purely potential character is the familiar distinction between substantial change and accidental change or, as he phrases

---

existences (*esse simpliciter*) both to matter and to form. Since *esse simpliciter* as it appears in that passage also signifies actual rather than potential existence, Godfrey's doctrine there is in agreement with that of Q 10, q. 9. See PB 4.13: "Descendendo vero ad distinctionem partium essentialium hominis quae sunt forma et materia, ex hoc non sunt ponenda in ipso plura esse existentiae simpliciter, quia illud numeratur solum secundum formam quae est idem quod actus et essentia simpliciter. Unde materia non habet esse simpliciter nisi esse formae; quia, licet materia non sit purum non ens cui nullo modo conveniat esse, non est tamen sic ens quod ei secundum se conveniat tale esse quod possit dici esse simpliciter, quia non est nisi pura potentia in genere substantiae ad esse simpliciter quod est a forma substantiali."

[34] PB 4.341. For a somewhat fuller explanation of this usage of potency, see Q 9, q. 12 (PB 4.251 – 52). There Godfrey explicitly introduces the notion of dispositions, something that he only includes by implication in the discussion in Q 10, q. 9.

[35] PB 4.341. Also see Q 9, q. 12 (PB 4.251). Compare with the distinction proposed by Siger of Brabant cited above in n. 3 of this chapter, and the text from Thomas's *Commentary* on *I Sent.* as cited in n. 20. All three, that is, Thomas, Siger, and Godfrey, appear to have in mind the same distinction.

it, between unqualified generation and qualified generation or alteration. He accepts as an undeniable fact attested to by sense experience that certain natural entities change into or become others or, in other words, that they undergo substantial change. And in reasoning that is ultimately inspired by Aristotle's procedure in the *Physics,* he briefly recalls that a contrary cannot directly and of itself become its contrary. If one thing changes into and becomes another and opposite thing, this can only be because both in some way share in something real that is common to them.[36]

Godfrey insists that in the case of unqualified or substantial change this common factor or subject cannot of itself enjoy any actuality. Otherwise the being to be produced would not arise from being in potency, but from being which was already actualized. In that eventuality one would have accidental change (qualified generation or alteration), but not truly substantial change (unqualified generation). And Godfrey himself would also contend that the newly produced being would not enjoy essential unity in itself. Consequently, he continues, one must posit as the subject of such change something that is purely potential, that is to say, prime matter. Only in this way can one safeguard the substantial character of such change and the essential unity of the new composite. This composite will consist of matter whereby it (the composite) is in potency to become still something else, and of form whereby it actually is this composite.[37]

Godfrey stresses the point that it is not really prime matter itself that undergoes change or becomes. It is rather the former composite which enjoyed potential being by reason of matter and actual being by reason of its form that has now become a new composite. Neither the matter nor the form of any such composite is to be regarded as a being as such. The composite itself will enjoy essential unity precisely because it is composed of two factors or principles, one of which is pure potency, and the other act or form.[38] In support of this Godfrey cites a passage from Aristotle's *Metaphysics* and from Averroes's commentary on the same.[39] And to illustrate this he suggests that if water should become fire, the entire fire including its matter and form will have been previously but potentially present in the water, and this by reason of the latter's matter. Through the process of substantial change this same composite, the fire, will now be realized in actuality.[40]

---

[36] PB 4.337–38. For Aristotle see *Physics* I, cc. 7–9.

[37] PB 4.337–39.

[38] PB 4.338.

[39] See *Metaphysics* VIII, c. 6 (1045a 20–33). For Averroes see *In VIII Met.* (Vol. 8, fol. 224ra). Godfrey's citation of Averroes is practically verbatim. See PB 4.338.

[40] PB 4.338.

In the above context Godfrey has closely connected matter-form composition and the purely potential character of prime matter with the fact of substantial change. In other contexts he sometimes reasons in reverse fashion. All that is composed of prime matter and of substantial form must be capable of substantial change.[41] As we shall see, he also maintains that where there is no possibility for substantial change, there can be no prime matter.[42] In sum, according to Godfrey not only is the fact of substantial change a clear-cut argument for the presence of prime matter in such a changeable entity; the presence of prime matter within a given entity implies that it can undergo such change.

C. THE POSSIBILITY OF THE EXISTENCE OF PRIME MATTER APART FROM ANY FORM

As we have now seen, according to Godfrey prime matter includes no actuality in itself but is pure potentiality. His answer to the present question follows almost automatically from this. But before presenting this answer in Quodlibet 1, q. 4, he refers to the opinion of a well-known *doctor* whose memory should be held in honor and who frequently stated that matter cannot exist without form. Godfrey refers to certain ones who constantly attack him by defaming his person and by heaping opprobrium upon his teaching rather than by reasoned argumentation.[43] So true is this, continues Godfrey, that

---

[41] See Q 15, q. 10 (PB 14.56): ". . . et ideo, cum in inferioribus habere materiam communem sit causa generationis et corruptionis, iudicant quod omnia illa quae communicant cum istis in hoc [quod] est habere materiam communem, sunt generabilia et corruptibilia."

[42] See Q 3, q. 3 (PB 2.184): "Ubi autem non potest esse transmutatio secundum substantiam, nec est materia quae est in potentia ad substantiam." Also see Q 5, q. 2 (PB 3.11): "Idem etiam dicit primo de Generatione quod quae communicant in materia sunt ad invicem transmutabilia, ex quo potest argui a destructione consequentis: quae non sunt ad invicem transmutabilia non communicant in materia." Hoffmans sees this as a reference to *De Generatione* 1, c. 4 (PB 3.407), but it appears to be an interpretation rather than a literal citation. For Godfrey's defense of this as Aristotle's doctrine see PB 3.11 – 12.

[43] ". . . aliqui doctrinam non modicum fructuosam cuiusdam doctoris famosi, cuius memoria cum laudibus esse debet, ut in pluribus impugnantes, vel deinde contra dicta sua procedentes, ad diffamationem personae pariter et doctrinae opprobria magis quam rationes inducere consueverunt" (PB 2.7). Godfrey's friendly reference to Thomas here reminds one of his more extended defense of Aquinas's teaching against the 1277 prohibitions in his Q 12, q. 5 of the mid-1290s (PB 5.100 – 04). For more on that discussion see our "The Condemnations of 1270 and 1277 at Paris," pp. 195 – 96, n. 61; and see Ch. X below, pp. 382 – 85.

they charge that Thomas's opinion on this point—it is clearly Thomas that Godfrey has in mind—is not only false but even erroneous from the theological standpoint. They maintain that the essence of an accident is surely more dependent upon its subject than the essence of matter upon form. But since in the Eucharist accidents can be immediately sustained in being by God apart from any subject, no believer should assert that matter cannot exist without some form.[44] Interestingly, Henry of Ghent presents a similar opening argument in favor of the claim that matter can exist without form in his Quodlibet 1, q. 10 and appears to accept a more nuanced version of the same in the corpus of his reply. There he comments that those who deny that matter can exist without form by divine power would with greater reason deny that any accident can exist without its subject, were it not clear from the teaching of faith that such does happen in the Eucharist.[45]

Whether or not Godfrey means to imply that Henry himself had charged Thomas with theological error in denying that matter can exist without any form, it is clear from the subsequent part of his discussion that he is presenting Henry's argumentation. There he almost literally reproduces some of Henry's reasoning in Quodlibet 1, q. 10, to which reference has been made above.[46] In brief, as Godfrey presents his position, Henry maintains that matter is not so close to nothingness or so potential as to preclude it from being a thing and a nature that differs essentially from form. Nor does it receive its entity from its form, but directly from God as its efficient cause. Hence, by God's creating activity matter may be conserved in being even when it is without

---

[44] ". . . dicunt quod hoc non solum est falsum, sed est erroneum" (PB 2.7). See pp. 7–8.

[45] See *op. cit.*, fol. 8r, 8v. In the latter context Henry remarks: "Simpliciter ergo dicendum quod actione divina supernaturali materia potest per se subsistere nuda ab omni forma, et hoc multo magis quam accidentia, ut dicit ratio ad hoc inducta. Unde qui modo negant materiam dei actione posse stare sine forma, nisi esset clarum quod fide tenendum est quod accidentia subsistunt sine subiecto in sacramento altaris, multo magis negarent dei actione accidens posse stare sine subiecto." But for explicit reference to Thomas's position as "erroneous" see William de la Mare's *Correctorium Fratris Thomae*. After appealing to the fact that God preserves an accident without its subject in the Eucharist in order to defend his ability to make matter exist without any form, William comments: "unde omnes magistri concordaverunt nuper quod erroneum est dicere quod Deus non potest dare esse actu materiae sine forma" (in *Le correctorium Corruptorii 'Quare,'* P. Glorieux, ed. [Le Saulchoir, Kain, 1927], p. 114). Henry's Quodlibet 1 dates from 1276, William's *Correctorium* ca. 1278–1280, and Godfrey's Quodlibet 1 from 1285. On William's *Correctorium* see Glorieux, "Pro et contra Thomam. Un survol de cinquante années," in *Sapientiae Procerum Amore, Studia Anselmiana* 63 (1974), pp. 261–62.

[46] Compare Godfrey, PB 2.8 with Henry's text, fol. 8v, 9r. For fuller presentation of Henry's position see above in this chapter pp. 263–64.

any form, granted that it is proper for it to exist together with its form in the composite.[47]

Godfrey himself reasons from the nature of matter as pure potentiality to the conclusion that it cannot exist apart from some form. To say that it is only potency or potential being is to imply that it is not something to which it can pertain to exist in itself.[48] Again, as we have seen him reasoning in Quodlibet 10, q. 9, something essentially one cannot result from the unity of two actualities. Given this, one must concede the purely potential character of prime matter.[49] As he observes in Quodlibet 14, q. 5, both matter and (corporeal) form are principles of being rather than beings in themselves. If this is so, neither matter nor form can be reduced from nonbeing to being in such fashion as to exist as a being in itself. Such can happen only to the composite being of which both are principles.[50] In other words, Godfrey is in full agreement with Aquinas on this point that prime matter, because of its purely potential character, cannot exist apart from some form, not even by divine power.

D. THE POSSIBILITY OF DIFFERENT KINDS OF PRIME MATTER

During Godfrey's days as a student and then as a Master at Paris the theory of universal hylemorphism or universal matter-form composition was widely held. Thus, in addition to the matter-form composition of corporeal entities in this world, spiritual realities were thought by many to be composed of a kind of matter and of form. This would apply both to separate substances such as angels and to the human soul. Only God would be entirely free from any and all such composition. Moreover, according to the prevailing physical and astronomical science of that time, heavenly bodies were thought to be incorruptible. In order to account for this some scholastic thinkers, most notably Thomas Aquinas, postulated a different kind of prime matter in them, a kind that does not carry with it the possible corruption of the resulting composite. With these positions in mind, we shall now consider Godfrey's views with respect to: (1) matter-form composition in angels; (2) matter-form composition in the human soul; (3) matter-form composition of the heavenly bodies.

---

[47] PB 2.8.

[48] PB 2.8–9.

[49] PB 4.337.

[50] PB 5.404–05. See the text cited above in n. 28.

1. Matter-Form Composition in Angels

Thomas Aquinas is well known for his rejection of universal hylemorphism and, hand in hand with this, of matter-form composition in separate intelligences or angels. Both in early works and in his more mature treatments he traces this theory back to the *Fons vitae* of the Spanish Jewish philosopher, Avicebron (Ibn Gabirol), whose treatise had been translated from Arabic into Latin in the twelfth century.[51] Already in his *De ente et essentia* Thomas proposes his own theory of the essence-existence composition of angels as an alternative way of safeguarding their nonsimple character. His critique of Avicebron becomes considerably more detailed in his later *De substantiis separatis*.[52] Since Thomas's views on this question have been studied in detail by others,[53] it will be sufficient here for us to recall that one of his reasons for rejecting matter-form composition in angelic entities is their nature as intelligences. Thomas judges it impossible for a corporeal or material entity to perform truly intellectual operations. Matter-form composition is incompatible with the necessary freedom from matter required for an intelligence or an intellectual power.[54]

It should be noted in passing that Thomas's denial of matter-form composition to angels and his theory of the individuation of material entities led

---

[51] Ed. by Cl. Baeumker in *Beiträge zur Geschichte der Philosophie des Mittelalters* 1, 2–4 (1892–1895). On Avicebron's universal hylemorphism see A. Forest, *La structure métaphysique du concret . . .* , pp. 109–10; F. Brunner, *Platonisme et Aristotélisme. La critique d'Ibn Gabirol par saint Thomas d'Aquin* (Louvain-Paris, 1965), pp. 33–61. See p. 53 for his comments on a number of earlier interpretations. For Thomas's attribution of this theory to Avicebron see his *De ente . . .* , c. 4 (ed. Roland-Gosselin, p. 30); *In II Sent.*, d. 3, q. 1, a. 1 (ed. Mandonnet, p. 86); *Treatise on Separate Substances,* c. 5 (ed. Lescoe, p. 56).

[52] See *De ente . . .* , (*ed. cit.*, pp. 34–35). Cf. *In II Sent.*, d. 3, q. 1, a. 1 (*ed. cit.*, pp. 87–88). See *Treatise on Separate Substances,* c. 6 (*ed. cit.*, pp. 61–68); c. 8 (pp. 74–82).

[53] See Brunner, *op. cit.*, pp. 37–61. Also see J. Guttmann, *Das Verhältniss des Thomas von Aquino zum Judenthum und zur jüdischen Litteratur* (Göttingen, 1891), pp. 16–30; M. Wittmann, *Die Stellung des hl. Thomas von Aquin zu Avencebrol, Beiträge zur Geschichte der Philosophie des Mittelalters* 3, 3 (1900), esp. pp. 33–55; A. Forest, *op. cit.*, pp. 116–20.

[54] See, for instance, *De ente . . .* , pp. 31–32; *In II Sent.*, d. 3, q. 1, a. 1, p. 86; ST I, q. 50, a. 2. Although this particular argument does not play a major role in Thomas's refutation of Avicebron in his *Treatise on Separate Substances,* it does enter into his effort in ch. 7 to show that there cannot be a single "matter" for spiritual and corporeal substances. See pp. 69–70, and also J. Collins, *The Thomistic Philosophy of the Angels* (Washington, D.C., 1947), p. 64. Collins comments on the possible presence of irony in Thomas's argumentation here. See ch. 2 of the same for Thomas's polemic against universal hylemorphism.

him to conclude that there can only be one angel in any given species.[55] We shall see more of this problem in Ch. IX while considering Godfrey's views on the individuation of material substances. But this particular conclusion, that there can only be one angel within a given species, was also defended by Siger of Brabant and by Boethius of Dacia, and would be included among the propositions condemned by Stephen Tempier in 1277.[56]

Thomas's rejection of matter-form composition in angels put him at odds with many of his contemporaries, especially among the Franciscans. Bonaventure is perhaps the best known defender of universal hylemorphism, but this doctrine is to be found in other Franciscans such as Roger Bacon, John Peckham, and a few years after Thomas's death in 1274 in William de la Mare, then in Richard of Middleton, and at the turn of the fourteenth century, in Gonsalvus of Spain, to name but a few.[57] Early in the thirteenth century

---

[55] See *De ente . . .* , pp. 33 – 34. On this and for other passages see Collins, *op. cit.*, pp. 93 – 102.

[56] See *Chartularium*, pr. 81 and 96; Mandonnet numbering, pr. 43 and 42. On these see R. Hissette, *Enquête sur les 219 articles . . .* , pp. 82 – 87, where he gives further references to Thomas, as well as to Siger and Boethius. Also see our "The Condemnations of 1270 and 1277 at Paris," p. 188.

[57] For general discussions of this see E. Kleineidam, *Das Problem der hylomorphen Zusammensetzung der geistigen Substanzen im 13. Jahrhundert, behandelt bis Thomas von Aquin* (Breslau, 1930); Lottin, "La composition hylémorphique des substances spirituelles," *Revue Néoscolastique de Philosophie* 34 (1932), pp. 21 – 41. For this in Bonaventure also see Gilson, *La philosophie de saint Bonaventure*, 3rd ed. (Paris, 1953), pp. 198 – 201 (on angels), pp. 255 – 56 (on human souls); A. Forest, *La structure métaphysique . . .* , pp. 116 – 19; J. F. Quinn, *The Historical Constitution of St. Bonaventure's Philosophy* (Toronto, 1973), pp. 139 – 50 (on matter in the human soul and in the angel), pp. 159 – 64 (on Thomas's critique); R. Macken, "Le statut de la matière première chez Bonaventure," in *Bonaventura. Studien zu seiner Wirkungsgeschichte, Franziskanische Forschungen* 28 (1976), pp. 99 – 101. On Bacon see Th. Crowley, *Roger Bacon. The Problem of the Soul in his Philosophical Commentaries* (Louvain-Dublin, 1950), pp. 81 – 91. As Crowley shows, Bacon had already developed this position in works dating from his early teaching career in the Arts Faculty at Paris, that is, ca. 1241 – 1245 (see p. 73). For this in Peckham see his *Tractatus de anima*, G. Melani, ed. (Florence, 1948), pp. 47 – 48, 61 – 63 (for discussion of his text). For William see *Le correctorium Corruptorii "Quare,"* pp. 49 – 52 (agst. Thomas, ST I, q. 50, a. 2), pp. 118 – 21 (on matter-form composition of human soul agst. Thomas, ST I, q. 75, a. 5). On Richard see Hocedez, *Richard de Middleton* (Louvain-Paris, 1925), pp. 190 – 99; D. E. Sharp, *Franciscan Philosophy at Oxford in the Thirteenth Century* (London, 1930), pp. 262 – 63. For Gonsalvus see his *Quaestiones disputatae et de quodlibet*, L. Amorós, ed. (Quaracchi, Florence, 1935), pp. 204, 213 – 21. For the interrelationship between Gonsalvus's *Disputed Questions* and Godfrey's Q 15, see our discussion in this chapter below under "Matter-Form Composition in the Human Soul."

it had been criticized by William of Auvergne and in Thomas's own time by Albert the Great.[58] Siger of Brabant, Henry of Ghent, and Giles of Rome were also opposed to it.[59]

There is some disagreement among contemporary scholars as to whether it is really Avicebron who is the major source for thirteenth-century theories of universal hylemorphism or whether these should rather be traced back to Augustine. While Avicebron's influence is stressed by many such as Théry, Forest, Crowley, F. Brunner, and Van Steenberghen, R. Zavalloni tends to assign the greater influence to St. Augustine.[60] Thirteenth-century testimony also appears to be divided on this point. Thus, Roger Bacon does not refer this doctrine to Augustine at all in his early development of his own version of the same.[61] Thomas, as we have seen, explicitly ascribes it to Avicebron and both exposes and criticizes the latter's development of it in detail. Later in the century, Giles of Rome will question its presence in Augustine. But Thomas of York had insisted that it is to be found there, as will Gonsalvus of Spain at the turn of the century.[62] One might surmise that during the latter quarter of the century defenders of universal hylemorphism tended to stress its Augustinian antecedents in order to lend greater authority to it, especially so in the wake of their reaction against both the Thomistic form of Aristotelianism and the radical Aristotelianism that had been condemned at Paris in 1270 and 1277.[63]

---

[58] On William's critique see Roland-Gosselin's account in his *Le "De ente et essentia" de s. Thomas d'Aquin,* pp. 71 – 74; A. Forest, *op. cit.,* 121 – 23. On Albert see Roland-Gosselin, *op. cit.,* pp. 90, 97, 101; Kleineidam, *Das Problem der hylomorphen Zusammensetzung* . . . , pp. 51 – 57; Forest, *op. cit.,* pp. 123 – 26; Lottin, *Psychologie et morale* . . . , Vol. 1, pp. 444 – 46. This section (pp. 427 – 60) corrects and completes the article cited in n. 57.

[59] On Siger see Van Steenberghen, *Maître Siger* . . . , pp. 282 – 92. For Henry see Q 4, q. 16, fol. 130v – 131r. Also see Paulus, *Henri de Gand* . . . , p. 216 and n. 1. For Giles see his *Theoremata de esse et essentia,* Th. XIX, pp. 128 – 29; Quodlibet 1, q. 8, pp. 17 – 19.

[60] See G. Théry, "L'Augustinisme médiéval et le problème de l'unité de la forme substantielle," *Acta Hebdomadae Augustinianae-Thomisticae* (Turin-Rome, 1931), pp. 145 – 46; Forest, *op. cit.,* ch. 4; Brunner, *op. cit.,* pp. 34 – 37; Crowley, *op. cit.,* pp. 82, 90; Van Steenberghen, *La philosophie au XIIIe siècle,* pp. 46 – 47, 150, 245 – 46, 249; Zavalloni, *op. cit.,* p. 422.

[61] See Crowley, *op cit.,* p. 91.

[62] Zavalloni, pp. 442 – 43. For Gonsalvus see his *Quaestiones disputatae* . . . , q. 11, *ed. cit.,* p. 221. But some twenty years before, Henry of Ghent explicitly attributes universal hylemorphism to Avicebron. See his Q 4, q. 16 (fol. 130v), dating from 1279.

[63] See Crowley, *op cit.,* p. 82.

Godfrey explicitly addresses himself to this topic in Quodlibet 3, q. 3, where he seeks to determine whether angels are composed of matter and form.[64] After recalling a number of the arguments usually offered in support of matter-form composition in angels, Godfrey acknowledges that one may take the term matter broadly so as to apply it to any potency. He then distinguishes between two different kinds of potency. The first, potency for certain accidental perfections and operations, is present in every creature. The second is a potency for substantial form whereby something enjoys substantial existence. This second kind of potency, pure potentiality, is properly referred to as prime matter or as *hyle*. While potency or "matter" in the first sense is to be assigned to angels insofar as their substance serves as the subject for certain accidental perfections, Godfrey denies that matter in the strict sense, prime matter, is to be found in them.[65]

His first major reason for rejecting the presence of prime matter in angels follows from the nature of matter itself and the incorruptible character of angels. Prime matter is not of itself more determined to one substantial form than to another. Nor can one distinguish between different kinds of prime matter. Just as pure nonbeing cannot be divided from itself, so too prime matter, pure potentiality, contains nothing within itself to enable one instance of it to differ in kind from another. Such would require some degree of actuality within prime matter, something that would be contrary to its nature as pure potentiality.[66] In other words, Godfrey has already undermined the possibility of distinguishing between different kinds of prime matter, whether between spiritual prime matter and corporeal prime matter or whether between different kinds of corporeal prime matter. The former distinction had been proposed by certain defenders of universal hylemorphism, while the latter, as we shall see, is used by Aquinas in his effort to account for the incorruptible character of heavenly bodies.[67]

---

[64] "Utrum natura angelica sit composita ex vera materia et vera forma" (PB 2.179).

[65] For these arguments see PB 2.180–81; also see the short version, PB 2.307. For the distinction between the two kinds of potency, potency *simpliciter* and potency *secundum quid* see PB 2.182 and PB 2.307 (short version). For some variant readings for the abridgement of Q 3, q. 3 as found in Florence *Bibl. nat. ms.* II.II.182 and in *Borghese* 298 see A. Pattin "La structure de l'être fini selon Bernard d'Auvergne, O.P.," *Tijdschrift voor Filosofie* 24 (1962), p. 703.

[66] PB 2.182–83, 308 (short version).

[67] See Gonsalvus of Spain, *Quaestiones disputatae* . . . , q. 11, *ed. cit.*, p. 204, for reference to this division of opinion among defenders of universal hylemorphism. He himself regards as more probable the claim that prime matter is one and the same in kind whether present in corporeal or incorporeal things. See *ed. cit.*, p. 204, n. 1 for a citation from Richard of Middleton wherein he defends different kinds of matter for spirits, for corruptible corporeal things, and for incorruptible corporeals. See

Nor will Godfrey permit one to escape from this conclusion by appealing to diversity in the kinds of forms to which matter is ordered in order to allow for different kinds of prime matter itself. Thus, one might argue that the prime matter of angels differs from that of corporeal entities simply by reason of the different kinds of forms to which they are ordered. Godfrey counters that if mere relationship to generically different kinds of forms were sufficient to account for different kinds of matter, then relationship to specifically different kinds of forms would result in specifically different kinds of matter. This he rejects as false, presumably because it is the unity in kind of prime matter as realized in different corporeal entities that allows for them to change into other corporeal entities even of different species.[68]

Godfrey immediately appeals to the unity-in-kind of prime matter in order to complete his first argument against matter-form composition of angels. Just as it is because corporeal entities share in one and the same kind of prime matter that they can change into one another, it will follow that angels too could be changed into one another if they were composed of matter and form. At the very least, spiritual matter as realized in different angels would have to be one in kind.[69] (Godfrey could, of course, here insist that spiritual matter and corporeal matter would also be one in kind.)[70] And then, in reasoning that we have seen before in Godfrey, he concludes that since prime matter itself renders something capable of substantial change, where there is no capacity for such change there can be no prime matter. Nor will it do for someone to suggest that certain matter-form composites are not capable of undergoing substantial change because the capacity of their matter for form has been completely filled by their particular substantial form. According to Godfrey, it is of the very nature of prime matter or pure potentiality to tend towards or to "desire" any other substantial form that is capable in any way of perfecting it.[71]

Hocedez, *Richard de Middleton*, pp. 190–91.

[68] PB 2.183, 308 (short version). He also reasons that since any such relation will add nothing to the essence of matter and will presuppose it, it can hardly differentiate matter into different kinds.

[69] PB 2.183, 308 (short version). In the longer version he argues that the matter of all corporeals is not only one in kind but even one in number insofar as it is viewed in itself ("una secundum rationem et etiam secundum rem etiam numeralem quantum est de se"). Such would also be true of the matter of spirits (see p. 183). For more on the unity enjoyed by matter see Ch. IX.

[70] Were this to be granted, he could then object that spiritual entities could be changed into corporeal entities and vice versa. But he does not judge it necessary to go to such lengths here to make his point.

[71] PB 2.183–84, and PB 2.308 (short version). See the texts cited in note 42.

Godfrey's second reason for rejecting matter-form composition in angels is based on their nature as intelligences and thus reminds one of Thomas's similar argumentation against the same.[72] Because the act of understanding is a perfect kind of act whereby something is grasped in abstraction from individuating conditions, the power capable of such activity must be so perfect and separate from matter that its essence cannot be material. Just as that which is material or purely potential cannot be understood in itself, much less could something truly material be an intelligence in and of itself. Thus, if the human intellect were simply the perfection of matter in such fashion that it could in no way exist apart from matter, it would be incapable of understanding. It is because of its immaterial nature and its capacity to exist apart from anything material that it can receive intelligible species in itself. But if an angel were composed of matter and form, then its intellect, that in which its intelligible species are received, would also be so composed.[73] Godfrey assumes that this would be so presumably because, according to the terms of universal hylemorphism, everything created, whether corporeal or spiritual, would be composed of matter and form, including angelic intellects.[74]

In concluding this discussion of matter-form composition in angels, Godfrey refers in passing both to one of the major arguments offered by defenders of the same and to what he regards as an unsuccessful reply to that argument. Many argue in favor of matter-form composition in angels in order to defend their composite character and thus to distinguish them from the divine simplicity. As we have seen above, Thomas Aquinas had accounted for this by appealing to his theory of composition of essence and existence in all creatures, including angels.[75] But as we have also seen, Godfrey rejects both the validity of this argument for matter-form composition in angels and any effort to meet it by appealing to essence-existence composition. It is not by having recourse to composition of essence and existence or of matter and form or

---

[72] See n. 54.

[73] PB 2.184–85. Underlying Godfrey's thinking here is his conviction that if an intellect were composed of matter and form it could only receive in a material way (". . . ita esset quid imperfectum . . . quantum ad hoc quod nihil recipere posset nisi materialiter," p. 184). Also see PB 2.308 (short version).

[74] ". . . tunc illud in quo primo et per se reciperetur species intelligibilis, esset compositum ex forma et materia vera" (PB 2.185). Also see PB 2.308: ". . . quia forma angeli non ponitur separabilis a tali materia sicut anima separabilis est a materia corporali."

[75] For this argumentation see PB 2.180 ("Circa primum . . .") and PB 2.307 (short version). On Thomas see above in this chapter, p. 275.

of any really distinct factors that one safeguards the nonsimple character of such creatures. Otherwise, one could do so simply by appealing to their substance-accident composition. As Godfrey here suggests in passing and as he explains in Quodlibet 3, q. 1 and in greater detail in Quodlibet 7, q. 7, one may regard an angelic essence as potential insofar as it falls short of the actuality of God, or for that matter of any other more perfect angel, and as actual insofar as it is compared with any less perfect being. This logical composition of potentiality and actuality, as we have styled it, suffices according to Godfrey for one to maintain the nonsimple character of any such creature.[76] If Godfrey is in agreement with Thomas in rejecting matter-form composition in angels, therefore, he differs from him in accounting for their nonsimplicity.

2. *Matter-Form Composition in the Human Soul*

Godfrey considers this issue in Quodlibet 15, q. 10, where he wonders whether the soul can inform two matters.[77] As we have already indicated above in the Introduction to this study, it was partly on the strength of apparent references in this discussion to Gonsalvus of Spain's Disputed Question 11 of 1302/1303 that Glorieux eventually dated this in 1303/1304 and concluded that it was Godfrey's final Quodlibet. As we have also indicated there, San Cristóbal-Sebastián acknowledged this interdependence between Godfrey's Quodlibet 15 and Gonsalvus's Disputed Question 11, but argued that it runs in the opposite direction. Gonsalvus would have cited Godfrey and hence this would not be Godfrey's final Quodlibet but would, in fact, be one of his earliest, dating from Christmas 1286.[78] Our own investigation of this has led us to support Glorieux in his conclusions and to offer more detailed textual evidence for the same.[79] Hence, we shall assume here that Godfrey's primary target in Quodlibet 15 is indeed Gonsalvus of Spain. And as we have already indicated, Gonsalvus not only defends matter-form composition in spiritual realities in his Disputed Question 11, but proposes as the more probable version of this theory that which assigns only one kind of matter to spiritual and to corporeal realities as well as to corruptible and incorruptible corporeal beings.[80]

---

[76] See PB 2.186 and 309 (short version). Also see Ch. II, pp. 91–97.

[77] "Utrum anima possit perficere duas materias" (PB 14.50).

[78] See in our Introduction, p. xxvii.

[79] See our "Godfrey of Fontaines: the Date of Quodlibet 15," pp. 322–32, 338–52.

[80] See *Quaestiones disputatae* . . . , q. 11, p. 204, pp. 219ff. Also see p. 194.

In Quodlibet 15, q. 10 Godfrey first refers in general to the opposed position insofar as it entails the claim that the soul or at least the form of the soul can perfect two different matters. Thus the separated soul will still include matter as an intrinsic part and will continue to perfect it. At the same time it will perfect corporeal matter so long as it is united with its body.[81] Gonsalvus explicitly defends this position and acknowledges that the soul is therefore separable from its extrinsic matter, that is, from the body, but not from its intrinsic matter within the natural course of events.[82]

Godfrey immediately offers a general argument in support of his own position, that is, that it is impossible for the soul to include matter as an intrinsic part of itself and therefore, that it is not possible for the soul to inform two matters, this intrinsic matter plus corporeal matter. In order to establish this he reasons that if something is entirely form and actuality, it cannot admit of matter as a part of itself. But such is the nature of the soul. Hence, there can be no matter in the soul.[83]

In proof of the major of this argument Godfrey explains that to say that something is entirely such (form and act in the present discussion) as he is here using this expression is to signify that it is such in terms of all that is included in its essence. To admit, then, that prime matter could be included within the essence of the soul would be to suggest that that which is entirely form and act (the soul) would at the same time be pure potentiality. This, remarks Godfrey, is entirely impossible, except perhaps, he adds rather scornfully, for those for whom all impossible things are to be regarded as possible.[84]

It remains for him to establish the minor of his argument—to show that the soul of itself is entirely form and act. In support of this he offers three fairly extended arguments. First of all, he reasons that if one maintains that the soul is not of itself entirely form and actuality but includes some matter that differs from corporeal matter, one must explain the relationship between the soul's intrinsic matter and corporeal matter. If one denies that they enjoy any kind of unity apart from the fact that they both happen to be informed by one and the same form, one will thereby reduce man himself to the status of an accidental composite with no greater unity than that of a pile of stones. But if one argues that there is some fundamental kind of unity between the two matters themselves, then one fares no better. Such unity might be re-

---

[81] PB 14.50.
[82] *Op. cit.*, pp. 194–96.
[83] PB 14.50
[84] PB 14.50–51.

garded as essential. But then there would not really be two matters, but only one. Or such unity might be thought to occur by "information," in that one matter would inform another. This Godfrey rejects as impossible, since pure potency would then be treated as if it were actuality insofar as one instance of the same, one matter, would inform another. (Godfrey here assumes that prime matter is pure potentiality, something that many of his opponents would not concede.) Or one might settle for unity by continuity. But this would be to assume that both matters were quantified and corporeal so as to be able to enter into continuity with one another, which would be to admit that there is really one matter in man.[85]

As a second argument in support of his contention that the soul is entirely form and actuality, Godfrey again reasons from the possible relationship and distinction between the types of matter it would have to inform if it were to include matter as an intrinsic part of itself. Either these two matters would be essentially distinct from one another of themselves, or they would be distinguished by reason of their quantity and position, or else because only one would be quantified while the other would not be. To the first of these suggestions Godfrey counters that if the two matters in question were essentially distinct of themselves, they could not both be actualized by a substantial form or act of one and the same kind. If they were distinguished solely by reason of their different quantities and positions, then one would have in fact made of the noncorporeal matter a corporeal matter. But if it be contended that they differ only insofar as only one of these matters is quantified, then, wonders Godfrey, how is one to account for the nonquantified character of the other? One can hardly say that it is nonquantified of itself since, according to Gonsalvus, all matter is of one and the same kind. But one cannot account for the nonquantified character of the one matter by appealing to the form since, by hypothesis, it would be the same form that actualized both. Hence, quantity would have to be present in both.[86] Finally, in rather derisive terms Godfrey rejects any suggestion that one matter might differ from the other simply because it is nobler or purer.[87]

In his final argument to show that the soul is entirely form and actuality Godfrey returns to the by now familiar theme that if the soul were composed of such matter and form it would be corruptible. He rejects, of course, any implication that the soul is corruptible and, in support of the antecedent in

---

[85] PB 14.51.

[86] PB 14.51 – 52.

[87] PB 14.52. Godfrey's impatience with the opposed position is evident throughout this discussion, but perhaps nowhere more so than in this immediate context.

this reasoning, recalls that if a thing's form is separable from its matter, then it is corruptible. He insists that the form of the soul would be separable from the soul's matter, even within the natural order. He recalls that according to the theory in question all matter is of one and the same kind. Hence, just as corporeal matter can be separated from the form of the soul, so could any other matter that is intrinsic to the soul.[88]

Godfrey then briefly considers and refutes some counterarguments offered by some to show that matter-form composition need not imply the corruptible character of the composite. As we have shown in another context, it is likely that he here has in mind specific counterarguments taken from Gonsalvus's Disputed Question 11.[89] And in the next section of this same Quodlibet 15, q. 10 Godfrey specifically addresses himself to a series of arguments in support of matter-form composition of spiritual entities. It is in his presentation of these arguments that one finds the greatest evidence pointing to Godfrey's direct knowledge and usage of Gonsalvus's Disputed Question. In the final part of his discussion Godfrey responds to each of these arguments in turn and thereby reinforces his conclusion that it is impossible for the soul to include matter as an intrinsic part of itself and, therefore, that it is impossible for the soul to perfect two different matters.[90] Rather than reproduce each of these arguments together with Godfrey's replies, we shall here limit ourselves to one of these, both because of its philosophical interest in itself and because Godfrey has obviously borrowed this argument from Gonsalvus in order to refute it.

According to Gonsalvus's second argument as it appears in his text and as it is reproduced by Godfrey, that which contributes to the perfection of substance as such insofar as it is to be distinguished from accidental being must certainly be assigned to nobler and more perfect beings such as those that are incorruptible. But this is matter. In order to establish this point, that it is matter that contributes to the perfection of substance as substance, the argument recalls that it pertains to substance to serve as the support or foundation for accidents. But the primary role in standing under or serving as a support for accidents in the case of composite beings is to be attributed to matter and not to the composite as such. Otherwise, one would have already

---

[88] PB 14.52 – 53.

[89] PB 14.53. Compare with Gonsalvus, *ed. cit.*, pp. 205 – 07. On this see our "Godfrey of Fontaines: the Date of Quodlibet 15," pp. 311 – 15.

[90] See PB 14.53 – 55 for the arguments and pp. 55 – 56 for Godfrey's rebuttal. For these in Gonsalvus see pp. 214 – 17 (for arguments 1 through 4) and pp. 207 – 08 for another argument that seems to correspond to another found in Godfrey (p. 54). On this see our "Godfrey of Fontaines: the Date of Quodlibet 15," pp. 322 – 32.

conceded the point that only composites can support accidents and, therefore, that every subsisting creature including angels is a composite. The primary role in supporting accidents cannot be attributed to form as form because, if that were true, every form would have to support accidents (according to Gonsalvus) or subsist (according to Godfrey's version of the argument). But such a consequence cannot be admitted.[91] Hence, it will follow that one must allow for matter-form composition of angels and of the human soul in order to account for the presence of accidents therein.

Godfrey's reply to this argument is quite succinct. He simply denies that it is matter that contributes to the perfection of all created substances insofar as they are substances. This is true only of material entities. And even in these, matter is their less perfect contributing principle. In other words, Godfrey criticizes the argument for assuming that which remains to be proven, that is, that all created substances are composed of matter and form, and for misconstruing the proper relationship between matter and form in composites.[92] In sum, in this final quodlibetal discussion of 1303/1304 Godfrey remains steadfast in his refusal to allow for matter-form composition of souls or of any spiritual entity. The fact that the theory had recently been defended by Gonsalvus of Spain may have occasioned the query leading to Godfrey's discussion of this in this Quodlibet. In any event, he is no more sympathetic to Gonsalvus's presentation of universal hylemorphism than he was to any of its earlier defenders.

3. Matter-Form Composition of the Heavenly Bodies

As we have already mentioned above in passing, the incorruptible character of the heavenly bodies was generally accepted in Godfrey's time. One important source for thirteenth-century discussions of this was, of course, Aristotle. Thus, in Bk. I of his *De caelo* the Stagirite distinguishes two simple local motions that correspond to two simple geometrical lines, that is to say, the straight and the circular. Straight local motion itself may either be away from the center of the universe (upward) or towards that center (downward).[93] If upward motion is natural for the elements of fire and air, and downward for those of water and earth, Aristotle also argues for a natural circular mo-

---

[91] For Gonsalvus see *ed. cit.*, pp. 214 – 15; for Godfrey, PB 14.53 – 54. For presentation of these texts in parallel columns see our "Godfrey of Fontaines . . . ," pp. 324 – 25.

[92] PB 14.55.

[93] *De caelo* I, c.2 (268b 17–24). On this see T. Litt, *Les corps célestes dans l'univers de saint Thomas d'Aquin* (Louvain-Paris, 1963), p. 44.

tion. Finding circular motion unnatural for the elements, he reasons that there must be some other simple body for which such motion is natural—a body that is beyond those found on earth and which is different and separate from them. Such are, according to Aristotle, the heavenly spheres or the heavenly bodies.[94] Each such sphere is hollow and moves with circular motion, but without losing its place or location as a whole. Such a body will not possess qualities such as lightness or heaviness, nor be subject to any kind of violent motion. It will admit of no contrary, since there can be no motion that is contrary to the circular. Hence, it will be ungenerated and incorruptible, free from increase and alteration, and eternal.[95]

Thomas Aquinas is familiar with this Aristotelian teaching and accepts much of it. (He will not, of course, defend the *de facto* eternity of the universe and of motion as proposed by Aristotle.) Since his teaching on the incorruptible character of the heavenly bodies has been presented in detail by T. Litt, we shall here content ourselves with reference to an important text from his *Summa theologiae*, I, q. 66, a. 2.[96] There he reasons that precisely because a heavenly body enjoys a motion that is different from the natural motion of the elements, it follows that it must differ in nature from them. And just as circular motion, which is natural to a heavenly body, admits of no contrariety, so too, a heavenly body itself must lack contrariety. Such is not true, he continues, of earthly bodies—that is to say, of the elements. But because generation and corruption presuppose contrariety, it will follow that a heavenly body is incorruptible. Important for our purposes here is Thomas's unqualified acceptance of the incorruptible character of the heavenly bodies. As Litt remarks, on many other occasions Thomas simply mentions their incorruptibility as if it were so evident as to need no proof.[97]

Still, if one bears in mind the Aristotelian theory of matter, form, and privation as principles of change, one might wonder how it is possible to assign matter-form composition to a heavenly body and still maintain its incorruptible character. Thomas was well aware of this difficulty, as had been Averroes. On a number of occasions Thomas reports Averroes's position. According to Aquinas, Averroes resolved this problem by denying matter in the proper sense to heavenly bodies—that is to say, prime matter such as that of terrestial elements and bodies. And in an early presentation of this position in his *Commentary* on Bk II of the *Sentences*, Thomas describes this part of

---

[94] *De caelo* I, c. 2 (268b 30–269b 17). Also see Litt, *op. cit.*, pp. 44–45.
[95] See Litt, *op. cit.*, pp. 44–46. See *De caelo* I, cc. 3–4; II, c. 3 (286a 3).
[96] See Litt, *op. cit.*, pp. 46–53; pp. 262–63.
[97] *Op. cit.*, p. 52.

Averroes's theory as more probable.[98] But in other contexts Thomas also interprets Averroes as holding that while a heavenly body lacks matter-form composition in the proper sense, it may be described as actually existing matter which is in potency only with respect to presence in place (*ubi*) and which receives its soul as its form only as its moving principle, not as that which communicates being to it.[99]

Thomas constantly rejects this denial that heavenly bodies are really composed of matter and form. While defending the presence of matter and form in such bodies, he maintains that their matter differs in kind from that of earthly elements and bodies. Thus the matter of a heavenly body is in potency to only one form, the one that actually informs it, so much so that it is not corruptible and not in potency to any other form. In brief, then, Thomas resolves this apparent dilemma by postulating two different kinds of matter, the kind appropriate to earthly bodies which does carry with it the capacity for further change and hence corruptibility, and another and higher kind that is present only in heavenly bodies and that does not entail corruptibility.[100]

Litt has singled this out as one striking illustration of a case where Thomas's understanding of the heavenly bodies did influence his philosophical thinking, in that he allowed for two different kinds of prime matter and for a matter-form composite that would not be corruptible.[101] While Godfrey

---

[98] See *In II Sent.*, d. 12, q. 1, a. 1 (ed. Mandonnet, pp. 302–03). For Averroes see *In I De caelo,* text. 20 (Venice, 1562), Vol. 5, fol. 15rab. Insofar as Averroes denies that matter of the same kind is common to heavenly and terrestrial bodies, Thomas describes his position as more probable and more in agreement with Aristotle's position in *Metaphysics* XII (p. 303). For Aristotle see *Metaphysics* XII, c. 2 (I069b 24–26), where he observes that eternal things that are not generable but movable do not have matter for generation but only for motion in terms of place. But Averroes also states that a heavenly body is not composed of matter and form as are the simple elements and that it is simple ("non est compositum ex materia et forma, sicut sunt quatuor corpora simplicia, et quod est simplex"). See fol. 15ra.

[99] See *In VIII Phys.*, lect. 21, n. 1152; ST I, q. 66, a. 2; *De spiritualibus creaturis,* a. 6, ad 2; *In I De caelo,* lect. 6 (R.M. Spiazzi, ed. [Turin-Rome, 1952]), n. 63 (where he hesitates as to Averroes's real meaning: if he merely denies that a heavenly body has the kind of matter that entails the capacity for nonbeing, he is correct; but not if he denies that it has any matter in the proper sense). For Averroes also see *In XII Met.*, Vol. 8, fol. 296vb–297ra; *In VIII Phys.,* Vol. 4, fol. 432rab.

[100] For thirty-seven texts ranging throughout Thomas's career see Litt, pp. 59–79. In these texts Thomas repeatedly defends the presence of matter-form composition in the heavenly bodies and the difference between the kind of matter found there and in earthly elements and bodies. See pp. 86–87 for a difficult text from *In de Trin.*, Q. 5, a. 4, ad 4.

[101] *Op. cit.*, p. 6.

devotes far less attention to the structure of the heavenly bodies and to this general question than does Thomas, he too was aware of the same difficulty. As already noted, he strongly insists on the purely potential character of prime matter. He also insists that wherever one finds matter-form composition *in the proper sense, one must allow for the corruptible character of that* composite.

In Quodlibet 5, q. 2, Godfrey addresses himself to this theme in the course of attempting to determine whether or not God can make an incorruptible body from the matter of one that is corruptible.[102] He begins his reply by allowing that such may be possible according to those who maintain that God can separate in reality all things that are essentially diverse—for instance, motion from any moving body, matter from form, or whiteness from quantity. Thus they might also contend that God can unite any being with any other being and any form with any matter, so as to produce the form of an angel or the form of the heaven in the matter of an element or of any other corruptible body in an incorruptible way. Godfrey himself does not see how such things are possible, although he acknowledges that God can do all that does not involve contradiction and that he himself does not understand all that God can do.[103]

Godfrey counters that it seems to be contradictory to suggest that God could introduce into matter a form that subsists in itself and has no essential relationship to matter in such fashion that it would then be essentially ordered to matter. So too, he judges it contradictory to hold that God could introduce a form into matter in such a way that it could not be separated from that matter. Matter by its very nature is designed to be subject to all material forms so that when it is in fact informed by one, it has a natural capacity and "desire" (*appetitus*) for others. This appetite to be subject to other forms is, argues Godfrey, inseparable from matter as such. Hence, to hold that matter could receive a form in inseparable and incorruptible fashion would be to *maintain that the matter could be separated from its given form (by reason* of its natural aptitude to be subject to other forms) and that it could not be (according to the hypothesis).[104] And then, speaking more generally, he returns to a theme we have seen in him before. It is impossible for any truly and naturally incorruptible body to contain matter intrinsically, if one understands by matter that which excludes all actuality and is pure potentiality.

---

[102] "Utrum Deus possit ex materia corruptibilis producere aliquod corpus incorruptibile" (PB 3.7).

[103] PB 3.7–8.

[104] PB 3.8.

By definition such matter is that by reason of which a thing or composite has the capacity for being and for nonbeing and is, therefore, naturally corruptible.[105]

He then turns to a theory which appears to be that defended by Aquinas. According to this view it is true that the presence of the prime matter known as *hyle,* which is proper to generable and corruptible things, necessarily entails the possibility for corruption of that in which it is present. But this is not true of the kind of matter found in heavenly bodies. The latter kind of matter differs because it is ordered to a special kind of form which is, as it were, so universal and perfect that it excludes any possibility of that matter's being ordered towards or receiving another form.[106] Godfrey flatly rejects this suggestion and argues that matter as such includes no actuality of itself and that, as pure potentiality, it cannot be divided into different kinds. Nor can its capacity and desire for forms be exhausted by any single form. In fact, says Godfrey, matter's potentiality may be described as infinite in this sense, that no matter how perfect the given form that actualizes it, it always retains its capacity for others.[107]

Godfrey then cites Averroes's *Commentary* on Bk I of the *De caelo* to this effect, that if there were any matter in the heavens in the sense of a potency for being, then nature would have been frustrated. Since the proper "operation" of such a potency is corruption and generation, or substantial change, this capacity would never be realized in heavenly bodies.[108] Godfrey concludes, along with Averroes, that it is unfitting to hold that the same kind of matter is present in the heavens and in corruptible things.[109] Here he seems to have forgotten Thomas's theory and to have returned to the original opinion according to which God could unite certain forms in inseparable fashion with matter.

---

[105] PB 3.8 – 9.

[106] PB 3.9. For Thomas see, for instance, among the many texts cited by Litt, *De veritate,* q. 8, a. 15 (Litt, p. 62); SCG II, c. 98 (Litt, p. 64); ST I, q. 84, a. 3, ad 1 (Litt, p. 68); *In I De caelo,* lect. 6, n. 63 (Litt, pp. 79 – 80). For the same see Giles of Rome, Quodlibet 1, q. 8, p. 18ab; and q. 12, p. 26a. Giles's Quodlibet 1 dates from 1286 (Glorieux, *La littérature quodlibétique. . . ,* Vol. 1, p. 141), hence not too long before Godfrey's Q 5 of 1288. But compare this with Giles's *Quaestiones metaphysicales* VIII, q. 3 (Venice, 1501), fol. 34r – 34v. And for other texts where Giles rejects different kinds of matter see Suárez, "La metafísica de Egidio Romano . . . ," pp. 294 – 95.

[107] PB 3.9.

[108] PB 3.9. For Averroes see *In I De caelo, ed. cit.,* fol. 15rab.

[109] PB 3.10.

Throughout the remainder of Quodlibet 5, q. 2, he strengthens his case against that position. Thus, he appeals to Aristotle's teaching concerning prime matter, privation, and the contrary—that is, the form contrary to the form to be generated, as developed in *Physics* I. These three, he contends, are always found together.[110] Prime matter is always subject to a given substantial form, but while united with one it remains capable of receiving others. Hence, it always remains in privation with respect to these other forms. It is for this reason, he insists, that things that share in the same kind of matter may be changed into one another.[111] But in Quodlibet 9, q. 7, Godfrey touches on this problem again.[112] Once more he refers to the theory according to which the matter of the heavenly bodies would differ, and differ generically, from that of the elements. And once more he reasons that because matter is pure potentiality, it is impossible to introduce any differentiation in kind into it. Viewed as pure potentiality it is equally potential with respect to any (corporeal) form.[113]

In this same context in Quodlibet 9, q. 7, Godfrey offers as more probable an alternative solution. He had, of course, rejected the possible presence of one and the same kind of matter in corruptible and incorruptible bodies. He has now reiterated his inability to admit of different kinds of prime matter. And so he concludes with obvious dependency upon Averroes that it is better to say that there is no matter, properly speaking, in heavenly bodies. Since heavenly bodies are not in potency to nonbeing—in other words, since they are incorruptible—there can be no matter in them. To allow for the presence of matter in them would be to admit that they are generable and corruptible.[114]

On this particular point, therefore, Godfrey has steadfastly refused to compromise the purely potential character of prime matter. Given this, he has been forced to eliminate the possibility that any naturally incorruptible entity

---

[110] PB 3.10. See Aristotle, *Physics* I, c. 7. Note Godfrey's comment: ". . . ista tria sunt ab invicem omnino inseparabilia, scilicet materia prima, et privatio, et contrarium sive forma contraria formae generandae, quia ubicumque est unum istorum sunt alia duo."

[111] PB 3.10–11. See his concluding remarks on p. 12 where he again insists that it is contradictory to hold that there is matter in the heavens of the same kind as that of the elements and that heavenly bodies are nonetheless incorruptible.

[112] In Q 9, q. 7, Godfrey asks: "Utrum possint esse duo entia specifice differentia aequaliter se habentia ad primum principium" (PB 4.231).

[113] PB 4.233. On the point that difference in matter will result in generic differentiation in terms of a natural genus see Thomas, *In de Trin.*, Q. 4, a. 2 (ed. Decker, pp. 141–42); also see Giles of Rome, Quodlibet 1, q. 8, p. 18ab.

[114] PB 4.233. There he literally cites Averroes, *In I Phys.*, Vol. 4, fol. 45rab.

could be composed of matter and form. Thomas's defense of a second kind of matter in heavenly bodies has also been rejected as unacceptable, since it, too, in Godfrey's eyes, does violence to the purely potential character of matter. Almost inevitably, he has been forced into the strange if courageous conclusion that there is no prime matter in heavenly bodies—a conclusion that he cautiously labels "more probable."

Chapter VIII.

Substantial Form and the Composite

In the present chapter we shall concentrate on Godfrey's understanding of substantial form insofar as it is realized in composite entities. Two issues relating to this were widely controverted during the latter part of the thirteenth century. The first has to do with the origin of substantial forms, that is to say, with that from which they originate in the process of substantial change. Augustine's theory of seminal reasons (*rationes seminales*) was also frequently connected with this discussion. The second is concerned with the number of substantial forms present in any given substantial composite: is there only one substantial form therein, or more than one? Theological issues were often cited in connection with this. Hence, this chapter itself will be divided into four major parts: A. The Origin of Substantial Forms; B. Dispositions and *Rationes Seminales*; C. Unicity vs. Plurality of Substantial Forms; D. Theological Difficulties.

A. THE ORIGIN OF SUBSTANTIAL FORMS

In considering this question Godfrey carefully distinguishes between the situation of the human intellective soul, on the one hand, and that of substantial forms as realized in purely material entities, on the other. As one would expect, he holds for direct divine creation of intellective human souls. In other words, the intellective or spiritual soul in man is not "educed" from any preexisting potentiality in matter nor even from any preexisting seminal reason (*ratio seminalis*). But this is not to deny that in the normal course of events the material and receiving principle for such a soul will be properly disposed or prepared to receive that soul itself. Every substantial form below the human soul is material and immersed in matter. Even the intellectual soul is designed by its very nature to communicate being to its matter and to exist in union with it. Still, contends Godfrey, it can exist in itself apart from its matter. Such is not true of less perfect substantial forms. They cannot exist apart from matter.[1] Given this understanding of purely material substantial forms, the question remains: How is one to account for their origin? Is one to appeal to direct creation of such forms by God? Or is one to suggest that they have actually preexisted as such in some fashion in the matter of the old composite from which the new one is to be generated?

Already in his early Quodlibet 2, q. 6 Godfrey indicates that he will accept neither of these suggestions and that he espouses the theory according to which such forms are educed from the potentiality of matter.[2] As he explains in Quodlibet 11, q. 2, it is not merely the form that is directly generated in the process of substantial change, but the composite. Given this, one might say that the matter and the form found in the composite are also generated in some way. But with reference to this Godfrey introduces a distinction. The form in the composite is generated with respect to its essence, since it did not preexist except in the potentiality of the matter. But the matter is not generated as regards its essence, since it did preexist under a different substantial form in the previous composite entity. Hence, the matter as informed by the new substantial form differs from that same matter when it was informed by the previous substantial form only in terms of its actuality (*esse*), not in terms of its essence. In this later treatment, therefore, that is, ca. 1295/96, Godfrey will not allow for any actual preexistence of a corporeal substantial form.[3]

---

[1] See Q 2, q. 6 (PB 2.90–92). See in particular: ". . . medium autem inter haec extrema videtur esse intellectiva forma in quantum est actus dans esse materiae in quo communicat cum aliis formis materialibus, non tamen sic materiae immersa et ab ea comprehensa vel dependens quin quantum est de se nata sit per se subsistere . . ." (p. 90); ". . . ita omnis forma inferior intellectiva est omnino materialis et omnino immersa materiae, et de potentia materiae per generationem educibilis . . ." (p. 91); "Sed omnis forma alia ab intellectu talis est quod non est nata habere esse in materia per creationem, sed per eductionem de potentia materiae ipsius transmutatione . . ." (p. 92).

[2] See note 1.

[3] PB 5.10. Note in particular: "Quamvis enim verum sit quod compositum per se generatur et in composito non solum forma, sed etiam materia generatur, tamen aliter et aliter; quia forma in composito sic generatur quantum ad eius essentiam quod secundum nullam entitatem suam praeerat nisi in potentia alterius . . . sed manet una et eadem materia differens secundum suam essentiam ab entitate formae sub formis

In the still later Quodlibet 14, q. 5 of 1298/99, Godfrey considers this same problem in greater detail. This time he prefaces his discussion with a brief historical survey of earlier responses to the same issue. He notes that certain thinkers were so impressed by the fact that the form of a newly produced substance does not preexist as such or in terms of its own entity that they concluded that it must be created at the end of the generative process. This creative function, continues Godfrey, is assigned by them to certain "Givers of forms" (*datores formarum*), although he acknowledges that they differ in explaining this final point. As had Thomas Aquinas in a similar context, Godfrey attributes this theory to Plato and to Avicenna.[4]

Godfrey then presents another theory that is diametrically opposed to the first one. Defenders of this position rejected the possibility of creation in the proper sense. Hence, observing the constant variation in things of the physical world and assuming that forms could not exist in any way before the completion of the generative process without actually existing, they concluded that all things are in some way present in all things. Thus, physical objects really consist of minute particles, each of which is a complete entity in itself including its own matter and form, and free from generation and corruption. There is really no generation or corruption in the proper sense, but such appears to occur because of the varying degrees in which these minute particles are united together or separated from one another in forming larger objects.[5] Thomas Aquinas and Bonaventure had assigned a similar position to Anaxagoras, although Godfrey's presentation varies slightly from theirs. Since Thomas himself explicitly depends upon Aristotle's *Physics* for his knowledge of Anaxagoras's position, it is likely that Godfrey, too, ultimately derives his awareness of it from that same source.[6]

Godfrey remarks that, if one bears in mind the simplicity of forms considered in themselves, there seems to be no possible intermediary position between these two extremes. Either one will have to admit of actual preexistence of forms in matter along with the second position or one will have to hold that forms do not preexist in any way and fall back on a doctrine of direct creation of all corporeal forms in order to account for generation. But since neither position is in itself acceptable, as Aristotle had pointed out on

---

contrariis; et sic differens a se ipsa non secundum essentiam sed secundum esse."

4 PB 5.405. For Thomas see *In II Sent.*, d. 1, q. 1, a. 4, ad 4 (ed. Mandonnet, T. 2, p. 27). Also see *De veritate*, q. 11, a. 1 (for this in Avicenna).

5 PB 5.405 – 06.

6 For Bonaventure see *In II Sent.*, d. 7, p. 2, a. 2, q. 1 (Quaracchi ed., Vol. 2, pp. 197ff.); for Thomas see *In II Sent.*, *loc. cit.*, pp. 26 – 27; for Aristotle see *Physics* I, c. 4.

many occasions, he himself proposed an intermediary solution. In agreement with the first position, Aristotle maintained that such forms do not formally preexist as such prior to the completion of the generative process. But he differed from that position by holding that forms do preexist potentially by reason of the preexisting matter.[7]

Godfrey then refers to another position that represents itself as the true intermediary between the above extremes and at the same time claims to be that of Aristotle. Although he does not name its defender, a number of practically verbatim citations leave no doubt that Godfrey here has in mind James of Viterbo, especially the discusssion in his Quodlibet 2, q. 5. According to James, it is not enough for one to maintain that before the completion of the process of generation a new form exists only virtually within the potency of matter or of the generating agent. A twofold mode of being pertains to form, one potential and the other actual. James's position differs from the first theory presented above, the creationist view, in that he holds that the form to be produced preexists in terms of its proper entity and formally. But James differs from the second position by denying that the form preexists according to its actual mode of being.[8] He maintains that a potency and its corresponding actuality need not bespeak different things (*res*), but only different modes of existing for one and the same thing—in this case, the form itself. These different modes, actual being and potential being, may be contrasted as perfection and imperfection, or as determination and indetermination, or as form or species and the absence of the same (*informitas*).[9]

In support of his contention that a form really preexists prior to the completion of the generative process, James appeals to texts from Averroes's *Commentary on Metaphysics* VIII and on *Metaphysics* XII. In each case, argues James, transition from potency to act is not presented as a passing

[7] PB 5.406. Here Godfrey gives no reference to specific Aristotelian passages.

[8] For Godfrey's presentation see PB 5.406 – 07. For James see Quodlibet 2, q. 5 (E. Ypma, ed., Vol. 2, p. 65:208–214), which is almost literally reproduced by Godfrey on p. 407.

[9] For Godfrey, see PB 5.407, where he reproduces James's text, *op. cit.*, p. 70:386–392. Much of Godfrey's citation of James here is verbatim. Somewhat farther on in the same general context James identifies form insofar as it exists in potency as an "aptitudo ad formam in actu, vel praeparatio, vel habilitas, vel via" (see p. 71:408–09). For Godfrey's explicit reference to what must also be James's theory of *aptitudines* see his Q 13, q. 3 (PB 5.191 – 92; 199 – 200). For more on James's theory see Casado, "El pensamiento filosófico del beato Santiago de Viterbo," *La Ciudad de Dios* 164 (1952), pp. 309 – 13.

from one thing to another but rather as the acquisition of a new mode of being by one and the same thing.[10]

Godfrey also presents in abbreviated fashion some of James's more extended argumentation. For instance, James reasons that since act and potency divide every genus and every species of being, an act and its corresponding potency must also be found within the same genus and the same species. Thus, actual fire and potential fire will belong to the same genus and species. But this could not be unless a form in potency and a form in act were one and the same thing (*res*).[11] Again, potential being falls between actual being and total nonbeing. But that which is intermediary must share in some way in both extremes. Wherefore, just as whiteness in act and the negation of whiteness are both distinct from matter, so too, potential whiteness must be something distinct from matter.[12] In other words, James's point is that the potential form, potential whiteness, must enjoy some reality in distinction from that of matter, presumably because it is the same thing (*res*) as the actual whiteness it will become once it is actualized or takes on its actual mode of being. Again, contends James, if one denies that a form preexists in terms of its potential mode of being, one will have to appeal to direct creation of the same in order to account for its production. In that eventuality, nothing but matter would preexist and, since the essence of form is distinct from that of matter, the form could only arise from nothingness.[13]

Godfrey is not sympathetic to James's proposed solution. Not only does he judge it to be contrary to the minds of Aristotle and of Averroes. He also regards its falsity and impossibility as even more obvious than that of the first two positions.[14] As to Aristotle's view, Godfrey counters that if the Stagirite had ever meant to imply that a corporeal form preexists in the way suggested

---

[10] For Godfrey see PB 5.407. For Averroes see *In VIII Met.* (Vol. 8, fol. 224ra): "Est igitur hic aliquid unum, quod primo est in potentia et post transfertur de potentia in actum. Translatio enim eius non largitur ei multitudinem sed perfectionem in esse." For James's citation of this see *op. cit.*, p. 72:444–46. Godfrey also cites Averroes's *Commentary on Metaphysics* XII: ". . . agens apud Aristotelem non est congregans inter duo in rei veritate, sed extrahens illud, quod est in potentia, ad actum" (Vol. 8, fol. 304va), almost exactly reproduced by Godfrey on p. 407. For James's apparent reference to this same text see p. 77:620–24.

[11] PB 5.407, where Godfrey refers to and literally reproduces part of James's third argument (*op. cit.*, p. 74:508–13).

[12] PB 5.407, where Godfrey summarizes James's fourth argument (*op. cit.*, p. 74:514–20).

[13] PB 5.407–08, where Godfrey summarizes and literally cites in part James's fifth argument (*op. cit.*, pp. 75:545–50, 76:564–69).

[14] PB 5.408.

by James—that is, formally and in terms of its own entity and nature—he would surely have said as much somewhere in his writings. When Aristotle acknowledges that such a form preexists potentially, he surely does not mean to imply that it preexists in its own nature and formally, as James would have it. In analogous fashion, light does not exist in its own entity or nature in darkened air prior to the latter's being illuminated by a shining body. Hence, for Aristotle, if any form does formally exist in matter in terms of its own entity or nature, it cannot be described as such a form in potency, but is actually such. Moreover, any composite in which both matter and form are present in terms of their proper entities cannot be described as that composite potentially but will actually be such.[15]

Godfrey recalls that according to Aristotle material substances consist of two intrinsic principles, one known as potency without any qualification, or matter, and the other as act without any qualification, or form. Just as it is impossible to maintain that prime matter is present in something in terms of its proper entity without acknowledging that that thing itself is thereby in potency, so is it impossible to assign substantial form in its proper entity to such a thing without acknowledging that it is thereby in act. If prime matter is potency and thus stands between absolute nonbeing and unqualified being, form is that whereby something enjoys actuality. And if one cannot descend below prime matter in the hierarchy of being without arriving at absolute nothingness, one cannot rise above it without arriving at actuality (*actus simpliciter*).[16]

Godfrey also rejects James's suggestion that form may be said to enjoy two modes of being, one potential and one actual. Just as it would be absurd to suggest that for Aristotle matter enjoys two modes of being, one potential and one actual, so is it equally absurd to hold that form enjoys these two modes of being. If the potentiality of matter is identical with the matter itself and is not something superadded to it, the actuality of form is identical with the form itself and is not some real mode that would be superadded to it.[17] There can be no question, then, in Godfrey's eyes, of suggesting that one and the same substantial form could exist under two different modes of being, potential being and actual being. If form is realized as such or as form, it is also realized as actual. This will be true of the lowest substantial form as well as of the highest.[18]

---

[15] *Ibid.*

[16] PB 5.408–09.

[17] PB 5.409.

[18] PB 5.409–10. Here Godfrey also rejects James's contrast between form in its actual mode of being and its potential mode of being as between perfection and

Godfrey hearkens back to Aristotle's discussion in *Physics* I of matter and the contraries, where the Stagirite shows that matter differs from the contrary forms it is capable of receiving. *Mutatis mutandis*, Godfrey himself reasons that according to James's theory the essence of the form itself would be indifferent to its potential and actual modes of being. Hence, it would really differ from them. But it would then follow that generation does not result in the production of a new form in the new composite, but only of a new mode of being for the same form. In other words, James's theory would, contends Godfrey, reduce substantial change to the level of a modal and accidental change.[19] Godfrey finds this charge reinforced by James's contention that the two modes of form pertain not to the genus or predicament of substance but rather to that of quality, with the potential mode of form belonging to the second species of quality and its actual mode to the first species.[20]

According to Aristotle, as Godfrey interprets him, form does not preexist in matter in terms of its own entity. Prior to the completion of the process of generation, matter preexists. The form to be produced may be said to preexist only in this sense that the matter itself is a potency which may be changed so as to result in the generation of a composite, which composite itself will include both matter and the new form. Aristotle avoids falling into the creationist position by holding that the newly generated composite is produced from something that remains intrinsic to it, that is, its potential or material principle. But for something to be produced from something that remains intrinsic to it, it must consist of two factors or principles, one of which preexists as that from which the composite is to be produced and the other which cannot preexist as such since it remains to be generated with the composite. The former, of course, is prime matter and the latter substantial form. It is in this sense that the form may be said to preexist in potency, but not formally in terms of its own entity or nature.[21]

Godfrey turns to Aristotle's *Metaphysics* VII for confirmation. There, in an effort to avoid either of the two extreme positions mentioned above, creationism and the view according to which all things actually preexist prior to their apparent generation, Aristotle builds his position on two fundamental

---

imperfection, or as between determination and indetermination, or as between form (or formality) and the absence of the same (*informitas*). See in this chapter p. 296 and n. 9. For Godfrey there is no real distinction between the perfection or imperfection of a form and that form itself. See p. 410: ". . . sed alietas quam important non est nisi quaedam alietas rationis quae convenit formae uni ex habitudine vel comparatione secundum rationem ad aliam."

[19] PB 5.410–11. For Aristotle see *Physics* I, cc. 7–9.

[20] PB 5.411. For James see *op. cit.*, p. 79:687–94.

[21] PB 5.411.

propositions: (1) it is neither matter nor form that is generated *per se* but the composite; (2) whatever is generated is generated from something that is intrinsic to it or a part of itself. From these two principles Aristotle concludes, reports Godfrey, that the composite is generated from the matter that is a part of itself and thereby avoids the creationist problem. Hence, Aristotle can state: "Obviously, then, the *species* (*εἶδος*), or whatever one should call the form (*μορφήν*) present in a sensible thing, is not made, nor is there any generation of it."[22]

Godfrey also cites Averroes's commentary on the above passage from *Metaphysics* VII, ch. 8, as well as some of his discussion of ch. 7. Thus Averroes observes that that which is generated cannot be described as being simply one, that is, as form alone, since it is rather the composite consisting of matter, form, and the preceding privation that is generated, properly speaking. Generation takes place when a generating principle changes matter sufficiently so as to produce a new form therein. In other words, the matter from which the agent produces the composite does not itself remain under the same dispositions in the new and in the old composite. Otherwise, the generating principle would not produce the new composite but only its form.[23]

In sum, insists Godfrey, both Aristotle and Averroes avoid the creationist position by holding that in the process of generation matter itself is in some way changed by an agent so as to become the new composite. They do not, repeats Godfrey, ever suggest that the form of the newly generated composite preexists as such or formally in the matter of the former composite. In fact, comments Godfrey, Aristotle would deny that the form existed even in potency if there were no preexisting matter, since he rejects the very possibility of creation or of the production of something from nothing. Given the reality of matter, however, Aristotle holds that a given form enjoys potential being only in this sense that such matter itself is capable of being changed into a new composite. Since this composite will consist of the preexisting matter and of a new form, the new form comes into being only with the production of the composite.[24] Because of this understanding of Aristotle's theory of the eduction of forms from the potentiality of matter, one can readily understand

---

[22] PB 5.411–12. For Godfrey's citation from Aristotle note: ". . . palam ergo quod nec species aut quodcumque oportet vocare in sensibili formam non fit, nec est eius generatio." For Aristotle see *Metaphysics* VII, c. 8 (1033b 5–6) for the text just cited, and cc. 7–8 for general discussion and the two propositions singled out by Godfrey.

[23] PB 5.412. For Averroes see *In VII Met.*, fol. 176vb (on the text cited in n. 22 above); fol. 176ra (on ch. 7). Godfrey literally cites from these passages in Averroes.

[24] PB 5.412–13.

why Godfrey rejects James's theory as being contrary to the minds both of Aristotle and of Averroes.

Godfrey has also pronounced the falsity and impossibility of James's position as even more evident than that of the two original positions—the creationist and that which assigns actual preexistence to forms by holding that all things exist in all things (*latitatio formarum*). Granted that most of the philosophers did reject the possibility of creation, still, counters Godfrey, its possibility should not be denied. And according to Catholic belief, creation has in fact occurred. Once one concedes the possibility of creation, it is not so immediately evident that one must reject the creation of any given form by God or even by some separate spiritual creature in order to account for generation. Again, as regards the second position, its falsity is not so immediately evident as is that of James's theory. Thus, we often experience a mixture or a mixed body which really consists of a multitude of actually distinct entities without our being immediately aware of each of these distinctive entities as such. Hence, each of these positions has been defended by reputable philosophers, something that cannot be said for James's theory. This must be, suggests Godfrey, because the intrinsic contradiction of his position is so immediately obvious.[25]

In order to show that James's position is indeed self-contradictory Godfrey charges that it entails describing a form or that which has a form as being and nonbeing or as existing and as not existing at one and the same time.[26] Thus, to hold that form is only potentially present in matter is not to describe it or that in which it is present as being without qualification but rather as nonbeing, granted that it is potential being. But to suggest that such a form is really present in matter in terms of its proper nature or entity is to posit the existence of a matter-form composite and thus to assign unqualified being to it. This follows, insists Godfrey, because the very reality of form is a kind of actuality. Hence, to say that form is really present in matter but only under a potential mode of being is to imply that form, actuality, is not actuality but only a kind of potentiality or that form and act are not form and act.[27] Godfrey does point out that one may assign two modes of being to the composite as such, one potential and one actual. Thus, given the existence of matter from which a composite may be formed, one may say that the composite enjoys only potential being. Once that composite has actually been produced, of course, it will then enjoy actual being.[28]

---

[25] PB 5.413 – 14.
[26] PB 5.414.
[27] *Ibid.*
[28] PB 5.415.

Godfrey also contends that James's theory implies that one and the same thing is generated and yet is not generated at one and the same time. Thus, the form of the thing to be generated will really be present in the preexisting matter, according to James's position. But given this, contends Godfrey, the *terminus ad quem* of the generative process will not differ from the *terminus a quo*. In each case one will be dealing with the same matter-form composite and as a consequence there will be no true generation even when such is allegedly occurring. James would, of course, argue that generation really takes place because the form will have taken on a new mode of being, actual being. Because no new predicamental reality (*res*) will have been acquired, Godfrey denies that true change will have occurred. James's proposed transition from a potential mode to an actual mode of one and the same form is not, in Godfrey's eyes, truly change. Godfrey also charges that it is a mere figment of the imagination for one to suggest that there can be any ontological intermediary between purely logical being, on the one hand, and predicamental being, on the other. But such appears to be the status of James's modes.[29]

After having concluded that James's position is both contrary to the minds of Aristotle and of Averroes and intrinsically self-contradictory, Godfrey returns to a key text from the Commentator offered by James in defense of his view. In his *Commentary on Metaphysics* VIII Averroes had observed that a material composite enjoys unity because that which was first in potency then passes from potency to act. This transition does not introduce multiplicity but perfection into the (composite) whole, which is then one in act.[30] As we have already intimated, James interprets this as implying that the transition from potency to act involved in generation is not, according to Averroes, a passing from one thing (*res*) to another but simply the acquisition of a new mode of being by one and the same thing (the form). If any new thing (*res*) were acquired as a result of the change, there would be more things after that change than before.[31]

Godfrey counters that Averroes's purpose in this passage is to show that the definition of a matter-form composite is really one because that which is defined, the composite, itself enjoys essential unity. It is not composed of two essences but of two essential principles, each of which depends upon the other.[32] Thus, as Averroes himself states in his *Commentary on Physics* II,

---

[29] PB 5.415–16.

[30] PB 5.417–18. For this text in Averroes see n. 10 in this chapter.

[31] See p. 296 in the present chapter. For James see p. 72:442–51.

[32] ". . . quia etiam diffinitum, scilicet compositum ex talibus duobus est unum

matter and form are co-causes of one another.[33] But, protests Godfrey, Averroes does not wish to deny in the passage under consideration that some new entity or *res* has now come into being which previously existed only in potency. By stating that what was first in potency is now realized in actuality, Averroes simply means that the entire composite as it now exists in actuality does not include anything more than it previously possessed in potentiality. Godfrey does acknowledge that the potential composite differs from the actual composite, not as that which is simply one differs from that which is manifold, but rather as that which is imperfect differs from that which is perfect.[34]

Finally, Godfrey refers to the various arguments drawn from James's text to which reference has been made above. James had reasoned that because an act and its corresponding potency must belong to the same species, a form in act and that form in potency must be one and the same reality.[35] Godfrey counters that being in act and the corresponding being in potency belong to the same species, not univocally and without qualification, but only analogically. This is to say that they will pertain to the same species only as that which actually possesses a specific form, on the one hand, and that which does not yet possess that form but is capable of so doing, on the other hand. Thus, the name and the definition of the species can be applied without qualification only to that which is actually present in that species, and to that which is potentially present therein only with certain qualifications. To account for the merely potential presence of something in a species, therefore, one need not assign any preexisting reality or entity to its form.[36]

James had also reasoned that because potential being falls between actual being and complete nonbeing it must share in some way in both extremes. And just as actual whiteness and the negation of whiteness are both distinct from matter, so too potential whiteness must be distinct from matter. In presenting this argument we understood James to be suggesting thereby that a potential form, potential whiteness, for instance, must therefore enjoy some reality in distinction from that of its matter. Hence, it will preexist in the

---

simpliciter sive unum secundum essentiam simplicem quidem sic quod non constituitur ex duabus essentiis, sed ex duobus talibus *principiis essentialibus* quorum unum dependet ex alio secundum essentiam et esse, sicut materia quae est potentia et forma quae est actus . . ." (PB 5.418). (Italics ours to highlight Godfrey's explicit usage here of the notion of "principles" of being to describe matter and form.)

[33] *In II Phys.*, Vol. 4 (fol. 79rb, c. 81), to which Godfrey may be referring here, as Hoffmans suggests (PB 5.425). If so, the citation is not literal.

[34] PB 5.418 – 19.

[35] See p. 297 and n. 11.

[36] PB 5.420.

matter according to its potential mode of being.[37] Godfrey turns the tables on James here by arguing that just as potential being must enjoy some reality so as to be distinguished from absolute nothingness, so too must it be devoid of all actuality if it is to be distinguished from the terminus of the generative process, the actual form in the actual composite. Given this, concludes Godfrey, such a potential being is really not distinct from matter prior to its actual production. Matter alone is that whereby something is truly in potency and matter itself falls between nothingness and actual being.[38]

James had also contended that one must assign preexisting reality or entity to the form in order to avoid having to appeal to direct creation of the new form in generation.[39] Godfrey counters by repeating that, properly speaking, the new form is neither created nor generated. It is rather the composite that is generated. And since the matter of the composite did preexist, one need not conclude that it (the composite) was produced from nothingness. But, James might still object, from whence comes the form? Godfrey insists that it is really the composite that is generated and comes into being. Since the new composite consists both of matter and form, its form will arise from that same principle from which the composite itself is produced, that is to say, from the preexisting matter.[40] In other words, it is educed from the potentiality of matter.

Before concluding this section of Ch.VIII we would like to call the reader's attention to two other discussions of this general problem which appear in the abbreviated version of Godfrey's Disputed Questions preserved in the Vatican manuscript *Borghese 122*. Although neither of these is attributed to Godfrey by the table of *Borghese 164*,[41] both are assigned to him by that found at the end of *Borghese 122*.[42] In order to avoid confusion with those questions mentioned in the table of *Borghese 164* whose numbering we have been following when citing Godfrey's other Disputed Questions, we shall simply refer to these two as *Disputed Question* 11 (Bo 122) and *Disputed Question* 12 (Bo 122) respectively.[43]

---

[37] See p. 297 and the references in n. 12.

[38] PB 5.425.

[39] See p. 297 and the references in n. 13.

[40] PB 5.425–26.

[41] See our reference to this table in the Introduction, p. xxx.

[42] See *Vatican lat. Borghese 122*, fol. 175ra: "Quaestiones Godefridi disputatae et abbreviatae;" and fol. 175rb: "Utrum in subiecto virtutis sit aliqua aptitudo quae transmutetur in actualitatem virtutis ita quod ipsamet fiat virtus completa;" and "Utrum in anima praeexistat aliquid virtutis inducendae, et idem est quaerere utrum in materia praeexistat aliquid formae inducendae."

[43] For the first of these (11) see *Borgh. 122*, fol. 164va–165vb, and continuing

In *Disputed Question* 11 (Bo 122) Godfrey wonders whether in a subject which receives a given virtue there is some preexisting aptitude that is itself changed into the actuality of that virtue. In *Disputed Question* 12 (Bo 122) roughly the same issue is raised: Does anything belonging to a virtue that is to be introduced into the soul already preexist there? In both contexts the question is quickly broadened so as to lead to an inquiry about the possible preexistence of any form that is to be introduced into matter.[44] And in both Questions Godfrey lists and refutes a number of unacceptable theories.[45] One of the positions described in the first Question maintains that that which preexists in addition to matter and from which the newly produced form becomes is the very essence of that form, but only as realized according to its potential degree. This particular theory reminds one of James of Viterbo's position, since it maintains that it is essentially the same form which was first present in potentiality which is subsequently realized in actuality.[46]

---

on fol. 155rb – 155va; for the second see fol. 165vb – 166vb. On this see Pelzer, PB 14.283. As Pelzer also notes (p. 288, nn. 1 and 2), the corpus of question 12 is reproduced together with Hervé of Nedellec's *Tractatus de virtutibus* in certain manuscripts, especially in *Vat. lat. 1076* (fol. 47rb – 48vb). Also see his "Godefroid de Fontaines. Les manuscrits . . . ," *Revue Néo-Scolastique de Philosophie* 20 (1913), pp. 526 – 30, where he had rejected these as Godfrey's *Disputed Questions*, a judgment which he has reversed in his 1937 study (PB 14.285 – 89). The first of these is also contained in *Bruges 491*, fol. 232ra – 233rb, although it remains incomplete in both manuscripts. Since it seems to know of and to refute James's theory, but in lesser detail and with less obvious textual dependency than is true of Quodlibet 14, q. 5, we are inclined to place it in the mid-1290s, that is, after James's Quodlibet 2 of 1294 (or 1293), but before Godfrey's more masterful discussion in Quodlibet 14, q. 5 of 1298/1299. Since *Disputed Question* 12 (Bo 122) may possibly also know of James's position, it may, perhaps, be given a similar dating. On the date for James's Quodlibet 2 see Ypma, *Jacobi de Viterbio, O.E.S.A. Disputatio prima de quolibet*, p. vi. Ypma assigns James's four Quodlibets to the years 1293–96. Hence, Quodlibet 2 would presumably fall in 1294. If James's first Quodlibet dates from ca. Easter 1293, a possibility we have proposed elsewhere, then his Quodlibet 2 could fall into the Advent session of 1293 as well. See our "The Dating of James of Viterbo's . . . ," pp. 380 – 83.

[44] Fol. 164va and *Bruges 491*, fol. 232ra (q. 11); fol. 165vb (q. 12).

[45] In *Disputed Question* 11 he distinguishes four general positions among the "ancients" (*Borgh. 122*, fol. 164va–vb; *Bruges 491*, fol. 232ra–rb), and then four different positions among the "moderns" (see *Borgh. 122*, fol. 164vb, but read with *Bruges 491*, fol. 232rb): "Sic et apud modernos sunt quattuor opiniones quarum tres ponunt formam produci et fieri per se ex aliquo sibi proprio quod est in subiecto formae. Quarta autem ponit formam fieri ex aliquo non quod sit ipsius formae aliquid ita quod ipsum fit aliquid vel immutetur postea in formam." For his exposition and critique of three unacceptable positions see *Disputed Question* 12 (*Borgh. 122*, fol. 165vb – 166rb).

[46] *Borgh. 122*, fol. 164vb; *Bruges 491*, fol. 232rb.

Rather than dwell upon Godfrey's somewhat lengthy refutations of the various unacceptable positions,[47] it will be of greater value for us to mention certain elements of the positive doctrine that emerges from these texts, especially from *Disputed Question* 11 (Bo 122). There, too, he defends the opinion according to which nothing belonging to the entity of a new form that is to be generated preexists as such in matter. Once more Godfrey insists that it is not the form that becomes or is generated, but the composite. Hence, one should not ask from whence comes the form but rather from whence comes the composite. The potential composite includes two factors, only one of which really preexists as such, namely, its matter. Its form is only potentially present in the preexisting matter, not really and not actually.[48]

Godfrey concludes this part of the same Question by offering an interesting division of the different kinds of production. If something is brought into being without being produced from something that is a part of itself or from any seminal reason, its production is really creation. If it is brought into being together with the production of something else of which it is an intrinsic part, but without its being derived from any preexisting seminal reason, and if it is of such a nature as to be able to exist by itself after its production, it too may be said to be created, although somewhat less properly. Here Godfrey has in mind the origin of the human intellect. He then proposes a third kind of production whereby something is not produced from any preexisting

---

[47] For his critique of the three unacceptable "modern" positions in *Disputed Question* 11 see *Borgh. 122*, fol. 164vb – 165va; *Bruges 491*, fol. 232rb – 233ra. For his critique of unacceptable positions in *Disputed Question* 12 see *Borgh. 122*, fol. 165vb–166rb. (The second theory described and refuted here may be that of James.)

[48] See *Borgh. 122*, fol. 165va; *Bruges 491*, fol. 233ra: "Restat ergo [omitted in Bo.] quarta opinio quod scilicet [omitted in Bo.] in materia non praeexistit aliquid [Br: aliud] ex quo forma fiat vel quod transmutetur in actualitatem formae. Circa quod est intelligendum quod forma non fit per se quia nec forma [omitted in Bo.] habet esse per se sed solum compositum, et ideo solum compositum fit per se. . . . Nunc autem in composito duo sunt, scilicet materia et forma, per quorum unum [omitted in Bo.] est in actu et [omitted in Br.] per aliud vero est [vero est: omitted in Bo.] in potentia . . . sed totum compositum est in potentia ratione materiae [add. by Bo: unius et] solius ita quod compositum in potentia duo includit, quorum unum existit realiter, scilicet materia, sed alterum solum potentialiter existens in illo quod existit realiter. Sic quia materia potest dici totum compositum inquantum est unum principiorum constituentium compositum secundum actualitatem, alterum autem [Bo: vel] secundum potentialitatem. Sed post generationem non dicitur totum sed pars quaedam totius secundum actum, licet ante generationem posset dici totum in potentia." See *Borgh. 122*, fol. 165va and *Bruges 491*, fol. 233rb (where one reads "Metaphysics XII") for another reference to the passage from Averroes's Commentary on *Metaphysics* VIII to which reference was made above.

seminal reason and is not capable of existing in itself. This kind of production is illustrated by the introduction of grace into the soul and is still less properly called creation. Finally, there is the production of the kind of form which cannot exist of itself and which is produced from some preexisting seminal reason. This is properly referred to as generation and can be described as creation only if one wishes to extend the latter term to any production of a form that does not result from a preexisting part of that same form.[49]

B. DISPOSITIONS AND *RATIONES SEMINALES*

Reference has just been made to Godfrey's usage of the expression "seminal reason" in *Disputed Question* 11 (Bo 122). There he has described generation as entailing the production of a form (along with its composite, to be sure) from some preexisting seminal reason.[50] At the same time, he has strongly rejected any theory that would suggest that the corporeal form of a composite which is to be generated preexists in terms of its own entity and in distinction from that of the preexisting matter. It would seem, therefore, that some clarification as to his understanding of seminal reasons is needed.

If Godfrey accounts for the origin of purely corporeal forms by appealing to their eduction from the potentiality of matter, as he clearly does, he also insists that this eduction of forms normally takes place according to a certain order. As he succinctly phrases it in Quodlibet 9, q. 12, it is not anything whatsoever that comes from anything whatsoever, but one determined thing that comes from another.[51] In other words, one must account for the fact that a substance such as wine may change into vinegar without the converse being true. In order to explain this, he observes that one may consider the capacity of matter in two different ways. One may simply view matter in itself as pure potentiality and, to that extent, as capable of receiving any material form from

---

[49] See *Borgh. 122*, fol. 165va; *Bruges 491*, fol. 233rb. The Bruges text of this question ends here, but gives a reference to Augustine's *De Trinitate*, Bk. 3, c. 13, for discussion of *rationes seminales*.

[50] For this text see *Borgh. 122*, fol. 165va – vb; *Bruges 491*, fol. 233rb: "Productio autem formae quae non est nata per se esse et fit ex aliqua ratione seminali praeexistente dicitur proprie generatio et nullo modo creatio nisi creationem voces productionem cuiuscumque formae non ex aliquo quod est pars sui. Sic enim potest dici creatio et potest dici quod agens naturale producendo formam creat." As we have indicated in the preceding note, *Bruges 491* then continues: "De rationibus seminalibus quaere libro tertio *De Trinitate*, cap. 13."

[51] ". . . quia non quidlibet fit ex quolibet, sed determinatum ex determinato." (PB 4.252).

any agent. So considered, the potency of matter is identical with the very reality (*substantia*) of the matter and admits of no variation in its capacity to receive one form or another. But matter may also be viewed insofar as it is proximately capable of being actualized by certain forms rather than by others. So considered, matter's capacity for form includes not only prime matter as such but some disposition towards certain determined forms resulting from the fact that it is already informed by another determined form. Thus it is because a given instance of matter is now informed by the form of wine that it is capable of becoming vinegar rather than something else such as a rock. But the form of vinegar does not dispose its matter in such fashion that it could immediately be changed into wine. A series of other forms would have to be introduced therein through a series of changes in order to prepare the matter.[52]

In this same context Godfrey refers to the dispositions which prepare matter for one kind of form rather than another as being akin in some way to seminal reasons.[53] This parallelism between dispositions and seminal reasons is developed at greater length in Quodlibet 2, q. 6.[54] There he has just observed that the forms of simple elements, on the one hand, and the intellective soul, on the other, seem to mark the extremes of the kinds of forms that can inform prime matter. Even if one defends the reality of some kind of form of corporeity in all bodies, continues Godfrey, matter will not exist under any such form unless it is also actualized by an elemental form.[55] And if the heaven exercises some control over these extremes, whether by disposing for and introducing such forms as with corporeal forms, or at least by disposing for them as with the intellective soul, then it will also have some control over intermediate forms as well. According to the natural order, less perfect forms dispose for those that are more perfect. Thus, the forms of elements dispose matter for the reception of the forms of mixtures, the forms of mixtures for living forms, living forms for sensitive forms, etc.[56]

At this point one might wonder whether Godfrey has not simply identified less perfect forms with dispositions insofar as they, the less perfect forms, prepare matter to receive more perfect forms. But shortly thereafter and still

---

[52] PB 4.251 – 52.

[53] "Et dispositiones sic materiam habilitantes aliquo modo dicuntur habere rationem eius quod dicitur ratio seminalis" (PB 4.252).

[54] In Q 2, q. 6 Godfrey considers this question: "Utrum in materia prima, virtute supernaturalis agentis possit fieri forma et species ad quam non est in potentia naturali" (PB 2.89).

[55] PB 2.90 – 91.

[56] PB 2.91. Also see PB 2.92.

within the same context he refers to the forms of elements and to the dispositions that follow upon them. This would suggest that both less perfect forms and certain dispositions that follow upon them prepare matter for the reception of more perfect forms and hence that the term disposition may be applied both to less perfect substantial forms themselves and to accidental qualities that share in this preparing or disposing role.[57]

Both in this discussion in Quodlibet 2, q. 6 and in other contexts Godfrey distinguishes the ways in which matter is in potency to receive forms from purely natural agents including the heaven, on the one hand, and from God the First Mover, on the other. Here he cites Augustine to this effect, that with respect to the heaven and, presumably, therefore, with respect to all lower agents, matter is not immediately capable of receiving any form whatsoever. Such can occur only in accord with a certain order such as that to which we have referred above and in accord with the different dispositions or *rationes seminales* present in given instances of matter. Thus, from the seed of a bean a purely natural agent such as the heaven cannot immediately produce an olive. But with respect to divine agency, matter is in potency in such fashion that regardless what particular dispositions may exist in it at any given moment, God can immediately introduce any form into it that matter as such is capable of receiving. God does not have to respect the order of natural dispositions.[58] Hence, one may distinguish in matter the natural potency that it enjoys by reason of those seminal reasons that are present therein and the obediential potency that it enjoys only with respect to the divine Agent.[59]

In this discussion of matter's capacity to receive forms from purely natural agents only in accord with the dispositions or *rationes seminales* that are already present within it, Godfrey has consciously both used the Augustinian expression and cited Augustine himself. Has he thereby equated dispositions and seminal reasons? He does here refer to these "seminal reasons" as being "set in" (*inditae*) matter in some way and thus once more echoes Augustine's

---

[57] "Et quia forte [formae] elementares et dispositiones istas consequentes non possunt disponere ad formam perfectiorem quam est anima intellectiva" (PB 2.91). Shortly before this Godfrey observes: "Quare cum formae praecedentes primo, scilicet ordine naturali in materia existentes sint dispositiones ad formas perfectiores . . ." (*ibid.*). For confirmation of this see Q 13, q. 3 (PB 5.205).

[58] PB 2.93. For Augustine see *De Genesi ad litteram* IX, c. 17 (PL 34.406).

[59] "Et secundum hoc distinguitur in materia quaedam potentia naturalis secundum rationes seminales aliquo modo inditas materiae, quaedam oboedientialis secundum rationes causales ei non inditas, sed in virtute divina existentes" (PB 2.93). For this same distinction also see Q 9, q. 12 (PB 4.252). Also see *Disputed Question* 12 (Bo 122) as cited in n. 69 of this chapter.

language.[60] While he continues to defend the purely potential character of prime matter, he contrasts its potency, which is in fact identical with matter itself, and these "superadded dispositions which are known as seminal reasons."[61] If one were to judge solely from this discussion in Quodlibet 2, q. 6, one might be tempted to conclude that Godfrey has combined an Augustinian doctrine of seminal reasons with his more Aristotelian understanding of prime matter as pure potentiality.

To the extent, however, that one presents seminal reasons as active potencies which are concreated with and preexist in matter and suggests that it is from these that new forms are produced, Godfrey will strenuously object.[62] Such a position would run counter to his emphasis on the purely potential character of prime matter. And to the degree that seminal reasons are understood in such fashion that their presence in matter minimizes the role of created efficient causes in the process of generation, Godfrey will also react negatively.[63] Hence, one finds him only likening dispositions to seminal

---

[60] See the text cited in n. 59 and compare with Augustine's *De Genesi ad litteram* IX, c. 17 (PL 34.406): "Super hunc autem motum cursumque rerum naturalem potestas Creatoris habet apud se posse de his omnibus facere aliud, quam eorum quasi seminales rationes habent, non tamen id quod non in eis posuit ut de his fieri vel ab ipso possit. . . . Horum et talium modorum rationes non tantum in Deo sunt, sed ab illo etiam rebus creatis inditae atque concreatae." Godfrey also cites a major part of this text (*ibid.*).

[61] ". . . sed oportet coadesse aliquas dispositiones superadditas quae dicuntur rationes seminales" (PB 2.94). On the purely potential character of prime matter see in this same question: ". . . materia quae est simpliciter et pura potentia . . ." (PB 2.90).

[62] In his *History of Christian Philosophy* Gilson describes Augustine's doctrine: "The created world was big with their 'seminal reasons,' that is with the seeds, or germs, of future beings . . ." (p. 73). On p. 592 Gilson comments: "A consequence of the doctrine of the seminal reasons is to reduce to a bare minimum the efficacy of secondary efficient causes." On Augustine's doctrine also see Gilson, *The Christian Philosophy of Saint Augustine* (New York, 1960), pp. 206–09. On Bonaventure's doctrine of seminal reasons see in particular *In II Sent.*, d. 7, p. 2, a. 2, q. 1 (Vol. 2, pp. 197–99); d. 18, a. 1, q. 2 (Vol. 2, pp. 436–37). On this see A. Pegis, *St. Thomas and the Problem of the Soul in the Thirteenth Century* (Toronto, 1934), pp. 47–48; J. F. Quinn, *The Historical Constitution of St. Bonaventure's Philosophy*, pp. 106–09 (see p. 109, n. 15, for other secondary sources). As we shall indicate immediately below, it is especially against James's version of seminal reasons that Godfrey objects.

[63] Even in his sympathetic discussion of seminal reasons in Q 2, q. 6 Godfrey will not minimize the need for the action of created efficient causes: ". . . sed appetitum suum proprium quasi sequendo, pervenit ad id quod intendit, licet non nisi virtute agentis principalis" (PB 2.94). Also see the final sentence in the passage from *Disputed Question* 11 (Bo 122) cited in n. 50.

reasons in Quodlibet 9, q. 12, but apparently without identifying them.[64] His hostility to at least one version of seminal reasons becomes more apparent in his Quodlibet 13, q. 3, undoubtedly because of the interpretation presented by James of Viterbo in the 1290s. Not only does James refer to them as certain *aptitudines* which preexist entitatively in matter according to their potential mode of being prior to their actual realization as forms as a result of substantial change;[65] he also assigns to certain *aptitudines* some degree of self-actualization in the order of formal causality.[66] In Quodlibet 13, q. 3 Godfrey rejects James's position on both counts. The last-mentioned part of his theory would, in Godfrey's opinion, among other things, seriously undermine the Aristotelian theory of and division of the four causes.[67] And as

---

[64] See PB 4.252 and the text cited in note 53.

[65] For this see James's Quodlibet 2, q. 5, pp. 65:195 – 89:996 plus our discussion of the same theory in section A of this chapter. In this context James clearly presents his forms that preexist according to their potential *esse* as seminal reasons. See, for instance, p. 89:994–96: "Et sic patet primum principale quod proponebatur declarandum circa rationes seminales, videlicet quod in materia praeexistere oportet exordium formae, et quod dici potest huiusmodi exordium ratio seminalis." Immediately thereafter he cites the need for some active principle as well if one is to account for change. He distinguishes two kinds of active principles: 1) that which acts by way of inclination, such as a form preexisting in its potential being in matter, since by reason of it matter is inclined towards actuality; 2) that which serves as a principle of transmutation. Both are required if one is to account fully for the eduction of any form from potency to act. And if the first type is clearly a seminal reason, he also suggests that this name be applied to the second as well, but less properly so, apparently. See pp. 89:997 – 90:1044; also p. 95:1194 – 1210. For a good resumé of his thinking on this also see Quodlibet 3, q. 10 (pp. 148:91 – 149:141). On James's doctrine of seminal reasons see Casado, "El pensamiento filosófico . . . ," pp. 312 – 14.

[66] As we have indicated in Ch. IV (n. 82) James applies his understanding of *aptitudo* both to the intellect and to the will in order to account for the fact that each can move itself *formaliter* though not *efficienter*. See our references there to James's Quodlibet 1, q. 12 and Quodlibet 1, q. 7. In Q 13, q. 3, Godfrey connects these two aspects of James's thought and rejects both: ". . . similiter ergo posito quod in materia sit aliquid tale quod sic dicitur ratio seminalis vel inchoatio formae vel aptitudo vel quocumque modo aliter, tamen non videtur aliqua necessitas ponendi quod ultra actionem agentis efficienter sit actio ipsius subiecti cum tali aptitudine agentis formaliter" (PB 5.200). He goes on to observe that it would be enough if they (James) were content with defending their view of the preexistence of forms (*de inchoatione formarum*), which position in itself Godfrey finds unreasonable. But, he continues, they compound the difficulty by proposing something else that is clearly unfitting: "scilicet quod subiectum cum tali aptitudine vere et proprie agat formaliter ad hoc quod potentialitas illa transeat in actualitatem; et hoc non solum quantum ad formas accidentales, sed etiam quantum ad substantiales" (*ibid.*).

[67] See PB 5.191 – 92 (for more on Godfrey's understanding of James's theory); for

has been indicated in the opening section of this chapter, the first-mentioned point is refuted by Godfrey in great detail, especially in Quodlibet 14, q. 5.[68]

Even though in certain contexts Godfrey has found it helpful to refer to dispositions as if they were seminal reasons, we conclude that he does not wish to imply thereby that they are active "seeds" in the sense of self-realizing potentialities. In fact, in *Disputed Question* 12 (Bo 122), after having distinguished between active and passive potencies, he observes that passive potencies may in turn be taken in two different ways. One may regard as a passive potency any subject of a form that unites with that form so as to constitute a unity. But one may also regard as a passive potency that which disposes a subject in order to prepare it to receive something from a given agent. Thus, the softness of wax disposes it to receive an imprint from a seal.[69] We assume, therefore, that for Godfrey dispositions, whether active or passive, simply prepare a given instance of matter to receive a given kind of form from a distinctive agent. They do not themselves become that new form nor do they produce it as such. Godfrey's appeal to the Augustinian terminology of seminal reasons in order to illustrate his understanding of dispositions in Quodlibet 2, q. 6 may have been an effort on his part to arrive at some accommodation, at least in terms of terminology, with some of his Neo-Augustinian contemporaries. By having stressed the purely potential character of prime matter he had already distanced himself from their understanding of matter. But the danger of possible misunderstanding resulting from this analogy between dispositions and seminal reasons appears to have become greater in Godfrey's eyes in later years, especially in his discussions in Quodlibet 13 and Quodlibet 14.

One problem still remains, however. In the text from *Disputed Question* 11 (Bo 122) to which reference was made above a form is said to become from or be made from a "seminal reason."[70] This cannot imply any preexisting entity on the part of the form itself, of course, since Godfrey has

---

his refutation see PB 5.200–01. Also see our Ch. IV, pp. 197–99.

[68] See in this chapter pp. 297–304.

[69] ". . . quia potentiarum quaedam est activa, quaedam passiva. Passiva autem dupliciter accipitur: uno modo pro eo quod est subiectum formae faciens unum cum ea per se, et isto modo quantitas est potentia per quam aliquid est figurabile quia nulla res potest esse subiectum figurae nisi per quantitatem; alio modo pro eo quod subiectum disponit ad patiendum a tali agente sicut mollities cerae disponit eam ut sit a sigillo per impressionem, et talis potentia distinguitur, quia quaedam dicitur naturalis sicut humiditas vel mollities quae disponunt materiam ad patiendum ab agente naturali; alia obedientialis, illud scilicet per quod ipsum subiectum natum est obedire Deo ad hoc quod de eo fiat quod Deus vult" (fol. 166rb–va).

[70] See the text cited in n. 50.

already in this very *Disputed Question* eliminated this by rejecting the three unacceptable "modern" theories. How, then, is one to understand this statement?

It may be that Godfrey is simply referring here once more to the need for previous dispositions to prepare matter to receive a given form. He does not appear to assign any active causing of the new form to these seminal reasons, since in this same passage he also requires a distinct natural agent to account for the generation of the new form. Still, his language is unfortunate for it seems to imply that the form is produced *from* the seminal reason. Strictly speaking, according to his usual position the new form is not produced or educed from the previous dispositions present in matter but from matter itself. Or it may be that he is simply using the expression "seminal reason" rather loosely so as to point to the need for preexisting matter from which the form is to be produced in the process of change. If so, the language is unusual when compared with Godfrey's other texts and somewhat puzzling in itself. The possibility of some textual corruption or omission can hardly be ruled out. The text ends abruptly at this point in both manuscripts, although it appears to resume again at another point in the *Borghese* manuscript.[71] And it should be recalled that in these *Disputed Questions* we have only an abbreviated version of the original discussion and quite possibly an abbreviated version of a *reportatio*.[72]

Finally, in Quodlibet 2, q. 7, in the course of discussing the problem of unicity of substantial form in man, Godfrey clearly defends the need for previous dispositions in matter in order for it to be prepared to receive a spiritual soul. The latter will be directly concreated by God in his production of the composite, man.[73] Even in this case, Godfrey maintains that in the

---

[71] For the apparent continuation of this in *Borghese 122* see fol. 155rb–va. See Pelzer, PB 14.283. Unfortunately, the continued text remains unfinished and casts no new light on our immediate problem. One wonders whether some further precisions with respect to the terminology of seminal reasons might not have been included in the complete version, but this can only be a matter of speculation in the absence of such a completed text.

[72] Hence, greatest weight should be assigned to the discussions in Quodlibets 9, 13, and 14, then to that of Quodlibet 2, and finally to the *Disputed Questions*. This does not preclude, of course, some development in Godfrey's attitude towards the language of "seminal reasons" from Q 2 until the later Quodlibetal discussions. But we must leave undetermined the precise place of *Disputed Question* 11 in any such development.

[73] PB 2.126–27. See in particular: "Et quia virtus naturalis agentis deficit respectu compositi perfecti per animam intellectivam et respectu ipsius animae, Deus . . . quasi vice agentis naturalis, efficit compositum quod est homo, animam rationalem non per se sed in materia disposita concreando" (PB 2.127).

normal course of events a gradual and successive preparation of matter through prior dispositions is required for it to be properly disposed to receive a higher form. Granted that in the generation of a man a purely natural agent cannot produce the new and spiritual soul, nonetheless, these preceding natural dispositions which result from purely natural agency do prepare for reception of that soul. Then God, as it were, takes the place of any natural agent and introduces the spiritual soul into the disposed matter. Godfrey acknowledges that God could dispense with this procedure and immediately infuse a spiritual soul into previously undisposed matter. But he does not do so and this, observes Godfrey, is only fitting since in this case God takes the place of the natural agent.[74]

Interestingly enough, in this discussion Godfrey never refers to these previous dispositions as "seminal reasons," an omission which is all the more striking in light of his likening the two in the immediately preceding question, that is, in Quodlibet 2, q. 6. This might lead one to believe that he was not that strongly committed to any identification of the two even in Quodlibet 2, q. 6 itself. Be that as it may, reference to Godfrey's Quodlibet 2, q. 7 may serve as a point of transition to our next topic.

C. UNICITY VS. PLURALITY OF SUBSTANTIAL FORM IN MAN

As is well known to students of medieval philosophy and theology, this topic was heatedly debated during the 1270s and 1280s at both Paris and Oxford. Thus, one recent historian of this controversy, R. Zavalloni, has suggested that it reached its peak in the years between 1277 and 1287 and diminished in intensity for some years thereafter, only to revive again at the beginning of the fourteenth century.[75] This is not to deny that the problem

---

[74] See PB 2.127–28. See in particular: "Quia non obstante quod posset animam intellectivam inducere in materia nuda quae fuisset sub quacumque forma secundum suam omnipotentiam, quia tamen non agit in huiusmodi actione nisi quasi vice agentis naturalis, ideo agit sicut etiam alia agentia secundum dispositionem materiae" (PB 2.128).

[75] See his *Richard de Mediavilla et la controverse sur la pluralité des formes* (Louvain, 1951), p. 213. On the controversy during this time also see Gilson, *History of Christian Philosophy* . . . , pp. 416–20; F. J. Roensch, *Early Thomistic School* (Dubuque, Iowa, 1964) for frequent discussion of this; Van Steenberghen, *La philosophie au XIIIe siècle*, pp. 488–93; Th. Schneider, *Die Einheit des Menschen. Die anthropologische Formel "anima forma corporis" im sogenannten Korrektorienstreit und bei Petrus Johannis Olivi. Ein Beitrag zur Vorgeschichte des Konzils von Vienne* (Münster, 1973), especially helpful on the controversy within the *Correctorium* lit-

was known to earlier Latin thinkers of the thirteenth century and that it was passed on to them by various non-Christian philosophical sources including Avicenna, Avicebron, Dominic Gundisalvi, and, of course, Aristotle.[76] In fact, Zavalloni goes so far as to suggest that each of these opposed traditions, that defending unicity of substantial form and that holding for plurality of forms, may be regarded as a different but unequally developed form of Aristotelianism.[77] He also remarks that the theory of unicity of form as developed by Thomas Aquinas marks a more authentic kind of Aristotelianism.[78] According to Aquinas himself and according to certain recent scholars the thirteenth-century position defending plurality of forms is heavily indebted to Avicebron.[79] Avicenna is cited as an early source for the theory of unicity of form by Callus and others, while Zavalloni sees in him an important source for the opposed pluralistic thesis.[80] But Zavalloni also tends to minimize Avicebron's influence in the development of the plurality position.[81]

---

erature including William de la Mare's attack on Aquinas (*Correctorium fratris Thomae*) and the various defenses of Aquinas occasioned by the same.

[76] On the origins of this controversy see D. A. Callus, "The Origins of the Problem of the Unity of Form," in *The Dignity of Science*, J. A. Weisheipl, ed. (The Thomist Press, U.S.A., 1961), pp. 121–49. There Callus gives appropriate references to Avicenna (pp. 127–28); Gundissalinus (Gundisalvi) as a channel for the Avicennian position (pp. 128–33); Avicebron, as "the main true source from which the pluralist theory has come down to the Schoolmen" (p. 134); Gundissalinus again as a channel for Avicebron's theory (pp. 135–36). Also see Zavalloni, *op. cit.*, pp. 384–419, on pre-Thomistic thought on the soul and the body, and pp. 420–30 on Jewish-Arabic sources for the pluralist position.

[77] *Op. cit.*, pp. 472–74, where he acknowledges his fundamental agreement with Van Steenberghen on this point. For Van Steenberghen's continued agreement with Zavalloni on this see *La philosophie au XIIIe siècle*, p. 492.

[78] *Op. cit.*, p. 473.

[79] As presented by Thomas, Avicebron postulates plurality of forms to correspond to the order of genera and species in which a given entity shares. See, for instance, Thomas's *Quodlibet* 11, q. 5; *De spiritualibus creaturis*, a. 3c; *In II De anima*, 1. 1 (n. 225). For this doctrine in Avicebron and its close connection there with his defense of universal hylemorphism see Callus, *op. cit.*, pp. 134–35; Zavalloni, pp. 421–22; Brunner, *Platonisme et Aristotélisme* . . . , pp. 64–78, both for an exposition and to some degree a defense of Avicebron against Thomas's critique.

[80] Both Avicenna and Aristotle are credited with defending unicity of substantial form by Giles of Rome in his *Errores philosophorum*, J. Koch, ed. (Milwaukee, 1944), pp. 8, 11 (Aristotle); pp. 24–26, 34 (Avicenna). On this see Callus, pp. 127–28; Forest, *La structure métaphysique* . . . , pp. 193–94; Zavalloni, *op. cit.*, pp. 423–28.

[81] *Op. cit.*, p. 422. Van Steenberghen is of the opinion that Zavalloni has underestimated the historical importance of Avicebron on this matter. See *La philosophie au XIIIe siècle*, pp. 491–92.

As regards the issue itself, at the risk of some oversimplification, one may phrase it in the following terms. In any matter-form composite is only one substantial form to be admitted or more than one—one, for instance, to account for the fact that it is a corporeal entity, another to explain its vegetative activities if it also enjoys plant life, another to account for its sensitive activities if it is also an animal, and so on?[82] And if one decides for plurality of substantial forms in material beings, will such be true of all material substances or only of certain types, such as men? Or again, is one to account for the enduring presence of certain elemental characteristics in a "mixture," a compound material substance, by positing a plurality of forms therein, or will the single substantial form of that compound substance suffice?

One can readily gather from the above that the problem and any proposed solution will have far-reaching ramifications on the level of metaphysics and natural philosophy. Defenders of unity of form (or unicity as we prefer to call it) will insist that to the extent that a given entity enjoys substantial unity and is, therefore, truly one being, it can admit of only one substantial form. Any other superadded form can only be accidental, not substantial.[83] Defenders of plurality of forms will obviously disagree. According to them, plurality of forms can be reconciled with the essential unity of a composite being.

The problem was also thought to have important theological ramifications, especially in terms of its application to man and to the human nature of Christ. For example, if one defends unicity of substantial form and if death involves separation of the intellective soul and hence of that single substantial form from the body, what is one to say of Christ's body during the time that it remained in the tomb? Without its soul and substantial form how could it continue to be united with the Word during that period, the *sacrum triduum*?[84] Or as the question would sometimes be phrased by various participants in

---

[82] This is not to suggest that this was the only form of pluralism advanced during the thirteenth century. As our immediately following remarks will indicate and as will become clearer from our discussion below of Godfrey's knowledge of and reaction to various pluralistic theories, there was considerable variety within that general tradition.

[83] Zavalloni has listed certain arguments common to defenders of unicity of substantial form and classified them as 1) metaphysical, 2) physical, 3) psychological, 4) logical, 5) theological. As he indicates, the argumentation just mentioned in our text falls under the metaphysical. See *op. cit.*, pp. 255–61.

[84] For this see Zavalloni, *op. cit.*, p. 317. In addition he lists a series of theological objections frequently raised by opponents of unicity of form. Unicity of form would compromise, it was charged: the transmission of original sin; transubstantiation; the cult of relics; the substantial identity of risen bodies; the divine maternity of Mary (see pp. 317–19).

the debate, was the body of Christ during its stay in the tomb numerically identical with that of the living Christ?[85]

Theological implications, especially those seemingly following from unicity of substantial form, undoubtedly did much to exacerbate the situation during Thomas's final years at Paris and thereafter. By his time, as is generally acknowledged, the plurality position in one form or another was widely held.[86] He himself, of course, stands out as the foremost defender of unicity of substantial form.[87] A few years after his death his position was effectively exposed and defended by Giles of Lessines and, at about the same time, though only after considerable evolution in his personal thinking on the subject, by Giles of Rome as well.[88] While there is no reference to unicity of

---

[85] See Thomas's recurring discussion of this in Quodlibets 2 (Christmas 1269), 3 (Easter 1270), 4 (Easter 1271), and again in ST III, q. 50, a. 5, ad 1. On this and on certain changes at least in Thomas's terminology see Zavalloni, *op. cit.*, pp. 267–68; also see Van Steenberghen, "Le 'De quindecim problematibus' d'Albert le Grand," repr. in his *Introduction à l'étude de la philosophie médiévale* (Louvain, 1974), pp. 450–52. Also see Godfrey, Q 3, q. 5: "Utrum dicere quod corpus Christi mortuum et alterius hominis mortuum fuerit corpus aequivoce sit erroneum" (PB 2.194).

[86] After distinguishing carefully between the problem of plurality of souls and that of plurality of forms, Zavalloni concludes that all of the scholastics belonging to the generation prior to that of Aquinas defended under one version or another plurality of forms. Against Aimé Forest he maintains that Albert did not defend unicity of form, granted that he upheld the simplicity and unicity of the soul. See *op. cit.*, pp. 404–19. For Van Steenberghen's subsequent agreement with this claim see his *La philosophie au XIIIe siècle*, p. 491. But for a list of twentieth-century scholars who deny the traditional character of the pluralistic position see Zavalloni, p. 384, n. 5. There he cites G. Théry, R.-M. Martin, Lottin, Copleston, and Callus.

[87] According to Zavalloni the doctrine of unicity of substantial form really originates with Aquinas. He does not deny, of course, that the path had been prepared by others, but does maintain that none of Thomas's predecessors in fact arrived at the unicity position (*op. cit.*, p. 419). For Thomas's own theory see Zavalloni, pp. 261–72. On the evidence for a certain degree of development in Thomas's position see pp. 262–66. Such seems to be indicated by his (Thomas's) admission of a certain form of corporeity (*corporeitas*) in his *In I Sent.*, d. 8, q. 5, a. 2. But for a denial that Thomas ever wavered in his defense of the unicity position see Schneider, *Die Einheit des Menschen . . .*, pp. 16–17. Schneider is heavily influenced by P. Denis, "Le premier enseignement de saint Thomas sur l'unité de la forme substantielle," *Archives d'Histoire Doctrinale et Littéraire du Moyen Age* 21 (1954), pp. 139–64. For more on Thomas's position and many of the texts see Schneider, pp. 16–21.

[88] See *Le Traité 'De unitate formae' de Gilles de Lessines*, M. De Wulf, ed. (Louvain, 1901); and Zavalloni, pp. 278–82. This treatise dates from 1278, approximately from the same period as Giles of Rome's important *Contra gradus et pluralitatem formarum*, often referred to as *De gradibus formarum*, that is to say, 1277–78.

form in the propositions condemned at Paris in 1270 and 1277, the impression seems to have circulated there for a decade or so after 1276 that this position had been condemned as "heretical and erroneous" by an assembly of the Paris Masters in the Theology Faculty. Only some ten years thereafter would Henry of Ghent, one of those responsible for conveying this impression, be forced to acknowledge that such a condemnation had not, in fact, taken place.[89]

See Zavalloni, pp. 223–24, 272–78, 489–91. On Giles of Rome's evolution on this question also see Hocedez, *Richard de Middleton*, pp. 460–77.

[89] For the charge that Thomas's teaching on unicity of form had been rejected by the Paris Masters of Theology as erroneous (contrary to faith) see William de la Mare's *Correctorium* . . . , a. 27 (p. 115), a. 32 (p. 145), a. 90 (p. 372). Also see Zavalloni, p. 490, n. 17, for texts from Matthew of Aquasparta. For a valuable discussion of Henry's role in propagating this belief that Thomas's position had been condemned as heretical and erroneous and his efforts to justify this charge in the original version of his Q 10, q. 5 of Christmas 1286, see L. Hödl, "Neue Nachrichten über die Pariser Verurteilungen der thomasischen Formlehre," *Scholastik* 39 (1964), pp. 178–96. There Hödl has reproduced the relevant portions of the original text as it is preserved in a manuscript eventually left by Godfrey himself to the Sorbonne (Paris, *Bibl. Nat. lat.* 15.350, fol. 170va–171va). According to this manuscript someone, apparently Henry himself, deleted from the final version of this question his belabored effort to justify his having regarded the unicity theory as heretical and erroneous. The deleted explanation does not appear in the 1518 printed Paris edition either. In brief, Henry here refers to a meeting of the Masters held in 1276 wherein all present with but two exceptions agreed that the position asserting unicity of substantial form in man is *false*. Henry recalls that in 1285 at the request of Pope Honorius IV the faculty again considered certain articles, including this one, and that with two exceptions and a third expressing doubt all the Masters once more rejected unicity of form as *false*. Having now been reminded that to reject something as false is not as such to condemn it as *heretical* and *erroneous*, Henry counters that since the position in question was regarded as false by the Masters because of its ramifications for certain matters of faith, by implication it was also condemned as heretical and erroneous. As added support he recalls that in 1276 he himself had been personally admonished by the Papal Legate, Simon of Brion, to defend plurality of forms in man in his lecturing since, in the Legate's own words: ". . . in causa fidei nemini parcerem." In 1286, however, Henry had been placed in a difficult situation by a letter signed by twelve members of the Theology Faculty. None of them could recall that the unicity theory had been condemned as heretical and erroneous during their time in Paris (*op. cit.*, pp. 183–85). Moreover, in Q 3, q. 5, also of Christmas 1286, Godfrey refers to this same letter and in scathing terms wonders how one man (Henry) could claim that this position had been condemned as heretical or erroneous (PB 2.207–08). After all of this Henry could no longer maintain that the unicity thesis had been so condemned at Paris. This may account for the deletion of his attempted self-justification from the final version of Q 10, q. 5. Some of the events reported there by Henry also may account for the fact that in his Quodlibet 1 of 1276 he had

At Oxford, however, in March 1277 the conservative Dominican Archbishop of Canterbury, Robert Kilwardby, condemned a series of thirty propositions touching on the fields of grammar, logic, and natural philosophy, and including a number which seem to rest on or presuppose Thomas's doctrine of unicity of substantial form.[90] His successor in that see, the Franciscan, John Peckham, had long opposed the doctrine of unicity of form and in 1284 renewed Kilwardby's prohibition at Oxford. In 1286 as part of his response to the continued defense of the unicity thesis by the Dominican, Richard Knapwell, Peckham issued a new series of prohibited propositions explicitly having to do with unicity of form.[91] With this background in mind, one can understand why this topic would be regarded by Godfrey as extremely sensitive when he addressed himself to it in his Quodlibet 2, q. 7 of Easter 1286, and when he returned to it again in Quodlibet 3, q. 5 of Christmas of that same year.

Although much of Godfrey's lengthy discussion in Quodlibet 2, q. 7 is highly philosophical, he is not unaware of the theological issues at stake. Towards the end of this question he returns to them in some detail and

---

been at least open to unicity of form in man, but refused to defend this in Q 2 of 1277. Ever afterwards he would oppose it. On his general position see below and Zavalloni, pp. 287–96; also, Hödl, *op. cit.*, pp. 189–90, 195.

[90] For these see *Chartularium* . . . , T. 1, pp. 558–59. For those more or less touching on unicity of form see: *In naturalibus*, prop. 7, 12, 13. Prop. 12 reads: "Item quod vegetativa, sensitiva et intellectiva sint una forma simplex." On this see D. Callus, *The Condemnation of St. Thomas at Oxford*, The Aquinas Society of London. Aquinas Papers (Oxford, 1946); W. A. Hinnebusch, *The History of the Dominican Order, II: Intellectual and Cultural Life to 1500* (Staten Island, N. Y., 1973), pp. 149–50; T. Crowley, "John Pecham, O.F.M., Archbishop of Canterbury, versus the New Aristotelianism," *Bulletin of the John Rylands Library* 33 (1950), pp. 242–55, especially, pp. 248–49; G. Leff, *Paris and Oxford Universities in the Thirteenth and Fourteenth Centuries* (New York, 1968), pp. 290–94; Schneider, *Die Einheit des Menschen* . . . , pp. 77–79; Zavalloni, pp. 218–19. Also see D. Douie, *Archbishop Pecham* (Oxford, 1952), pp. 272–301.

[91] See Crowley, "John Pecham . . . ," pp. 249–55; Callus, *The Condemnation of St. Thomas* . . . ; Schneider, *op. cit.*, pp. 95–101; Glorieux, "Comment les thèses thomistes furent proscrites à Oxford (1284–1286)," *Revue thomiste* 32 (1927), pp. 259–91; F. Pelster, "Die Sätze der Londoner Verurteilung von 1286 und die Schriften des Magister Richard von Knapwell OP," *Archivum Fratrum Praedicatorum* 16 (1946), pp. 83–106; Zavalloni, pp. 219–21. For the text of the 1286 prohibited propositions see *Ioannes Pecham, Registrum epistolarum*, C. T. Martin, ed., T. III (London, 1885), pp. 921ff., reproduced in Zavalloni, p. 220, n. 25. Proposition 8 merits quotation here: "Octavus est quod in homine est tantum una forma, scilicet anima rationalis, et nulla alia forma substantialis; ex qua opinione sequi videntur omnes haereses supradictae."

explicitly takes up the issue relating to the body of Christ in the tomb again in Quodlibet 3, q. 5. We shall examine his philosophical consideration of this problem in the present section of this chapter and his theological analysis of the same in the final part of this chapter. And since in Quodlibet 2, q. 7 he specifically addresses himself to the question of unicity vs. plurality of substantial form in man, we shall concentrate on his position with respect to this.[92] Enough will be said in his discussion of this topic to give one a fairly precise indication as to his view on plurality of forms in nonhuman material entities as well.

Central to Godfrey's philosophical analysis of this problem is his conviction that two entities cannot unite to constitute a being that enjoys essential unity unless one is pure potentiality and the other its first substantial act. This conviction plays an essential role in his defense of the purely potential character of prime matter.[93] One might expect him to move rather easily from this to the conclusion that there can be but one substantial form in any given substance, even in man. But, as will become clear from his discussion in Quodlibet 2, q. 7 and elsewhere, while Godfrey's philosophical preferences certainly point to this conclusion, he will hesitate to give unqualified support to the theory of unicity of substantial form in man. Undoubtedly, theological concerns such as those referred to above and to be investigated in greater detail below account for much of his caution in this matter.

In Quodlibet 2, q. 7 Godfrey presents three general positions, each of which in some way defends plurality of forms in man. According to the first position, because man belongs to a given species within a given genus, one must postulate substantial forms in him to correspond both to his genus and to his specific difference. According to a second position, because man is also a material being, plurality of forms must be realized in him in order to account for the fact that the elements are present in his body, and still another form to account for the fact that these elements unite to constitute a mixture or compound. Finally, there is another theory that maintains that because man is not merely material but in some way immaterial and incorruptible, in addition to a material, corruptible, and "natural" form one must also posit in him another immaterial, incorruptible, and "supernatural" form.[94] Since Godfrey considers and then refutes each of these theories in turn, we shall now follow this same order in presenting his discussion.

---

[92] "Utrum homo habeat esse ab una forma substantiali vel a pluribus" (PB 2.95).
[93] See Ch. VII, p. 268.
[94] PB 2.96–97.

1. The First Theory

Hocedez and Zavalloni have both suggested that in his presentation and refutation of this first position Godfrey has in mind Richard of Middleton's version of the theory, especially as proposed in the latter's *Disputed Question* 39.[95] As Godfrey understands this position, it rests upon the following contention. If something belongs to a given species it must be composed of genus and difference. But since the difference implies something in addition to the genus, in any such entity there must be forms corresponding both to the genus and the difference. In anticipation of the obvious objection that defenders of unicity of form might raise, exponents of this position maintain that they too can safeguard the essential unity of the resulting being. Even though according to this position prime matter enjoys some minimum degree of actuality, it can still unite with form to constitute something that is essentially one. Hence, the form corresponding to the genus in a given entity may be regarded as something that is still imperfect and in potency to another form, the completing and perfecting form implied by the difference. In other words, the first and generic form will combine with matter so as to constitute an incomplete and imperfect composite that is still in potency with respect to the completing form corresponding to the difference.[96]

It is true that Aristotle writes in *Metaphysics* VII that a being that is essentially one cannot result from two beings in act. But the present theory would restrict this dictum to two instances of completed act.[97] In the present situation a being that is essentially one can result, because it arises from a combination of incompleted act (the composite of matter and the generic

---

[95] Hocedez, *Richard de Middleton*, pp. 420–24; Zavalloni, *op. cit.*, pp. 235–41. There Zavalloni specifies that Godfrey did not know of Richard's *De gradu formarum* and notes that neither in his exposition nor in his refutation of the pluralistic theory (the first theory) does Godfrey refer to plurality of forms in mixtures or in animals, something that Richard does discuss in the last mentioned treatise (*op. cit.*, p. 235). However, as we shall observe farther on, it seems to us that the first theory as presented by Godfrey does, at least by implication, defend plurality of forms in all material entities, not merely in man. As regards Godfrey's exposition of the second theory, which defends plurality of forms in mixtures, Zavalloni remarks that he there refers to fairly widespread views such as those found in the *Correctorium* literature without making any specific reference to Richard.

[96] PB 2.97.

[97] For Aristotle see *Metaphysics* VII, c. 13 (1039a 3–5). According to Godfrey's citation: ". . . ex duobus actibus vel entibus in actu non fit aliquid unum per se . . ." (PB 2.97).

form) and completing act (the specific form). In fact this specific form viewed as completing act not only serves as the form of the difference but in some way even as that of the genus. Since the generic form does not communicate that degree of being and actuality whereby the composite enjoys unqualified and complete being, it does not even provide complete and unqualified membership in a given genus, for instance, that of substance or that of body, but only incomplete substantial or corporeal being. Such being must be completed by the specific form. To say anything else would be to suggest that the composite was already constituted as a complete substance by its first form. Then its specific form would be something superadded, accidental, and nonessential to the composite entity.[98]

As regards man's metaphysical structure, according to this theory it is man's intellective form that accounts for his presence in the species man and at the same time perfects his being within the genus substance. Thus, the intellective form does not communicate substantial being or corporeal being to man as such but rather a perfecting and completing of his substantial and corporeal being. Hence, given the plurality of forms in man, according to this theory one can still safeguard his essential unity. One form, the generic, unites with matter so as to serve as something potential, as a kind of matter as it were, with respect to the final and perfecting form. Granted the minimum degree of actuality implied by matter according to this theory and the greater degree implied by the first form (that corresponding to the genus), these still stand in potency to the ultimate and completing form, the intellective.[99]

As Godfrey also points out, this theory maintains that nature never permits matter to exist only under the first and generic form, but continually proceeds onward to that completing and specific form to which matter is in potency. So too, according to the natural course of events the process of corruption does not come to a halt with a resolution back to the proximate matter for the intellective form, that is, the composite consisting of matter and the generic form. Corpses do not enjoy a stable and permanent being as such but are subject to further resolution and corruption. In the case of Christ's body in the tomb, however, this further process of corruption was prevented by divine intervention. Only his intellective form (and soul) was separated from his body, according to this version of the plurality-of-forms position.[100]

---

[98] PB 2.98.

[99] PB 2.98.

[100] PB 2.98–99. Here in what is almost an aside Godfrey comments that the above logic should also lead one to defend plurality of forms within accidents as well as substances. An accident such as whiteness may also be regarded as being composed of a genus and species (p. 99). Presumably, he is proposing this as a counterargument based on a *reductio ad absurdum*.

Godfrey then presents a long series of arguments that may be offered against this version of plurality of forms. Only a few will be considered insofar as they are representative. First of all, it may be argued that as regards membership in a genus, that which is most general pertains to a given being by reason of that same ultimate form through which it enjoys its specific being rather than by means of any other form which is alleged to preexist and coexist in the generated being. Thus, a horse more truly subsists by reason of the soul whereby it has its specific being than by any other form that might be imagined to be present in it. Hence, it is by reason of this same specific form that it is also a substance. But such would not be the case if the horse's sensitive soul were distinct from the form that makes of it a substance (its substantiality). It must be by reason of one and the same form that it is a horse, an animal, and a substance.[101]

If one were to insist that it is by one form that something is a horse and by reason of another that it is an animal or a sensible being, the form that accounts for its specific being (as a horse) could hardly be less perfect than that which accounts for its generic being (as an animal or a sensible thing). Given this, the form that accounts for its specific being as a horse will either be its sensitive soul or something nobler than that soul. But this would lead to the absurd conclusion that there are two sensitive souls in a given animal, or what is even worse, to the position that one of these is more perfect than the sensitive soul. This could only be a rational soul and form, something that must not be assigned to any mere animal. And if one acknowledges that it is through one and the same form that something is both a horse and an animal, that is, enjoys both its specific and generic being, then one can hardly deny that it also enjoys its substantial being by reason of that same form. Such a denial would lead to the unhappy consequence that the form by reason of which it is a horse and an animal is not really a substantial form at all, since only that form which confers substantial being is truly a substantial form.[102]

Again, reasons Godfrey, if the generic form or substantiality only confers some formal but incomplete substantiality, then the specific form, if it really differs from the former as the theory in question would have it, will not render the substantiality of that first form any more perfect. Thus, a form of corporeity added to the first substantiality or first form will not render that substantiality any more complete. It will simply account for the fact that the

---

[101] PB 2.99.

[102] PB 2.99. See the corrections for this text as listed on p. 355 by the editors. Even with these corrections the text is somewhat difficult and reflects, in our opinion, its nature as a *reportatio*.

total being enjoys some other perfection in addition to its substantiality. So too the proposed final completing specific form will not render perfect or complete the prior substantiality. In fact, it will confer no substantiality at all unless one admits that it is of itself and essentially a kind of substantiality. But if it is, it will then unite with the first form to produce a new substance consisting of two formal and actual substantialities, something that Godfrey would reject as impossible.[103]

And if one seeks to escape from this dilemma by countering that the specific form is really not a determined kind of substantiality, then not only will it (the specific form) fail to complete the substantiality of the first and generic form. It will be unable to unite with it so as to constitute a being that is essentially one. As Godfrey phrases it, a substance does not arise from the union of substantiality and nonsubstantiality.[104] In other words, the general thrust of this line of criticism is that this version of the plurality thesis must ultimately compromise the substantial unity of the composite and hence of man as well.

In order to press the point that it is by reason of one and the same form that a given thing belongs to its genus and its species, Godfrey draws an analogy between substantial forms and numbers. Just as number does not bespeak a form that is really distinct from the forms of the different species of number, so it seems that there can be no genus in the order of reality without some proximate species. Hence, no distinctive generic form need be postulated apart from that implied by a given species or difference. (As regards number, Godfrey observes that it is impossible for there to be a discrete multitude which is neither odd nor even.)[105] At this juncture Godfrey is, in effect, raising the charge of exaggerated realism against the theory in question. He points out that a genus enjoys unity in the conceptual order, but not in the order of reality. Taking his cue from a remark by Themistius in his *Commentary on the De anima,* he contrasts genus and species in this respect. A generic concept is grounded on only a tenuous similarity between a number of individuals, presumably individuals that differ in species. But one's idea or concept of a species presupposes some nature or form found in things themselves.[106] It is this conceptual similarity that enables the logician

---

[103] PB 2.100.

[104] PB 2.101.

[105] PB 2.102–03. For other texts where Godfrey likens the differing degrees of being to number see Ch. III, n. 133.

[106] For Themistius see *Commentaire sur le traité de l'âme d'Aristote,* G. Verbeke, ed. (Louvain, 1957), pp. 8–9: "Genus quidem enim conceptus est sine hypostasi summatim collectus ex tenui singularium similitudine (et aut omnino nihil est genus aut multo posterius singularibus), species autem natura quaedam vult esse et forma."

to predicate genus univocally of its species. But the natural philosopher, who is directly concerned with studying real being, maintains that genus is predicated in some way in equivocal fashion, not purely univocally, and this because there is no one form or nature in reality to correspond to one's generic concept.[107] Hence, Godfrey's point is this: there is no justification for postulating a distinctive form in material entities such as men in order to account for or to correspond to one's generic concept. The single form which accounts for their presence in their species will suffice.

Another interesting objection is based on the assumption that there is a fundamental difference between mathematical abstraction and logical abstraction. The former is the abstraction of a form, presumably the form of quantity, from sensible matter, while the latter is rather the abstraction of a universal from a particular. According to this objection, if genus and species point to distinct forms in reality, then in each type of abstraction that which is abstracted, the form of quantity in the one case and the universal or generic form in the other, will really differ from that from which it is abstracted.[108] Godfrey's point here is that logical abstraction would then be the same as mathematical abstraction, since it too would involve the abstraction of a form, that of the genus.

But for Godfrey the most compelling metaphysical reason for rejecting this theory of plurality of forms in a given substance is his contention that it would destroy that substance's essential unity. A being that is essentially one cannot result from the union of different beings in act. Because forms as such are simple, the various forms within a given being as envisioned by this theory will really differ from one another. Hence, any entity that includes two or more of these can be one only in the way in which an accidental aggregate is one.[109] Moreover, the definition of any such being would lack essential unity.[110] Godfrey rejects the claim that this difficulty can be overcome by the proposal that the generic form with its matter is still only something incomplete and can, therefore, unite with the specific form to constitute

---

We have added the parentheses to indicate the section missing from Godfrey's quotation (PB 2.103).

[107] PB 2.103. On Godfrey's critique of this version of pluralism for its "Platonic realism" see A. Pegis, *St. Thomas and the Problem of the Soul* (Toronto, 1934), pp. 59–60, n. 71.

[108] PB 2.105.

[109] PB 2.105.

[110] *Ibid.* Godfrey there refers to Aristotle's discussion of definition, genus, and differentiae in *Metaphysics* VII, c. 12 (1038a 1–9). He also cites Averroes's *Commentary* on the same. See *In VII Met.*, fol. 196va; also, fol. 194va.

something that is essentially one. On the contrary, he contends that since each and every substantial form communicates the act of substantial being (*actus essendi*), the proposed composite entity will itself then include more than one substantial act and will constitute not one but more than one substance.[111]

Godfrey acknowledges, of course, that something that is essentially one can result from the union of prime matter and substantial form. But this is because matter does not of itself imply any actuality but is pure potentiality. Just as there can be nothing intermediary between prime matter and absolute nonbeing, so too there can be no intermediary between prime matter and unqualified or substantial being. Hence, any substantial form, no matter how imperfect it may be when compared with other forms, cannot fail to communicate substantial being to matter once it actually informs it.[112]

In this discussion Godfrey obviously sees a close connection between the view that prime matter is pure potentiality and that which defends unicity of substantial form in any corporeal entity. As we have indicated in the preceding chapter, he strongly defends the first point, the purely potential character of prime matter. Not surprisingly, therefore, he concludes that the theory of plurality of forms now under consideration lacks any solid foundation.[113] He also comments that if one rejects the purely potential character of prime matter and assigns to it some actuality in itself, then it will not unite with its substantial form to constitute a being that is essentially one. In sum, whether one assigns some minimum degree of actuality to matter or whether one defends its purely potential character but still maintains that it is first informed by an "incomplete" substantial form, one will have undermined the possibility of any essential union between that matter and the final or so-called completing substantial form. One will have nothing more than an accidental aggregate of more basic entities.[114]

In concluding our consideration of Godfrey's treatment of this first version of plurality of forms, we should observe that while he has presented it within the general context of the question of unicity vs. plurality of forms in man,

---

[111] PB 2.106.

[112] PB 2.107.

[113] PB 2.107–08. Here he cites with approval from Averroes's *De substantia orbis* c. 1 (Venice, 1562), Vol. 9, fol. 3vab. From that citation note in particular, according to Godfrey's version: ". . . unam enim formam habere nisi unum subiectum est impossibile. Quod enim est in actu non recipit aliquid quod est in actu secundum quod est in actu. . . . Unde natura huiusmodi subiecti recipientis formas substantiales scilicet primae materiae necesse est esse naturam potentiae . . . et ideo nullam habet formam propriam et naturam existentiae in actu, sed eius substantia est esse in posse . . ." (PB 2.108).

[114] PB 2.108.

the theory in question evidently defends plurality of forms in other material substances as well.

2. *The Second Theory*

According to this second theory, because man is a "mixed being," that is to say, a compound substance formed of the basic elements, one must admit of plurality of substantial forms in him. This follows, it is contended, because the elements in some way remain in mixed bodies. While the elements themselves are simple bodies with simple forms, mixtures are composed or compound bodies, or else have forms that are in some way composed. Hence, in addition to the forms of the elements that remain within the body of man, there must be some more complete and higher form which is neither an element nor reducible to the elements.[115] Nor will it suffice for one to counter that the elements themselves undergo corruption as regards their substantial actualities when they unite to form a mixed body, and hence, that there is only one simple form in such a body, one which is really distinct from those of the previously existing elements. This suggestion will not do justice to Aristotle's definition of an element in *Metaphysics* V as that of which something is composed which remains within that thing.[116] In addition, if the elements are in fact corrupted when a mixture is formed, then there will be no difference between generation, on the one hand, and mixing (*mixtio*) or the process whereby a mixture is formed, on the other.[117]

According to this theory, the forms of the elements are the most incomplete and imperfect of all substantial forms, so much so in fact that in some way they are intermediary between complete substantial forms and those that are purely accidental. It is contended that in some way they admit of contrariety with respect to one another and also that they are capable of admitting of greater or lesser. Hence, they endure in a mixed body, though neither in completed actuality nor in mere potentiality, but, as it were, in some intermediary stage between actuality and potentiality. Defenders of this theory also cite a text from Averroes's *Commentary on the De caelo* as well as one from John Damascene's *De fide orthodoxa* in support of their position.[118]

---

[115] PB 2.109.

[116] *Ibid.* For Aristotle see *Metaphysics* V, c. 3 (1014a 26–27). Godfrey's citation here is not completely literal.

[117] PB 2.109.

[118] PB 2.109–10. For John Damascene see his *De fide orthodoxa,* III, c. 16 (equals cap. 60 in the Burgundio translation), E. Buytaert, ed. (St. Bonaventure, N. Y.,

Godfrey is obviously most troubled by the text from Averroes, but maintains that it must be interpreted in such fashion as to accord with the Commentator's assertion that there is only one substantial form in a composite. Rather than understand him as implying that the substantial forms of elements remain in a mixture even though they are imperfect when compared with other forms, Godfrey proposes another interpetation. A mixture comes into being when the elements involved undergo corruption both in terms of their accidental and substantial being and when an appropriate agent produces a new substance, a mixture, together with some intermediary quality which in some way falls between the qualities of the mixed elements. Thus, this new quality will differ from the former ones not in degree (by intension or remission) but in species.[119]

One may hold that the elements remain virtually in the single form of the mixture and that the elemental qualities are virtually present in the new intermediary quality which may also be described as virtually many.[120] One may also say that the mixture is more composed than are the simple elements from which it was formed for this same reason, this virtual presence of the forms of the elements and the simple elemental qualities. This is not to imply, warns Godfrey, that the new intermediary quality itself consists of really distinct parts, but only of virtual parts that are logically distinct. In the same way, he continues, just as the elements are virtually present in the form of a mixture, so too are the elements and the form of the mixture virtually present in the vegetative form of a plant, and all of these virtually present in the single soul of a brute animal.[121]

In sum, then, Godfrey sees no need to defend plurality of forms in material entities because of the presence—virtual presence to be precise—of elements or elemental qualities in mixtures. Once more he seems to have in mind and

---

1955), p. 247:56–57. In Godfrey's text the passage reads: "necesse est hominem dicere ad minus compositum esse ex quinque naturis, id est ex quattuor elementis et anima" (PB 2.110). For Averroes see *In De caelo* III, com. 67 (Venice, 1562), Vol. 5, fol. 227rab; also cited in PB 2.110, n. 1.

[119] Godfrey recognizes that Averroes's text might well be interpreted in the first way. See PB 2.111: "Et ideo non videtur tenendum esse quod videtur sonare littera Commentatoris. . . ." For such an understanding of Averroes see Thomas, *Quaestiones disputatae de anima,* a. 9, ad 10; Forest, *op. cit.,* pp. 198–99. For Thomas's original sympathy with this position and eventual rejection of it see *ibid.* On Godfrey's interpretation of Averroes's text also see Zavalloni, *op. cit.,* pp. 301–02.

[120] PB 2.111. Godfrey's solution reminds one of that eventually adopted by Aquinas. See *Qu. disp. de anima,* a. 9, ad 10; ST I, q. 76, a. 4, ad 4; Forest, pp. 198–99.

[121] PB 2.111. Cf. Q 10, q. 10 (PB 4.344), 1st par.

to have refuted a theory that would defend plurality of forms in all material entities, not merely in man. In fact, one suspects that his division between the first theory and the second is somewhat artificial. Thus a pluralist might well combine them, as Richard of Middleton seems to have done.[122] Godfrey's purpose in so presenting them appears to be to show that they are grounded on different reasons, that is to say, on the fact that material entities fall into genera and species, and on the alleged continuing existence of elements and elemental qualities in mixtures.

3. The Third Theory

In presenting this third theory Godfrey appears to have a specific representative and defender of the same in mind, Henry of Ghent, the frequent target of his philosophical critique as we have by now so often seen. Reference has already been made above to the fact that Henry's position evolved after 1276. If he was noncommital on this question in his Quodlibet 1, q. 4 of 1276 while discussing the theological issue of the continued identity of Christ's body in the tomb, by 1277 in his Quodlibet 2, q. 2 he had already adopted some version of the plurality thesis.[123] This development, of course, is not surprising in light of his later report about his intervening meeting with the Bishop of Paris, the Papal Legate, and others, and the Legate's admonishment that Henry defend plurality of forms in man in his subsequent lectures.[124] In the discussion in Quodlibet 2, Henry distinguishes between the way of nature and the way of faith. According to the first, one must hold that in man the rational soul is united to matter by means of a natural form drawn from the potency of matter. According to the second, one must ac-

[122] See, for instance, his *De gradu formarum* (Zavalloni, p. 130), where he posits five substantial forms in every mixed body below man, that is, the four incomplete elementary forms and the completing form of the mixture, and at least six in man, namely, the four elementary forms, the sensitive soul, and the intellective soul which completes the whole. Also see Zavalloni, pp. 364–66.

[123] See Henry's Q 1, q. 4 ("Utrum corpus Christi in sepulchro habuit aliquam formam substantialem qua informabatur anima eius ab ipso separata"), fol. 2r–3r, especially 2v–3r; Q 2, q. 2 ("Utrum anima Christi separata, remansit aliqua forma in ipso corpore eius"), fol. 29r–30v.

[124] See in this chapter, n. 89; also Hödl, "Neue Nachrichten über die Pariser . . . ," p. 184 for Henry's text: "Iam enim X annis cum quidam notati fuerint Parisius, quasi posuissent quod in homine non esset forma substantialis nisi anima rationalis, et ego eodem tempore in dubio reliquissem in prima disputatione mea de quolibet, quaestione an plures formae ponendae essent in homine vel unica tantum . . ."

knowledge that in Christ this form remained in matter when his soul was separated from his body, and this in order to safeguard the numerical identity of Christ's body on the cross and in the tomb.[125]

In Quodlibet 3, q. 6 of Easter 1278, Henry formulates his position with greater precision. He had developed his proposed solution in order to do justice to the fact that human generation is due to two different kinds of agency, human and divine. Defenders of unicity of form undercut the human agency in man's origin since, according to them, the single substantial form, man's soul, comes from without as a result of divine agency. But defenders of pluralism multiply forms even in those cases where only one kind of agency is involved, as in subhuman generation. Henry views his own position as intermediary between these two since it is only in man that he admits of more than one substantial form, and even here, only of two.[126] As he develops this position in greater detail in Quodlibet 4, q. 13 of 1279, philosophical argumentation points to unicity of form in all composites other than man. But theology requires duality of substantial forms in the case of man.[127] Again he offers arguments drawn from the way of nature and from the data of faith to support this "dualistic" view of man.[128] Since two agencies are involved in the generation of man, two distinct substantial forms must correspond to these different agencies. The one form will be due to purely human agency and will be drawn from the potentiality of matter. The other, the spiritual and rational soul, will be created directly by God.[129] As regards the arguments based on faith, Henry contends that one must maintain the numerical identity of the living and dead body of Christ. Hence, a distinct substantial form must have remained there during the period when his intellectual soul was separated from his body. Henry also argues in support of

---

[125] *Op. cit.*, fol. 29v–30r. On this see Zavalloni, *op. cit.*, pp. 292–93.

[126] In Q 3, q. 6 Henry asks: "Utrum vegetativa et sensitiva in Christo infusae erant cum intellectiva vel erant eductae de potentia materiae" (fol. 53r). See Zavalloni, pp. 293–94. In Henry see especially fol. 54r.

[127] Q 4, q. 13 considers this question: "Utrum in quidditate rerum sensibilium materialium cadunt plures formae substantiales re differentes" (fol. 104v–115r). For analysis of this question see Zavalloni, *op. cit.*, pp. 288–92; Bayerschmidt, *op. cit.*, pp. 219–29; A. Maurer, "Henry of Ghent and the Unity of Man," *Mediaeval Studies* 10 (1948), pp. 12–14.

[128] See *op. cit.*, fol. 108v: "Sed oportet contra eos procedere duplici alia via: una a priori et a causa, arguendo ostensive ex eis quae in operibus naturae convincimus; altera vero a posteriori et ab effectu, arguendo ad impossibile ex eis quae in operibus gratiae ex fide tenemus."

[129] Fol. 108v–109v. Also see G. Fioravanti, "*Forma* ed *esse* in Enrico di Gand. . . ," *Annali della scuola normale superiore di Pisa* 5 (1975), pp. 987–96.

the same from certain implications that follow, in his opinion, from the doctrine of the Eucharist.[130]

In exposing Henry's position in his own Quodlibet 2, q. 7, Godfrey highlights Henry's appeal to the twofold agency involved in man's generation. Man's nature is intermediary between the purely material and corruptible and the purely spiritual and incorruptible. Hence, he must be brought into being by two agents, one natural and one "supernatural." Given this, and since only one of these agents requires preexisting matter for its action, these diverse actions must terminate in different forms. As Godfrey presents the position, once the matter has been sufficiently disposed to receive the new form that will result from human agency, then it is also disposed to receive its "supernatural" form. As one single subject the matter then stands in proximate potency to receive both of these forms at one and the same time.[131] And just as one will not become present to matter without the other, so too, neither is designed to communicate being to the human supposit and to subsist without the other. Still, the two forms do not communicate distinct subsistences, but one and the same subsistence. The form educed from the potency of matter serves as a disposition which prepares the matter in the order of nature to receive the intellective soul. But it unites with the same soul as if they were one form in order to perfect matter and to give to the supposit only one subsistence.[132]

If one should object to Henry that there can only be one existence in a given substance, he will reply that this is true of that existence which is subsistence (*esse suppositi*) but not of the being proper to nature (*esse naturae*). While it is true that form communicates *esse*, this applies only to the being proper to nature (*esse naturae*), not to subsistence. But one cannot extend this solution to purely corporeal entities. In all such entities apart from man there can be only one substantial form. Each such form will perfect matter and communicate subsistence to it as well. Because man's intellective soul is not educed from the potentiality of matter whereas his other substantial form is, the two are ordered to perfect matter according to the same degree

---

[130] *Op. cit.*, fol. 109v – 112v.

[131] PB 2.112, where Godfrey almost literally cites Henry's Q 4, q. 13 (fol. 112v). Note in particular the following where Godfrey cites Henry's text almost verbatim: ". . . cum iam facta est dispositio quae est necessitas in materia ad susceptionem illius formae naturalis quae producenda est de potentia materiae, simul facta est necessitas ad susceptionem formae supernaturalis, et tanquam unum subiectum facta est materia unica habilitate potentiali proxima susceptiva duarum dictarum formarum simul et in eodem instanti." The close textual dependency continues in the following context as well.

[132] For Godfrey see PB 2.112. For the same in Henry see *op. cit.*, fol. 112v – 113r.

of its receptive capacity, and so much so that one will not perfect matter without the other or at least not until corruption ensues. Given this, neither form alone will constitute with matter a composite or supposit.[133] Granted that the two forms differ in kind, still they inform one and the same matter according to the same degree of perfectibility and thus may be said to be more truly of the same order than any other two natural forms.[134]

Godfrey prefaces his criticism of Henry's position with the remark that the difficulties already raised against other versions of plurality of forms also appear to apply to this particular theory.[135] He then presents a long series of objections, only a few of which space will permit us to consider here. He begins by raising what is his most fundamental difficulty on the metaphysical level with all forms of pluralism. Two substantial forms cannot combine to constitute a being that is substantially one, not even in the case of man. It is of the very essence of form to communicate actual being. Henry's "natural" form is itself a kind of actual nature in the line of substance—in other words, a substantial form. Nor can Henry escape from this dilemma by suggesting that the corporeal form unites with the "supernatural" or spiritual form as if they were one so as to constitute only one substance. Insofar as the first-mentioned form enjoys actual entity distinct from the potency of prime matter, the composite must receive some actuality from it. Hence, both this form as well as the spiritual one will communicate substantial being to the human composite, thereby destroying man's essential or substantial unity.[136]

Nor will Godfrey permit Henry to meet this difficulty by suggesting that there are two kinds of substantial forms, those that give substantial being without combining with any other substantial form and those that do not. Only the human soul and the form of corporeity as realized in man would illustrate the second type in that together they would actualize only one potentiality in matter and thus communicate only one substantial being.[137] First of all, counters Godfrey, this suggestion begs the question, since it assumes what remains to be proven, that is, that matter as realized in man can be ordered to and perfected by different substantial forms at one and the same time.[138] Secondly, one could equally well apply this same reasoning to

133 PB 2.113 (Godfrey); fol. 113r and 113v (Henry).

134 PB 2.114.

135 PB 2.114.

136 PB 2.114–15. See in particular: "Sed, ut pluries dictum est, illud in quo sunt plures formae dantes esse in actu non potest esse aliquod unum per se" (PB 2.115).

137 PB 2.115.

138 *Ibid.*

other corporeal substances and postulate in each of them duality of substantial forms, something that Henry refuses to do. Thus, one might argue that no such substantial form taken singly and by itself can inform prime matter and communicate substantial being, but that the two forms can do this when they are taken jointly. And one might make a particular case for this contention with respect to forms that stand in some kind of ordered relationship to one another.[139]

Henry may reply that while prime matter cannot be simultaneously ordered to more than one substantial form that has been educed from the potentiality of matter because each of these would fulfill that matter's capacity, still it can be ordered to two different forms when only one of them is educed from matter. To this Godfrey counters that there is no reason for one to hold that man's form of corporeity will not as completely fulfill matter's capacity as any other form that is educed from matter. Moreover, the form that is not educed from matter, that is, the human soul, must be no less capable of fulfilling matter's capacity than any other substantial form that is so educed. Insofar as any form is substantial, it belongs to it to fulfill the potentiality of a given instance of matter and to communicate substantial being. With this, Godfrey undermines Henry's contention that in man matter serves as a single subject with a single capacity for two distinct substantial forms.[140]

Even though Henry admits that in man one substantial form will not communicate being without the other, some role must be assigned to each form. While the form of corporeity will not dispose for the spiritual form by any temporal priority, it seems that it must first dispose for it in the order of nature. If so, then it cannot be said that the two forms inform matter with equal immediacy.[141] Rather, one will immediately perfect matter and the other, the spiritual form, will do so only by means of the former. Otherwise no disposing role could be assigned to the form of corporeity. But it can only dispose insofar as it is in itself actuality. The familiar objection reappears. Since both forms according to Henry do communicate some kind of being of nature (*esse naturae*), how can he avoid admitting that each also communicates substantial being and hence substantial existence and subsistence? And then, how can he avoid acknowledging that they will result in two substances, thereby reducing man to the level of an accidental aggregate? This concern with safeguarding man's essential unity is obviously of paramount importance in Godfrey's eyes.[142] He expresses the same concern by

---

[139] PB 2.115–16.
[140] PB 2.116.
[141] PB 2.117–18.
[142] PB 2.118.

suggesting that according to Henry's theory the spiritual form will presuppose the other form in the order of nature and therefore will only be superadded to it in the manner of an accidental form. This follows because any form that perfects matter which is already to some extent actualized can only do so as an accidental form.[143]

Godfrey concludes this philosophical evaluation of Henry's position with the observation that the strongest argument against plurality of forms in other entities also seems to apply to man. In every case the first form would give substantial being and the second only some kind of accidental being. Just as one cannot subtract anything from the potentiality of matter without reducing it to nothingness, so too one cannot add any actuality to it without producing an actual and substantial being. Hence, any further actuality that is added to that first form, such as a spiritual soul, will not give substantial being to man, but only some kind of accidental being.[144]

At this point Godfrey offers an interesting comment. If one still finds it necessary to defend duality of forms in man, one coming from within and one coming from without because of the two kinds of agency involved in his generation, Godfrey suggests that the form that is produced from within and from the potentiality of matter should be the sensitive form. Here he appears once more to have Henry in mind and to be offering an improvement upon his theory. In Quodlibet 3, q. 6 Henry had considered this problem and had concluded that the vegetative and sensitive principles in man are not to be identified with the form that is educed from matter but rather with that which is introduced from without by God. In other words, the vegetative and sensitive principles are created with the rational soul. They do not together with the rational soul constitute three souls or even three forms, but one spiritual form and soul endowed with these three powers.[145]

Godfrey takes exception to this, even within the perspective of Henry's theory. According to Henry's own doctrine of unicity of form in brutes (and all other subhuman entities), it is one form that accounts for the fact that a brute is a mixture and also enjoys vegetative and sensitive life. The same should also obtain in man, suggests Godfrey, *mutatis mutandis*. The distinct spiritual form will not account for man's vegetative and sensitive activities. Godfrey returns to this point in Quodlibet 10, q. 10. There he wonders

---

[143] *Ibid.* See in particular: ". . . omnis forma perficiens materiam, non ut est nuda potentia ad esse simpliciter, sed ut est aliquo modo in actu, est forma accidentalis, sive materia possit habere esse in illo actu primo sine isto sive non."

[144] PB 2.122. For further arguments against Henry's position see PB 2.118 – 22.

[145] PB 2.122 – 23. For Henry on this see *op. cit.*, fol. 54r – 54v. Also see Zavalloni, *op. cit.*, pp. 295 – 96.

whether those who defend plurality of forms in man must also postulate plurality of souls in him.[146] Once more he refers to Henry's position according to which there is plurality of forms in man alone, and this due to the two-fold agency involved in his production. Without committing himself there either to unicity or to plurality of forms, among the pluralist positions he obviously favors Henry's position. Once more he observes that the major difficulty militating against its acceptance arises from the fact that the reasons leading one to deny plurality of forms in other entities also seem to apply to man.[147]

But if one wishes to defend this dualist position with respect to man, Godfrey argues that one should not maintain that the intellective form also contains the vegetative and sensitive powers and thus that there are two forms but only one soul in him. Just as the form of the mixture is educed from the potency of matter according to this theory, Henry should also admit the same of the vegetative and sensitive principles in man. Hence, if Godfrey were to defend duality of forms in man he would do so in this way, that is, by holding that the vegetative and sensitive principles are contained in the single form that is educed from matter and which also accounts for man's being a mixed body, and that the intellective form and soul alone is introduced from without. Hence, there would be two souls as well as two forms in man, the intellective and the sensitive.[148]

In Quodlibet 2, q. 7 Godfrey proposes to rank the various positions on plurality of forms in man in terms of their degree of probability. (He appears to defend unicity of form in other corporeal beings.)[149] He acknowledges that it is difficult to defend either unicity or plurality of forms in man, but that the objections raised against plurality seem to be weightier. In fact, the strongest objections that can be presented against the unicity position may also be urged against the plurality theories. This is so because these arise from the fact that the intellective soul is thought to be an immaterial substance which is in some way independent from matter and yet unites with prime matter in such fashion as to give substantial existence to a corporeal and extended composite. This, comments Godfrey, is extremely difficult to explain according to any of the positions under consideration.[150]

---

146 PB 2.123. For Q 10, q. 10 see PB 4.343: "Utrum secundum ponentes in homine plures formas substantiales oportet ponere in ipso plures animas." In brief, his answer is in the affirmative. See PB 4.347.

147 PB 4.344.

148 PB 4.345, 347.

149 See PB 2.125: ". . . licet in homine vel in quibuscumque viventibus non sit nisi una forma, sicut nec in aliis sive mixtis sive simplicibus corporibus."

150 PB 2.123–24.

Thus, those philosophers who have defended only one substantial form in man have attempted to account for the intellect's union with the body in different ways. Alexander of Aphrodisias seems to have viewed the possible intellect as a material power and thus as the potency of a corporeal substance or corporeal form. Others have held that the intellect exists in separation from the body and is conjoined to it in some way through its operation, but that it is only one in itself. Here Godfrey has in mind Averroes's theory of one separate and unique possible intellect for all mankind, a position which he immediately dismisses as erroneous.[151] Not quite so obviously erroneous but still unacceptable would be a position according to which the highest sensitive form in man is substantially united to matter and communicates substantial being to him. Intellective souls would be multiplied numerically just as are individual men, but without being united to them substantially. These intellects would simply communicate their particular acts of understanding, willing, meriting, etc., to individual men.[152]

But if one must hold, as Godfrey certainly does, that the rational soul communicates to man both his substantial and specific being, then the difficulty in accounting for this remains.[153] In brief, as Godfrey sees it, the problem concerning unicity vs. plurality of substantial form in man arises from the need to account for the fact that he is both a material and spiritual being and still essentially one. Given all of this, he suggests that it is easier to maintain that there is only one substantial form in man. Once more he observes that the arguments militating against plurality of forms in other entities also seem to obtain with respect to man. Thus, if one insists that there is some additional "natural" form that communicates being to man in distinction from his intellective soul, it would seem to follow that the intellect itself could not fulfill this function of communicating being but would have to be one and separate from all men.[154] Once more one would have fallen into the Averroistic position.

---

[151] PB 2.124. For Alexander see his *De intellectu et intellecto* which had been excerpted from his *De anima* and circulated independently in a Latin translation. For the text see G. Théry, *Autour du décret de 1210: II. Alexandre d'Aphrodise* (Le Saulchoir, Kain, 1926) pp. 74–82. Also see E. Gilson, "Les sources gréco-arabes de l'augustinisme avicennisant," *Archives d'Histoire Doctrinale et Littéraire du Moyen Age* 4 (1929), pp. 7–15. For Averroes see his *In III de anima*, c. 5, F. Stuart Crawford, ed. (Cambridge, Mass., 1953), pp. 401–07. For Averroes's critique of Alexander see pp. 393–95.

[152] PB 2.124.

[153] *Ibid.*

[154] *Ibid.*

With all of this in mind, Godfrey ranks the various theories considered above as follows. That which defends unicity of form in all entities is more probable. Those which defend plurality of forms in all material entities are more improbable. That which defends duality of forms in man alone is less improbable, since it postulates that which is less probable (plurality of forms) in fewer beings and since man is obviously quite different from other material composites. But this third theory is more difficult to defend since it must contend with objections raised by each of the other positions, unicity of form in all and plurality of forms in all.[155]

In his considerably later Quodlibet 10, q. 10 Godfrey again comments on the difficulty involved in arriving at any definitive solution with respect to this issue. He continues to regard as more probable among the plurality positions the one which restricts this to man, but with the precision to which reference has been made above. He acknowledges that he had previously maintained and still maintains that unicity of substantial form in man may be defended as probable. But he refuses to commit himself definitively either to unicity or to duality of forms in man.[156] Given his conviction that a material being that is substantially one cannot arise but from the union of prime matter and the single substantial form that communicates to it its first substantial act, one might wonder why Godfrey refuses to adopt the unicity theory more decisively.[157] So hesitant is he, in fact, that Zavalloni has described his

---

155 *Ibid.* ". . . videtur probabilior positio quae ponit tantum unam in omnibus, improbabilior quae plures in omnibus, minus improbabilis autem quae tantum in homine ponit plures . . ."

156 See PB 4.344. See in particular: "Et ideo semper fuit perplexitas circa hominem de hoc articulo et apud philosophos et apud theologos catholicos propter ignorantiam naturae rationalis animae et modi quo unibilis est materiae. Propter quod ego etiam super hoc nec scio nec audeo aliquid diffinire, licet mihi visum fuerit alias et adhuc videatur circa istum articulum quod probabiliter possit sustineri quod non sit nisi una forma substantialis in homine, scilicet anima rationalis omnes praecedentes virtute continens." Also see PB 4.347. "Quamvis autem non asseram in homine plures formas esse nec etiam contrarium . . ."

157 Note the following comment in Godfrey's Q 6, q. 14: "Sed quia circa hoc sunt diversae opiniones, cum quidam ponunt plures formas substantiales simul in eodem, quod non videtur posse esse, quia sicut materia in genere substantiae est ens in potentia simpliciter, ita etiam quaelibet forma substantialis est actus simpliciter et ideo dat esse simpliciter; propter quod videtur quod unum ens simpliciter non possit habere nisi unam formam quae sit de genere substantiae" (PB 3.248). In this discussion ("Utrum anima humana tota producitur in esse in fine generationis") Godfrey goes on to answer the question under the supposition that there is only one substantial form in man. For some reason he does not find it necessary to express any reservations about that position in this context. See PB 3.247–49.

position on this matter as "skeptical."[158] Be that as it may, philosophical and especially metaphysical considerations certainly made him favor the doctrine of unicity of form in man. But, as we shall now see, theological concerns seem to have prevented him from taking a more definite stand.

D. THEOLOGICAL DIFFICULTIES

In Quodlibet 2, q. 7 Godfrey introduces his consideration of some of these theological issues with a call for moderation. He observes that certain arguments have been introduced into this discussion insofar as they are alleged to touch on matters of faith. But he remarks that it is not immediately obvious that all of these issues do pertain to the faith. Hence, one should not lightly assert that this or that position is contrary to faith. As Godfrey also notes, objections of this kind had been raised in particular against the theory of unicity of substantial form in man. But insofar as he himself can determine, this doctrine has not been shown to be contrary to faith. Given this, he maintains that it can be defended as at least probable in itself. Still, he will not reject the opposed position (which defends plurality of forms in man) as either impossible or erroneous.[159] While he regards unicity of form in man as probable and while he is prepared to defend unicity of form in all other material entities, he would accept the doctrine of plurality of forms in man should more convincing argumentation be offered for it or should some future determination by the Church concerning the body of Christ or some other religious doctrine require this.[160]

He then turns to certain objections against the doctrine of unicity of form in man to which he had referred at the beginning of Quodlibet 2, q. 7. According to some this doctrine runs counter to sense experience, to reason, and

---

[158] *Op. cit.*, pp. 296–97. Zavalloni comments that Godfrey's attitude is marked by a certain skepticism both on the metaphysical and psychological levels, although it is more definite on the cosmological level. Zavalloni recognizes that the primary reason for his perplexity is theological. Gilson is more reluctant to style Godfrey's position "skepticism." See his *History of Christian Philosophy* . . . , pp. 419–20. He, too, stresses Godfrey's theological concerns in this issue. Also see De Wulf, *Un théologien-philosophe* . . . , pp. 114–15; Bayerschmidt, *op. cit.*, pp. 277–78.

[159] PB 2.125–26.

[160] PB 2.126. Note in particular: ". . . ideo etiam volo asserere in aliis ab homine non posse esse nisi unam formam, paratus tenere determinate in homine esse plures formas, si appareant aliae rationes efficaciores, vel si ex determinatione Ecclesiae determinetur aliquid circa corpus Christi esse tenendum quod nondum est determinatum . . ."

to faith. In considering each of these charges Godfrey now connects the first and the third with alleged difficulties pertaining to the faith. As regards the first point, it is argued that sense experience indicates that the same accidents are present in a dead body as were in it when it was living. Thus, the same accidents must remain in the living and in the dead body of Christ. But this seems to presuppose that some substantial form remains the same in both.[161]

Godfrey acknowledges that some maintain that certain common accidents do remain numerically the same before and after the substantial change of their subject. But he rejects this as unlikely and rather proposes that when a new substantial form is introduced into matter, numerically distinct accidents must also be introduced. The cause responsible for the generation of the new substantial composite and for the corruption of the preceding one will also account for the coming into being of these new accidents. For Godfrey this is consistent with his doctrine on the need for and the role of previous dispositions in preparing matter to receive a new substantial form. Granted that there is a resolution to prime matter (according to the doctrine of unicity of form) in the course of substantial change, the previous dispositions will have prepared matter to receive a new form sufficiently like the preceding one to support similar but not numerically identical accidents.[162]

Before turning to the third objection, one that is properly theological, Godfrey considers the second charge, that the doctrine of unicity of form is contrary to reason. In this particular argument it is contended that distinct forms must correspond to the distinct agencies involved in man's generation, the divine and the human.[163] The reader will, of course, recognize the thinking of Henry of Ghent. Against this contention Godfrey counters that one may preserve a role for each level of agency within the theory of unicity of form. The natural or human agent will prepare for the coming of the spiritual soul by disposing the preexisting matter. But since of themselves such agents are incapable of producing a spiritual soul, God then intervenes and, by taking the place, as it were, of any purely natural agent, produces the composite man by concreating the rational soul in the matter which has been properly disposed.[164]

In cases of purely material generation it is true that while producing a new matter-form composite a natural agent also corrupts the preceding substantial form and the accompanying accidents. In the generation of man, however,

---

[161] PB 2.96, 126.

[162] PB 2.126. Also see Ch. V, Corollary 2, for Godfrey's denial that numerically one and the same accident can exist in different subjects in the natural order.

[163] See PB 2.96.

[164] PB 2.127.

God himself does this in this way, that in the course of producing the composite of matter and the soul, *per accidens* he also corrupts the preceding imperfect composite of matter and the previous substantial form. Godfrey is concerned with assuring that even in the production of man the generation of one composite does involve the corruption of the preceding one. In addition, he wishes to show that a proper role for human agency has also been preserved, and assigns to this the introduction of dispositions which prepare matter to receive the intellective or rational soul. He also suggests that purely natural agency then introduces certain new accidental dispositions into the newly generated human composite which will inhere therein as in their proper subject. Those dispositions and accidents which pertain to man only by reason of his spiritual soul, on the other hand, will be due to the divine cause of that soul itself.[165]

The third objection is strictly theological. If there is only one substantial form in man, then during the time that Christ's body was in the tomb it would not have been numerically identical with his living body.[166] Reference has already been made above to the sensitive nature of this issue during the controversy concerning plurality of forms in man. Godfrey begins his rebuttal of this objection against unicity of form in man with the comment that all the religious authorities that may be cited in favor of the continued identity of the living and dead body of Christ should be applied in the same way to other men as well. Thus, since both Christ and the thieves on the cross died at approximately the same time, Godfrey does not think it proper to suggest that the dead body of Christ differed in species from the dead bodies of the thieves. All of these bodies were identical in species when living. Here he is urging that one be consistent. One should not insist that Christ's body was numerically one and the same when living and dead unless one will admit this of all others as well.[167]

Moreover, continues Godfrey, one need not appeal to a form of corporeity

---

[165] PB 2.127–28. See PB 2.129–31 for further discussion of philosophical difficulties that might be raised against unicity of form in man.

[166] For the objection see PB 2.96. In that same context Godfrey also refers to another objection against the unicity position allegedly following from the doctrine of the Eucharist. If there is only one substantial form in Christ, then the substance of bread will be changed into matter alone in the Eucharist or else into the composite of matter and the soul. But the soul will be said to be present therein only *per concomitantiam*. For Godfrey's rather brief reply to this see PB 2.133. Also see Bayerschmidt, *Die Seins-und Formmetaphysik. . .* , pp. 271–72. This alleged difficulty is obviously far less serious in Godfrey's eyes than the one having to do with the identity of Christ's body when living and when dead.

[167] PB 2.131.

that would be common to the living and dead body of Christ in order to account for the fact that it did not undergo corruption in the tomb. His body might have been preserved from corruption in the same way the bodies of certain saints have been. Or, since the time between Christ's death and resurrection was relatively brief and since his body had been anointed with certain preservatives, one might suggest that it was preserved even without appealing to any such miracle.[168]

But, one might counter, how is one to avoid the conclusion that during the *sacrum triduum* a new form was introduced into the matter of Christ's body and hence that during that period a new hypostatic union obtained, one between his separated soul and the Word, and another between this new composite of form and matter and the Word? Godfrey agrees that one must not hold that during this period Christ assumed a new nature. But he does not find it unacceptable to admit that during this time a new kind of union was in some way perfected, though not a new assumption of nature. Thus, all would admit that much new matter was added to Christ's body through nourishment since the moment of his conception in Mary's womb. This is not to say that such nourishment was in itself assumed by the Word, but only that it was united to that preexisting matter which was a part of the assumed human nature and hence united to the divine supposit. So, too, one might hold, according to the doctrine of unicity of form, that the single soul or form and the matter which it perfected during Christ's life remained united to the Word during the period in the tomb, even though a new form was also introduced into that matter during its separation from his (Christ's) soul. Since this new form would have been united to matter only as the perfection of that matter which was directly and primarily united with the Word, then, by way of consequence the new form would also be so united.[169]

In this context Godfrey takes care to indicate that he does not propose the above as definitive, but only wishes to comment that he does not see why the question at issue cannot be so explained. He judges it as impossible for the living and dead body of Christ or of any other man to be numerically identical as it would be for wine and vinegar to be numerically the same. Just as vinegar does not contain the same substantial form as the wine from which it was produced, so too the same substantial form cannot be found in a dead body as in a living one unless one is willing to admit that it is the

---

[168] PB 2.131. See in particular: "Nulla ergo videtur necessitas hoc ponendi specialiter in Christo, esto quod in eo sint duae formae, si in aliis hoc non ponatur."

[169] PB 2.131–32. Also see Bayerschmidt, *op. cit.*, pp. 269–70. For the same see Q 3, q. 5 (PB 2.209–11).

form of the living and the dead simultaneously. And if, according to the doctrine of unicity of substantial form, the body of Christ was not numerically one and the same when living and when dead by reason of one and the same substantial form, it would still be one in another sense by reason of its continuing union with the divine supposit.[170]

Godfrey returns to this same problem in Quodlibet 3, q. 5, where he wonders whether it is erroneous to state that the dead body of Christ and those of other deceased persons are to be described as bodies only equivocally, that is, as differing not merely numerically from one another but even in species.[171] Once more Godfrey urges that this point be discussed with moderation and notes its connection with the dispute concerning unicity vs. plurality of forms in man. One must beware of presenting as certain and necessary on theological grounds something that is, in fact, still open to discussion by believers. But he also comments that if something is clearly determined as following from the faith, then it must be defended as certain no matter how greatly it differs from what philosophers have held on the same point.[172]

Godfrey observes that the doctrine of unicity of substantial form in man and hence in Christ is thought by some to be contrary to faith, and by others to be in harmony with it. In his discussion in Quodlibet 2, q. 7, earlier in this same year, 1286, he had as he here recalls, refused to define or determine either position (unicity or plurality) as true or to reject either as false or impossible. He had only maintained that the doctrine which defends unicity of form in man as well as in all other composite entities may be defended as probable and that the arguments to the contrary may also be resolved in probable fashion.[173] Since the strongest arguments offered by some for unicity of form in other entities also seem to apply to man, Godfrey now comments that just as he neither asserted nor now asserts that there is only one form in man, so too he neither has asserted nor now asserts that there is only one substantial form in other entities![174] This final observation is surprising in

---

[170] PB 2.132.

[171] "Utrum dicere quod corpus Christi mortuum et alterius hominis mortuum fuerit corpus aequivoce sit erroneum" (PB 2.194). For the short version of this question see PB 2.312–16.

[172] See PB 2.195–96.

[173] PB 2.197.

[174] "Et quia potissimae et efficacissimae rationes quibus ab aliquibus ponitur tantum una forma in igne vel in lapide eandem habent efficaciam in homine et in quocumque alio composito, ideo sicut non asserui quod in homine non sit nisi una forma substantialis nec assero, ita etiam nec asserui nec assero quod in aliis non sit nisi una

light of fairly clear indications in Quodlibet 2, q. 7 that he does there defend unicity of form in nonhuman material entities.[175] One wonders whether Godfrey's memory of his earlier statements has become clouded or whether there is perhaps some textual problem, since in both questions we are restricted to *reportationes* of his lectures. In any event, in Quodlibet 3, q. 5 he continues to be extremely cautious about the doctrine of unicity of form in man and protests his willingness to embrace whichever opinion may eventually be established by convincing argumentation or else by the authority of the Church. He obviously regards the question as still open, theologically speaking, at least in Paris, and this in spite of his awareness of John Peckham's most recent condemnation of unicity of form in his role as Archbishop of Canterbury (April 30, 1286).[176]

As regards the particular point under consideration in Quodlibet 3, q. 5 (whether the body of Christ and that of the dead thief, for instance, differed in species), Godfrey comments that it must be held as certain that Christ was truly and perfectly man and therefore of the same nature as other men. Hence, because human nature bespeaks a composite of body or matter and of rational soul or form, just as Christ's soul was specifically the same as the souls of other men, so too was his body, at least when living. Accordingly, it would seem during the separation of his soul from his body that his body would still agree in species with the bodies of other deceased men, granted that it was miraculously preserved from corruption during its period in the tomb. He can think of no religious authority that would compel one to deny this

---

forma substantialis; nam non video quin dictae rationes eandem efficaciam habeant in omnibus" (PB 2.197).

[175] See the texts cited above in notes 149 and 160. In the latter text, in particular, Godfrey clearly defends unicity of form in nonhuman beings even though he would be prepared to embrace plurality of forms in man if convincing argumentation could be offered for it or if some future judgment by the Church should require it.

[176] PB 2.197–99. See p. 198 for an obvious reference to one of the articles condemned by Peckham in 1286, according to which one who wishes to teach unity of substantial form and the related articles is not bound to bow to the authority of the Pope or of Gregory or of Augustine or of similar figures or of any teacher, but only to that of the Bible and to necessary argumentation. Although such a view has been imputed to a certain Valens (Richard Knapwell), Godfrey comments that he has heard from that man's own mouth that he never stated or thought any such thing. For Peckham's revised and definitive text see his *Registrum* . . . , ed. Martin, T. III, p. 923, art. 7, and Zavalloni, p. 221, n. 25. On Godfrey's reference to Knapwell see Schneider, *Die Einheit des Menschen*, p. 99. It seems that Richard must have stopped at Paris in 1286 on his way to appeal his case in Rome. Also see Pelster, "Die Sätze . . . ," pp. 99–100; F. Roensch, *Early Thomistic School*, p. 38 and for further references, n. 107 (p. 67).

specific identity between Christ's body in the tomb and those of other dead men, and hence that would force one to conclude that some substantial form remained in Christ's body during that period which would not remain in the body of another deceased person.[177]

Whether one defends unicity of form in man or some version of plurality of forms therein, Godfrey contends that this same conclusion still follows. The dead body of Christ was one in species with the dead body of any other person. According to the unicity position, at the moment of death another substantial form would necessarily be introduced into prime matter, and this would apply both to Christ's body and to that of all other deceased men. But in the case of Christ any further process of corruption would have been prevented by special divine intervention.[178]

When Godfrey now considers this question within the context of theories that defend plurality of forms, he is especially troubled by one aspect of Henry of Ghent's position. According to Henry there are two substantial forms in man, to be sure, and at the moment of death both of these cease to be present. Not only is the intellective soul separated from the body, but the purely material form of corporeity also ceases to inform matter. But in the case of Christ's death, an exception would have occurred. Due to special divine intervention, the corporeal form would have continued to inform his matter during the *sacrum triduum*, something that is not true of other dead bodies. This, of course, implies that Christ's body while in the tomb would not be specifically the same as the bodies of other deceased persons. This position is already apparent in Henry's earlier discussions such as Quodlibet 4, q. 13, but it is interesting to observe that during the same Quodlibetal period when Godfrey was defending his Quodlibet 3, q. 5, that is, Christmas 1286, Henry presented it again in his own Quodlibet 10, q. 5.[179]

Godfrey fears that this exception, whereby the form of corporeity of Christ's body would have remained during the period in the tomb, will undermine the truly natural character of Christ's death. In fact, according to Henry's theory the purely corporeal or "natural" form is itself a disposition

---

[177] PB 2.199–201. Also see Bayerschmidt, *op. cit.*, pp. 273–74.

[178] PB 2.200–01. Note in particular: "Sed hac forma eiusdem speciei in diversis mortuis introducta, in uno potest virtute divina miraculose conservari ne etiam putrescere incipiat, cum in alio in continenti tendat ad putrefactionem, sicut dicitur de Christo respectu aliorum" (*ibid.*).

[179] For Henry's Quodlibet 4, q. 13, in addition to the references above in nn. 127–130 see fol. 113v–114r, and Bayerschmidt, *op. cit.*, pp. 228–29. For his Quodlibet 10, q. 5 see *op. cit.*, fol. 403v–413r. On this see Bayerschmidt, *op. cit.*, pp. 245–52.

towards the spiritual or "supernatural" form. To suggest that the former was preserved in Christ's body in the tomb without the latter is, therefore, to hold that it was in some way preserved in a manner contrary to its nature, in an unnatural state.[180] If, on the other hand, one admits with most pluralists that it is not necessary for the form that is immediately prior to the human soul to undergo corruption at the very moment when the soul is separated from the body, one may say the same of Christ. Granted that in other cases there will be a tendency for further corruption to set in after a period of time, in the case of Christ such would not have occurred during the *sacrum triduum*. Hence, during that time his dead body would still belong to the same species as the bodies of others recently deceased.[181] Though Godfrey has some difficulties with this version of pluralism, as regards the present issue he judges it to be less irrational in itself and to involve fewer impossibilities or unintelligible aspects than Henry's theory. Both according to this version of pluralism and according to the doctrine of unicity of form, Christ's body, when dead, was still one in species with the bodies of others recently deceased. Hence, Godfrey regards this view as more conformed to the faith than that of Henry, according to which the bodies in question would differ in species.[182]

Godfrey realizes, of course, that defenders of unicity of form in man will deny that Christ's body in the tomb was numerically identical with his living body. But they will say the same of any other corpse as well. Defenders of the general pluralistic position will defend the numerical identity of the living and dead body of Christ, as of any other human being, for a certain period after death. He is aware of Peckham's condemnation not only of unicity of form in man, but also of the view that the living and dead bodies of other men are not numerically identical.[183] After some interesting exegesis of Peckham's text, he points out that neither of these positions has been condemned as heretical and erroneous at Paris. It is here, in the passage to which ref-

---

[180] PB 2.202; 314–15 (short version). For further argumentation against Henry's position see PB 2.202–04 and 314–15 (short version); and Bayerschmidt, pp. 274–75.

[181] PB 2.204 and 314 (short version).

[182] PB 2.205 and 315 (short version).

[183] For discussion of these propositions see PB 2.205–07. Also see pp. 313–14 (short version). Godfrey here has in mind article 6 (which would deny that the dead body of any saint or any other man, before it is changed by putrefaction into dust or the elements, is numerically identical with the corresponding living body); article 8 (according to which there is only one substantial form in man, the rational soul); and article 2 (according to which at his death a new substantial form was introduced into Christ's body). For these see Peckham's *Registrum* . . . , pp. 921–23; Zavalloni, *op. cit.*, pp. 220–21.

erence has been made above, that he sharply rebukes Henry for having asserted that these articles had been so condemned there.[184]

As regards Henry's position, Godfrey comments that only one of these two views can be correct, either that which asserts that Christ's body in death belonged to the same species as did the bodies of other deceased persons at that time or the position that denies this. Hence, the other view will be false and, since it touches on a matter of faith, erroneous in the objective order. But since it is not yet clear as to which view is true and which false, no one should be condemned as culpably heretical or erroneous for defending either position.[185]

And now, in an apparent shift from his earlier and fairly sympathetic treatment of Henry's defense of duality of forms in man in Quodlibet 2, q. 7, Godfrey comments that if he were to defend plurality of forms in man he would do so in the more common way, that is, by holding for the continued numerical identity of the living and dead body in every case, not merely in the case of Christ.[186] In Quodlibet 5, q. 5 he continues to be critical of Henry's theory and his denial that Christ's body in the tomb was specifically the same as the dead bodies of others.[187] The reasons for this apparent shift with respect to Henry's position are obviously theological. By the time of his later Quodlibet 10, q. 10, Godfrey has again become more sympathetic to Henry's defense of duality of forms in man, but only with the suggested change according to which the form that comes from within and from the potentiality of matter is also the sensitive form and soul. There he is not explicitly concerned with the theological issue about the similarity between Christ's body and the bodies of others who are deceased.[188] In short, when

---

[184] PB 2.207–08; p. 314 (short version). Also see in this chapter, n. 89.

[185] PB 2.208.

[186] PB 2.209; p. 316 (short version). Note his comment in the latter context: "Et si tenerem pluralitatem formarum in eodem libentius tenerem illam quae ponit plures sic quod naturaliter una separata manet alia et in Christo et in aliis, quam illam quae ponit ambas in omnibus aliis a Christo simul desinere esse, in Christo autem solo alteram retineri alia separata."

[187] PB 3.19–20. Q 5, q. 5 is addressed to this question: "Utrum incorruptionis corporis Christi fuit causa acceleratio resurrectionis vel conservatio miraculosa alicuius formae quae prius erat in corpore vivo" (PB 3.17).

[188] See in this chapter p. 335 and notes 146–48. See in particular his remarks with reference to Henry's position: "Et quantum ad hoc utique est ista positio multum probabilis . . ." (PB 4.344); and then with reference to his corrected version of Henry's position: "Quamvis autem non asseram in homine plures formas esse nec etiam contrarium, tamen si ponerem in homine plures formas ad hunc modum ponendi, sicut puto, si possem libentius declinarem, quia magis videtur rationi et auctoritati concordari" (PB 4.347).

the theological concern is paramount in his mind, as in the discussions in Quodlibets 3 and 5, Godfrey tends to be even more critical of Henry's position. But when he focuses attention on the problem of unicity of form as such, he is somewhat more sympathetic to Henry's dualistic view of man.

While Godfrey's personal philosophical sympathies surely lie with the doctrine of unicity of form in man and in all else, his theological preoccupations clearly prevented him from giving unqualified assent to that position. On this point, then, real or imagined theological difficulties do seem to have exercised an inhibiting role on his philosophy, and this in spite of the fact that he strongly argued for one's freedom to defend unicity of form at Paris. The fact that he had to establish this right, as it were, rose from his opponents' contention that this position was heretical and erroneous. And even though he successfully challenged any claim that it had ever been so condemned at Paris, the local prohibitions at Oxford in 1277, 1284, and especially 1286, and the highly charged atmosphere surrounding the debate at Paris made of it a sensitive issue indeed. When one recalls that Giles of Rome had been "exiled" from the Paris Theology Faculty from 1278 until 1285 or thereabouts, and that ecclesiastical condemnation for heresy would entail loss of one's chair at the University, one can appreciate some of the extrinsic reasons for Godfrey's hesitation. Still, we have no reason to doubt his sincerity when he contends that the evidence, especially theological, is simply not sufficiently strong to enable him to decide this question definitively.

Chapter IX.

The Problem of Individuation

As will be recalled from our discussion in Ch. VI, Godfrey suggests in Quodlibet 7, q. 5 that one may distinguish between nature and supposit in two different ways. One may compare them as that which is signified by an abstract term, after the manner of a simple form, and that which is signified by the corresponding concrete term and as something composed. But one may also compare them as that which is signified by a general or universal term (nature) on the one hand, and by a singular or individual term, on the other. To ask whether supposit adds anything to nature when they are compared in the first way is to raise the problem of subsistence. To ask this when they are compared in the second way is to take up the problem of individuation.[1]

The fact that Godfrey differentiates between these two ways of contrasting nature and supposit is significant, for it shows that he also differentiates between the problem of subsistence and that of individuation. Not all of his contemporaries distinguished them quite so clearly. Witness, for instance, Henry of Ghent.[2] In Ch. VI we considered Godfrey's solution to the problem

[1] PB 3.300–01. Also see in our text, Ch. VI, pp. 227–28.

[2] See Paulus, *Henri de Gand . . .* , Ch. VI ("La nature, le suppôt et l'individuation"), especially pp. 329, 337–38, 341, 349, 356ff.

of subsistence. In the present chapter we shall concentrate on his discussion of the problem of individuation and his efforts to arrive at a metaphysical solution for the same.

Briefly stated, the problem amounts to this. What is the precise relationship, on the one hand, between a universal and specific nature, such as humanity or man and, on the other, the many individuals in which this nature is realized, such as this humanity or this man? Or in other words, how is one to account for the fact that a given specific and universal nature, such as man, can in fact be realized in many different individuals, each of which may be described as *a* man? One may regard it as another version of the classical problem of the One and the Many, but only as applied to the possibility of many individuals within a given class or species, not simply to the possibility of many beings within the unity of being itself. For Godfrey and many of his contemporaries the problem of individuation is particularly pressing with respect to material entities. Here, they were convinced, one finds many instances of numerical multiplication of individuals within species. Certain thinkers such as Aquinas denied that there are numerically distinct individuals within angelic species. And a word will be said later about Godfrey's views on that topic. But for the present, since he certainly agrees with his contemporaries that there may be many individuals within a given species of material entities, how is he to account for this? One can hardly identify the individual and the species on this level, of course, for that would be to fly in the face of the evidence indicating that there are numerically distinct individuals within such species. Thus one may ask, as does Godfrey, what it is that the supposit (meaning the individual) adds to the species?[3] In considering his discussion of this problem, therefore, we shall proceed according to the following order: A. The Formal Principle of Individuation; B. The Role of Quantity in Individuation; C. Individuation, Separated Souls, and Angels.

A. THE FORMAL PRINCIPLE OF INDIVIDUATION

There is considerable lack of agreement among twentieth-century scholars as to Godfrey's personal opinion on this matter. Roland-Gosselin suggests that he distinguishes between a substantial principle of individuality and an accidental one, and that for him this substantial principle is the substantial form of the composite being. He wonders whether Godfrey has failed to grasp fully the distinction between substantial unity and numerical unity.[4]

---

[3] PB 3.318–19.

[4] See his discussion in *Le "De ente et essentia" de S. Thomas d'Aquin*, p. 129.

Hocedez finds this latter distinction clarified by Godfrey's "disciple" in this discussion, that is to say, Peter of Auvergne. For the latter the form is the principle of essential unity, while quantity is the principle that distinguishes individuals among themselves and thus accounts for their numerical unity. But, according to Hocedez, Peter and Godfrey are in fundamental agreement.[5] According to De Wulf, Godfrey identifies the principle of individuation with the form.[6] But a more recent writer, Arway, suggests that De Wulf himself has here failed to distinguish between the problem of individuality and that of individuation. As regards the latter, Godfrey would have agreed with Thomas Aquinas in proposing matter as signed by dimensive quantity as the principle of individuation.[7] Evidently, there is some confusion as to Godfrey's mind on this matter and some need for clarification.

Although it is not our intent here to rewrite the history of the problem of individuation, we tend to agree with those according to whom Aristotle locates the principle or reason for the individuation of material entities in their matter. At the same time it is clear that he did not work out his theory in any detailed fashion.[8] Both Avicenna and Averroes appear to fall within this same general Aristotelian tradition with respect to this question, even though there are considerable differences between their respective solutions. Thus, while Avicenna appeals both to a form of corporeity and to determined dimensions in order to explain how matter is always capable of being considered as extended, Averroes rejects this explanation and rather has recourse to undetermined dimensions. But both have difficulty with the same problem, that is, to explain, if individuation takes place by reason of matter, how such matter can account for distinct substantial forms within the same species.[9] Thomas Aquinas's position has been carefully studied and much debated by

[5] See Hocedez, "Une question inédite de Pierre d'Auvergne sur l'individuation," *Revue Néoscolastique de Philosophie* 36 (1934), pp. 356–58.

[6] See his *Un théologien-philosophe . . .* , pp. 119–20; *idem, Histoire de la philosophie médiévale*, 6th ed., Vol. 2 (Louvain, 1936), pp. 294–95.

[7] "A Half Century of Research on Godfrey . . . ," pp. 205–06 and n. 36.

[8] On this see the remarks by Paulus in his *Henri de Gand . . .* , pp. 330–31 and his references on p. 331, n. 1 to De Corte's critique of efforts to assign to Aristotle a theory of individuation by reason of form. See M. De Corte, *La doctrine de l'intelligence chez Aristote* (Paris, 1934), pp. 198–224; Roland-Gosselin, *Le "De ente et essentia" de S. Thomas . . .* , pp. 51–55; I. Klinger, *Das Prinzip der Individuation bei Thomas von Aquin* (Vier-Türme-Verlag Münsterschwarzach, 1964), pp. 15–16.

[9] See Roland-Gosselin, *op. cit.*, pp. 59–66 (Avicenna), pp. 67–70 (Averroes); Forest, *La structure métaphysique du concret . . .* , pp. 240–43; Klinger, *Das Prinzip . . .* , pp. 16–27 (Avicenna), pp. 27–30 (Averroes).

recent scholars. There seems to be evidence of development in his thinking or at least in his terminology with respect to one aspect of his position, that is, his attitude towards the Avicennian notion of determined dimensions and the Averroistic appeal to undetermined dimensions. But he, too, clearly assigns an important role to matter in his efforts to account for individuation and struggles to explain how matter, being purely potential and undivided in itself, can be prepared to receive and distinguish substantial forms of the same species.[10]

As regards Godfrey's own approach to this issue, reference has already been made to his suggestion that when one contrasts that which is signified by a universal term and that which is signified by a concrete and singular term, one is in position to examine the problem of individuation. In this case one views that which is signified by the universal as in some way one in the conceptual order, but as capable of being participated in by various individuals. And for one to ask what it is that the individual adds to the universal when they are so contrasted is for one to inquire after the cause of individuation. Godfrey proposes to concentrate on this problem insofar as it arises with respect to material entities. By an individual he here means a particular subject (*suppositum*) that shares in such a common or universal nature, which nature either actually is or at least can be realized in other individuals.[11] Or as Godfrey also explains somewhat farther on in his discussion, one may refer to the individual as he here understands it as first substance, that is, as that which is substance in the primary and principal way and which exists in itself independently of one's understanding of it. It is of this that substance is per se and directly predicated. By species, on the other hand, one may understand second substance which is affirmed of first substance and is said to be realized in it although not as in a subject (as would be true of accidents). The difficulty, then, consists in this, to determine the precise relationship

---

[10] See Roland-Gosselin, *op. cit.*, pp. 104 – 26; Forest, *op. cit.*, pp. 243 – 57; J. Bobik, "La doctrine de saint Thomas sur l'individuation des substances corporelles," *Revue philosophique de Louvain* 51 (1953), pp. 5 – 41; *idem*, "Dimensions in the Individuation of Bodily Substances," *Philosophical Studies* 4 (1954), pp. 60 – 79. Bobik contends that there is really no opposition between Thomas's appeal to *dimensiones interminatae* on certain occasions and to *dimensiones determinatae* on others. But cf. Klinger, *op. cit.*, pp. 44 – 82, 121 – 25. For one of Thomas's finest developments of the problem see his *In De Trinitate*, Q. 4, a. 2 (B. Decker, ed., [Leiden, 1959]), pp. 142 – 43. In this text, however, he opts for undetermined dimensions (*dimensiones interminatae*) rather than determined (*terminatae*) dimensions in explaining how matter becomes *this* designated matter.

[11] PB 3.318 – 19.

between this common nature, or second substance, on the one hand, and its realization in first substance or in the individual, on the other.[12]

Closely connected with Godfrey's discussion of this problem is the distinction which he proposes, as we have already seen in Ch. I, between transcendental unity and numerical unity in the strict sense.[13] Attention to this distinction is not only crucial if one is to understand Godfrey's solution to the problem of individuation, but will, in our opinion, eliminate some of the confusion as to whether he has recourse to form or to matter or to quantity in his proposed explanation. As will be recalled from our earlier consideration of this, in Quodlibet 6, q. 16 Godfrey distinguishes between the kind of unity that is convertible with being and the kind that serves as a principle of number. He suggests that every unity may be regarded as a principle of number in some way, since multitude itself implies some kind of number. Nonetheless, in here describing the second kind of unity as a principle of number, Godfrey has in mind specifically the kind of number that is based on discrete quantity and thus falls into the genus quantity.[14]

In order to avoid confusion, therefore, and in accord with a terminological precision which we introduced into the discussion in Ch. I, we shall refer to numerical unity in the broad sense (the kind that is convertible with being) and numerical unity in the strict sense (the kind that is grounded on quantity). The first type of unity is usually described as transcendental or ontological, and this because it is to be found wherever being itself is found or, in other words, because it is convertible with being. Not only will this kind of unity (transcendental or ontological) apply to every subsisting substance, but also to every accident as well. Moreover, should one maintain that each angel is a species unto itself and thereby reject the possibility of numerical multiplicity of individuals within angelic species, every such angel will still enjoy ontological or transcendental unity. As will be recalled, Godfrey holds that it is by reason of its form that any being enjoys such ontological or transcendental unity since it is by reason of its form that it is what it is, undivided in itself, and divided from all else.[15]

The second type of unity, numerical unity in the strict sense, is not transcendental and not convertible with being, since it is present only in those entities which possess continuous quantity. And it is only by division of such continuous quantity that parts of the same class or species can arise and

---

[12] PB 3.320.
[13] See Ch. I, pp. 25 – 26.
[14] PB 3.256.
[15] PB 3.257.

hence, substances of the same class or species. Thus it is only because different parts of quantity differ from one another that numerically distinct members of the same species, for instance, numerically distinct stones, can be realized. But if substance must be subject to quantity in order to enjoy numerical unity and thus be multiplied within the same species, quantity does not receive its own numerical unity from something else superadded to it. Indeed, comments Godfrey, just as the parts into which quantity is divided are by their very nature the extension in which substance participates, so too these same parts of quantity are of themselves the numerical multiplicity (accidental multiplicity, as Godfrey here phrases it) in which substance only participates. Thus while accidental multiplicity is essential to quantity, it can be realized in other things only by something added to their essential being, that is to say, by reason of quantity.[16]

Godfrey's point here is to show that while substance must depend on quantity in order to enjoy numerical unity in the strict sense (strictly numerical unity) and thus to be multiplied numerically, such pertains to quantity by its very nature. As Godfrey himself puts it, in the case of quantity numerical unity taken broadly (transcendental or ontological unity) and strictly numerical unity do not differ really but only logically. For the essential or transcendental unity which quantity possesses of itself is or accounts for the strictly numerical and therefore accidental unity of the substance in which it inheres.[17] Godfrey can hardly maintain any other position, of course, without falling into an infinite regress. Thus, if quantity did not enjoy strictly numerical unity by its very nature, it would depend on something superadded for this and that in turn upon something else, *ad infinitum*.[18]

In this discussion of transcendental unity and strictly numerical unity Godfrey has given some important clues for a proper understanding of his explanation of the individuation of material substances. Thus he has assigned transcendental unity, the unity that is convertible with being, to every substance and, for that matter, to accidents as well. A given entity will enjoy this kind of unity, not by reason of something further that is superadded, but

---

[16] PB 3.258.

[17] PB 3.258–59. Note in particular: "Sed in quantitate non differunt realiter, sed solum secundum rationem unum quod convertitur cum ente et quod est principium numeri, quia ipsum quod est essentialiter continuitas et partibilitas quaedam secundum se indivisum quid et divisum ab aliis et sic est unum sua tali unitate essentiali ut participatur ab alio, scilicet a substantia cui accidit, est unitas accidentalis illi; unde, quod est unitas essentialis in quantitate secundum se est unitas accidentalis in substantia cui accidit."

[18] See PB 3.258.

of itself. And since in a matter-form composite it is really form that determines the matter and renders the essence definable and communicates being, he does not hesitate to suggest that it is by reason of its form that such a being enjoys transcendental unity, unity of being. But in order for a given substance to enjoy strictly numerical or "accidental" unity, it must also be quantified. Since numerical distinction of one substance from another presupposes the numerical identity of each, it is clear that Godfrey will have to appeal to quantity to account for this. In sum, then, in light of the discussion in Quodlibet 6, q. 16, it seems that Godfrey will have to turn to quantity or to matter as quantified if he is to account for numerical multiplicity of individuals within a given species or, in other words, if he is to resolve the problem of individuation.

With this background in mind we are now in position to turn once more to Quodlibet 7, q. 5. Godfrey begins his discussion with the observation that since the various individuals within a given species share in the same common or specific nature, they can hardly be differentiated by reason of that which they have in common. In other words, it seems that in addition to the nature which is implied by their membership in a given species, such individuals will include something else as well, something that will individuate that nature in each individual. Just as a genus cannot be divided into different species except by the addition of some difference that pertains to the essence of each species, it would seem to follow that a given species cannot be divided into different individuals unless each of these individuals includes something in addition to the specific nature itself. Otherwise, nothing will be found in one individual that is not also included in another, which is to say that the different individuals will not really differ from one another.[19]

Furthermore, continues Godfrey, if something must be added to the specific nature to account for the fact that it is realized in different individuals, it would seem that this superadded factor can only be something accidental. In other words, something accidental will be the principle or cause of individuation. Various authorities may be cited to this same effect, such as Porphyry, Boethius, John Damascene, and Avicenna.[20] And if this is true, it

---

[19] PB 3.318–19.

[20] PB 3.319–20. Godfrey simply refers to Porphyry without naming the work from which his citation is taken and then to Boethius's Commentary. In his Q 5, q. 8 Henry of Ghent also cites these same passages in connection with the view according to which individuals of the same species differ only by reason of accidents (*op. cit.*, fol. 165r). Godfrey's editors (PB 3.411, 412) refer the reader to Porphyry's *Commentary on the Categories* (*In Categorias Scholia in Aristotelem*), Ch. Brandis, ed. (Berlin, 1836), pp. 2a–3, and for Boethius to PL 64.105–06. Paulus also presents

will follow that the quiddity, on the one hand, and that which has such a quiddity, on the other, really differ. But this would be to imply that nature and supposit, as they are here being contrasted, also really differ and hence that there is real distinction between second substance and the corresponding first substance.[21]

On the other hand, a host of arguments militate against this suggestion that something accidental might serve as the principle of individuation. For instance, the individual or first substance is no more an accidental aggregate (*ens per accidens*) than is the species or second substance. Otherwise, the first substance or individual would not fall directly into the genus, substance, and second substance could not be essentially predicated of it. Again, individual accidents seem to be posterior to and superadded to substance. Hence, they presuppose an individuated substance insofar as they inhere in it as in their subject. Also, if one must appeal to accidents to account for the individuation of substance, how is one to avoid having recourse to additional accidents to account for the individuation of the prior accidents themselves *ad infinitum*? And, finally, there is the obvious objection that if one grounds the individuation of substances on something accidental, one thereby reduces the distinction between different substances within the same species to the purely accidental level.[22]

After presenting these and other arguments against the contention that something accidental might serve as the principle of individuation, Godfrey acknowledges that if such a function could be attributed to any accident, that accident could only be quantity. Thus other accidents, whiteness, for instance, do not seem to differ numerically from one another within the same species of themselves, but only insofar as they exist in a given surface and are extended by the extension of that same surface. Because of this they are understood to be capable of having different parts of the same kind in different parts of that surface or to be individuated. So too, if one examines material substance, matter as included therein does not of itself include anything to account for the fact that something can admit of different parts of the same

---

some references to Porphyry's *Isagoge* and to Boethius's Commentary on this (see *Henri de Gand* . . . , p. 333, n. 3). In the same respective contexts both Godfrey and Henry cite Boethius's *De Trinitate*, for which see ch. 1 in *The Theological Tractates*, Stewart – Rand, ed. (Cambridge, Mass., 1968), p. 6, 24 – 25. They then both refer to Damascene's *De duabus naturis et una persona Christi*, for which see his *De duabus in Christo voluntatibus*, PG 95.130; and to Avicenna's *Metaphysics* V, for which see *op. cit.*, fol. 89rb.

[21] PB 3.320.

[22] PB 3.320 – 21.

kind or be individuated. Matter of itself is one and indivisible. The same seems to be true of any given substantial form. It is only insofar as one views a given substantial form as received in quantified or extended matter that one can explain the fact that individual instances of that form may be received in different parts of that matter. Hence, it would seem that the strictly numerical differentiation and the individuation both of substances and of accidents in some way rests upon quantity.[23]

But Godfrey also finds this suggestion unacceptable. If quantity is really the cause of individuation, it can only be such by serving as its efficient or final or material or formal cause. He quickly dismisses any suggestion that quantity is the efficient or the final cause of individuation. It cannot serve as its material cause because the subject or substance composed of matter and substantial form is itself the matter or material cause of quantity, its accident, and not vice versa.[24] But perhaps quantity is the formal cause of individuation? This suggestion will not do since it would then follow that the formal principle that differentiates one individual substance from another within the same species is only something accidental. In that case the two individuals would not differ substantially from one another, but only accidentally. They would be two in terms of quantity, or on the accidental level, but not in terms of their substantial reality. They would not be two but only one substance.[25] In other words, Godfrey fears that one will fall into a kind of monism of the species if one proposes quantity as the cause of individuation. This he cannot admit since he is convinced that two individual members of the same species, such as Socrates and Plato, differ not only in terms of quantity but also in terms of substance. As he also phrases it, if two things are accidentally distinct from one another, one accidental form will not be formally identical with the other. So too, if two substances really differ from one another, then the substantial form of one cannot be formally identical with that of the other.[26] And as he has argued above, it seems that accidents must be individuated by their respective substances rather than vice versa. But if this is so, how can quantity formally individuate the substance in which it inheres? For substance itself is prior, at least in the order of reality, to quantity.[27]

At this point Godfrey appears to have reached an impasse. On the one hand, he has denied that the principle of individuation can be the essential

---

[23] PB 3.322.

[24] PB 3.322.

[25] PB 3.322–23.

[26] PB 3.323.

[27] *Ibid.*

nature that is common to all individual members of a given species. On the other hand, he has now eliminated the possibility of making any accident, even quantity, the principle of individuation. He now recalls that there are individual immaterial substances as well as individual material ones. It is clear enough that in immaterial beings there can be no appeal to quantity to account for the fact that they are individuals. Hence, the cause of their individuation is rather the indivision of their form into other forms of the same kind. Given this, he now suggests that even in material beings that form whereby the individual is what it is and subsists is also its principle of individuation. For something is undivided and one in itself through that whereby it is what it is. And in material entities this is still their form.[28]

It will be recalled from our discussion above of Godfrey's Quodlibet 6, q. 16 that he there maintains that substantial form is the principle of transcendental or ontological unity, that is to say, the unity convertible with being. He has now proposed form as the principle of individuation as well. This undividedness from itself or ontological unity which a composite substance enjoys by reason of its form is prior in the order of nature to any of its accidents. Hence it is also prior to any kind of division that might pertain to that substance by reason of an accident. And insofar as matter is in potency to the form whereby it exists in act, matter, too, is in potency to this same undividedness that comes to the composite by reason of its form. To that extent, continues Godfrey, matter, too, is a principle of individuation insofar as it is a kind of principle, that is, a subject, for its substantial form.[29]

Now, in line with the doctrine he had presented in Quodlibet 6, q. 16, Godfrey concentrates in Quodlibet 7, q. 5 on the fact that material substances may be multiplied within their species. Granted that material substance considered simply in itself is undivided into many individuals of the same kind or species, it is capable of such division, and this insofar as it is in potency to quantity. Thus, just as it is rendered quantified by means of the accident quantity, so too it is divided into many such substances within the same species by means of this same accident. Godfrey recalls that strictly numerical unity arises from quantity. Hence, that is numerically one which is undivided in terms of that nature whereby it is distinguished from others within the same species. But the principle whereby something enjoys such numerical unity in the strict sense is quantity.[30]

---

[28] PB 3.323–24.
[29] PB 3.324.
[30] *Ibid.*

With this background in mind, Godfrey distinguishes between the principle of strictly numerical unity, on the one hand, and the principle of individuation, on the other. While quantity is the principle of numerical unity in the strict sense, it is rather the substantial form whereby something exists in reality that serves as its principle of individuation. Hence, as regards material entities one cannot identify the principle of individuation and the principle of strictly numerical unity. In purely immaterial substances the form is the principle of individuation, to be sure. But since such substances do not enjoy strictly numerical unity, there is no principle of such numerical unity in them. In material substances, on the other hand, there is both individuation and strictly numerical unity.[31] Corresponding to these, as we have seen, are two distinct principles, substantial form and quantity.

B. THE ROLE OF QUANTITY IN INDIVIDUATION

It follows from the above, then, that Godfrey not only appeals to the substantial form of a material substance to account for its ontological or transcendental unity. Since material entities are multiplied within their species, the substantial form of any such being will also serve as its formal principle of individuation. For it is by reason of its form that each such individual is undivided in itself and divided from all others. And if quantity is the principle of strictly numerical unity in any such being, quantity will also play some role in individuation.

Godfrey now attempts to determine more precisely the function of quantity in the individuation of material substances. He has, of course, refused to make of it the formal principle of individuation. Nor, as we have seen, will he permit one to regard quantity as the material cause of individuation. Still, in order for numerically distinct substantial forms of the same kind to be received into matter, matter itself must be divided. And it is quantity that renders matter divisible. It is because of this that such substances not only differ ontologically or transcendentally from one another through the multiplication of the kind of unity that is convertible with being, but also numerically and accidentally through the multiplication of strictly numerical unity, the unity that results from quantity. With this in mind Godfrey now suggests that quantity's role in individuation must in some way be reduced to that of matter insofar as quantity itself prepares or disposes matter to be divided into different parts. In other words, it seems that quantity serves as a material dispositive cause of individuation.[32]

---

[31] *Ibid.*

[32] PB 3.325–26.

Godfrey finds support both in Aristotle and in Averroes for this contention that matter is in some way the cause of such distinction and individuation.[33] But, as Averroes points out in his *De substantia orbis*, because matter is of itself indivisible, it cannot receive different forms unless it is rendered divisible by something else that is divisible of itself, that is to say, quantity.[34] In other words, it is only insofar as matter is understood to be subject to quantity that it enjoys extension and divisibility into parts of the same kind. And it is only insofar as matter itself is extended and divided into parts that numerically different forms of the same kind or species can be received therein or that such forms can be numerically differentiated from one another. And it is only because of this, of course, that such composite entities can be individuated. Godfrey concludes that quantity's role in such division of matter and hence, in individuation, reduces to the realm of material causality. This is not to say that quantity itself is the material cause either of the composite or of individuation, but rather that quantity disposes matter so as to render it extended, divisible, and capable of accounting for the extension and division of the resulting composite entity.[35]

Godfrey must now introduce some additional clarifications. One might think that he is assigning priority to quantity and dimensions vis à vis matter in his account of individuation and therefore that they exist "before" the matter-form composite does in which they inhere. In addressing himself to this issue he refers both to undetermined and to determined dimensions. And this raises the question as to which kind of dimensions enter into individuation.

As regards the first point, Godfrey denies that dimensions are presupposed in matter in such fashion as to be prior in nature either to the matter itself or to the form of the individuated composite entity. They are prior to matter only in the sense that they are required in order to allow for matter's divisibility into different parts of the same kind. In order to clarify this he recalls that two different causes may be prior to one another according to different orders of causality at one and the same time. Thus matter as present in a given composite may be regarded as prior to substantial form insofar as it receives the form and is presupposed by it. Hence matter is prior in the order

---

[33] PB 3.326. For Aristotle see *Metaphysics* XII, c. 8 (1074a 33–34); *Metaphysics* VII, c. 8 (1034a 6–8), instead of *Metaphysics* V, as Godfrey's text states. Godfrey also cites Averroes's commentary on the passage from *Metaphysics* VII, for which see *In VII Met.*, Vol. 8, fol. 178va.

[34] See PB 3.326, where Godfrey refers to the *De substantia orbis*, c. 1 (Venice, 1562), Vol. 9, fol. 3vb–4ra.

[35] PB 3.326.

of material causality. But the form itself is prior in nature to matter insofar as it is nobler and more perfect and insofar as it gives being to matter. In other words, form is prior in the order of formal causality. So too, reasons Godfrey, undetermined dimensions may be viewed as prior to the substantial form insofar as matter itself is presupposed by the form in the order of material causality and insofar as it is only by reason of quantity (and dimensions) that matter can be prepared to receive different forms of the same type.[36]

Immediately thereafter Godfrey remarks that the same will be true of a given corporeal composite that is in fact actualized by its substantial form. Its matter will be rendered divisible only insofar as it is subject to quantity and to dimensions, to be sure, but to *determined* dimensions. Again his main concern is to show that insofar as an accident such as quantity with its determined dimensions formally causes a given effect, here the division of matter into parts, then it may be regarded as prior to matter in that order, formal causality. But insofar as this particular matter-form composite is the subject of this same quantity and its determined dimensions, then the composite will be prior to quantity and its determined dimensions in the order of material causality.[37]

By undetermined dimensions Godfrey presumably has in mind the three dimensions without any further specification as to their precise limits. In accounting for the original divisibility of matter that is required for it to receive and to individuate a given substantial form in distinction from all other substantial forms of the same species, he has appealed to these undetermined dimensions. As he explains in Quodlibet 11, q. 3, undetermined quantity or undetermined dimensions will be sufficient to render matter divisible into different parts capable of receiving different substantial forms.[38] Averroes's appeal to undetermined dimensions may have influenced him on

[36] PB 3.327. Here, in language that reminds one of Averroes, Godfrey seems to be viewing prime matter abstractly and in itself, as it would be if it lacked all form. So considered it is undivided. In order for it to be divided it must be rendered divisible by quantity and thus must be viewed as subject to quantity and dimensions, but to undetermined dimensions. This is not to imply that it ever exists as such without some substantial form but as actualized by undetermined dimensions. See PB 3.327–28. Also see Q 11, q. 3 (PB 5.13–14). See his citation on p. 327 of Averroes's *De substantia orbis, ed. cit.*, fol. 3vb–4ra. On this in Averroes see Roland-Gosselin, *op. cit.*, pp. 68–69.

[37] PB 3.327. See PB 3.335, 336.

[38] See PB 5.13–15. Note in particular: "Dicitur autem indeterminata, quia ad hoc solum requiritur in materia ut eam simpliciter reddat divisibilem et plurificabilem non sic determinate vel sic" (PB 5.13).

this question.[39] And Godfrey may have realized that the given dimensions of any material composite may vary considerably during that body's duration. As Aquinas had remarked in his *Commentary* on the *De Trinitate* of Boethius, were one to appeal to determined dimensions to account for the individuation of a given material body, one might thereby compromise the continuing numerical identity of that body.[40] Nonetheless, dimensions are always in fact realized in a given entity as *these* dimensions, that is, as of this given length and this given width and this given depth, hence as determined. Thus when Godfrey concentrates on a given material substance insofar as it exists as this individual substance, he refers to its dimensions as determined.[41]

As regards the causes of individuation, Godfrey has obviously assigned an important role to quantity. But he has insisted throughout this discussion that it cannot be regarded as the formal cause of individuation. Its formal cause is rather the substantial form that exists in one substance as undivided in itself and as divided and distinguished from forms found in other individual members of the same species. The material cause of individuation is matter, to be sure; not simply of itself, however, but only insofar as it is disposed by undetermined quantity (quantity under undetermined dimensions) so as to be divisible into different parts of the same kind. The efficient cause of individuation is the agent that produces from properly disposed matter something that is undivided in itself and divided from all others of the same species.[42] While quantity is not the formal cause of individuation, it is the formal cause of matter's divisibility into different parts of the same kind. As regards individuation, therefore, quantity's causality is mediate rather than immediate. And it apparently is of the material dispositive order, for it enters into individuation as such only by enabling matter to serve as the material cause of the same.[43]

Two problems remain for Godfrey in his account of individuation. Since he has assigned some role to quantity therein, how is he to avoid reducing the difference between different substances of one and the same species to the purely accidental level? Secondly, since he initiated this discussion by contrasting nature and supposit as the universal and the individual, must he not acknowledge that supposit when understood as signifying the individual adds something real to nature when the latter is taken as signifying the universal?

---

[39] See his reference to Averroes's *De substantia orbis* in Q 7, q. 5 as indicated above in n. 36, and to the "Commentator" again in Q 11, q. 3 (PB 5.13).

[40] See his *In de Trinitate*, Qu. 4, a. 2 (ed. Decker), p. 143:10–14.

[41] See PB 3.335.

[42] PB 3.328–29.

[43] See PB 3.325–26. Also see PB 3.336.

As regards the first point, Godfrey is well aware of the difficulty. He has agreed with Averroes's remark in his *De substantia orbis* that one must appeal to quantity in order to account for the fact that matter may be divided into different parts and thereby receive different forms of one and the same species. Nonetheless, one such resulting composite substance will differ from another of the same species not only accidentally but formally and substantially. This follows, reasons Godfrey, because such a substance is really extended and divided from all others both with respect to its matter and its form. In his assertion that such a substance differs from others within the same species substantially (*substantialiter*), Godfrey apparently wishes to stress the point that it is numerically distinct from the others not merely in terms of its quantity but in terms of its substantial reality, including both its matter and its substantial form. Hence its substance is not numerically identical with the substance of the others.[44]

Godfrey has also referred to such substances as differing from one another formally (*formaliter*). One might conclude from such a remark that if two such individuals differ formally, they cannot belong to the same species. Godfrey replies that if two things differ in terms of their forms when the latter are viewed simply in and of themselves, then the two entities will also differ in species. But if two beings differ in terms of their forms only according to the being which such forms enjoy as received in matter and not insofar as they are viewed in themselves apart from matter, then they will differ in number, to be sure, but not in species.[45] In sum, as regards the first difficulty, Godfrey insists that two material substances which belong to the same species differ numerically from one another, and in such fashion that they may also be said to differ substantially and formally. This is really to make the point that one such substance is not to be identified with any other, since the first is this individual substance with its own matter and its own form. Nevertheless, since the same kind of substantial form will be present in both, they will not differ specifically.[46]

Finally, as regards the second difficulty, when supposit is taken as signifying an individual within the genus substance or as first substance, it will not include anything in its essential content (*ratio*) that does not pertain to

---

[44] ". . . partes divisae substantiae sunt substantiae plures formaliter et differentes substantialiter. . . . Quamvis ergo substantia extensionem et divisibilitatem praedictam habeat formaliter a quantitate quae est accidens, tamen, quia ipsa substantia quantum ad materiam et formam realiter extenditur et etiam dividitur . . . vere et etiam realiter habent partes substantiae differentiam substantialem formaliter formalitate substantiae" (PB 3.328).

[45] PB 3.332.

[46] PB 3.332–33.

the essential content of substance as such. Granted that the individual substance will not enjoy actual existence apart from its quantity, its quantity is not included within its essential content. Consequently, reasons Godfrey, it seems to follow that whatever nature denotes primarily and directly when it is signified by a universal term will also be denoted by the term "supposit" when the latter is taken as expressing a corresponding individual substance. And this will be true whether nature and supposit, when contrasted as the universal and the individual, are compared as the abstract and the abstract (as humanity and Socrates-ness, for instance), or as the concrete and the concrete (as man and as Socrates, for example). Thus, just as the term "humanity" signifies something consisting of flesh and bones without also signifying those undetermined accidents such as quantity and quality with which it must be conjoined in reality, so too "this humanity" or "Socrates-ness" signifies something consisting of a determined soul and body without also signifying the determined accidents with which it must be united in reality. The same holds for the terms "man" and "Socrates." Those determined accidents without which the individual, Socrates, can never exist in reality are not included within his essential content any more than the corresponding undetermined accidents are included within the essential content or definition of the species, man.[47]

The above follows, insists Godfrey, because the species or second substance is predicated of the individual or first substance *per se* and essentially. He turns to Aristotle's *Metaphysics* VII for added support for his position. In things which exist *per se* there is no distinction between the quiddity or essence, on the one hand, and that which has the quiddity or essence, that is to say, the individual, on the other. It is clear, continues Godfrey, that in the text in question Aristotle means by that which has quiddity first substance or the supposit and by the quiddity itself the species or definition which is an expression of the essence of that species. In other words, the substance which is described as quiddity and the substance which is referred to as an individual are really one and the same. Hence, when nature and supposit are compared as the universal and the individual, the supposit or the individual does not add anything real to nature or the universal in terms of its direct and primary meaning or its denotation.[48]

C. INDIVIDUATION, SEPARATED SOULS, AND ANGELS

Against the background of Godfrey's account of the individuation of material substances, difficulties would seem to arise for him both with respect

---

[47] PB 3.329–30.

[48] PB 3.330. See *Metaphysics* VII, c. 6, especially 1031b 18ff.

to separated souls and angels. As we have seen in Ch. VII, Godfrey rejects the presence of matter either in the separated soul or in the angel.[49] But in the present discussion he has appealed to matter as subject to quantity in order to allow for individuation in the sense that this implies numerical multiplicity of individuals within species. One might wonder how he is to account for numerical differentiation and individuation of the human soul in its state of separation from the body. And one might also wonder whether he defends numerical multiplicity of angels within species.

As regards the first question, the numerical differentiation and individuation of the human soul in its state of separation from the body, Godfrey does, of course, defend the survival of the individual soul, a point which has already been discussed in some detail in Ch. VI. Granted that the separated soul does not enjoy the fullness of its natural perfection in its state of separation, it does, according to Godfrey, retain its natural aptitude and inclination to exist in its body.[50] He also touches on this issue in Quodlibet 6, q. 16. Because of its natural inclination for its body, the separated soul is not to be regarded as on a par with separate substances such as angels. Human souls were originally created as forms of their given bodies and multiplied and individuated accordingly. Godfrey insists that in their state of separation such souls retain the numerical differentiation and individuation they originally enjoyed when united with their bodies, even though he concedes that it is difficult to understand and explain fully how this happens.[51]

In his final Quodlibet 15, q. 10 Godfrey briefly returns to this issue again, this time in the course of refuting one of Gonsalvus of Spain's arguments for matter-form composition of souls. Without such composition, reasons Gonsalvus, separated souls would not be numerically distinct from one another.[52]

---

[49] On matter-form composition in angels and separated souls see Ch. VII-D, pp. 278–85.

[50] See Ch. VI-C, pp. 246–49.

[51] PB 3.256: ". . . sicut etiam anima rationalis separata non est sic pure ens metaphysicum, sicut intelligentiae vel angeli, propter naturalem habitudinem et inclinationem ad corpus naturale quod includit dispositiones materiales et naturales . . ." Also: "Hoc tamen non obstante, ponuntur plures animae numero differentes; sed hoc dicitur fieri ex eo quod diversorum corporum numero differentium sunt formae cum quibus etiam huiusmodi individuationem sive numeralem distinctionem consequuntur" (PB 3.259). Also see: "Quantumcumque tamen sit difficile hoc intelligere, tamen de animabus simpliciter hoc est tenendum" (*ibid.*).

[52] For Godfrey's presentation of this argument see PB 14.54. Both in Godfrey's text and in Gonsalvus's exposition of the same in his *Disputed Question* 11 this is only a small part of a longer and more complicated argument. For Gonsalvus see *Quaestiones disputatae . . . , ed. cit.*, pp. 215–16, and for a discussion of the same in both Gonsalvus and Godfrey see our "Godfrey of Fontaines: the Date of Quodlibet 15," pp. 326–28.

In reply to this Godfrey comments, first of all, that numerical plurality (and therefore individuation, presumably) does not result from matter except insofar as the latter is quantified. In order to account for the continued numerical differentiation of separated souls, Godfrey then proposes two alternatives. One might account for this by appealing to the different relationships of such souls to different instances of matter as diversified by quantity. Presumably, he means by this that such relationships or inclinations endure within the separated souls themselves. Or one might account for this by postulating a certain potentiality within every such form, that is, any form that is designed by nature to inform matter. By reason of this potentiality within such a form or soul the latter would have been and would continue to be numerically differentiated, individuated, and multiplied.[53] Godfrey's explanation is extremely brief, to be sure, and he expresses no special preference for one explanation over the other. He appears to be content that either will suffice to account for the continued individuation of the human soul after death and that neither requires that one postulate any kind of spiritual matter in the soul. But his failure to go into this matter in greater detail here is not too surprising in light of his earlier reference in Quodlibet 6, q. 16 to the difficulty involved in understanding this issue.

Even this explanation will be of no help in the case of separate substances or angels, as Godfrey is well aware. Thus in Quodlibet 6, q. 16 he observes that it is even more difficult to understand how there can be many angels which differ only numerically rather than specifically than it is to account for numerical multiplicity of separated souls. Nonetheless, he remarks that one must not deny that angels or separate substances can be multiplied within the same species because of a certain prohibited article. Here he is clearly referring to Stephen Tempier's condemnation of 1277.[54] And in Quodlibet 7, q. 5 he observes in passing that one cannot account for the individuation or the multiplication of separate entities within the same species by appealing to the complex explanation he had given there of individuation of material substances. He limits himself in passing to the observation that he does not

---

[53] PB 14.55. Note in particular: ". . . dicendum quod non differunt numero per materiam remanentem in animabus separatis, sed vel per habitudinem ad diversas materias per quantitatem diversificatas, vel per hoc quod in omni forma quae nata est esse in materia est potentialitas per quam nata est habere talem plurificationem."

[54] Immediately following the last quotation cited in n. 51 above Godfrey comments: "sed magis est difficile intelligere quomodo possunt esse plures angeli numero differentes; quod tamen hoc sit possibile non est omnino negandum secundum quod dicit quidam articulus quo contrarium condemnatur" (PB 3.259).

know whether such can be accounted for in some other way, although he does not deny that such may be possible.[55]

In brief, by rejecting any kind of matter-form composition in angels and separate substances, Godfrey would seem to have undermined any possibility of allowing for numerical multiplication of such beings within species. But two of the propositions condemned by Stephen Tempier in 1277 directly bear upon this. Thus, according to proposition 96, God cannot multiply individuals within a given species without matter. And according to proposition 81, because intelligences do not include matter within their being, God cannot produce many intelligences within the same species.[56] As we have already indicated in Ch. VII, Thomas Aquinas, Siger of Brabant, and Boethius of Dacia had all maintained that there can only be one angel within a given species.[57] In light of the two condemned articles to which reference has just been made, one can readily understand why Godfrey is reluctant to deny the possibility of numerical multiplicity of angels within species. At the same time, he has made it abundantly clear that he does not understand how one could account for this.

That this continued to be a stormy issue after the 1277 condemnation becomes even more manifest when one turns to Henry of Ghent and to Giles of Rome. In his Quodlibet 2, q. 8, debated only some months after Tempier's condemnation of March 7, 1277, Henry cites the two above-mentioned articles while arguing against the view that forms can be multiplied only by reason of matter. He also refers to article 191, according to which the claim that forms are only divided from one another by reason of matter is to be rejected as erroneous unless this be restricted to forms that are educed from the potentiality of matter.[58]

Giles of Rome was forced to come to grips with this same issue not too long after his readmission to the Paris Theology Faculty in 1285. In his Quodlibet 2, q. 7 of 1287, he prefaces his reply to the question as to whether

---

[55] "Ex his etiam patet quod in separatis a materia quantitati subiecta non potest esse individuatio sive divisio speciei vel formae specificae in plura individua solo numero differentia dicto modo. Si autem possit fieri alio modo non intelligo; sed tamen non nego" (PB 3.329).

[56] See *Chartularium* . . . , pr. 81: "Quod, quia intelligentiae non habent materiam, Deus non posset facere plures eiusdem speciei" (Mandonnet, pr. 43); *Chartularium* . . . , pr. 96: "Quod Deus non potest multiplicare individua sub una specie sine materia" (Mandonnet, pr. 42).

[57] See Ch. VII, p. 276 and n. 56.

[58] See *ed. cit.*, Vol. 1, fol. 33v. Also see Paulus, *Henri de Gand* . . . , pp. 348–49.

God can produce many angels within the same species by citing condemned proposition 81, to which reference has been made above. He comments that it would have been better had such condemned articles been drawn up with more careful deliberation and he hopes that sounder judgment will still be applied to them at some future date. But for the present he proposes to defend the position implied by the condemnation of the article in question.[59]

In his reply he first suggests that while according to the present dispensation it would not be fitting for God to multiply individual angels within species, he does not wish to deny that God could do this according to another order of things.[60] He suggests that such might occur if the form of a separate substance were realized only according to its imperfect being rather than according to its perfect fullness of being. Thus, just as a corporeal form may be regarded as limited and restricted by reason of the matter in which it is received, so too, according to Giles's proposed solution, an angelic form might enjoy only limited and restricted being by reason of God, its extrinsic cause. This would happen simply because God failed to communicate to this form the fullness of being of which it is capable.[61] Granted that this does not happen according to the present order of things, Giles suggests that it could happen in another order by reason of God's absolute power.[62] He is aware that this effort to allow for the possibility of multiplicity of angels within species is somewhat forced, even adding that he himself does not fully approve of it. He evidently does not wish to challenge Tempier's condemnation of the article in question, and proposes his explanation not as something that must be accepted as true, but rather to stimulate the minds of his readers.[63]

From the above it is clear enough that neither Giles nor Godfrey was convinced on philosophical grounds that separate substances or angels can be multiplied within species. Neither was prepared, however, to challenge

---

[59] See his *Quodlibeta* (Louvain, 1646), p. 65a. Note in particular: "Optandum vero foret, quod maturiori consilio tales articuli fuissent ordinati; et adhuc sperandum quod forte de iis in posterum sit habendum consilium sanius. Hinc in praesenti, quantum possumus, et ut possumus, articulum sustinemus."

[60] See *op. cit.*, p. 65b.

[61] *Op. cit.*, p. 68ab.

[62] *Op. cit.*, p. 69a. See in particular: "Non est autem secundum naturae cursum, sed est ex Dei potentia absoluta, quod restringatur in esse ex parte Dei tribuentis esse. Unde dicimus quod Deus per absolutam potentiam hoc poterit facere."

[63] *Ibid.* Note his comment: "hanc autem evasionem non omnino adhuc approbamus. . . . Dicimus ergo esse possibile quod articulus dicit. Modum tamen datum magis posuimus ad exercitandum legentium mentes quam ad id quod dictum est pertinaciter asserendum." For further discussion of this also see Paulus, *Henri de Gand* . . . , pp. 350–51.

directly Tempier's action of 1277, at least not in the texts to which reference has been made. A few years thereafter, in his Quodlibet 12, q. 10 of 1296/97, Godfrey singles out propositions 96 and 81 along with a number of others condemned by Tempier in 1277.[64] He cites these as illustrations of condemned articles which are theologically defensible in themselves, since they have been proposed by many Catholic teachers *(doctores)*. He also includes them among those which are thought to have been taken from the writings of Thomas Aquinas, whose doctrine he commends.[65] At the time of this later discussion, Godfrey obviously views the position which rejects the possibility of numerical multiplication of angels within species as theologically defensible in itself. And as we have already observed, it is to this same conclusion that his philosophical explanation of the individuation of material substances surely points.

---

[64] PB 5.101.

[65] PB 5.101, 102–103. For fuller discussion of Godfrey's reaction to the 1277 prohibitions in Q 12, q. 5 and his defense of Aquinas therein see our Ch. X, pp. 382–85.

Chapter X.

Concluding Remarks

Our exposition of Godfrey's metaphysical thought has now come to an end. In this concluding chapter we should like, first of all, to recall some of the salient points of his metaphysics and, secondly, to locate him somewhat more precisely within his general intellectual milieu. In the opening pages of Chapter I we suggested that if there is one theme that continually recurs throughout his discussion of metaphysical topics and, we might add, in any number of different contexts, it is his particular development of the Aristotelian doctrine of act and potency.[1] There, after presenting his description of the nature and subject of metaphysics, we considered his views as to how being itself is to be divided. Most important for our purposes was his division of real being into actual being and potential being, along with his insistence that something may enjoy the latter by reason of some preexisting intrinsic cause and, or perhaps only, by reason of some preexisting extrinsic cause. In that same chapter we also examined his theory of analogy of being and his discussion of the transcendentals.

In considering his rejection of either real or intentional distinction between essence and existence in Chapter II, we again encountered his personal understanding of and application of the metaphysics of act and potency. Godfrey denies that one need postulate any kind of real distinction and composition

[1] See p. 2.

of essence and existence in creatures, including angelic beings, in order to differentiate them from God and to account for their contingent and composite character. Instead, he appeals to an unusual kind of act-potency "composition" in spiritual entities. Compared to God and therefore viewed as less perfect than the divine, any such being may be regarded as potential. But when compared with a less perfect being, any such being may be regarded as enjoying perfection and actuality. Hence its act-potency composition is assured. As we have already suggested, this solution marks an interesting combination of certain Aristotelian and Neoplatonic elements. It had already been foreshadowed by Siger of Brabant, although Godfrey himself develops it more fully. In addition to using it as a focal point for his own metaphysics of essence and existence in creatures, especially spiritual ones, Godfrey also turns to it in order to be enabled to place angelic beings in a logical genus, *though not in a natural one*.

Within this same Chapter II we also found Godfrey appealing to various features of his metaphysics of act and potency in order to refute certain arguments offered by Giles of Rome in defense of real distinction between essence and existence, as well as others presented by Henry of Ghent in his defense of intentional distinction between them. For instance, Godfrey insists that one cannot understand an essence as actual and as not existing at one and the same time. Hence one should not conclude to real distinction between essence and existence in order to account for knowledge of something as not existing. One may understand a given essence as only potentially existing, to be sure; but then one will recognize it as merely potential in terms of its essence as well. Nor should one appeal to Henry's unusual metaphysics of essential being in order to account for the possibility of knowledge of not-yet existent possibles. Insofar as such an entity enjoys real but potential being by reason of some preexisting cause, whether intrinsic or extrinsic, it can be known in terms of such a cause or causes. The possibility of such knowledge does not require either intentional or real distinction between its essence and existence.

In Chapter III we considered a number of features of Godfrey's metaphysics of divine creative causality. In connection with this we first examined his views regarding the possibility of philosophical knowledge of God's existence. If he assigns some place to physical argumentation for the existence of the divine, he clearly regards this as in need of completion by metaphysical reasoning. His carefully elaborated discussion of the different steps involved in arriving at some knowledge as to what God is or of the divine essence may be regarded as another application of his metaphysics of act and potency. This involves a gradual movement from awareness that is more general and confused (or potential) to that which is more particular and exact and determined (or actual). In discussing the divine attributes he also wonders whether awareness, even divine awareness, of the various divine attributes presupposes some reference to really distinct pure perfections as realized or realizable in creatures.

In Chapter III we next turned to a consideration of Godfrey's philosophical analysis of the procession of creatures from God. Somewhat surprisingly, he admits of distinct divine ideas to correspond to the different species of creatures, but not to correspond to numerically distinct individuals within such species. For once he agrees, at least in part, with Henry of Ghent. But such agreement quickly disappears when he turns to Henry's account of the procession of creatures from God. Once more Godfrey is uncompromising in his criticism and rejection of Henry's theory of essential being and his way of correlating divine formal and divine efficient causality. In refuting Henry and in developing his own position, Godfrey frequently has recourse to his division of being into actual being and potential being. Thus he accounts for the ontological status of a not-yet existent possible simply by applying his distinction between purely cognitive being, on the one hand, and real potential being, on the other. This same distinction enables him to account for the difference between a true and genuine possible and a mere chimera. In addition to its cognitive being, such a possible will also enjoy real but potential being from all eternity, and this by reason of God, who from eternity has the power to bring it into actual being. And as we have already noted, Godfrey is convinced that his theory is sufficient to enable him to account for the possibility of there being knowledge of such nonexistent possibles.

In addition, Godfrey criticizes Henry's theory for mistakenly assuming that an intelligent being, in this case God, could serve as formal exemplary cause of something from all eternity without at the same time also functioning as its efficient cause. Not only this, but Henry's position should lead him to the conclusion that creatures are not really created from nothing. And, according to Godfrey, by assigning eternal essential being to creatures, Henry has in fact compromised his own denial that creatures could be created from eternity. As far as Godfrey himself is concerned, the impossibility of an eternally created universe cannot be demonstrated, though he does not claim that one can demonstrate its possibility.

The second major part of our study, devoted to Godfrey's metaphysics of substance and accident, introduced us to a number of additional applications of his metaphysics of act and potency. In Chapter IV we considered his general understanding of both substance and accident and their mutual interrelationship. Since substance serves in two roles for Godfrey, that is, as center of existence in itself and as support or subject for accidents, it may be regarded as potential vis à vis its corresponding accidents when it is considered in relation to them. He also suggests that one may describe substance as participating in its accidental perfections. This is not to deny, of course, that substance may be realized only in its first or primary role, that is to say, as a center of existence in itself. But such is in fact true only of the divine substance.

In discussing the causal relationship between substance and accident, Godfrey refuses to admit that a substance may be the immediate and efficient cause of any accident that inheres in it. To admit of such a possibility would, in his eyes, seriously compromise the "act-potency axiom," according to which nothing can be in act and potency at one and the same time with respect to the same thing. Not only does Godfrey offer detailed argumentation in support of this axiom. He defends its universal application. Man's spiritual activities are no exception.

In brief, Godfrey maintains that the efficient cause of proper accidents is really the same efficient cause that produces the substantial essence from which they flow. This substantial essence in turn serves as their subject or material cause, to be sure, but not as their efficient cause. Some other efficient cause must be introduced in order to account for the origin and reality of variable or transient accidents, especially of immanent operations such as intellection and volition. Such activities or operations may be viewed as inhering in a created substance mediately, that is to say, by means of other accidents, powers such as the intellect and the will. These powers are, according to Godfrey, really distinct from the essence of the soul, since an act and its proximate potency or power should correspond in genus. But, Godfrey concludes, the efficient cause of immanent operations such as intellection and volition can only be the object that is understood or willed.

His defense of this final point places him squarely within the intellectualistic tradition as regards any philosophical account of the interrelationship between intellect and will in the act of choice. In rejecting any kind of voluntaristic explanation, he pits himself against Henry of Ghent in particular and is much more sympathetic with positions already foreshadowed by Siger of Brabant and by Thomas Aquinas[1]. But in assigning efficient causality in volition to the object as presented to the will by the intellect, he has clearly gone beyond the letter of Aquinas's texts, even though he may, as Lottin has contended, have remained true to their spirit.[2] James of Viterbo's unusual theory of "aptitudes" receives no more sympathetic treatment from Godfrey than does Henry's claim that a spiritual being can reduce itself from virtual act to formal act.

Godfrey's contention that individual existences must be admitted to correspond to individual accidental essences was examined in Chapter V. His

---

[2] *Psychologie et morale . . .*, T. 1, pp. 331–39.

position here follows almost inevitably from his defense of real identity of substantial essence and existence in creatures. Having refused to allow for real distinction between them on the level of substance, he would not be expected to distinguish an accident's essence from its existence. On this point he clearly differs from Giles of Rome and from one position that has been assigned by certain recent commentators to Thomas Aquinas. Godfrey also maintains that even if one defends real distinction between substantial essence and existence, multiplicity of accidental existences is still to be conceded. Admission of a plurality of existences within a created entity, one substantial and the others accidental, will not compromise the unity of that being, according to Godfrey. Nor does he hesitate to admit that it will follow from this that one existence (substantial) may be said to participate in another (accidental), just as substance itself may be said to participate in its accidental perfections. Insofar as his own identification of essence and existence in creatures is itself an application of his metaphysics of act and potency and insofar as he correlates substance and accident as potency and act, his defense of distinctive accidental existences may be viewed as another application of his thinking on act and potency.

In his discussion of the relationship between nature and supposit (see Ch. VI), Godfrey introduces an important precision. Granted that they differ as something considered abstractly differs from that same thing when it is considered concretely, still, in terms of its direct and primary meaning, supposit adds nothing real to nature. But when considered in terms of its secondary meaning or connotation, then supposit does connote something more than nature, that is, those accidents without which a created nature will never be realized in concrete existence, together with the exclusion of any other subject in which the supposit might inhere or with which it might join as a part. This difference in the *modi significandi* of the terms "nature" and "supposit" suffices for Godfrey to account for the fact that nature cannot be predicated of supposit on the creaturely level. It also enables him to allow for the fact that actions may be attributed to the supposit, but not to nature.

As regards a theological issue centering around the hypostatic union, Godfrey's position appears to anticipate one developed shortly thereafter by Duns Scotus. Precisely because Christ's human nature is united with the divine supposit or the Word, it lacks that independence in existence which is required for an individuated nature to be a supposit or person. But if the human nature were ever to be separated from the divine supposit and were to continue in existence, then the human nature itself would become a human supposit. Certain points of similarity between Godfrey's way of correlating nature and supposit and James of Viterbo's views on the essence-existence relationship were also noted.

Given this theory of subsistence, Godfrey concludes that the human soul when separated from the body will not enjoy the full perfection of a supposit or person. In its separated state it will still be ordered toward and retain a natural inclination for its body, and will, therefore, only enjoy an imperfect mode of subsisting. If a man's entire actual being (*esse*) is retained by his separated soul, such is not true of his potential being, or his matter.

Godfrey's metaphysics of the human person (rational supposit) as well as his defense of real identity of essence and existence in creatures control his answer to another theological matter, the question whether there is only one substantial existence in Christ. Evidently quite familiar with the positions defended by Thomas Aquinas, Giles of Rome, and Henry of Ghent with respect to this, Godfrey assigns to Christ two existences, but only one subsistence. And, in conscious departure from Aquinas, he insists that one may say that Christ is indeed one according to the masculine gender (*unus*), but many according to the neuter gender (*plura*). While his own rejection of real distinction of essence and existence in creatures inevitably leads him to defend duality of existences in Christ, he maintains that such would obtain even if essence and existence were really distinct. Existences must be multiplied even as essences are. Hence, he holds that when the Word assumed a human nature it also assumed a new and human existence. This existence will not be subsistence, of course, so long as the human nature is united with the Word.

In his analysis of the nature of prime matter (see Ch. VII), Godfrey defends what we have referred to as the purer Aristotelian position. By this we have in mind the view that prime matter is pure potentiality and enjoys no actuality in and of itself. On this point, Godfrey falls within the general tradition developed by Thomas Aquinas and defended by Giles of Rome and in the main, by Siger of Brabant. Following from this is Godfrey's contention that prime matter, because it is pure potentiality, can never exist in itself apart from some substantial form, not even by divine power. Godfrey, of course, fits this view of matter and its union with form into his general doctrine on the essence-existence relationship. He closely connects the presence of prime matter in any corporeal entity with the possibility that such a being may undergo substantial change. So true is this that, as we have also seen, he is unwilling to admit with Aquinas that there could be incorruptible bodies that are composed of form and a special kind of matter. He rather inclines to agree with Averroes that it is better to hold that there is no matter in the strict sense in heavenly bodies.

In refusing to assign any degree of actuality to prime matter itself and in denying that prime matter could ever exist apart from some substantial form, Godfrey again appears to have as his primary target Henry of Ghent. And once more he is also siding against the more general Neo-Augustinian tradition of his time and is again applying quite rigidly his understanding of the metaphysics of act and potency, this time to the matter-form relationship.

Following from this is his rejection of matter-form composition in any purely spiritual entity, whether angelic or the human soul. Universal hylemorphism must be rejected. But denial of matter-form composition to spiritual entities must not be interpreted as implying any kind of real distinction between essence and existence therein, as Thomas and Giles had proposed. In his final Quodlibet 15 Godfrey still argues forcefully against Gonsalvus of Spain's defense of matter-form composition in the human soul.

In Chapter VIII we concentrated on Godfrey's analysis of the nature of substantial form itself. Throughout his discussion of this certain difficulties reappear, difficulties which arise from the generally accepted view of his time that man is in some way both material and spiritual. Thus, in discussing the origin of substantial forms, Godfrey distinguishes between the situation of the human intellective soul, on the one hand, and that of purely corporeal substantial forms, on the other. If the former can originate only by direct divine creation, the latter are, according to Godfrey, in some way educed from the preexisting potentiality of matter. In explaining the last-mentioned point, Godfrey denies that these corporeal forms actually preexist as such either in matter or in any kind of seminal reason. Here he is especially critical of the modified version of seminal reasons proposed by James of Viterbo. According to James, a form does not actually preexist in matter, to be sure, but does preexist in terms of its proper entity and "formally." In Godfrey's eyes, such an interpretation, a classic illustration of Neo-Augustinianism in our opinion, cannot be reconciled with Aristotle's understanding of the nature of prime matter or his general thinking on act and potency.

In Chapter VIII we also examined in some detail Godfrey's defense of the need for dispositions which are required, at least in the purely natural order, to prepare matter for the reception of one kind of substantial form rather than another. His occasional use of the terminology "seminal reasons" in order to illustrate or even to describe such dispositions raises certain problems of interpretation, but it seems evident enough that he does not accept the Augustinian doctrine of seminal reasons in any strict sense of the term. He rather appears to have on occasion attempted to accommodate this language to his own theory of previous dispositions. Dispositions are not to be interpreted as implying either the actual or the formal preexistence of a form which is to be produced by being educed from the potentiality of matter. They simply prepare a given instance of matter to receive a given kind of form from a given kind of agent. They are also needed in order to prepare matter for reception of the spiritual soul directly from God. Even though God could infuse such a soul into previously undisposed matter, he does not do so.

In this same Chapter VIII we considered Godfrey's position with respect to the then hotly contested issue of unicity versus plurality of substantial forms in corporeal entities, and especially in man. Both philosophical and theological concerns entered into many discussions of this in Godfrey's time. As regards his philosophical preferences, Godfrey's metaphysics of act and potency once more heavily influences him. Two principles or factors cannot unite to constitute a being that is essentially one unless one of these is pure potentiality and the other its first substantial act. This same conviction also enters into his insistence that prime matter is pure potentiality. And it now positively disposes him to defend unicity of substantial form in all material entities, including man. Thus it serves as a leading principle in his detailed criticism of three different versions of plurality of forms then being advanced, as emerges from his discussion in Quodlibet 2, q. 7. Neither the fact that differing levels of perfection are united in more complex material entities, nor the enduring presence of elemental qualities in mixed bodies compels Godfrey to admit of plurality of substantial forms in such beings. And against Henry's defense of duality of substantial forms in man he raises many objections, the most important and most metaphysical being the one just mentioned. Two different substantial forms cannot unite with matter to constitute a being that is substantially and essentially one, not even in the case of man.

Given his sharp criticism of all versions of plurality of forms, one would expect Godfrey to conclude by defending unicity of substantial form in all corporeal entities. And yet he hesitates to do so with respect to man. He traces this hesitation back, on the philosophical level, to the difficulty in accounting for the fact that man is both a spiritual and material being, and at the same time, essentially and substantially one. He does present as more probable the view that defends unicity of form in all entities, including man. Theological difficulties also account in large measure for Godfrey's hesitation to adopt definitively the unicity theory in man, even though he argues strongly for one's theological freedom to defend this position. But if the doctrine of unicity of form in man should be shown at some future date to be contrary to the faith, he would then be prepared to accept some version of plurality. It seems likely enough that he would have adopted the unicity position even in man but for these theological concerns and considerations.

In Chapter IX we considered Godfrey's efforts to determine more precisely the respective roles of form, matter, and quantity in accounting for the individuation of material entities. His distinction between numerical unity in the strict sense and numerical unity in the broad sense (transcendental unity) serves him well here. It is by reason of its form that any given being enjoys transcendental or ontological unity. Strictly numerical unity is realized only in material beings, and then only insofar as they are quantified. Still, Godfrey refuses to acknowledge that quantity itself is the formal cause of individuation, even though it is the principle of strictly numerical unity. It is rather a material thing's substantial form which serves as its formal principle of individuation. Quantity is a material dispositive cause of individuation, since it renders matter itself divisible into numerically distinct parts which can therefore receive different substantial forms of the same kind.

In light of this brief recapitulation and in light of the previous nine chapters of this study, some further observations are now in order. First of all, as we have already observed in the opening lines of this concluding chapter, Godfrey's metaphysics might well be described as one that ultimately rests on the act-potency theory. Repeated illustrations of this have now been offered, and one must commend him for his ingenuity in developing so many new and varied applications of the metaphysics of act and potency and for his consistent employment of the same. His constant appeal to this in rejecting argumentation either for real or for intentional distinction between essence and existence and in developing his own positive metaphysics of essence and existence is one outstanding example of this. And it was so recognized by others, for instance by Walter Burley, who, writing in 1301, not only attributes this doctrine to Godfrey, but accepts it as the correct approach to the essence-existence question.[3] Godfrey's rigid application of the act-potency axiom to human action, especially to human volition, is another illustration of the same.

Secondly, it has been necessary for us to turn to Godfrey's Quodlibets and Disputed Questions in order to recover his metaphysical thought. Given the nature of such Questions, and especially of the Quodlibets, it has been interesting and even surprising for us to discover so complete and so consistent a metaphysics emerging therefrom. For, as we have often indicated above, the particular questions proposed for discussion in quodlibetal debates could and often did range over any number of issues, both philosophical and theological. On many occasions the topics proposed for Godfrey's consideration were strictly philosophical, and this in spite of the fact that he conducted these in his capacity as a Master of Theology. On other occasions, of course, the questions raised were theological. But even within the latter contexts Godfrey often judges it necessary to introduce a considerable amount of metaphysical thinking before attempting to resolve the theological issue. And to that extent discussions of the latter kind have also proved to be valuable sources for us in our efforts to recapture his metaphysical thought. In addition, it should be

---

[3] See S. Brown, "Walter Burley's *Quaestiones in Librum Perihermeneias*," *Franciscan Studies* 34 (1974), pp. 200–01 (for the dating); pp. 271–72 (for Burley's appeal to Godfrey's division of being in terms of act and potency in support of the view that "esse est idem quod essentia" and his apparent agreement with Godfrey on this: " . . . et haec est positio Magistri Godefridi quam credo esse veram"). But if his remarks on p. 273 imply his defense of intentional distinction between essence and existence, he is there in disagreement with Godfrey (see 4.42).

recalled that his Quodlibets range over a period of almost twenty years, that is to say, from 1285 until 1303/04. Nonetheless, this variety in terms of context and in terms of time notwithstanding, a remarkably consistent and, in our opinion, an intrinsically powerful metaphysical system is contained in these texts and, in many of its essentials, even in Godfrey's earlier Quodlibets, especially in those dating from 1286–1287. In fact, it was because so many of his fundamental metaphysical positions had already been formulated in his own mind by that time that he could repeatedly and consistently appeal to them in later years in discussing both philosophical and theological topics.

As regards more important influences upon Godfrey's metaphysics, Aristotle surely stands out as the most dominant, often as commented upon and developed by Averroes. Neoplatonic influences are also in evidence, especially the *Liber de causis* and Proclus's *Elementatio theologica* and, to a lesser degree, Avicenna. As we approach the more immediate intellectual background for Godfrey's own philosophizing, it may be helpful for us to distinguish, along with Van Steenberghen, three general philosophical currents which had appeared at Paris by 1270 or thereabouts.[4] One of these is the radical form of Aristotelianism developed by Siger of Brabant, Boethius of Dacia, and others within the Arts Faculty there in the 1260s and onward into the 1270s. A second is the distinctive philosophical approach then being elaborated by Thomas Aquinas. Each of these two currents is heavily Aristotelian in inspiration, of course, granted the presence of Neoplatonic elements in each as well.

But in addition to these, what one might describe as a Neo-Augustinian way of philosophizing was developing at this time. Ultimately inspired by Bonaventure, its true founder seems to have been John Peckham. Continued in one direction by William de la Mare and other Franciscan thinkers and in another and distinctive way by Henry of Ghent,[5] it finds still a third expression in the teaching of James of Viterbo at Paris in the 1290s. To refer to it as Neo-Augustinian is not to deny that much of its vocabulary and even much of its teaching is still heavily influenced by Aristotle. But certain doctrinal excesses on the part of Siger and others in the Arts Faculty, on the one hand,

---

[4] See our "The Condemnations . . . ," pp. 173–74.

[5] On this see Van Steenberghen, *La philosophie au XIIIe siècle*, pp. 456–71, 495–500. In the latter context he also cites as representative of the Neo-Augustinian position (at least in metaphysics) Richard of Middleton, William of Ware (to a lesser extent), and Peter John Olivi and at Oxford, Roger Marston. Granted that James of Viterbo's approach to metaphysical thought is not reducible to that of the Franciscan thinkers of this movement or to that of Henry of Ghent, it seems to us to be appropriate to include him within this general Neo-Augustinian movement.

and certain doctrinal innovations introduced by Thomas Aquinas in his usage of Aristotle within the Theology Faculty, on the other, had aroused considerable opposition by 1270, and especially by 1277, and had led to a strong and conservative reaction against each of these forms of Aristotelianism. In part inspiring and in part strengthened by Stephen Tempier's sweeping condemnation of 219 propositions in 1277, this Neo-Augustinian philosophical movement obviously enjoyed considerable support during Godfrey's days at Paris, both as a student and then as a Master of Theology.

As regards Godfrey's personal metaphysical thought, it cannot be reduced to any one of the three above-mentioned philosophical movements. Nevertheless, he is evidently far more sympathetic to Siger's way of philosophizing and to that of Aquinas than to that of the Neo-Augustinians. One need only recall his constant opposition to Henry of Ghent on point after point, or his criticisms of various positions developed by James of Viterbo, or in the opening years of the fourteenth century, his critique of the Franciscan, Gonsalvus of Spain. Thus in defending the purely potential character of prime matter, or in denying that prime matter can ever exist apart from some substantial form even by divine power, or in rejecting matter-form composition in spirits, or in defending real distinction between the soul and its powers, or in criticizing James's seminal reasons, he is obviously distancing himself from one or other expression of the Neo-Augustinian current. And to that extent, of course, he has more in common with Siger and the radical Aristotelians and with Aquinas.

Not only is this the case, but as we have pointed out on a number of occasions, there is reason to believe that both Siger and Aquinas exercised some positive influence on Godfrey's thinking on various points. For instance, in denying real distinction between essence and existence he is in agreement with Aristotle and with Averroes, to be sure, but also with Siger. His theory of act-potency "composition" of spiritual creatures reminds one of a position at least foreshadowed by Siger, granted that Godfrey develops it far more fully. His discussion of the possibility of an eternally created universe is clearly indebted to Thomas's *De aeternitate mundi*. And it is likely that in his defense of real distinction between the soul and its powers he is also heavily influenced by Aquinas.

Godfrey will never follow Aristotle or Averroes or any of the radical Aristotelians into doctrinally heterodox positions, to be sure. At the same time, on many points he also clearly differs with Aquinas. Consider, for instance, his rejection of real composition of essence and *esse* in creatures, or his defense of plurality of existences in Christ, or his denial that there are distinctive divine ideas to correspond to individuals within species, or his refusal to admit that heavenly bodies can be incorruptible and still be composed of matter and form.

It seems clear, then, that Godfrey developed his own version of Aristotelianism, and this in spite of the severe blow dealt both to the Aristotelianism of Siger and his colleagues in the Arts Faculty and to that of Aquinas by Tempier's condemnation of March 7, 1277. Frequent enough reference has been made to this event to indicate that Godfrey was well aware of it and that on occasion he judged it necessary to take it into account while presenting some of his own favored philosophical positions.[6] On the one hand, the obvious impetus given to the Neo-Augustinian current by Tempier's action did not deter Godfrey from working out and from publicly teaching and defending his own metaphysics at Paris from 1285 until 1303 or 1304. And that metaphysics is, in our opinion, a purer form of Aristotelianism and somewhat less indebted to Neoplatonism than that of Aquinas himself. On the other hand, the aftermath of the 1277 condemnation obviously had some effect on Godfrey's handling of certain sensitive issues. Witness his explanation of the individuation of material substances and his denial of matter-form composition in angels. These two positions would seemingly undermine the possibility of there being many angels or separate substances within the same species. But as we have indicated in the concluding pages of Chapter IX, he does not dare go quite so far, because of two propositions expressly condemned by Tempier.[7]

In his Quodlibet 12, q. 5 of 1296 or 1297, Godfrey explicitly addresses himself to a number of Tempier's prohibited articles. Since the particular articles which he there considers were thought to have been defended by Thomas, Godfrey's sensitive discussion of these is revealing both for what it tells us about his assessment of the continuing prohibition of the same and for what it indicates about his attitude toward Aquinas. His remarks are all the more interesting since Godfrey himself was hardly a Thomist. In this question he addresses himself to the following issue: "Does the Bishop of Paris sin because he fails to correct certain articles that were condemned by his predecessor?"[8] Godfrey attempts to show that many of the articles condemned by

---

[6] For these see the *Index*, under "Condemnation of 1277, Paris."

[7] See pp. 367–69.

[8] "Utrum Episcopus parisiensis peccet in hoc quod omittit corrigere quosdam articulos a praedecessore suo condemnatos" (PB 5.100). For more on this see De Wulf, *Un théologien-philosophe* . . . , pp. 42–49 (also on Quodlibet 12, q. 6: "Utrum liceat doctori praecipue theologico recusare quaestionem sibi positam cuius veritas manifestata per determinationem doctoris offenderet aliquos divites et potentes" [PB 5.105–07]). Also see M.-H. Laurent, "Godefroid de Fontaines et la condamnation de 1277," *Revue thomiste* 35 (1930), pp. 273–81; N. F. Gaughan, "Godfrey of Fontaines—An Independent Thinker," *American Ecclesiastical Review* 157 (1967), pp. 43–54, especially pp. 52–53.

Tempier should be corrected, that is to say, should no longer be condemned. That which impedes the progress of students, which is an occasion of scandal among them, and which works to the detriment of truly useful teaching, should be corrected. But such is true of the continuing condemnation of many of these articles.[9]

Godfrey's overriding thesis here is that when a matter is truly uncertain and of such nature that either side can be defended without obvious harm to the faith, it should be left open for discussion. And as regards a number of the condemned articles, Godfrey insists that they are still open to dispute. To illustrate this he considers articles 96 and 81, according to which God cannot multiply individuals within a species without matter, and God cannot produce many intelligences in the same species since they lack matter. These are, observes Godfrey, still open to discussion, for they have been defended by many Catholic teachers.[10] The same is to be said of article 124, according to which it is improper to maintain that some intellects are nobler than others because, since such diversity could not come from the side of the body, it would have to come from the side of the intellect. In other instances Godfrey defends prohibited positions by showing that Tempier had also condemned their contradictory. Hence, concludes Godfrey, condemnation of the above articles and of others like them impedes students in their search for knowledge.[11]

He also complains that prohibition of such articles has been an occasion of scandal both for teachers and for students.[12] Finally, he comments that

---

[9] PB 5.100.

[10] PB 5.101. For these see Ch. IX, p. 367, and n. 56.

[11] For article 124 in Mandonnet see pr. 147. As illustrations of prohibited articles which seem to exclude one another Godfrey cites pr. 36 (Mandonnet, 9): "quod Deum in hac mortali vita possumus intelligere per essentiam" and pr. 215 (Mandonnet, 10): "quod de Deo non potest cognosci nisi quia est vel ipsum esse." Also, pr. 204 (Mandonnet, 55), which he here summarizes: "quod error est dicere quod substantiae separatae sunt alicubi et moventur de loco ad locum per operationem, si intelligatur sine operatione substantiam angeli non esse in loco nec transire de loco ad locum" and pr. 219 (Mandonnet, 54): "quod dicere quod substantiae separatae nusquam sunt secundum substantiam est error, si intelligatur ita quod substantia angeli non sit in loco; si autem intelligatur ita quod substantia sit ratio essendi in loco, verum est." See PB 5.101–02. He also singles out propositions 129 (Mandonnet, 169), 130 (Mandonnet, 166), 160 (Mandonnet, 101), 163 (Mandonnet, 163).

[12] Here Godfrey comments that it is often necessary to explain some of the above and others like them in a sense that, while not contrary either to truth or to the meaning they should have had for those who originally promulgated them, is surely contrary to the letter of the text. Given this, some who are less expert in such matters think that those who so explain them are subject to excommunication and delate them

prohibition of these has done no small harm to the teaching of that "most reverend and most excellent teacher, Brother Thomas." The above-mentioned articles and others like them seem to have been taken from his writings. Seeing this, many of the simple believe that his teaching is to be rejected as erroneous. Students themselves are thereby harmed, since this discourages them from studying his doctrine. This Godfrey regrets because, as he himself phrases it: "With all due respect for certain teachers, with the exception of the teaching of the saints themselves and of those whose sayings have been accepted as authorities, the aforementioned teaching (Thomas's) must be regarded as of greater usefulness and as more praiseworthy than all others."[13]

Given all of this, continues Godfrey, it is hardly commendable for a great teacher, in the course of determining a difficult question, to seek added support for his position by citing the prohibition of the above-mentioned articles. (The implication is, of course, that such had happened at Paris.)[14] And finally he returns to the opening question: What of the present Bishop of Paris, who has not corrected the prohibited articles in question? Godfrey observes that the Bishop is eminent in the fields of canon and civil law and has some knowledge of theology. But since he is not really expert in the latter, he would need the advice of Masters in Theology in order to correct these articles. Because these Masters themselves are in disagreement about these matters, the Bishop can be excused to some extent for not now correcting them. But since the penalty attached to them by Tempier could easily be removed without endangering peace and since this would be of benefit to many, Godfrey does not so readily excuse him for failing to do this. Still, he does not dare condemn him, but notes again that the articles in question should be corrected.[15]

---

to the Chancellor or the Bishop. Such behavior, Godfrey wryly comments, causes considerable division among the students (PB 5.102). His remarks indicate that the following lines of Tempier's condemnation continued to be taken seriously, at least by some: ". . . excommunicantes omnes illos, qui dictos errores vel aliquem ex illis dogmatizaverint, aut deffendere seu sustinere presumpserint quoquomodo, necnon et auditores, nisi infra vii dies nobis vel cancellario Parisiensi duxerint revelandum" (*Chartularium*, I, p. 543; Mandonnet, p. 176).

[13] ". . . quia, salva reverentia aliquorum doctorum, excepta doctrina sanctorum, et eorum quorum dicta pro auctoritatibus allegantur, praedicta doctrina inter ceteras videtur utilior et laudabilior reputanda, ut vere doctori qui hanc doctrinam scripsit, possit dici in singulari illud quod Dominus dixit in plurali apostolis, Matth., quinto: 'Vos estis sal terrae'; et cetera, sub hac forma: 'Tu es sal terrae, quod si sal evanuerit, in quo salietur'?" (PB 5.103). On this also see Glorieux, "Pro et contra Thomam: Un survol de cinquante années," in *Sapientiae procerum amore . . .*, *Studia Anselmiana* 63 (Rome, 1974), pp. 276–77.

[14] PB 5.103. Here he also points out that the prohibition is purely local in its binding force: ". . . cum istae leges non habeant vim ligandi nisi in uno solo loco."

[15] *Ibid.*

We do not know whether Godfrey's remarks resulted in any reprimand from the Bishop or the Chancery in Paris. It is interesting to observe that during the following academic year he hesitates to take a position with respect to the question of angelic presence in place because of the continuing prohibition of certain articles relating to this, articles which appear to stand in contradiction to one another.[16] In any event, his remarks in Quodlibet 12, q. 5 are a revealing expression of his disapproval of the continuing condemnation of positions that are still open to theological discussion. And his words of tribute to Aquinas speak for themselves.

If we may conclude by returning once more to Godfrey's personal achievement, his metaphysics stands out, in our opinion, as the most striking and most powerful form of a purer kind of Aristotelianism to be developed at Paris during the period between the death of Thomas Aquinas in 1274 and the highly original synthesis created by John Duns Scotus at Oxford and Paris around the turn of the fourteenth century. This remark is in no way intended to denigrate from the relative merit to be assigned to the metaphysical thought of others at Paris during that time such as Henry of Ghent, Giles of Rome, or James of Viterbo. But it should be clear enough from what we have now seen that none of these was as Aristotelian in his metaphysics as was Godfrey. Thus we have felt justified in including both Henry and James within the Neo-Augustinian movement of that time. And one need only recall the importance assigned by Giles to the theory of real distinction between essence and existence within his own metaphysics to appreciate how far removed he is from Aristotle on that central point. At the same time, as we have previously indicated, not even Godfrey's metaphysical thought is purely Aristotelian, since important Neoplatonic influences are also discernible therein.

Isolated instances of Godfrey's influence on subsequent thinkers could also be cited. Witness, for instance, reference to and frequently enough criticism of Godfridian positions by Duns Scotus.[17] Bernard of Auvergne's attacks

---

[16] See Q 13, q. 4 (PB 5.221): "De argumento ad oppositum non est ad praesens multum curandum, declarando scilicet si angelus est in loco et quomodo est in loco . . . . Hoc etiam est difficile determinare propter articulos circa hoc condemnatos, quia contrarii videntur ad invicem; et contra quos nihil intendo dicere propter periculum excommunicationis." See propositions 204 and 219 as cited above in note 11, from Godfrey's Q 12, q. 5.

[17] For Scotus's knowledge of and criticism of Godfrey's understanding and application of the act-potency axiom, see Effler, *John Duns Scotus . . .*, pp. 92–97, 149–55. For Scotus's explicit criticism of his application of this to intellection and his understanding of the role of the phantasm in human cognition also see O. Lacombe, "La critique des théories de la connaissance chez Duns Scot," *Revue thomiste* 35 (1930), pp. 150–57; Gilson, *Jean Duns Scot. Introduction à ses positions fon-*

against Godfrey's Quodlibets are also well known.[18] Walter Burley's approval of Godfrey's views on essence and existence has been mentioned. The anonymous author of the doctrinal table edited by Hocedez was evidently one of Godfrey's admirers.[19] John of Pouilly, Peter of Auvergne, and Gerard of Bologna have also been included among the latter.[20] But any definitive pronouncement as to the extent of Godfrey's influence on subsequent philosophical generations would be premature at this time. It is our hope that the present study will be of assistance to students of early fourteenth-century metaphysical thought in their continuing effort to identify more adequately thirteenth-century influences upon thinkers of immediate concern to them. It is our suspicion that Godfrey will frequently enough appear among these.

damentales (Paris, 1952), pp. 526–28. For other references in Scotus to Godfrey see the helpful notes provided by the editors of the various volumes of the Vatican edition.

[18] On his refutation of Godfrey's Quodlibets see Stella, "Teologi e teologia . . . , pp. 171–214; Pattin, "La structure de l'être fini . . . ," pp. 672–75; 678–81 (for citations by later thinkers of his *impugnationes* against Godfrey and against Henry of Ghent, among which those by Capreolus are especially numerous); 689–708 (for his critique of Godfrey's views on essence and existence).

[19] See Introduction, p. xii, n.5.

[20] Arway, "A Half Century of Research . . . ," p. 202. See, for instance, Godfrey's influence on Peter of Auvergne's theory of individuation as developed by the latter in his Quodlibet 2, q. 5 and as indicated by Hocedez in his "Une Question inédite de Pierre d'Auvergne sur l'individuation," pp. 356–58 and pp. 370–79 (for an edition of Peter's text). Hocedez also notes that by the time of this Quodlibet (1297) Peter had come to accept Godfrey's position on the essence-existence relationship (p. 362). For an edition of Peter's discussion of this point in his Quodlibet 2, q. 4 see A. Monahan, "*Quaestiones in Metaphysicam* Petri de Alvernia," in *Nine Mediaeval Thinkers*, J. R. O'Donnell, ed. (Toronto, 1955), pp. 177–81.

Select Bibliography

PRINTED SOURCES

Albertson, J. "The *Esse* of Accidents According to St. Thomas." *The Modern Schoolman* 30 (1953), pp. 265–78.

[Alexander of Aphrodisias]. *De intellectu et intellecto,* ed. C. Théry. *Autour du décret de 1210: Alexandre d'Aphrodise*. Le Saulchoir, Kain, 1926, pp. 74–82.

[Algazel]. "*Logica Algazelis:* Introduction and Critical Text," ed. Ch. Lohr. *Traditio* 21 (1965), pp. 223–90.

[Anonymous]. "La table des divergences et innovations doctrinales de Godefroid de Fontaines," ed. J. Hoffmans. *Revue Néoscolastique de Philosophie* 36 (1934), pp. 412–36.

[Anselm]. *Monologium,* in *Sancti Anselmi opera omnia,* ed. F. S. Schmitt. Vol. 1, Edinburgh, 1946.

Antweiler, A. *Die Anfangslosigkeit der Welt nach Thomas von Aquin und Kant.* 2 vols., Trier, 1961.

[Aristotle]. *Aristoteles graece, ex recensione Bekkeri.* Berlin, 1831.

———. *Aristotle's Metaphysics. A Revised Text with Introduction and Commentary,* ed. W. D. Ross. Oxford, 1924.

———. *The Basic Works of Aristotle,* ed. R. McKeon. New York, 1941.

Arway, R. J. "A Half Century of Research on Godfrey of Fontaines." *The New Scholasticism* 36 (1962), pp. 192–218.

[Augustine]. Opera omnia. PL 32–46.

———. *Ad Nebridium, Epist. XIV.* CSEL 34.1.

———. *De Civitate Dei.* CCSL 47, 48.

———. *De diversis quaestionibus.* CCSL 44A.

———. *De trinitate.* CCSL 50; 50a. Also see *Oeuvres de Saint Augustin,* Vol. 16, Paris, 1955.

[Averroes]. *Aristotelis opera cum Averrois commentariis.* Venice, 1562–1574.

———. *In Aristotelis de anima libros,* ed. F. Stuart Crawford. Cambridge, Mass., 1953.

[Avicebron]. *Avencebrolis (Ibn Gebirol) Fons Vitae ex Arabico in Latinum translatus ab Iohanne Hispano et Dominico Gundissalino,* ed. Cl. Baeumker. *Beiträge zur Geschichte der Philosophie des Mittelalters* 1.2–4 (1892–1895).

[Avicenna]. *Avicennae perhypatetici philosophi ac medicorum facile primi opera.* Venice, 1508.

Balič, C. "Henricus de Harcley et Ioannes Duns Scotus." *Mélanges offerts à Etienne Gilson.* Toronto-Paris, 1959, pp. 93–112.

———. "The Life and Works of John Duns Scotus." *Studies in Philosophy and the History of Philosophy.* Vol. 3: *John Duns Scotus, 1265–1965* (Washington, D.C., 1965), pp. 1–27.

Bayerschmidt, P. *Die Seins-und Formmetaphysik des Heinrich von Gent in ihrer Anwendung auf die Christologie.* Münster i. W., 1941.

Bazán, B. "Le dialogue philosophique entre Siger de Brabant et Thomas d'Aquin. A propos d'un ouvrage récent de E. H. Wéber." *Revue philosophique de Louvain* 72 (1974), pp. 53–155.

Behler, E. *Die Ewigkeit der Welt. . . Erste Teil: Die problemstellung in der Arabischen und Jüdischen Philosophie des Mittelalters.* Munich, 1965.

Benes, J. "Valor 'possibilium' apud S. Thomam, Henricum Gandavensem, B. Iacobum de Viterbio." *Divus Thomas* (Piacenza) 29 (1926), pp. 612–34; 30 (1927), pp. 94–117, 335–55.

Bobik, J. "La doctrine de saint Thomas sur l'individuation des substances corporelles." *Revue philosophique de Louvain* 51 (1953), pp. 5–41.

———. "Dimensions in the Individuation of Bodily Substances." *Philosophical Studies* 4 (1954), pp. 60–79.

[Boethius]. *In librum de interpretatione.* PL 64.

———. *Boethii Philosophiae Consolatio.* CCSL 94.

———. *Boethius. The Theological Tractates. The Consolation of Philosophy,* ed. H.F. Stewart–E.K. Rand. Cambridge, Mass., 1968.

[Boethius of Dacia]. *Un Traité récemment découvert de Boèce de Dacie De mundi aeternitate,* ed. G. Sajó. Budapest, 1954.

———. *Boetii de Dacia. Tractatus de aeternitate mundi,* ed. G. Sajó. Berlin, 1964.

———. *Boethii Daci Opera. Modi significandi sive Quaestiones super Priscianum maiorem,* ed. by J. Pinborg and H. Roos with S. Skovgaard Jensen. *Corpus Philosophorum Danicorum Medii Aevi.* Vol. 4.1, Hauniae, 1969.

———. *Boethii Daci Opera. Opuscula de aeternitate mundi, de summo bono, de somniis,* ed. N. Green Pedersen. *Corpus Philosophorum Danicorum Medii Aevi.* Vol. 6.2, Hauniae, 1976.

Bonansea, B. "The Question of an Eternal World in the Teaching of St. Bonaventure." *Franciscan Studies* 34 (1974), pp. 7–33.

———. "The Impossibility of Creation from Eternity According to St. Bonaventure." *Proceedings of the American Catholic Philosophical Association* 48 (1974), pp. 121–35.

[Bonaventure]. *Doctoris Seraphici S. Bonaventurae . . . Opera Omnia.* 10 vols., Quaracchi, 1882–1902.

Brady, I. "John Pecham and the Background of Aquinas's *De Aeternitate Mundi,*" in *St. Thomas Aquinas 1274–1974. Commemorative Studies.* Toronto, 1974. Vol. 2, pp. 141–78.

Braswell, B. "Godfrey of Fontaines' Abridgement of Boetius of Dacia's 'Quaestiones supra librum Topicorum Aristotelis'." *Mediaeval Studies* 26 (1964), pp. 304–14.

Brown, S. "Avicenna and the Unity of the Concept of Being: The Interpretations of Henry of Ghent, Duns Scotus, Gerard of Bologna and Peter Aureoli." *Franciscan Studies* 25 (1965), pp. 117–50.

Bruni, G. *Le opere di Egidio Romano*. Florence, 1936.

Brunner, F. *Platonisme et Aristotélisme. La critique d'Ibn Gabirol par saint Thomas d'Aquin*. Louvain-Paris, 1965.

Callus, D. *The Condemnation of St. Thomas at Oxford*. The Aquinas Society of London. Oxford, 1946.

———. "The Origins of the Problem of the Unity of Form." in *The Dignity of Science*, ed. by J.A. Weisheipl. The Thomist Press, U.S.A., 1961, pp. 121–49.

Carlo, Wm. *The Ultimate Reducibility of Essence to Existence in Existential Metaphysics*. The Hague, 1966.

Casado, F. "El pensamiento filosófico del Beato Santiago de Viterbo." *La Ciudad de Dios* 163 (1951), pp. 437–54; 164 (1952), pp. 301–31; 165 (1953), pp. 103–44, 283–302, 489–500.

Chossat, M. "L'Averroïsme de saint Thomas. Note sur la distinction d'essence et d'existence à la fin du XIIIe siècle." *Archives de Philosophie* 9 (1932), pp. 129 [465] –177 [513].

Collins, J. *The Thomistic Philosophy of the Angels*. Washington, D.C., 1947.

Congar, Y. "Aspects ecclésiologiques de la querelle entre mendiants et séculiers dans la seconde moitié du XIIIe siècle et le début du XIVe." *Archives d'Histoire Doctrinale et Littéraire du Moyen Age* 28 (1961), pp. 35–151.

Crowley, Th. *Roger Bacon. The Problem of the Soul in his Philosophical Commentaries*. Louvain-Dublin, 1950.

———. "John Pecham, O.F.M., Archbishop of Canterbury, versus the New Aristotelianism." *Bulletin of the John Rylands Library* 33 (1950), pp. 242–55.

Cunningham, F. "Distinction According to St. Thomas." *The New Scholasticism* 36 (1962), pp. 279–312.

———. "Textos de Santo Tomas sobre el esse y esencia." *Pensamiento* 20 (1964), pp. 283–306.

———. "Some Presuppositions in Henry of Ghent." *Pensamiento* 25 (1969), pp. 103–43.

———. "The 'Real Distinction' in John Quidort." *Journal of the History of Philosophy* 8 (1970), pp. 9–28.

de Blic, J. "L'intellectualisme moral chez deux aristotéliciens de la fin du XIIIe siècle." *Miscellanea moralia in honorem ex. Dom. Arthur Janssen, Ephemeridum theologicarum Lovaniensium Bibliotheca*. Ser. I, Vol. 2 (Louvain, 1948), pp. 45–76.

De Corte, M. "La causalité du premier moteur dans la philosophie aristotélicienne." *Revue d'Histoire de la Philosophie* 5 (1931), pp. 105–46.

———. *La doctrine de l'intelligence chez Aristote*. Paris, 1934.

de Finance, J. *Etre et agir dans la philosophie de saint Thomas*. 2nd ed., Rome, 1960.

de Lagarde, G. "La philosophie sociale d'Henri de Gand et de Godefroid de Fontaines." *Archives d'Histoire Doctrinale et Littéraire du Moyen Age* 14 (1943–1945), pp. 73–142.

———. *La naissance de l'esprit laïque au déclin du moyen âge*. 2nd ed., Vol. 2, Louvain, 1958.

Delorme, F. "Autour d'un apocryphe scotiste. Le *De rerum principio* et Godefroy de Fontaines." *La France franciscaine* 8 (1925), pp. 279–95.

del Prado, N. *De veritate fundamentali philosophiae Christianae*. Fribourg, 1911.

Denifle, H. and Chatelain, A. *Chartularium Universitatis Parisiensis*. T. 1, Paris, 1889; T. 2, Paris, 1891.

Denis P. "Le premier enseignement de saint Thomas sur l'unité de la forme substantielle." *Archives d'Histoire Doctrinale et Littéraire du Moyen Age* 21 (1954), pp. 139–64.

De Poorter, A. *Catalogue des manuscrits de la Bibliothèque publique de la ville de Bruges*. Paris, 1934.

De Raeymaeker, L. *Metaphysica Generalis*. T. 1, Louvain, 1931; T. 2, Louvain, 1932.

———. "La profonde originalité de la métaphysique de saint Thomas d'Aquin." *Die Metaphysik im Mittelalter, Miscellanea Mediaevalia* 2 (1963), pp. 14–29.

De Wulf, M. *Un théologien-philosophe du XIII*[e] *siècle. Etude sur la vie, les oeuvres et l'influence de Godefroid de Fontaines*. Brussels, 1904.

———. "Un preux de la parole au XIIIe siècle." *Revue Néoscolastique de Philosophie* 11 (1904), pp. 416–32.

———. *Histoire de la Philosophie en Belgique*. Brussels, 1910.

———. L'intellectualisme de Godefroid de Fontaines d'après le Quodlibet VI, q. 15." *Beiträge zur Geschichte der Philosophie des Mittelalters*, Supplementband I (1913), pp. 287–96.

———. *Histoire de la philosophie médiévale*. 6th ed., Vol. 2, Louvain, 1936.

[Dionysius (Pseudo)]. *De divinis nominibus*. PG 3.

Doig, J. "Science première et science universelle dans le 'Commentaire de la métaphysique' de saint Thomas d'Aquin." *Revue philosophique de Louvain* 63 (1965), pp. 41–96.

———. *Aquinas on Metaphysics. A historico-doctrinal study of the Commentary on the Metaphysics*. The Hague, 1972.

Douie, D. *Archbishop Pecham*. Oxford, 1952.

———. *The Conflict Between the Seculars and the Mendicants at the University of Paris in the Thirteenth Century*. London, 1954.

Duin, J.J. *La doctrine de la providence dans les écrits de Siger de Brabant*. Louvain, 1954.

———. "La bibliothèque philosophique de Godefroid de Fontaines." *Estudios Lulianos* 3 (1959), pp. 21–36; 137–60.

Dunphy, W. "The *Quinque Viae* and some Parisian Professors of Philosophy." *St. Thomas Aquinas 1274–1974. Commemorative Studies*. Toronto, 1974. Vol. 2, pp. 73–104.

Düring, I. *Aristoteles*. Heidelberg, 1966.

Effler, R. *John Duns Scotus and the Principle "Omne quod movetur ab alio movetur"*. St. Bonaventure, N.Y., 1962.

Ehrle, F. "Beiträge zu den Biographien berühmter Scholastiker. I. Heinrich von Gent." *Archiv für Literatur-und Kirchengeschichte* 1 (1885), pp. 365–401; 507–08.

Fabro, C. *La nozione metafisica di partecipazione*. 2nd ed., Turin, 1950.

Forest, A. *La structure métaphysique du concret selon saint Thomas d'Aquin*. Paris, 1931.

Gál, G. "Gulielmi de Ware, O.F.M. Doctrina philosophica per summa capita proposita." *Franciscan Studies* 14 (1954), pp. 265–92.

Gaughan, N.F. "Godfrey of Fontaines—An Independent Thinker." *American Ecclesiastical Review* 157 (1967), pp. 43–54.

Gauthier, R.-A. "Trois commentaires 'averroïstes' sur l'Ethique à Nicomaque." *Archives d'Histoire Doctrinale et Littéraire du Moyen Age* 16 (1947–1948), pp. 187–336.

[Giles of Lessines]. *Le Traité 'De unitate formae' de Gilles de Lessines*, ed. M. De Wulf. PB 1, Louvain, 1901.

[Giles of Rome]. *Theoremata de corpore Christi*. Bologna, 1481.
———. *Quaestiones metaphysicales Clarissimi Doctoris Egidii Romani ordinis Sancti Augustini*. Venice, 1501; repr. Frankfurt/Main, 1966.
———. *Egidius Romanus. De esse et essentia, De mensura angelorum, et De cognitione angelorum*. Venice, 1503; repr. Frankfurt/Main, 1968.
———. *Commentarius in Primum Sententiarum*. Venice, 1521.
———. *In Secundum Librum Sententiarum*. Venice, 1581.
———. *B. Aegidii Columnae Romani, Ordinis Eremitarum S. Augustini . . . Quodlibeta*. Louvain, 1646; repr. Frankfurt/Main, 1966.
———. *De compositione angelorum*, partially edited by D. Trapp, in "Aegidii Romani de doctrina modorum." *Angelicum* 12 (1935), pp. 449–501.
———. *Aegidii Romani Theoremata de esse et essentia. Texte précédé d'une introduction historique et critique*, ed. E. Hocedez. Louvain, 1930.
———. *Errores philosophorum*, ed. J. Koch. Milwaukee, 1944.
Gilson, E. "Avicenne et le point de départ de Duns Scot." *Archives d'Histoire Doctrinale et Littéraire du Moyen Age* 2 (1927), pp. 89–149.
———. "Le sources gréco-arabes de l'augustinisme avicennisant." *Archives d'Histoire Doctrinale et Littéraire du Moyen Age* 4 (1929), pp. 5–149.
———. "La notion d'existence chez Guillaume d'Auvergne." *Archives d'Histoire Doctrinale et Littéraire du Moyen Age* 15 (1946), pp. 55–91.
———. "L'objet de la métaphysique selon Duns Scot." *Mediaeval Studies* 10 (1948), pp. 21–92.
———. *The Spirit of Mediaeval Philosophy*. London, 1950.
———. *Being and Some Philosophers*. 2nd ed., Toronto, 1952.
———. *Jean Duns Scot. Introduction à ses positions fondamentales*. Paris, 1952.
———. *La philosophie de saint Bonaventure*. 3rd ed., Paris, 1953.
———. *History of Christian Philosophy in the Middle Ages*. New York, 1955.
———. *The Christian Philosophy of St. Thomas Aquinas*. New York, 1956.
———. *The Christian Philosophy of Saint Augustine*. New York, 1960.
Girardi, G. *Metafisica della causa esemplare in San Tommaso d'Aquino*. Turin, 1954.
Glorieux, P. *La littérature quodlibétique de 1260 à 1320*. Vol. 1, Paris, 1925; Vol. 2, Paris, 1935.
———. "Comment les thèses thomistes furent proscrites à Oxford (1284–1286)." *Revue thomiste* 32 (1927), pp. 259–91.
———. "Un recueil scolaire de Godefroid de Fontaines." *Recherches de Théologie ancienne et médiévale* 3 (1931), pp. 37–53.
———. *Répertoire des maîtres en théologie de Paris au XIIIe siècle*. 2 vols., Paris, 1933.
———. "Le Quodlibet et ses procédés rédactionnels." *Divus Thomas* (Piacenza) 42 (1939), pp. 61–93.
———. "Notations brèves sur Godefroid de Fontaines." *Recherches de Théologie ancienne et médiévale* 11 (1939), pp. 168–73.
———. "Où en est la question Quodlibet?" *Revue du Moyen Age Latin* 2 (1946), pp. 405–14.
———. "Saint Thomas et l'accroissement de la béatitude." *Recherches de Théologie ancienne et médiévale* 17 (1950), pp. 121–25.
———. "Quodlibeti." *Enciclopedia Cattolica*, Vol. 10 (Vatican City, 1953), col. 436–38.
———. *Aux origines de la Sorbonne. I: Robert de Sorbon*. Paris, 1966.
———. "L'Enseignement au Moyen Age. Techniques et méthodes en usage à la Faculté de Théologie de Paris au XIIIe siècle." *Archives d'Histoire Doctrinale et Littéraire du Moyen Age* 35 (1968), pp. 65–186.

———. "Pro et contra Thomam. Un survol de cinquante années." *Sapientiae Procerum Amore, Studia Anselmiana* 63 (1974), pp. 255–87.

[Godfrey of Fontaines]. *Les quatre premiers Quodlibets de Godefroid de Fontaines*, ed. M. De Wulf and A. Pelzer. PB 2, Louvain, 1904.

———. *Les Quodlibets cinq, six et sept*, ed. M. De Wulf and J. Hoffmans. PB 3, Louvain, 1914.

———. *Le huitième Quodlibet, Le neuvième Quodlibet, Le dixième Quodlibet*, ed. J. Hoffmans. PB 4, Louvain, 1924, 1928, 1931.

———. *Les Quodlibets onze et douze, Les Quodlibets treize et quatorze*, ed. J. Hoffmans. PB 5, Louvain, 1932, 1935.

———. *Le Quodlibet XV et trois Questions ordinaires de Godefroid de Fontaines*, ed. O. Lottin. *Etude sur les manuscrits des Quodlibets*, by J. Hoffmans and A. Pelzer. PB 14, Louvain, 1937.

———. *Disputed Questions*. For a listing of those which have been edited either in whole or in part see *Introduction*, pp. xxxi–xxxii.

———. "Le Sermon de Godefroid de Fontaines pour le deuxième dimanche après l'Epiphanie," ed. P. Tihon. *Recherches de Théologie ancienne et médiévale* 32 (1965), pp. 43–53.

———. *Scholia on the Summa Contra Gentiles*, ed. P. Uccelli. *S. Thomae Aquinatis Summa de Veritate Catholicae Fidei Contra Gentiles*. Rome, 1878, "Appendix," pp. 1–31. On their authenticity see *Introduction*, pp. xxxiii–xxxiv.

Goichon, A.-M. *La distinction de l'essence et de l'existence d'après Ibn Sina (Avicenne)*. Paris, 1937.

Gómez Caffarena, J. "Cronología de la 'Suma' de Enrique de Gante por relación a sus 'Quodlibetos'," *Gregorianum* 38 (1957), pp. 116–33.

———. *Ser participado y ser subsistente en la metafísica de Enrique de Gante*. Rome, 1958.

[Gonsalvus of Spain]. *Quaestiones disputatae et de quodlibet*, ed. L. Amorós. Ad Claras Aquas, Florence, 1935.

Grabmann, M. "Die Eröterung der Frage, ob die Kirche besser durch einen guten Juristen oder durch einen Theologen regiert werde, bei Gottfried von Fontaines († nach 1306) und Augustinus Triumphus von Ancona († nach 1328)." *Festschrift Eduard Eichmann zum 70. Geburtstag*. Paderborn, 1940, pp. 1–19.

———. "Doctrina S. Thomae de distinctione reali inter essentiam et esse ex documentis ineditis saeculi XIII illustratur." *Acta hebdomadae Thomisticae Romae celebratae 19–25 Novembris 1923 in laudem S. Thomae Aquinatis*. Rome, 1924, pp. 131–90.

———. *Die theologische Erkenntnis- und Einleitungslehre des heiligen Thomas von Aquin*. Freiburg in der Schweiz, 1948.

Gutiérrez, D. *De B. Iacobi Viterbiensis O.E.S.A. vita, operibus, et doctrina theologica*. Rome, 1939.

Guttmann, J. *Das Verhältniss des Thomas von Aquino zum Judenthum und zur jüdischen Literatur*. Göttingen, 1891.

[Henry of Ghent]. *Quodlibeta Magistri Henrici Goethals a Gandavo doctoris Solemnis*. 2 vols., with continuous pagination, Paris, 1518; repr. Louvain, 1961.

———. *Henrici de Gandavo Quodlibet I*, ed. R. Macken. Louvain-Leiden, 1979.

———. *Summae quaestionum ordinariarum*. 2 vols., Paris, 1520; repr. St. Bonaventure, N.Y., 1953.

Hinnebusch, W.A. *The History of the Dominican Order, II: Intellectual and Cultural Life to 1500*. Staten Island, N.Y., 1973.

Hissette, R. "Boèce de Dacie et les Questions sur la Physique du Clm 9559." *Recherches de Théologie ancienne et médiévale* 39 (1972), pp. 71–81.

———. *Enquête sur les 219 articles condamnés à Paris le 7 mars 1277*. Louvain-Paris, 1977.

Hocedez, E. "Gilles de Rome et Henri de Gand sur la distinction réelle (1276 – 1287)." *Gregorianum* 8 (1927), pp. 358 – 84.

———. "Le premier quodlibet d'Henri de Gand (1276)." *Gregorianum* 9 (1928), pp. 92 – 117.

———. "Deux questions touchant la distinction réelle entre l'essence et l'existence." *Gregorianum* 10 (1929), pp. 365 – 86 .

———. "La condamnation de Gilles de Rome." *Recherches de Théologie ancienne et médiévale* 4 (1932), pp. 34 – 58.

———. *Quaestio de unico esse in Christo a doctoribus saeculi XIII disputata, Textus et Documenta. Series Theologica* 14, Rome, 1933.

———. "Une question inédite de Pierre d'Auvergne sur l'individuation." *Revue Néoscolastique de Philosophie* 36 (1934), pp. 355 – 86.

Hödl, L. "Neue Begriffe und neue Wege der Seinserkenntnis im Schul- und Einflussbereich des Heinrich von Gent." *Die Metaphysik im Mittelalter, Miscellanea Mediaevalia* 2 (1963), pp. 607 – 15.

———. "Neue Nachrichten über die Pariser Verurteilung der thomasischen Formlehre." *Scholastik* 39 (1964), pp. 178 – 96.

Hoeres, W. *Der Wille als reine Vollkommenheit nach Duns Scotus*. Munich, 1962.

———. "Wesen und Dasein bei Heinrich von Gent und Duns Scotus." *Franziskanische Studien* 47 (1965), pp. 121 – 86.

[James of Viterbo]. *Jacobi de Viterbio O.E.S.A., Disputatio prima de quolibet*, ed. E. Ypma. Würzburg, 1968.

———. *Jacobi de Viterbio O.E.S.A., Disputatio secunda de quolibet*, ed. E. Ypma. Würzburg, 1969.

———. *Jacobi de Viterbio O.E.S.A., Disputatio tertia de quolibet*, ed. E. Ypma. Würzburg, 1973.

[John Damascene]. *De fide orthodoxa*, ed. E. Buytaert. St. Bonaventure, N.Y., 1955.

[John Duns Scotus]. *Opera omnia*. Vivès ed., Paris, 1891 – 1895.

———. *Opera omnia*. Vatican City, 1950—.

———. *Cuestiones Cuodlibetales (Obras del Doctor Sutil Juan Duns Escoto)*, ed. and tr. by F. Alluntis. Madrid, 1968.

[John Peckham]. *Joannes Pecham. Registrum epistolarum*, ed. C. T. Martin. T. III, London, 1885.

———. *Tractatus de anima*, ed. G. Melani. Florence, 1948.

Kleineidam, E. *Das Problem der hylomorphen Zusammensetzung der geistigen Substanzen im 13. Jahrhundert, behandelt bis Thomas von Aquin*. Breslau, 1930.

Klinger, I. *Das Prinzip der Individuation bei Thomas von Aquin*. Vier-Türme-Münsterschwarzach, 1964.

König, E. "Aristoteles' erste Philosophie als universale Wissenschaft von den ARXAI." *Archiv für Geschichte der Philosophie* 52 (1970), pp. 225 – 46.

Kovach, F. "The Question of the Eternity of the World in St. Bonaventure and St. Thomas—A Critical Analysis." *Bonaventure and Aquinas*, ed. R. Shahan and F. Kovach (Norman, Oklahoma, 1976), pp. 155 – 86.

Künzle, P. *Das Verhältnis der Seele zu ihren Potenzen. Problemgeschichtliche Untersuchungen von Augustin bis und mit Thomas von Aquin*. Fribourg, Switzerland, 1956.

Lacombe, O. "La critique des théories de la connaissance chez Duns Scot." *Revue thomiste* 35 (1930), pp. 24 – 47; 144 – 57; 217 – 35.

Langevin, P.E. "Nécessité ou liberté, chez Godefroid de Fontaines." *Sciences Ecclésiastiques* 12 (1960), pp. 175 – 203.

Lapierre, M.J. "Aquinas' Interpretation of Anselm's Definition of Truth." *Sciences Ecclésiastiques* 18 (1966), pp. 413–41.

Laurent, M.-H. "Godefroid de Fontaines et la condamnation de 1277." *Revue thomiste* 35 (1930), pp. 273–81.

Lefèvre, Ch. "Siger de Brabant a-t-il influencé saint Thomas?" *Mélanges de science religieuse* 31 (1974), pp. 203–15.

Leff, G. *Paris and Oxford Universities in the Thirteenth and Fourteenth Centuries.* New York, 1968.

Litt, Th. *Les corps célestes dans l'univers de saint Thomas d'Aquin.* Louvain-Paris, 1963.

Lobato, A. *De influxu Avicennae in theoria cognitionis Sancti Thomae Aquinatis.* Granada, 1956.

Lottin, O. "La composition hylémorphique des substances spirituelles." *Revue Néoscolastique de Philosophie* 34 (1932), pp. 21–41.

———. "Une question quodlibétique inconnue de Godefroid de Fontaines." *Revue d'Histoire Ecclésiastique* 30 (1934), pp. 852–59.

———. *Psychologie et morale au XIIe et XIIIe siècles.* 6 Tomes, Gembloux, 1942–1960.

———. "Le libre arbitre chez Godefroid de Fontaines." *Revue Néoscolastique de Philosophie* 40 (1937), pp. 213–41.

———. "Le thomisme de Godefroid de Fontaines en matière de libre arbitre." *Revue Néoscolastique de Philosophie* 40 (1937), pp. 554–73.

Macken, R. "De radicale tijdelijkheid van het schepsel volgens Hendrik van Gent." *Tijdschrift voor Filosofie* 31 (1969), pp. 519–71.

———. "La temporalité radicale de la créature selon Henri de Gand." *Recherches de Théologie ancienne et médiévale* 38 (1971), pp. 211–72.

———. "La volonté humaine, faculté plus élevée que l'intelligence selon Henri de Gand." *Recherches de Théologie ancienne et médiévale* 42 (1975), pp. 5–51.

———. "Le statut de la matière première chez Bonaventure." in *Bonaventura. Studien zu seiner Wirkungsgeschichte, Franziskanische Forschungen* 28 (1976), pp. 94–103.

———. "Subsistance de la matière première selon Henri de Gand." *San Bonaventura, Maestro di vita francescana e di sapienza cristiana (Atti del Congresso internazionale per il VII centenario di San Bonaventura da Bagnoregio).* T. 3 (Rome, 1976), pp. 107–15.

———. "Heinrich von Gent im Gespräch mit seinen Zeitgenossen über die menschliche Freiheit." *Franziskanische Studien* 59 (1977), pp. 125–82.

———. "Le statut de la matière première dans la philosophie d'Henri de Gand." *Recherches de Théologie ancienne et médiévale* 46 (1979), pp. 130–82.

Mahoney, E.P. "Metaphysical Foundations of Hierarchy of Being According to Some Medieval and Renaissance Philosophers." *Ancient and Medieval Philosophies of Existence*, ed. P. Morewedge (New York, forthcoming).

Maier, A. *Zwei Grundprobleme der scholastischen Naturphilosophie. Das Problem der intensiven Grösse. Die Impetustheorie.* 2nd ed., Rome, 1951.

Mandonnet, P. "La carrière scolaire de Gilles de Rome." *Revue des sciences philosophiques et théologiques* 4 (1910), pp. 480–99.

———. *Siger de Brabant et l'Averroïsme latin au XIIIe siècle.* 2nd ed., 2 vols., Louvain, 1911, 1908.

Martel, B. *La psychologie de Gonsalve d'Espagne.* Montréal-Paris, 1968.

Maurer, A. "*Esse* and *Essentia* in the Metaphysics of Siger of Brabant." *Mediaeval Studies* 8 (1946), pp. 68–86.

______. "Henry of Ghent and the Unity of Man." *Mediaeval Studies* 10 (1948), pp. 1–20.

______. "*Ens Diminutum*: A Note on its Origin and Meaning." *Mediaeval Studies* 12 (1950), pp. 216–22.

McMahon, F., "The *Esse* of Accidents: A Discussion." *The Modern Schoolman* 31 (1954), pp. 125–30. See pp. 130–32 for a reply by J. Albertson.

McMahon, F., and Phelan, G. "The *Esse* of Accidents." *The New Scholasticism* 43 (1969), pp. 143–48.

Meehan, F.X. *Efficient Causality in Aristotle and St. Thomas*. Washington, D.C., 1940.

Morewedge, P. "Philosophical Analysis and Ibn Sīnā's 'Essence-Existence' Distinction." *Journal of the American Oriental Society* 92 (1972), pp. 425–35.

[Moses Maimonides]. *Dux Neutrorum seu dubiorum*. Paris, 1520; repr. Frankfurt/Main, 1964.

______. *The Guide of the Perplexed*. Chicago, 1963.

Mühlen, H. *Sein und Person nach Johann Duns Scot*. Werl/Westf., 1954.

Nash, P. "Giles of Rome, Auditor and Critic of St. Thomas." *The Modern Schoolman* 28 (1950–51), pp. 1–20.

______. "Giles of Rome on Boethius' 'Diversum est esse et id quod est'," *Mediaeval Studies* 12 (1950), pp. 57–91.

______. "The Accidentality of Esse According to Giles of Rome." *Gregorianum* 38 (1957), pp. 103–15.

______. "Giles of Rome." *New Catholic Encyclopedia* 6 (1967), pp. 484–85.

Neumann, B. *Der Mensch und die himmlische Seligkeit nach der Lehre Gottfrieds von Fontaines*. Limburg/Lahn, 1958.

O'Brien, A.J. "Duns Scotus' Teaching on the Distinction Between Essence and Existence." *The New Scholasticism* 38 (1964), pp. 61–77.

Oeing-Hanhoff, L. *Ens et unum convertuntur. Stellung und Gehalt des Grundsatzes in der Philosophie des hl. Thomas von Aquin*. Münster, 1953.

Owens, J. "The Conclusion of the Prima Via." *The Modern Schoolman* 30 (1953), pp. 33–53; 109–21; 203–15.

______. *The Doctrine of Being in the Aristotelian Metaphysics*. 2nd printing, Toronto, 1957.

______. "Quiddity and Real Distinction in St. Thomas Aquinas." *Mediaeval Studies* 27 (1965), pp. 1–22.

______. "Aquinas and the Proof from the 'Physics'," *Mediaeval Studies* 28 (1966), pp. 119–50.

Patfoort, A. *L'unité d'être dans le Christ d'après s. Thomas*. Paris, 1964.

Pattin, A. "Gilles de Rome, O.E.S.A. (ca. 1243–1316) et la distinction réelle de l'essence et de l'existence." *Revue de l'Université d'Ottawa* 23 (1953), pp. 80*–116*.

______. "La structure de l'être fini selon Bernard d'Auvergne, O.P." *Tijdschrift voor Filosofie* 24 (1962), pp. 668–737.

Paulus, J. "La théorie du premier moteur chez Aristote." *Revue de Philosophie* n.s. 4 (1933), pp. 259–94; 394–424.

______. "Le caractère métaphysique des preuves thomistes de l'existence de Dieu." *Archives d'Histoire Doctrinale et Littéraire du Moyen Age* 9 (1934), pp. 143–53.

______. *Henri de Gand. Essai sur les tendances de sa métaphysique*. Paris, 1938.

______. "Les disputes d'Henri de Gand et de Gilles de Rome sur la distinction de l'essence et de l'existence." *Archives d'Histoire Doctrinale et Littéraire du Moyen Age* 13 (1940–1942), pp. 323–58.

———. "Henry of Ghent." *New Catholic Encyclopedia* 6 (1967), pp. 1035–37.

Pegis, A. *St. Thomas and the Problem of the Soul in the Thirteenth Century*. Toronto, 1934.

———. "St. Thomas and the Coherence of the Aristotelian Theology." *Mediaeval Studies* 35 (1973), pp. 67–117.

Pelster, F. "La Quaestio disputata de saint Thomas 'De unione Verbi incarnati'," *Archives de Philosophie* 3 (1925), pp. 198–245.

———. "Die Sätze der Londoner Verurteilung von 1286 und die Schriften des Magister Richard von Knapwell O.P." *Archivum Fratrum Praedicatorum* 16 (1946), pp. 83–106.

———. "Das Wachstum der Seligkeit nach der Auferstehung. Um die Auslegung von S. th. 1, 2, q. 4 a. 5 ad 5." *Scholastik* 27 (1952), pp. 561–63.

Pelzer, A. "Godefroid de Fontaines. Les manuscrits de ses Quodlibets conservés à la Vaticane et dans quelques autres bibliothèques." *Revue Néoscolastique de Philosophie* 20 (1913), pp. 365–88; 491–532.

Peter, C. *Participated Eternity in the Vision of God*. Rome, 1964.

Pinborg, J. "Zur Philosophie des Boethius de Dacia. Ein Überblick." *Studia Mediewistyczne* 15 (1974), pp. 165–85.

Plotnik, W. "Transubstantiation in the Eucharistic Theology of Giles of Rome, Henry of Ghent, and Godfrey of Fontaines." *Wahrheit und Verkündigung. Michael Schmaus zum 70. Geburtstag*, Vol. 2 (München-Paderborn-Wien, 1967), pp. 1073–86.

[Proclus]. *The Elements of Theology*, ed. E.R. Dodds. 2nd ed., Oxford, 1963.

———. "Procli Elementatio theologica translata a Guilelmo de Moerbeke," ed. C. Vansteenkiste. *Tijdschrift voor Philosophie* 13 (1951), pp. 263–302; 491–531.

Quinn, J. *The Historical Constitution of St. Bonaventure's Philosophy*. Toronto, 1973.

Rahman, F. "Essence and Existence in Avicenna." *Mediaeval and Renaissance Studies* 4 (1958), pp. 1–16.

[Richard of Middleton]. *De gradu formarum*, ed. by R. Zavalloni in his *Richard de Mediavilla . . .* , pp. 35–169.

Roensch, F. *Early Thomistic School*. Dubuque, 1964.

Royce, J. "St. Thomas and the Definition of Active Potency." *The New Scholasticism* 34 (1960), pp. 431–37.

Ruello, F. *La notion de vérité chez Saint Albert le Grand et Saint Thomas d'Aquin de 1243 à 1254*. Louvain-Paris, 1969.

———. "Les fondements de la liberté humaine selon Jacques de Viterbe O.E.S.A. Disputatio 1ª de Quolibet, q. 7 (1293)." *Augustiniana* 24 (1974), pp. 283–347; 25 (1975), pp. 114–42.

Rüssmann, H. *Zur Ideenlehre der Hochscholastik unter besonderer Berücksichtigung des Heinrich von Gent, Gottfried von Fontaines und Jakob von Viterbo*. Freiburg im Breisgau, 1938.

Sajó, G. "Boetius de Dacia und seine philosophische Bedeutung." *Die Metaphysik im Mittelalter, Miscellanea Mediaevalia* 2 (1963), pp. 454–63.

San Cristóbal-Sebastián, A. *Controversias acerca de la voluntad desde 1270 a 1300 (Estudio histórico-doctrinal)*. Madrid, 1958.

Schneider, Th. *Die Einheit des Menschen. Die anthropologische Formel "anima forma corporis" im sogenannten Korrektorienstreit und bei Petrus Johannis Olivi. Ein Beitrag zur Vorgeschichte des Konzils von Vienne*. Münster, 1973.

Schöllgen, W. *Das Problem der Willensfreiheit bei Heinrich von Gent und Herveus Natalis*. Düsseldorf, 1927.

Schweizer, O. *Person und Hypostatische Union bei Thomas von Aquin*. Fribourg, Switzerland, 1957.

Seiler, L. "La notion de personne selon Scot. Ses principales applications en Christologie." *La France franciscaine* 20 (1937), pp. 209–48.

Sharp, D.E. *Franciscan Philosophy at Oxford in the Thirteenth Century*. London, 1930.

Siemiatkowska, Z.K. "Avant l'exil de Gilles de Rome. Au sujet d'une dispute sur les 'Theoremata de esse et essentia' de Gilles de Rome." *Mediaevalia Philosophica Polonorum* 7 (1960), pp. 3–67.

[Siger of Brabant]. *Siger de Brabant. Questions sur la Métaphysique*, ed. C.A. Graiff. Louvain, 1948.

———. "Die *Questiones metaphysice tres* des Siger von Brabant," ed. J. Vennebusch. *Archiv für Geschichte der Philosophie* 48 (1966), pp. 175–89.

———. *Les Quaestiones super librum de causis de Siger de Brabant*, ed. A. Marlasca. Louvain-Paris, 1972.

———. *Siger de Brabant. Quaestiones in tertium de anima, De anima intellectiva, De aeternitate mundi*, ed. B. Bazán. Louvain-Paris, 1972.

———. *Siger de Brabant. Ecrits de logique, de morale et de physique*, ed. B. Bazán. Louvain-Paris, 1974.

[Simplicius]. *Simplicius. Commentaire sur les catégories d'Aristote. Traduction de Guillaume de Moerbeke*, ed. A. Pattin. T. 1, Louvain, 1971.

Sokolowski, R. "Matter, Elements, and Substance in Aristotle," *Journal of the History of Philosophy* 8 (1970), pp. 263–88.

Stadter, E. *Psychologie und Metaphysik der menschlichen Freiheit. Die ideengeschichtliche Entwicklung zwischen Bonaventura und Duns Scotus*. München-Paderborn-Wien, 1971.

Stella, P. "Teologi e teologia nelle 'Reprobationes' di Bernardo d'Auvergne ai Quodlibeti di Goffredo di Fontaines." *Salesianum* 19 (1957), pp. 171–214.

Stohr, A. "Die Hauptrichtungen der spekulativen Trinitätslehre in der Theologie des 13. Jahrhunderts." *Tübinger Theologische Quartalschrift* 106 (1925), pp. 113–35.

———. "Des Gottfried von Fontaines Stellung in der Trinitätslehre." *Zeitschrift für katholische Theologie* 50 (1926), pp. 177–95.

Suárez, G. "El pensamiento de Egidio Romano en torno a la distinción de esencia y existencia," *La Ciencia Tomista* 75 (1948), pp. 66–99; 230–72.

———. "La metafísica de Egidio Romano a la luz de las 24 tesis tomistas." *La Ciudad de Dios* 161 (1949), pp. 93–130; 269–309.

Sweeney, L. "Existence/Essence in Thomas Aquinas's Early Writings." *Proceedings of the American Catholic Philosophical Association* 37 (1963), pp. 97–131.

[Themistius]. *Commentaire sur le traité de l'âme d'Aristote: Traduction de Guillaume de Moerbeke*, ed. G. Verbeke. Louvain, 1957.

Théry, G. "L'Augustinisme médiéval et le problème de l'unité de la forme substantielle." *Acta Hebdomadae Augustinianae-Thomisticae* (Turin-Rome, 1931), pp. 140–200.

[Thomas Aquinas]. *Scriptum super libros sententiarum*, ed. P. Mandonnet and M. Moos. 4 vols., Paris, 1929–1947.

———. *Summa Contra Gentiles*, ed. Leonina manualis. Rome, 1934.

———. *Le 'De ente et essentia' de s. Thomas d'Aquin*, ed. M.-D. Roland Gosselin. Paris, 1948.

———. *Opuscula omnia*, ed. J. Perrier. Vol. 1, Paris, 1949.

———. *In duodecim libros Metaphysicorum Aristotelis expositio*, ed. M.-R. Cathala and R.M. Spiazzi. Turin-Rome, 1950.

———. *Quaestiones disputatae*, ed. R. Spiazzi et al. 2 vols., Turin-Rome, 1953.
———. *Opuscula philosophica*, ed. R. Spiazzi. Turin-Rome, 1954.
———. *Opuscula theologica*, ed. R. Verardo, R. Spiazzi, M. Calcaterra. 2 vols., Turin-Rome, 1954.
———. *Quaestiones quodlibetales*, ed. R. Spiazzi. Turin-Rome, 1956.
———. *In Aristotelis librum De anima commentarium*, ed. A. Pirotta. Turin-Rome, 1959.
———. *Sancti Thomae de Aquino expositio super librum Boethii de Trinitate*, ed. B. Decker. Leiden, 1959.
———. *Saint Thomas Aquinas. Treatise on Separate Substances*, ed. F. J. Lescoe. West Hartford, Conn., 1963.
———. *Sancti Thomae de Aquino opera omnia*, Leonine edition. Rome, 1882—.
Tihon, P. *Foi et théologie selon Godefroid de Fontaines*. Paris-Bruges, 1966.
Trapé, G. "Il Platonismo di Egidio Romano." *Aquinas* 7 (1964), pp. 309–44.
———. "Il Neoplatonismo di Egidio Romano nel commento al 'De causis'." *Aquinas* 9 (1966), pp. 49–86.
———. "La dottrina della partecipazione in Egidio Romano." *Aquinas* 10 (1967), pp. 170–93.
———. "Caratteristiche dell' 'esse' partecipato in Egidio Romano." *Lateranum* 34 (1968), pp. 351–68.
———. "Causalità e partecipazione in Egidio Romano." *Augustinianum* 9 (1969), pp. 91–117.
———. "L' 'esse' partecipato e distinzione reale in Egidio Romano." *Aquinas* 12 (1969), pp. 443–68.
Trapp, D. "Aegidii Romani de doctrina modorum." *Angelicum* 12 (1935), pp. 449–501.
Vande Wiele, J. "Le problème de la vérité ontologique dans la philosophie de saint Thomas." *Revue philosophique de Louvain* 52 (1954), pp. 521–71.
Van Steenberghen, F. "La composition constitutive de l'être fini." *Revue Néoscolastique de Philosophie* 41 (1938), pp. 489–518.
———. *Siger de Brabant d'après ses oeuvres inédites*. Vol. 2. *Siger dans l'histoire de l'Aristotélisme*. Louvain, 1942.
———. *La philosophie au XIIIe siècle*. Louvain-Paris, 1966.
———. "Saint Bonaventure contre l'éternité du monde," in *S. Bonaventura 1274–1974*, T. 3 (Grottaferrata, 1973), pp. 259–87.
———. "Le 'De quindecim problematibus' d'Albert le Grand," in his *Introduction à l'étude de la philosophie médiévale* (Louvain-Paris, 1974), pp. 433–55.
———. *Maître Siger de Brabant*. Louvain-Paris, 1977.
———. "Le mythe d'un monde éternel." *Revue philosophique de Louvain* 76 (1978), pp. 157–79.
[Walter of Bruges]. *Quaestiones disputatae du B. Gauthier de Bruges*, ed. E. Longpré. PB 10, Louvain, 1928.
[Walter Burley]. "Walter Burley's *Quaestiones in Librum Perihermeneias*," ed. S. Brown. *Franciscan Studies* 34 (1974), pp. 200–95.
Wéber, E.-H. *La controverse de 1270 à l'Université de Paris et son retentissement sur la pensée de s. Thomas d'Aquin*. Paris, 1970.
———. "Les discussions de 1270 à l'Université de Paris et leur influence sur la pensée philosophique de s. Thomas d'Aquin." *Die Auseinandersetzungen an der Pariser Universität im XIII. Jahrhundert, Miscellanea Mediaevalia* 10 (1976), pp. 285–316.

Weisheipl, J. *Friar Thomas d'Aquino: His Life, Thought, and Work.* New York, 1974.

[William de la Mare]. *Correctorium Fratris Thomae,* in *Le correctorium Corruptorii 'Quare'*, ed. P. Glorieux. Le Saulchoir, Kain, 1927.

Wilpert, P. "Ein Compendium des 13. Jahrhunderts (Gottfried von Fontaines als Abbreviator)." *Mittellatèinisches Jahrbuch* 2 (1965), pp. 165–80.

Winandy, J. "Le Quodlibet II, art. 4 de saint Thomas et la notion de suppôt." *Ephemerides theologicae Lovanienses* 11 (1934), pp. 5–29.

Wippel, J.F. "Godfrey of Fontaines and the Real Distinction between Essence and Existence." *Traditio* 20 (1964), pp. 385–410.

______. "Godfrey of Fontaines." *New Catholic Encyclopedia* 6 (1967), pp. 577–78.

______. "Godfrey of Fontaines: The Date of Quodlibet 15." *Franciscan Studies* 31 (1971), pp. 300–69.

______. "Godfrey of Fontaines and the Act-Potency Axiom." *Journal of the History of Philosophy* 11 (1973), pp. 299–317.

______. "Godfrey of Fontaines: Disputed Questions 9, 10 and 12." *Franciscan Studies* 33 (1973), pp. 351–72.

______. "The Dating of James of Viterbo's Quodlibet I and Godfrey of Fontaines' Quodlibet VIII." *Augustiniana* 24 (1974), pp. 348–86.

______. "Godfrey of Fontaines and Henry of Ghent's Theory of Intentional Distinction between Essence and Existence." *Sapientiae procerum amore. Mélanges Médiévistes offerts à Dom Jean-Pierre Müller O.S.B., Studia Anselmiana* 63 (Rome, 1974), pp. 289–321.

______. "The Condemnations of 1270 and 1277 at Paris." *The Journal of Medieval and Renaissance Studies* 7 (1977), pp. 169–201.

______. "Aquinas's Route to the Real Distinction: A Note on *De ente et essentia,* c. 4." *The Thomist* 43 (1979), pp. 279–95.

______. "The Relationship between Essence and Existence in Late Thirteenth-Century Thought: Giles of Rome, Henry of Ghent, Godfrey of Fontaines, and James of Viterbo." *Ancient and Medieval Philosophies of Existence,* ed. by P. Morewedge (New York, forthcoming).

______. "Did Thomas Aquinas Defend the Possibility of an Eternally Created World? (The *De aeternitate mundi* Revisited)," *Journal of the History of Philosophy* (forthcoming).

Wittmann, M. *Die Stellung des hl. Thomas von Aquin zu Avencebrol. Beiträge zur Geschichte der Philosophie des Mittelalters* 3, 3 (1900).

Wolter, A.B. "The Formal Distinction." *Studies in Philosophy and the History of Philosophy,* Vol. 3: *John Duns Scotus, 1265–1965* (Washington, D.C., 1965), pp. 45–60.

______. "Thc Ockhamist Critiquc." *The Concept of Matter in Greek and Medieval Philosophy,* ed. by E. McMullin (Notre Dame, Ind., 1965), pp. 124–46.

Xiberta, B. "Les Qüestions ordinàries de Godofred de Fontaines retrobades parcialment en un manuscrit de Barcelona." *Criterion* 4 (1928), pp. 339–42.

Ypma, E. *La Formation des Professeurs chez les Ermites de Saint-Augustin de 1256 à 1354.* Paris, 1956.

______. "Recherches sur la carrière scolaire et la bibliothèque de Jacques de Viterbe † 1308." *Augustiniana* 24 (1974), pp. 247–82.

______. "Recherches sur la productivité littéraire de Jacques de Viterbe jusqu'à 1300." *Augustiniana* 25 (1975), pp. 223–82.

Zavalloni, R. *Richard de Mediavilla et la controverse sur la pluralité des formes*. Louvain, 1951.

Zimmermann, A. *Ontologie oder Metaphysik? Die Diskussion über den Gegenstand der Metaphysik im 13. und 14. Jahrhundert, Texte und Untersuchungen*. Leiden-Köln, 1965.

———. *Ein Kommentar zur Physik des Aristoteles aus der Pariser Artistenfakultät um 1273*. Berlin, 1968.

Zwaenepoel, J.P. *Les Quaestiones in Librum de causis attribuées à Henri de Gand*. Louvain-Paris, 1974.

MANUSCRIPTS

Paris: Bibl. Nat. lat. 15.350.
Paris: Bibl. Nat. lat. 15.819.
Paris: Bibl. Nat. lat. 16.096.
Paris: Bibl. Nat. lat. 16.297.
Vatican: Borgh. 122.
Vatican: Borgh. 164.
Vatican: lat. 1032.
Bruges: Stadsbibliot. 491.

Index of Names

Index of Topics